Modern Urban and Regional Economics

SECOND EDITION

Philip McCann

OXFORD
UNIVERSITY PRESS

OXFORD

UNIVERSITY PRESS

Great Clarendon Street, Oxford, OX2 6DP,
United Kingdom

Oxford University Press is a department of the University of Oxford.
It furthers the University's objective of excellence in research, scholarship,
and education by publishing worldwide. Oxford is a registered trade mark of
Oxford University Press in the UK and in certain other countries

British Library Cataloguing in Publication Data

Data available

ISBN 978-0-19-958200-6

Printed in Great Britain by
Ashford Colour Press Ltd, Gosport, Hampshire

To my parents Kath and Joe, and to my family

About the Author

Philip McCann holds the University of Groningen Endowed Chair of Economic Geography in the Faculty of Spatial Sciences at the University of Groningen, The Netherlands. He is Adjunct Professor of Economics at the University of Waikato in New Zealand, and a former Professor of Urban and Regional Economics at the University of Reading, UK.

During 2010–2013 Philip McCann was Special Adviser to the European Commissioner for Regional Policy, Johannes Hahn, advising on all aspects of the reform of EU Cohesion Policy. He also acts as an adviser to OECD and to various government departments in several countries, as well as being a member of the steering committees of national and international research commissions.

Educated at Cambridge University, Philip McCann has published numerous journal articles, books, and book chapters over two decades, and won various international awards for his research. He has previously held long-term visiting professorships at University of Pennsylvania, USA, University of Tsukuba, Japan, Ritsumeikan University, Japan, and Thammasat University, Thailand, as well as short-term visiting positions at Bocconi University, Italy, Cornell University, USA, and University of Barcelona, Spain.

Philip McCann is also co-editor of *Papers in Regional Science*, *Spatial Economic Analysis*, and *Review of Urban and Regional Development Studies*.

Acknowledgements

My thanks go to the editorial team at Oxford University Press who have always been supportive and professional in everything they do, making the arduous process of writing a book such as this as straightforward as possible. I am also very grateful for the significant amount of work undertaken by five anonymous reviewers whose detailed insights, comments, and criticisms on each chapter greatly improved the book.

My thanks also go to the numerous scholars and teachers from all over the world who have kindly provided me with excellent ideas and suggestions for this second book, almost all of which I hope I have managed to include.

Finally, I am forever grateful for the many friends and family who have supported me in my work.

Contents

List of figures

List of tables

Introduction

The logic and organization of the book

The front cover of this book provides a wonderful example of why urban and regional economics is such an exciting and important subject to study. The building featured is the Bank of China Tower building in Hong Kong, and for me it is one of the most elegant modern buildings in the world. The building is the home of various international corporations providing knowledge-based financial services with enormous investments in China. Yet, as a book-cover image, the building succinctly captures the urban and regional transformations evident in the modern global context. Hong Kong is one of the most dynamic cities in the world. Located in the heart of the rapidly expanding global super-region of South and East Asia, less than five decades ago Hong Kong was a centre for low-value-added manufacturing. Hong Kong is now one of the major global centres of finance and trade and in commercial terms it is a meeting point and melting pot of east and west, north and south. The wonderful building therefore is also a symbol of the transformations we have witnessed in the global economy during the last twenty years.

When the first edition of *Urban and Regional Economics* was published in 2001, we were still little more than a decade on from the fall of the Berlin Wall, the creation of the European Union and its Single Market, seven years from the founding of the North American Free Trade Agreement (NAFTA), and only a decade from creation of the world wide web in its modern sense. The global economic changes wrought by these transformations were still only emerging and as such were still relatively little understood. Today the situation is radically different. Since the Millennium, enormous strides have been made in terms of urban and regional data provision and urban and regional theoretical analysis. These empirical and theoretical developments have significantly increased our awareness and understanding of the role played by cities and regions in the global economy, and, in turn, the impacts of the global economic changes on cities and regions. The debates surrounding cities and regions have nowadays also broadened to include issues such as creativity, institutions, well-being, social capital, and sustainability, and cities and regions are seen to be central to all such discussion. Whereas once urban and regional issues were seen by many economists to be a minor avenue of research, nowadays many of the most important international institutions including the World Bank, the OECD, the European Commission, and the United Nations are all grappling with the economic challenges and possibilities associated with regions and cities.

The novelty and originality of the 2001 edition of this textbook was to treat urban and regional economic issues in an integrated manner, drawing out the links and differences between the various model approaches. The intention was to make the book accessible to economists, geographers, regional planners, business and management students, and also public policy-makers. The book was structured around a series of models presented in a manner which would allow the issues to be taught and applied irrespective of which part of the world the reader inhabited. The fact that the sales of the book have been more or less equally distributed across the globe, as well as being translated into Chinese, Greek, Korean, and Japanese, suggests that it was successful in terms of these objectives.

This new edition of the textbook adopts exactly the same approach as the earlier edition. However, it has been re-titled as *Modern Urban and Regional Economics*, and this is in order to signal the novel features of this new edition, which is quite different to the first book in several key respects. The new edition aims to achieve two objectives. First, it seeks to update all the traditional analytical discussions in the light of the new thinking, the new models, and the new empirics that have emerged over the last decade. Second, it seeks to position these theoretical and empirical developments in the much broader and transforming global context in which today's cities and regions find themselves. The book comprises ten chapters. Each chapter takes a particular theme and discusses the various ways in which we are able to ask and answer questions related to the topic in question. The discussions operate at different levels, with the first seven chapters discussing the ways in which we analyse the spatial behaviour and urban and regional impacts of firms, people, land markets, inter-firm linkages, and technology. The last three chapters take a much broader historical, geographical, and institutional approach to examine the broader underlying changes that affect cities, regions, and the urban and regional policy challenges faced in the modern economy. Given the different levels at which these groups of chapters operate, the book is split into two parts, entitled Urban and regional economic models and methods, and Globalization: cities, regions, and economic policy. Part I deals with various aspects of urban and regional economic analysis, while Part II discusses the broader themes relating to the changing context in which regions and cities nowadays find themselves.

Chapter 1 discusses the various theoretical ways we can understand the location behaviour of individual firms. Chapter 2 employs these arguments to explain why groups of firms and activities are often located together in cities, urban agglomerations, and industrial clusters. However, we also know that firms differ greatly in their location patterns and are often found to be distributed across widely different spatial scales. Chapter 3 therefore examines these broader patterns of location and dispersion, allowing for the fact that different firms face different pressures and advantages from being clustered or located apart from each other, and uncovers some regularities and systematic features underpinning the relationships between spatial concentration and dispersion. Where clustering leads to the growth of a city, once an urban area has arisen at a particular location, Chapter 4 explains how the urban land market works and how local land allocations are determined. Chapters 5–7 then adopt a more macro-approach to discussions of various regional economic issues that are generally understood primarily in macroeconomic terms. Chapter 5 discusses multiplier analysis and the ways in which the linkages between firms and activities in a local area affect the overall output of an area. Chapter 6 explains the response of spatial labour markets to local demand and supply changes, and discusses the particular problems associated with local labour market adjustments and interregional migration flows. Chapter 7 then integrates the arguments in each of the previous chapters in order to discuss the various approaches we have to analyse regional growth behaviour. As with Chapters 2–4, Chapters 5–7, which deal with these more macroeconomic issues, are underpinned by explicitly spatial considerations. This allows us to identify the differences between analysis of economic phenomena at the urban or regional level and analysis at the national macroeconomic level.

Part II takes a much broader panoramic approach to understanding the impacts of globalization on cities, regions, and the policy challenges and possibilities associated with these changes. Chapter 8 discusses the historical relationship between urbanization, industrialization, and wealth in the context of four centuries of globalization processes. The intention here is to explain why studying cities and regions is so important for understanding national growth, and how these relationships have changed during different time periods, right up to the present day. What is important here is to understand that the long-term historical trends linking the growth of cities and densely populated regions to the growth of the national economy heavily influence the twentieth-century logic and construction of the models discussed in Chapters 1–7. Yet, in terms of the relationships between cities, regions, and national economies, the twentieth century itself was a period of dramatic twists and turns, in which many of these relationships were either broken or refashioned in different ways in different parts of the world. Some of these twists and turns now have profound impacts on the ways in which we are able to use the models examined in Chapters 1–7 in the modern economy, because the underlying context in which such models can be applied may differ significantly in different places. In order to investigate these issues, Chapter 9 examines the major urban and regional changes that have arisen during the modern era of globalization which began in the late 1980s, and considers these changes in the light of the long-run trends discussed in Chapter 8. As we will see, the enormous global changes experienced since the late 1980s have fundamentally altered the long-run historical relationships between cities, regions, and nations in ways that we are only now beginning to understand better. An awareness of these changes is essential in order to understand how best to use the models discussed in Chapters 1–7 for analysing contemporary phenomena. At the same time, these changes have also led to new debates and controversies regarding regional and urban policy, debates that are sufficiently profound and influential that they are now taking place at the highest levels of international economic policy-making. These debates are examined in Chapter 10, which discusses in detail the nature of, and the justification for, urban and regional economic policy in the context of modern globalization. Chapter 10 explains how we can use the urban and regional economic models and methods described in Part I of this book in order to understand, predict, and target the impacts of various types of urban and regional policies. These discussions also highlight the limitations of our current understanding, and point out possible directions for further research.

As we will see in Part II of the book, the impacts of modern globalization on cities and regions have been profound, while in turn cities and regions have been in the vanguard of modern globalization processes. The emerging awareness of these relationships over the last decade has shaped entirely new discourses within politics and policy-making the world over. Many of these discussions are valuable, but not all are accurate. A genuine understanding of these processes therefore requires a strong grounding in the theoretical models while at the same time an awareness of the fundamentally changing context in which these models need to be positioned and interpreted. It is hoped that a good awareness of both the models and methods, along with the current global context, will help us best achieve the desired outcomes of public policy initiatives that contain urban and regional elements. This book aims to provide both this theoretical grounding and also a real awareness of the evolving global context. No other textbook dealing with urban or regional issues sets these squarely in today's global context, and no text on globalization deals explicitly with the analytics of cities and regions. This new version of the book is therefore genuinely new.

Why study urban and regional economics?

All economic phenomena take place within geographical space. Economic issues invariably involve either questions concerning the place specificity of particular activities, or alternatively, questions relating to the overcoming of space and geographical distance. For example, all commodities are traded at various market locations. However, in order to reach the appropriate market locations, goods have to be transported and delivered across space. Similarly, service activities take place at particular locations, and the knowledge and information required to carry out the activity must be transmitted or acquired across geographical space. In each case, the costs incurred in these spatial transactions will themselves partly determine the price and cost conditions at each market location. Yet the reasons why particular markets are located at particular places are also economic questions, and as we will see in this book, the nature and behaviour of markets depend somewhat on their location. Market performance therefore partly depends on geography. At the same time, the economic performance of a particular area also depends on the nature and performance of the various markets located within the area. Acknowledging that geography plays a role in determining economic behaviour, many discussions about the performance of particular local, urban, or regional economies are, in fact, fundamentally questions about the relationships between geography and the economy. Geography and economics are usually interrelated issues.

For many years before the 1990s, spatial questions were all too often ignored by economists and economic policy-makers. This is partly a problem of education. In most textbook discussions, the whole economic system is assumed to take place on a pinhead (Isard 1965). While for a long time there have been many urban economists, regional scientists, and economic geographers who have been explicitly concerned with spatial economic phenomena, for many years the majority of geographical issues were subsumed by Ricardian theories of comparative advantage and international trade. In the post-war Bretton Woods world of relatively closed economies and currency convertability restrictions, such assumptions may have appeared to many economists to be acceptable. However, in the modern era of free trade areas such as the North American Free Trade Agreement (NAFTA), new information and communications technologies, currency convertibility, the EU Single Market and the euro, rapidly increasing capital and labour mobility, and the enormous city-region growth of the newly emerging BRIICS countries of Brazil, Russia, India, Indonesia, China and South Africa, many of these traditional assumptions can no longer be justified. These recent developments have highlighted the fact that competition between regions is often more important and more complex then competition between individual countries. Indeed, much international competition is actually dominated by competition between particular regions in different countries, rather than between whole countries. In each of these cases, the nature of the sub-national and super-national competitive relationships between various regions depends on the spatial distribution of industrial activities. Geography is an essential element of the economic system, and the economics of urban and regional behaviour are just as important as that of national behaviour. The role of geography in the economy and the importance of the regional economic behaviour provide the motivation and justification for studying urban and regional economics.

Since the early 1990s there has been an enormous increase in interest is spatial economic questions within the world of academic research and public policy-making. Testament to this comes from highly influential work on urban and regional issues undertaken during recent years by the World Bank, the OECD, the European Commission, and the United Nations, as well as the major changes in policy-thinking in many countries regarding the critical role in growth played by cities and regions. In part, this has been because of the new institutional and technological developments mentioned above, which have highlighted the need for explicit considerations of space in economic discussions. The writings of Paul Krugman and Michael Porter, among others, have also brought the importance of spatial economic issues to the attention of wider audiences within the international economics, business and management fields. The work of these authors has led to significant developments in our understanding of the relationships between space and the economy. However, there is a long and broad tradition of spatial economic analysis, the origins of which pre-date both of these authors. Building on the original seminal works of authors discussed in this book, a huge number of authors have subsequently provided many fundamental insights into the complex nature of the relationships between geography and space. A consideration of these insights and the analytical techniques thereby developed is essential in order to provide a comprehensive understanding of the nature and workings of the modern spatial economy.

Traditionally spatial economic analysis has broadly been split into two sub-fields, namely urban economics and regional economics. These are by no means mutually exclusive categories and many analyses will fall into both categories. The distinction between these two categories has arisen as a result of asking slightly different questions. Urban economics, by definition, is generally concerned with asking questions about the nature and workings of the economy of the city. As such, the models and techniques developed within this field are primarily designed to analyse phenomena that are confined within the limits of a single city. Regional economics, on the other hand, tends to ask questions related to larger spatial areas than single cities, and the models and analytical techniques developed generally reflect this broader spatial perspective. In essence, urban economics tends to emphasize issues or relationships operating primarily at a place, whereas regional economics tends to emphasize issues or relationships operating primarily between places. Moreover, the the central questions of regional economics therefore focus on the reasons why individual spatial parts of the same country or of groups of adjacent countries behave differently to one another, whereas the central questions in urban economics tend to ignore areas which are primarily rural or primarily a mixture of smaller urban and rural localities. However, as we will see in this book, there are many issues which can be analysed within either field, such as questions relating to the locations of cities, the location of firms, or the migration behaviour of labour. In each urban or regional case, the choice of the appropriate analytical approach to adopt or the techniques to employ will in part be determined by the particular real-world context we are considering and the data that are available.

For the purposes of this book, an urban area is defined as a single continuous and contiguous area of urban development and built environment. The central questions of urban economics therefore focus on the workings of the individual city. The definition of a region is rather more complex, because areas can be defined as individual regions in terms of their topography, climate, economy, culture, or administrative structure. For the purposes of this book we define regions in terms of spatial units. A region is defined here as a spatial area that is larger than a single urban area, but that is different the spatial definition of a single nation. In general, we assume that regions are smaller than individual countries, but in this book we also explore the many cases where regions are larger than nations. For example, the spatial classifications of urban and regional areas adopted here are by no means definitive. For example, some individual urban areas such as Los Angeles and Tokyo can be regarded as major regions in their own right. At the same time, some regional areas cut across national boundaries. For example, the economy of Detroit and some parts of Western Ontario are largely the same regional economy. Similarly, the economy of Seattle can be considered to be broadly part of the same regional economy as Vancouver, British Columbia. Meanwhile, in Europe, the southern part of Netherlands can be regarded as being largely part of the same regional economy as parts of northern and eastern Belgium and the Nordrhein-Westfalen area of Germany. Furthermore, regions can also vary enormously either in geographical or population size. For example, the south-west region of the USA is the spatial size of the whole of Western Europe, while the Tokyo–Kanto regional population is larger than the whole population of Scandinavia.

Although many spatial economic topics can be analysed within either an urban or a regional economics framework, this is not to say that the spatial unit of analysis, whether it is a single city or a multi-city region, is an arbitrary choice. Some economic phenomena primarily affect localized individual urban areas, whereas the impacts of certain other economic phenomena are generally felt over much larger regional areas. The appropriate geographical area of analysis will therefore depend on the nature and spatial extent of the economic phenomena. At the same time, regions and cities are both valid areas for economic analysis because economic policy is often implemented at these levels. Individual urban metropolitan governments have a role to play in determining transportation and land-use policies within the confines of the individual city, and some of the financing of such policies will be raised by local city taxation. The analysis of the impacts of such schemes must be made at the level of the individual urban area. Similarly, inter-urban transportation and land-use policies will have impacts on all the cities within a region. As such, the regions comprising the groups of cities become the appropriate areas of analysis, as the effects of such schemes may be rather different between the individual cities. As we will see in this book, the choice of the area of analysis will determine the models we employ and also how the results we generate are to be interpreted.

For analytical simplicity, in Chapters 1–7 of this book, which develop the various urban and regional economic models, we will therefore initially adopt the convention that regions are smaller than individual countries and larger than individual urban areas, with the additional assumption that a country is an area with a common currency and free internal capital and labour mobility. We then relax this assumption in Chapters 8–10 and allow for regions spanning national borders when we discuss the role of cities and regions in the modern era of globalization.

Aims and objectives of the book

The object of this book is to provide an integrated approach to urban and regional economics, such that students are able to understand the broad range of relationships between economics and geography. Through an appreciation of these relationships, students will come to understand the location-specific nature of many urban and regional economics issues. An understanding of the relationships between economics and geography will also better inform us of the long-run impacts of continuing economic integration across nations. This understanding will, in turn, it is hoped, encourage our future economic policy-makers to make explicit consideration of the geographical aspects of economic policies, irrespective of whether they are government or corporate decision-makers. In the modern era of rapid communications technologies, decreasing trade barriers, increasing international labour mobility and currency convergence, geography and economics must be discussed together. By adopting such an integrated approach, this book is somewhat different to many of the urban and regional economics undergraduate textbooks currently available. Urban economics books often tend to focus their discussions at the level of the individual urban area, with the object of their analysis being the urban land market. The explicitly spatial economic analysis generally takes place within the context of the individual urban area, and the analysis tends to be entirely microeconomic. The implications of the local urban economic phenomena for other cities and areas are often ignored. Regional economics texts, on the other hand, often tend to underplay the spatial aspects of economic behaviour, and instead adopt more of a macroeconomic approach to regional behaviour. Yet this approach ignores both the spatial microeconomic foundations of regional behaviour, and also the effects of urban economic behaviour on the wider regional economies. The logic of this book is therefore to overcome many of the limitations of existing textbooks by adopting both microeconomic and macroeconomic approaches to the discussions of both urban and regional economies, within an explicitly spatial framework.

This book is aimed specifically at intermediate-level students, such as third- or fourth-year under-graduates or first-year postgraduates. The book is also written as a textbook which is accessible to a wide range of students from economics, business and management, urban planning or geography. The only requirement in order for a student to read this book comfortably is that he/she must have taken introductory micro- and macroeconomics classes. All the material in the book is explained with the aid of numerous diagrams and tables, and each of the topics can be understood simply by reading the main text alone and following the diagrams carefully. For more advanced students, mathematical appendices to each chapter provide formal proofs of the key conclusions of each chapter. These appendices will be particularly appropriate for economics students or for postgraduate students of all disciplines studying urban and regional economics for the first time. The overall intention of this book is therefore to introduce the study of urban and regional economics to a wide range of students. Those students who continue on to postgraduate work will subsequently be equipped to read more advanced material. Alternatively, those students who progress into employment positions that involve economic analysis and decision-making will be better able to understand the spatial impacts of their decisions.

Part I

Urban and Regional Economic Models and Methods

Industrial location: the location of the firm in theory

1.1 Introduction

In this chapter we introduce the basic building blocks of firm location theory. The models are introduced and explained primarily by means of diagrams, with mathematic treatment reserved largely for the appendices. We begin by a providing detailed analysis of the Weber (1909) model, in many ways the fundamental building blocks of microeconomic firm locational analysis, which is constructed in the context of fixed production factor relationships. The chapter then extends the Weber approach by examining the insights derived from the Moses (1958) model, which deals with issues of input factor substitution. Additional location production models are also discussed, including the concept of extension of distance costs from simply that of transport costs to total logistics costs, which incorporates the costs associated with time and the frequency of interaction. Taken together, these location-production models allow us to uncover some general analytical insights regarding the interactions between location and production behaviour. The chapter then moves on to consider how the geography and spatial delineation of a market influences firm location choices. A detailed analysis of the Hotelling (1929) model demonstrates that location behaviour and firm strategy are intertwined, and that the nature of this relationship also depends on the market pricing structures possible. Price competition and spatial clustering are seen to be largely incompatible under various situations, due to the risks associated with price wars. Possible solutions to these problems emerge from both the Hotelling (1929) model and the more general Salop (1979) model and centre on the role played by non-price competition behaviour. In particular, product variety and product quality competition are found to offer reasons why firm clustering is widely observed.

1.2 Classical and neoclassical models of location

The level of output and activity of an area depends on the total quantities of factor inputs employed in the area, and the wealth of an area depends on the total payments received by those factors. Observation suggests that some regions exhibit dense concentrations of factors, with large numbers of people and investment located in the same area, whereas other regions exhibit sparse populations and low levels of investment. At the same time, observation also suggests that people are paid different wages in different areas, while land prices vary significantly between locations. Therefore, in order to understand the economic performance of a region it is necessary to understand why particular quantities of factors are employed in that area, and why the factors there earn the particular rewards that they do.

Production factor inputs are usually defined in terms of three broad types, namely capital, labour, and land, and the factor payments earned by these factors in the production process are profits, wages, and rents, respectively. In some analyses of the production process, additional factor inputs are also identified, such as entrepreneurship and technology. However, in our initial discussion of the causes and reasons for particular types of industrial location behaviour, we will not initially distinguish these additional factors from the broad factor groups. We include entrepreneurship in our description of labour, and technology in our description of capital. Later in our discussion of the causes and reasons for particular types of industrial location behaviour, we will also investigate the additional issues associated with entrepreneurship and technology. In this chapter we will concentrate on the determinants of spatial variations in capital investment, and in later sections of the book we will focus on spatial variations in labour stocks, and variations in land prices.

We start our analysis by asking the question: what determines the level and type of capital invested in a particular region? When talking about capital, our most basic unit of microeconomic analysis is the capital embodied in the firm. In order to understand the level of capital investment in an area it is necessary to ask why particular firms are located there and why the particular levels and types of investment in the area are as they are. These are the questions addressed by industrial location theory. We begin by discussing three classical and neoclassical models of industrial location behaviour, namely the Weber model, the Moses model, and the Hotelling model. Each of these models provides us with different insights into the fundamental reasons for, and the consequences of, industrial location behaviour. After analysing each of these models in detail, we will discuss two alternative approaches to analysing industrial location behaviour, namely the behavioural approach and the evolutionary approach. A broad understanding of these various approaches to industrial location behaviour will then allow us to discuss the concept of agglomeration economies.

1.2.1 The Weber location-production model

Our starting point is to adopt the approach to industrial locational analysis originally derived from the nineteenth-century German mathematician Laundhart (1885), but which was formalized and publicized beyond Germany by Alfred Weber (1909). For our analysis to proceed we assume that the firm is defined at a point in space; the firm is therefore viewed as a single establishment. We also adopt the standard microeconomic assumption that the firm aims to maximize its profits. Assuming the profit-maximizing rationale for the firm, the question of where a firm will locate therefore becomes the question of at which location a firm will maximize its profits. In order to answer this question we will begin by using the simplest two-dimensional spatial figure, namely a triangle. This very simple type of two-dimensional approach will subsequently be extended to more general spatial forms.

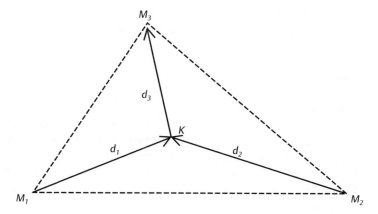

Figure 1.1 Weber location-production triangle

The model described by Figure 1.1 is often described as a Weber location-production triangle, in which case the firm consumes two inputs in order to produce a single output.
Notation for use with Figures 1.1 to 1.12.

d_1, d_2 distance travelled by input goods 1 and 2, respectively, to the firm at k

d_3 distance travelled by the output produced by the firm to the market

m_1, m_2 weight (tons) of material of input goods 1 and 2 consumed by the firm

m_3 weight of output good 3 produced by the firm

p_1, p_2 prices per ton of the input goods 1 and 2 at their points of production

p_3 price per ton of the output good 3 at the market location

M_1, M_2 production locations of input goods 1 and 2

M_3 market location for the output good 3

t_1, t_2 transport rates per ton-mile (or per ton-kilometre) for hauling input goods 1 and 2

t_3 transport rates per ton-mile (or per ton-kilometre) for hauling output goods 3

K the location of the firm

We assume that the firm consumes material inputs 1 and 2, which are then combined by the firm in order to produce an output commodity 3. In the Weber location-production model, we assume that the coefficients of production are fixed, in that there is a fixed relationship between the quantities of each input required in order to produce a single unit of the output. Our production function therefore takes the general form

$$m_3 = f(k_1 m_1, k_2 m_2) \tag{1.1}$$

In the very simplest case $k_1 = k_2 = 1$, in which case our production function becomes

$$m_3 = f(m_1, m_2) \tag{1.2}$$

This represents a situation where the quantity of the output good 3 produced is equal to the combined weight of the inputs 1 and 2. In other words, for the purposes of our analysis here, we can rewrite (1.2) as

$$m_3 = m_1 + m_2 \tag{1.3}$$

The production locations of the input sources of 1 and 2, defined as M_1 and M_2, are given, as is the location of the output market M_3, at which output good 3 is sold. The prices per ton of the inputs 1 and 2 are given as p_1 and p_2, at the points of production M_1 and M_2, respectively. The price per ton of the output good 3 at the market location M_3 is given as p_3. As such, the firm is a price taker. Moreover, we assume that the firm is able to sell unlimited quantities of output 3 at the given price p_3, as in perfect competition. The transport rates are given as t_1, t_2, and t_3, and these transport rates represent the costs of transporting one ton of each commodity 1, 2, and 3, respectively, over one mile or one kilometre. Finally, the distances d_1, d_2, and d_3 represent the distances over which each of the goods 1, 2, and 3 are shipped.

We also assume that the input production factors of labour and capital are freely available everywhere at factor prices and qualities that do not change with location, and that land is homogeneous. In other words, the price and quality of labour is assumed to be equal everywhere, as is the cost and quality of capital, and the quality and rental price of land. However, there is no reason to suppose that the prices of labour, capital, and land are equal to each other. We simply assume that all locations exhibit the same attributes in terms of their production factor availability. Space is therefore assumed to be homogeneous.

If the firm is able to locate anywhere, then assuming the firm is rational, the firm will locate at whichever location it can earn maximum profits. Given that the prices of all the input and output goods are exogenously set, and the prices of production factors are invariant with respect to space, the only issue which will alter the relative profitability of different locations is the distance of any particular location from the input source and output market points. The reason for this is that different locations will incur different costs of transporting inputs from their production points to the location of the firm, and outputs from the location of the firm to the market point.

If the price per unit of output p_3 is fixed, the location that ensures maximum profits are earned by the firm is the location at which the total input plus output transport costs are minimized, *ceteris paribus*. This is known as the *Weber optimum location*. Finding the Weber optimum location involves comparing the relative total input plus output transport costs at each location. The Weber optimum location, will be the particular location at which the sum (*TC*) of these costs is minimized. The cost condition that determines the Weber optimum location can be described as

$$TC = Min \sum_{t=1}^{3} m_i t_i d_i \tag{1.4}$$

where the subscript i refers to the particular weights, transport rates, and distances over which goods are shipped to and from each location point K. With actual values corresponding to each of the spatial and non-spatial parameters, it is possible to calculate the total production plus transportation costs incurred by the firm associated with being at any arbitrary location K. Given our assumptions that the firm will behave so as to maximize its profits, the minimum cost location will be the actual chosen location of the firm.

In his original analysis Weber characterized the problem of the optimum location in terms of a mechanical analogy. He described a two-dimensional triangular system of pulleys with weights called a Varignon Frame. In this system, the locations of the pulleys reflect the locations of input source and output market points, and the weights attached to each string passing over each of the pulleys correspond to the transport costs associated with each shipment. The point at which the strings are all knotted together represents the location of the firm. In some case, the knot will settle at a location inside the triangle, whereas in other cases the knot will settle at one of the corners. This suggests that the optimum location will sometimes be inside the Weber triangle, whereas in other cases the optimum location will be at one of the corners. Nowadays, rather than using such mechanical devices, the optimum location can be calculated using computers. However, although it is always possible to calculate the optimum location of the firm in each particular case, of interest to us here is to understand how the location of the Weber optimum will itself be affected by the levels of, and changes in, any of the parameters described above. In order to explain this, we adopt a hypothetical example.

1.2.2 The location effect of input transport costs

Let us imagine that Figure 1.1 represents a firm that produces automobiles from inputs of steel and plastic. The output good 3 is defined as automobiles and these are sold at the market point M_3. We can assume that input 1 is steel and input 2 is plastic, and these are produced at locations M_1 and M_2, respectively. If the firm produces a car weighing 2 tons from 1 ton of steel and 1 ton of plastic, and the fixed transport rate for steel t_1 is half that for plastic t_2 (given that plastic is much less dense than steel, and transport rates are normally charged with respect to product bulk), the firm will locate relatively close to the source of the plastic production. In other words, the firm will locate close to M_2. The reason is that the firm will wish to reduce the higher total transport costs associated with shipping plastic inputs relative to steel inputs, *ceteris paribus*. The firm can do this by reducing the value of d_2 relative to d_1. On the other hand, if the firm has a different production function, such that it produces a car weighing 2 tons from 1.5 tons of steel and 0.5 tons of plastic, then even with the same values for the fixed transport rates t_1 and t_2 as in the previous case, the firm will now be incurring higher total transport costs associated with steel shipments, *ceteris paribus*. The reason for this is that although plastic is twice as expensive to ship per kilometre as steel, the total quantity of steel being shipped is three times that of plastic. The result is that the firm can reduce its total input transport costs by reducing the value of d_1 relative to d_2. The optimum location of the firm will now tend towards the location of production for the steel input M_1.

Within this Weber framework, we can compare the effects of different production function relationships on the location behaviour of the firm. For example, we can imagine that the two types of production function relationships described above, one which is relatively plastic intensive, and one which is relatively steel intensive, actually refer to the different production functions exhibited by two different competing automobile producers. Firm A

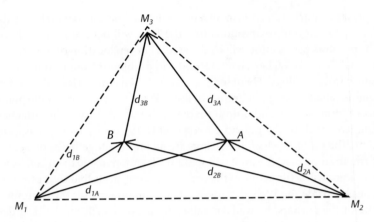

Figure 1.2 Relative input transport costs and location

exhibits the plastic-intensive production function, and firm B exhibits the steel-intensive production function. As we see in Figure 1.2, from the argument above we know that firm A will locate relatively close to M_2, the source of plastic, while firm B will locate relatively close to M_1, the source of steel. This is because, if we were to consider the case where steel and plastic inputs were shipped over identical distances, i.e. $d_{1A} = d_{2A}$, for firm A the total transport costs associated with plastic transportation would be greater than those associated with steel transportation. It therefore has an incentive to reduce the higher costs associated with plastic shipments by reducing d_{2A} and increasing d_{1B}. Alternatively, for firm B, for identical input shipment distances, i.e. $d_{1B} = d_{2B}$, the total transport costs associated with steel transportation would be greater than those associated with plastic transportation. It therefore has an incentive to reduce the higher transport costs associated with steel by reducing d_{1B} and increasing d_{2B}.

1.2.3 The location effect of output transport costs

Until now we have only considered the transport cost pull of the input sources on the location decision of the firm. However, the market itself will display a pull effect on the location behaviour of the firm. We can imagine the case of a power-generating plant which burns coal and coke, produced at M_1 and M_2, respectively, in order to produce electricity. We can regard the output of the plant as having zero weight or bulk. The output transportation costs of shipping electricity can be regarded as effectively zero, given that the only costs associated with distance will be the negligible costs of booster stations. In this case, the market point of the plant, whether it is a city or a region, will play no role in the decision of where to locate the plant. As such, the optimal location of the plant will be somewhere along the line joining M_1 and M_2. The optimal location problem therefore becomes a one-dimensional location problem. A discussion of this type of problem is given in Appendix 1.1.

In most situations, however, the output of the firm is costly to transport due to the weight and bulk of the output product. Different output weight and bulk will affect the

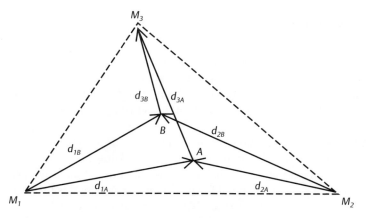

Figure 1.3 Relative output transport costs and location

optimum location of the firm relative to the location of the market and the inputs. Once again, we can illustrate this point by using our hypothetical example above of two automobile producer firms, A and B, each consuming inputs of steel and plastic. However, in this case we can imagine a situation where the input production functions of both firms are the same. In other words, the relative input combinations for each firm, given as m_1/m_1, are the same. If both firms pay the same respective transport rates t_1 and t_2 for each input shipped, the relative locational pull of each input will be identical for each firm. However, in this situation we also assume that the firms differ in terms of their technical efficiency, in that firm A discards 70 per cent of the inputs during the production process, whereas firm B discards only 40 per cent of the inputs during the production process. Consequently, the total output weight m_3 of firm B is twice as great as that of firm A, for any total weight of inputs consumed. This greater output weight will encourage firm B to move closer towards the market point and further away from the inputs points than firm A. As seen in Figure 1.3, firm B will therefore be more market oriented than firm A in its location behaviour.

A more common situation in which similar firms exhibit different location behaviour with respect to the market is where the density of the product changes through the production process at different rates for each of the producers. For example, we can imagine our two automobile firms A and B producing identical weights of output from identical total weights of inputs. Here, the production functions of both firms are therefore the same. However, we can also assume that firm A specializes in the production of small vehicles suited to urban traffic, while firm B produces large four-wheel-drive vehicles suitable for rough terrain. As we have already seen, transport rates also depend on the bulk of the product, and products which have a high density will exhibit lower unit transport costs than products with a low density. In this situation firm B produces goods which are very bulky, whereas firm A produces goods which are relatively dense. Therefore the output of firm B will be more expensive to transport than that of firm A, and this will encourage firm B to move closer to the market than firm A. Once again, as seen in Figure 1.3, firm B will be more market oriented than firm A.

1.2.4 **The location effect of varying factor prices**

Our analysis so far has proceeded on the assumption that labour and land prices are identical across all locations, although in reality we know that factor prices vary significantly over space. The Weber approach also allows us to consider how factor price variations across space will affect the location behaviour of the firm. In order to understand this, it is necessary for us to identify the factor price conditions under which a firm will look for alternative locations.

We assume that the firm is still consuming inputs from M_1 and M_2 and producing an output for the market at M_3. Under these conditions, we know that the Weber optimum K^* is the minimum transport cost location of the firm, and that if all factor prices are equal across space this will be the location of the firm. Our starting point is therefore to consider the factor price variations, relative to the Weber optimum K^* which will encourage a firm to move elsewhere. In order to do this, it is first necessary for us to construct a contour map on our Weber triangle, as described by Figure 1.3. These contours are known as *isodapanes*.

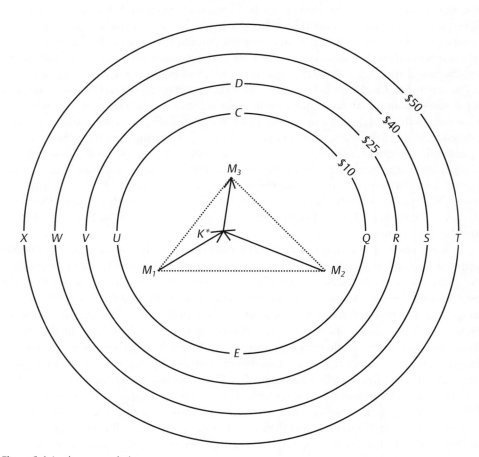

Figure 1.4 Isodapane analysis

On a standard geographical map each contour links all the locations with the same altitude. On the other hand, each isodapane contour in a Weber map links all the locations which exhibit the same increase in total input plus output transport costs, per unit of output m_3 produced, relative to the Weber optimum location K^*. Increasing isodapanes therefore reflect increased total input plus output transport costs, per unit of output m_3 produced, relative to the Weber optimum K^*. As the location of the firm moves away from the Weber optimum in any direction, the firm incurs increasing transport costs relative to the Weber optimum. In other words, the locations become less and less efficient, and the firm exhibits successively lower profits, *ceteris paribus*. We can also say that the firm incurs successively greater opportunity costs as it moves further away from the Weber optimum. If factor prices are equal across space, locations further away from the Weber optimum will become successively less desirable locations for investment. Therefore we need to ask by how much do *local* factor prices need to fall relative to the Weber optimum location K^* in order for the firm to move there?

If we take the case of location R, we can ask by how much factor prices at R need to fall relative to the Weber optimum K^* in order for the firm to move from K^* to R. As we see from Figure 1.4, R is on the $25 isodapanes. If the costs of the labour and land factor inputs required to produce one unit of output m_3 at R are $20 less than at K^*, it will not be in the interests of the firm to move from K^* to R. The reason is that the fall in local factor input prices associated with a move from K^* to R will not be sufficient to compensate for the increased total transport costs as we move away from the Weber optimum. If the firm were to move from K^* to R under these circumstances, it would experience profits which were $5 unit of output m_3 less than at K^*. On the other hand, if the local labour and land prices per unit of output as R are $30 less than at K^*, it will be in the interest of the firm to move. This is because the reduction in the local input factor costs associated with a move from K^* to R will now more than compensate for the increase in total transportation costs incurred by the move. If the firm were to move from K^* to R under these circumstances, it would experience profits which were $5 per unit of output m_3 greater than at K^*. This type of analysis can be applied to any alternative locations, such as Q, R, S, and T, in order to determine whether a firm should move and to which location.

For example, location Q is on the $10 isodapane, R is on the $25 isodapane, S is on the $40 isodapane, and T is on the $50 isodapane. Let us assume that the costs of the labour and land factor inputs required to produce one unit of output m_3, at Q, R, S, and T, are less than the factor costs at K^* by amounts of $12, $20, $35, and $55, respectively. We can determine that the alternative locations Q and T are superior locations to K^*, in that both will provide greater profits than K^*, whereas R and S are inferior locations in that they exhibit reduced profits relative to K^*. However, of these superior alternatives, T is the better location because profits here are $5 per unit of output greater than at K^*, whereas those at Q are only $2 greater. With this particular spatial distribution of local labour and land prices, location T is the optimum location of the firm. T is a superior location to the Weber optimum location at which total transport costs were minimized because the lower local factor input prices more than compensate for the increased total transport costs associated with the location of T.

This type of approach also allows us to ask and answer a very important question; how will local wages and land prices have to vary over space in order for the firm's profits to be the same for all locations? This can be analysed by modifying Figure 1.4. We can construct Figure 1.5 by employing Figure 1.4, but then altering it by drawing a line from K^* eastwards

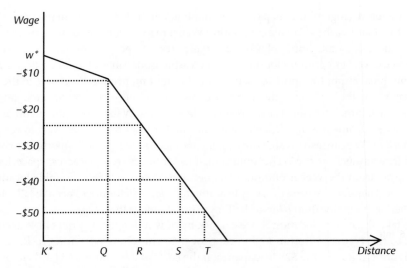

Figure 1.5 Distance-isodapane equilibrium labour prices

which passes through Q, R, S, T. This line is defined in terms of geographical distance. We can then observe how the isodapanes intercept this line.

From the above example, we know that location Q is on the $10 isodapane, R is on the $25 isodapane, S is on the $40 isodapane, and T is on the $50 isodapane. The firm's profits will be the same in all locations if the local labour and land factor input prices at each location exactly compensate for the increased total transport costs associated with each location. Therefore in Figure 1.5 this allows us to plot the labour and land price gradient with respect to distance, which ensures equal profits are made at all locations east of K^*, assuming the wage at K^* is w^*. We can repeat the exercise by drawing a line from K^* which passes west through U, V, W, and X, and plotting the local factor prices which will ensure the firm makes profits equal to at K^* at all locations west of K^*. Combining this information allows us to construct the interregional factor price curve for our particular firm which ensures that it makes equal profits at all locations in the east–west direction. This is shown in Figure 1.6.

This slope of the line is the interregional *equilibrium* factor price gradient for this particular firm along this particular axis. This equilibrium factor price gradient describes the variation in local factor prices, which ensures that the firm will be *indifferent* between locations. The firm is indifferent between locations along the east–west line because the profits it can earn are the same everywhere along this line. As such, from the point of view of this firm, all locations along the east–west line are *perfect substitutes* for each other.

In principle, we can also construct similar factor price gradients for movements in any other direction away from K^*, such as movements passing through locations C, D or E, in order to generate a two-dimensional equilibrium factor price map of the whole spatial economy.

The idea that locations can be perfect substitutes for each other, from the point of view of a firm's profitability, is important in terms of understanding the spatial patterns of industrial

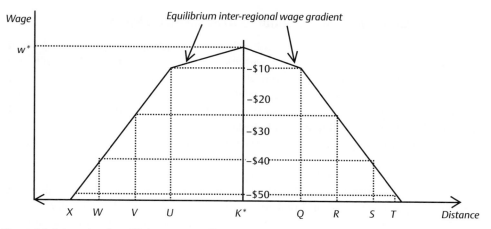

Figure 1.6 Interregional equilibrium wage gradient

investment. For example, if a multinational manufacturing firm is looking for a new production site in order to develop its business in a new area, the likelihood of it going to any particular location will depend on the firm's estimate of the profits it can earn at that location. From the isodapane analysis of our Weber location-production model here, we know that the locations of key input sources such as M_1 and M_2, and market points such as M_3, will automatically mean that some locations are more profitable than others, with the Weber optimum being the most profitable location, *ceteris paribus*. Therefore, in order to make other locations attractive for investment, local factor prices have to fall relative to the Weber optimum. The attractiveness of any particular location as a new investment location for the firm will depend on the extent to which the local factor price falls can compensate for the increased transport (opportunity) costs associated with any suboptimal geographical location. If all local factor prices are interregional equilibrium prices, as described by Figure 1.6, the firm will be indifferent between locations. Under these circumstances, the firm will be equally likely to build its new production facility at any location. In other words, the probability of investment will be equal for all locations. Over large numbers of firms with similar input requirements and similar output markets to this particular firm, the level of investment in any location should be the same as in all locations. On the other hand, if wages are not in equilibrium over space, certain areas will automatically appear more attractive as locations for investment, thereby increasing the probability of investment there.

Geography confers different competitive advantages on different locations, which can only be compensated for by variations in local factor prices. However, in the above example, the equilibrium relationship between local factor prices and distance was only applicable to the particular firm in question here. This is because the interregional factor price gradient was calculated with respect to the Weber optimum of this particular firm. As we have seen, different firms will exhibit different Weber optimum locations, and this implies that different equilibrium interregional factor price gradients will exist for different types of firms exhibiting different transport costs, different production functions, and, finally, different input and output locations.

1.2.5 The location effect of new input sources and new markets

Our analysis has so far discussed the locational effect of different transport costs, different production functions, and the resulting conditions under which a firm will be willing to move to alternative locations. We will now discuss the question of different input and output locations and the conditions under which a firm will search for alternatives. In the examples above, it was possible to use isodapane analysis to identify the factor price conditions under which a firm will move from one location to another. However, this process of movement itself may engender changes in the input sources employed and the output markets served.

In Figure 1.7 we can consider the situation where the firm relocates from K^* to F in response to the lower factor prices at F, which more than compensate for the additional input and output transport costs involving in consuming steel and plastic inputs from M_1 and M_2, and serving a market at M_3. Location F has therefore been determined as the new optimum location with respect to M_1, M_2, and M_3. However, in moving from K^* to F, it may be that alternative suppliers of identical inputs now become available. For example, the

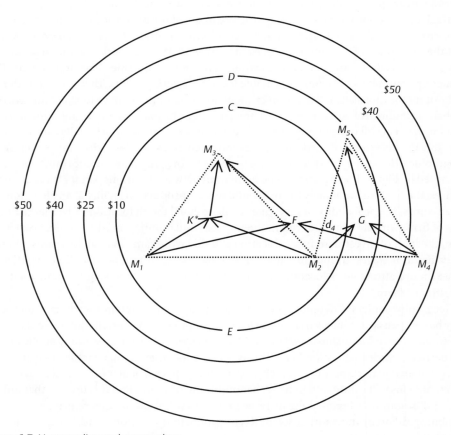

Figure 1.7 New suppliers and new markets

input supply location M_4 may be able to supply exactly the same steel input as M_1 but from a location whose distance from M_4 to F, which we denote as d_4, is now much smaller than the distance d_1 from M_1 to F. Assuming the delivered price at location F of the steel input produced at M_4 is less than that of the input produced at M_1, i.e. $(p_4 + t_4 d_4) < (p_1 + t_1 d_1)$, the firm will substitute input supplier M_4 for M_1. This will produce a new Weber location-production problem, with the points M_4, M_2, and M_3 as the spatial reference points. This change in input suppliers will also imply that a new Weber optimum can be found, and that a new series of equilibrium local factor input prices can be calculated with respect to the new Weber optimum location.

With the points M_4, M_2, and M_3 as the spatial reference points, the new Weber optimum is G. At point G, it becomes advantageous for the firm to serve market point M_5, rather than M_3. This is because M_5 is nearer to G than M_3, and $(p_5 - t_5 d_5) > (p_3 - t_3 d_3)$. Therefore the firm makes a greater profit from selling automobiles to market M_5 than to market M_3. The firm could switch markets completely from M_3 M_5. Alternatively, it could decide to supply both markets M_3 and M_5. Under these conditions, it may be that a new optimum location of H arises, in which the firm at H buys from two supplier locations M_4 to M_2, and sells at two market locations, M_3 and M_5. More complex arrangements are possible. For example, in order to guarantee sufficient supplies of steel inputs for the newly expanded automobile market of $(M_3 + M_5)$, the firm may decide to continue to purchase steel from both M_1 and M_4, as well as purchasing plastic from M_2. Now we have a Weber location-production problem with M_1, M_2, M_3, M_4, and M_5 as spatial reference points. Once again, this will move the Weber optimum away from point H, and will also alter the interregional equilibrium wage gradient.

This type of geometrical arrangement, in which a firm has multiple input sources and multiple output market locations, is the norm for firms in reality. Although our analysis here has been developed primarily with only two input source locations and one output market location, the Weber location-production arguments and the associated isodapane analysis are perfectly applicable to the case of firms with multiple input and output locations. The reason for employing the triangular case of the two input locations and one output market location is that this particular spatial structure is simply the easiest two-dimensional model to explain. The model is designed to help us understand the advantages which geography confers on particular locations as sites for investment. A first key feature of the Weber model is therefore that it allows us to understand the factor price conditions under which other areas will become more attractive as locations for investment. Secondly, the model allows us to see location as an evolutionary process, in which changes in factor prices can engender changes in location behaviour, which themselves can change the supply linkages between suppliers, firms, and markets. Industrial location problems are inherently evolutionary in their nature as firms respond to new markets and products by changing their locations, and by changing the people they buy from and the people they sell to. All of these are spatial issues.

There is one final issue relating to the Weber model which needs to be addressed. In reality, firms are constantly changing their input suppliers and output markets in response to changes in input and output market prices. From our Weber analysis, these changes will also imply that the optimum location of the firm is continuously changing, and that in order to ensure the profitability of any particular location the equilibrium interregional factor price gradient must also be continuously changing. However, observation tells us that firms in reality do not move very frequently, and this raises the question of the extent to which the Weber model is a useful analytical tool to describe industrial location behaviour.

The reason why firms are not continuously moving is that the relocation process itself usually incurs very significant costs, such as the dismantling of equipment, the moving of people, and the hiring of new staff. Part of the transactions costs associated with relocation are also related to information and uncertainty, which are topics we will deal with later in the chapter. However, within the above framework we can easily incorporate these relocation costs by including the annualized cost of these one-off relocation costs into our isodapane model. The existence of these additional costs simply implies that firms will only move when the factor cost advantages of alternative locations also compensate for these additional relocation costs as well as the increased transport costs. In other words, the equilibrium interregional wage gradient will be even steeper than under the situation where such costs are negligible. The Weber model therefore still allows us to identify the optimum location, and consequently the profit-maximizing behaviour of the firm in space, even in situations where relocation costs are significant. The observation that firms do not move frequently does not limit the applicability of the Weber model to real-world phenomena.

The one major location issue which the Weber model does not address is that of the relationship between input substitution and location behaviour. In order to understand this relationship, we now turn to a discussion of the Moses location-production model.

1.3 The Moses location-production model

The Weber model assumes that the quantities of each input consumed, m_1 and m_2, are fixed per unit of output m_3 produced. However, we know from standard microeconomic analysis that substitution is a characteristic feature of firm behaviour, and that efficiency conditions mean that firms will substitute in favour of relatively cheaper inputs, *ceteris paribus*. Substitution behaviour was first incorporated coherently into the Weber analysis by Moses (1958), and in order to see how substitution behaviour affects the location behaviour of the firm, we discuss here the main features and conclusions of the Moses approach.

In Figure 1.8, we construct an arc IJ in our triangle M_1, M_2, M_3, which is at a constant distance d_3 from the market point M_3. If we constrain our firm to locate along this arc, the distance from the location of the firm K to the market M_3 will no longer be a variable. Therefore we can analyse the locational pull on the firm of changes only in the delivered prices of the inputs produced at M_1 and M_2.

For example, if the firm is located at I, the delivered price of input 1, given as $(p_1 + t_1 d_1)$, will be a minimum, because the distance d_1, from M_1 to I, will be a minimum. Similarly, the delivered price of input 2, given as $(p_2 + t_2 d_2)$, will be a maximum, because the distance d_2, from M_2 to I, will be a maximum. The delivered price ratio, given as $(p_1 + t_1 d_1)/(p_2 + t_2 d_2)$, will therefore be a minimum at location I. On the other hand, if the firm now moves to J, the delivered price of input 1 will be a maximum, because the distance d_1, from M_1 to J, will be a maximum. At the same time, the delivered price of input 2 will be a minimum, because the distance d_2, from M_2 to I, will be a minimum. Therefore the delivered price ratio, $(p_1 + t_1 d_1)/(p_2 + t_2 d_2)$, will be a maximum at location J.

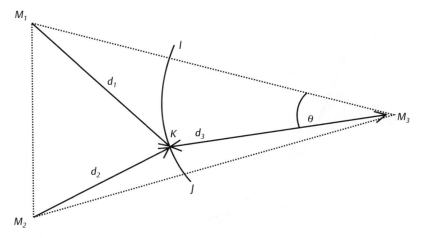

Figure 1.8 Weber–Moses triangle

In standard microeconomic approaches to firm efficiency, the optimal input combination is determined by finding the point at which the highest isoquant attainable is tangent to the budget constraint. In this standard approach, the slope of the budget constraint is determined by the relative prices of the goods. From the above argument, we can draw the budget constraints at locations I and J as shown in Figure 1.9, which represent equal total expenditure on inputs at each location. The delivered price ratios at locations I and J are given by the ratio of the tangents of the angles α_I/β_I and α_J/β_J, respectively.

Yet this argument is also applicable to all locations along the arc IJ. If there are different delivered price ratios for different locations, this implies that for given source prices of the

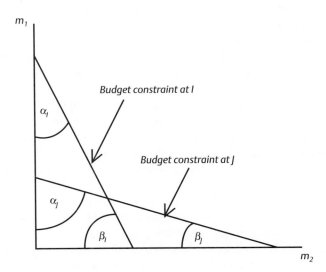

Figure 1.9 Budget constraints at the end points I and J

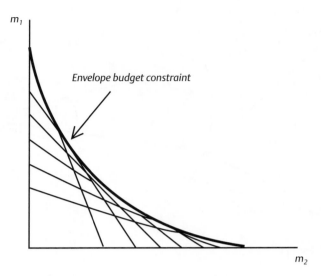

Figure 1.10 The envelope budget constraint

inputs p_1 and p_2, the slope of the budget constraints at each location along IJ must be different. As we move along the arc IJ from I to J, the delivered price ratio increases, and for every location along the arc IJ there is a unique delivered price ratio. This means that the usual approach to analysing microeconomic efficiency is not applicable to the firm in space, and must be adapted to incorporate the effects of location on the slope of the budget constraint. In order to do this we must construct the *envelope* budget constraint, which just contains all of the budget constraints associated with each of the locations along the arc IJ. This is done by drawing each of the budget constraints for each of the location points on the arc IJ, as in Figure 1.10, and the outer limits of this set of individual budget constraints will define the envelope budget constraint.

The Moses argument is that we can now apply standard efficiency conditions to this model by finding the point at which the envelope budget constraint is tangent to the highest isoquant attainable. This is shown in Figure 1.11, where the point of maximum efficiency is at $E^\star$.

At $E^\star$, the optimum input combinations are given as $m_1^\star$ and $m_2^\star$. However, $E^\star$ also represents an *optimum location* $K^\star$. The reason is that the optimum input combination is found at a particular point on the envelope budget constraint. Yet every point on the budget constraint also represents a unique location. Therefore the optimum input mix and the optimum location of the firm are always jointly determined. One is never without the other. This is a profound insight. Where input substitution is possible, all location problems become production problems and all production problems become location problems.

We can illustrate the argument with an example. In our Weber–Moses triangle, we can imagine that a road building programme takes place in the area around location M_1, the effect of which is generally to reduce the value of t_1 for all shipments of goods from this location, relative to all other locations. If all the other parameters remain constant, this will imply that the delivered price ratio $(p_1 + t_1 d_1)/(p_2 + t_2 d_2)$, at all locations along IJ, will fall.

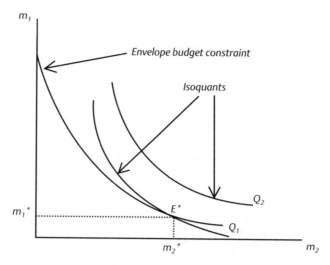

Figure 1.11 Location-production optimum

In other words, the slope of each budget constraint becomes steeper, *ceteris paribus*, and the envelope budget constraint also becomes steeper and shifts upwards to the left. Strictly speaking, in accordance with the income effect, the envelope will also shift outwards to the right, because the price of the input has fallen. However, in this discussion we focus only on the substitution effect of the change in slope of the envelope. For a given set of production isoquants, the optimum production combination will change from that represented by E^*.

As we see in Figure 1.12, at the new optimum E', the optimum input mix is now m_1' and m_2'. The reason is that the firm substitutes in favour of input 1, which is now relatively cheaper than before, and away from input 2, which is now relatively more expensive than before. In doing so, the firm increases the relative quantities of input 1 it consumes and reduces the relative quantities of input 2 it consumes. However, this also implies that at the original location K^*, the firm now incurs increasing total transport costs ($m_1t_1d_1$) for input 1 relative to the total transport costs ($m_2t_2d_2$) for input 2. Therefore the firm will move towards M_1, the source of input 1, in order to reduce these costs. The new optimum location of the firm K' is closer to M_1 than E^*, and so the firm moves towards M_1.

The area around M_1 benefits in two different ways. First, the relative quantity of goods produced by the area around M_1 which is purchased by the firm increases. This increases regional output for the area. Second, the firm itself locates in the vicinity of M_1, thereby increasing the levels of industrial investment in the area.

Exactly the same result would have arisen in the case where, instead of a road building programme, there had been a fall in the local wages at M_1, which reduced the source price p_1, relative to all other locations. Once again, the fall in the delivered price ratio at all locations leads to substitution in favour of the cheaper good and also relocation towards M_1.

We can contrast this Moses result with that of the Weber model. In the simple Weber model, if the transport rate t_1 falls, *ceteris paribus*, the effect on the location of the firm is to move the locational optimum *away* from M_1. The reason is that input 2 now becomes relatively more expensive to transport, and because the coefficients of production are fixed,

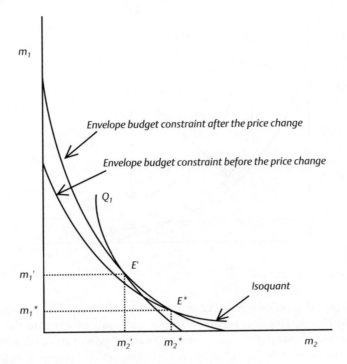

Figure 1.12 A change in the location-production optimum

such that the relative quantities of m_1 and m_2 consumed remain the same, the firm will move towards the source of input 2 in order to reduce the total transport costs. The difference between the location-production results of the two models is that in the Weber model the fixed coefficients mean that no input substitution is possible, whereas in the Moses model of variable coefficients, input substitution is possible. In the latter case, the input substitution behaviour alters the relative total transport costs and consequently the optimum location behaviour of the firm. In reality, there is a continuum of possible location effects, dependent on the technical substitution possibilities. In situations where the elasticities of substitution are zero or very low, the results will tend to mimic those of the Weber model, whereas in situations where the elasticities of substitution are high, the results will tend towards those produced by the conclusions of the Moses model.

A second feature of the Moses model is that it allows us to examine the effect of returns to scale on the location-production behaviour of the firm. In particular, we can ask: how will the optimum location of the firm be affected by changes in the level of output of the firm? In order to answer this, in Figure 1.13 we construct a series of envelope budget constraints, represented by the dotted lines, which correspond to different levels of total expenditure on inputs. Envelope budget constraints further to the right imply greater total expenditure levels on inputs. An isoquant map, represented by the solid curves, can now be combined with the envelope map. We can also apply the Moses argument, which states that the optimum point for each level of output and input expenditure is where each particular envelope is tangent to the highest isoquant, to the case of different output levels. By joining all the

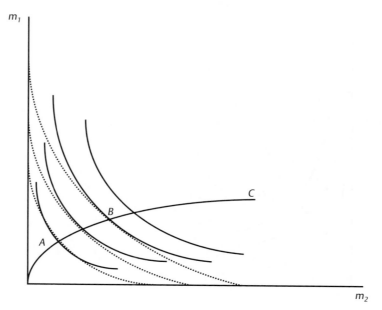

Figure 1.13 Output changes and location-production behaviour

points of tangency we construct a line *ABC*, which is an output expansion path. Yet this output expansion path is different from the usual form of an expansion path. Each point on the expansion path defines a particular optimum input combination. However, each point on the expansion path also defines an optimum location.

If the expansion path is curved downward, such as in the case of *ABC* in Figure 1.13, it implies that, as the output of the firm increases, and the total quantity of inputs consumed increases, the optimum input mix changes relatively in favour of input 2. The optimum ratio of m_1/m_2 falls and the optimum location of the firm moves towards M_2. Alternatively, if the expansion path were to curve upwards, this would mean that as the output of the firm increased, the optimum input combination would change in favour of input 1. As the optimum ratio of m_1/m_2 increases, the optimum location of the firm would move towards the market for m_1.

This argument immediately leads to the conclusion that if the expansion path is a straight line from the origin, such as *FGH* in Figure 1.14, both the optimum input mix and also the optimum location of the firm will remain constant as output expands, *ceteris paribus*. The actual slope of the expansion path is not important, except that it implies a different optimum location. All that is required to ensure that, once the firm has found its optimum location it will always remain at this optimum location as output changes, is that the production function of the firm exhibits a straight line expansion path from the origin. This is the basic Moses result.

This basic Moses result holds in the case where the firm is constrained to locate on the arc *IJ* at a fixed distance from the market. However, in the more general case where the distance from the market is also part of the location problem, the optimum location of the firm will be independent of the level of output, as long as both the production function of the firm

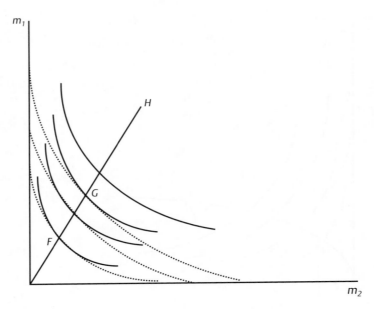

Figure 1.14 The independent of output optimum location solution

and the transportation technology of the firm exhibit constant returns to scale. The Weber fixed-coefficients production function will satisfy the Moses requirement. However, there are other more general types of production function allowing for input substitution, which also satisfy this requirement. These results are detailed in Appendix 1.2.

The Moses result can be viewed somewhat as the spatial equivalent of the firm in perfect competition. The firm is a price taker, and once it has determined its optimum production technique and optimum location, the firm will not change its behaviour, *ceteris paribus*. In other words, unless there are external changes in technology which alter the production function relationships, or changes in transportation technology which alter relative transport costs, or externally determined changes in the location of input goods sources and output market points, the firm will always remain at the same location employing the same input–output production techniques. It would be wrong, however, to view these spatial results as implying that the spatial economy is essentially static. From our Weber model discussion we see that the spatial economy exhibits evolutionary characteristics. These evolutionary features arise because firms continually search for new optimum locations in response to factor price changes, new input supplier and new market output locations. Whether firms actually relocate in response to these search processes is an issue discussed in Chapter 2. However, the key insights of the Weber and Moses models are that production behaviour and location behaviour are completely intertwined issues. Often this point is overlooked in textbook discussions of industrial economics and the theory of the firm. This is largely because location adds an extra dimension to the optimization problems, making the analysis somewhat more complex.

Additional complexity, but also a much richer set of locational insights relating to output prices and the value added during the production process, can be incorporated into

BOX 1.1 The logistics-costs model

There are a couple of possible limitations to the applicability of the Weber–Moses framework to real-world phenomena that need to be considered at this point. The first limitation is that the market price or revenue of the output good plays no role in the determination of the optimum location of the firm in either model. In the Weber model, the optimum location is determined solely by the transportation costs associated with the input and output goods, whereas in the Moses model, the input prices do play a role in the optimum location. In neither model does the market price have any effect on the determination of the optimum location. The second limitation of this framework is the emphasis on transport costs as a locational issue. In reality, transport costs tend to be only a very small percentage of total costs for most firms.

Both these Weber–Moses model weaknesses can be largely reconciled within a similar analytical framework by employing a broader description of distance-transport costs, which include the costs of time and frequency. These total *logistics costs* also include all the inventory purchasing and carrying costs associated with transportation (McCann 1993, 1997, 1998). Employing this *logistics-costs* approach, it can be demonstrated both that market price and market sales revenue play a crucial role in determining the optimum location, and also that distance costs are very significant. In particular, as we see in Appendix 1.3, the higher-value-adding activities will tend to be more market oriented than lower-value adding activities, and will also tend to be less sensitive to interregional labour price changes. As such, market areas will tend to be surrounded by higher-value activities or activities further up the value chain, whereas supply sources will tend to be surrounded more by lower-value-adding activities or firms lower down the supply chain. At the same time, total logistics costs can also be shown to be very much more significant than transport costs alone, because each of the inventory purchasing and carrying cost components can be shown to be functions of distance. A final point here is that the total logistics-costs approach can also be employed to account for the economies of distance and scale generally observed in transport pricing (McCann 2001) and discussed in Appendix 1.1.

Further extensions to these location-production problems can also be developed using facility-location modelling techniques (ReVelle 1987). These models build on the insights of the models discussed here, and are used to determine the optimum location in complex spatial contexts in which location or factor substitution possibilities are limited due to the operation of various constraints. These models often employ linear programming techniques and can be used for deciding on the ideal location for different kinds of investments such as retail establishments, as well as various kinds of public facilities such as hospitals, libraries, and schools. While these techniques are beyond the scope of this book, they offer powerful tools for both commerce and public policy, and demonstrate the importance of locational issues in economic, commercial, and public policy arenas.

these Weker–Moses types of location-production models when the costs of time and frequency are included in the analysis, as in the logistics-costs location-production discussed in Box 1.1.

1.4 Market area analysis: spatial monopoly power

In our analysis so far we have assumed that the market location is simply a point in space. However, taking geography and space seriously in our models of firm behaviour also requires that we investigate the explicitly spatial nature of market areas. Market areas frequently differ over space, due to differences in spatial population densities, differences in income distributions across space, and differences in consumer demand across space according to regional variations in consumer tastes. However, even if there were no spatial variations in population densities, income distributions, and consumer demand patterns, space would still be an important competitive issue. The reason is that geography and space can confer *monopoly power* on firms, which encourages firms to engage in spatial competition in order to try to acquire monopoly power through location behaviour. In order to see this we can adopt the approach first used by Palander (1935).

In Figure 1.15, we have two firms A and B located at points A and B along a one-dimensional market area defined by O–L. We assume that both firms are producing an identical product. The production costs p_a of firm A at location A can be represented by the vertical distance a, and the production costs p_b of firm B at location B can be represented by the vertical distance b. As we see, firm A is more efficient than firm B. The transport costs faced by each firm as we move in any direction from the location of the firm are represented by the slopes of the transport rate functions. As we see here, the transport rates for the two firms in this case are identical, i.e. $t_a = t_b$. For any location at a distance d_a away from firm A, the delivered price of the good is given as $(p_a + t_a d_a)$, and for any location at a distance d_b away from firm B, the delivered price of the good is given as $(p_b + t_b d_b)$.

If we assume that consumers are evenly distributed along the line OL, and we also assume that consumers, being rational, will buy from the firm which is able to supply at that particular location at the lowest delivered price, the total market area will be divided into two sectors, OX and XL. The reason for this is that between O and X the delivered price of firm A, given as $(p_a + t_a d_a)$, is always lower than that of firm B. On the other hand, at all locations between X and L the delivered price of firm B, given as $(p_b + t_b d_b)$, is always lower than that

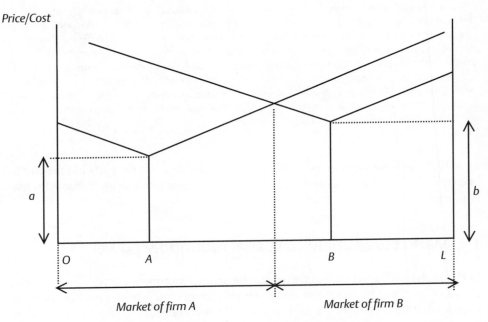

Figure 1.15 Spatial market areas: a one-dimensional model with equal transport rates

of firm A. Although firm A is more efficient than firm B, and although both firms produce an identical product, firm A does not gain all of the market. The reason is that location gives each firm some monopoly power over the area around itself. Firm A cannot capture all of firm B's market, even though it is more efficient than firm B, because the transport costs associated with shipping goods to market locations close to firm B increase the delivered price $(p_a + t_a d_a)$ to an uncompetitive level in market locations close to firm B. In terms of selling to consumers in the vicinity of firm B, firm A is unsuccessful simply because it is too far away. On the other hand, for sales in this area, firm B is successful simply because it is in the right location, even though it is less efficient in production.

This type of analysis can be extended to allow for differences in transport rates between firms as well as differences in production costs. In Figure 1.16 (a) and (b), we see that market areas can be divided up in a variety of ways in situations where the production costs and transport rates vary between the firms. Generally, the size of a firm's market area will be larger the lower are the production costs of the firm and the lower are the transport rates faced by the firm. However, only in the case where transport rates are zero is a lower production price sufficient to ensure a firm captures all of the market. The reason is that the existence of transport costs allows less efficient firms such as firm B to survive by providing each firm with some monopoly power over particular market areas. In general, the areas over which firms have some monopoly power are the areas in which the firms are located. For example, Figure 1.16(b) can be regarded as representing a case such as a local bakery, where firm B maintains a very small local market area in the face of competition from a national bakery, firm A, which produces at a much lower unit production costs and transports in large low-cost shipments.

Monopoly power refers to the ability of the firm to increase the production price of the good p_a or p_b, and yet maintain some market share. In general, the greater the monopoly power of the firm, the steeper the firm's downward-sloping demand curve. In many textbook descriptions of monopoly or monopolistic power, the slope of the firm's downward-sloping demand curve is viewed as being dependent on brand loyalty, associated with advertising and marketing. However, location is also an important way in which many firms acquire monopoly power. The reason is that transport costs are a form of transactions costs, and from the theory of the firm we know that the existence of transactions costs such as tariffs and taxes can provide protection for some inefficient firms. Geography acts in a similar manner, because the costs of overcoming space in order to carry out market exchanges incur transport-transactions costs. In the context of Figures 1.15 and 1.16, there are two general rules governing the extent to which distance costs provide a firm with spatial monopoly power:

(i) The greater the values of the transport rates t_a and t_b, the lower will be the fall in the market area of the firm, and the greater will be the monopoly power of the firm, for any marginal increase in the price of either p_a or p_b, ceteris paribus.

(ii) The further apart the firms, the lower will be the fall in the market area of the firm, and the greater will be the monopoly power of the firm, for any marginal increase in the price of either p_a or p_b, ceteris paribus.

Therefore firms which are located at a great distance from each other, and which face significant transport costs, will consequently exhibit significant local spatial monopoly power.

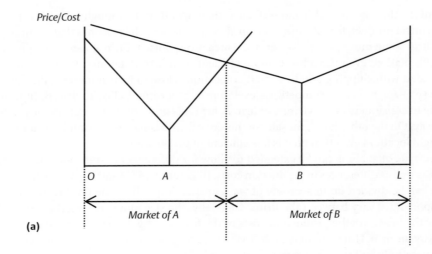

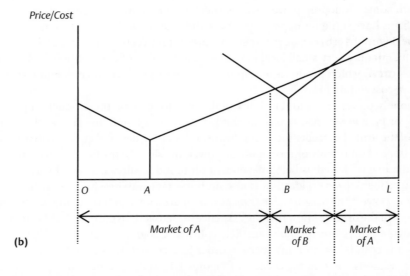

Figure 1.16 Spatial market areas: one-dimensional models with varying transport rates and production costs

1.4.1 The Hotelling model of spatial competition

The existence of spatial monopoly power provides an incentive for firms to use location as a competitive weapon in order to acquire greater monopoly power. This is particularly important in industries where firms do not compete primarily in terms of price, but instead engage in non-price competition, such as product quality competition. In competitive environments characterized by oligopoly, the interdependence of firms in the determination of output quantities and market share is also a result of locational considerations, as well as interdependence in terms of pricing decisions. The simplest demonstration of this is the

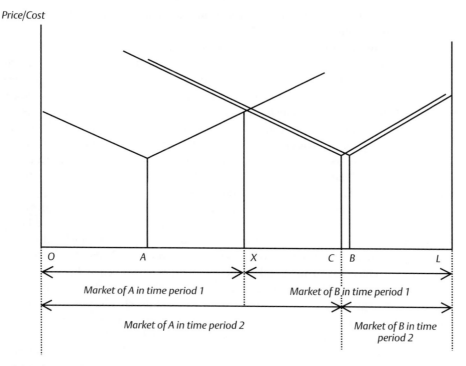

Price/Cost

O   A   X   C B   L

Market of A in time period 1

Market of B in time period 1

Market of A in time period 2

Market of B in time period 2

Figure 1.17 The Hotelling location game

Hotelling (1929) model, which describes firms' spatial interdependence within the context of a locational game.

In Figure 1.17 we adapt Figure 1.15 to the case where both the production costs and transport rates of firm A and firm B are identical. In other words, $p_a = p_b$ and $t_a = t_b$, and we assume that these prices do not change. As before, we assume that consumers are evenly distributed along OL and we also introduce the assumption that the demand of consumers is perfectly inelastic, such that all consumers consume a fixed quantity per time period irrespective of the price. In terms of firm strategy we assume that each firm makes a competitive decision on the basis of the assumption that its competitor firm will not change its behaviour. In the game theory literature this particular set of rules describing the nature of the competitive environment is known as 'Cournot conjectures'. Given that the firms are not competing in terms of their production prices, which are assumed to be fixed, each firm can only adjust its location in order to acquire greater market share. If the firms react to each other in sequential time periods, the location result can be predicted easily.

If we assume that the firms A and B are initially located at one-quarter and three-quarters of the way along the market, respectively, firm A will have monopoly power over OX and firm B will have monopoly power over XL. In this case, both firms will have identical market shares. In time period 1 firm A will therefore move from its original location to a location at C, just to the left of B. In this way firm A will increase its market share from OX to a new maximum value of *OC*. Firm *B* will still retain market share over *BL*, although its market share is now at a minimum.

Firm *B* will now assume that firm *A* will maintain its location at *C*, and so in time period 2, firm *B* will move just to the left of *C*. In time period 3, firm *A* will respond by moving to the left of firm *B*, and this process will continue until both firms are located at *X*, in the middle of the market. Once both firms are located at *X*, neither firm has any incentive to change its location behaviour, because any location change will involve a reduction in market share relative to their location at *X*. In game theory, any situation in which neither firm has any incentive to change its behaviour is known as a 'Nash equilibrium'. The locational result in which both firms are located at the centre of the market is the Nash equilibrium for this particular locational game. Consequently, once the firms reach this point they no longer continue to move. This is the Hotelling result. The details of this are given in Appendix 1.4.

At the conclusion of the Hotelling game we see that the market share of both firms located at *X* will be half of the market, exactly the same as at the start of the location game. However, from Figure 1.18 we see that the Hotelling result leads to a fall in consumer welfare relative to the original situation. Given that consumers all consume a fixed quantity per time period of the good produced by firms *A* and *B*, there is no substitution effect between the goods produced by firms *A* and *B* and other consumption goods. Therefore the change in the delivered prices at the each location will accurately reflect the change in welfare of the consumers at each location. The net effect of these welfare gains and losses can be represented by the areas under the delivered price curves, which are arrived at by comparing the delivered prices at the respective locations at the start and the end of the Hotelling location game.

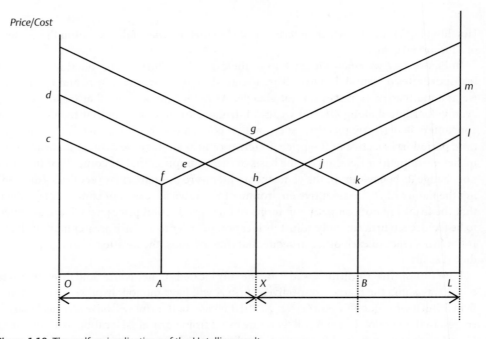

Figure 1.18 The welfare implications of the Hotelling result

The consumers who are located in the centre of the market benefit by generally reduced delivered prices, represented by *eghj* in Figure 1.18, whereas those located at the edges of the market lose by generally higher delivered prices, represented by (*defc*) + (*jklm*) in Figure 1.18. The gain in lower prices for the central consumers is outweighed by the increase in prices for the more peripheral consumers. The net effect is therefore a social welfare loss.

In one-dimensional space discussed here, the Hotelling result holds for two firms. Meanwhile, in the two-dimensional case, the Hotelling result holds for the case of three firms. However, beyond these numbers, there is no stable equilibrium result as firms keep changing their location.

1.4.2 Price competition, quality competition, and product space

Even in the one-dimensional case described above, the Hotelling result only holds as long as the firms do not compete in terms of prices. If price competition is also a possibility, there is no Hotelling result (d'Aspremont et al. 1979). In Figure 1.19, we can consider the situation where firm *A* lowers its production price marginally in time period 1 when both firms are located at *X*. In time period 2 firm *A* gains all of the market. From our Cournot conjectures, firm *B* now assumes that firm *A* will maintain both its new lower price and its location at *X*. Therefore in time period 3 firm *B* also lowers its market price below that of firm *A*, and now gains all of the market. This process will continue and the long-run Nash equilibrium of this price war is that both firms will end up selling at zero profit while still being located at point

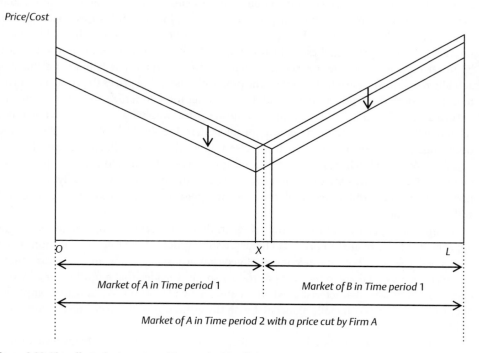

Figure 1.19 The effect of price competition on the Hotelling result

X. If the marginal costs of production are zero, the prices will fall to zero, whereas if the production costs are not zero but rather are positive, the long-run result of the Hotelling co-location competition will be to drive prices down to the marginal costs of production, which is the typical equilibrium result of a competitive market.

The Hotelling model is implicitly about monopoly power, with firms able to use location as a means of generating monopoly power over a certain portion of their market. Moreover, the greater is their localized monopoly power, the greater will be the possibilities for the firm to raise additional revenues by employing monopoly practices such as price discrimination. Therefore, in a situation where prices could spiral downwards due to the Bertrand problem, each firm has some incentive to move away from its competitor in order to maintain monopoly power, and consequently positive profits, over some of the market area. However, neither firm has an incentive to move away first, because if it does, the other firm will then be able to maintain its current prices at the centre of the market and dominate a larger market area than the firm which moved away from the centre. Therefore, unless there is some way in which the firms can mutually agree to move away from each other, a price war becomes inevitable, with disastrous consequences for both firms. This relationship between the co-location of competing activities and the problem of a price war is known as the 'Bertrand problem'.

Competitor firms will consequently only locate next to each other in situations in which price competition is ruled out either by mutual agreement or by other forms of non-price competition. Yet, in these types of non-price competitive situations, the spatial clustering of competitor firms is a natural process. Many types of shops and showrooms, for example, such as those for clothing, electronics goods, automobiles, restaurants, and furniture, compete in industries dominated by non-price competition. In these industries prices are used to indicate product quality, and to indicate the types of consumers for whom the good is intended. As such, prices in these industries tend to be fixed. Firms are unwilling to compete by lowering prices because this suggests that the product quality is falling, and this may actually have an adverse effect on sales. The practice of ascribing prices to products in order to indicate both the product quality and the consumer for whom the product is intended is known as 'price placing', and the problem of lower prices implying lower product quality is related to the famous 'market for lemons' problem described by Akerlof (1970). At the same time, engaging in non-price competition also implies that the products are not identical, and therefore the Hotelling result would appear not to be relevant. However, in many cases of non-price competition, the differences between the products are largely superficial, involving primarily differences in packaging and appearance. The products in essence will still be identical.

An interesting analytical issue now arises, in that our discussion of location strategies appears also to be related to product characteristics. Indeed, the Hotelling location model which is developed above in the context of geographical space can be more or less equivalently applied by analogy to the case of product space. The idea that a product or service is basically a bundle of characteristics which a consumer will pay for according to their preferences and tastes was originally associated with the groundbreaking consumer theory work of Lancaster (1971).

Following this logic, we can reconsider the space defined by *OL* as now being transformed into a product characteristics space, in which products exhibit a range of characteristics which can be ordered from O to L. Firms compete for customers by adjusting product characteristics, and in product space, exactly as with geographical space, the competition between the firms ensures that both competing firms produce products which are very close to each other in terms of product characteristics, as well as very close to each other geographically. As such, the locational proximity of the firms in the case of geographical space is also mirrored by the similarity of the competing products' features in terms of characteristics space. The same Hotelling equilibrium locational result holds in both notions of space, and this gives rise to what is known as the 'Hotelling paradox'. This refers to the observation that in order to avoid the Bertrand problem, the mutual interdependence of firms often gives rise to firms producing basically the same product (in characteristics space), and selling them at the same location (in geographical space), while at the same time using non-price competition to make these products appears the most different to each other. In these situations, firms will naturally tend to cluster together in space, and this is exactly how retail parks and central city shopping areas arise, along with rows of showrooms in the same street for the same generic good, such as is often the case with the sales of furniture, automobiles, flowers, shrubs and garden equipment, fabrics, white-ware goods and electronics, among many other examples.

On the other hand, where firms produce identical products in which non-price competition is extremely difficult, such as the market for gasoline, firms will not cluster together in space. Oil companies which own or franchise out gasoline retail stations will mutually agree not to locate their outlets too close to their competitors, in order to guarantee some market monopoly power for each station in its immediate vicinity. The only time at which gasoline stations will be located close to each other on the same highway is where they are separated from each other by a central reservation, median barrier, or major junction. In these cases, the stations are effectively separated from each other and customers are denied the choice between the stations, because they are unable to easily switch sides of the road. Therefore, the stations can be considered as not being located together, but rather located away from each other.

The Hotelling result therefore provides us with two important sets of analytical conclusions. First, for competitor firms producing the same type of product and which also engage in non-price competition, the spatial competition for markets may encourage such firms to locate next to each other. In other words, spatial industrial clustering can arise naturally where price competition is not paramount. This is particularly important in many examples of retailing. Moreover, in this situation, the market will be split more or less equally between all the firms in the spatial cluster. This ensures that no firm will be any worse off than its competitor due to an inferior location. On the other hand, for firms which produce more or less identical products for which non-price competition is very difficult to engage in, and in which there are no information problems, spatial competition will encourage such firms to move away from each other. The result of this process is industrial dispersion. Second, from a welfare point of view, consumers located close to a spatial cluster of firms will tend to experience a welfare gain relative to those located at a great distance away. The reason for this is that the costs of consuming the goods produced by the firms will tend to be much lower for those who are located close to the firms than for those who are located at a distance away. This is an important observation concerning the advantages of being located so as to benefit from agglomeration economies, a topic which we will discuss in Chapter 2.

The general conclusion of the Hotelling model is that if firms are physically located together in geographical space, then the Bertrand problem can only be avoided if firms are able to ensure that no price competition operates. Assuming that cartel behaviour is illegal, then the problem with this is that the situation is always on a knife-edge if the competing products are still basically very close substitutes for each other, even if lots of branding and marketing is taking place in order to persuade consumers otherwise. This is because there is always the danger that consumers eventually come to realize that the competing products are indeed very close substitutes for each other, such that the whole local equilibrium once again becomes unstable and subject to the Bertrand problem. Unless alternative means can be found which limit the ability of consumers to switch between producers, such as in the case of the gasoline station example above, this implies that a stable outcome is only really possible if the firms move away exactly as d'Aspremont et al. (1979) demonstrated, or if the products are fundamentally different, in which case the firms may not actually be competing for the same consumers.

A problem with this argument, however, is that we routinely observe firms clustered together selling similar or often almost identical goods, and this is particularly noticeable in the case of retail activities. The knife-edge unstable position implied by the pure Hotelling model and its requisite mechanisms for inhibiting consumer switching do not appear to be realistic, particularly given that typical consumer retail behaviour involves multiple switching, even in a single shopping trip. In order to understand this it is necessary to extend the insights of the pure Hotelling model by applying a largely analogous framework where the geographical location space is reinterpreted in terms of non-finite product space. This is most famously modelled in the case of a circular (non finite) product space using the Salop (1979) model discussed in Box 1.2, in which the interactions between spatial competition and product competition in determining the degree of monopoly power are analysed.

BOX 1.2 The Salop (1979) model of product location

In the Salop (1979) model, the interactions between product space and geographical space are examined. In particular, the conditions under which spatial monopoly power are generated are investigated. A key novelty of the approach provided by the Salop model is that if consumers have different preferences, this implies that the optimum 'location' of each consumer in product space is different. As such, the more consumers there are at a particular geographical location, the more the product space competition relates to multiple product space locations, rather than just one product space location, as is the case with the Hotelling model.

In Figure 1.20, the vertical line represents the consumption utility. The Salop model assumes that product space is not finite, and that each consumer has a different optimal location, defined by the highest point on the utility 'pyramid', with the level of utility falling away with increasing product space 'distance' from the optimum, as depicted by the downward slopes of the utility functions. Under these conditions, if each variety is 'located' at the product space at the peak of the pyramid, the firm will have a monopoly of those customers whose preferences are 'located' in the same product space range. In other words, the monopoly product space for each firm is given by $2d_m$, and within each respective monopoly product space there is no competition.

In the case of a competitive environment in which competing brand varieties are close to each other, as we see in Figure 1.21, the monopoly product space associated with each brand is now only $2d_c$, which

BOX 1.2 Continued

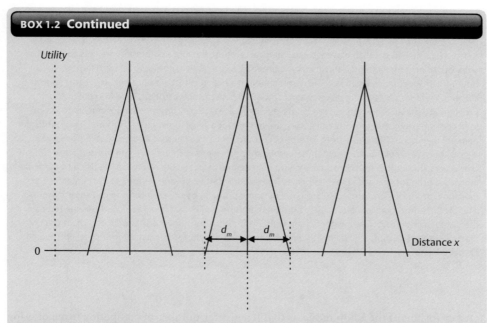

Figure 1.20 Monopoly region Salop model

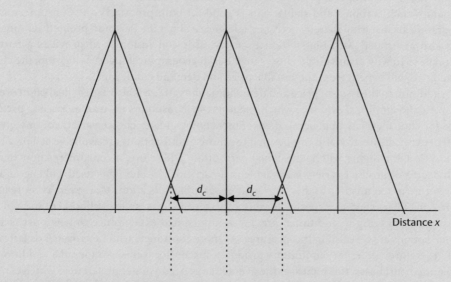

Figure 1.21 Competitive region Salop model

is less than $2d_m$. The actual market space dominated by each firm will therefore also depend on the price it offers for its output, with consumers 'located' in the area of competition now able to switch between brands according to the relationship between their preferences and the prices.

BOX 1.2 **Continued**

The more varieties available at each geographical location, the more consumers are able to switch in response to price movements, and also the more retailers are able to compete across difference optimum product space locations. The combination of a high product variety allied with geographical clustering provides a powerful defence against the Bertrand problem, not only because the product proliferation provides customers with increased possibilities for consumer switching, but also because such consumer switching means that a price movement for a single firm's variety has much less effect on demand in general. This is true both for a price rise and for a price fall, and as such, local demand in aggregate is very inelastic, the greater the number of price-elastic producers. From the perspective of consumers, this implies that consumers have a high degree of 'protection' from a price rise by a particular individual producer because the possibilities for switching between varieties are greater. Similarly, the individual producers are 'protected' from the Bertrand problem by the clustering, because the system as a whole becomes more stable. The Salop model therefore implies that geographical clustering reduces the instability risks associated with price movements for both consumers and producers. The more that places with a greater range of competing product varieties are clustered, the more stable will be overall demand levels.

A key insight of the Salop model is that if a greater number of competing firms offering alternative varieties are located at the same geographical location, the Salop arguments also imply that more local competition between product varieties will lead to a local market demand which is robust and stable. This is good for both producers and consumers, and geographical clustering thereby becomes a defence against the Bertrand problem, as long as it is also associated with high product variety. This conclusion itself provides a partial rationale as to why firms should cluster together in geographical space: as a group, the clustered firms will benefit from these stable price and demand conditions.

In addition to the issue of price and demand stability, there is also a great deal of theoretical work and empirical evidence which suggests that consumers have an increasing preference for choice variety in general. If consumers enjoy greater choice variety for any given level of expenditure, this also implies that the more brand options are available at a particular location, the higher will be the consumers' utility. Therefore, if consumers know that a high degree of product variety is available in a particular locality, this itself will encourage more of them to consume at this particular geographical location. Moreover, as more and more consumers shop at a specific location, this also increases the likelihood of individual consumers engaging in additional previously unplanned expenditure as new purchasing choice options are revealed in the local area. As more consumers with heterogeneous tastes—and therefore different optimum product space 'locations'—undertake additional unplanned purchases, this increases the overall range of consumer preferences which can be catered for by the geographical cluster. If the local geographical cluster can sustain more competing producers, while still allowing the individual producers to maintain approximately the same degree of characteristics distance between brands varieties which are adjacent in product space, then individual firms' profits will remain largely the same. If, however, a growing market also leads to a relatively greater degree of additional geographical clustering of firms, then the average characteristics distance between the producers will fall, individual firm profits will be squeezed, and consumers will benefit even more. This itself will thereby encourage even more local unplanned additional consumption.

These arguments, which emphasize the links between choice and variety, also underpin the agglomeration arguments associated with the new economic geography (NEG) models discussed in Chapter 3. Either way, the *ex post* result of these types of processes associated with clustering is that consumers will on average spend more than they had planned *ex ante*, and the benefits of these additional expenditures will be distributed approximately evenly between all of the geographically clustered producers, as long as the characteristics distance between all adjacent producers is approximately even. The geographical clustering of competing differentiated brand producers can therefore facilitate the growth of the overall local market space, as well as providing for greater overall market and price stability. These inter-relationships of product variety, price stability, and the growth of a local market all provide a clear rationale as to why firms should cluster together in space. In addition, as we see in Urban and Regional Example 1.1, there are even some cases where price competition and clustering are compatible.

One final point concerning this Palander and Hotelling type of spatial market analysis is the criticism that, in many real-world cases, individual firms charge the same delivered price for a given product at all locations. As such, spatial markets are not divided according to delivered prices, which vary with location. On the other hand, where delivered prices are invariant with respect to distance within a given market area, this implies that the marginal profitability of each delivery will be different according to the location of the customer. This is because the transport costs of outputs must be absorbed by the firm, thereby reducing the net marginal profits from sales as the delivery distance increases. In other words, the profits

---

 Urban and Regional Example 1.1   Price fluctuations and clustering

When applying the widely applicable insights of the Hotelling and Salop frameworks to the real world, we need to be aware that there are some other exceptions where price competition and spatial clustering are also compatible. An example here is the case where prices are not predictable and are continually changing, such as in the case of many fresh-produce food markets, flower markets, legalized gambling activities such as on-course horseracing bookmakers, auctions, and many types of financial and commodity brokerage markets. In these markets purchases have to be made almost instantly in the face on ongoing and rapid price changes, and as soon as product prices and availability reach a level close to the preferences of the consumer, the consumer has to move quickly to secure a deal. In these situations, although price competition is very keen and firms may indeed gain from short-term first-mover advantages, customer inertia limited information, in the face of rapid and frequent price changes it is actually perfectly rational for spatial clustering to occur. The reason is that in these types of markets, the clustering of competitors minimizes the information costs and search costs on the part of the potential customers. The co-location of retailing activities in this case is justified, as with the case of non-price retail competition, because this may encourage customers to buy more goods in general than they would otherwise if they were not presented with a broad range of consumption alternatives and the relevant price information about them. As such, all firms in the cluster are expected to gain, and co-location ensures that all firms benefit more or less equally. These arguments are related primarily to the questions of information, clustering and externalities discussed initially in Chapter 2.

associated with deliveries to nearby customers will be much higher than those for deliveries to distant customers. As such, for any given spatial distribution of markets, the location of the firm will still determine the overall profitability of the firm. Moreover, as we see in Appendix 1.3 and Appendix 1.4, even for uniform delivered prices firms are able to employ changes in the quality of service, such as changes in delivery frequencies, in order to mimic the spatial price effects of situations in which customers pay the transport charges in addition to the quoted source prices.

1.5 Conclusions

The foregoing discussion suggests that we can use classical and neoclassical models of firm location behaviour to consider the spatial behaviour of firms operating under different circumstances and also with different objectives. We see that input factor prices, factor substitution, and market prices are all critical aspects of location behaviour. Indeed, all location problems are also production problems, and vice versa, and these interrelationships begin to account for why geography is so important for economics. The analysis of market areas, in which location strategy, output strategy, and pricing strategy are all seen to be interrelated, further reinforces this general point. The role of product quality and variety emerges as an essential aspect of location behaviour and these issues are examined in more detail in Chapter 2, which deals with the phenomenon of industrial agglomeration and clustering.

Discussion questions

1.1 How does the location of input sources and output markets determine the location behaviour of the firm?

1.2 To what extent are firm-locational changes dependent on the input substitution characteristics of the firm's production function?

1.3 How do changes in local land prices and labour prices affect firm location behaviour?

1.4 Explain how firm location changes are linked to changes in the potential input and output market locations.

1.5 In what ways does space confer monopoly power?

1.6 What role can location play in the competitive strategy of firms, and how are location and price strategies interrelated?

1.7 What role do logistics costs play in determining firm location behaviour?

1.8 What role does product differentiation play in location behaviour?

Appendix 1.1 The one-dimension location problem

Within the Weber framework, we can summarize the relative strength of the transportation 'pull' towards any particular input source point. If, at any particular location,

$\Delta(m_1t_1d_1) > -\Delta(m_2t_2d_2)$ as the firm moves away from input source 1 and towards input source 2 (where Δ represents a marginal change), the firm should move towards input source 1. This is because the marginal increase in the total transport costs for the shipment of input 1 is greater than the marginal fall in the total transport costs for the shipment of input 2. Alternatively, if $\Delta(m_1t_1d_1) < -\Delta(m_2t_2d_2)$, the firm will move closer towards input source 2. In the situation where $\Delta(m_1t_1d_1) = -\Delta(m_2t_2d_2)$, the firm can move in either direction, and will be indifferent between adjacent locations.

Within the Weber triangle, we can imagine a situation where the output good is weightless, such as in the case of the electricity generated by a power station which consumes inputs of coal and coke from M_1 and M_2, respectively. In this case, the plant will be constrained to locate along the line joining M_1 and M_2. Here, the location problem becomes a one-dimensional problem. Initially we can analyse the situation where the transport rates are constant.

In this situation, any small change, denoted here by Δ, in the input shipment distance d_1 will be associated with an equal and opposite change in the input shipment distance d_2. If $\Delta(m_1t_1d_1) > -\Delta(m_2t_2d_2)$, at any location along the line joining M_1 and M_2, as the firm moves away from input source 1, the firm will locate at M_1. Alternatively, if $\Delta(m_1t_1d_1) < -\Delta(m_2t_2d_2)$, at any location along the line joining M_1 and M_2, as the firm moves away from input source 1, the firm will locate at M_2. The reason for this is that if m_1, t_1, m_2, and t_2 are fixed, the only cause of change in the total transport costs for each input shipment is the change in the relative distances, which are always equal and opposite in this case. Therefore the inequality which holds at any particular point on the line M_1M_2 will hold at all points on the line. This will encourage the firm to continue to move in the same direction. The optimum location behaviour of the firm is therefore to locate at the particular end-point M_1 or M_2, which has the lowest total transport costs. As we see in Figure A.1.1.1, in a one-dimensional space such as the line joining M_1 and M_2, where transport rates are constant, there is always an

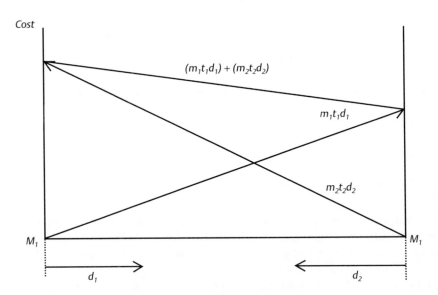

Figure A.1.1.1 One-dimensional location problem with constant transport rates

end-point optimal location solution, in this case at M_2. In microeconomics this is called a corner solution, because the optimum location will never be between, or interior to, the end-points M_1 and M_2.

The situation becomes somewhat more complicated where the transport rates change with the distance of haulage. Transport rates per ton-kilometre normally fall with increasing haulage distance, implying that the total input transport costs increase by less than proportionately with distance. On the other hand, in some circumstances transport rates per ton-kilometre increase with distance, implying that total transport costs increase by more than proportionately with distance. In these situations, we must also consider the effect of the change in transport rates with changes in distance, as the distance itself changes. As above, an optimal location for the firm will only be at an interior location, i.e. between the end-points M_1 and M_2, where the marginal increase in the total transport costs for the shipment of input 1, as we move away from M_1, is equal to the marginal fall in the total transport costs for the shipment of input 2. If we denote the total transport costs associated with the input shipment of good 1 as $TC_1 = (m_1 t_1 d_1)$, and those associated with the input shipment of good 2 as $TC_2 = (m_2 t_2 d_2)$, the condition for an optimum location internal to M_1 and M_2 is where $\Delta TC_1 = -\Delta TC_2$, for a small location change. In order to identify such a situation it is necessary to use calculus to observe the first and second derivative of each of the relationships between total transport costs and distance in the situation where transport rates vary with haulage distance.

We can specify $T(d_1) = t_1(d_1)d_1$ and $T(d_2) = t_2(d_2)d_2$ as representing the change in the total transport costs associated with a marginal change in d_1 and d_2, allowing for changes in the per unit transport rates as the distance changes. Assuming a marginal change in d_1 and a marginal decrease in d_2 we can write:

$$\Delta TC_1 = \partial(TC_1)/\partial d_1 = m_1(\partial T_1/\partial d_1)$$

and

$$\Delta TC_2 = (\partial(TC_2)/\partial d_2)(\partial d_1/\partial d_2) = -m_2(\partial T_2/\partial d_2)$$

The first-order conditions for the inner optimum locations are given by:

$$m_1(\partial T_1/\partial d_1) = m_2(\partial T_2/\partial d_2)$$

and the second-order condition is given as:

$$m_1(\partial^2 T_1/\partial d_1^2) + m_2(\partial^2 T_2/\partial d_2^2) > 0$$

In other words, the transport costs associated with at least one of the inputs must be increasing by more than proportionately with distance, as distance increases, in order for there to be an optimum location between M_1 and M_2. We can see this in Figure A.1.1.2, where the interior optimum is at d^*.

On the other hand, if transport rates exhibit economies of distance, i.e. $(\partial^2 T_1/\partial d^2{}_1)$ and $(\partial^2 T_2/\partial d_2^2)$ are negative, or fixed transport rates i.e. $(\partial t_1/\partial d_1)$ and $(\partial t_2/\partial d_2)$ are zero,

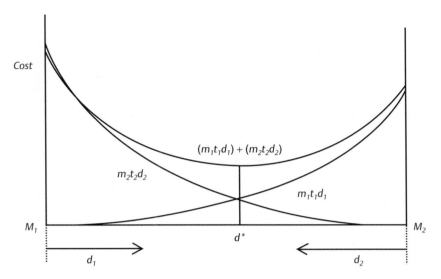

Figure A.1.1.2 One-dimensional location problem with increasing transport rates

there is no interior solution. As we see in Figures A.1.1.3 and A.1.1.1, in these cases, which are the usual two situations, the optimal location will always be at an end-point such as M_1 and M_2. In A.1.1.3 the optimum location is at M_1 whereas in A.1.1.1 it is at M_2.

The final possibility is where there are trans-shipments costs associated with the loading and unloading of goods at ports or terminals. In these situations, the 'terminal' costs associated with these trans-shipments points may alter the transport rates in a variety of ways. Optimal locations with terminal costs can be either at end-points or at interior locations. As we see in Figures A.1.1.4 to A.1.1.6, the optimal location will depend on the structure of the transport costs.

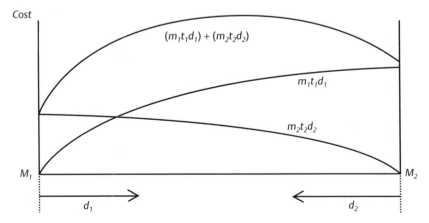

Figure A.1.1.3 One-dimensional location problem with decreasing transport rates

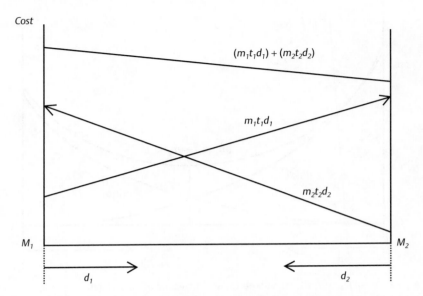

Figure A.1.1.4 One-dimensional location problems with terminal costs and linear transport rates

In Figure A.1.1.4 the transport rates are constant, although not equal to each other, and both transport cost functions exhibit terminal costs. In this case, the optimal location which minimizes total transport costs is at the end-point M_2.

In Figure A.1.1.5, the transport rates are falling with distance, such that total transport costs are concave with distance, although they are not equal to each other. Both transport

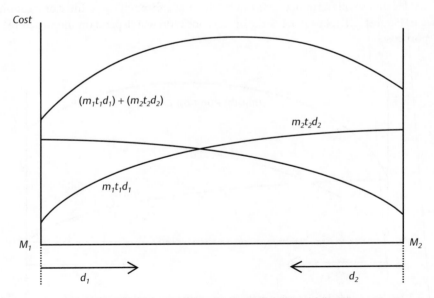

Figure A.1.1.5 One-dimensional location problems with terminal costs and falling transport rates

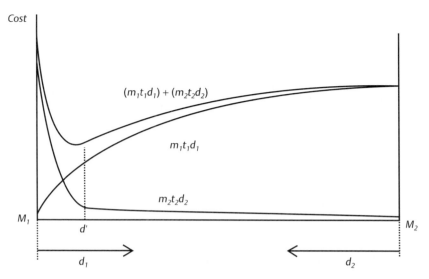

Figure A.1.1.6 One-dimensional location problems with terminal costs and increasing and decreasing transport rates

cost functions exhibit terminal costs. In this case, the optimal location which minimizes total transport costs is at the end-point M_1.

In Figure A.1.1.6, one of the transport rates is falling with distance, whereas the other is increasing with distance. Both transport cost functions exhibit terminal costs. In this case, the optimal location which minimizes total transport costs is at the interior location d'. The classic proof of the one-dimensional location problem is given by Sakashita (1968).

Appendix 1.2 The general solution to the Weber–Moses problem

We can write the profit (π) function of the firm as

$$\pi = p_3 m_3 - (p_1 + t_1 d_1)m_1 - (p_1 + t_1 d_1)m_1 - t_3 d_3 m_3 \tag{A.1.2.1}$$

Any profit maximization production-location point will need to satisfy the optimization conditions both with respect to the input combinations, m_1 and m_2, and also the locational coordinates. In our Weber–Moses triangle (Figure 1.8) we can define the locational coordinates in terms of two variables, namely the angle θ and the output shipment distance d_3. Any changes in the input distances d_1 and d_2 can be defined in terms of changes in these two variables. For an optimum location-production result, the partial derivatives of the profit function with respect to the four variables m_1, m_2, θ, and d_3 must be equal to zero. Following Miller and Jensen (1978), by partial differentiation, the first-order conditions for profit maximization are

$$\frac{\partial(\pi)}{\partial m_1} = -(p_1 + t_1 d_1) - m_1 d_1\left(\frac{\partial t_1}{\partial m_1}\right) - t_3 d_3\left(\frac{\partial m_3}{\partial m_1}\right) - m_3 d_3\left(\frac{\partial t_3}{\partial m_3}\right)\left(\frac{\partial m_3}{\partial m_1}\right) = 0 \tag{A.1.2.2}$$

justification for this is that moving goods over space takes time, and between individual shipments firms must hold inventories of goods to maintain supplies. The holding of these inventories itself incurs costs, so the firm must consider the relationship between the costs of moving goods and the costs of not moving them, i.e. holding inventories. If we include all the costs associated with the holding of inventories plus the shipment of input good i over space, we can define the total logistics costs of the input shipments per time period as

$$TLC_i = \frac{m_i}{Q_i} S_i + \frac{IQ_i(p_i + t_i d_i)}{2} + m_i t_i d_i \qquad (A.1.3.1)$$

where the parameters m, p, t, d are the same as in the above sections, and

Q_i weight of an individual input shipment

S_i procurement costs of inputs

I holding cost coefficient of input inventories

The first terms on the right-hand side of (A.1.3.1) represents the ordering and procurement costs which are incurred each time an input shipment is received, but which are independent of the shipment size. In manufacturing firms, these costs will also include machinery set-up costs, and can be shown to very significant. As these costs are independent of the shipment size but are incurred each time an input shipment is received, the total ordering costs are a multiple of the shipment frequency, i.e. the number of shipments per time period. The second term on the right hand side represents the inventory capital holding costs, which are a function of the average value of inventories held per time period. These costs are the capital interest plus insurance costs associated with holding inventories. Assuming that we consume inventories at a constant rate, and that stocks are replenished in a timely manner such that our inventory levels stay constant, these costs can be seen to be a function of the delivered price of the goods. In other words, inventory costs are a function of transport costs. Finally, the third term on the right-hand side of (A.1.3.1) represents the familiar transport costs term used above.

Using a similar logic we can also define the logistics costs associated with shipments of output goods, denoted with the subscript 'o', as

$$TLC_o = \frac{m_o}{Q_o} S_o + \frac{IQ_o(p_o - t_o d_{oi})}{2} + m_o t_o d_o \qquad (A.1.3.2)$$

In this case, the capital costs associated with holding inventories are the opportunity costs of output revenue which are incurred by not shipping outputs in a continuous manner and selling them at the market price of p_o.

For both input and output goods, the aim of the firm is to determine the optimum shipment size Q^* which minimizes the sum of the total logistics costs for any given locational arrangement of input supply points and output markets. However, this is not as straightforward as it might initially appear, because it can be shown that while the optimal shipment size Q^* is a function of the transport rates, transport rates are also a function of the optimal shipment size. In order to circumvent these problems, the definition of transport rates must be re-specified to allow for discrete shipments. While the details of this problem are beyond the scope of this book (McCann 1993, 1998, 2001), it can be demonstrated under very general conditions that the optimal shipment size (McCann 2001), and therefore the optimal average weight of inventories $Q^*/2$ to be held, is a positive function of the distance of the shipment, and the transport costs associated with the shipment. This also implies that the ordering costs, which are an inverse multiple of the size of Q, are also a function of the transport costs. The combined sum of all the interrelated components of total logistics costs can be shown to be a concave function of distance transport costs (McCann 1998), with distance cost curves similar in shape to those in Figure A.1.1.5.

By employing this broader logistics-costs description of the costs associated with transporting goods over geographical distances, we can now re-evaluate the Weber–Moses problem within a logistics-costs framework. Under very general conditions (McCann 1993, 1998), we can show that there is no solution to the independent of output optimum location problem. Moreover, as we see in Figure A.1.3.1, as the value-added by a firm increases, the optimum location of the firm K^* moves towards the market.

As the value-added by the firm increases, or the higher up the input–output value chain is the firm, the steeper is the negatively sloping interregional equilibrium wage gradient, which would allow a firm to move away from a central market point (McCann 1997, 1998). We can see this in Figure A.1.3.2, in which the point M represents a location containing both markets and input source points.

The interregional equilibrium wage gradient associated with total logistics costs, rather than simply transport costs, becomes steeper, i.e. it changes form R_1 to R_2, as the value-added by the firm increases, or as the firm moves up the value-adding chain. In other words, in order to encourage a firm to move away from a Weber optimum location at M where wages are w_M, interregional wage differences will need to be greater in order for a high-value-adding firm to relocate. On the other hand, a low value-adding firm, or a firm lower down the value-adding input–output chain, will be able to move in response to relatively minor interregional wage differences (McCann 1997, 1998). Moreover, in Appendix 3.4,

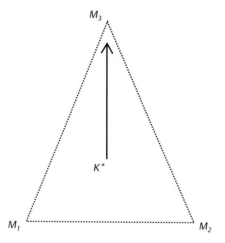

Figure A.1.3.1 Logistics-costs optimum location and value-added by the firm

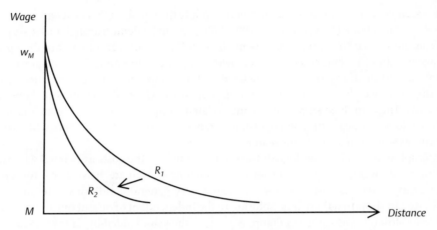

Figure A.1.3.2 Interregional equilibrium wage gradient associated with logistics costs

knowing that the optimum shipment size Q^* is inversely related to the trip frequency f, we are able to show that the interregional equilibrium wage gradient must be convex with respect to distance, as in Figure A.1.3.2.

The overall location-production conclusions to come out of the logistics-costs approach to the Weber–Moses framework is therefore that high-value-adding firms tend to be both more market–oriented, and much less responsive to regional wage differences, i.e. they are much less footloose than low-value-adding firms.

Appendix 1.4 The Hotelling location game

Before a Hotelling game of spatial competition takes place along a market OL, as we see in Figure A.1.4.1, we assume that we have two firms A and B, with A located to the left of B. The distance from O to A is denoted as a, and the distance from L to B is denoted as b. The distance from O to the market boundary is denoted as x', and the total distance OL is denoted as d. In order for this duopoly to exist there must be three conditions satisfied. The first condition is that a consumer located at point O must always buy from firm A. In other words, the delivered price of the output of A at O must always be less than the delivered price of the output of B at O. This can be written as

$$P_A + t_A a < p_B + t_B(d - b) \tag{A.1.4.1}$$

Second, a consumer located at point L must always buy from firm B. In other words, the delivered price of the output of B at L must always be less than the delivered price of the output of A at L. This can be written as

$$p_B + t_B b < p_A + t_A(d - a) \tag{A.1.4.2}$$

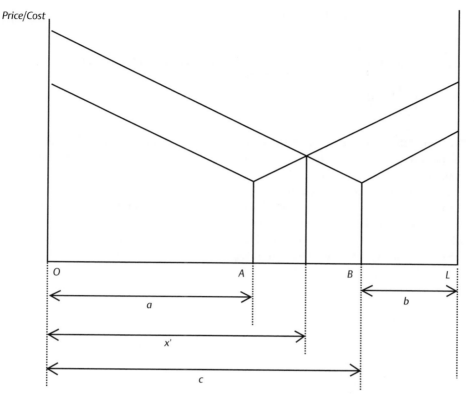

Figure A.1.4.1 The Hotelling spatial framework

At the same time, thirdly, there must also be an indifferent consumer at a distance x' somewhere between A and B. For this indifferent consumer the delivered prices must be the same. In other words

$$p_A + t_A(x' - a) = p_B + t_B(d - b - x') \tag{A.1.4.3}$$

If we set $t_A = t_B$, then rearranging equation (A.1.4.3) gives

$$P_A - P_B + 2tx' - ta - td + tb = 0 \tag{A.1.4.4}$$

If the transport rates t_A and t_B for the two firms are the same, and the source prices, p_A and p_B, of the two firms are also the same, we have

$$x' = \frac{a + d - b}{2} \tag{A.1.4.5}$$

The value of x' given in equation (A.1.4.5) represents the size of the market captured by firm A, and the size of the market captured by firm B can thus be represented as

$$d - x' = d - \left(\frac{a + d - b}{2} \right) = \frac{b + d - a}{2} \qquad (A.1.4.6)$$

Recalling from Figure A.1.4.1 that $c = (d - b)$, we can rewrite (A.1.4.5) as

$$x' = \frac{a + d - (d - c)}{2} = \frac{a + c}{2}$$

As such, if the transport rates are the same and also the product source prices are the same, the boundary between the two firms is exactly half-way between the two firms, and is independent of the transport rates, as we would expect.

For a given source production price p_A, known as a 'mill' price, the market revenue of firm A depends on maximizing the value of x'. From (A.1.4.5) and the arguments in section 1.4.1, we see that this is achieved by increasing a and reducing b as much as possible, while still ensuring that firm A is to the left of firm B. This location change then triggers the leap-frogging behaviour described in section 1.4.1.

2 Agglomeration and clustering

2.1 Introduction

In Chapter 1 we discussed the theoretical issues which affect the location behaviour of the individual firm. Each of the models presented provides us with a way of analysing the particular microeconomic effects on firm location behaviour, of various influences such as transport costs, local factor prices, production and substitution possibilities, market structure, and competition. In reality the actual location behaviour of the firm is a result of a complex mix of each of these influences. Therefore this leaves us with the problem of determining which particular influences are the dominant influences in which situations. Unfortunately, without information on the individual firm and industry, however, the various microeconomic models above do not lead to any systematic conclusion as to whether optimal firm location behaviour is more likely to result in industrial clustering or in industrial dispersion. Yet, in describing the generally observable features of industrial location behaviour, two particular features do stand out.

The first generally observed feature of industrial location behaviour is that most industrial activities tend to be clustered together in space, and the reasons for this clustering behaviour are examined in this chapter. Most productive and commercial activities do take place in the immediate vicinity of other such activities, and such clusters may take a variety of forms, including industrial parks, small towns, or major cities. However, as we have discussed in Chapter 1, firms make different location choices based on their production and cost functions, the spatial delineation of their markets, and their competitive strategies. Moreover, firm clustering obviously often leads to congestion costs and higher land prices. Yet, in spite of these different location-production choices and congestion costs, the general observation that industrial clustering is widespread is indeed valid. As such, this observation raises the important question of why it is exactly that activities are generally grouped together geographically, and the reasons why firms are often clustered together in space is the central issue discussed in this chapter.

The second generally observed feature of industrial location behaviour, which will be discussed in detail in Chapter 3, is that there appears to be a size distribution of spatial clusters, with different ranges of activities taking place in different clusters. Some activities are typically dispersed over large areas, with goods being shipped generally over large distances, while others are more geographically concentrated. These differences in the degree of dispersion also give rise to regularities in the patterns of clusters. In particular, within an individual country or market area, there will usually be a single largest city cluster which exhibits almost all types of activities, followed by larger numbers of other smaller clusters which increase in number as their individual size falls. The smaller clusters will tend to exhibit a smaller range of activities taking place within them than the larger clusters. These observations are collectively known as an 'urban hierarchy', and the particular reasons for the development of such a system of cities are discussed in Chapter 3. Instead, this chapter will focus specifically on the issues explaining why activities cluster together in space.

In sections 2.2 to 2.5 of this chapter, we will discuss in detail the various arguments and explanations as to why industrial activities are often observed to be clustered geographically. The arguments in sections 2.2 and 2.3 centre on the role played by knowledge spillovers, labour markets, and economies of scale in fostering agglomeration. Moving beyond simply agglomeration, section 2.4 examines the transactions costs relationships underpinning a broader range of different types of clusters, and section 2.5 discusses the role played by both creativity and consumption in fostering urban agglomeration and clustering, in particular. Yet these explanations all suggest a level of information availability, awareness, and rationality on the part of individual firms and people, such that collectively their individual decisions give rise to agglomerations and clusters. For this reason section 2.6 raises the question of how clusters do actually arise in an environment of limited information, conflicting goals, and uncertainty, and here we see that evolutionary processes become central to the discussion. Not surprisingly, these evolutionary processes also reappear as a critical element in Chapter 7 where we discuss regional growth.

2.2 Industrial clustering: returns to scale and geography

Industrial clustering refers to the observation that all types of commercial activities—manufacturing, services, resource-based industries—are frequently observed to be grouped together in space. In attempting to explain this observation, it is necessary to employ the notion that economies of scale can be place specific. To see this, we can consider the spatial outcomes of the alternative hypothetical case where all firms achieve constant returns to scale. If, for whatever reason, a large group of such firms in the same sector or a range of sectors ends up being located in the same place, the result of this clustering will be a large level of investment at that particular location. These firms will require land and space for their activities, and the high demand for land at the particular location will force up its price. If everything else is unchanged, and if the firms all achieve constant returns to scale, the increase in the price of land will reduce the profitability of all the firms at that location. Similarly, the increase in the local land price will mean that the living costs of the labour employed will also go up. In order to maintain the local labour supply the firms will also have to increase wages. Once again, this will reduce the profitability of all the firms in the area. The reduced profits will mean that firms located here will be less competitive than their competitors located elsewhere and will struggle to survive in the market. Some firms will move away to alternative locations while others will simply go out of business. Eventually the cluster will disappear. This hypothetical example is, however, inconsistent with the general observation that most activity clusters continue to exist.

On the other hand, let us imagine a situation where each of the firms in the same locality achieves significant external economies of scale precisely because of the large number of firms located in the area. In this situation, the high level of investment in the local area will still imply high local land prices and high labour prices as before. However, the difference now is that these increased factor prices may be more than compensated for by the increased efficiency on the part of each firm. The result of this will be even higher profitability for all the local firms, even though the local factor prices may be higher than elsewhere. Other firms from other areas may now also consider moving into our area, contributing to a further growth in the levels of local investment, factor prices, and firm profitability. This in-migration of new firms will lead to a cumulative process of local growth.

This hypothetical example is consistent with the observation that most activity clusters continue to exist. However, in reality, the growth of local clusters tends not to be a process which is continuously cumulative, as in the latter example. The reason for this is that this would imply that all activity would end up at one location! Therefore, in order to discuss the existence of spatial industrial clusters, it is necessary to employ the notion that place-specific economies of scale do exist, but also to acknowledge that there may be limits to such effects.

2.3 Agglomeration economies

Location-specific economies of scale are generally known as agglomeration economies. The existence of agglomeration economies was acknowledged by classical authors such as Weber, but it was Alfred Marshall who first provided a detailed description of the sources of these economies. In Marshall's (1890, 1920) schema, these economies are generally understood to be external economies, which are independent of a single firm, but which accrue to all of the firms located in the same area. A good description of the Marshall approach is given by Krugman (1991). However, as well as Marshall's description of the sources of agglomeration economies, there is also Hoover's (1937, 1948) classification of types of agglomeration economies. Hoover's description is a somewhat different characterization to that of Marshall, but it shares some elements, and given that both approaches are frequently adopted, it is necessary to be explicit about their differences.

2.3.1 The sources of agglomeration economies

Marshall (1890, 1920) observed that firms often continue to cluster successfully in the same locations. From our example above, this implies that increasing returns to scale must be achieved by the firms in the cluster. Marshall provided three reasons why such economies of scale might be achieved. In other words, he identified three possible sources or origins of such economies of scale. These are knowledge spillovers, local non-traded inputs, and a local skilled labour pool.

(i) Knowledge spillovers

If many firms in the same industry are grouped together in the same location, it implies that the employees of any one particular firm have relatively easy access to employees from other local firms. This easy access can be either through the facility to have frequent direct face-to-face contact in business meetings, or alternatively though frequent informal contacts such as lunch meetings, sports activities, or other such social occasions. The important point about such informal meetings is that they allow tacit information to be shared between the participants. Tacit knowledge is knowledge or information which is incomplete and which is shared on a non-market basis, and can relate to issues such as new products, personnel, technology, and market trends. The participants in such meetings will each give information which is partial in order to acquire other information which is also partial. This process of the mutual trading of information allows each of the market participants to build up a more coherent picture of the overall market environment, thereby improving their ability to compete in the market. The more such participants there are in the local area, the more complete a picture can be assembled by each participant. The advantage of spatial clustering in this case is therefore that proximity maximizes the mutual accessibility of all individuals within the cluster, thereby improving the knowledge and information available to all local participants. In market environments characterized by rapidly changing information, such clustering affords the agglomerated firms an information advantage relative to all other firms, and the extent of this advantage depends directly on the number of such firms which are located in the same area.

Good examples of this are the international financial markets, which are centred on highly concentrated areas such as Wall Street, New York, the City of London, and the Marunouchi district of Tokyo. In this sector, international financial market information is changing by the minute. Managers have to make important decisions on a daily basis, and these decisions often involve rapid negotiations with other participants within the banking syndicates of which each financial institution is a part. Immediate access to market participants is essential.

(ii) Non-traded local inputs

In situations where many firms in the same industry are grouped together in the same area, there will be possibilities for certain specialist inputs to be provided to the group, in a more efficient manner than would be the case if all the firms were dispersed. These inputs are described as 'non-traded' in order to distinguish them from consumed inputs of the type described in the Weber and Moses models. For example, if we once again take the case of the financial markets, areas such as Wall Street and the City of London have many specialist legal firms and software firms, whose only role is to provide specialist services to the international financial sector. The provision of such specialist services is very expensive. However, where there are many firms within the industry which are located at the same place, the average cost of this service provision to each market participant will be low. The reason is that the costs of setting up such services will be spread over a large number of local customer firms. Similarly, in automotive engineering clusters in city-regions such as Detroit, Michigan, Nagoya, Japan, Stuttgart, Germany, and Turin,

Italy, there are specialist testing firms. Their only role is to test the accuracy and safety of industrial components, using highly specialized and expensive equipment. The cost of employing such equipment would be prohibitive to most market participants, but the fact that a large number of firms within the same sector that require such testing services are also located at the same place allows the costs to be spread across the group. A second type of non-traded local input is that of specialist local infrastructure. In the City of London there is a specialist dedicated wide-band fibre-optic cable system which is designed to allow the maximum possible flows of data between the local financial institutions, while excluding the general public. Access to the system comes about only through location in the City. All the local market participants benefit from the specialist infrastructure, and the cost of it is spread across all the beneficiaries. As above, the costs of the non-traded local inputs to each firm within the group will fall as more firms join the cluster.

(iii) Local skilled labour pool

The third source of agglomeration economies is the existence of a specialized local labour pool. This allows firms to reduce their labour acquisition costs, and there are two aspects to this. The first is that firms require sufficient quantities of labour to respond to market conditions. Therefore, if market demand conditions improve rapidly, a firm will wish to expand its labour force quickly, and will need to undertake a search process to acquire the workers. Secondly, the firm will also need to ensure that the employees are able to carry out the tasks correctly. In many sectors the costs of training labour and skills acquisition can be extremely high. This is because workers will need to be provided with specialist courses and instruction. Also, the opportunity costs involved with the time involved in these training activities can be extremely high. However, if a firm is located in an area which already has a large local pool of workers with the specialist skills required by the particular industry, the costs to the firm of expanding its workforce will be relatively low. This is because the firm will have to undertake little or no retraining activities. For industries in which skills-acquisition costs are high, or in which the opportunity costs of time are significant due to rapidly changing market conditions, a local pool of skilled workers will therefore be of great benefit. The labour acquisition costs on the part of the firms, which include both the search costs and the retraining costs, will be reduced relative to firms in dispersed locations.

These three sources of agglomeration economies have been succinctly captured by Duranton and Puga (2004), who describe them as processes of *learning, sharing, and matching*. This very neat formulation allows us to see agglomeration not as a static phenomenon, but as a dynamic phenomenon of simultaneous processes of interaction. Together, these three sources of agglomeration economies can allow firms within a cluster to experience economies of scale which are external to any single firm, but which are internal to the group. The key feature of each of these sources of agglomeration economies is that spatial clustering reduces knowledge and information transactions costs. Clustering therefore increases the likelihood that the appropriate information will be transmitted, that the specialist requisite services will be provided, and the appropriately skilled labour will be available, at that location, relative to other more dispersed locations.

2.3.2 **The types of agglomeration economies**

The sources of agglomeration economies described above allow firms within the same industry which are clustered together in space to achieve localized external economies of scale. However, in many areas, groups of firms in different industries can be clustered together geographically. For example, major cities may contain hundreds of industrial clusters. The exact nature of the agglomeration economies may therefore be different in different locations. In order to describe the particular nature of agglomeration economies in any particular area, economists often adopt a classification which was first employed by Ohlin (1933) and Hoover (1937, 1948). This classification splits agglomeration economies into three types, namely internal returns to scale, localization economies, and urbanization economies.

(i) **Internal returns to scale**

Some firms achieve significant economies of scale in their production simply by reason of their size. These economies of scale are regarded as being internal to the firm, in that the efficiency gains are explicitly deemed to be a result of the size of the individual firm. As such, these internal economies do not concur with the Marshall description above of economies of agglomeration as being external. Yet the notion of economies of scale here is explicitly spatial in that it is assumed that the internal economies of scale are generated because a large level of investment takes place at one particular location, rather than across a range of different locations. A large factory, such as the Fiat automobile plant in Turin, or the Boeing Everett hangar in Seattle, requires a large quantity of capital and a large labour force to be located at the same place. These internal production economies of scale are therefore associated with a high spatial concentration of both investment and people. As such, large stocks of factors are clustered together in space, although in this case they are within the definition of a single firm. However, the point is that the internal economies of scale are location specific.

(ii) **Economies of localization**

Localization economies are the agglomeration economies which accrue to a group of firms within the same industrial sector located at the same place. For example, in the case of Seattle, there are many firms that produce specialist aerospace components supplied directly to Boeing. Similarly, in automobile clusters such as in Detroit, Michigan, Stuttgart, Germany, and Nagoya, Japan, there are many firms producing specialist supplies for the major automobile-producing firms. There are several ways in which the local supply firms can benefit from close proximity to their major customer firms, which are the firms achieving internal returns to scale. According to Marshall's first source of agglomeration economies, the supply firms may benefit from frequent information exchanges with the customer firms, thereby increasing the mutual understanding and familiarity of these firms at different stages within the production process. Sometimes this will also involve exchanges of personnel and consultants. These activities can facilitate product development in markets where the risks are high. Also, as with Marshall's two other sources of agglomeration economies described above, the firms in the same sector can benefit from specialist non-traded local services and a skilled local labour pool. Each of Marshall's sources of agglomeration can therefore contribute to localization economies, the definition of which is therefore that they accrue within a particular industrial sector.

(iii) Economies of urbanization

Urbanization economies are those economies of agglomeration which accrue to firms across different sectors (Jacobs 1960). For example, in the case of the cities mentioned above, namely Seattle, Detroit, Stuttgart, and Nagoya, the economy of each of these cities is centred around a single plant or a group of very large plants, each of which exhibits internal returns to scale. Around these plants are many supplier firms, and the group of customer and supplier firms together achieve localization economies. However, each of these cities is much larger than simply the single sector of aerospace in Seattle, and the automobile sector in Detroit, Stuttgart, and Nagoya. In order for other activities to continue to be clustered in these cities, they must also experience economies of scale. For example, all the people who live and work in the sectors achieving localization economies will require legal, real-estate, retail, educational, health care and leisure services. Similarly, the firms themselves may require services such as marketing, advertising, catering, packaging, transportation, real estate, and security, among others. These various activities, although not directly related to the sector experiencing internal returns to scale and localization economies, will still cluster in the local economy in order to provide services for the firms and employees of this sector. This clustering is in response to the large local market possibilities which exist. However, as before, these firms will experience increased local factor prices, which must be compensated by economies of scale if the clustering is to continue. The agglomeration economies experienced by these other sectors are termed urbanization economies.

Following on the from the seminal papers of Glaeser et al. (1992) and Henderson et al. (1995), there have been many discussions using urban and regional data from many countries regarding the extent to which diversity or specialization is more advantageous for growth. Many studies support the advantages of diversity over specialization, although, as a whole, the evidence is still rather inconclusive (de Groot et al. 2009). Part of the problem is that many knowledge activities and transactions transcend individual industries, sectors, or technologies, and therefore identifying and classifying these effects is very difficult (Mameli et al. 2008).

In the Hoover typology, internal returns to scale are firm-specific economies of agglomeration, localization economies are industry-specific economies of agglomeration, and urbanization economies are city-specific economies of agglomeration. As we see in Urban and Regional Example 2.1, the difference here between the three classes of agglomeration economies therefore depends on the definition of the boundaries of the firms and the sectors.

These definitional changes do not always simply reflect changes in firm boundaries or changes in firm ownership. In some cases, the change in definition of agglomeration economies may also indicate more fundamental changes in the nature of the interactions taking place between firms, and in many cases these changes can actually be driven largely by the

Urban and Regional Example 2.1   Changes in firm boundaries

For example, the difference between the location-specific internal returns to scale and localization economies in part depends on the boundaries of the individual firm within an individual sector. To see this, we can consider a case where a group of separate firms within the same industry are clustered together and experience localization economies. If this group is subsequently all bought cut by a single firm, any economies of scale they achieve due to spatial proximity will now be counted as internal to the individual firm. An example here would be the early growth of General Motors in Detroit. The change in the firm boundaries due to the change in the ownership structure does not of itself alter the fact that location-specific economies of scale are operating at this particular place. On the other hand, we can consider the opposite case where a large location-specific activity is fragmented. For example, a chemicals complex at Teeside in the UK was formerly entirely owned by a single firm, ICI. Subsequently, parts of the plant were sold to other chemicals firms such as DuPont, although the various parts of the complex continued to produce for each other as before. What previously would have been counted as internal returns to scale would now be classified as localization economies. As before, however, the change in the ownership structure will not fundamentally alter the fact that location-specific economies of scale are operating at this particular place. A similar argument also applies to the situation where firms sell off parts of their operations to firms in other industries. These changes appear as increased urbanization economies, because these ownership changes will mean that the plants will now be defined as representing a variety of industries, rather than a single industry.

changes of ownership. Indeed, ownership reorganization is a key feature of most forms of industrial restructuring, and if the ownership changes are associated with beneficial changes in the competitive and cooperative relationships between firms (Saxenian 1994), these ownership changes will be associated with genuine agglomeration impulses. We will deal with the features of different types of agglomeration and clustering and the relationships between firms in section 2.4. Before this however, Box 2.1 reviews a range of other descriptions of industrial clusters, all of which play an important role in contemporary discussion if industrial clustering.

BOX 2.1 Alternative descriptions of industrial clusters

As well as the classic Marshall and Hoover descriptions of agglomeration economies, there is a range of other models which discuss particular aspects of industrial clustering. Each of these models is also regularly adopted by analysts to describe various types of clusters, so we will briefly discuss them here. They are the three long-established models known as the growth pole model, the incubator model, and the product cycle model, as well as two more recent models, the Porter model (1990, 1998) and the new industrial areas model (Scott 1988).

The growth pole model

The growth pole model was originally associated with the work of Perroux (1950), although it employed some of the ideas of Schumpeter (1934). Perroux described economic relationships in terms of monetary space, in which there are certain polarities regarding financial transactions. In other words, the decisions made by key large firms have major financial implications for other firms which are linked to the key firm through customer–supplier relationships. Perroux described these key large firms as 'growth poles', and the decisions they make which affect other firms relate primarily to issues such as innovation. The concept was translated into spatial planning terms primarily by Boudeville (1966), in which it was argued that the spatial behaviour of an area will be affected by the location behaviour of certain major firms or plants. For example, if large firm investments or public investment projects are implemented at a particular location, this location-specific investment can act as a focus for local growth. Other local firms may be able to use the advantage of proximity in order to increase their local sales to the new investment, thereby generating localized growth in the hinterland of the investment. These beneficial effects, however, will take time to develop. For example, as we saw in section 3.1, the immediate effect of a large location-specific investment may be an increase in local factor prices. This may reduce local efficiency in the short run and also lead to some localized crowding-out effects. In the growth pole literature these negative local effects are collectively known as 'backwash effects'. However, as the positive economic aspects of the growth pole begin to take effect, the beneficial 'spread effects' are assumed to dominate the negative backwash effects within the hinterland region, thereby engendering positive local growth over the long run. The major point raised by the growth pole model is that large innovative firms or investment activities will tend to have significant impacts on the local development of industrial clusters. Innovation alone may not be of such significance, nor will size alone, although a combination of the two may engender significant local growth effects. The weakness of the approach, however, is the lack of any coherent analysis of the costs and benefits of such investment schemes. Good reviews of this literature are provided by (Richardson 1978; Parr 1999a,b).

The incubator model

The incubator model is associated with the work of Chinitz (1961, 1964) and was derived from observations of the industrial structure of Pittsburgh and New York. At the time Pittsburgh was dominated by a small number of very large firms and a small number of sectors—primarily coal and steel. In contrast, New York contained a wide variety of different sectors, and was less dominated by particular large firms. The argument of Chinitz is that industrial clusters which are highly diversified, and which contain a range of types of industries and firm sizes, will act as superior 'incubators' for the development and growth of new firms. The reason for this is that in such an environment, there will be a variety of local business services available to these small firms which will facilitate their growth. On the other hand, in industrial clusters dominated primarily by large firms, many of these requisite services will not be available because the large firms will be able to supply such activities internally, or on the basis of log-term contracts with a limited number of suppliers and customers. These arguments have been extended more recently by Duranton and Puga (2001), who examine the incubator advantages of 'nursery' cities. Chinitz's argument is important because it suggests that the issues of firm ownership structure, as discussed in section 3.2.2, may also play an independent role in affecting the growth of the cluster. In particular, a larger diversity of local sectors, firm sizes, and firm types may be important for the growth of the cluster, as it provides greater potential opportunities for firms to find new market niches. The Chinitz argument therefore suggests that diversified regions offer greater growth potential for newly emerging technologies and firms.

The product cycle model

The product cycle model is associated with the work of Vernon (1960, 1966) and is one of the approaches most frequently used to describe the qualitative aspects of spatial investment patterns. The most common use of the product cycle model has been in discussions of international investment flows (Vernon 1966), although the origins of the theory are actually found in observations of city clusters (Vernon 1960). Vernon's argument is that firms will separate activities by location according to the stage in the life cycle of the product, which in turn is reflected by the activities of the particular plant. For example, in high-level industrial clusters, such as in dominant central cities, firms will tend to locate

BOX 2.1 Continued

information-intensive activities such as research and development and high-level decision-making, which together relate to the early stages of the life cycle of the product. The reason is that these activities require large knowledge inputs, and, in particular, knowledge which is generally non-standardized. The non-standardized nature of the product or process is precisely due to the newness of the product or technique. Following the Marshall argument above, these activities may therefore benefit from the informal knowledge and information spillovers associated with localized clustering. Meanwhile, highly skilled employees will also be required to carry out such activities, and, once again, from the Marshall argument, it may be consistently easier to find these workers in such clustered areas. On the other hand, once a product and the associated production process have been designed, tested, and developed, the firm will be able to issue a blueprint or template which documents all the aspects of the production of the product or service and also the detailed specification of its delivery mechanisms. This information will now be available to other branches of the firm's organization. The information regarding the product is thus standardized and, as production increases, the product becomes 'mature'; in other words, it is no longer so novel. Over time, the production techniques tend to become better understood and relatively easier to carry out. As this happens, the requirement for knowledge inputs and highly skilled labour tends to fall, with the result that the firm can move the production process to other lower-cost and lower-skilled areas. The product-cycle argument therefore implies that more geographically peripheral areas, which tend to exhibit lower labour costs and lower labour skills, will also tend to have plants producing more mature, less novel, and more standardized products (Markusen 1985). The result is that there will tend to be a clear separation of activity types between central city-regions and more peripheral areas. The important observation of the product-cycle model is that there may therefore emerge a qualitative distinction between the types of activities which take place at the economic centre or at the periphery of any geographical area. As we will see in Chapter 9, the evidence of the recent era of globalization suggests that the spaces over which these differences often emerge is now global as well as regional.

The Porter model

Within the business management community there has been much interest in the arguments of Porter (1990, 1998 a,b). Porter focuses on the concept of *competitiveness*, a concept which is broader than just profitability, because it relates to all the elements and manifestation of the processes of profit creation. Porter's arguments on competitive advantages were initially developed within a firm and industry-based approach (Porter 1985), but his arguments were subsequently translated into an urban and regional setting. In terms of urban and regional issues, Porter (1990) argues that clustering may act as an alternative organizational form to the standard markets and hierarchies dichotomy associated with the work of Williamson (1975). He argues that clustering provides individual firms with another way of organizing their transactions in an environment of rapidly changing information and technology. This particular form of spatial industrial organization maximizes the transfer of technology, knowledge, and information flows between the firms, and is particularly important in the case of small firms which rely mainly on external sources of information and technology. However, the key point of Porter's argument is that proximity also engenders mutual visibility between competitors. In others words, firms are able to observe the competitive developments of each other, and this visibility itself acts as a spur to all firms to continue to improve their own individual competitiveness. The proximity of many suppliers, customers, and related institutions or organizations also helps built the cluster, but Porter's (1990) crucial point is that transparency drives competition and competition drives *innovation*.

Innovation is not invention. Innovation is the translating of new ideas, new designs, new inventions, and new concepts into new marketable and commercially viable products and services. The three fundamental features of all innovations are newness, improvement, and reduction of risk (Gordon and McCann 2005). Firms attempt to overcome long-term risk by trying to develop monopoly positions over competitors, and this is the motivation for innovation. In order to do this they strive to develop novel products or services which are commercially viable, but the determination as to whether a new product or service is commercially viable depends on whether the customers in the market perceive the product or service to be an improvement on existing offerings, given the prices being charged. As such, it is not only novelty that drives growth, but the flows of knowledge between potential suppliers and customers. The mutual transparency associated with clustering fosters both the striving for novelty and the generation of the requisite knowledge flows for market selection processes to operate efficiently. The Porter (1990) approach closely relates to the Alchian (1950) adapting–adopting issues discussed in Section 2.6. However, the Porter (1990) arguments represent a much more dynamic approach, emphasizing that localized competition drives innovation, which in turn increases the competitiveness and growth of the cluster as a whole. Porter's arguments are rather different in origin to many of the other urban and regional economic approaches examined in this book, in that he makes almost no assumptions about the nature of the representative firm, the properties of market equilibrium conditions, or the properties of production factors such as diminishing marginal returns and factor substitutibility. His arguments derive primarily from numerous case studies of the behaviour of firms and industries.

The new industrial areas model

The new industrial areas model, or new industrial spaces model, derives primarily from a series of observations within the field of urban planning and geography (Scott 1988). Certain industrial clusters, such as the electronics cluster in Silicon Valley (Saxenian 1994), the electronics and biotechnology cluster in Cambridge, UK (Keeble and Wilkinson 1999), and the small-firm manufacturing industry of the Emilia-Romagna region of Italy, have shown themselves to be major centres of innovation (Breschi and Malerba 2005; Becattini et al. 2009). These observations have led to suggestions from many observers that industries which are made up of spatial networks or clusters of small firms tend to be more highly innovative than industries comprising mainly large firms (Saxenian 1994), because such environments provide the appropriate 'milieux' for such innovations to take place (Aydalot and Keeble 1988). In particular, as well as Marshall's classic sources of agglomeration economies, it is also argued that networks of important business relationships operate between local decision-makers which allow for risk-taking. These relationships are perceived to depend on strong mutual trust between the participants, and are assumed to have developed partly due to geographical proximity. The reasons why these arrangements are argued to work is that the people trust each other not to engage in opportunistic behaviour, but rather to lean towards cooperative types of relationship. There is clear evidence in favour of these arguments from a small number of European countries (Becattini et al. 2009). At the same time, however, there is little or no consensus among observers concerning the applicability of these arguments to other countries or regions (Suarez-Villa and Walrod 1997; Simmie 1988; Arita and McCann 2000). What is evident is that the relationships between firm size, innovation, and industrial clustering highlighted by this literature have led to a great deal of interest among public policy planners. The primary motive for this is the belief that understanding this relationship may improve public policy initiatives to foster such developments elsewhere (Castells and Hall 1994).

2.4 Clusters, firm types, and the nature of transactions

A problem with discussing the nature of, and reasons for, industrial clustering is that it is very difficult both empirically and theoretically to distinguish between each of the above reasons for, and descriptions of, industrial clustering. From an empirical point of view, distinguishing between urbanization economies and localization economies is notoriously difficult (Glaeser et al. 1992; Henderson et al. 1995), because many industrial clusters such as cities will contain all types of clusters both within and across a range of sectors. From a theoretical perspective, the Marshall description is important in allowing us to understand the sources of agglomeration economies within an individual industry sector, while the Hoover approach is important from the point of view of identifying the particular firms and sectors which experience these agglomeration economies. However, it may appear that the distinction between the three Hoover classifications is rather arbitrary, given that mergers and acquisitions mean that firms are frequently changing ownership and sectors. Moreover, the relationship between the Marshall and Hoover classifications may be further complicated by each of the issues raised by the growth pole, the incubator, the product cycle, the Porter, and the new industrial area models. Yet there are clear differences between the types of industrial clusters which exist in reality, according to the nature of relations between the firms within the individual clusters and the particular features they exhibit (Gordon and McCann 2000).

In order to understand these relations, it is necessary for us to focus on the characteristics of firms which exist in the cluster, and the transactions which take place within the cluster. Adopting this approach, we see that there are three broad typologies of spatial industrial clusters, as defined in terms of the features they exhibit (Gordon and McCann 2000). These are the *pure agglomeration,* the *industrial complex,* and the *social network.* The key feature which distinguishes each of these different ideal types of spatial industrial cluster is the nature of the relations between the firms within the cluster. The characteristics of each of the cluster types are listed in Table 2.1, and as we see, the three ideal types of clusters are all quite different. In reality, all spatial clusters will contain characteristics of one or more of these ideal types, although one type will tend to be dominant in each cluster. Therefore, from an empirical point of view or from a public policy perspective which seeks to influence the behaviour of the cluster, it is necessary to determine which of these particular ideal types of industrial cluster most accurately reflects the characteristics and behaviour of any particular cluster.

Table 2.1 Industrial clusters

Characteristics	Pure agglomeration	Industrial complex	Social network
firm size	atomistic	some firms are large	variable
characteristics of relations	non-identifiable	Identifiable	trust
	fragmented	stable trading	loyalty
	unstable		joint lobbying
			joint ventures
			non-opportunistic
membership	open	closed	partially open
access to cluster	rental payments	internal investment	history
	location necessary	location necessary	experience
			location necessary but not sufficient
space outcomes	rent appreciation	no effect on rents	partial rental capitalisation
notion of space	Urban	local but not urban	local but not urban
example of cluster	competitive urban economy	steel or chemicals production complex	new industrial areas
analytical approaches	models of pure agglomeration	location-production theory input–output analysis	social network theory (Granovetter)

In the model of pure agglomeration, inter-firm relations are inherently transient. Firms are essentially atomistic, in the sense of having no market power, and they will continuously change their relations with other firms and customers in response to market arbitrage opportunities, thereby leading to intense local competition. As such, there is no loyalty between firms, nor are any particular relations long term. The external benefits of clustering accrue to all local firms simply by reason of their local presence, the price of which is the local real-estate market rent. There are no free-riders, access to the cluster is open, and consequently it is the growth in the local real-estate rents which is the indicator of the cluster's performance. This idealized type is best represented by the Marshall model, and the localization and urbanization economies of Hoover, but also contains elements of the Porter, Chinitz, and Vernon models. The notion of space in these models is essentially urban space in that this type of clustering only exists within individual cities.

The industrial complex is characterized primarily by long-term stable and predictable relations between the firms in the cluster. This type of cluster is most commonly observed in industries such as steel and chemicals, and is the type of spatial cluster typically discussed by classical (Weber 1909) and neoclassical (Moses 1958) location-production models, representing a fusion of locational analysis with input–output analysis (Isard and Kuenne 1953). Component firms within the spatial grouping each undertake significant long-term investments, particularly in terms of physical capital and local real estate, in order to become part of the grouping. Access to the group is therefore severely restricted both by high entry and exit costs, and the rationale for spatial clustering in these types of industries is that proximity is required primarily in order to minimize inter-firm transport transactions costs. Rental appreciation is not a feature of the cluster, because the land which has already been purchased by the firms is not for sale. This ideal type of cluster more closely reflects the internal returns to scale argument of Hoover and aspects of the growth pole model of Perroux than the other cluster types. The notion of space in the industrial complex is local, but not necessarily urban, in that these types of complexes can exist either within or outside an individual city.

The third type of spatial industrial cluster is the social network model. This is associated primarily with the work of Granovetter (1973, 1985, 1991, 1992), and is a response to the hierarchies model of Williamson (1975). The social network model argues that mutual trust relations between key decision-making agents in different organizations may be at least as important as decision-making hierarchies within individual organizations. These trust relations will be manifested by a variety of features, such as joint lobbying, joint ventures, informal alliances, and reciprocal arrangements regarding trading relationships. However, the key feature of such trust relations is an absence of opportunism, in that individual firms will not fear reprisals after any reorganization of inter-firm relations. Inter-firm cooperative relations may therefore differ significantly from the organizational boundaries associated with individual firms, and these relations may be continually reconstituted. All these behavioural features rely on a common culture of mutual trust, the development of which depends largely on a shared history and experience of the decision-making agents. This social network model is essentially aspatial, but from the point of view of geography, it can be argued that spatial proximity will tend to foster such trust relations, thereby leading to a local business environment of confidence, risk-taking, and cooperation. Spatial proximity is necessary but not sufficient to acquire access to the network. As such, membership of the network is only partially open, in that local rental payments will not guarantee access, although they will improve the chances of access. The social network model therefore contains elements of both the Porter model (1990, 1998) and the new industrial areas model (Scott 1988), and has been employed to describe the characteristics and performance of areas such as Silicon Valley and the Emilia-Romagna area of Italy. In this model space is once again local, but not necessarily urban.

When we consider the fundamentally different nature of each of these cluster types, there are two major issues which immediately arise. Firstly, there is the question of whether there are any risks associated with locating in a cluster which might deter firms from doing so, and secondly, there is the question as to how to identify empirically the dominant features and logic of the cluster.

On the first point regarding the potential risks associated with locating in a cluster, the major issues here relate to the risks of experiencing what are known as unintended knowledge outflows (Grindley and Teece 1997). From the agglomeration arguments we know that one of the reasons why firms might wish to co-locate is to benefit from knowledge spillovers. From the perspective of the individual firms the positive and beneficial aspects of knowledge spillovers are knowledge inflows from other firms. However, where firms undertaking R&D have privately developed novel ideas or techniques on which they wish to build new products or services, in general their wish will be to keep such knowledge secret until it can be protected by patents, licences, copyrights, and the like. Such firms will want to avoid unintended knowledge spillovers to other firms, or in other words unintended knowledge outflows. Otherwise the potential competitive advantages afforded by this proprietary knowledge and proprietary assets will be lost. Tight firm boundaries and long-term legal contracts are the standard technique for avoiding such unintended knowledge outflows, exactly in accordance with the markets and hierarchies argument of Williamson (1975) underpinning the organizational logic of the industrial complex. The industrial complex model therefore allows for large-scale R&D to be undertaken with the risk of such unintended knowledge outflows occurring. In the case of the social network model the risks associated with unintended knowledge outflows are controlled by the shared norms and values of the network, the foundations of which are built on a code of non-opportunism. In the case of the pure agglomeration model, there are really no means by which such unintended knowledge outflows can be limited. The point about this argument is that it is not automatic that firms will wish to cluster together in space (see Urban and Regional Example 2.2).

What we see is that whether firms are clustered together depends on the knowledge advantages of clustering versus the knowledge disadvantages of clustering, and these issues are just as pertinent to small companies as they are to large companies. The only proprietary asset that many small companies have is a novel idea, product, or technology. For these firms the risks of clustering can be very real because if knowledge about the novel idea, product, or technology unintentionally leaks out to competing firms, the *raison d'être* of the firm disappears. However, these firms are often too small to fully pursue their idea alone and therefore they must take on board the risks associated with sharing knowledge and information with potential suppliers, customers, or collaborators, all of whom could become competitors. As such, the risks of clustering are not just limited to large firms, but also arise for small firms. What becomes clear is that while there are advantages associated

Urban and Regional Example 2.2   To cluster or not to cluster?

Whether a firm wishes to co-locate with other firms depends on the balance between the positive benefits from received knowledge inflows, which are a public good, and the potential losses associated with unintended knowledge outflows. In markets where product life cycles are very short, such as in international finance or in some of the Silicon Valley components of the semiconductor industry (Saxenian 1994), for many firms the only way to acquire the relevant market knowledge is by very frequent face-to-face contact, which can only be afforded by proximity (McCann 2005). Where the need for such high-frequency interactions is less, firms have much more flexibility to move away from each other if they wish.

Where secrecy is absolutely paramount due to the enormous costs of R&D, as is the case in pharmaceuticals or in many non-Silicon Valley parts of the semiconductor industry (McCann and Arita 2006), a very different location approach is often adopted by firms. In some cases firms will choose to pursue internal R&D within a closed environment while developing little or no linkages with the surrounding regional economy, or even in effect becoming 'islands' of innovation (Simmie 1988). Alternatively, firms may even choose to move away from other firms in the same industry. In both cases, the aim of the firm is to remove the risks of unintended knowledge outflows, as these are regarded as being too costly relative to the benefits of knowledge inflows.

with agglomeration, as outlined above, there are also disadvantages associated with clustering that go well beyond the issues of congestion or rising land prices.

On the second point regarding empirical observation, as we have already noted, all industrial clusters will contain features of one or more of these ideal types. However, determining the major features of any particular cluster will require us to consider which of these particular types is dominant. The reason is that empirically each of these cluster types will have different manifestations. For example, in the pure model of agglomeration, the dominant feature will be an appreciation in local real-estate values, with no particular purchasing or decision-making linkages being evident between local firms. Discussions of the strength of local purchasing or decision-making linkages, or the types of local alliances undertaken by firms, will not indicate agglomeration behaviour. On the other hand, in the case of the industrial complex there will be no real-estate effects, but the dominant feature will be a stability of both purchasing and decision-making linkages. However, measuring the scale of such linkages is less important than measuring the duration of the linkages. Finally, in the network model, although the market environment will be highly competitive, the dominant feature of the firm relations will be a willingness to undertake a variety of informal collective and cooperative activities which cut across organizational boundaries, such as joint lobbying, or inter-firm credit availability. Measuring real-estate appreciation or the strength of local purchasing linkages will not tell us very much. Industrial clusters are therefore of a variety of types, the observation and measurement of which is also a complicated topic.

Linking these individual types of clusters to economic growth and development is also complex. It is clear from the data that both innovation and entrepreneurship are related to agglomeration (Acs 2002; Van Oort 2004). However, the arguments here also imply that innovation may just as easily be related to industrial complexes and social networks as to agglomeration, because each of these three broad types represents a different way of solving the problems related to the generation, exchange, acquisition, and exploitation of knowledge. In order examine how these cluster types are related to innovation processes, Iammarino and McCann (2006) develop a cluster–innovation taxonomy which explicitly links a slightly extended version of the Gordon and McCann (2000) cluster typologies outlined here to a famous innovation-system classification scheme known as the Pavitt (1984) taxonomy. While the detailed issues arising from the Iammarino and McCann (2006) approach are beyond the scope of this book, the important point to note here is that the different forms of clusters are all related to innovation, but the ways in which we can empirically observe these relationships are very different. Simple observations of the spatial clustering of firms cannot be taken at face value as evidence of agglomeration, because their reasons for locating in the same place may have little or nothing to do with knowledge spillovers (McCann 1995a). In order to identify the relationships between firm location behaviour, knowledge, and innovation, it is nearly always necessary to complement the use of secondary empirical data sources with the use of primary survey and case-study type evidence on the nature of the industrial transactions and interrelationships operating between the firms, in a manner akin to the Porter (1990) approach.

2.5 People clustering: creativity and urban consumption

As well as the various industrial clustering arguments described here, over recent years two other closely related explanations of the advantages of urban clustering have also emerged. However, these explanations are somewhat different from those described so far, because they focus on the advantages of *people* clustering in urban areas, rather than firm clustering, and these explanations are the creative class hypothesis (Florida 2002, 2005) and the consumer city hypothesis (Glaeser et al. 2001; Glaeser and Gottlieb 2006).

The creative class hypothesis was originally developed by Richard Florida (2002, 2005), who sought to explain how and why clusters of certain types of people, rather than firms, were so important for regional growth. Florida's argument in its original form (Florida 2002) examined the performance of places populated with diverse and often rather unconventional and unorthodox communities, and his initial observations (Florida 2002) centred on places such as San Francisco, a city with a long history of social innovation and social tolerance. The central tenet of the creativity hypothesis is that places which are tolerant of cultural diversity and cultural differences are also environments which are ideally suited for fostering unconventional approaches to the development of novel ideas, systems, products, or services. This unconventionality itself is argued to enable and encourage experimentation, innovation, and entrepreneurial behaviour of all different forms. Florida (2002) argues that the natural outcome of this culture of tolerance is an environment of creativity, which is manifested in the form of various types of creative outputs in art, theatre, and media, as well as in terms of novel business concepts and new technology and investment ideas. As such, his original argument is that in these types of environments artistic creativity will also be associated with commercial dynamism, and the creativity of the community will therefore be manifested in different ways.

Florida also argued (Florida 2002, 2005) that people with these requisite creative personalities and skills will increasingly move to culturally tolerant places, in search of both creative employment and commercial opportunities but also in search of a particular lifestyle, which is tolerant of unconventionality. The in-migration of creative people also drives further innovation in the tolerant and creative regions, both via local competition effects and also via innovation-creation effects. In contrast, regions that are intolerant of cultural diversity will increasingly lose these creative people, and consequently they will also lose the commercial dynamism associated with these people.

In many ways Florida's arguments echo some of the explanations for the success of the Dutch Republic during the seventeenth-century 'Golden Age', which posit that the flowering burst of economic ingenuity in an environment of religious tolerance allowed for inflows of Jews, Huguenots, and Catholics seeking refuge from religious intolerance in other countries. Even explanations for the nineteenth-century growth of some of the US coast cities contain some of this logic. Moreover, it will become clear that the Florida arguments are also in some ways related to the bridging and bonding (Putnam 1996) dimensions of social capital, as discussed in Chapter 7. Indeed, as we will see in Chapter 7, some authors actually refer to *creative capital* as a distinct entity in its own right.

A related argument is that of the consumer city hypothesis (Glaeser et al. 2001; Glaeser and Gottlieb 2006), which posits that high-skilled and high-income people will increasingly migrate towards cities offering high-quality amenities, such as opera houses, theatres, museums, culinary outputs, and so on. This argument conceives of the modern city as a place of leisure as well as work, where high-income workers consume highly income-elastic goods and services produced in these particular types of urban environments. This argument is related to the amenity-migration arguments discussed in Chapter 6, although the emphasis of the amenity-migration models is on the importance of natural environmental amenities while the consumer city hypothesis here emphasizes the importance of human-produced urban amenities. The consumer city hypothesis is also closely related to the urban gentrification arguments discussed in Chapters 4 and 10.

A point of overlap between these two models comes from the fact that artistic and culinary outputs produced by creative people concentrated in urban areas are exactly the types of highly income-elastic human-produced goods consumed by high-income workers in urban areas. Various papers (Comunian et al. 2010; Abreu et al. 2012) have demonstrated recently that the average wages earned by creative workers working in artistic activities tend to be lower than those of equivalently skilled workers working in other activities. In part this reflects a more skewed wage distribution among creative–artistic occupations than other activities, but, even allowing for this, it appears that creative workers are willing to accept lower wages, presumably because some of the rewards to their labour are in the form of job satisfaction. However, this observation suggests that the major beneficiaries of these creative processes are not the creative workers themselves, but the high-income consumers working in the city and enjoying the high-quality creative services and amenities on offer in the city, exactly as argued by the consumer city hypothesis.

Our understanding of these issues is still developing and there are both supporting and dissenting voices (Caves 2000; Scott 2000; Markusen 2006) on these matters. What is important for our purposes, however, is to recognize that urban clustering is not simply about firms, nor where it relates to labour is it purely about matching. It also appears to be related to interactions of people, and in particular to social aspects of interactions, which facilitate the generation and the spreading of new ideas.

2.6 Limited information, uncertainty, and the evolution of clusters

The models discussed in Chapter 1 and also in the earlier parts of this chapter rely largely on the assumption that firms and individuals are basically rational, and the behaviour of firms and individuals predicated on this rationality is sufficient to generate clusters. Yet this argument itself has three implicit dimensions. First, it is assumed that firms and individuals either know, or the price mechanism will quickly reveal, the locations where the potential profitability advantages are greater for their particular activities. Second, it is assumed that firms and individuals will act on this information and use their location behaviour in order to maximize their profits. Third, the cumulative effect of such individual choices is that agglomerations and clusters will naturally emerge.

In reality, however, the information available to firms and individuals is often rather limited, and different firms will often have different information available to them. For these reasons, some commentators have argued that firms cannot and do not make rational decisions in order to maximize their profits. Rather, they argue that firms make decisions in order to achieve goals other than simply profit maximization. Therefore, from the perspective of both individual and aggregate group location behaviour, this critique might suggest that the underlying motivation of our location, clustering, and agglomeration models would need to be reconsidered. In particular, the ways in which agglomerations and clusters arise in environments of uncertainty and limited information may need to be reconsidered. This critique, which is important to understand, has three themes: bounded rationality, conflicting goals, and relocation costs. The first two themes discussed in Box 2.2 can be grouped

BOX 2.2 Behavioural theories and bounded rationality

Where firms face limited information, Baumol (1959) has argued that they will focus on sales revenue maximization as the short-run objective of their decision-making. One reason for this is that sales revenue maximization implies the maximum market share for the firm in the short run. Where information is limited, current market share is deemed by many observers to be the best indicator of a firm's long-run performance, because it provides a measure of the monopoly power of the firm. The logic of this approach is that the greater the market share of the firm, the greater the current monopoly power of the firm, and the greater will be the firm's long-run ability to deter potential competitors through defensive tactics such as limit-pricing and cross-subsidizing. From the perspective of location models, this may imply that the firm will make location decisions primarily in order to ensure maximum sales revenue rather than maximum profits. In the Hotelling model described in Chapter 1, these two objectives coincide. However, if the costs of production or transportation faced by the firm were to vary with location along the line *OL* in Figure 1.17, as they can do in the Weber and Moses type models, the two objectives of sales maximization and profit maximization may not coincide at the same location point in the Hotelling model. The eventual location result will therefore depend on which particular performance measure the firm adopts and chooses to maximize.

The second critique of profit maximization as the decision-making goal of the firm is that of 'conflicting goals'. This critique is most closely associated with the work of Cyert and March (1963). The argument here is that in a world of imperfect information, the separation of ownership from decision-making in most major modern firms means that business objectives are frequently pursued which are different from simply profit maximization. Only shareholders have a desire for maximum profits in the short run. On the other hand, in modern multi-activity, multi-level, multi-plant and multi-national firm organizations, corporate decisions are the result of the many individual decisions made by a complex hierarchy of people, each with particular business objectives, and many of which are different from profit maximization. The reason is that the performance of different employees within a company is measured in different ways. For example, the directors' performance may be evaluated primarily by the firm's market share, whereas the sales manager's performance may be evaluated by sales growth. Similarly, the production manager's performance may be evaluated primarily by inventory throughput efficiency, whereas the personnel officer may be evaluated according to the number of days lost through industrial disputes. Given that each of these different decision-makers is evaluated on different criteria, the success, promotion, and consequently the wages earned by each of these workers will be evaluated differently. Therefore the objectives pursued by different employees may be quite different from profit maximization. Under these conditions, the 'conflicting goals' critique suggests that firms will aim to 'satisfice'. In other words, the firms will aim to achieve a satisfactory level of performance across a range of measures. In particular, the firm will initially aim to achieve a level of profit sufficient to avoid both shareholder interference in directors' activities and also to avoid the threat of a takeover. Once this objective is achieved, the other various goals of the firm can be satisfied. For example, the firm may aim to achieve market share levels as high as possible without jeopardizing the efficiency cost gains associated with production and logistics operations. Equally, employees' pay may be increased in order to encourage firm loyalty. The point here is that the overall objective of the firm can be specified in various ways.

In Figure 2.1, the firm's total profit function $T\pi$ is constructed as the difference between the total revenue function TR and the total cost function TC. The firm may choose to produce at output levels Q_1, Q_2, and Q_3, which represent the minimum cost output, the maximum profit output, and the maximum revenue output levels, respectively. All these levels of output produce a profit level sufficient to maintain a firm's independence π_s, but only one of these output levels Q_2 is the profit maximization level of output.

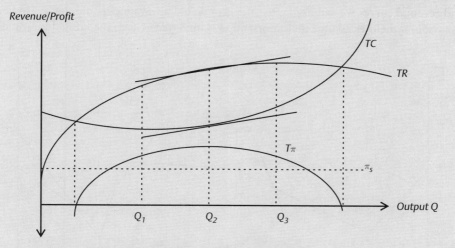

Figure 2.1 Profit maximizing, revenue maximizing, and profit satisficing

under the general heading of *Behavioural Theories*, and these arguments are not fundamentally geographical in nature, nor were they originally directed at location models in particular. In contrast, the third theme is essentially an explicitly spatial question.

The arguments concerning 'bounded rationality' are most closely associated with Simon (1952, 1959). This critique concerns the fact that firms in the real world face limited information, and this limited information itself limits firms' ability to be 'rational' in the sense assumed in microeconomics textbooks. These arguments are a more general critique of rationality within microeconomics as a whole. However, they have been argued to be particularly appropriate to the question of industrial location behaviour. The reason is that information concerning space and location is very limited, due to the inherent heterogeneity of land, real estate, and local economic environments. Therefore, when considering location issues, it would appear that the ability of the firm to be 'rational' is very much 'bounded' by the limited information available to it. In these circumstances, decisions guided by straightforward profit maximization behaviour appear to be beyond the ability of the firm. Therefore location models based on this assumption seem to oversimplify the location issue. Location behaviour may be determined primarily by other objectives than simply profit maximization, as discussed in Box 2.2.

The behavioural arguments imply that firms do not necessarily have the ability or the desire to make decisions which are explicitly aimed at maximizing short-term profits. Applying this argument to geography means that if we are faced with a set of spatial total cost and revenue curves, such as those described by Figure 2.2, the firm will make different location decisions, according to whether it is aiming to maximize profits in the short run or whether it is aiming to earn satisfactory profits in the short run along with achieving some other goals. For example, in Figure 2.2, if the firm is aiming to maximize profits in the short run it will locate at point *P*. On the other hand, if it is aiming to maximize sales it will locate at *S*, and if it is aiming to minimize production costs and to maximize production efficiency it will locate at *C*. If the firm had perfect information regarding these different spatial cost and revenue curves we can argue that the firm would always move to point *P*. However, behavioural theories assume that information is imperfect. Given the limited information

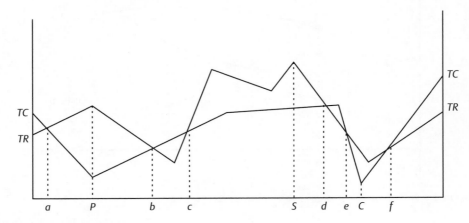

Figure 2.2 Spatial cost and revenue curves

available and the conflicting goals within the organization, the actual location behaviour of the firm will depend on which is its particular dominant objective.

The third critique of the classical and neo classical location models comes from the question of relocation costs. Relocation costs are the costs incurred every time a firm relocates. The models described above all assume that location is a costless exercise. However, relocation costs can be very significant, comprising the costs of the real-estate site search and acquisition, the dismantling, moving, and reconstruction of existing facilities, the construction of new facilities, and the hiring and training of the new labour employed. These significant transactions costs, along with imperfect information and conflicting goals, will mean that firms are unlikely to move in response to small variations in factor prices or market revenues. In Figure 2.2, the areas in which positive profits are made, i.e. where $TR > TC$, are known as 'spatial margins of profitability' (Rawstron 1958), and are represented by the areas between locations a and b, c and d, and e and f. The relationship between marginal location change and the profitability of the firm in these areas is given by $\partial(TR - TC)/\partial d$, and this is represented by the differences in the slopes of the spatial revenue and spatial cost functions as location changes. In the spatial margins of profitability in which the slopes of the spatial revenue and spatial cost functions are very shallow, the marginal benefit to the firm of relocation will be very low. Therefore, in the presence of high relocation costs the firm will not move to a superior location even if it knows which alternative is superior. In conditions of imperfect information and bounded rationality, conflicting goals, and significant relocation costs, the behavioural approach would argue that once a firm has chosen a location, it will tend to maintain its location as long as profits are positive, and not use relocation as a competitive weapon. Rather the firm will attempt to reorganize its factor allocations and activities among its current set of existing plants. At the same time, the firm will focus primarily on other price and non-price issues as competitive weapons, and the relocation of a plant, or the reorganization of multi-plant activities which involves either the closing or opening of a plant, will only be a last resort strategy. On the other hand, where relocation costs are insignificant, the firm will take advantage of spatial revenue and spatial cost differences and will be able to move to superior locations as a competitive strategy.

One obvious weakness of the behavioural critiques is that, unlike the classical and neo-classical location models discussed in Chapter 1, the behavioural theories do not of themselves indicate why a firm chooses a particular location in the first place. In this sense the behavioural approach is not prescriptive. However, the applicability of the location behaviour insights offered by the classical models and theories to real-world situations does need to be interpreted in the light of the behavioural critique, because uncertainty, bounded rationality, imperfect information, conflicting goals, and relocation costs are all features particularly characteristic of the spatial economy. Indeed, as a whole, the application of the behavioural critique to spatial behaviour suggests that observed spatial patterns are not necessarily reflective of optimum location behaviour, but rather sub-optimal adjustments to restricted alternatives. This critique provides an explanation as to why firm location behaviour may not be so responsive to the available optimization possibilities, and why aggregate spatial investment patterns in general may be very slow to adjust to the emerging profitability opportunities. This obviously also puts into question the validity of many of our models which assume that clusters and agglomerations will arise naturally in response to price signals. This is important because we implicitly assume that firms and individuals will voluntarily move and congregate where agglomeration advantages are on offer. Indeed, if the behavioural arguments provide a powerful critique of the ability of firms in the real world to act rationally in terms of location behaviour, then it would also appear *prima facie* to question our assumptions as to how agglomerations and clusters arise in the first place.

These difficulties can be overcome by considering the evolutionary argument of Alchian (1950). Alchian's argument is that the behaviour of firms in conditions of uncertainty can be understood by discussing the relationship between a firm and its environment, whereby a firm's environment is understood to encompass all the agents, information, and institutions competing and collaborating in the particular set of markets in which the firm operates. In Alchian's argument, we can characterize the uncertain economy by two broad types of environments. One is an 'adoptive' environment and the other is an 'adaptive' environment. These two classifications are not mutually exclusive, but serve as the two extreme stylized types, between which the real economy will exist.

In the 'adoptive' environment, all firms are more or less identical in that no firm has any particular or systematic information advantage over any other firm. However, they will have differences in their ability to survive, but these differences are often unrevealed or unknown *ex ante*. The results of the competitive process will imply *ex post* that some firms will be successful while others will not, although *ex ante*, no firms had any *a priori* knowledge that their products or techniques would be superior to those of their competitors. This characterization of the economy is Darwinian, in that the environment 'adopts' the firms which were better suited to the needs of the economy, even though the firms had no particular knowledge beforehand that this was the case. In statistical terms, in any given time period in the 'adoptive' environment, the probability of a particular single firm making a successful strategic decision is identical to that of all the other individual firms.

On the other hand, in the 'adaptive' environment, some individual firms are able to gather and analyse market information, simply by reason of their size. Large firms in general are able to utilize resources in order acquire and process information relating to their market environment, and the purpose of these information-gathering activities by the firms is to subsequently use the information to their own advantage, relative to their competitors. In statistical terms, therefore, in any given time period in the 'adaptive' environment, the probability of a particular firm making a profitable strategic decision is increased by reason of its size.

In the real world of heterogeneous firms and imperfect information, smaller firms will tend to perceive themselves to be at an information disadvantage relative to larger firms. Therefore they will tend to make decisions which mimic or dovetail with those of the larger firms, in matters such as styles, protocols, formats, and technology. In part this is because they perceive the market leaders to be the best barometers of market conditions, and also because the behaviour of the market leaders itself often contributes significantly to the overall economic environment simply by reason of their size. By copying the behaviour of the larger firms the small firms therefore perceive that they will maximize the likelihood of their own success. The result is that large firms tend to overcome uncertainty by information gathering and analysis, and small firms tend to overcome uncertainty by imitation.

This type of leader–follower behaviour is common in models of oligopoly and uncertainty. However, this behaviour is particularly pertinent to questions of location. In environments of uncertainty, larger firms will generally have the information and financial resources to make more considered location decisions than small firms. Major firms will be able to make location decisions more akin to those described by the Weber, Moses, and Hotelling models of Chapter 1, given that they will generally have sufficient resources to evaluate the cost and revenue implications of their location choice. These large firms will attempt to make rational and optimal decisions, and the results of their location choices can be analysed by the types of classical and neo classical models described above. On the other hand, small firms will generally be located where their founders were initially resident. There will have been no explicit initial location decision as such when the firm began operating. Often such small firms are entrepreneurial start-ups, whereby founders who were previously working for large firms decide to set up a new business in a related field, in many cases selling goods and services back to the large firm for which they previously worked, as well as accessing new markets. The geographical distribution and also the technological profile of such 'spin-offs' therefore tends to closely mirror that of the established firms, and gives rise to the evolution (Arthur 1991; Boschma and Martin 2010) of localized clusters of small and large firms, often in related technological fields (Frenken et al. 2007). As we will see in Chapter 7, this technological relatedness is a fundamental aspect of regional growth.

Over time, increasing competition means that location will eventually become a decision-making issue even for small firms as they develop and grow. As such, in subsequent location decisions, many small firms will tend to choose to open new establishments close to other large firms located in different market areas. Similarly, there is much evidence to suggest that large multi-plant firms grow by means of the establishment of new ventures, in particular already well-established spatial concentrations of firms (Delgado et al. 2010). This itself favours further concentration. Therefore, for small firms which are risk averse, these clustering strategies are particularly good strategies, because as we see from the Hotelling model, locating close to competitor firms ensures that an individual firm's market share is no lower than that of an equivalent firm. Moreover, the Salop (1979) argument suggests that clustering acts as also partial defence against the instability associated with price movements. The clustering of small firms around major firms is therefore very commonly observed. As such, imitation also takes place in terms of the foundation or relocation of new establishments, as well as the location behaviour of established firms.

2.7 Conclusions

This question of industrial clustering is the topic of Chapter 3, in which we discuss agglomeration economies, the growth of cities and urban hierarchies, and centre–periphery relationships.

Many activities are clustered together in space, giving rise to the formation of cities. This process of industrial clustering, however, typically leads to an increased demand for local land and consequently local real-estate prices will tend to increase, as will local labour prices. These increases in the prices of local factor inputs will therefore reduce profits, *ceteris paribus*, thereby reducing the attractiveness of the area as a location for the firms, unless certain countervailing features exist that more than compensate for the increased local factor costs. These countervailing features are generally understood to be agglomeration economies.

Following on from Marshall's (1890) insights as to the sources of agglomeration and the Ohlin–Hoover approach to classifying agglomeration effects, various other related reasons for the growth of cities have been proposed by a range of authors. The common element of all of these approaches is that the generation, acquisition, and transfer of knowledge is a key component of all aspects of industrial clustering. However, as our transactions costs approach has also demonstrated, the actual mechanisms by which these are achieved differ between different types of cluster. Understanding the types of cluster is critical for identifying the knowledge spillover processes which are economized on by the formation of a cluster, and vice versa. Yet, while these various analyses explain why clusters may arise, they do not explain exactly how they may arise in an environment of limited information, risk, and uncertainty. Here, a discussion of the behavioural critique suggests that the leader–follower behaviour typical of many industries will tend to encourage small firms to cluster together in space close to larger firms. Such behaviour underpins an evolutionary process of cluster formation, in which clusters and cities are seen to arise naturally, even in the context of less-than-perfect information. That is not to say, however, that agglomeration processes are linear and indefinite. In contrast, we also observe not only that many activities are geographically dispersed, but also that many clusters and cities are also dispersed. Indeed, the spatial economy appears to be characterized by both geographical concentration and geographical dispersion, and the balance between these two features produces a system of cities, an urban hierarchy. It is to these issues that we turn in Chapter 3.

Discussion questions

2.1 What are the three major sources of agglomeration economies and how do they operate?

2.2 Explain the three major types of agglomeration effects. What difficulties are there in identifying these different classifications?

2.3 What other descriptions and mechanisms of industrial clustering do we have?

2.4 Using a transactions costs framework, explain the role and contribution of knowledge, uncertainty, and trust in different types of industrial clusters.

2.5 Which examples of industrial clusters from your country best reflect each of the different types of clusters you have discussed?

2.6 What role do creativity and consumption play in clustering?

2.7 What insights are provided for industrial location analysis by behavioural theories of firm behaviour?

2.8 Explain the ways in which evolutionary processes of adaptation and adoption to the competitive environment are important for firm location behaviour.

3 The spatial distribution of activities

3.1 Introduction to industrial dispersal

All the arguments in Chapter 2 have attempted to explain and classify why it is that firms are so often clustered together in space. However, observation also tells us that not all activities are located together. For example, activities in primary industries tend to be spatially dispersed. Quarrying, drilling, and mining take place only in particular areas where the appropriate minerals can be extracted economically, and the geological conditions may require that such activities take place only in a dispersed spatial pattern of locations. Similarly, agricultural activities as a whole tend to be distributed rather evenly over space, simply because of the requirement of land as an input to the agricultural production process. At the same time, there are also many commercial and industrial activities which also tend to be dispersed. As we saw in Chapter 1, oligopolistic environments in which price competition is a major feature will tend to encourage competitor firms to move away from each other. Such firms are often observed to deliver products and services over large distances to their customers and from locations which are far from the locations of their immediate competitors. Similarly, cities and industrial clusters are often scattered over large distances, with some regions contain a several cities while other regions containing few densely populated settlements. What is noticeable, however, is that these patterns of industrial dispersion have a microeconomic logic to them, while at the wider level of the spatial pattern of the 'system of cities', these patterns of industrial dispersal also display particular regularities, known as the urban hierarchy.

Section 3.2 discusses the neoclassical arguments accounting for the industrial dispersal of individual firms and microeconomic regularities often observed. Section 3.3 discusses the two major classical approaches to the formation of the urban hierarchy, namely the Christaller and Löschian models. Section 3.4 then discusses the insights regarding the evolution of systems-of-cities generated by a more recent and highly influential school of models, known collectively as 'new economic geography' (NEG). Section 3.5 discusses the regularities evident in the interregional distribution of cities and section 3.6 provides a review of some alternative ways of measuring industrial dispersion and concentration, diversity and specialization.

then we have

$$r = \frac{\alpha^2}{(x - \alpha)^2} \tag{3.3}$$

which, as we see in Appendix 3.2, rearranges to

$$\alpha = \frac{x\sqrt{r}}{1 + \sqrt{r}} \tag{3.4}$$

The actual location of the market boundary between the two retail centres will be dependent on the relative 'pulls' of the markets and the factors inhibiting the overcoming of distance.

The pull of the market is the relative attractiveness of the market as a location for purchasing, and in Reilly's approach, the attractiveness of the retail location, represented by the size of the retail centre, depends on the variety of goods which can be purchased at the same location. In other words, a larger centre implies that a greater variety of goods can be purchased on each trip to the centre. Implicit in Reilly's approach here is a notion of purchasing economies of scope, in that a single journey to a single centre will partially or completely substitute for many individual journeys to purchase a range of products. The greater the variety of goods available at the retail centre, the greater will be the attractiveness of purchasing from there, even from a significant distance. At the same time, Reilly's approach also assumes that the marginal costs of overcoming distance become successively greater as distance increases. This could be represented by, for example, an increasing marginal disutility of travel time. Obviously, if the retail centres are the same size the value of r will be 1, and $\alpha = x/2$. As such, in this unique case the market boundary will be equidistant between the two markets. More generally, however, the different distances between retail centres and their market area boundaries will be determined by the interaction of the relative attractiveness of the centre in terms of the possible economies of scope, and the accessibility of the centre, which depends on distance.

Although Reilly's market area approach is a simple empirical rule of thumb, it does provide us with a fundamental insight into the nature of market areas. Goods will be purchased over greater market areas, and consequently also shipped over greater geographical distances, from centres which produce a greater variety of goods, *ceteris paribus*. This observation therefore suggests that the greater urbanization economies associated with larger cities will also imply larger hinterland market areas, and larger shipment distances for the goods produced in the city. In contrast, more local market areas with short-distance goods shipments will tend to be dominated by purchases of a lower variety of goods.

3.2.3 Linkage analysis and value–weight ratios

While the Reilly arguments emphasize the consumption economies available at particular retail centres, the agglomeration and clustering arguments discussed in Chapter 2 emphasize the production economies available at particular centres. The agglomeration and clustering arguments assume that that the production of high-value, non-standardized, highly customized and newer goods and services requires greater inputs of knowledge, information, skills, and technology inputs than for lower-value goods and services, and that these inputs tend to be more readily available in major urban areas than in smaller centres. The knowledge and technology required in producing and marketing high-value non-standardized products means that high-value products tend to be produced in a smaller number of locations and by a smaller number of producers than low-value standardized products, whose production using less knowledge-intensive inputs is widely dispersed. This smaller number of locations for the production of high-value goods and services relative to low value products is itself sufficient to ensure that higher-value goods tend to exhibit greater market areas and longer shipment distances than lower value goods.

Following the Reilly arguments, we can also reinterpret these observations in terms of the characteristics of the products produced, whereby the relationship between the value of the product and the distances over which high-value products are captured in terms of product value–weight ratios or value–bulk ratios. High-value goods are defined as being high value–weight ratio or high value–bulk ratio goods. In other words the value per tonne of the good is high or the value per cubic metre is high. This approach assumes that the unit weight or unit volume of a product can be used as a denominator or a numeraire for measuring the value of something, and high-value products generally exhibit very high value–weight ratios. The reason this is important is because transport costs are partly charged according to the weight or bulk volume of the good being shipped, as well as the shipment distance. The simple argument here is therefore that the transport costs involved in moving high value–weight or high value–bulk ratio goods are very low as a percentage of the price of the good and are likely to remain so even over long distances, whereas for low value–weight ratio or low value–bulk ratio goods the transport costs are likely to become a high percentage of the price of the good very quickly, even over short distances.

This type of thinking therefore suggests that we are likely to see high value–weight ratio or high value–bulk ratio goods typically shipped over long distances, while low value–weight ratio or low value–bulk ratio goods will typically be shipped over short distances. Moreover, to the extent that the major production locations of high-value goods also tend to be in the larger and dominant urban centres, which are relatively few in number, the value–weight ratio linkage conclusions outlined above will be even further reinforced. In general, we would expect to see the average purchasing linkage distance for high value–weight ratio and high value–bulk ratio goods being higher than for lower value–weight ratio goods, many of which will simply be purchased locally.

These arguments have traditionally been widely used in the empirical geographical literature, by adapting them slightly to facilitate measurement into what are known as 'linkage' analyses, which examine the types of commodity flows across space and between firms. Using this linkage methodology, historically one of the most common findings of traditional linkage analysis is that there is a relationship between the delivery distance and the nature of the products being transported. In particular, the higher the value–weight ratio of the product, the greater will be the average distance of shipment (Lever 1972, 1974; Hoare 1975; Marshall 1987). The general 'rule of thumb' justification for this observation used primarily by geographers is that high-value products can be transported over large distances because the high value of the product can absorb long-distance transportation costs.

On the other hand, for low-value products, the transport costs will be very high relative to the value of the good even over short distances, thereby restricting the distance over which these goods can be shipped. For example, a very small weight or small volume of micropro- cessors exhibits a much higher value than the same weight or volume of processed food products.

While linkage arguments can sometimes be very useful, in general there are, however, three weaknesses with these simple linkage arguments. The first of these weaknesses is not too problematic, while the next two represent more fundamental analytical difficulties.

First, large urban centres are not the only production locations for high-value goods, and major centres are also the production locations for many low value goods as well as for high-value goods. However, if large urban centres are the source locations of a high variety of goods, spanning the range from low- to high-value goods, it is clear that the market areas of major urban centres will tend to be much larger than those for the small centres, whose product ranges are much smaller. As such, high-value products will tend to be delivered over long distances, and to the extent that high-values are reflected in high value–weight ratios, this implies that high value–weigh ratio products will tend to be shipped over the longer distances on average, given the smaller number of production locations.

The second, and more fundamental, problem is that many service sector 'products' are without either weight or bulk. As such, value–weight or value–bulk ratios mean little in this context. As we see in Chapter 9, this is a particularly important issue in the context of the current phase of globalization with the rise of what is known as the 'weightless economy' (Quah 2001), in which the provision of services, and in particular services which are primar- ily delivered electronically, has grown rapidly. Traditional linkage analysis measures were based on manufacturing and processing industries in a period when such sectors domi- nated. Today this is no longer the case in many advanced countries, and these traditional value–weight and value–bulk linkage measures are largely incapable of capturing many aspects of the emerging weightless activities. This is because the weight or volume denomi- nator term in all such value–weight or value–bulk ratios when applied to the weightless economy would be zero, and all such ratios would therefore be infinite, rendering them useless for capturing the competitive nuances between the different parts of these service industries. While the traditional linkage approaches may still be of some use in discussions regarding manufacturing and processing sectors, their more general usefulness may be increasingly limited.

The third problem, which is more technical and represents a fundamental analytical problem, is discussed in Box 3.1, and relates to the relationship between the value product and the required return to investments.

All the issues discussed in this chapter so far provide reasons why many activities are geographically dispersed, and why many transactions take place over large distances. As such, these arguments and observations are largely in contrast to those discussed in Chapter 2, all of which emphasizes agglomeration, concentration, and clustering. The spatial econ- omy as a whole therefore comprizes on the one hand, mechanisms, forces, and issues which encourage industrial clustering and agglomeration, and on the other hand, mechanisms, forces, and processes which encourage industrial dispersal. The balance between these two countervailing tendencies will generate the actual observed spatial patterns of cities and regions, and these are the issues to which we now turn.

BOX 3.1 Problems with value–weight ratio explanations of linkages

As we have just seen, it is frequently argued that high value–weight ratio products are shipped across much longer distances than lower value–weigh ratio products, and a common justification for this argument is that high-value products can absorb long distance transportation costs. On the other hand, for low-value products, the transport costs will be very high relative to the value of the good even over short distances, thereby restricting the distance over which these goods can be shipped. For example, high value–weight Japanese, Korean, or Taiwanese electronics goods are shipped to markets all over the world, whereas many low value–weight ratio vegetables tend to be produced and sold locally. This argument, however, is rather weak, and there are many exceptions to this principle. For example, this argument cannot explain why so many low-value agricultural and dairy products are shipped over enormous distances from New Zealand to the rest of the world. Nor can the argument explain why low-value clothing and toys are shipped over enormous distances from developing countries to industrialized nations. At the same time, it cannot explain why so many high-value products are shipped over short distances between various countries within a common market area, such as the European Union.

The major problem with this simple value–weight ratio linkage argument is that it implicitly assumes that the quantities of all capital invested in any production process, and the quantity of all outputs produced by any production process, are approximately equal. We can see this if we consider that the revenue earned by the firm from the sales of its products is necessary to cover all the costs of its production. However, the performance of any particular production activity is defined not in terms of the total profits earned, but in terms of the rate of return, which is given as the total profits divided by the capital initially invested. The denominator term is the quantity of capital initially invested and not the weight of output produced. Only if the total weight of output produced is identical can the total profits earned be compared between any two production activities. Moreover, in terms of the rate of return, only if the quantities of capital initially invested are also identical can the rate of return be compared between any two activities. In order to understand the general patterns of linkage lengths it is therefore also necessary to consider the total quantities of output produced and the total quantities of capital invested. Simple value–weight ratios can be very misleading.

3.3 Urban hierarchies and classical central place theory

Chapters 1 and 2 and the above sections of this chapter describe the many theoretical reasons behind both the spatial clustering and the spatial dispersion of industrial activities. However, in reality the mix of these simultaneous tendencies towards either clustering or dispersion does not appear to produce a spatial pattern which is entirely random. Observations from many countries suggest that there is a certain regularity in the spatial patterns of activity, and this regularity has two aspects. First, the spatial distribution of cities exhibits certain typical features, and second, the numerical distribution of such cities also exhibits certain typical features. Nations tend to be dominated by one or two primal cities, generally located in the centre of the major populated regions of the country. These cities will tend to be the production locations of most of the outputs produced by the economy. Other more peripheral regions will tend to be focused around successively smaller cities which dominate less populated hinterland areas. These smaller cities will also tend to produce a smaller range of outputs than the primal cities. At the same time, as the size of the individual city falls, the number of such cities generally increases. The result is that both the size and spatial distribution of the urban centres exhibit something of a hierarchical pyramidal pattern, as depicted in Figure 3.1.

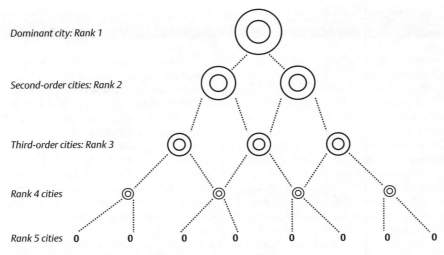

Figure 3.1 The spatial and hierarchical organization of the urban system

The dominant city, which has the largest population, is defined as the city with the highest rank-ordering. The next group of similar-sized cities is defined as the second level in the rank ordering of city sizes, and the subsequent group of smaller similar-sized cities as comprising the third level in the rank-ordering of the urban hierarchy. Exactly why the national–regional economy should exhibit such a spatial hierarchical pattern is the subject of much debate, and traditionally has been the focus of an area of research known as 'central place' theory. In the following sections we will discuss three different approaches to central-place theory. Initially we will discuss the two classical approaches set within a two-dimensional framework, namely those of Christaller (1933) and Lösch (1954), and in section 3.4 we introduce the more recent 'new economic geography' approach to such questions, which follows the work primarily of Krugman (1991 a, b) and Fujita et al. (1999a).

3.3.1 The Christaller approach to central places

The first general discussion of the urban system came from a German scholar, Walter Christaller (1933, 1966), whose work was based on observations of the spatial distributions of cities and towns in Southern Germany. The Christaller model of central places is consequently primarily inductive rather than deductive, in the sense that the model is based more on observation of reality rather than on the extrapolation of any schema constructed from first principles (Parr 2002).

The Christaller system assumes that there is a hierarchy of N different goods $g = (1,2,...N)$, a hierarchy of N different market areas levels, $m = (1,2,....N)$, and a hierarchy of N different level urban centres, $u = (1,2,....N)$. Higher-order goods provide for larger spatial market areas, and it is assumed that there is a direct correspondence between the hierarchical position of each good and the size of its spatial market area. In other words, a good of level $g = 2$ will exhibit a spatial market of area $m = 2$, and a good of level $g = 3$ will exhibit a spatial market of area $m = 3$. Moreover, it is assumed that for an evenly distributed rural population, the relative size of the market area for a good of one level and a good of the level immediately below it is always a constant, given as k. In other words, the ratio

now ask: what will be the ideal spatial landscape in the case in which the economy is characterized by a range of types of firms?

The demand curves for different firms and the price elasticity of demand of the goods produced by the various firms will be different according to the different types of goods they produce. The result of this is that the market areas for different types of goods will also be different according to the characteristics of the individual demand curves. Allowing for the caveats discussed in section 3.7.2, we can assume that high-value products tend to be price inelastic, due to product quality and product heterogeneity, whereas low-value products tend to be highly price elastic due to product homogeneity. Therefore, in general, firms producing goods whose demand curves are highly price elastic will tend to exhibit small market areas. The reason is that the demand for the product will be very sensitive to the transport cost mark-up on the source price of the good, with demand falling sharply over even small delivery distances. On the other hand, goods whose demand curves are highly price inelastic will be relatively insensitive to transport cost mark-ups. The result of this is that demand will fall only slowly with increasing delivery distance, thereby tending to increase the market area. At the same time, different firms producing different goods will also exhibit different supply cost curves, and it is the interrelationship of the demand curves and the supply curves which will determine the actual sizes of the individual hexagonal market areas. The ideal Löschian hexagonal spatial pattern will therefore be different for different types of firms. Firms producing highly price elastic goods, such as many agricultural commodities, will tend to exhibit small hexagonal market areas and be located at many points, whereas firms producing low price-elastic goods will tend to exhibit larger hexagonal spatial areas and be located at fewer points.

In a situation such as this, where the economy is made up of a variety of firms producing a variety of products, and where the spatial economy exhibits a variety of hexagonal market area patterns, the Löschian argument is that the most efficient economic landscape is one where the maximum number of firms is located at the same point. The logic of this argument is that the maximum number of firms located at the same point will allow agglomeration economies to take place within each of the sets of firms which are located at the same place.

The mathematics and geometry of the Löschian argument and results are beyond the scope of this book, although the general conclusions of Lösch are quite straightforward. As we see in Figure 3.7, Lösch concludes that the economy of any spatial area will tend to be dominated by a central primal city, the hinterland of which will be characterized by smaller settlements and alternating areas of industrial concentration and dispersion. The rationale and justification for Lösch's actual conclusions have been the source of much debate (Beavon 1977; Parr 2002). Other small market area shapes, which allow for all the market spaces to be covered include triangles and squares, are also possible in the Löschian-type framework, but hexagons are the most efficient for servicing a market in terms of both transport costs and delivered prices (Beavon 1977).

Overall, Parr (2002) concludes that the primary contribution of Lösch's work is to show that industrial concentration and urbanization can arise independently of local peculiarity or particularity.

The classical approaches to urban hierarchies and central places represented by the work of both Christaller and Lösch were landmarks in the history of urban and regional economics, and both systems of analysis represented major breakthroughs at their time. Yet, in comparison to today's modern microeconomics, and in particular in comparison with modern general equilibrium frameworks of analysis, these classical approaches over time are increasingly seen

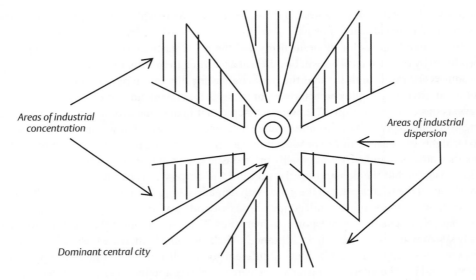

Figure 3.7 The Löschian ideal landscape

to exhibit major limitations. These limitations relate primarily to the rather restrictive geometrical features imposed on the analysis, and the rather restrictive nature of some of the assumptions required in order to generate the spatial pattern regularities. Moreover, in these classical approaches, little room is allowed for the roles played by labour mobility, consumption patterns, or trade creation in driving the evolution of the spatial economy, and few insights are therefore provided regarding processes of interregional convergence and divergence. These issues are all central to the new generation of models which emerged in the 1990s, a school of analysis known collectively as 'new economic geography', or NEG for short.

3.4 New economic geography (NEG)

The fact that industrial concentration and urbanization can arise independently of local peculiarity or particularity is a phenomenon which both underpins and also arises out of a research agenda known as 'new economic geography', or NEG for short. The origins of NEG are most closely associated with the work of Nobel Laureate Paul Krugman, who adapted and translated ideas, insights and techniques from international economics to geography (Krugman 1991a,b). Krugman's landmark 1991 publications sparked off a surge in the development of new analytical techniques and empirical approaches to understanding the economics of geography. Along with Krugman's key co-authors, most notably Masahisa Fujita and Anthony Venables, as well as a long list of other researchers, NEG scholars have provided some major analytical and empirical breakthroughs in urban and regional economics. The number of papers, books, and analytical contributions made by this research tradition is so large that it has now become a whole sub-field of spatial economics in its own right. Fortunately there are now many excellent books (Fujita and Thisse 2002; Baldwin et al. 2003; Henderson and Thisse 2004; Combes et al. 2008; Brakman et al. 2009) from which the interested reader can gain a detailed understanding of the major insights generated by the very large and very technical literature emerging from the NEG tradition. However, rather than examining a particular individual NEG model, for our purposes here it is important to sketch out the major features of the NEG tradition and to position and link these with the other major issues examined in the broad field of urban and regional economics.

New economic geography models, hence forward referred to as NEG models, contain a small number of basic building blocks. The first is the relationship between size and variety. NEG models work on the assumption that product diversity increases the welfare of individuals and households by increasing the range of consumers' choices and consumption opportunities on offer. At the same time, product variety also increases a firm's production efficiency by increasing the range of a firm's factor input and market output choices or opportunities. Importantly, within NEG the setting where size and variety come together is the urban area, the city, and the justification for this setting is based on the agglomeration arguments discussed in this chapter.

The second element within these models is factor migration. Labour is able to move to different degrees in different NEG models, some of which allow for zero migration and some for high levels of mobility depending on whether the labour is working in the production of agricultural goods or manufactured goods. In many industries producing human-produced goods rather than land-based agricultural goods we often observe increasing returns to scale rather than constant returns to scale. Once again, in an NEG setting size comes together with product variety and also labour inputs in an urban setting, in a city. A greater number of local labour inputs drives down local wages and allows firm's to operate more efficiently. Taken together, within NEG models cities are seen as the interface where production economies of scale, welfare in consumption, and efficiency in production all come together.

The third and final element in the basic NEG schema is the particular way that the costs of overcoming distance are incorporated into the framework. For technical modelling reasons these are generally defined in a form known as 'iceberg' transportation costs. Appendix 3.3 provides a more technical description of the basic elements contained in the original explicitly spatial NEG models and a more complete description of how these are understood to operate in an explicitly spatial setting. However, at this point what is important to note for our purposes is that in an NEG general equilibrium setting the combination of urban scale-related production efficiencies, partial labour mobility, and distance costs together gives rise to both centripetal forces promoting spatial concentration and centrifugal forces promoting dispersion. The observed spatial distribution of economic activities is seen to depend on the balance between these two opposing forces, and the outcomes are that in some regions economic activity is dispersed and in other regions it is spatially concentrated.

Theoretical NEG models tend to fall into two broad types, namely those which are aspatial and those which are spatial. NEG models which are largely aspatial in nature tend to be closer to international trade models in that they do not model geographical distance explicitly, but rather discuss distance costs within an iceberg transport costs setting as being variously 'high' or 'low'. This formulation allows all trade-related costs incurred in crossing borders, including trade tariffs and customs duties as well as transport costs, to be treated in an aggregated and consistent manner. On the other hand, the spatial NEG models do explicitly model distance using a distance-varying iceberg specification.

There are many different insights generated by NEG models, but for our purposes it is useful to highlight and summarize two key insights, one of which is associated with an aspatial NEG model and one of which is associated with a spatial NEG model.

In terms of aspatial models, one of the most important NEG insights is provided by the model of Krugman and Venables (1995). Their model analyses the situation of two neighbouring economies, one of which is large and contains a large agglomeration and one of which is small and contains only small urban areas. Both countries or both regions are assumed to produce two sets of outputs, one of which is agricultural goods produced under constant returns to scale, and the other of which is manufactured goods produced under increasing returns to scale. If the economies are largely closed to each other because trade costs are very high, Krugman and Venables (1995) demonstrate that all countries or regions exhibit similar production patterns. The reason is that high trade costs act as a trade barrier, thereby encouraging local production and a tendency towards autarky. However, as trade costs begin to fall an increasing centre–periphery divergence forms in that the agglomeration advantages of the large country or region begin to dominate while the small country or region declines. If production factors are mobile, then capital and labour will shift towards the larger country and away from the small country. The reason is that the large country has a much stronger 'home-market' effect, in that the larger domestic market provides a platform for greater domestic levels of competition, product variety, and scale, all of which are linked via agglomeration processes. The scale-productivity advantages of the large country with a large home market and large agglomerations only disappear as trade costs fall towards zero. If trade costs are close to zero, then there is little or no location advantage and the benefits of agglomeration more or less disappear. In this case investment can just as easily take place anywhere and convergence between the countries or regions starts to re-occur. The relationship between the level of trade costs and the degree of spatial concentration of economic activities is represented by an invented-U shape, in which both very high and very low trade costs are associated with very low spatial concentration of activities, while a large range of intermediate levels of trade costs is associated with high levels of spatial concentration.

In terms of the explicitly spatial NEG models discussed in detail in Appendix 3.3, the evolving spatial distribution of activities within an NEG framework (Fujita et al. 1999a,b) can be shown under fairly general conditions to reflect both the types of urban hierarchy patterns described by Christaller (1933) and Lösch (1944), and also the rank-size rule pattern of urban distributions discussed below. The cities emerge at discrete points in space interspersed with areas of no urban development, rather than as a continuum of urban developments across space. The reason for this is that in the immediate hinterland around a city there are few or no possibilities for competing via commercial developments because the nearby city dominates the local market area. This is known as a 'shadow effect'. It is only at a significant distance away from the city that the costs of distance provide enough 'protection' from the city producers for firms to invest profitably. The role which distance plays in conferring local monopoly power and allowing less efficient producers to survive has already been discussed in Chapter 2. The one-dimensional simulations of Fujita et al. (1999a,b) have been extended to two-dimensional simulations by Stelder (2002, 2005), and these clearly demonstrate that clustering and dispersion are natural outcomes of spatial competition processes.

The theoretical developments in NEG have been rather more significant than the empirical developments. The major empirical developments in NEG relate to the ways in which market potential can be estimated. Market potential is traditionally measured as Harris (1954) market potential, in which the sizes of the different markets which can be accessed from a point are weighted according to the distance and then aggregated together. NEG models extend this approach (Redding and Venables 2004) by also including the impacts of competition, variety, and wages into the system. While the use of these approaches is becoming more widespread, the results of these models are found to be very sensitive to the actual specifications employed, and the reasons for this are related to the particular ways in which transport costs are defined in these models (Bosker and Garretsen 2010).

At this point it is fair to say that in general the contributions of NEG are greater in terms of theoretical insights than in terms of empirical developments, and whether the balance changes over time remains to be seen. Certainly, there are increasing numbers of spatial econometric models incorporating NEG frameworks into their analysis (Fingleton 2005), but the primary impact of NEG is in terms of analytical insights.

3.5 Empirical regularities of the urban system: the rank-size rule

Observations from many countries suggest that there appears to be something of a regularity to the size distribution of the cities within a country, a regularity which NEG model simulations have also been able to generate (Fujita et al. 1999a,b). This apparent regularity is often discussed in terms of what is known as the rank-size rule.

As with any economic observation of distributions we can write a very general description of a distribution function as $f(x)$, whereby $f(x)$ shows the frequency with which a variable X takes a given value x in the sample or population. If X is continuous, the cumulative distribution which shows the number of observations not greater than x can be written (Chiang 1984) as

$$F(x) = \int_0^x f(x)dx \tag{3.5}$$

In the case of cities, as we have already mentioned, most cities within a country will tend to be small, with successively larger cities being progressively smaller in number. The result of this is that a frequency distribution $F(x)$ of urban areas, ranked according to the size (x) of the individual urban area, will tend to be skewed to the left. Yet as we shall see in Chapters 8 and 9, very large urban areas play a crucial role in the behaviour and performance of the overall economy, due primarily to the presence of agglomeration economies. The result of this is that urban and regional economics tends to place a greater emphasis on the behaviour and performance of these large urban clusters, which are relatively few in number. For this reason, city-size distributions are measured from the right-hand side of the distribution. In other words, if the total number of urban areas is given as T, the city-size distribution function $R(x)$ is defined as $R(x) = T - F(x)$. The city-size function $R(x)$ therefore describes the number of urban areas which are greater in size than x. As the actual city-size distribution is skewed, we employ a non-linear function. Within urban and regional economics, the usual functional form of the city-size distribution is a modified version of the Pareto-income distribution function (Mills 1972; Mills and Hamilton 1994), given as

$$R(x) = Mx^{-a} \tag{3.6}$$

where M is the population of the dominant metropolitan area. For any country, the size distribution of the urban areas can be estimated econometrically by taking a natural log transformation of this function. In other words we estimate the function:

$$ln\ R(x) = ln\ M - a\ ln\ x \tag{3.7}$$

On the basis of many empirical observations, however, a simple common assumption is that the value of a is close to 1. In other words, our city-size distribution function is given as

$$R(x) = Mx^{-1} \tag{3.8}$$

where x is the individual city size, and $R(x)$ is the rank order of the particular city within the urban hierarchy. The situation in which the value of a in equation (3.7) is assumed to be close to 1 is known as the simple rank-size rule or Zipf's (1949) law.

Zipf's law produces a distribution of urban centres which corresponds to the patterns observed in Figure. 3.8, and this is a pattern which has been observed in many countries. Assuming that the slope is equal to −1, the simple rank-size rule can be rewritten as

$$xR(x) = M \tag{3.9}$$

which states that the size of the individual city multiplied by its rank order is a constant M, where M is defined as the population of the largest urban centre in the country. For the largest metropolitan area, the population will be M and its rank order will be 1. For the second-rank urban areas, the population will be approximately half that of the dominant city, and for the third-rank urban areas the populations will be approximately one-third that of the dominant city. Obviously, the rank-size rule is neither a rule nor a law, but it is a useful approximation in many countries.

While advanced countries often closely correspond to Zipf's law across much of their urban hierarchies, in Box 3.2 we see that in some countries the size of the largest and primal

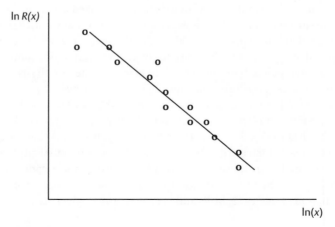

Figure 3.8 Zipf's law city size distribution

BOX 3.2 Empirical observations of the rank-size distributions

The size distribution of urban centres in many countries corresponds fairly closely to the rank-size rule when measured across all cities. However, at the upper end of the urban hierarchy, we often observe that the primal cities are too large, or too small, relative to what would be predicted on the basis of Zipf's law. For example, using the OECD (2012) definition of metropolitan areas, calculated according to the density of employment and residential distributions along with commuting patterns, we see that the largest city in the USA is New York, with a population of 18.6 million. The second-largest city in USA is Los Angeles, with a population of 17.03 million, the third-largest city is Chicago with a population of 9.39 million, and the fourth-largest city is San Francisco, with 9.27 million. The third and fourth cities together add up to the size of with the primal city, and are also just larger than the second city. This suggests that, on the basis of a very simple and literal interpretation of Zipf's law, the second-largest city of the USA, Los Angeles, is too large. Similar patterns regarding the relationship between the size of the largest and the second-largest cities also hold in the case of Spain and Australia.

For Italy, the largest city is Rome, with 4.09 million followed by Milan with 3.92 and Naples with 3.07, and Turin with 2.28 million. The fact that the four largest cities in Italy are of similar size suggests that the very largest cities may be too small according to a simple reading of Zipf's law. Similarly, Sweden's three largest cities, Stockholm (1.81 million), Gothenburg (1.49), and Malmo (1.13 million), are all more or less the same size, and as we see in Table 5.1, the same is true for the three largest cities of the Netherlands.

In marked contrast, using the same OECD (2012) method of calculation shows that the size of the UK's largest city, London, is 14.51 million, while the combined size of the next four cities of Leeds–Bradford (2.79 million), Manchester (2.58 million), Birmingham (2.32 million), and Glasgow (1.79 million) are very much smaller than London. Similarly, for France the size of the largest city, Paris, is 11.69 million, while the combined size of the next four cities of Lille (2.56 million), Lyon (2.28 million), Marseille (1.97 million), and Lens (1.46 million) is also much less than that of Paris. On a much smaller scale similar skewed patterns also exist in Denmark, Ireland, and New Zealand.

Many countries in the newly industrializing and developing parts of the world also exhibit urban distributions which at the top of the urban system are very different from the rank-size distribution. As we will see in Chapter 9, mega-cities are typical at the top of the urban system of many developing countries, whose size is far above what would be predicted on a simple and literal reading of Zipf's law. The most notable case is probably Thailand, where the Thai capital of Bangkok is somewhere between forty and seventy times larger than the second-order urban centres, depending on the spatial definition used (Kittiprapas and McCann 1999).

cities are often well above or well below what would be predicted on the basis of Zipf's law. As we see in Chapter 8, primal cities which are well above what would be predicted by Zipf's law are common, particularly in the newly industrializing and developing world, while primal cities which are below what would have been predicted by Zipf's law are typical in many advanced economies. However, once these very largest cities are removed, even in these countries the rest of the urban system usually corresponds fairly closely to a rank-size distribution. In general, therefore, when we consider all the urban areas in a country, the rank-size rule does seem to hold reasonably well as an approximation.

In spite of the available data and the many observations which are compatible with the rank-size rule, the reasons why this regularity holds are still not entirely clear. There is as yet no overall consensus as to whether the rank-size distribution is a result of economic processes or statistical processes. The long-run simulation results of Fujita et al. (1999a,b), discussed in Appendix 3.3, suggest that the rank-size rule does indeed approximate to the long-run spatial distribution of a mature spatial system. This would suggest that the rule might be the result of long-run general equilibrium economic processes. In contrast, Gabaix (1999a,b) demonstrates that the rank-size rule could also be a natural statistical outcome of a growth process in which random growth shocks are independent of the size of the urban area. As such, this argument suggests that the rank-size 'rule' or Zipf's 'law' is in essence a statistical artefact, and is actually commonly observed in other areas of nature and science. What does appear to be the case, however, is that the distribution remains robust even allowing for the complex patterns of growth and decline across cities (Duranton 2007).

The debate as to whether the rank-size rule is primarily a result of economic or statistical processes has implications which relate in particular to countries undergoing rapid industrial and regional transformations. In Chapter 1 we observed that there are nowadays major differences between the urban distributions of the industrialized and newly industrializing economies and those of many of the advanced economies in that many of these countries are dominated by enormous cities, some of which are many times larger than the next city. If the rank-size rule is indeed the result of long-run economic processes, this would suggest that the highly skewed urban distributions within many newly industrializing economies are something of a transition phenomenon, and that as their economies continue to develop and grow, their urban systems will naturally tend to move towards the rank-size spatial distribution associated with industrialized economies. However, caution needs to be exercised with such interpretations because, as we have already noted, at the moment it is accepted that the rank-size rule is neither a rule nor a law. Moreover, depending on the slope coefficients we employ in equation (3.7), a variety of rank-size relationships is possible. If the observations are primarily statistical rather than economic, then very little can be inferred regarding the long-run development of the urban system of newly industrializing economies. Either way, whether there is indeed any long-run adjustment of the urban system in developing countries towards to something closer to the patterns evident in advanced economies is also likely to depend on many other issues will be further examined in detail in Chapters 8 and 9, on the basis of the analytical arguments developed in Chapters 1 to 7.

As we have seen in this chapter and in Chapter 2, different sizes of cities are associated with different degrees of specialization and diversity, concentration, and diversification, and there is a range of empirical techniques available for capturing these variations, some of which are discussed in Box 3.3.

BOX 3.3 Measuring spatial concentration and regional diversification

The extent to which industrial activities are spatially concentrated or dispersed across the various regions of an economy can be discussed from two broad perspectives. The first approach is to measure the extent to which a given national industry is evenly distributed spatially across the national urban system. The second approach is to take a given region and to consider the relative contribution of each industry to the regional industrial structure.

In the first approach, the most direct method of measuring the extent to which a given national industry is evenly distributed spatially across the national urban system comes from what is known as the spatial Gini index (Krugman 1991a; Audretsch and Feldman 1996). The spatial Gini index of industrial spatial concentration captures the degree to which a particular industry's spatial distribution reflects that of the national urban hierarchy. In other words, the index can be used to measure the extent to which an industry tends to cluster in space. Higher values of the index indicate that the industry in question tends to cluster in a small number of locations. As such, from the arguments in sections 3.2 to 3.6 of this chapter, in cases where the spatial Gini index is a high-value, we would suggest that such an industry tends to benefit from agglomeration economies. Alternatively, where the index value approaches zero, we would expect that the industry tends not to benefit from clustering.

The spatial Gini index is defined as

$$G_i = \sum_{r=1}^{m} (s_{ir} - x_r)^2$$
(3.10)

where

G   spatial Gini

s_{ir} share of industry sector i's national employment in each region r

x_r the share of aggregate national employment in each region r

Following Black and Henderson (1999), expression (3.10) can be rewritten as

$$G_i = \sum_{r=1}^{m} \left[\frac{E_{ir}}{E_{in}} - \frac{E_r}{E_n} \right]^2$$
(3.11)

where

E_{ir} employment in sector i in region r
E_{in} employment in sector i in country n
E_r employment in region r
E_n employment in country n

The spatial Gini index of industrial spatial concentration is therefore given by the sum over all regions of the squared deviations of each region's share of total national manufacturing. Where an industry is evenly distributed across the urban system, such that its spatial distribution exactly mirrors that of the urban hierarchy, the value of G will be zero. Alternatively, as the industry tends towards being more spatially concentrated, the spatial Gini index tends towards a maximum value of two. However, given that the deviations are squared, the index tends to be dominated by the two or three largest cities (Black and Henderson 1999).

The second approach to considering the extent to which industries are clustered or dispersed across space is to take a given region and to consider the relative contribution of each industry to the regional industrial structure. This approach provides us with a range of measures of the specialization, or alternatively of the diversity, of individual regions rather than industries.

Duranton and Puga (2000) suggest that the simplest method of capturing regional industrial diversity is simply to compute

$$RDI_r = \frac{1}{\sum_i |s_{ir} - s_{in}|}$$
(3.12)

where RDI_r is the relative diversity index of the region r, s_{ir} represents the share of industry i in region r, and s_{in} represents the share of industry i in the national economy n. For an individual region, equation (3.12)

BOX 3.3 Continued

represents the inverse of the summed differences between each regional and national industrial share. Using the same notation as in equation (3.11), in terms of employment equation (3.12) can be rewritten as

$$RDI_r = \frac{1}{\sum_i \left| \dfrac{E_{ir}}{E_r} - \dfrac{E_{in}}{E_n} \right|} \qquad (3.13)$$

The value of the relative diversity index increases as the regional employment distribution approaches that of the national economy.

A very similar index of regional specialization comes from Blair (1995, p. 113). Once again, using the notation of equation (3.11), the index of regional specialization can be defined as

$$IRS_r = \sum_i \alpha \left[\frac{E_{ir}}{E_r} - \frac{E_{in}}{E_n} \right] \qquad (3.14)$$

where α takes the value of one if $E_{ir}\backslash E_r > E_{in}\backslash E_n$, and α takes the value of zero otherwise. The index of regional specialization is calculated as the sum of all of the positive differences between the regional industrial employment shares and the national industrial employment shares.

Amiti (1998) proposed an alternative regional specialization index in which the location quotients (see Chapter 5 for a detailed discussion of location quotients) of each of a region's industries are ranked in descending order. The cumulative sum of the location quotient numerator terms is plotted against the cumulative sum of the denominator terms. The regional specialization Gini coefficient is then calculated as twice the area between the plotted line and the 45 degree line. There are also various other indices of specialization and diversity which have been proposed and employed by analysts (Dewhurst and McCann 2002). However, while most of the indices provide largely similar rankings, in some cases they can provide very different rankings even for the same spatial data (Dewhurst and McCann 2002) as well as for different data sets. It is important, therefore, to ensure a careful interpretation of these types of indices, and the use of more than one index is often a sensible approach.

3.6 The structure and interpretation of regional data

The reason that we wish to measure issues of regional diversity, regional specialization, and regional concentration is that the relationships between geographical structure and economic structure contribute to all the regional economic adjustment and growth processes captured in the various chapters of this book. As yet, however, there is no overall consensus as to whether specialization (Henderson et al. 1995) or diversity (Glaeser et al. 1992; Combes 2000) is better for the long-run growth of a region (De Groot et al. 2009), because it appears to depend on the context. In particular, the degree of a region's diversity or specialization is often observed to play a different role in different locations and different time periods. We know that large cities tend to be diversified, and the strong growth performance of many large cities since the late 1980s would therefore suggest that diversity is an advantage for many of the reasons outlined in this chapter. However, as we will also see in Chapter 8, more recent evidence from the OECD suggests that many smaller and less densely populated regions are now exhibiting stronger growth than many large urban areas, evidence which would appear to point to the advantages of specialization over diversification in many cases. Following Christaller (1933), Lösch (1954), and Fujita et al. (1999), an urban-systems type of approach would suggest that it is the relationship between different types of places, each of which plays a different role in the economy, which is critical. However, exactly how we might demonstrate this empirically is a difficult problem.

The structure and interpretation of spatial data is a major field in its own right, and a set of topics beyond the scope of this book. However, for those readers interested in exploring this field there are some excellent books on spatial economics (LeSage and Pace 2009; Anselin 1988), geographically weighted regression models (Fotheringham et al. 2000, 2002), and other methods of spatial data and computational analysis (Batty 2005).

Yet the technical issues involved in interpreting spatial data are not trivial. All spatial data suffer from an underlying statistical problem known as the modifiable areal unit problem—MAUP (Openshaw and Taylor 1979). The problem arises because even though economic activities are distributed in space, the empirical analysis of these data is heavily affected by the cartographical boundaries of the sub-units of the area being analysed. For example, given the spatial distribution of the activities in the US economy, we can represent the spatial distribution of these activities by reporting data according to the fifty US states. Alternatively we could report the data at the level of the more than three thousand US counties. What we observe is that the indices of regional specialization, concentration, or diversity change while the actual geographical distribution of economic activities remains unchanged. Similarly, we could redraw the cartographical boundaries of the states or counties so that the average size of the areas remains unchanged while their shapes change. Once again, the indices of specialization, diversity, or concentration are seen to change for no actual changes in the spatial distribution of activities (Menon 2012). The reason why the MAUP exists is because the spatial data generated depend on the definition of the cartographical sub-units into which the overall economy is disaggregated.

A similar, but also quite distinct, problem from MAUP exists in terms of using data classified at different hierarchical levels (Van Oort 2004) of sectoral decomposition or aggregation (Mameli et al. 2008) even for exactly the same spatial units. For example, if total economic output is broken down into ten industries or sectors, the regional indices of specialization, concentration, or diversity will differ from the case where total economic activity is broken down into fifty industries or sectors, for exactly the same cartographical units. Moreover, the difficulties associated with using and interpreting spatial data do not end there. Other indices have been developed to measure the spatial concentration or dispersion of activities while allowing and controlling for the observations of clustering which are for statistical reasons unrelated to actual firm location behaviour or choices. For example, indices have been developed to control for the fact that some observed patterns of employment clustering and dispersion may simply be the result of the distribution of firm sizes with small numbers of large firms and large numbers of small firms (Ellison and Glaeser 1997; Maurel and S'Edillot 1999; Guimarães et al. 2007). Other indices have also been developed to control for the effects of the drawing of cartographical boundaries (Duranton and Overman 2005) and the effects of shared linkages between industries (Ellison et al. 2010). In each of these cases, the aim of these indices is to account for the degree of spatial clustering which occurs in addition to what would be expected on the basis of the definitions of firms, areas, or industries.

3.7 **Conclusions**

This chapter has discussed the various reasons why the spatial pattern of industrial activity exhibits both concentration and dispersion. Different industries will exhibit different spatial patterns, according to the extent to which they benefit from spatial proximity. There is a variety of potential benefits from spatial industrial clustering, the impacts of which will be different for different firms in different locations. However, at the same time, in other different industrial sectors and firms there will be a preference for the dispersal of firms. As we have seen, the underlying reasons why particular industries tend to benefit from spatial concentration or dispersion are many and varied, and, at present, there is no full consensus on these issues. Yet these various patterns of spatial industrial concentration and dispersion do tend to give rise to a hierarchical pattern of urban centres, the regularity of which can be captured by a range of empirical measures. Understanding the economics within these urban centres and clusters and also the economic relationships between these centres and clusters are central topics within urban and regional economics.

Discussion questions

3.1 Explain how pricing behaviour can lead to firm dispersion.

3.2 Explain why simple product value–weight ratios or value–bulk ratio indices are often misleading indicators of location and firm linkage patterns.

3.3 Discuss the Christaller and Lösch frameworks for explain the structure of urban hierarchies.

3.4 In what ways do the 'new economic geography' models differ from traditional central place models?

3.5 What is the relationship between urban size, the number of cities, and urban diversity or specialization?

3.6 How can we measure each of these issues?

3.7 Explain the ideas underlying the rank-size rule and Zipf's law.

3.8 To what extent do the urban patterns in your own country reflect the 'rules' or 'laws' of city-size distributions?

Appendix 3.1 Spatial monopoly and price discrimination

In standard microeconomic arguments of third-degree price discrimination in which a firm sells the same good in different markets, it is always argued that a firm will price-discriminate so as to equate the marginal revenue earned in each market. We can also apply the same logic to the case where market areas are differentiated by location explicitly as a function of the distance over which the goods are shipped. The total revenue TR can be defined as $TR = PQ$, where P is the price of the good and Q is the quantity produced. Therefore the marginal revenue can be defined as

$$MR = \frac{\partial(TR)}{\partial Q} = P + \frac{\partial P}{\partial Q}Q \qquad\qquad (A.3.1.1)$$

which can be rewritten as

$$MR = \frac{\partial(TR)}{\partial Q} = P + \frac{\partial P}{\partial Q}Q\left(\frac{P}{P}\right) \qquad\qquad (A.3.1.2)$$

which gives

$$MR = \frac{\partial(TR)}{\partial Q} = P + \left(\frac{\partial P}{P}\right)\left(\frac{Q}{\partial Q}\right)P \qquad\qquad (A.3.1.3)$$

Therefore, remembering that

$$-\frac{\partial Q/Q}{\partial P/P} = e \qquad\qquad (A.3.1.4)$$

where e is the price elasticity of demand, we have

$$MR = P\left(1 - \frac{1}{e}\right) \qquad\qquad (A.3.1.5)$$

With this general aspatial expression for marginal revenue, we can now consider the distance costs which will eat into any revenue earned at any location. Following Greenhut (1970) and Greenhut and Ohta (1975), if we define distance costs as td, where d is the distance and t is the transport rate, the theory of third-degree price discrimination suggests that the marginal revenue net of transport costs gained at all locations should be the same. In other words, the value of $(MR - td)$ for all locations should be the same. If we set the net marginal revenue at any given value k, such that $(MR - td) = k$, this implies that k is invariant with respect to d. Therefore

$$MR - td = P\left(1 - \frac{1}{e}\right) - td = k \qquad\qquad (A.3.1.6)$$

holds for all locations. If we set $t = 1$ for simplicity, this can be rewritten as

$$k = P - Pe^{-1} - d \qquad\qquad (A.3.1.7)$$

which gives the distance of the market boundary α from retail location *A* (Richardson 1978). More complete two-dimensional descriptions of Reilly's law can be found in Hoover and Giarratani (1985) and Parr (1997) in which the shapes of the market areas are described.

Appendix 3.3 The NEG model of the urban–regional economy

The two central-place approaches discussed in section 3.7 are set explicitly within a two-dimensional spatial framework. However, there is a sense in which these two approaches are rather static, in that the historical evolution of these ideal spatial urban systems is ignored. In both of the above models it is implicitly assumed that the spatial outcomes of the competitive market process will automatically converge towards something close to the ideal landscape. Yet, until recently, these assumptions have not been tested. Many new insights have been provided by the recent area of research commonly known as 'new economic geography' (NEG), which follows the work primarily of Krugman (1991a,b; 1993), Fujita and Krugman (1995), and Fujita et al. (1999a,b). The models developed within this particular research programme have attempted to generate and simulate Christaller-type general equilibrium results within a monopolistic competition framework. The analyses are set in one-dimensional space, and the models are based on a set of simple assumptions regarding the costs of distance, the utility of consumers, and the productivity of manufacturing and agriculture. While a detailed analysis of this particular research field is well beyond the scope of this book, following Krugman (1991a,b) and Fujita et al. (1999b), the basic tenets of the original explicitly spatial NEG models are outlined here.

There are three basic assumptions upon which these complex new economic geography models are built. These assumptions relate to the welfare effects associated with product variety, the productivity of manufacturing, and finally the costs of transporting goods.

In terms of welfare effects, the NEG models assume that the economy is split into two sectors, namely agriculture and manufacturing. Manufacturing industry is assumed to produce a variety of outputs under monopolistically competitive conditions, whereas agriculture is assumed to produce a homogeneous product under conditions of perfect competition. All consumers are assumed to have the same tastes, defined by the simple Cobb–Douglas utility function:

$$U = M^\mu A^{1-\mu} \tag{A.3.3.1}$$

where *M* is the composite index of consumption of manufactured goods, *A* is the consumption of agricultural goods, and μ is the expenditure share of manufactured goods. However, embedded within this utility function is a sub-utility function which describes the aggregate demand for the variety of manufactured products. This function is based on the monopolistic functional form first employed by Dixit and Stiglitz (1977), and is given as

$$M = \left[\sum_{i=1}^{n} (m_i)^\rho \right]^{1/\rho} \tag{A.3.3.2}$$

where m_i represents the consumption of each individual variety of manufactured good, and ρ is a parameter with a range between zero and one, representing the strength of the consumer preference for product variety among n manufactured goods. If ρ is close to one, the different goods are almost perfect substitutes for each other, and the demand curve for each firm tends towards the horizontal. On the other hand, the closer ρ is to zero, the greater is the consumer preference for product variety, and the more price inelastic is the demand curve for any individual firm. If we set $\sigma = 1/(1 - \rho)$, and assume that there is a continuum of n varieties of manufactured goods, we can write the demand function for manufactured goods as a CES (constant elasticity of substitution) function

$$M = \left[\int_0^n m_i^{(\sigma-1/\sigma)} di \right]^{\frac{\sigma}{\sigma-1}} \tag{A.3.3.3}$$

where σ represents the elasticity of substitution between any two varieties of manufactured good, varying between infinity for perfect substitutes and unity for highly differentiated products. Fujita et al. (1999, pp. 46–48) show that if the prices of the individual manufactured goods m_i are defined as p_i, the general cost of living index, which defines the minimum costs of purchasing a single unit of the composite manufactured good M, can be defined as

$$C_m = \left[\int_0^n p_i^{(1-\sigma)} di \right]^{\frac{1}{1-\sigma}} \tag{A.3.3.4}$$

If the number of product varieties available increases, the fact that consumers value product variety means that the cost of attaining any given level of utility falls. Therefore, the cost of living falls. We can see this because if all manufactured goods are sold at the same price P_m, equation (A.3.3.4) reduces to

$$C_m = P_m n^{1/(1-\sigma)} \tag{A.3.3.5}$$

In other words, as the number of varieties n of manufactured products increases, the fall in the cost of living is greater for lower values of the elasticity of substitution σ. Similarly, for a given elasticity of substitution σ, the cost of living is inversely proportional to the number of product varieties.

In terms of the productivity of firms, it is assumed that agriculture exhibits constant returns to scale and is a perfectly competitive economy. On the other hand, manufacturing is assumed to exhibit increasing returns to scale of the form

$$L_m = a + bX_m \tag{A.3.3.6}$$

where L_m represents the labour employed by each manufacturing firm, and X_m represents the manufactured output of the firm. This simple specification of increasing returns to scale implies that, for each firm, the labour required to produce any level of output exhibits both a fixed overhead component, independent of the level of output, and a variable component directly related to the level of output. The existence of increasing returns to scale, along with consumers' preference for product variety, means that each firm will produce a single unique good. In this monopolistically competitive environment, the number of firms therefore will be the same as the number of products produced.

From the perspective of the monopolistic producers, the perceived elasticity of demand for their own product is σ. Therefore the output price mark-up on their marginal cost can be expressed as

$$p_i(1 - 1/\sigma) = bw_m = MC \tag{A.3.3.7}$$

where w_m is the wage for manufacturing labour and p_i is the output price. This gives

$$p_i = \left(\frac{\sigma}{\sigma - 1}\right) bw_m \tag{A.3.3.8}$$

With zero profits, we know that price equals marginal cost. Therefore the ratio of $\sigma/(\sigma - 1)$ acts also as an index of economies of scale, as well as being a parameter of consumer preference for variety. Assuming freedom of entry within the monopolistically competitive environment leads to zero profits, then the revenue must equal costs. In notation,

$$p_i^* X_m = w_m(a + bX_m) \tag{A.3.3.9}$$

where p_i^* is the equilibrium output price. Combining (A.3.3.8) with (A.3.3.9) we have

$$X_m^* = \frac{a(\sigma - 1)}{b} \tag{A.3.3.10}$$

where X_m^* is the profit-maximizing equilibrium level of output of the firm, and the equilibrium labour demand L_m^* for the firm is thus

$$L_m^* = a + b\frac{a(\sigma - 1)}{b} = a\sigma \tag{A.3.3.11}$$

If there are L_M workers in a region, the number of manufactured goods produced in the region will therefore be

$$n = \frac{L_M}{L_m^*} = \frac{L_M}{a + bX_m^*} = \frac{L_M}{a\sigma} \tag{A.3.3.12}$$

As such, in this particular formulation, the number of varieties of outputs produced in a region, and consequently the number of firms in the region producing the outputs, can all be expressed simply in terms of the variety of goods available.

The third central element of the NEG approach is the particular way in which distance costs are modelled. Distance costs are defined in terms of 'iceberg' transport costs, an approach previously employed by Samuelson (1952) and Mundell (1957). The iceberg analogy comes from the idea that the transport costs involved in towing an iceberg can be understood as causing an iceberg to melt during the journey. The costs of overcoming distance are therefore regarded as 'eating into' the quantity of the good being shipped, and the consequent decay or shrinking of the good thereby ensures that only a fraction of the good actually arrives at any particular location. In the Krugman–Fujita approach, the iceberg specification of distance costs is applied more generally to all goods shipments. Assuming a constant rate of decay for each unit of distance travelled, given as τ, where $0 < \tau < 1$, iceberg transport costs can be described generally as

$$P_{id} = P_i e^{-\tau d} \qquad\qquad (A.3.3.13)$$

where P_i is the source f.o.b. price per ton of the good, τ is the constant rate of decay of the good with respect to the distance d, and P_{id} is the delivered price of the quantity of good actually delivered at the distance d. This description of distance costs implies that the costs of distance are a function of the value of the good produced, because the level of decay is proportional to the source price of the good. At the same time, we see that the greater the haulage distance, the greater will be the level of decay, and consequently the smaller will be the quantity of goods actually delivered. Therefore, in order to ensure that a given quantity of good is actually delivered at any particular location, the total quantity of goods purchased at the source location must increase as the delivery distance increases, in order to offset the process of goods-decay. In other words, for any given source value of the good, the total level of goods expenditure increases with haulage distance at a rate proportional to $e^{\tau d}$. The iceberg transport costs associated with delivering a given weight of product at any given distance can therefore be understood to increase exponentially with distance, as described by Figure A.3.3.1.

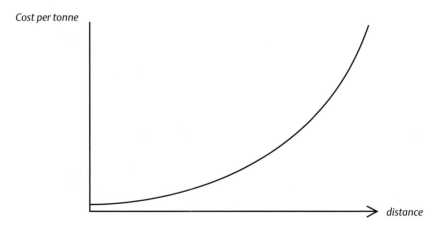

Figure A.3.3.1 Iceberg transport costs and haulage distance

If we compare Figure A.3.3.1 with the distance-transport cost functions discussed in the appendices to Chapter 2, we see that the behaviour of iceberg transport costs employed in NEG models with respect to distance is very different from the types of transport cost functions typically employed in location theory models (McCann 2005; Fingleton and McCann 2007). As we have seen in Chapter 1, the general form of transport cost functions employed in location theory models are either linear or concave with distance. Concave transport costs functions reflect the usual empirical observations of distance costs (McCann 2001) derived from the distance-frequency optimization problems, either on the basis of the logistics costs argument discussed in Chapter 1 (McCann 1993) or in terms of the relationship between distance and knowledge-acquisition costs (McCann 2007). The theoretical and empirical implications of these differences in the transport cost functions between NEG and classical location theory are discussed elsewhere (McCann 2005, Fingleton and McCann 2007).

The NEG models integrate these three issues, namely product variety competition, economies of scale, and transport costs within place-specific considerations, within a framework of labour mobility. Labour moves between locations according to real wages, which, as usual, are defined as nominal wages deflated by the local cost of living index. The nominal wages paid to workers are higher the better the access of (i.e. the closer is) a firm to a market, the greater the local market income, and the lower the level of local product competition. Conversely, the cost of living increases according to the geographic distance, and the lack of local product competition. Large cities with a wide range of manufacturing activities producing a high variety of products will be relatively inexpensive to live in, in real terms, because the high variety of goods locally available will allow any given level of utility to be achieved at lower real cost. At the same time, these areas will also produce goods at relatively low cost because of the intense local competition, thereby allowing large market areas to be captured. However, the point about the exponential form of the iceberg transport cost function is that the market area tends towards being finite, subject to the source prices of the goods. Therefore some small cities, or cities which are geographically peripheral with low product competition and high source prices, will still be able to capture small local market areas. The role of distance-transport costs is therefore to act as a counterbalance to the effect of localized increasing returns to scale in the major cities. Within this integrated framework, the NEG models show how cities can naturally grow and decline as national and international market areas expand. In particular, these models suggest how Christaller-type urban hierarchies, approximating to the rank-size rule, can be a natural response to economic development over time.

Appendix 3.4 The Löschian demand function

If we consider Figure 3.3, in which the market demand of the firm is defined in one-dimensional terms, we see that the quantity demanded Q is a function of the delivered price of the good. As such, if we denote distance as d we can write in very general terms that

$$Q = f(p + tL) \qquad\qquad\qquad (A.3.4.1)$$

where p is the source price of the good, t is the transport rate per kilometre, and L is the haulage distance in the Löschian framework. The total market sales of the firm are therefore given by the sum of all the individual demands at each location. This can be written as

$$Q = \int_0^D f(p + tL)L\,d \qquad (A.3.4.2)$$

where D is the distance to the edge of the market.

Equation (A.3.4.2) is the integral of each of the individual demands along the one-dimensional spatial plane moving away from the firm's production point in one direction only. However, in order to consider the firm's demand in a two-dimensional spatial plane, it is necessary for us to consider the demand defined by equation (A.2.4.2) for movements in any direction away from the firm's production location.

From Figure 3.1 we see how the Löschian spatial market area for the firm without adjacent competitors is defined. If we modify Figure 3.4 to give Figure A.3.4.1, we can see how the two-dimensional spatial market is can be conceived of as comprizing of segments. The total area of the spatial market is defined by that particular portion of the total circular market which the firm has. In Figure A.3.4.1, the market segment is defined by the angle θ. If the firm only has a one-dimensional market along the east–west line, the angle θ will be zero degrees. Alternatively, if the firm has half of the circular spatial market, the angle θ will be 180 degrees, or π radians. In the case of the Löschian spatial market where there are no adjacent competitors, the firm has all the circular spatial market, such that the angle θ will be 360 degrees or 2π radians.

In order to find the total market revenue for the firm it is therefore also necessary to calculate the firm's market demand function, given by equation (A.3.4.2), as a function of the

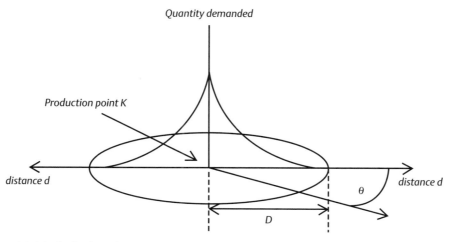

Figure A.3.4.1 The firm's market area in the Löschian framework

This fixed coefficients von Thunen model will then be extended to a more general variable coefficients model, known as a 'bid-rent' model. The bid-rent model, which allows for substitution behaviour between land and other production or consumption factors, is the orthodox model of the urban economy. We will see that applying conventional production and consumption theory to the bid-rent model provides us with a range of conclusions regarding the distribution of urban land, the location of urban activities and people, and the land prices charged at each location.

4.2 The von Thunen model

In order to construct a von Thunen model, we assume that there is a specific market point located at M, at which all agricultural goods are traded, and we assume that all land is owned by absentee landlords. We assume that all farmers producing the same agricultural good exhibit the same production technology and the same fixed production coefficients. We assume that land is of identical quality at all locations and also that there is freedom of entry into the agricultural market. Therefore any production locations which can be shown to be profitable will result in the agricultural land at that particular location being used for production.

For example, let us assume that a farmer growing wheat can produce one ton of wheat from one hectare of land, by combining one hectare of land with one unit of non-land inputs. Non-land inputs will be a combination of any of the factor inputs employed except land, such as human labour, animal labour, or human-produced capital inputs such as agricultural machinery. As long as these factor relationships are fixed, it becomes quite straightforward for us to consider how much rent the wheat farmer will be willing to pay for a hectare of land, depending on its location.

In order to see this, we can assume that the price of a ton of wheat at the market location M is $100, and that the transport cost t of bringing wheat to the market is $1 per ton-mile or per ton-kilometre. As we see from Figure 4.1, if the farmer is located immediately adjacent to M, the haulage distance d from the production location to the market M will be zero. As such, the farmer will incur no transport costs, and all $100 sales revenue can be spent on payments to the land and non-land production factor inputs. If the non-land inputs require payments of $50, the maximum rent the farmer can pay for a hectare of land immediately adjacent to M will be $50. At a distance of 20 kilometres, the maximum the farmer will be able to pay for a hectare of land is $30, while at a distance of 50 kilometres, the maximum the farmer will be able to pay for a hectare of land will be zero. Beyond 50 kilometres, there will be no wheat produced and sold at M. The reason is that the market price of the wheat will not cover the costs of producing plus transporting the wheat to the market from beyond this distance. As such, the von Thunen model predicts that there will be a negative land-rent gradient, in which land prices will fall directly with haulage distance, in order to exactly compensate for higher distance transport costs. At the same time, the von Thunen model also predicts that there will be a finite limit to the spatial extent over which wheat will be produced for sale at the market M, beyond which no production will take place.

This basic argument can now be extended to allow for changes in the price of the good, or changes in the rewards to the factors. For example, in Figure 4.2, if we imagine that the

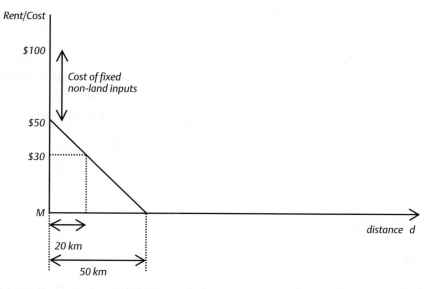

Figure 4.1 Von Thunen land-rent gradient

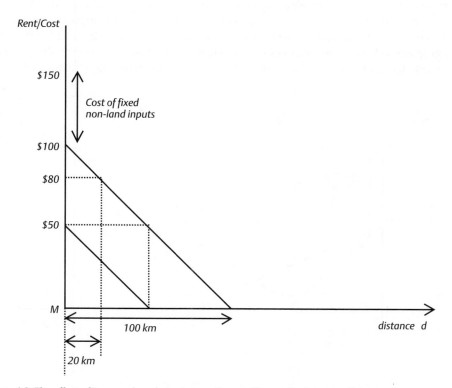

Figure 4.2 The effect of increased market prices on the von Thunen land-rent gradient

market price of wheat increases from $100 to $150 per ton, this now implies that the maximum the farmer will be willing to pay for a hectare of land immediately adjacent to M is $100. The intercept of the land-rent gradient therefore moves upwards from $50 to $100. At a distance of 20 kilometres from M, the farmer will be willing to pay $80 rent for the hectare of land, and at 50 kilometres from M the farmer will now be willing to pay $50 rent per hectare. Moreover, the maximum land rent will now equal zero at a distance of 100 kilometres, rather than at 50 kilometres as was previously the case. As such, the distance limit of the land cultivated for wheat production and sale at M will have increased by 50 kilometres from 50 kilometres to 100 kilometres. Within this limit, the maximum possible rents payable to land at all locations have increased. An increase in the market price therefore brings forth an increase in the quantity of land brought under cultivation and a consequent increase in the quantity of output produced and sold, just as we would expect from basic demand and supply theory.

Exactly the same result as above will also arise if the required payments for the non-land inputs fall from $50 to zero, with a fixed market output value of $100. In this case, the fall in the payments to non-land inputs will be exactly compensated for by greater payments to the land inputs.

The effect of changes in the transport rates is slightly different from changes in the output market prices or changes in the non-land factor payments. This can be explained with the help of Figure 4.3. For a market price of $100, and non-land input payments of $50, the maximum the farmer will be able to pay for land immediately adjacent to M will be $50, irrespective of the transport rate. The reason for this is that the total transport costs incurred by the farmer at a distance $d = 0$ from M are always zero. As such, the intercept of the land-rent gradient will remain at $50, irrespective of the transport rate. If, however, the transport rate t falls from $1 per ton-kilometre to $0.5 per ton-kilometre, the maximum rent the

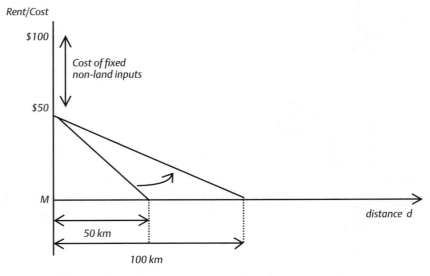

Figure 4.3 The effect of reduced transport rates on the von Thunen land-rent gradient

farmer will now be able to pay at a distance of 20 kilometres from M will be $40. Meanwhile, at a distance of 60 kilometres the farmer will be able to pay a maximum of $20, and the maximum land rent will now equal zero at a distance of 100 kilometres. Once again, the distance limit of the land which is brought under cultivation to produce wheat for sale at M has increased from 50 kilometres to 100 kilometres. At the same time, within this limit, the maximum possible rents payable to land at all locations have increased, except for the land which is immediately adjacent to the market. The relationship between rental values and the quantity of land employed is therefore slightly different between the case of changes in transport rates and the cases of changes in either the output market prices or the non-land factor payments. Each of the potential changes in the quantity of land used and the maximum rents payable, described above, will obviously be reversed for equal and opposite changes in the respective cost parameters.

In the von Thunen model, we treat land as simply a factor input in the production process, just like any other production factor, except for the fact that land payments are viewed as being residual. This assumption is based on the approach of Ricardo (1821) and means that rental payments to land are distributed only after all other non-land factors and transport costs have been paid. The maximum rents per hectare generated by the von Thunen model can therefore be described thus:

$$\frac{Land\ rent}{per\ hectare} = \frac{Output\ revenue}{per\ hectare} - \frac{Non\text{-}land\ payments}{per\ hectare} - \frac{Transport\ costs}{per\ hectare}$$

In the models above, for simplicity we have assumed that a single hectare of land is employed in the production of wheat. However, if we relax this assumption and allow for different quantities of land to be employed, with non-land inputs being employed in the equivalent fixed proportion levels, a more general description of the von Thunen land rent payable is

$$Land\ rent\ per\ unit\ area \times Land\ area = Output\ revenue - Non\text{-}land\ payments$$
$$- Transport costs$$

Land rent per unit area, such as per square metre or per hectare, multiplied by the land area is simply the residual from the total output revenue after all transport costs and non-land inputs have been paid. Therefore the land rent per unit area is the residual from the total output revenue after all transport costs and non-land inputs have been paid, divided by the land area employed, S.

The slope of the negative land-price gradient with respect to distance is given by the change in the land rent per unit area. This is given by $-t/S$. This can be understood as that, for any small increase change in distance Δd, the increase in total transport costs $t\Delta d$ must be compensated for by falls in the rent payable to the total land area employed, S. Therefore, if Δd is approximately zero, the rent per unit area must fall at a rate of $-t/S$. A formal proof of this is given in Appendix 4.1. As well as this we can also derive the distance to the outer limit of the area under cultivation. In Appendix 4.1.1 we show that, as we have seen in the above example, this is positively related to the market output price, and negatively related to both the transport rate and the level of non-land payments.

4.2.1 Land competition in the von Thunen model

With this analytical framework, we can now consider the question of competition for land in the von Thunen model. We can imagine that there are two types of farmers, one producing wheat as above, and the other producing barley. We assume that the non-land input costs for the production of both crops are the same at $50 and that both crops require one hectare of land to be cultivated to produce one ton of output. As before, we assume that the price of a ton of wheat at the market location M is $100, and that the transport cost t of bringing wheat to the market is $1 per ton-mile or per ton-kilometre. The maximum rental values for the land producing wheat fall from a value of $50 per hectare immediately adjacent to M, to a value of zero at a distance of 50 kilometres. At the same time, we can assume that the market price of one ton of barley at M is $150 and the transport cost t of bringing wheat to the market is $2.5 per ton-mile or per ton-kilometre. Under these conditions, the maximum rental values for the land producing barley fall from $100, at locations immediately adjacent to M, down to zero at a distance of 40 kilometres. If there is competition for land, we can assume that the land will be allocated according to whichever usage is able to pay the highest rents at any particular location. This assumption is also based on the approach of Ricardo (1821).

As we see from Figure 4.4, the land close to the market will be employed in the production of barley, and the land further away from the market will be employed in the production of wheat. The outer limit of the area under cultivation will be 50 kilometres. As we see in Appendix 4.1.2, we can calculate the distance at which the land use changes as 33 km, simply by calculating the distance at which the rental price for the two crops is equal.

If the transport rate on barley falls to $1 per ton-kilometre, the area of land employed in the production of barley will now extend to 100 kilometres from M. In other words, all the land around the market M will be employed in the production of barley. As such, the production of wheat will no longer be competitive in the vicinity of M, and all the land will be transferred to a single use. A similar result will arise if, the given the original transport rates, the market price of wheat simply rose to $150. In this case, all the land within a distance of 100 kilometres of M will be transferred to the production of wheat.

If we consider the results of the one-dimensional model in terms of a two-dimensional plane, it is clear that the von Thunen model predicts that the land will be allocated between competing uses in terms of concentric rings around the market point M. In the above example, the result will be two concentric rings, with barley production close to the market, and wheat production in a ring of land outside the barley-producing area. We can obviously extend this type of argument to more than two competing land uses, in which case the land will be divided up into a series of three or more concentric zones.

Implicit in these types of arguments are three Ricardian assumptions, two of which have already been mentioned. The first is that land rent is treated as a residual, and the second is that land is allocated according to its most profitable use, or alternatively to the highest bidder, at that location. The third assumption is that the supply of land at any location is a fixed quantity. In other words, we assume land supply is perfectly inelastic. This question of land supply and also land ownership will be dealt with later in the chapter. For the moment, however, we will accept the second and third Ricardian assumptions, but develop the von Thunen-type approach into a broader more orthodox type of model in which land payments

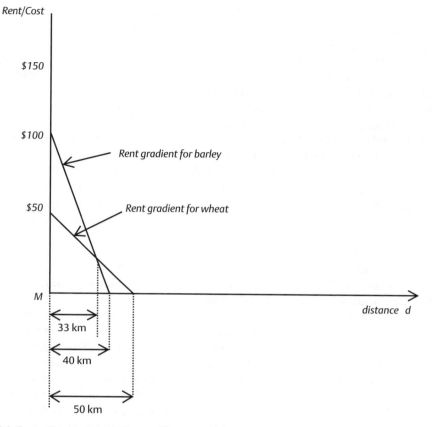

Figure 4.4 Competing land uses in the von Thunen model

are not viewed simply as a residual. Rather, in this broader type of model, known as a 'bid-rent' model, we assume that land and non-land production factors can be treated as mutually substitutable inputs. This allows us to discuss land use within a mainstream microeconomic framework.

4.3 The bid-rent model for a firm

The bid-rent model, associated primarily with the work of Alonso (1964, 1971), and subsequently developed by a series of authors such as Mills (1969, 1970), Muth (1969), and Evans (1973), attempts to cast the von Thunen type of framework in a broader setting, which is more easily related to other areas of microeconomics. In order to do this, the bid-rent model adopts largely the same basic approach as the von Thunen model, but includes one major difference. As we have just indicated, the difference is that whereas in the von Thunen model the land and non-land production factor relationships are fixed, in the bid-rent model land and non-land production factors are assumed to be mutually substitutable inputs, irrespective of whether the firm produces an agricultural or a manufactured good. In terms of the relationship between the fixed coefficients von Thunen model and the variable coefficients bid-rent model, there is something of a parallel here between the relationship of the fixed coefficients Weber model and the variable coefficients Moses model outlined in Chapter 1. The variable coefficients bid-rent model is much broader than the fixed coefficients von Thunen model, and provides a wider range of insights.

In order to understand the bid-rent model, we will once again assume that there is a market point located at M at which all goods are traded. However, although land is assumed to be of identical quality at all locations, we will now also assume that land and non-land production factors are mutually substitutable. Under these conditions, for a firm producing a particular good, we can ask the firm what it would be willing to pay per unit area, such as per square metre, per acre or per hectare, in order to be located at any particular distance away from M, while still achieving a certain profit level. Assuming that the transportation of goods to the market M incurs transport costs, we would expect the rents payable by the firm to fall with increasing distance. As we saw above, for a fixed transport rate per ton-kilometre, in the von Thunen model the rent gradient is a negatively sloped straight line. However, in the case of a bid-rent curve, the rents payable by the firm will fall with distance, but at a decreasing rate. In other words, as we see in Figure 4.5, the bid-rent gradient describes a rental slope which is both negative and convex to the origin M.

In order to understand the reasons for this observation, we need to reconsider the question of factor substitution. In standard microeconomic production theory, in the case where a firm employs two production factor inputs, such as capital and labour, a firm will equate the slope of the budget constraint with the slope of the maximum attainable isoquant. If the price of one of the production factors falls, thereby making it relatively cheap in comparison to the other factor, the firm will rearrange its consumption of factors by substituting in favour of the relatively cheap factor and away from the relatively expensive factor. The firm will continue to substitute its factors until once again the slope of the budget line is equal to the slope of the highest attainable isoquant.

In the case of a bid-rent curve we construct the rents payable by the firm which will allow the firm to produce at the same level of profitability, irrespective of the distance from M. However, we know from our von Thunen model that as we move further away from M, the

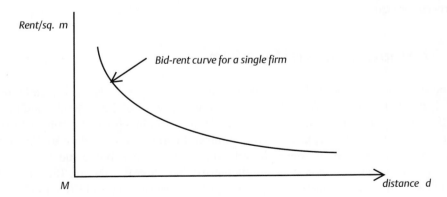

Figure 4.5 Bid-rent curve for an individual firm

price of land must fall. Assuming that the price of non-land inputs stays constant irrespective of distance, this means that the price of land must fall relative to the price of non-land inputs, as the distance from M increases. Production theory suggests the firm will substitute in favour of land and away from non-land inputs, as the firm moves away from M. Moreover, as the distance from M increases, the firm should continue progressively to substitute in favour of land. Alternatively, given that the price of land increases as we move towards the market point M, the firm should progressively substitute away from land and in favour of non-land inputs, as the firm moves closer to the market M. This means that if the firm consumes the optimum amount of factor inputs for each location, given the particular relative prices of land and non-land factor inputs at each location, it will consume both different relative and absolute quantities of land and non-land inputs at each location. Close to the market the firm will consume small parcels of land and large quantities of non-land inputs, whereas far away from the market the firm will consume large areas of land and small quantities of non-land inputs. Therefore, as the firm moves away from the market, the non-land/land consumption ratio will fall, whereas as the firm moves closer to the market, the non-land/land consumption ratio will rise.

As with the von Thunen model, the negative slope of the bid-rent curve with respect to distance is given by the change in the land rent payable per unit area. The slope of the bid-rent curve is given by $-t/S$. Although this initially appears to be the same result as in the von Thunen model, it is fundamentally different in the sense that in the case of the bid-rent curve, the land area S is not fixed, but rather it increases with increasing distance. If the transport rate t is constant, the negative slope of the bid-rent curve must become shallower with distance, because the value of S will be increasing. The result of this substitution behaviour is that the bid-rent curve for the firm with substitutable factor inputs is convex to the origin, as we see in Figure 4.5. The reason for this is simply that the slopes of the production isoquants, along which the factor substitution takes place, are also convex. A proof of this is given in Appendix 4.2.

A second feature of bid-rent analysis is that the higher the position of the bid-rent curve, the lower the profitability of the individual firm. In other words, in Figure 4.6, the firm profitability π associated with bid-rent curve BR_1, which we can write as $\pi(BR_1)$, is less than that associated with bid-rent curve BR_2, which in turn is less than that associated with BR_3. In

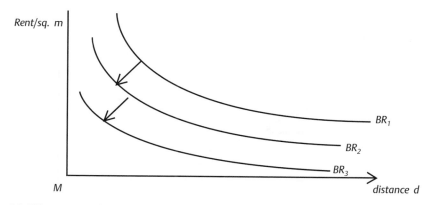

Figure 4.6 Bid-rent curves for an individual firm

Figure 4.6, therefore, $\pi(BR_1) < \pi(BR_2) < \pi(BR_3)$. The reason for this is that, given a firm's budget constraint, the lower the prices of the land consumed for any given sales revenue, the greater the profitability of the firm. In general, however, we adopt the convention that firms will pay rents such as to ensure that net utility is zero. This is because our assumptions of freedom of entry into the land market would suggest that if some sectors are systematically making profits in excess of other sectors, investment flows will move into the most profitable sectors and away from the less profitable sectors, thereby tending to equate profit rates across sectors with those of normal or zero profits. The result of this is that the bid-rent curves of firms and industries will tend to reflect the normal or zero profit conditions.

If there are competing producers, some of whom exhibit fixed coefficients of production in which factor substitution is not possible, as in the von Thunen model, and others for whom land and non-land inputs are mutually substitutable according to the bid-rent argument, land will always be allocated to the flexible producer. We can see this in Figure 4.7 if we compare two producers producing the same output quantity which sells at the same price per ton at the market M. We can imagine a point at a distance D from M at which a rent per square metre R_D payable by both firms is just sufficient for both firms to earn zero profits. At this point, if the land and non-land inputs employed by both firms are identical, the rent curves for each firm will coincide. However, as we move towards the market point M, the rents payable by the flexible firm will increase at a faster rate than those payable by the inflexible firm. The reason is that the flexible firm will progressively substitute non-land inputs for land as it moves closer to the market M, thereby reducing the total quantity of land consumed while increasing the rent per unit area. If there are sufficient numbers of competing producers of each type of firm, the flexible firms will occupy all the land around the market. Reversing the argument, a similar conclusion can be arrived at by assuming that the rent curves for the two types of firms coincide at the intercept M, with the same production coefficients. In this case, as we move away from M, the bid-rent curve of the flexible firms will be shallower than that of the fixed coefficients firms, thereby once again ensuring that the flexible firms will be able to pay higher land rents at all locations. The result of this argument is that where fixed and flexible production techniques are competing for land, in

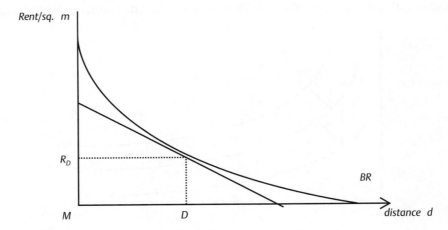

Figure 4.7 Rents payable for fixed and variable coefficients firms

in which there is competition for land between different activities, the land-rent gradient will be the envelope of the individual bid-rent curves.

In this type of model, the distance to the edge of the city is determined by the point at which it is profitable to convert agricultural land to urban land use. In other words, the distance to the edge of the city is determined by the point at which the rents payable by urban activities are just greater than those payable by the agricultural sector r_A. Assuming the profitability of agricultural land is given, irrespective of the distance to the particular city centre, the agricultural bid-rent curve will be horizontal, as given in Figure 4.7. However, even if the profitability of the agricultural land is dependent on location from the city centre, as in the von Thunen framework, we can assume that the agricultural bid-rent curve will be very shallow relative to the other sectors, whose performance is very much more dependent on accessibility to the particular city centre. As such, within a competitive environment, the distance to the edge of the city will still be determined by the point at which it is profitable to convert agricultural land to urban land use. In Figures 4.9 to 4.15 we assume for analytical and diagrammatic simplicity that r_A is given as zero, and therefore we concentrate only on the urban rent and urban land area.

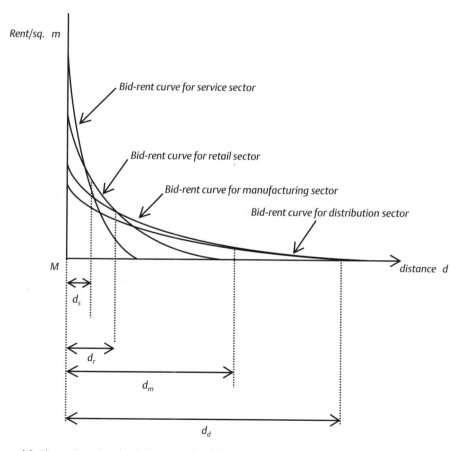

Figure 4.9 Alternative urban land allocations for different sectors

The actual land allocation results outlined in Figure 4.8 depend both on our assumptions of the relative preference for accessibility to the centre or edge of the city on the part of the different types of activities, and also on the particular way we have categorized the different activities. For example, in Figure 4.9 we can split up the retail and distribution sector in principle into two distinct groups, namely retail and distribution. In this case, we may hypothesize that retail activities will exhibit a relative preference for accessibility to central city locations in order to take advantage of any retail agglomeration effects. On the other hand, the distribution sector may have a relative preference for accessibility to the edge of the city for the reasons outlined above. As we see in Figure 4.9, under these assumptions the urban land still dominates the city centre with its outer fringe at d_s, but now the retailing activities are located immediately adjacent to the service activities, with their outer fringe at d_r. Outside these central areas, the manufacturing industry will tend to dominate the land in immediate proximity to the retailing sector with an outer fringe at d_m, and finally the distribution sector will once again be on the edge of the city with its outer fringe at a distance d_d on the city limit.

In principle, we can take this argument even further. For example, we can split up the retail sector into two groups, namely the traditional type of small- to medium-sized retail stores in which shops are relatively specialized in certain product ranges, and the large multi-product sales outlets which favour large-floorspace sales areas. In this case, we may argue that the former type of retail outlet will exhibit a higher preference for accessibility to the city centre, whereas the latter type will exhibit a higher preference for edge-of- city locations, in order to facilitate market access to the hinterland of the city. In this case, we would have the edge of the city areas dominated both by large-floorspace shopping malls along with distribution activities, while central areas would exhibit smaller, more specialized shops. Alternatively, we could split up the service sector into international business services and personal household services, or we could split the manufacturing sector into large-scale engineering or small-scale workshop activities. In each of these cases, the location preferences of the disaggregated sectors will tend to be different from those of the aggregate sectors discussed above. Therefore what we see is that our analytical description of a city in part depends on how we classify the different types of activities which are competing for land in the urban economy. However, although a city comprises many activities, there will be certain similarities in the preferences and behaviour of large groups of activities. Therefore we can simplify our analysis by treating groups of different activities as though they were part of a homogeneous individual group. The justification for this grouping may depend in part on observation and empirical evidence, and our assumptions may therefore be different for different cities in different countries. Different cities will exhibit different characteristics according to different preferences on the part of the firms in the city. There is therefore no ideal type of city structure, although the city structure exhibited by Figure 4.8 is frequently assumed to represent the simplest description of the most common type of urban land allocation.

4.4 The bid-rent model for a residential household

Within economics, the question of the allocation of urban land between residential households is discussed in more or less the same manner as the allocation of urban land between

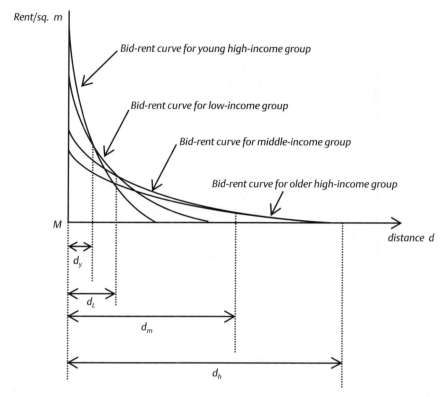

Figure 4.12 Residential urban land allocation with two different high-income groups

Specifically, the width of this area of land will have fallen from d_L to $(d_L - d_y)$. This implies that, for a given bid-rent curve, the low-income people will be occupying a smaller total area. In other words, if the population of this group remains the same, the average area occupied by individual households within this group will have fallen and the residential density will have increased. Given that individual utility is in part a function of the quantity of land consumed, the utility of the low-income group must therefore be reduced by the presence of the young high-income earners.

Apart from the way in which we categorize different groups, another possible way in which our model results may change is that our assumptions regarding the relative preferences for space and accessibility may not always be justified. For example, in some situations it may be that the income elasticity of demand for accessibility is generally greater than the income elasticity of demand for space. In this case, as we see in Figure 4.13, the urban land allocation will be reversed from that which is given in Figure 4.11, in that high-income earners will live in the city centre, with middle-income earners in immediately adjacent areas, and low-income groups located on the edge of the city. In Figure 4.13, the high-income earners will live between the city centre M and the outer fringe of their residence at a distance d_h from the city centre M. The middle-income earners will live immediately adjacent to the high-income earners between d_h and the outer fringe of their residence at a distance

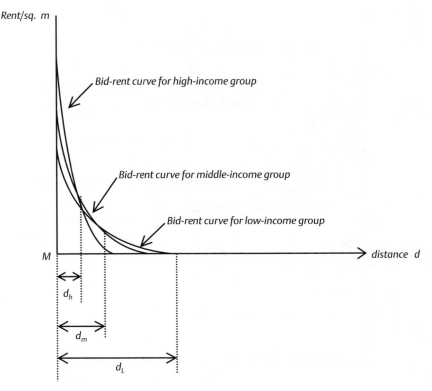

Figure 4.13 Residential land allocation with high relative preferences for accessibility

d_m from M. Finally, the low-income earners will occupy the land at the edge of the city between d_m and the urban fringe at a distance d_L from the city centre M. In this case, the city will tend to be very small in area, relative to the city described by Figure 4.11, and the residential density will be very high. This is because the outer fringe of the city will be defined with respect to the limited commuting transport costs payable by the lower-income groups. Cities which exhibit urban land allocations of this type are cities such as Bangkok and Manila, in which heavy traffic congestion due to insufficient infrastructure limits the ability of people to commute over anything other than short distances. The opportunity costs of travel time become very high for all wage earners, but particularly for higher income groups, which respond by purchasing land in the city centre.

4.4.2 The treatment of environment in the household bid-rent model

So far in our bid-rent analysis we have assumed that land at all locations is homogeneous, and differs only according to location. However, land at different locations will inevitably be associated with qualitatively different environments. When firms or individuals consume land at a particular location, they also consume the environmental amenities which are provided at that particular location. These amenities are often location specific, in that the quality of the environment can change as the location changes. This will be reflected in the

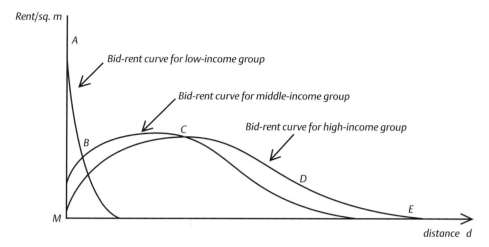

Figure 4.14 The effects of environmental variations on bid-rent curves

rent payable at each location by individuals, because implicitly they will be purchasing different bundles of environmental goods at different locations.

In order to see this, we can consider the example of the pollution generated by city-centre activities. In Figure 4.14 we can assume for simplicity that the city centre is the major source of urban environmental pollution, due to the generation of exhaust gases caused by local traffic, plus the presence of smoke from local factories and fumes from city-centre office ventilation systems. As we see in Figure 4.14, the low-income groups are constrained to remain close to the city because of their inability to pay high-distance commuting transport costs. On the other hand, the middle- and high-ncome households may be willing and able to pay higher rents over a range of locations in order to acquire land further away from the centre. The reason for this is that the natural environmental quality of land will increase with distance from the city centre, as it will suffer less from the harmful effects of pollution. For the middle- and high-income groups, the bid-rent curves will therefore be upward sloping over a large distance, because these groups will be willing to pay higher rents in order to avoid the pollution damage to their environment. However, beyond a certain distance the localized effects of the city-centre pollution will be negligible, and the behaviour of rents with respect to distance will be as predicted by the simple bid-rent model. The shape of the rent gradient *ABCDE* in Figure 4.14, which at first rises with distance and subsequently falls with distance, can be described as concave with distance between *B* and *D*, but convex between *A* and *B* and between *D* and *E*.

In reality, however, the relationship between environmental quality and the urban rental gradient may be much more complex than simply the generally concave rent gradient of Figure 4.14. The reason is that defining exactly what constitutes 'environment' is itself rather difficult. Urban environmental amenities may be considered to include leisure and entertainment facilities. If these are predominantly located in the city centre, this will tend to increase city-centre rents relative to those at more distant locations. Alternatively, increasing distance from the city centre may imply that the level of greenery and foliage increases, thereby improving the local environmental amenities. This will tend to reduce the negative

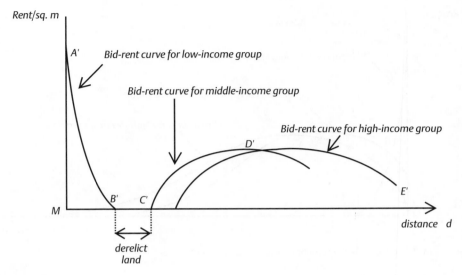

Figure 4.15 Derelict urban land

slope of the rent gradient with distance. Environment may also be considered from the point of view of social amenities. For example, low-income areas in city centres may be associated with certain social problems such as crime. In this case, as we see in Figure 4.15, it may be that the rent gradient $A'B'C'D'E'$ falls to zero in certain areas between B' and C', as higher-income groups prefer to pay a rent premium in order to isolate themselves from lower-income groups. The result of this is that there will be a band of derelict space which remains largely unoccupied by households. Similarly, in such cases, the poor security implications of locating in these areas may imply that firms will not wish to invest. The result will be an inner-city 'no-man's land', which is a phenomenon often observed in urban areas. Once again we can argue that this result is due to the relationship between the location of land and the qualitative characteristics of the local environment.

The point about all these observations is that the relationship between the rental gradient and the nature of the environment is not at all clear-cut. If there are environmental changes associated with location, the urban land-rent gradient may increase, fall or even change sign, as the distance from the city centre increases. See Appendix 4.2.2 for a formal discussion.

4.5 Alternative models of distance–land price convexity

The bid-rent model is the dominant model of land price–distance convexity, in terms of its popularity as an analytical approach. However, in reality the problems associated with isolating bid-rent functions from the effects of environmental variations, the weakness of the assumption of absentee landlords, and the fact that in most urban areas public transportation infrastructure allows low-income groups to commute over all the urban area, together may limit the applicability of the bid-rent approach. Therefore there are also alternative models of rent–gradient convexity and urban land allocation which do not rely on the bid-rent assumptions of factor substitution between land and non-land inputs. Box 4.1 discusses two types of models, each of which ascribes rent–gradient convexity to particular features of the urban land market not fully incorporated in the bid-rent model.

BOX 4.1 Alternative explanations of the convex relationship between land prices and distance

Two other analytical approaches, neither of which requires substitution behaviour of the type envisaged by the bid-rent model, suggest that land prices will be convex with distance. The first approach focuses on the role of asset price appreciation, and is primarily related to the role of housing markets. The second approach, which emphasizes the land use and location needs of firms and industry, is based on the transactions frequency choices faced by firms. Here we introduce both of these approaches, with more detailed discussions contained in the appendices.

Urban growth, property asset appreciation and land price–distance convexity

The bid-rent model assumes that all land is owned by absentee landlords. In some countries such as Japan, where the level of home ownership is rather low, such assumptions may be justified. However, in many countries, such as the UK, Canada, Italy, Australia and the USA, over three-quarters of the population own their own homes. The result of this is that land prices for residential properties, in particular, are generally not described in terms of rental values, but rather in terms of purchase prices. At the same time, this level of home ownership introduces another aspect into the behaviour of the urban property market, which is the ability to gain from the appreciation in the value of land, and this feature itself can alter the distance-rent gradient. Land exhibits the peculiar feature that it can be regarded either as a consumption good with utility-bearing qualities as assumed in the bid-rent model, or as a capital asset investment good. People will therefore purchase land according to whether they perceive land to be primarily a consumption or an investment good. From a macroeconomic perspective, at different times in the business cycle the dominant characteristic of land purchases may change, with the investment aspect of land tending to dominate during a period of rapid growth, and the consumption aspect of land dominating during a period of price stability or declining prices.

Over a long period of urban growth, however, the relationship between the price of land and the urban location is also in part determined by the relationship between the consumption and the investment values of land. The reason for this, as we will see shortly, is that the rate of rental growth is location dependent. Therefore, if we consider the asset value of landed property from the perspective of investing in property in order to generate rental income growth, the present value of the property, and consequently its current market price, will also depend on location. The argument in this section is therefore that the relationship between the distance from the city centre and the price of property can be convex due to the partially compensating effect of positive rental growth on the negative distance rent relationship. In order to see this, in this section we follow the arguments of Capozza and Helsey (1989) and DiPasquale and Wheaton (1996).

In the von Thunen model described by Figure 4.1, in which land is consumed in fixed individual quantities such that the density of land use is constant, and in which transport costs per kilometre are assumed to be fixed, the rental price payable at any particular location increases linearly as we move closer to the market point M. The reason that a higher rent is payable as we move closer to the market is that the rent is a compensation for reduced transport costs to the market, relative to more distant

BOX 4.1 Continued

locations. Under these conditions, if the land rent at the edge of the city is zero, for a unit area of land, the rent $r(d)$ can therefore be described as

$$r(d) = t(D - d) \tag{4.1}$$

where D is the distance to the edge of the city, t is the transport rate per kilometre, and d is the distance of the location of the land from the market or central business district point M. If, for some reason, the land price at the edge of the city r_D is greater than zero due to the level of agricultural rents, for example, the land rent per unit area would be given as

$$r(d) = t(D - d) + r_D \tag{4.2}$$

Following a similar argument, if the land is also developed with housing infrastructure, the rent per unit area of the developed property $R(d)$ will be given as

$$R(d) = t(D - d) + r_D + k \tag{4.3}$$

where k represents the annualized mortgage costs of constructing the housing infrastructure. Figure 4.16 is constructed by applying the logic of Figure 4.2 to equations (4.1)–(4.3), in the case where the land rent on the edge of the city r_D is greater than zero, and where the annualized costs of house building per square metre k are also included in the property rental value.

With this information, we can now consider the case where the rental gradient given in Figure 4.1 moves upwards and outwards according to a rise in the income earned at the market point M, as in Figure 4.2. If the wage income earned at the city centre M increases, the rent payable per unit area at M by a representative resident will increase from R_{M1} to R_{M2}. If this increase in city-centre wages attracts more people to the city, the area of a city will increase. As the population of the city increases from n_1 to

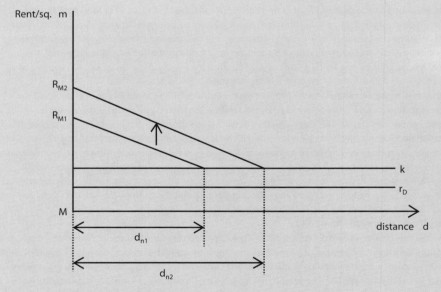

Figure 4.16 Income growth and city growth

BOX 4.1 Continued

n_2, the urban boundary will move outwards from d_{n1} to d_{n2}, as in Figure 4.16. In other words, the distance from the edge of the city to the central business district M, denoted as D in equation (4.1), increases. In an environment of growth, where the city expands over a long period, we can observe the behaviour of the property rental growth at any location by differentiating (4.3) with respect to D thus:

$$\frac{\partial R(d)}{\partial D} = t \qquad (4.4)$$

which, multiplying both sides by , $\partial D/R(d)$ gives

$$\frac{\partial R(d)}{R(d)} = \frac{t}{R(d)} \partial D \qquad (4.5)$$

We can rearrange this expression in terms of growth rates by multiplying the right-hand side by D/D thus:

$$\frac{\partial R(d)}{R(d)} = \frac{tD}{R(d)} \left(\frac{\partial D}{D} \right) \qquad (4.6)$$

Equation (4.6) tells us that at a given point in time, for a given rate of growth of the radius of the city ($\partial D/D$), the rate of growth of the property rental earnings will be higher where the property rent is the lowest. In other words, the rate of rental growth will be highest at the edge of the city, and will fall as we move towards the city centre and away from the urban boundary.

Equation (4.6) is specified in terms of the rent $R(d)$ of the property. However, in markets where land is purchased as an asset, the difference in rental growth across locations, described by equation (4.6), provides the possibility for differences in property purchase prices across locations due to differences in asset value appreciation, rather than simply according to transport costs. In Appendix 4.3.1 we show that as the rate of rental growth is higher the further away the property is away from the city centre, the greater will be the long-run capital gain from land purchases further away from the city centre. This increased capital gain associated with distance will partially offset the negative effect of increased distance on the property price. The property price–rent ratio will therefore increase with distance, and the result will be that the property-price gradient will be convex with the distance from the central business district.

A similar argument can be employed in a situation where a city is constrained in its spatial growth by geographical features such as mountains or lakes, or alternatively by severe land-use planning 'greenbelt' constraints, such as those employed in the UK, South Korea, and the Netherlands. This situation described by Figure 4.17 represents the case where the central business district wage incomes grow over time such that the city-centre wages payable increase from R_{M1} to R_{M2}, but the city is unable to expand beyond the distance limit d_P set by either a greenbelt planning policy or simply by the geography. As we see, for any given increase in wage incomes earned at the city centre, if the transport costs are linear with distance, the rental growth will be higher where rents are lower, and will consequently be the highest at the edge of the city. These differences in rental growth across locations once again provide for different capital gains associated with rental growth at different locations. As we see in Appendix 4.3.2, the result of this is that, as in the case above, the increased property price–rent ratio will increase with distance, and the property-price gradient will be convex with the distance from the central business district.

Trip frequency

A second approach to understanding the convex relationship between rental prices and the distance from the city centre is that of trip frequency. All the models discussed so far assume that the frequency of

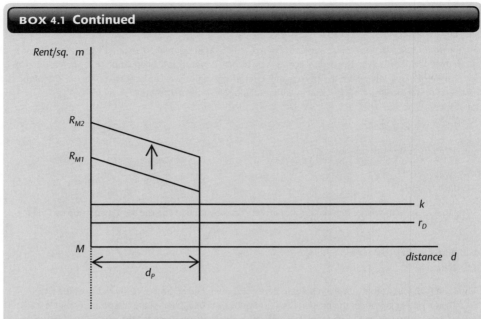

Figure 4.17 Income growth and city growth with spatial land constraints

trips from any location to the city centre is constant. Implicitly, we usually assume that all the people commute to the city centre each day for work. However, for many people employed in a wide variety of activities such as sales, retail, and distribution, the number of trips to a central business district may not be fixed. In these cases, the trip frequency itself may become a decision variable, and the rent payable at any location will therefore depend on the costs, in turn dependent on the frequency of trips. In such circumstances, the optimum trip frequency will depend on the balance between the costs of making a trip and the opportunity costs of not making a trip. As we see in Appendix 4.4, where trip frequency is also a decision variable, for a wide variety of cost relationships the rent-distance gradient can be shown to be convex, even when input factors exhibit fixed relationships (McCann 1995, 2007). This issue is more important than ever, because modern changes in working and organizational practices which are permitted by advanced information and communications technologies mean that commuting frequencies, shipment frequencies, and transactions frequencies are no longer largely fixed. The frequency of interaction is increasingly a decision-making variable which firms and individuals consider on a daily basis, yet these issues are almost entirely absent from traditional urban economic or housing models. However, they are included in models of location production (McCann 1993, 1995, 1998), models of innovation (McCann 2007), and models of international commuting (McCann et al. 2010).

4.6 Critiques of urban economic models

The models discussed in sections 4.2 to 4.5 are based on the assumptions that the city is monocentric, and that the fixed supply of land available at each location is supplied to the highest bidder at that location. Moreover, the fact that land is allocated according to its most profitable use means that the boundary between the edge of the city and its hinterland reflects the optimal size of the city. However, as with any economic model, the results of the models depend on the assumptions on which they are constructed. Therefore the real-world applicability of the models for assisting policy decisions must be considered carefully. There are several issues which need to be raised at this point in order to qualify some of the results of the standard models described above. These issues relate to the assumption of monocentricity, the questions of land supply and land ownership, the behaviour of the property developers, and finally the issue of the optimal size of the city.

4.6.1 Monocentricity

The simple models assume that the city is monocentric. In other words, these models assume that there is a single dominant spatial reference point, with respect to which all location and land-price decisions are made. In reality, however, large cities have many sub-centres, which act as local focal points for business and commercial activity. These sub-centres can often be viewed as local small-scale agglomerations, and the reasons for the existence of such sub-centres can be attributed to any of the issues discussed in Chapter 2. In cases such as this, as we see in Figure 4.18, the local rental prices may increase in the immediate vicinity of these sub-centres, such as C_1 and C_2 at a distance d_{c1} and d_{c2} from M, thereby complicating the simple downward-sloping distance–land price gradient described above. However, the existence of such sub-centres does not pose a major problem for our models. The reason is that we can consider the overall urban land-rent gradient as simply the envelope of two types of bid-rent gradients, namely those which are determined with respect to the major urban centre, and those which are determined primarily with respect to the urban sub-centre. The former are the bid-rent curves discussed above. The latter are the bid-rent curves of the firms or households whose activities serve specifically local customers, such as retail, food, and clothing establishments. In addition, if the existence of such sub-centres is associated

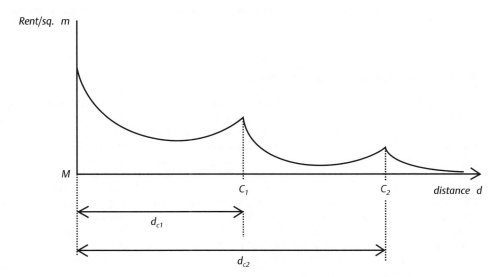

Figure 4.18 A multicentric city

with environmental variations, the issues discussed in section 4.4.2 will also become pertinent.

However, while the calculation of land prices and location will become more complex the greater the number of such urban sub-centres, the arguments outlined above do generally hold. The reason is that all cities have a dominant central business district with respect to which all urban land prices are at least partially determined. As we see in Figure 4.18, only the land prices immediately within the vicinity of the sub-centre will be determined primarily by demand for access to the sub-centre. Land prices at all other locations will be determined by the general urban bid-rent curves with respect to the city centre.

In the case described here it is clear that the polycentric urban structure described above still represents a single major conurbation. However, as Urban and Regional Example 4.1 makes clear, there are also cases where groups of cities exhibit similar types of polycentric characteristics.

Whatever the reasons for the emergence of polycentric city patterns, we can still point to the likely land-price outcomes. From our theoretical arguments, the combination of rental and land-price gradients in the polycentric system will generate multiple localized peaks associated with each urban centre. These will each be surrounded by downward-sloping land-price gradients, which intersect with the other downward-sloping land-price gradients associated with the adjacent urban centres within the polycentric system, in a manner largely akin to a standard urban model with many smaller sub-centres, as depicted in Figure 4.18. The overall level of the rent gradients will be determined by the density and economic performance of the region as a whole, and the three-dimensional topography of the land-price 'map' of the region will look something like the three-dimensional topography of a mountain range.

A final issue relates to the fact that in the monocentric city model of residential behaviour discussed in section 4.4 we assume that households commute to the city centre for work, whereas in the monocentric city model of firm urban location behaviour discussed in section 4.3 we assume that firms are dispersed across a broad area surrounding the central

 Urban and Regional Example 4.1   Polycentric city-regions

Recently, a literature has also evolved which focuses on 'polycentric' city-systems (Hall and Pain 2005), and this literature argues that in many urban regions, groups of highly networked cities provide for frequent commuting between alternative cities within the same broad region. Examples here might include the Randstad region of the Netherlands, incorporating cities such as Amsterdam, Rotterdam, Utrecht, and The Hague; the Ruhr region of Germany, including cities such as Essen, Wuppertal, Bochum, Duisburg, Dortmund, and Dusseldorf; and also the North of England, comprising cities such as Manchester, Liverpool, Sheffield, Leeds, and Newcastle. As yet, there is little theoretical work on the development and construction of these types of regions, and the thinking regarding these polycentric city-systems is largely driven by empirical observations of dense and frequent movements of people, goods and information between these centres. It may be that in some cases these patterns have developed in part because of land-use planning restrictions which limit the ability of the individual cities to fully merge. In other cases, it may just be an accident of history, related to the distribution of specialized industrial activities in previous eras.

business district. Clearly a more sophisticated approach requires that households are also able to find work locally in suburbs. However, if we assume that for suburban residents the transport costs to local suburban employment locations are approximately zero, then the trade-off for the household is between choosing employment in an adjacent suburban location with zero commuting costs and choosing employment at the CBD with its associated commuting costs. Importantly, the wages earned by the employee in the local suburban employment location, and therefore the household residential rents payable by this employee in the same location, will also reflect the profitability and land prices paid by the firm at that location, as determined by the bid-rent model of firm location described in section 4.3. Therefore, as long as the local commuting costs are approximately zero, the model conclusions still hold. In contrast, the simple argument would start to break down in cases where a very high proportion of employment is in suburban areas with only limited employment in the CBD. Examples here might be cities such as Los Angeles and Miami, but also many cities in the Netherlands.

4.6.2 Land supply and land ownership

One of the issues which complicates economic models of urban land allocation is the question of land supply. As we have seen, most models adopt the Ricardian assumption that a fixed supply land at each location is allocated to the highest bidder as soon as an alternative use becomes more profitable. In other words, land supply is assumed to be perfectly elastic at each location. However, the pattern of ownership of land may affect the nature of the supply of land, and there are two aspects to this: the first is the quantity of land held by each individual landowner; and the second is the time period of the tenure of the landowner.

In microeconomic analysis, we typically assume that a monopoly supplier who controls a high proportion of the market output will use his monopoly power to mark up the price of the goods above the marginal cost of supply. From the point of view of land supply, it is often argued that a similar phenomenon exists. In other words, a landowner who owns a high proportion of the land in a particular area will be able to force up the price of the land above the competitive market rate, thereby restricting development. This is the standard monopoly pricing argument applied to land markets. However, it is also possible to argue that the opposite may occur. In order to see this it is necessary to consider how the costs of land supply are determined. For a landowner, the costs of land holding are the opportunity costs of lost profits from land sales. This is the argument which has underlain our assumptions until now. In other words, for a landowner holding agricultural land, as soon as the opportunity cost of an alternative use is greater than the return on the current use of the land, the landowner will sell the land and its use will change. It may be, however, that the marginal cost of land supply is also a function of the quantity of land held and the time period over which the land is held. The argument here is that owners may ascribe subjective marginal 'attachment' value to the land (Dynarski 1986), which depends on both the quantity of land held and the time period of tenure. Attachment value here refers to any subjective utility ascribed to the ownership of the land, and as such the true opportunity cost of land holding will be the opportunity cost of the alternative profits, minus the attachment value. On the basis of the law of diminishing marginal utility, Evans (1983) argues that large landowners attribute either zero or low attachment value to any marginal parcel of land because they already have extensive landholdings. The result of this is that any such marginal parcel of land will be sold at the market price determined by the opportunity cost of land. On the other hand, according to the law of diminishing marginal utility, small landowners will tend to ascribe large attachment values to their land because any marginal land sale will entirely or substantially deplete their current land holding stocks. From the perspective of the landowners, this argument suggests that the opportunity cost of land sales in a given area will therefore tend to be inversely related to the size of the individual land holdings in that area. The result of this is that the more fragmented is the land ownership in any given area, the higher will tend to be the market price (Dynarski 1986). In an area with heterogeneous owners in terms of their landholdings, the price of land may differ between adjacent properties due to different attachment values on the part of landowners. The result of this is that land-market development will tend to be piecemeal.

A similar argument may be applied to the question of the length of tenure. Land holders who have owned a property for a long period may tend to have developed a larger attachment value to the property than land holders who have only owned the property for a short period. This inflated opportunity cost may inflate land prices above simply the best use value. Once again, in an area with heterogeneous owners in terms of the length of their current ownership tenure, the price of land may differ between adjacent properties due to different attachment values on the part of landowners. As before, the result of this is that land-market development will tend to be piecemeal.

Piecemeal urban development, particularly on the urban fringe, can also be explained in terms of information and pecuniary asymmetries between land buyers and sellers, and the existence of transaction costs. However, the point about all the arguments in this section is that the simple assumption that land supply is fixed in any location, and that land is simply supplied to the highest use value, is not always realistic. Other institutional issues surrounding land holding and land tenure must also be explored. These institutional issues will in addition include questions relating to the behaviour of property development firms. Such firms engage in land speculation, buying land in advance and often through intermediaries, in order to build up land holdings. These firms often make no attempt to supply land on the basis of the current market price, instead hoping to make greater profits on future development. The rationale for such behaviour can be understood on the one hand from the perspective of acquiring a monopoly supply position in a local market. This may allow the firm to force up the subsequent future sale price in an orthodox monopoly argument, as described above. On the other hand, in the case of land the determination and definition of a monopoly position is as much a question of location as it is a question of land area. Small land holdings in strategically crucial locations can provide monopoly power. In the case where a seller perceives that a large buyer wishes to buy a large area of local land in order to undertake a major development, the small seller may attempt to force up the market price in order to extract as much consumer surplus as possible from the buyer. However, where the potential buyers are all small, the seller will have little opportunity for such price mark-ups. The result of all these different types of interactions is that the market prices for land at any location may vary simply because of issues relating to industrial organization. For discussions of the behaviour of the property market see Evans (1985) and Ball et al. (1998).

4.6.3 **The optimal size of a city**

The arguments outlined in Chapter 2 imply that there is no optimal size for a city, but rather that there may be an optimal city-size distribution and urban spatial hierarchy. There is, however, an argument which suggests that the actual size of a city may systematically be greater than its optimum size (Alonso 1971). This argument is an adaptation of the theory of the firm and can be understood from Figure 4.19, in which the population of the city is drawn along the horizontal axis, and the costs and benefits of city are measured along the vertical axis.

In this argument it is assumed that the costs of city dwelling, which include both private and public costs, exhibit economies of scale over a certain range of city size. For example, such cost efficiencies may include urban agglomeration economies, plus economies of scale in the provision of public and social infrastructure. Beyond a certain size, however, it may be that a city begins to experience diseconomies of scale, associated with increased congestion and pollution. If the benefits of urban dwelling increase with city size, due to a greater variety of local employment and consumption opportunities, simple efficiency theory would suggest that the optimal size of the city should be at the point Q^*, where marginal costs equal marginal benefits and the net average benefits are maximized. However, the argument here is that the city will grow to a size of Q', at which total costs equal total benefits, and average costs AC equal average benefits AB. The reason for this is that if city growth is unregulated, the marginal migrant to the city will perceive the potential net benefits to migration to be positive at all city sizes below Q', and will ignore his own marginal contribution to the change in urban dwelling costs. Given that all migrants will ignore their own contribution to the change in urban costs, the resulting externality problem associated with large numbers of marginally erroneous individual calculations will mean that the city grows to Q' rather than Q^*.

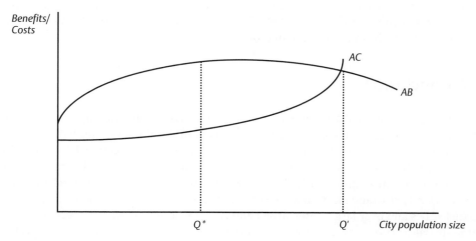

Figure 4.19 The optimum size of a city

The argument is similar in logic to the arguments underlying the over-congestion of certain roads (Button 1993). The main problem with the argument, however, is that it ignores the role of inter-urban migration, a topic discussed in detail in Chapter 6. However, at this point there are several issues which can be raised. From Chapter 3 we know that there may be an optimal distribution of city sizes. Therefore, if certain cities grow too large, the implication of this is that the profitability of locating in these cities will be less than in other cities. In principle, this will encourage out-migration from these cities to other urban areas which are at less than their optimal size. In equilibrium theory this inter-urban or interregional migration argument suggests that the process will continue until all urban areas are close to their optimum sizes. However, on the other hand, if interregional migration flows are driven primarily by average wages rather than marginal wages, as is discussed in Chapter 6, the result will be that destination regions often grow too large while the origin regions over-contract and become too small (Laurila 2011). This market failure argument reflected in Figure 4.19 can probably be best understood in terms of the nature of physical urban growth. When a city is expanding, a lack of regulation will tend to mean that the city grows too large. The city growth will be manifested in terms of an increasing area of land being transferred from agricultural to urban use and an associated increase in the infrastructure of the urban built environment. In-migration in response to average wages rather than marginal wages will mean that the city becomes over-congested, leading to negative environmental and social effects, as well as negative efficiency effects. At some point it may be the case that the negative externalities start to predominate, thereby deterring migration and leading to the reverse movements advocated by equilibrium arguments. As the effects of the excessive urban growth begin to manifest themselves over time, in terms of reduced urban profitability, efficiency, and welfare, the out-migration of activities and people now creates the problem of urban dereliction. Physical building infrastructure cannot be demolished and redeveloped costlessly and quickly, and this process of growth and decline can lead to the different types of environmental problems discussed in section 4.4.2, associated not with over-congestion and density, but with dereliction and under-development. As such, these market failure arguments are also applicable to discussions of the effects of growth and decline on the urban infrastructure, and the associated effects on local land prices, as well as to the question of the size of the individual urban economy.

4.7 Conclusions

The various institutional and industrial organization issues surrounding the supply of land discussed in sections 4.6 to 4.6.2 will affect land prices at the very local intra-urban level. However, along with the environmental issues discussed in section 4.4.2 and indirectly in section 4.6.3, and the possibility of urban sub-centres and polycentric structures discussed in section 4.6.1, the discussion implies that the actual relationship between land prices and location will be rather complex over both very small intra-urban spatial scales and over larger inter-urban and regional scales. As we have seen, over the large spatial scales of whole metropolitan urban areas or of groups of closely connected urban areas, the relationship between land prices and location will reflect the theoretical discussions in sections 4.2 to 4.5.3. In other words, land prices will tend to fall with distance from the city centre, but at a diminishing rate. From the point of view of this book, this result is important, because the larger spatial scale of the whole individual metropolitan area or regions featuring groups of connected urban areas is the spatial scale of most interest to us. The reason is that in this book we are primarily interested in the relationship between the urban economy as a whole and the regional and interregional economy as a whole.

Discussion questions

4.1 What are bid-rent curves? How can an analysis of bid-rent curves help us to understand the shape of urban land-price gradients?

4.2 How is urban land allocated between different competing income groups?

4.3 How is urban land allocated between competing firms?

4.4 How do urban land allocations differ between different types of cities in different countries?

4.5 What is the effect of environmental changes on bid-rent curves and urban rental gradients?

4.6 Apart from bid-rent analysis, what other ways are there of explaining the shape of urban land-price gradients?

4.7 Under what conditions will the actual size of the individual city differ from its optimum size?

4.8 Which cities in your country best reflect the theoretical monocentric model of urban land allocation and which ones appear to differ significantly from the standard model?

Appendix 4.1 The slope of the rent gradient in the von Thunen model

In the von Thunen framework we can define the total profit accruing to the farmer as

$$\pi(d) = pm - iK - rS - mtd \qquad \text{(A.4.1.1)}$$

where:

π price per ton of output at the market M

d haulage distance from the market M

i price per unit of non-land production inputs

K composite capital good of non-land production inputs

r rental price per unit area of land

m total quantity of output produced per time period

t transport rate per ton-kilometre

p price per ton of the good at the market

S land area employed

The profit per unit of output is thus given as

$$\frac{\pi(d)}{m} = p - i\frac{K}{m} - r\frac{S}{m} - td \qquad (A.4.1.2)$$

If we let $K_m = K/m$ and $S_m = S/m$, whereby K_m and S_m represent the quantities of composite capital and land inputs required to produce one ton of output, and we also denote $\pi_m = \pi(d)/m$, where π_m is the profit per unit of output, we have

$$\pi_m = p - iK_m - rS_m - td \qquad (A.4.1.3)$$

which can be rewritten as

$$\pi_m = (p - td) - iK_m - rS_m \qquad (A.4.1.4)$$

In other words, the profit per unit of output is the source price of the good at the point of production, given as the market price minus the transport costs, minus the total production factor payments. The maximum rent payable per unit area of land can be calculated by setting $\pi_m = 0$ thus:

$$\pi_m = (p - td) - iK_m - rS_m = 0 \qquad (A.4.1.5)$$

which can be rearranged to give

$$r = \frac{(p - td) - iK_m}{S_m} \qquad (A.4.1.6)$$

Equation (A.4.1.6) describes the maximum rent payable per unit area of land, as being the rent payable after all other factors and transport costs have been paid, which ensures that total profits are zero. The relationship between rents and distance can be found by differentiating (A.4.1.6) with respect to distance d thus:

$$\frac{\partial r}{\partial d} = -\frac{1}{S_m}\left[t + \frac{\partial t}{\partial d}d\right] \qquad (A.4.1.7)$$

If transport rates are constant, i.e. if $(\partial t/\partial d = 0$, then the rent-distance gradient is given by

$$\frac{\partial r}{\partial d} = -\frac{t}{S_m} \qquad (A.4.1.8)$$

exactly as discussed in section 4.2.

Appendix 4.1.1 Distance to the edge of the von Thunen area of cultivation

In order to calculate the distance to the edge of the area of cultivation, we simply set $r = 0$, thus:

$$0 = \frac{(p - td) - iK_m}{S_m} \tag{A.4.1.9}$$

which rearranges to

$$d = \frac{p - iK_m}{t} \tag{A.4.1.10}$$

The conclusions reached in section 4.2 can all be verified from this equation. By observing that the cross-partial derivative $(\partial d/\partial p)$ of equation (A.4.1.10) is positive, we see that the distance limit of cultivation increases as the market output price increases. Similarly, the cross-partial derivative $(\partial d/\partial t)$ is negative. Therefore, as transport rates increase, the distance limit of cultivation falls. Finally, the cross-partial derivatives $(\partial d/\partial t)$ and $(\partial d/\partial K_m)$ are also negative, which implies that as the payments to non-land production inputs increase, the distance limit of cultivation falls.

Appendix 4.1.2 Distance to a change of land use in the von Thunen model

In the case of competing land use, in order to calculate the distance at which the land use changes we simply set the rental prices in each production to be equal. From equation (A.4.1.6) the land rent in wheat production is given by

$$r = \frac{(100 - 1d) - 50}{1} \tag{A.4.1.11}$$

and the land rent in barley production is given by

$$r = \frac{(150 - 2.5d) - 50}{1} \tag{A.4.1.12}$$

Therefore, if the rents are equal between the two uses, we have

$$\frac{(100 - 1d) - 50}{1} = \frac{(150 - 2.5d) - 50}{1} \tag{A.4.1.13}$$

which gives $d = 33$, as we see in Figure 4.4.

Appendix 4.2 The slope of the bid-rent curve

The bid-rent curve assumes that the household or firm consumes land and non-land inputs in the optimum quantities for any location, given the particular price of land at each location. Moreover, we assume that the quantities and prices paid for the inputs ensure that the net utility of the individual is zero, and the net profitability of the firm is zero. The analysis of the two cases proceeds in more or less the same manner, with the only difference being that the household land consumption decision is modelled using a utility function, whereas the firm land consumption decision is modelled using a profit function. Therefore, here we will focus only on the case of the individual household residential location decision and the utility gained by such a decision. Within a bid-rent framework, we can write the utility function of an individual household as

$$U = U\big(K(d),\ S(d)\big) \tag{A.4.2.1}$$

where:

K composite capital good representing non-land inputs

S land area

The quantities of both land and non-land inputs consumed are assumed to be functions of distance d from the central business district.

As we see in Figure 4.10, individual or household utility in a bid-rent model varies according to the position of the bid-rent curve, with lower bid-rent curves implying higher utility. However, this results from the fact that utility is understood here in terms of a residual, leftover net utility surplus, after all the land and transport payments have been paid. This notion of net utility, whereby behaviour is determined by the utility surplus which is a residual, is akin to the understanding of utility in the Salop (1979) model outlined in Chapter 2. As such, in order to motivate these models we implicitly assume that there is an 'outside' good unrelated to this particular urban location model and which individual or households in our model are able to consume if they choose. In this case, given that individuals are able to migrate to other cities or regions, the appropriate outside good is the utility derived from the difference between the average income and the average living cost of all other location possibilities in all other cities. The implications of these migration possibilities will be discussed in Chapter 6. However, for our purposes here, it is sufficient to note that bid-rent analysis implies that individual urban location behaviour is determined by the surplus or net utility derived after factor payments are all accounted for.

Given these points, the bid-rent objective of the household is to maximize net utility subject to a given income budget constraint. This can be written as

$$Max\ U = U\big(K(d), S(d)\big)$$

subject to the budget constraint

$$Y - iK - rS - T \geq 0 \tag{A.4.2.2}$$

where:

Y budget constraint determined by the wage income

i price of non-land inputs

r rent per unit area of land

T transport costs

In a bid-rent model the price of land at each location must fall with distance, because of the transport-distance costs incurred in commuting to the urban centre. Therefore, in terms of efficiency analysis, at each location the household must consume land and non-land inputs in the particular quantities so as to equate the ratio of the marginal utilities from their consumption with their price ratio. The price ratio of non-land and land inputs is given by $-i/r$, and the ratio of the marginal utilities of non-land and land inputs is given by MU_K/MU_S. However, MU_K/MU_S is also equal to the marginal rate of substitution of land and non-land inputs, given as $\Delta S/\Delta K$, where Δ represents any marginal change in quantity of the inputs consumed. Therefore we have

$$-\frac{i}{r} = \frac{\Delta S}{\Delta K} \tag{A.4.2.3}$$

For any marginal change in inputs consumed associated with a change in the distance, we can write

$$-\frac{i}{r} = \frac{\Delta S}{\Delta K}\frac{\Delta d}{\Delta d} \tag{A.4.2.4}$$

which can be rearranged to give

$$i\frac{\Delta K}{\Delta d} + r\frac{\Delta S}{\Delta d} = 0 \tag{A.4.2.5}$$

However, equation (A.4.2.5) cannot be a complete description of the efficiency conditions a bid-rent function must fulfil, because the effect of distance changes on the costs of land and non-land inputs is not symmetrical. For a small change in distance Δd, the price of land r will fall by a small amount Δr. On the other hand, we assume that the price of non-land inputs i is independent of location. It therefore is necessary to specify each of these relationships as follows:

K is a function of distance $K = K(d)$

S is a function of distance and rent $S = S(d, r)$

r is a function of distance $r = r(d)$

i is independent of distance

T is a function of distance $T = td$, where T are total transport costs and t is the transport rate per kilometre

With the particular specifications we can now rewrite (A.4.2.2) as

$$Y - iK(d) - r(d)S(d,r) - td \geq 0 \tag{A.4.2.6}$$

which, if we set net utility to equal to zero, gives

$$Y = iK(d) - r(d)S(d,r) - td \tag{A.4.2.7}$$

Following Mills (1972), totally differentiating (A.4.2.7) with respect to distance such that residual surplus[1] is constant gives

$$\frac{dY}{dd} = i\left(\frac{\partial K}{\partial d}\right) + \left(\frac{\partial r}{\partial d}\right)S(d) + r(d)\left(\frac{\partial S}{\partial d}\right) + \left(\frac{\partial S}{\partial r}\frac{\partial r}{\partial d}\right) + \left(t + \frac{\partial t}{\partial d}d\right) = 0 \tag{A.4.2.8}$$

From (A.4.2.5) we know that

$$i\frac{\partial K}{\partial d} + r\frac{\partial S}{\partial d} = 0$$

Therefore

$$\left(\frac{\partial r}{\partial d}\right)S(d) + \left(\frac{\partial S}{\partial r}\frac{\partial r}{\partial d}\right) + \left(t + \frac{\partial t}{\partial d}d\right) = 0 \tag{A.4.2.9}$$

which rearranges to

$$\frac{\partial r}{\partial d} = -\frac{\left(t + \frac{\partial t}{\partial d}d\right)}{\left(S(d) + \frac{\partial S}{\partial r}\right)} \tag{A.4.2.10}$$

If total transport costs are a function of distance, the numerator term will always be positive. However, even if transport costs are constant with distance, such that if $(\partial t/\partial d)$ is zero, and the numerator term reduces simply to t, we still cannot yet determine the sign of (A.4.2.10) because $(\partial S/\partial r)$ is negative.

In order to unequivocally establish the sign of (A.4.2.10) is necessary to employ the Envelope Theorem (Takayama 1993). This theorem is used in situations where we assume that all variable inputs are employed at their optimal quantities, given the budget constraint and the prevailing prices. To employ the Envelope Theorem, it is necessary for us to distinguish between the variables which are direct and indirect functions of the distance.

The fall in the price of land will obviously alter the relative prices of the two inputs for a marginal increase in distance. This will cause a small increase ΔS in the optimum quantity of land to be purchased, and for a given budget constraint, will consequently also reduce by a small amount ΔK the optimum quantity of land to be consumed for any marginal increase in distance. What we see is that for any budget constraint, the quantity of

---

[1] The residual surplus is the utility from consumption minus the costs of consumption, and this is calculated with respect to other 'outside good' choice alternatives, in a manner akin to Salop (1979). The relevant 'outside good' in the case of an urban location choice is that of the best residual surplus achievable in a location in another urban area.

land consumed is an indirect function of the distance, because the quantity of land consumed is a direct function of the price of land, which itself is a direct function of the distance. At the same time, given the budget constraint, the quantity of non-land inputs consumed at any distance is an indirect function of the distance, because the quantity of non-land inputs consumed is a function of the quantity of land consumed at that distance, which itself is a function of the distance. This means we can rearrange and rewrite equation (A.3.2.7) as

$$r(d) = \frac{Y - iK^*(S, Y.d) - td}{S^*(Y, d, r)} \tag{A.4.2.11}$$

whereby S^* is the optimized quantity of land consumed, given the budget constraint, the distance and the price of land, and K^* is the optimized value of non-land composite capital inputs, given the budget constraint, the distance and the quantity of land employed. Applying the Envelope Theorem to (A.4.2.11), we assume that the values of the inputs S and K are always at their optimized values, S^* and K^*, for any given distance. This allows us to differentiate with respect to only those variables which are directly a function of distance. From (A.4.2.11) we see that the only such variable is the transport cost. Therefore

$$\frac{\partial r(d)}{\partial d} = -\frac{\left(t + \frac{\partial t}{\partial d} d \right)}{S^*} \tag{A.4.2.12}$$

which, if transport rates are constant, and the land is always consumed in optimum quantities, gives

$$\frac{\partial r}{\partial d} = -\frac{t}{S} \tag{A.4.2.13}$$

In other words, the Envelope Theorem tells us that for a marginal change in distance, the value of the indirect effect of $(\partial S/\partial r)$ in equation (A.4.2.10) is approximately zero, and only the direct effect of distance determines the bid-rent slope. The signs of equations (A.4.2.10) and (A.4.2.13) are unambiguously negative, and the value of the bid-rent slope is given by $-t/S$.

Appendix 4.2.1 The relative income elasticities of the demand for land and accessibility in the bid-rent model

We can assume that the total expenditure on both transport costs and land is a function of the income of the household. If transport rates are a constant function of distance, from (A.4.2.13) the equation of the bid-rent curve is given by

$$\frac{\partial r}{\partial d} = -\frac{t}{S} \tag{A.4.2.1.1}$$

To observe the effect of income changes on the bid-rent gradient we take the cross-partial derivatives of (A.4.2.1.1) with respect to income, thus:

$$\frac{\partial\left(\dfrac{\partial r}{\partial d}\right)}{\partial Y} = -\frac{1}{S}\left(\frac{\partial t}{\partial d}\right) + \frac{t}{S^2}\left(\frac{\partial S}{\partial Y}\right) \tag{A.4.2.1.2}$$

If (A.4.2.1.2) is positive, the bid-rent curve becomes shallower for higher income groups, as described by Figure 4.11. For the bid-rent curve to become shallower, therefore

$$\frac{t}{S^2}\left(\frac{\partial S}{\partial Y}\right) > \frac{1}{S}\left(\frac{\partial t}{\partial Y}\right) \tag{A.4.2.1.3}$$

which can be rewritten as

$$\left(\frac{1}{\partial Y}\right)\left(\frac{\partial S}{S}\right) > \left(\frac{1}{\partial Y}\right)\left(\frac{\partial t}{t}\right) \tag{A.4.2.1.4}$$

Therefore multiplying both sides by Y gives

$$\left(\frac{Y}{\partial Y}\right)\left(\frac{\partial S}{S}\right) > \left(\frac{Y}{\partial Y}\right)\left(\frac{\partial t}{t}\right) \tag{A.4.2.1.5}$$

which rearranges to

$$\frac{\left(\dfrac{\partial S}{S}\right)}{\left(\dfrac{Y}{\partial Y}\right)} > \frac{\left(\dfrac{\partial t}{t}\right)}{\left(\dfrac{Y}{\partial Y}\right)} \tag{A.4.2.1.6}$$

Therefore, from (A.4.2.1.6) the slope of the bid-rent curve will become shallower if the income elasticity of the demand for space is greater than the income elasticity of demand for reduced travel costs. Alternatively, reversing the inequality (A.4.2.1.6) such that the income elasticity of the demand for space is less than the income elasticity of demand for reduced travel costs implies that the bid-rent curve becomes steeper with increasing income, as in Figure 4.13.

Appendix 4.2.2 Environmental changes and bid-rent analysis

If environmental damage is caused by city-centre pollution, such that the quality of the environment increases with distance away from the city centre, we can write $E = f_e(d)$, whereby E represents environmental quality, and $f_e(d)$ describes the functional relationship between environmental quality and distance from the city centre. We assume that environmental quality is a location-specific public good, and that E is independent of the quantity of land consumed at a location. We can regard the effect of improved environment as increasing the utility of the household, for any given level of expenditure on land and non-land inputs. Therefore we can incorporate environmental quality within our utility function in general terms as

$$U = U\big(K(d), S(d), E(d)\big) \tag{A.4.2.2.1}$$

Following the argument in equation (A.4.2.11) above, we can therefore write

$$r(d) = \frac{Y - iK^*(S,Y,d) - td + Ed}{S^*(Y,d,r)} \tag{A.4.2.2.2}$$

which, once again differentiating with respect to d using the Envelope Theorem, gives

$$\frac{\partial r}{\partial d} = -\frac{\left(t + \dfrac{\partial t}{\partial d}d\right)}{S} + \frac{\dfrac{\partial E}{\partial d}}{S} \tag{A.4.2.2.3}$$

which gives

$$\frac{\partial r}{\partial d} = \frac{1}{S}\left[\frac{\partial E}{\partial d} - \left(t + \frac{\partial t}{\partial d}d\right)\right] \tag{A.4.2.2.4}$$

If the bracketed term in (A.4.2.2.4) is positive, the bid-rent curve will be upward sloping. In other words, if the monetary value of the improvement in the environment with respect to distance is greater than the increase in total transport costs with respect to distance, the bid-rent curve will be upward sloping. From the point of view of costs, the monetary value of the improvement in the environment can be understood in terms of the money that would be required in order to improve the current environment at the particular location to the required level. On the other hand, if the environmental improvements with respect to distance are less significant than the transport costs of distance, the slope of the bid-rent curve will still be negative, although shallower than would be the case with no environmental variations.

Appendix 4.3 Property asset appreciation and land price–distance convexity: the role of urban spatial growth

The argument here follows that of DiPasquale and Wheaton (1996). For any land-based asset held in perpetuity earning an annual rent of $R(t)$, discounted at a rate of i, the present value of the property is given as

$$PV = \int_0^\infty R(t)e^{-it}dt \tag{A.4.3.1}$$

which is an improper integral (Chiang 1984, ch. 13). If the rent payable at each time period is fixed, i.e. $R(t) = R$, equation (A.4.3.1.1) can be transformed by taking the limit of a proper integral, thus:

$$PV = \int_0^\infty Re^{-it} dt = \lim_{y \to \infty} \int_0^y Re^{-it} = \lim_{y \to \infty} \frac{R}{i}(1 - e^{-iy}) = \frac{R}{i} \qquad \text{(A.4.3.2)}$$

From equation (4.3) we have an expression for the rent payable for a unit size of property distributed at an even density around the central business district, given as

$$R(d) = t(D - d) + r_D + k \qquad \text{(4.3)}$$

Therefore, from (A.4.3.1.2), the present value of this property asset held in perpetuity paying the same rent as the current rent defined by equation (4.3) is given as

$$PV = \frac{t(D - d) + r_D + k}{i} = \left(\frac{tD}{i} - \frac{td}{i}\right) + \left(\frac{r_D}{i} + \frac{k}{i}\right) \qquad \text{(A.4.3.3)}$$

The first bracketed term on the right-hand side reflects the current location value of the property, in terms of the transport cost savings to the edge of the city, and the second bracketed term reflects the agricultural land plus construction value of the property, which we assume is independent of the location. In the case where a city grows in terms of the wage incomes payable at the city centre, the urban population and the city radius, we know from equation (4.6) that the growth in rents is greater for locations further away from the central business district. If we assume that the growth rate of the urban radius ($\partial D/d$) in the long run takes a constant value of h, the first term in the first bracket on the right-hand side of equation (A.4.3.1.3) can be rewritten as ($tD/i - h$). This is because as the city radius grows, the location value of any location interior to the city grows as the distance to the edge of the city increases. Therefore, assuming that $i > h$, the continually increasing transport cost saving from any location to the edge of the city partially compensates for the depreciating effect of the discounting on the future value of the location. Therefore we have

$$PV = \left(\frac{tD}{i - h} - \frac{td}{i}\right) + \left(\frac{r_D}{i} + \frac{k}{i}\right) \qquad \text{(A.4.3.4)}$$

which can be rewritten as

$$PV = \left(\frac{r_D}{i} + \frac{k}{i}\right) + \left(\frac{tD}{i} - \frac{td}{i}\right) + \left(\frac{tDh}{i(i - h)}\right) \qquad \text{(A.4.3.5)}$$

where

$$\left(\frac{tDh}{i(i - h)}\right) = \frac{tD}{i - h} - \frac{tD}{i} \qquad \text{(A.4.3.6)}$$

In other words, as we see from equation (A.4.3.1.5), in a situation of urban growth, the present value of the property is equal to the discounted value of the property given its current location relative to the edge of the city, plus the future growth in its location value.

Given that the present value of a property is its current market price, in order to understand the relationship between the price of the property P and the rent R of the property we can divide equation (A.4.3.1.5) by equation (4.3), thus:

$$\frac{P}{R} = \frac{\left(\frac{r_D}{i} + \frac{k}{i}\right) + \left(\frac{tD}{i} - \frac{td}{i}\right) + \left(\frac{tDh}{i(i-h)}\right)}{t(D-d) + rD + k} \tag{A.4.3.7}$$

which can be rearranged to give

$$\frac{P}{R} = \frac{(i-h)r_D + (i-h)k + (i-h)t(D-d) + tDh}{i(i-h)} \bigg/ t(D-d) + r_D + k \tag{A.4.3.8}$$

which from equation (4.3) simplifies to

$$\frac{P}{R} = \frac{(i-h)R + tDh}{i(i-h)R} = \frac{1}{i} + \frac{tDh}{i(i-h)R} \tag{A.4.3.9}$$

From equation (A.4.3.1.9) we see that the price–rent ratio increases as the rent falls. In other words, the further the location of the property from the central business district, the greater will be the price–rent ratio. Following the argument of equation (4.6), the reason for this is that more peripheral locations experience greater rental gains as a city grows, relative to central locations. On the other hand, if the city spatial growth h is zero, the price–rent ratio is given by $1/i$, and is therefore independent of location. Where cities do grow, the result of equation (A.4.3.1.9) is that even if transport costs are linear, and rents fall linearly with distance, the market price of properties will fall less than linearly with distance. More specifically, if the price–rent ratio increases with distance, property prices will be convex with distance.

Appendix 4.3.1 Property asset appreciation and land price–distance convexity: the role of income growth in a spatially constrained city

In the situation where a city is constrained in its spatial growth either by physical geographical restrictions or by land-use planning restrictions, the radius of the city can be viewed as being held constant. In this case, once the city has expanded to occupy all the available land, the agricultural rent will no longer be a determining factor in the urban rents. Therefore all rental values must be calculated with respect to the wage income Y earned at the city centre. Adopting the notation employed in section 4.5.1 and Appendix 4.3.1, and adapting equation (A.4.1.1.6) such that all measurements relate to a unit area size, i.e. $S = 1$, we can write an expression for urban property rents in a city of uniform density as

$$R(d) = Y - td - k \qquad \text{(A.4.3.1.1)}$$

Differentiating with respect to income Y gives $(\partial R / \partial Y) = 1$, and therefore $\partial R = \partial Y$. Dividing both sides by R, and multiplying ∂Y by Y/Y, we have

$$\frac{\partial R}{R} = \left(\frac{\partial Y}{Y} \right) \left(\frac{Y}{R} \right) \qquad \text{(A.4.3.1.2)}$$

From equation (A.4.3.2.2) we see that the rate of rental growth is inversely related to the share of income accounted for by rent R/Y. In other words, as we move away from the city centre, the rate of rental growth increases.

These different possibilities for rental appreciation will imply different relationships between property prices and property rents at each location. Following the approach of Appendix 4.3.1, we can write the present value of a property at any location as

$$PV = \frac{Y}{i - g} - \frac{td}{i} - \frac{k}{i} \qquad \text{(A.4.3.1.3)}$$

where g here represents the constant long-run rate of growth of city-centre wage incomes $\partial Y / Y$. The argument here is that, assuming $i > g$, the growth in incomes partially offsets the value-depreciating effects on future income of discounting. Equation (A.4.3.2.3) can be rearranged to give

$$PV = \frac{Yi - td(i - g) - k(i - g)}{i(i - g)} \qquad \text{(A.4.3.1.4)}$$

Given that the property market price P will be given by present value, we can therefore construct a price–rent ratio thus:

$$\frac{P}{R} = \frac{Yi - td(i - g) - k(i - g)}{i(i - g)} \bigg/ Y - td - k \qquad \text{(A.4.3.1.5)}$$

which rearranges to

$$\frac{P}{R} = \frac{Yi + (i - g)(-td - k)}{i(i - g)\left(Y - td - k\right)} \qquad \text{(A.4.3.1.6)}$$

Equation (A.4.3.2.6) can be rewritten as

$$\frac{P}{R} = \frac{Yi + (i - g)(R - Y)}{i(i - g)R} \qquad \text{(A.4.3.1.7)}$$

which can be rearranged to give

$$\frac{P}{R} = \frac{Yi}{i(i-g)R} + \frac{1}{i} - \frac{Y}{iR} \tag{A.4.3.1.8}$$

Therefore we have

$$\frac{P}{R} = \frac{1}{i} + \frac{Yg}{i(i-g)R} \tag{A.4.3.1.9}$$

From equation (A.4.3.2.9) we see that in the case of a city of uniform density which is spatially constrained, but which experiences incomes growth, the price–rent ratio of property increases for locations with lower rents. In other words, the price–rent ratio of a property increases with respect to the distance from the city centre, and the price–distance gradient is therefore convex. On the other hand, as with equation (A.4.3.1.9), if there is no income growth the price–rent ratio reduces to $1/i$, and is therefore independent of location.

The types of arguments discussed in Appendices 4.3.1 and 4.3.2 obviously assume that growth is correctly factored into the property prices. However, real-estate markets often exhibit major growth-expectation swings which result in what is known as 'over-shooting' and 'under-shooting'. These swings also have major effects on the capital liquidity made available by banks for housing finance, and the degree to which these monocentricity arguments are affected by shifts in expectations depends on the scale and duration of the over-shooting and under-shooting. Moreover, this is almost certainly not only a minor issue of misspecification, in that large movements in the property market associated with changing expectations are very much the drivers of property markets. Changing expectations heavily influence the availability of real-estate finance, which in turn influences the levels of construction and supply. However, given the time period involved in construction and development activities, real-estate markets tend to lag movements in the rest of the economy by a period of twelve to eighteen months, and also the real-estate asset prices tend to fluctuate more markedly than other financial markets (Ball et al. 1998).

Appendix 4.4 Optimum trip frequency and rent–gradient convexity

Following McCann (1995, 2007), we can set up a trip frequency optimization problem, in which a firm faces the cost minimization problem:

$$C = \varphi d^p f^n + \theta f^{-m} + rS \tag{A.4.4.1}$$

where:

d distance to the city centre

f frequency of journey

r rent per unit area

S land area

C total cost per time period

m, n, θ, ρ, ϕ, are positive constants, such that ϕd^{ρ} is the total distance costs per journey, and θ is the opportunity cost of less than continuous (i.e. f is less than infinite) face-to-face contact.

The first term in equation (A.4.4.1) reflects the fact that total transport costs per time period are a function of trip frequency, while the second term indicates that the opportunity cost of the lost market revenues of a firm may be negatively related to trip frequency. In other words, as trip frequency increases the firm will increase its market share up to a maximum when continuous face-to-face contact is maintained.

In a situation such as this, the firm must decide its optimum trip frequency. In order to calculate this, we differentiate with respect to f and set equal to zero, thus:

$$\frac{\partial C}{\partial f} = n\phi d^{\rho} f^{n-1} - m\theta f^{-m-1} = 0 \tag{A.4.4.2}$$

The second-order condition can be shown to be positive such that this is the expression for minimum costs (McCann 1995). Rearranging (A.4.4.2) gives

$$\frac{m\theta}{f^{m+1}} = n\phi d^{\rho} f^{n-1} \tag{A.4.4.3}$$

and thus

$$f^{n+m} = \frac{m\theta}{n\phi d^{\rho}} \tag{A.4.4.4}$$

Therefore the optimum trip frequency per time period F can be written as

$$F = \left(\frac{m\theta}{n\phi d^{\rho}} \right)^{\frac{1}{n+m}} \tag{A.4.4.5}$$

Consequently, what we see is that the optimum number of journeys per time period is inversely related to the distance of the firm from the city centre. In order to calculate the rent payable at each location, assuming that all trips are undertaken at the optimum frequency $f = F$, for each particular location, we can rewrite equation (A.4.4.1) thus:

$$C = \phi d^{\rho} F^{n} + \theta F^{-m} + rS \tag{A.4.4.6}$$

where $c = C$ when $f = F$. Differentiating with respect to d, setting to zero and applying the Envelope Theorem (Takayama 1985, pp. 137–41) gives

$$\frac{\partial C}{\partial d} = \rho \varphi d^{\rho-1} F^n + \frac{\partial r}{\partial d} S = 0 \qquad\qquad\text{(A.4.4.7)}$$

such that

$$\frac{\partial r}{\partial d} = \frac{-\rho \varphi d^{\rho-1} F^n}{S} \qquad\qquad\text{(A.4.4.8)}$$

From (A.4.4.5) we can write

$$F^n = \left(\frac{m\theta}{n\varphi d^{\rho}} \right)^{\frac{n}{n+m}} \qquad\qquad\text{(A.4.4.9)}$$

Therefore (A.4.4.8) can be rewritten as

$$\frac{\partial r}{\partial d} = -d^{\left(\frac{m\rho}{n+m}-1\right)} \left[\frac{\rho\varphi}{S} \left(\frac{m\theta}{n\varphi} \right)^{\frac{n}{n+m}} \right] \qquad\qquad\text{(A.4.4.10)}$$

Equation (A.4.4.10) is always convex in d as long as ρ is less than or equal to one. In other words, as long as total transport costs are less than linear (concave) or linear with distance, even where the land area of the firm or household is fixed, the rent gradient will still be convex with distance. The standard bid-rent result is achieved here even without substitution between land and non-land inputs. The point is that where trip frequency is itself a decision variable, as in the case of all transport, distribution, retail, and consumer shopping activities, plus all activities where the level of face-to-face contact affects the market share, the rent-gradient convexity is determined by the optimized trip frequency. This general argument can subsequently be applied to a range of different real-world examples (McCann 1995, 1998, 2007) with various alternative specifications of costs and factor quantities.

5 Regional specialization, trade, and multiplier analysis

5.1 Introduction

In Chapter 1 we discussed the question of the location behaviour of the individual firm. As we saw, the reasons for the spatial behaviour of firms depend both on the characteristics of the firm and on the characteristics of the various regions in which the firm could locate. Understanding industrial location behaviour then allowed us in Chapter 3 to explain the economic motivation for the growth of cities and industrial clusters. Our analysis focused on the issues which determine industrial clustering and industrial dispersion, and, in particular, on the various types of spillovers and links which take place between firms in the same area. In Chapter 4, the localized growth of an industrial cluster was then used as the basis of our comparative analysis of urban land prices and urban land distribution.

One of the issues raised by these arguments which has not yet been dealt with is the local impact of any local industry changes, such as industry expansion or contraction, or alternatively of the local impact of any local microeconomic changes, such as firm relocation, firm expansion, or firm closure. Following the arguments in Chapters 2 and 3, any firm relocation, firm expansion, or firm closure within a local economy must have consequences specific to the rest of local economy, as well as those consequences for the economy in general. The reason for this is that such changes will alter the demand for locally supplied factor inputs, and these demand changes will also engender further changes locally along the lines discussed in Chapter 3. As we will see in this chapter, the transmission of these effects will be mediated by the inter-firm linkages which exist in the local economy, plus the linkages which exist between the local firms and the suppliers of local factor inputs. In general we would expect the strength of these impacts to be broadly associated with the size of the change involved. In particular, where the individual firm involved is very large, any changes in the firm size or organization will have potentially major impacts on the local economy.

This type of argument can also be extended to the aggregate level where firm relocations, expansions, or contractions take place at the level of a local industry as a whole. Following the arguments in Chapters 2, 3, and 4, changes in the output and performance of an individual local industrial sector will have implications for other sectors in the local economy. However, from the arguments of Chapter 3, we would expect that the strength of these effects will depend on the extent to which the region is specialized in the activities of the sector in question. If a region is highly specialized in a particular industrial sector, the aggregate effect on the local economy of any changes in the performance of this sector would be expected to be relatively large. On the other hand, where a region is highly diversified, in the sense that it contains a wide variety of local industrial activities, we would expect that changes in the performance of an individual local sector would have a relatively smaller effect on the local economy. The local impacts of these changes can be analysed in terms of the aggregate effects of the individual microeconomic changes. This allows us to understand the relationship between a local region and a local industrial sector. The fortunes of an industrial sector and a local region therefore become interdependent.

The analysis of the impacts of industrial change on a host economy, through an assessment of the various linkages between firms and factor inputs, is known as *multiplier analysis*. This involves consideration of the regional trade patterns which exist both within and between regions. However, unlike countries, by definition, regions do not have the facility to collect continuous data on the level and patterns of their trade flows with other regions. Therefore, in the absence of regional trade data, it is necessary for us to employ measures which indirectly impute trade patterns to a region. The process of indirectly estimating regional trade patterns is done on the basis of observations of the regional industrial structure. Under various conditions, these observations allow us to impute regional trade patterns. With these imputed regional trade data we are then able to consider the regional effects of the expansion or contraction of a local regional industrial sector.

In this chapter we will initially deal with three different approaches to regional multiplier analysis. These approaches are economic base models, Keynesian regional income multipliers, and input–output analysis. While the models are somewhat different from each other, they each throw light on different aspects of the nature of the local impacts associated with industrial changes, and also on different aspects of the process by which such impacts are transmitted.

Each of these three model techniques is based on the two fundamental assumptions that, first, local factor prices are fixed, and second, that there are no local factor supply constraints. The first assumption implies that the marginal costs associated with a local output or employment expansion are constant. In other words, marginal costs and average costs are both equal to each other and fixed. At the same time, the second assumption implies that local output and employment can expand without facing any local capacity constraints. Taken together, these two assumptions imply that regional output or employment can increase indefinitely in a linear manner, in which average costs stay constant. Although these assumptions may appear unrealistic at first, they are useful for analytical purposes here in order to indicate the trade-linkage relationships between different industrial sectors within the same regional economy. The issues raised by changes in the local availability of factor inputs, or by changes in the local supply prices of factor inputs, will be discussed in Chapter 6. Moreover, as we will see in Chapter 8, in conditions of local unemployment there are many cases in which these assumptions, and the models constructed on them, can be defended as a basis for regional policy.

We will begin by discussing the economic base model, the most general of the three approaches. The economic base model will then be contrasted with the Keynesian regional income multiplier model. As we will see, the Keynesian regional multiplier is rather different from the Keynesian multiplier employed in national income models, but can be made compatible with the regional economic base model. Third, we will introduce the input–output approach to regional modelling. Although this is analytically the most sophisticated of the three multiplier techniques, in that it deals with interregional trade in a more comprehensive manner, this approach also benefits from the motivation and insights of the other two approaches. One final point we have not yet mentioned is that the process of indirectly estimating regional trade patterns, on the basis of observations of the regional industrial structure, is itself problematic. However, various measures of regional industrial diversity and specialization can be employed in order to facilitate this process. Therefore we will conclude the chapter by considering the difficulties associated with some of the techniques which are available for estimating regional trade patterns on the basis of observations of regional industrial structures. These issues will also be discussed in detail in Appendices 5.1–5.3.

5.2 The economic base model

The economic base model is conceived at the city-region level of aggregate analysis. Rather than analysing the impacts of industrial changes at a microeconomic level, the economic base model focuses on the links between aggregate sectors by characterizing a region as comprising two broad but distinct industrial sector-groupings. These two sector-groupings are knows as the *basic* sector, and the *non-basic* sector. The definition of these two groupings is that the basic sector is the sector whose performance depends primarily on economic conditions external to the local economy, while the non-basic sector is made up of the sectors whose performance depends primarily on the economic conditions internal to the local economy. The definition of external and internal dependence here relates to the location of the markets for the outputs of the sectors. Industries whose markets are national or global will tend to sell almost all their output outside the local city-region in which the industry is based. As such, the market demand for the output of this type of industry will be almost entirely dependent on market demand conditions outside the local economy. These industries are classified as *basic* industries, or sometimes as *export-base* industries. On the other hand, there are many sectors whose output tends to be accounted for almost entirely by local consumers. This is very typical in industries such as retailing, hospitality, and leisure, and activities such as legal services, real estate and consumer banking, education, health, and equipment maintenance, all of which tend to cater for households and small businesses. These industries comprise the *non-basic* sector, and in economic base terminology are also known as the *service* sector, although service here relates to the local orientation of demand, and is not to be confused with the definition of the tertiary sector.

In situations where regions are dominated by particular major industrial sectors, such as the automobile industries in Turin and Detroit, the aerospace industries in Everett-Seattle and Toulouse, and the international financial services industries in London and Frankfurt, the classification of the basic and non-basic sectors is a relatively easy matter, at least in principle. The basic sector will comprise the dominant exporting industry in the city-region, and the non-basic service sector will comprise all other sectors in the local area. On the other hand, as we will see shortly, for many cities or regions the distinction between the basic and non-basic sector is not so straightforward. Note here that we are defining exports in terms of selling outside of the city or region in which the industry is located. In other words, the definition of regional exports therefore includes both sales to customers in other parts of the same country as well as sales to customers in other countries.

In order to understand the economic base model, let us imagine we are dealing with an area where we can easily specify which local industries are basic and non-basic. The most common form of economic base models treats employment as a proxy for the level of output. In this case, the employment structure in the local economy can be defined by:

$$T = B + N \tag{5.1}$$

where:

T total regional employment

B basic employment

N non-basic employment

Equation (5.1) simply says that total employment in an area is the sum of the employment in the basic industry and the employment in the non-basic sectors. In the economic base approach, we assume that the output of the non-basic sector is determined by the performance of the local economy as a whole, whereas the performance of the basic sector is determined by factors exogenous to the local economy. As such, we can write $N = nT$, where n is a coefficient between zero and one representing the sensitivity of employment generation in the non-basic sector to the total level of employment generated in the region. Rewriting equation (5.1) gives

$$T = B + nT \tag{5.2}$$

which rearranges to

$$\frac{T}{B} = \frac{1}{1 - n} \tag{5.3}$$

The ratio T/B is called the economic base multiplier, and indicates the relationship between employment in the basic sector and employment in the total economy. The higher the ratio T/B, the greater the economic base multiplier. The economic base multiplier allows us to discuss the overall employment impacts associated with a change in the basic sector thus:

$$\Delta T = \frac{1}{1 - n} \Delta B \tag{5.4}$$

Therefore, for any change ΔB in the employment levels in the basic sector, total regional employment will increase by ΔT.

Implicit in this argument is the assumption that the total employment of the region is a function of the employment generated by the basic sector. The strength of this link between total regional employment and basic sector employment is indicated by $1/(1 - n)$, where n represents the strength or sensitivity of the linkage between the local economy and the locally oriented activities. That this is so can be understood in terms of our assumption that the performance of the local economy as a whole depends in part on the performance of the basic sector. At the same time, the employment generated by the basic sector will require inputs to be provided by the non-basic sector, which itself will generate further employment. The coefficient n can therefore be perceived as an expenditure-linkage parameter, reflecting the strength of demand by the basic sector for local non-basic inputs. The higher the value of n, the smaller the value of $(1 - n)$ and the greater the economic base multiplier $T/B = 1/(1 - n)$.

In areas in which local inter-firm linkages are very strong, the demand linkages between firms located in the same area will tend to be very high. In some of the industrial clustering situations described in Chapter 2, and in the cases mentioned above, such as Turin, Detroit, Toulouse, and Frankfurt, the employment growth in a dominant firm or industry associated with an output expansion will create enormous additional growth possibilities for local supplier firms in other sectors. These growth possibilities arise from the increased provision of inputs both to the basic firms themselves and also to the increased number of employees of those firms. In circumstances such as these, the value of n will tend to be high, and, consequently, the value of the economic base multiplier will also be high. On the other hand, there will be some areas in which the relationship between the basic and non-basic industries will be rather weak. For example, in many areas dominated by agricultural industries, the falling demand for labour associated with the increasing use of agricultural mechanization may mean that local increases in agricultural output will have relatively small impacts on local employment growth in other sectors. In this case, both the value of n and the value of the economic base multiplier will tend to be very low. The use of economic base models therefore tends to be associated primarily with city-regions dominated by urban concentrations of both population and production.

Obviously, the economic base relationship may be somewhat more complex that the simple description given in equation (5.3). The non-basic sector may not behave in an entirely linear manner in relation to the basic sector, in that a certain level of non-basic activity may be somewhat independent of the basic sector. In this case, our economic base model may look something like this:

$$T = B + (N_o + n_1 T) \tag{5.5}$$

where N_o represents the level of non-basic employment activity which is autonomous of the basic sector. This rearranges to

$$T = \frac{N_o}{1 - n_1} + \frac{B}{1 - n_1} \tag{5.6}$$

in which case we once again have

$$\Delta T = \frac{1}{1 - n_1} \Delta B \tag{5.7}$$

The result in equation (5.7) is the same as in equation (5.4). This implies that even if the non-basic sector is partly autonomous of the basic sector, in the situation where the marginal growth of the non-basic sector is constant with respect to the basic sector, the value of the economic base multiplier will be unaltered.

For practical purposes, models of the form described by equations (5.1) to (5.7) are useful for empirical purposes. The reason is that they are amenable to simple econometric estimation (Weiss and Gooding 1968) of the form

$$T = \alpha + \beta B + e \tag{5.8}$$

where the estimated values of α and β give us values for $N_o/(1 - n)$ and $1/(1 - n)$ respectively, in equation (5.6). In the simplest case outlined by equations (5.1) to (5.4), the value of $N_o/(1 - n)$ will be zero and $1/(1 - n)$ will be positive, whereas in the case where the non-basic sector is partly autonomous of the basic sector, the situation will be best described by equations (5.5) to (5.7).

It is also possible to conceive of situations in which the marginal relationship between the total employment change in the basic and non-basic sectors is not constant. For example, some of the agglomeration arguments discussed in Chapter 3 imply that the sensitivity coefficient n, which defines the strength of the linkage between the local basic and non-basic sectors, may itself be a function of the size of the local basic sector. Under these circumstances, it may be possible to describe the linkage between the sectors as something like

$$n = n_o + n_1 B \tag{5.9}$$

In this situation, we have

$$T = B + (n_o + n_1 B)T \tag{5.10}$$

which rearranges to

$$T = B\left(\frac{1 + n_1 T}{1 - n_o}\right) \tag{5.11}$$

and

$$\Delta T = \Delta B\left(\frac{1 + n_1 T}{1 - n_o}\right) \tag{5.12}$$

As we see in this case, the value of the economic base multiplier will increase with the size of the total level of employment in the region. The implication of this is that regional growth will become progressively more sensitive to growth in the basic sector as the size of the city-region increases. This scenario imposes much greater problems of empirical estimation than the previous models. Moreover, there is no reason to suppose it is indicative of generally continuing behaviour, as the limits to this explosive growth process will also depend on the arguments concerning the existence of diseconomies of agglomeration, as discussed in Chapter 3.

5.3 Identifying the basic and non-basic sectors

The argument in section 5.2 is based on the assumption that it is a relatively straightforward matter for us to decide which industrial activities comprise the regional basic sector, and which industrial activities comprise the regional non-basic sector. In other words, we assume it is easy for us to determine which local industrial sectors are primarily regional exporting sectors, and which local sectors are primarily non-exporting sectors. As we mentioned above, in some city-regions which are highly specialized in particular activities, such as Detroit, Turin, and Toulouse, it is quite easy in principle to identify the major local basic exporting industries simply from observation. However, even in urban regions like these it may be that there are many other industries which are basic in nature, but which are not easily identifiable as being so without additional information on the individual industries. Similarly, many regions appear not to be dominated by any particular single industry or group of industries. Areas such as these tend to be very highly diversified in terms of the industrial activities which are represented locally. Therefore determining what the basic and non-basic sectors are in these regions is not straightforward. Consequently, without prior knowledge, in the case of many regions, determining whether an industry is basic or non-basic is an inexact science.

There are three broad approaches to determining which local industrial sectors are the regional exporting sectors, namely the assumptions methods, the location quotient method, and the minimum requirements method. In the following sections we will deal with each of these three approaches in turn.

5.3.1 The assumptions method

The simplest approach to determining which local industrial sectors are basic and non-basic is to assume that all primary and secondary industries, which include all the extraction, agricultural, and manufacturing sectors, are basic in nature, and that all tertiary sectors are non-basic. This is known as the 'assumptions method'. This approach, however, must necessarily be inaccurate because many tertiary activities, such as financial services, are frequently nationally and internationally traded activities. As such, they will be non-basic in nature. Similarly, many agricultural activities, and also extraction activities such as quarrying, will tend to produce primarily for local markets, due to their relatively high transport costs. As such, many of these activities will be non-basic in nature. The simple basic and non-basic classification according to the assumptions method will therefore be subject to a large margin of error.

At the same time, there are many city-regions in which classification judgements based on experience and observation cannot easily identify basic and non-basic sectors. For example, in major cities such as New York, Paris, or London, the sheer number and variety of sectors means that identifying the basic and non-basic industries is almost impossible.

5.3.2 Location quotients

In situations such as these, where regional employment data are available, the most commonly used technique of basic and non-basic classification is to employ what are known as regional 'location quotients' (*LQs*). The location quotient *LQ* describes the employment share of any sector in any region, relative to the national share of employment in the sector. A regional location quotient LQ_{ir} is defined as the ratio of the regional proportion of employment *E* in a given sector *i* in a given region *r*, relative to the national *n* proportion of employment in the same given sector. A regional location quotient is given as

$$LQ_{ir} = \frac{E_{ir}}{E_r} \bigg/ \frac{E_{in}}{E_n} \tag{5.13}$$

where:

E_{ir} regional employment in sector *i*

E_r total employment in region *r*

E_{in} national employment in sector *i*

E_n total national employment

In terms of economic base analysis, the logic behind the *LQ* argument is that if a region has an employment share in any given sector greater than the national average, the region must be relatively specialized in the production of the output of that particular sector. In this case, $LQ_{ir} > 1$. If we assume for simplicity that, for any given industry sector, all regions have the same linear production functions, and we also assume that all regional household consumption functions are identical, then a location quotient which is greater than one will imply that the region must be a net exporter of the output of the particular sector. Conversely, a location quotient of less than one implies that a region is a net importer of the good in question. A location quotient of unity implies zero net regional trade flows.

On the basis of this argument, we would expect that the location quotients for the automotive sectors in cities such as Detroit and Turin will be greater than one, as these areas are relatively specialized in the automotive sector. At the same time, these areas are net exporters of automobiles, simply because the local economies of Detroit and Turin are small relative to the total markets of the local automotive sectors. Therefore, in these particular cases, the level of industrial specialization in these areas is taken as an indirect indicator of the level of their regional exports. Similarly, if the location quotient of a regional sector is less than the national average, the region must be a net importer of the goods produced by the sector. As an example, the level of employment in the whisky industry in England is almost zero, as almost all such UK employment is in Scotland. The location quotient for the whisky industry in all the regions of England will be close to zero, although whisky is consumed in large quantities in all regions of England. As such, the English regions are all net importers of whisky. On the other hand, the location quotient for the whisky industry in Scotland will be very much greater than one, because almost all of the UK output is produced in Scotland; Scotland is thus a net exporter of whisky.

This general location quotient argument can be applied to cities and regions in order to build up a picture of the regional importing and exporting patterns. Table 5.1 indicates the 2012 location quotient values for the aggregate industrial groupings within each of the three major cities of the Netherlands. These cities are Amsterdam, The Hague, and Rotterdam, and all three cities are similar in terms of size.

Table 5.1 City location quotient distributions

Sector	Location quotients					
	Amsterdam (FUR)	The Hague (FUR)	Rotterdam (FUR)	Amsterdam (municipality)	The Hague (municipality)	Rotterdam (municipality)
A Agriculture, forestry and fishery	0.35	0.48	0.68	0.01	0.30	0.06
B–E Energy and manufacturing	0.49	0.34	0.77	0.40	0.27	0.70
F Construction	0.50	0.63	1.27	0.39	0.48	0.84
G Wholesale and retail	0.90	0.72	0.97	0.78	0.56	0.70
H Transport and storage	1.57	0.68	1.56	0.76	0.77	1.74
I Hotels and restaurants	1.34	0.87	0.86	1.51	0.86	0.85
J Information and communication	1.71	1.64	0.77	1.93	1.58	0.85
K Financial intermediation	2.01	1.06	0.96	2.67	1.16	1.19
L&N Real estate. rental and other commercial services	1.28	1.12	1.11	1.12	1.18	1.19
M Knowledge-intensive business services	1.47	1.15	1.16	1.60	0.99	1.29
O Public administration	0.81	2.71	1.02	0.99	3.38	1.33
P Education	0.86	0.88	0.89	1.07	0.87	1.04
Q Health and social work	0.78	0.90	0.95	0.88	0.89	0.99
R Culture, recreation and other services	1.03	1.74	0.98	1.25	1.72	1.15

Source: Calculations kindly produced by Dr Martijn Burger, Erasmus University Rotterdam.

Table 5.1 provides the 2012 location quotient values for each of the three cities defined both at the wider functional urban region (FUR), which includes the travel to work area, and also at the level of the municipality, the local government area. As we see in Table 5.1, these three major urban agglomerations of Amsterdam, The Hague, and Rotterdam exhibit rather different industrial structures. Amsterdam is the centre of financial services within the Netherlands, with the result that its location quotient for the financial intermediation sector is 2.01 or 2.67, depending on whether we use the functional urban region or the municipality as the definition of the city. In contrast, The Hague is the location of all national government activities (even though Amsterdam is the official capital city), with the result that the location quotient values for the public administration sector are 2.71 and 3.38, depending on the city definition employed. Finally, as one of the world's largest ports, Rotterdam is obviously the transport and logistics centre of the Netherlands, and therefore the transport and storage sector exhibits location quotient values of 1.56 and 1.74 for the functional urban region and the municipality, respectively. Note that the wider Amsterdam region also exhibits many transport facilities, as reflected in the location quotient value of 1.57, but these are generally located outside the city itself, whereas in the case of Rotterdam they are in the city itself.

In contrast, in the case of the energy and manufacturing sector, all three cities exhibit location values which are significantly below one. As such, all three cities must import the outputs of these sectors from other regions of the Netherlands or other countries. Within the Netherlands, one of the major manufacturing centres is the city-region of Eindhoven while one of the major energy centres is the city of Groningen. The three major Dutch cities of Amsterdam, The Hague, and Rotterdam will import the outputs of these sectors both from these other smaller Dutch city-regions as well as from other regions across Europe and the wider global economy.

The same framework was first used by Lichtenberg (1960) as part of the first large-scale empirical and economic study of a major city, specifically in the case of the New York metropolitan study as discussed in Box 5.1.

5.3.3 Choosing between the alternative economic base approaches

In economic base models, the choice of technique adopted for determining the relative sizes of the basic and non-basic sectors will depend in part on the data which are available to us. The assumptions method is the most basic approach and relies on the least detailed sectoral employment information. The location quotient approach relies only on data for the region in question and national data, whereas the minimum requirements approach requires data on all regions. Unfortunately, these three techniques can give vastly different results. Therefore, because of the analytical problems with the minimum requirements technique discussed above and also in Appendix 5.2, the location quotient method is generally the most commonly used approach to determining the size of the regional basic and non-basic sectors.

Even if we are able to overcome the data problems discussed and to successfully identify the regional basic and non-basic sectors with a reasonable level of accuracy, a second issue which we have not yet discussed is the question of determining the value of the coefficient n in equation (5.2), where n represents the strength or sensitivity of the linkage between the

BOX 5.1 Using location quotients to calculate the economic base

The Lichtenberg approach

The location quotient argument presented here can now be applied directly to the problem of the economic base. For any city or region we can simply group together all those industrial sectors whose location quotients are greater than one, and categorize them as basic, and all sectors whose location quotients are less than or equal to one can be classified as non-basic. This is an exercise first carried out by Lichtenberg for the city of New York in 1954, a year in which the population of New York represented one-tenth of the total US population (Lichtenberg 1960; Hoover and Giarratani 1985). In order to understand the Lichtenberg approach, equation (5.13) above can be rearranged to give:

$$
\begin{aligned}
LQ_{ir} &= \left(\frac{E_{ir}}{E_r} \right) \left(\frac{E_n}{E_{in}} \right) \\
&= \left(\frac{E_{ir}}{E_{in}} \right) \left(\frac{E_n}{E_r} \right) \\
LQ_{ir} &= \left(\frac{E_{ir}}{E_{in}} \right) \bigg/ \left(\frac{E_r}{E_n} \right)
\end{aligned}
\tag{5.14}
$$

Equation (5.14) redefines the location quotient in terms of the ratio of the proportion of national sectoral employment in a region relative to the proportionate size of the region. In the case of New York, the city represented 10 per cent of the 1954 population. Therefore all New York industrial sectors which were found to account for more than 10 per cent of US national sectoral employment were assumed to be sectors which export goods and services to other parts of the national and international economy.

If we now apply the Lichtenberg logic to the case of the three Dutch cities described in Table 5.1, we can say that the logistics and transport sector is the major basic sector of Rotterdam, public administration for The Hague, and financial intermediation for Amsterdam. In addition, each of the other sectors with values greater than one will be included in the definition of the city economic base. A weakness of these location quotient approaches, however, is that the results generated depend on the level of industrial aggregation (Karaska 1968). Given that the description of the regional economy in terms of a simple dichotomy between basic and non-basic activities is a rather broad definitional approach, for large population regions location quotient estimates used for these purposes are only really meaningful at rather large levels of industrial aggregation, as in Table 5.1. Alternatively, the approach can work in small spatial areas in which the region is specialized in a relatively small number of activities.

The minimum requirements approach

The two major analytical weaknesses of the location quotient approach, even allowing for the issues of sufficient data availability and the problems of aggregation described above, are the assumptions of a common production function for each individual sector across all regions, and the assumption of a common household consumption function for all regions. As we see from Chapters 1–3, variations in spatial industrial patterns can arise due to geographical differences in demand conditions. This implies that there may be spatial differences in consumption patterns. Similarly, from Chapter 1 and Chapter 4 we see that industrial location behaviour can be associated with factor substitution, which itself will alter the relative quantities of individual factor inputs per unit of output produced. Each of these issues therefore calls into question the extent to which location quotients can really indicate the extent to which a regional sector is an exporting sector.

In response to these problems, a variation on the simple location quotient technique known as the 'minimum requirements' technique was proposed by Ullman and Dacey (1960). This alternative approach is based on the argument that because regional economies are much more open than national

BOX 5.1 Continued

economies, there is no theoretical reason why the national economy should be the most appropriate benchmark for assessing whether a regional sector is basic or non-basic. In order to take account of this, the minimum requirements method employs an index which compares the regional sectoral employment structure within a particular region with that of similar sized regions, rather than with respect to that of the country as a whole. For regions of similar sizes, the smallest share of sectoral employment in any single region within the appropriate size band is taken to represent the local sectoral consumption requirement for regions of that size. All regional sectoral employment shares greater than this are assumed to represent employment in regional exporting industries. On this argument, the minimum requirements location quotient $MRLQ$ can be represented by

$$MRLQ_{ir} = \frac{E_{ir}}{E_r} \bigg/ \frac{E_{im}}{E_m} \qquad (5.15)$$

where the subscript m represents the region with the minimum sectoral employment share. In principle, this method looks similar to the location quotient approach described by equation (5.13). As we see in Appendix 5.2, from the point of view of economic base studies, the attractiveness of the minimum requirements technique is that the basic/non-basic employment ratio is constant for all regions when summed across all sectors, although it is different for individual regional sectors. However, even apart from the problem of identifying the appropriate comparison regions, the analytical weakness of this approach is that it is not possible for a region to be a net importer of the output of any particular sector. The reason is that the $MRLQ$ value for any sector cannot be less than unity, because if a region's sectoral share were less than any alternative region of a similar size, the region in question would be taken as the minimum requirements benchmark region. All regions are therefore either net exporters or exhibit no net trade. This is obviously problematic. At the same time, in order to employ an economic base model of the form described by equations (5.1) to (5.8), it is not necessary for us to assume that all regions exhibit the same basic/non-basic employment ratio. All that is required is for the ratio to be fixed for the individual region in question.

size of the locally oriented sectors and the externally oriented activities within the local economy. From our discussions in Chapters 1–4, it is clear that these linkages could arise, first, due to direct expenditure on local factor inputs by the externallyoriented sectors. The Weber–Moses arguments of Chapter 1 indicate that firm location behaviour may sometimes be associated with strong local input purchasing linkages. This will be the case where the optimal location is a corner solution at an end point location. If the firms in question are primarily export-oriented firms with wide market areas, the result will be that a firm with a wide market area will exhibit strong local input purchasing. This will imply that the economic base linkage between the basic and non-basic sectors will be strong. At the same time, the agglomeration arguments of Chapter 2 suggest that there will be a second potential source of linkages between the basic and non-basic sectors. Additional linkages may arise due to information spillovers, whereby industrial clustering may lead to the improved flow of information between local firms. The implication here is that such improved information flows will improve the ability of locally oriented firms to respond to the input market needs of the local export-oriented firms, relative to more distant firms. This suggests that the locally oriented firms will maximize their share of the market for inputs supplied to the local basic sector by being better able to customize their outputs to best suit the needs of the basic sector. This will be done in part by investing in the most appropriate technology at the most appropriate time. The argument is therefore that this process of appropriate investing, in response to the improved local information flows associated with proximity, will itself strengthen the linkages between the basic and non-basic sectors.

These arguments provide us with two sources of linkages between the basic and non-basic sectors, namely the direct expenditure on factor inputs and intermediate goods by basic firms, and the additional investment linkages possibly associated with agglomeration arguments. Both of these linkages are monetary linkages. However, distinguishing between these two sources of linkages between the basic and non-basic sectors can be difficult. Therefore, evaluating the impact of growth in the basic sector on the local economy, while taking into account both of these effects, can also be difficult. One way of discussing these different effects is by constructing an expenditure multiplier in which these monetary linkages are explicitly distinguished at the local regional level. The easiest way of doing this is to construct a Keynesian regional multiplier.

5.4 Keynesian regional multiplier

A model which is similar in nature to the economic base multiplier, and which can be made largely compatible with it, is that of the Keynesian regional multiplier. The Keynesian regional multiplier is adapted from the standard Keynesian national income–expenditure multiplier model familiar in introductory and intermediate macroeconomic textbooks. Assuming that marginal and average input costs remain constant, and assuming that there are no capacity constraints within the economy, the standard Keynesian national income–expenditure multiplier model can be described as in Figure 5.1. In Figure 5.1, the change in income ΔY associated with any change in aggregate demand ΔAD can be described as $\Delta Y = k(\Delta AD)$, where k is the value of the multiplier. The multiplier therefore is given by the value of the ratio of the horizontal shift from Y_1 to Y_2, divided by the vertical shift from AD_1 to AD_2. In Figure 5.1, the successive rounds of expenditure are indicated by the converging income–expenditure path abc.

For a change in any of the individual components of aggregate demand, we can therefore multiply the individual change by the value of the multiplier to provide us with the overall income change, after all the successive rounds of expenditure have taken place. This income–expenditure process may be dynamic in the sense that successive rounds of expenditure may take place over several time periods. However, as we see in Appendix 5.1, it is quite straightforward to reconcile the simple static Keynesian income–expenditure model with a dynamic model incorporating time into the model, such that the conclusions here hold in either case.

We can now apply this broad logic to the case of a region. However, from the discussions in the previous sections, there are particular features of the local regional economy which are somewhat different from those exhibited by the national economy. The result is that the Keynesian regional multiplier is also somewhat different from the standard national Keynesian multiplier. In order to see this we can set up a simple set of expressions out of which we will construct our multiplier model.

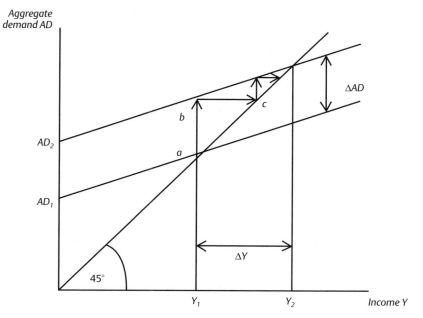

Figure 5.1 Keynesian income–expenditure multiplier model

The standard Keynesian income–aggregate demand expression can be applied to a region as

$$Y_r = C_r + I_r + G_r + X_r - M_r \qquad (5.16)$$

where Y_r represents regional income, C_r represents regional consumption, I_r is regional investment, G_r is regional government expenditure, X_r are regional exports, and M_r are imports. Each of the terms on the right-hand side of equation (5.16) represents an individual component of aggregate regional demand. These terms can be modified to show the relationship between them and the level of income.

Our first modification to the simple expression above is a standard linear consumption function, in which the level of regional consumption C_r is partly exogenous of regional income Y_r and partly a function of regional income. This is given as

$$C_r = \bar{C} + cY_r \qquad (5.17)$$

where:

$\bar{C}$ exogenous regional consumption

c regional marginal propensity to consume

In a regional income–expenditure model, the consumption specification given in (5.16) is the same as that in a national model.

Our second modification to the simple expression above is adapted from a standard linear import expenditure function, in which the level of regional imports M_r is partly exogenous of regional income Y_r and partly a function of regional income. This is given as

$$M_r = \bar{M} + mY_r \tag{5.18}$$

in which

$\bar{M}$ exogenous regional imports

m regional marginal propensity to import

In the case of a regional income–expenditure model, the definition of an import is expenditure on anything which is purchased from outside of the region, as well as outside of the country. In this way, the definition of regional imports is broader than that of national imports. This is the first major difference between the regional and national income–expenditure frameworks.

The income term Y_r in equations (5.17) and (5.18) is usually treated as the disposable income after tax. We can incorporate total regional taxation leakages T_r in a simple manner as

$$T_r = t \, Y_r \tag{5.19}$$

where t is the average regional tax rate, such that disposable income after tax is given as $Y_r(1 - t)$.

With equations (5.16) to (5.19) we are now able to provide an income–aggregate demand expression for regional income. Assuming for the moment, as many national income–expenditure models do, that regional private sector investment I_r, government regional expenditure G_r, and regional exports X_r are exogenous, we can substitute the information in equations (5.17) to (5.19) in equation (5.16) to give

$$Y_r = \bar{C} = cY_r(1 - t) = I_r + G_r + X_r - \bar{M} - mY_r(1 - t) \tag{5.20}$$

This can be rewritten as

$$Y_r - cY_r(1 - t) + mY_r(1 - t) = \bar{C} + I_r + G_r + X_r - \bar{M} \tag{5.21}$$

which rearranges to

$$Y_r = \frac{\bar{C} + I_r + G_r + X_r - \bar{M}}{1 - (c - m)(1 - t)} \tag{5.22}$$

The regional income Y_r is thus given as the sum of the exogenous components of aggregate demand multiplied by a regional multiplier k_r thus:

$$Y_r = k_r(\bar{C} + I_r + G_r + X_r - \bar{M}) \tag{5.23}$$

where

$$k_r = \frac{1}{1 - (c - m)(1 - t)} \tag{5.24}$$

The value of the regional multiplier k_r is seen to depend crucially on the value of the bracketed term $(c - m)$, which represents the difference between the marginal propensity to consume and the marginal propensity to import from outside the region. The term $(c - m)$ therefore represents the marginal propensity to consume locally produced goods. As the value of $(c - m)$ increases, the value of the regional multiplier increases, and as the value of $(c - m)$ falls, the value of the regional multiplier falls.

If we consider the effect of an increase in any one of the components of aggregate demand within the multiplier framework, we can write

$$\Delta Y_r = \frac{\Delta(\bar{C} + I_r + G_r + X_r - \bar{M})}{1 - (c - m)(1 - t)} \tag{5.25}$$

This suggests that the greater the regional value of the marginal propensity to consume locally produced goods, the greater the value of the regional multiplier, and the greater the increase in regional income. This observation fits well with the discussions in Chapters 1 and 2, in that regions with a strong supply of production factors and intermediate inputs will benefit greatly from any output increases on the part of the individual components of demand. The reason for this is that more of the income will be maintained within the region through successive rounds of expenditure between firms and local suppliers. On the other hand, regions characterized by firms which have very few local suppliers will tend to exhibit a high propensity to import m. The result will be that the marginal propensity to consume locally produced goods will tend to be very low, as will the value of the regional multiplier. The geography of inter-firm linkages therefore largely determines the value of the regional multiplier.

The regional multiplier expression given in (5.25) is not substantially different from simple national multiplier models, except for the geographical definition of imports. However, there is a second major difference between regional and national income multiplier frameworks, and this focuses on the question of investment. In standard national models investment is treated as being exogenous, as it is regarded as being dependent primarily on issues such as inflation, interest rates and expectations. As such, the level of investment is not regarded as being primarily dependent on the level of national income. However, within a regional framework the marginal propensity to invest in the local economy may be a function of local regional income. The reason for this is that local business confidence, and also the willingness of banks to provide loans to local businesses, may be dependent on the existing strength of the local economy, irrespective of national inflation expectations or interest rates (Dow 1982, 1987; Dow and Rodriguez-Fuentes 1997). The justification for this type of argument comes from the discussions of location and clustering in Chapters 1 and 2, in which clustering and proximity may improve flows of information between firms and between firms and consumers, and also may improve the efficiency of the local labour market, thereby increasing local income via agglomeration externalities.

In situations such as this we can assume that local investment levels are partly exogenous in that they are dependent on national economic conditions, and also partly dependent on the level of local regional income. We can therefore write regional investment income as

$$I_r = \bar{I} + iY_r(1 - t) \qquad (5.26)$$

where i is the local regional marginal propensity to invest in the local economy.

The third way in which regional income–expenditure flows are different from national flows is in terms of government expenditure. In national income–expenditure models government expenditure G is assumed to be exogenous of income, being dependent primarily on political issues. However, in the case of regions this is not so. Government expenditure in regions is in part dependent on the level of regional income. In particular, it can be argued that flows of government expenditure tend to be inversely related to the level of local regional income. For example, low-income areas often suffer from relatively high unemployment. In such cases, large flows of welfare benefits will tend to be directed into the regional economy. Similarly, low-income areas often are eligible for public subsidies from regional policy funds or urban policy schemes. On the other hand, high-income areas will receive relatively fewer public expenditure flows of the types just mentioned, because there will be less need for such flows. Government expenditure therefore acts as a partial stabilizer, countering changes in regional income. Therefore, in terms of regional income–expenditure models, the argument here suggests that public expenditure is in part an inverse function of local regional income. We can thus rewrite our government regional income–expenditure function as

$$Gr = \bar{G} - gY_r(1 - t) \qquad (5.27)$$

where minus g represents the marginal propensity of government expenditure to be withdrawn from the local economy as regional income increases.

Now, if we substitute equations (5.17), (5.18), (5.19), (5.26), and (5.27) into equation (5.16), we have

$$Y_r = \bar{C} + cY_r(1 - t) + (\bar{I} + iY_r) + (\bar{G} - gY_r) + X_r - \bar{M} - mY_r(1 - t) \qquad (5.28)$$

which, rearranged in a similar manner to equations (5.20) to (5.22), gives us

$$Y_r = \frac{\bar{C} + \bar{I} + \bar{G} + X_r - \bar{M}}{1 - \left[(c - m) + (i - g)\right](1 - t)} \qquad (5.29)$$

and

$$Y_r = k_r(\bar{C} + \bar{I} + \bar{G} + X_r - \bar{M}) \qquad (5.30)$$

where

$$k_r = \frac{1}{1 - \left[(c - m) + (i - g)\right](1 - t)} \qquad (5.31)$$

This expression is essentially the same as equation (5.22), except for the fact that the denominator term in equation (5.29) is broader than that in (5.22). In equation (5.29) the denominator term in square brackets contains an additional term $(i - g)$, as well as the term $(c - m)$, which is the marginal propensity to consume locally produced goods, and $(1 - t)$. This additional term $(i - g)$, which we can call the regional marginal (public plus private) propensity to invest in the local economy, reflects the total private local investment flows associated with local income levels, net of the public expenditure withdrawals associated with increasing regional income (Sinclair and Sutcliffe 1983; Black 1981). We assume that $i > g$, such that regional income growth is positively associated with overall public plus private sector investment growth. The type of multiplier model given by equation (5.31), which includes both the local customer–supplier expenditure linkages $(c - m)$ and the local investment linkages $(i - g)$, is sometimes known as a 'super' multiplier (McCombie and Thirlwall 1994).

As before, the justification for this type of model comes from the discussions in Chapter 2, in that business clustering in many cases is associated with increased regional income due to improved local information flows between customers, suppliers, and factor inputs. One of the features of areas characterized by such agglomeration economies is that there may be an associated increase in the entrepreneurial environment. In part this could be because of a greater general awareness of potential business investment opportunities, due to geographical proximity between market agents. At the same time, as we have seen, this could also imply that credit becomes more readily available for investment opportunities in already-buoyant economies. For all of these reasons we can assume that the marginal propensity to invest in the local economy will be positively related to the level of local regional income.

One final point we must consider concerns the regional propensity for government investment to be withdrawn from the region as regional income increases, as described by equation (5.27). As a region grows, the absolute levels of government expenditure in the region will tend to increase as greater levels of investment are required to provide and maintain local public infrastructure such as roads, schools, and hospitals. This suggests that the marginal propensity for government investment is a positive function of regional income. However, we can consider this effect as primarily a scale effect on public infrastructure investment in response to a growth in the local population. On the other hand, the effect described by equation (5.27) can be related to the income growth of either a stable or growing population, and relates both to the increasing out-transfer of welfare payment income, and also public infrastructure investment. In principle, equation (5.27) can be modified to take both of these effects into account thus:

$$G_r = \bar{G} + (g' - g'')Y_r(1 - t) \tag{5.32}$$

where g' represents the marginal propensity to increase government investment on local regional public infrastructure as regional income increases in line with regional population growth, and g'' represents the marginal propensity to withdraw government expenditure as regional income increases for any given level of regional population. In principle, equations (5.28) to (5.31) can be adjusted to take account of this modification. However, in countries with welfare systems and some element of regional policy, we can assume that $(g' - g'')$ is generally negative. Otherwise we would see that government expenditure serves to systematically increase regional income disparities rather than reduce them. Given that such a situation cannot be sustainable in the long run, we can assume that $(g' - g'')$ is negative. Therefore we can write $g = (g' - g'')$, where g represents the net marginal propensity of government expenditure to be withdrawn from the local economy as regional income increases. As such, our multiplier model equations (5.27) to (5.31) do not need to be altered.

5.5 Comparing the economic base and Keynesian regional multipliers

As was mentioned in section 5.1, although the economic base multiplier model and the Keynesian multiplier model are rather different conceptually from each other, they can be made more or less compatible. In order to see this, we can convert our income–expenditure multiplier expression (5.29) into an export base multiplier model, which is analogous to the economic base models discussed in section 5.2. To do this we simply separate the export income component of aggregate regional demand from the other domestic regional income components thus:

$$Y_r = \frac{X_r}{1 - \left[(c - m) + (i - g)\right](1 - t)} + \frac{\bar{C} + \bar{I} + \bar{G} - \bar{M}}{1 - \left[(c - m) + (i - g)\right](1 - t)} \tag{5.33}$$

The first term on the right-hand side of (5.33), which is our export base multiplier, reflects the economic base multiplier described in terms of income flows rather than employment numbers. The second term on the right-hand side of (5.33) describes the income–expenditure multiplier associated with specifically local activities. If we consider a change in regional exports ΔX_r, the corresponding change in regional income Y_r can be represented as

$$\Delta Y_r = \frac{\Delta X_r}{1 - \left[(c - m) + (i - g)\right](1 - t)} \tag{5.34}$$

Immediately we can see that equation (5.34) is the income–expenditure equivalent of our economic base equation (5.4), which was given as

$$\Delta T = \frac{1}{1 - n} \Delta B \tag{5.4}$$

The increase in export income ΔX_r in equation (5.34) is the equivalent of the employment increase in the basic sector ΔB in equation (5.4). Similarly, the basic/non-basic linkage coefficient n in equation (5.4) is the employment equivalent of the income–expenditure expression $[c - m + (i - g)](1 - t)$ in equation (5.34). The same argument can be extended to the relationship between the income–expenditure multiplier equation (5.33) and the economic base equation (5.6), which was given as

$$T = \frac{N_o}{1 - n_1} + \frac{B}{1 - n_1} \tag{5.6}$$

The second numerator term on the right-hand side of equation (5.33) is given as

$$(\bar{C} + \bar{I} + \bar{G} - \bar{M})$$

This term represents the exogenous levels of regional income which are independent of regional exports. By comparing (5.33) with (5.6) we can see that the second numerator term on the right-hand side of equation (5.33) is the income–expenditure equivalent of N_o, which in the economic base model represents the level of regional employment autonomous of exports. These comparisons therefore allow us to see that the employment linkages between the basic and non-basic sectors are mediated through the local expenditure linkages generated by the transactions between the two sectors. These expenditure linkages can be of the form of direct expenditure on locally produced intermediate inputs and local factor supplies, the strength of which is given by the marginal propensity to consume locally produced goods $(c - m)$. Additional induced expenditure can also be generated by increases in local investment, which are represented by the regional (public plus private) propensity to invest $(i - g)$.

The actual levels of exports and imports depend on a variety of geographical, technological, and historical factors, as discussed in Chapter 7. A region's current exports and imports depend in part on the economic history of the region as well as its economic geography, because today's products and services produced in the region are also a result of the activities undertaken in the region in the past. In addition, institutional issues are also important, as these lead to trade barriers. Gravity equation models, similar to those discussed in Chapter 6, are often used to estimate interregional trade allowing for such trade barriers (Anderson and van Wincoop 2003, 2004) in situations where the trade data are limited. However, such models are never a substitute for detailed input-out and multiplier models.

5.6 Impact analysis

At the aggregate regional level, the impacts of an increase in regional export activity, associated with a growth of the basic sector in general, can be analysed in a straightforward manner by observation of equation (5.34). Similarly, using the same approach, we can also observe the regional multiplier effects of a change in any of the regional domestic components of demand given in equation (5.30), simply by multiplying the change in the particular component of aggregate demand by the regional multiplier, as described in equation (5.31). At the micro level, however, the situation may be rather more complex.

We can imagine a situation where a firm which serves a wide geographical market area moves into a particular region. If the market area of the firm is much wider than that of the host region, it becomes immediately obvious that the exports of the region will increase due to the local presence of the immigrant firm. In the above expressions this implies that ΔX_r is positive. However, following the location theory arguments outlined in Chapter 1, a new firm may initially only have very weak links with the local economy in which it has located. This is because it may take time for a firm to develop strong linkages with the local economy. The manifestation of this will be that the firm's marginal propensity to consume locally produced goods may be much lower than the prevailing average regional marginal propensity to consume locally produced goods (Sinclair and Sutcliffe 1978, 1983). In a situation such as this, equation (5.33) will need to be adjusted to allow for two different expenditure effects associated with different types of linkages, and this is known as 'impact analysis'. The type of multiplier framework which accounts for this is known as an 'impact multiplier' and the method of construction of these impact multipliers, as described in Box 5.2, is known as 'impact analysis'.

Linkage expenditure patterns can be defined both in terms of geography and in terms of time. The geography of linkage patterns, as discussed in Chapters 1 and 2, will determine the value of the regional expenditure coefficients. However, this information will not tell us anything about the speed of such effects. In order to understand the temporal aspects of regional impact multipliers, all the models described by equations (5.16) to (5.37) can be made more sophisticated by splitting up the various rounds of the income–expenditure

---

BOX 5.2 Calculation of the impact multiplier

In impact analysis we attempt to evaluate the regional development effects of individual structural changes to a region, such as the immigration of a new large firm into a region, or the construction of a new infrastructure project within the region. Relative to standard multiplier models described by equations (5.16) to (5.31), impact multiplier models provide us with a more rigorous, but also rapid, way of estimating the regional multiplier in cases such as this, by distinguishing the expenditure linkages directly associated with the firm or project in question and those which are due to general regional expenditure patterns.

In terms of impact analysis, the first effect comes from the direct expenditure by the new immigrant firm on locally produced goods and services. The additional regional income accounted for by the new immigrant firm is represented by ΔX_r. We can think of this as the first-round income injection.

The second-round income injection can be considered to be the additional expenditure in the local economy by the new firm, which can be represented by $\Delta X_r(c_F - m_F)(1 - t_F)$, where c_F represents the firm's marginal propensity to consume, m_F represents the firm's marginal propensity to import, and t_F represents the firm's corporate tax rate.

This second-round expenditure injection into the local economy will itself then be subject to the regional multiplier represented by equation (5.31). These will be the third and subsequent rounds of income injections. These different stages can be described as

$$\Delta Y_r = \Delta X_r + \frac{\Delta X_r(c_F - m_F)(1 - t_F)}{1 - \left[(c - m) + (i - g)\right](1 - t)} \tag{5.35}$$

If we let

$$e_1 = (c_F - m_F)(1 - t_F)$$
$$e_2 = \left[(c - m) + (i - g)\right](1 - t)$$

we can write equation (5.35) as

$$\Delta Y_r = \Delta X_r\left(1 + \frac{e_1}{1 - e_2}\right) \tag{5.36}$$

which rearranges (Wilson 1977) to

$$\Delta Y_r = \Delta X_r\left(\frac{1 + e_1 - e_2}{1 - e_2}\right) \tag{5.37}$$

The impact analysis approaches described by equations (5.35)–(5.37) are useful in providing reasonably quick estimates to such regional structural changes.

process into discrete time periods. This allows us to integrate export base models with accelerator type models (Hartman and Seckler 1967). There are, however, analytical weaknesses inherent in all these types of Keynesian income–expenditure multiplier models, which we must consider. The problems concern the relationship between the values of the parameters contained in the coefficients e_1 and e_2, as a structural change of this sort takes place.

If a firm moves into an area, we know from our Weber analysis in Chapter 1 that the supply linkages of the firm are likely to be very different from those of the host region as a whole. In particular, the new firm's supply linkages will tend to be less localized than those of the firms or industries which have been located in the host region for a significant time period. Over time, the firm's local supply linkages, defined by e_1, may converge towards the regional average values, defined by e_2, as the firm seeks to employ more local suppliers. On the other hand, this may not be the case, either if firms are unable to find suitable local suppliers, or if corporate organizational concerns militate against the employment of local suppliers, instead requiring the firm to employ corporation-wide suppliers from other locations. If either of these latter situations occurs, the firm's regional linkage expenditure patterns, reflected in its marginal expenditure coefficients, may remain quite different from the regional linkage expenditure values. Over time, therefore, the immigration of the new firm may itself change the regional linkage values, and consequently the regional marginal expenditure values, averaged across all sectors. If the immigrant firm is very large relative to the size of the local economy, such as in the case of a newly opened automobile production plant, the regional expenditure coefficients may change very quickly. In some cases these changes may occur before all of the successive rounds of expenditure have had time to take place, in which case the value of the regional multiplier will itself have been changed by the immigration of the new firm.

The immigration of different types of firms into a region will therefore change the regional multiplier in different ways according to the particular linkage patterns of the firms in question. The reason for this is that firms of different types will exhibit different demand requirements for intermediate inputs and production factors. The demand requirements across the various sectors within the region will differ according to the expenditure patterns of the particular firm or sector we are observing. To address these problems coherently, it is therefore necessary for us to isolate each of the individual expenditure linkages between each of the sectors within the region, and between the region sectors and all other regions. Only then will we be able to identify and accurately estimate, the regional multiplier impact of any particular regional structural change. In order to do this, we must undertake what is known as regional input–output analysis.

5.7 Regional input–output analysis

The basic principle behind regional input–output analysis is to identify and disaggregate all the absolute flows of expenditure between different industries, between consumers and industries, and between industries and factor supplies, in order to reveal the underlying trading structure of the regional economy. These individual expenditure linkages are then defined in proportionate terms, and the aggregate pattern of these proportionate relationships is used to construct detailed regional multipliers. It therefore becomes possible to

Table 5.2 Regional expenditure flows

Sales of ($m)	Purchases of ($m)				
	Industry X	Industry Y	Industry Z	Final consumers	Total output
Industry X	–	–	70	30	100
Industry Y	20	–	80	100	200
Industry Z	20	80	–	200	300
Regional factor inputs	40	110	140	–	290
Regional imports	20	10	10	30	70
Total inputs	100	200	300	360	960

identify how the regional economy in general, and how each of the individual regional sectors, is affected by a change in the level of demand of one or more of the individual regional industrial sectors. As such, regional input–output analysis can avoid many of the analytical problems described in section 5.6 as long as sufficient updated input–output data are available, which is a point we will return to at the end of this section.

The first stage of a regional input–output analysis is to construct a regional trade flow table. In order to understand the logic of this we will use a numerical example employed by Thorne (1969), in which region R comprises three industrial sectors X, Y, and Z. Table 5.2 indicates the absolute values of the current output and expenditure on inputs by each of the three sectors X, Y, and Z, plus the expenditure by final consumers in the region on finished goods. As we see in Table 5.2, at the current levels of regional output, local industry X spends $20 million on inputs from each of the other local industrial sectors Y and Z, $20 million on regional imports, and $40 million on local regional inputs. The respective expenditure flows of each of the sectors Y and Z can also be seen by reading down the column values in Table 5.2. Similarly, local household consumers are seen to purchase $30 million worth of finished goods and services from local industry X, $100 million from local industry Y, $200 million from local industry Z, plus £30 million worth of finished goods and services produced outside the region. At the same time, we can interpret the pattern of sales by each sector across each of the other sectors and household consumers by reading across the columns from left to right. For example, local industry Z sells $20 million worth of outputs to local industry X, $80 million to local industry Y, and $200 million to local consumers. Meanwhile, local factor inputs supply factor services worth £40 million, $110 million, and $140 million to each of the local industries X, Y, and Z, respectively. These values represent the combined total wages, rent, and interest earned by the local labour, land, and capital suppliers employed in the activities of each of the local industries X, Y, and Z. The final column on the right-hand side provides the total output sales for each sector.

The second stage in the input–output analysis involves defining the disaggregated expenditure flows for each of the three industries and the final consumers as described in Table 5.2 in terms of their proportionate size. In order to do this we simply divide the expenditure value in each of the cells of Table 5.2 by the respective column total at the foot of each of the columns. For example, in Table 5.2 we see that local industry Y currently purchases $80 million worth of inputs from local industry Z. By dividing 80 by the respective column

Table 5.3 Regional expenditure coefficients

	Purchase coefficients of:			
	Industry X	Industry Y	Industry Z	Final consumers
Industry X	–	–	0.23	0.08
Industry Y	0.2	–	0.27	0.28
Industry Z	0.2	0.4	–	0.56
Regional factor inputs	0.4	0.55	0.47	–
Regional imports	0.2	0.05	0.03	0.08
Total inputs	1.0	1.0	1.0	1.0

total of 200, we see that the expenditure by industry Y on inputs from industry Z accounts for 0.4, i.e. 40 per cent, of the total input expenditure of industry Y. The value of 0.4 is defined as the regional expenditure coefficient of local industry Y's purchases of the output of local industry Z. By repeating this procedure for each of the cells in Table 5.2 we arrive at Table 5.3, which gives each of the individual regional expenditure coefficients for purchases by industries X, Y, and Z, as well as final household purchases. Table 5.3 can be considered a matrix of regional expenditure coefficients.

By means of Table 5.3 we can now consider the impact on the regional economy of an increase in the output demand of one of the local industrial sectors. For example, we can consider the situation where final consumers increase their consumption of the goods produced by local industry Z to $1000 million. In order to supply $1000 million worth of goods and services to final consumers, from Table 5.3 we know that local industry Z must also purchase 23 per cent of its inputs from local industry X (i.e. $0.23 \times 1000 = \$230$ million), 27 per cent of its inputs from local industry Y (i.e. $0.27 \times 1000 = \$270$ million), 47 per cent of its inputs (i.e. $0.47 \times 1000 = \$470$ million) from local factor suppliers, and 3 per cent of its inputs (i.e. $0.03 \times 230 = \$6.9$ million) as regional imports. Industry X in turn will then spend 20 per cent of its income on additional inputs from local industry Y (i.e. $0.2 \times 230 = \$46$ million), 20 per cent of its income on additional inputs from local industry Z (i.e. $0.2 \times 230 = \$46$ million), 40 per cent of its income on additional local factor supplies (i.e. $0.4 \times 230 = \$92$ million) and 20 per cent (i.e. $0.2 \times 230 = \$46$ million) on regional imports. Meanwhile, industry Y will spend 40 per cent of its income on additional inputs from local industry Z (i.e. $0.4 \times 270 = \$108$ million), 55 per cent of its income on additional local factor supplies (i.e. $0.55 \times 270 = \$148.5$ million), and 3 per cent of its income (i.e. $0.03 \times 270 = \$8.1$ million) on regional imports. Each of the three sectors in turn will continue to purchase additional inputs through the successive rounds of expenditure along the lines described in Appendix 5.1. Assuming that the expenditure coefficients remain constant through the successive rounds of expenditure, it is possible to calculate the total value of regional output and expenditure associated with local industry Z producing $1000 million worth of goods and services for local consumers.

Following Thorne (1969), the absolute output and expenditure values are given in Table 5.4. A final consumer demand of $1000 million for the output of local industry Z results in a total regional output of $2868 million, because of the successive rounds of

Table 5.4 Regional output and expenditure flows for consumer purchases of $1000 million from industry Z

Sales of ($m)	Purchases of ($m)				
	Industry X	Industry Y	Industry Z	Final consumers	Total output
Industry X	–	–	282	–	282
Industry Y	56	–	322	–	378
Industry Z	56	152	–	1000	1208
Regional factor inputs	113	207	564	–	884
Regional imports	57	19	40	–	116
Total inputs	282	378	1208	1000	2868

expenditure between each of the local industrial sectors. The value of the regional multiplier in this particular case is therefore total regional output divided by the particular output demand in question. In other words, the regional multiplier is given by $2868/1000 = 2.87$.

From Table 5.3 we see that each industry has a different pattern of regional expenditure, as reflected by the different values of the regional expenditure coefficients. However, once the initial demand stimulus has been transmitted to the supplying sectors, the pattern of purchasing through the successive rounds of expenditure remains constant. Yet what we immediately see from this example is that for any given level of final output, the actual value of the regional multiplier depends on the source of the initial output demand stimulus. For a fixed pattern of regional sectoral purchase coefficients, given in Table 5.3, the absolute value of the regional multiplier will depend crucially on the pattern of the first-round local purchases by the sector in which the initial demand stimulus arose. In the above case, if the output demand originated in local sector X, the value of the overall regional multiplier would have been much less, because sector X has a much higher propensity to import than either sector Y or sector Z. Therefore the first-round expenditure injection into the regional industrial system would have been much lower than in the above case.

On first inspection, the individual regional expenditure coefficients in each of the cells of Table 5.3 may appear to be the input–output equivalent of n in the economic base model (equation 5.3), and $(c - m)$ in the Keynesian multiplier model (equation 5.24). However, in the input–output case the individual regional expenditure coefficients of Table 5.3 refer only to a single expenditure linkage between one individual purchasing sector and one individual supply sector. On the other hand, the values of n in the economic base model and $(c - m)$ in the Keynesian multiplier model represent aggregate average regional expenditure values across all regional purchasing linkages. As we see in Appendix 5.3, the actual input–output equivalent of the economic base or Keynesian multiplier models is determined by calculating the inverse of the matrix of all the coefficients given in Table 5.3. It is this technique that allows us to calculate the values given in Table 5.4.

5.7.1 Additional comments on regional input–output analysis

The input–output multiplier is equivalent to, but much more precise and flexible than, either the economic base multiplier (T/B in equation 5.3) or the Keynesian regional multiplier (k_r in equation 5.24). One reason is that the input–output multiplier automatically incorporates all the issues raised by impact analysis, as discussed in section 5.6 above, concerning the fact that the first-round impact coefficient values (given as e_1 in equation 5.36) will depend on the source of the demand stimulus, and will be different from the regional expenditure coefficients of the successive rounds of local expenditure (given as e_2 in equation 5.36).

Second, the basic input–output model described here can be further modified to be made more directly comparable with the economic base (Billings 1969) and Keynesian regional multiplier models by splitting up final consumer demand into a local and a non-local component. In other words, by isolating whether a demand stimulus originates primarily from outside of the region or within the region, we can consider the extent to which the region behaves as an export base, along the lines described in sections 5.5 and 5.6. In the example above, we can consider the situation where the region very much exhibits an export base type of structure by imagining that almost all of the final consumer demand is external to the region. In this case, the input–output structure described by Tables 5.2 to 5.4 will represent an economic base model. To a large extent it will also represent a Keynesian regional multiplier, except for the induced investment expenditure effects. As well as using this technique to consider the local effects of a regional export stimulus, we can also use it to investigate the regional multiplier effects of the immigration of a new firm into a region, by considering the first and subsequent rounds of expenditure directly and indirectly generated by the new firm.

Third, the technique can be extended to construct a system of interregional input–output tables, in which trade flows between all sectors and across all regions are explicitly distinguished from trade flows between all sectors within individual regions. This allows interregional trade feedback effects to be analysed (Miller 1998), in which mutual trading relationships between the regions mean that a demand stimulus in one region generates an increased demand impact in a second region, which itself leads to an increased demand in the first region. Moreover, such models can be made dynamic in the sense that demand changes over time can be simulated.

Although the principle behind the regional input–output model is quite straightforward, in practice, however, the use of such techniques is much more complicated because the construction of regional input–output tables is itself a very difficult task. The reason is that without borders or a customs administration system, regions are not able to collect detailed trade statistics of flows of goods and services to and from other regions. Nor are they able to collect detailed internal trade statistics between sectors within the domestic economy. Therefore we have little or no direct information as to the input–output coefficients which will enter each cell in a regional input–output table such as Table 5.3. In a very few cases such as Scotland and Wales regional input–output data are constructed fairly frequently from extremely large and detailed surveys carried out by government agencies. However, in most other cases such surveys are not possible. In these more usual situations where updated surveys are not available, the construction of regional input–output tables is therefore carried out in an indirect manner. In order to do this, there are two standard practices. The first approach is employed where no updated national input–output table exists. In this approach regional trade flows are estimated on the basis of regional sectoral employment distributions, which are calculated using location quotient techniques. In the second approach, where updated national input–output tables do exist, regional trade estimates are produced by adjusting the national input–output coefficients. The details of the techniques employed are discussed in Appendix 5.2. In situations where it is possible to test the accuracy of regional input–output tables constructed on the basis of these indirect approaches with actual regional trade survey data, the results suggest that there is often a high degree of error. In particular, as we see in Appendix 5.2.2, regional trade estimates arrived at on the basis of location quotients generally tend to overestimate local multiplier values.

A final analytical issue relating to input–output analysis, but which also relates to the economic base and Keynesian regional multiplier models, concerns the realism of the assumption of the stability of the input–output coefficients through the successive rounds of expenditure. All three models are based on the assumption that the regional expenditure coefficients remain stable throughout the successive rounds of local expenditure. In other words, we assume that the marginal and average costs of production remain equal and constant as output expands. Furthermore, we also assume that all production functions are linear, in the sense that all input expenditure coefficients remain fixed, and that the relationship between inputs and outputs exhibits constant returns to scale. (Such production functions are referred to as linear input–output functions, or alternatively as Leontief functions, after the founder of input–output analysis, Wassily Leontief (1953). Taken together, these assumptions amount to saying that the prices of any factor inputs which are specifically local, such as labour and land prices, are invariant with the level of output.

In situations in which there are unemployed resources, and in particular in situations in which there is a pool of unemployed local labour at the prevailing regional wage rate, the input–output assumptions concerning constant marginal and average costs would appear to be good approximations of the real world. In these situations, the regional input–output model can be made compatible with, and provide extensions to, the Keynesian regional multiplier model (Hewings et al. 1999). Moreover, demographic changes in the composition of the local labour supply can also be made compatible with such assumptions (Batey and Madden 1981; Batey et al. 2001). On the other hand, where supply constraints become evident, the prices of the various local inputs will begin to rise. This may lead to some factor substitution effects, thereby contravening our multiplier assumptions. The extent to which the accuracy of our multiplier model is affected will therefore depend on the extent to which our linearity assumptions are violated across all regional sectors.

5.8 Conclusions

The question of regional industrial specialization, which was first introduced in Chapter 2, has implications for the pattern of trade which a region engages in. In particular, spatial industrial clustering implies that a region is relatively specialized in the production of the outputs of the locally clustered sector. The result is that the industrial sectors which are clustered in certain regions tend to provide the major exports for the regions in which they are located. Conversely, the majority of a region's imports will tend to come from the sectors which have a relatively low level of employment in the region. As we have seen in this chapter, the regional trade patterns which result from these patterns of regional industrial specialization have implications for the relationship between the externally oriented regional export sectors and the locally oriented regional industrial sectors. These relationships are manifested in terms of employment and expenditure linkages, the structure of which can be understood in terms of regional multipliers. The basic observation to come out of these multiplier models is that a demand increase in one regional export sector will have even greater impacts for overall regional demand.

We have discussed the three broad approaches to identifying regional multipliers, namely the economic base model, the Keynesian regional multiplier model, and regional input–output analysis. These three approaches to regional multiplier analysis allow us to analyse the contribution of regional exports to the successive rounds of income and expenditure which remain in the local economy. Of the three techniques, the economic base model is seen to be analytically the simplest approach, in which estimates of the basic and non-basic sectors are most commonly made on the basis of regional industrial employment distributions. The Keynesian regional multiplier model adopts a different perspective in that it focuses on the issues which determine the nature of the monetary flows involved in each of the successive rounds of income and expenditure. As we have seen, however, the economic base model and the Keynesian regional multiplier model can be made more or less compatible, at least in analytical terms, in that local sectoral employment linkages will be mediated through local money expenditure linkages. Meanwhile, the input–output approach is much more comprehensive than the other two approaches, and avoids many of the analytical problems associated with the two techniques.

On the other hand, all three approaches suffer from the same two basic problems. The first is the issue of data availability, and the limitations of the various techniques for overcoming data availability problems. The second problem is the question of the assumption of constant regional average and marginal costs with excess regional capacity. As we have seen, in situations where there is excess labour supply, such assumptions can be justified. In particular, these approaches can be very useful in analysing the impacts of the policies adopted for rejuvenating under-performing regions. These issues will be dealt with in detail as part of our regional policy discussions in Chapter 7. At the same time, as we will see in Chapter 6, these models can also throw some light on the downward adjustment mechanisms of regions which experience adverse demand shocks. On the other hand, where labour supply prices are changing, such as in situations in which there are local labour supply constraints, or alternatively where interregional labour migration is a major feature, regional multiplier models may exhibit rather greater limitations. These various issues surrounding the regional demand and supply of local labour are the central topics discussed in Chapter 6.

Discussion questions

5.1 What types of urban and regional economies are most suited to an economic-base type of analysis?

5.2 What empirical measures can we adopt for estimating basic and non-basic industries?

5.3 Within a Keynesian regional multiplier framework, examine the role played by the marginal propensity to consume locally produced goods in determining regional income.

5.4 Explain the concept of a 'super multiplier'.

5.5 How can a Keynesian regional multiplier framework be made consistent with an economic base model?

5.6 How is the structure of the regional multiplier affected by the types of firms which locate in a region?

5.7 What are the advantages of input–output techniques over other regional multiplier approaches?

5.8 Which regions in your own country reflect a classical export-base economic structure?

Appendix 5.1 The simple static and dynamic Keynesian multiplier models

We can construct a simple static Keynesian income–expenditure model thus:

$$Y = A \tag{A.5.1.1}$$

and

$$AE = C + I \tag{A.5.1.2}$$

where:

Y income

AE aggregate expenditure

C consumption

I exogenous investment

If we define consumption C as

$$C = \bar{C} + cY \tag{A.5.1.3}$$

where $\bar{C}$ represents the exogenous component of income, from (A.5.1.3) we can therefore rewrite (A.5.1.2) as

$$AE = \bar{C} + cY + I = Y \tag{A.5.1.4}$$

which rearranges to

$$Y = \frac{\bar{C} + I}{1 - c} = \frac{AE}{1 - c} \tag{A.5.1.5}$$

where the numerator term represent the exogenous components of income. Now, if for example exogenous investment increases by ΔI, the multiplier effect can be described as $\Delta Y = k(\Delta AE) = k(\Delta I)$, where the value of the multiplier k is given by

$$k = \frac{1}{1 - c} \tag{A.5.1.6}$$

Table A.5.1 Successive time-period rounds of expenditure

	Change in I	Change in C	Change in Y
First-period round of expenditure	ΔI	0	
Second-period round of expenditure	0	$c\Delta I$	$c\Delta I$
Third-period round of expenditure	0	$c^2\Delta I$	$c^2\Delta I$
nth-period round of expenditure	0	$c^{n-1}\Delta I$	$c^{n-1}\Delta I$

This simple static version of the Keynesian income–expenditure multiplier can also be defined in simple dynamic terms by assuming that current consumption is a function of the income in the previous time period thus:

$$C_t = \bar{C} + cY_{t-1} \tag{A.5.1.7}$$

If we also assume that the inter-temporal equilibrium is defined by $Y_t = Y_{t+1}$, we can write

$$C_t = \bar{C} + cY_t \tag{A.5.1.8}$$

Following Levacic and Rebmann (1982 p. 23), the successive rounds of the income–expenditure process can now be described with the help of Table A.5.1.

The total change in income over each of the successive time periods and rounds of expenditure can thus be given as

$$\Delta Y = \Delta I + c\Delta I + c^2\Delta I + \ldots c^{n-1}\Delta I$$
$$= \Delta I(1 + c + c^2 + \ldots c^{n-1}) \tag{A.5.1.9}$$

which, multiplying both sides by $(1 - c)$, gives

$$\Delta Y(1 - c) = \Delta I(1 - c^n) \tag{A.5.1.10}$$

As $n \to \infty$, $c^n \to 0$. Therefore, as above, we can write $\Delta Y = k(\Delta AE) = k(\Delta I)$, where the value of the multiplier k is given by

$$k = \frac{1}{1 - c} \tag{A.5.1.6}$$

The successive rounds of the income–expenditure process therefore take place though time, but the overall effect on income of a change in any of the components of demand can be described as in Figure 5.1.

Appendix 5.2 The relationship between the alternative forms and uses of location quotients in the construction of regional input–output tables

There are two approaches to using employment data in the construction of regional input–output tables. The first approach is where no updated national input–output tables exist, and the second approach is where such tables do exist.

Appendix 5.2.1 Estimating regional trade using location quotients where an updated national input–output table is not available

In cases where updated national input–output tables are not available, the absence of regional trade data means that the construction of sub-national regional input–output tables is typically based on indirect methods of estimating regional trade flows. Once the trade flows between sectors have been calculated, it is quite straightforward to calculate the regional input–output expenditure coefficients. The most common method is based on the observation of regional employment patterns. Comparing regional sectoral employment shares with those of the national economy allows us to construct an index of net regional sectoral trade, under various assumptions. As we saw in section 5.3.2, this index is known as a location quotient (LQ) and from equation (5.13) its simplest form can be represented as

$$LQ_{ir} = \frac{E_{ir}/E_r}{E_{in}/E_n} = \frac{E_{ir}}{E_{in}} \div \frac{E_r}{E_n} \tag{A.5.2.1}$$

where E_{ir} and E_{in} represent the total employment levels accounted for by sector i in region r and in the nation n, and E_r and E_n represent the total employment levels of the region and nation, respectively. In general terms, this approach posits that:

(a) the greater is the LQ above unity, the larger will be the regions net sectoral exports;

(b) the greater is the LQ below unity, the larger will be the regions net sectoral imports;

(c) for an LQ of unity, the region is neither a net exporter nor a net importer.

However, four assumptions are required for this index to give an accurate measure of net regional sectoral trade (Norcliffe 1983). These are that:

(i)   per capita sectoral productivity levels are invariant with respect to location;

(ii) per capita consumption levels and patterns are invariant with respect to location;

(iii) the national economy exhibits no net exports or imports for any sector;

(iv) there is no interregional cross-hauling for any sector, such that for any regional sector which is an exporter, all local consumption of the output of that sector is accounted for by the local industry.

Where these conditions are met, for a region which is a net exporter of the output of sector i, the actual relationship between the LQ_{ir} and the level of regional sectoral export X_{ir} employment can be written as (Isserman 1977a, 1980)

$$X_{ir} = (1 - 1/LQ_{ir})E_{ir} = \left(\frac{E_{ir}}{E_{in}} - \frac{E_r}{E_n} \right)E_{in} \qquad \forall LQ_{ir} > 1 \tag{A.5.2.2}$$

which can be converted to give net regional sectoral export values by substituting national sectoral output P_{in} for national sectoral employment E_{in} (Norcliffe 1983) thus

$$X_{ir} = (1 - 1/LQ_{ir})P_{ir} = \left(\frac{E_{ir}}{E_{in}} - \frac{E_r}{E_n} \right)P_{in} \qquad \forall LQ_{ir} > 1 \tag{A.5.2.3}$$

In the case where a region is a net importer of the output of sector i, assumptions (i)–(iv) allow us to describe the level of regional sectoral employment generated in all other regions in order to produce imports M_{ir} for our region as

$$M_{ir} = -(1 - 1/LQ_{ir})E_{ir} = \left(\frac{E_r}{E_n} - \frac{E_{ir}}{E_{in}} \right)E_{in} \qquad \forall LQ_{ir} < 1 \tag{A.5.2.4}$$

which once again can be converted to give net regional sectoral import values for our region as

$$M_{ir} = -(1 - 1/LQ_{ir})P_{ir} = \left(\frac{E_r}{E_n} - \frac{E_{ir}}{E_{in}} \right)P_{in} \qquad \forall LQ_{ir} < 1 \tag{A.5.2.5}$$

Given our assumptions (i)–(iv), the principle behind the simple LQ method is that the total level of regional production in any particular sector can be described as being proportionate to the relative contribution of regional to national sectoral employment. At the same time, the total regional consumption of the output of any particular sector is defined as being in proportion to the size of the region. The net regional sectoral trade flows are assumed to be defined by the differences in these values. If a region is calculated as having an LQ which is greater than or equal to unity, we assume that, within a regional input–output framework, the input expenditure coefficient for that particular activity is assumed to be one. On the other hand, for regional LQ values of less than one, the region will be assumed to be a net importer of the goods. In these cases, the regional input–output expenditure coefficients are assumed to be proportional to the regional LQ values of less than one.

In the simple LQ approach the regional consumption of the output of sector i is assumed to be a function of the regional population expenditure, defined by the total regional level of employment. However, even allowing for appropriate regional consumption adjustments it is arguable that, in many sectors, there is no reason why the size of a region per se should have any bearing on regional consumption levels. This is true in the case of many intra-industry transactions not involving final household demand. In these cases, regional sectoral demand is more likely to be related to the local level of activity of the various industrial purchasing sectors within the region rather than to population levels as a whole. In order to account for the interregional spatial variation in intra-industry sectoral demand we can construct a cross-industry location quotient ($CILQ$) which is calculated as the ratio of the LQ of the supplying sector i over that of the purchasing sector j. Substituting the $CILQ$ for the simple LQ in equations (A.5.2.2) and (A.5.2.3) gives us

$$X_{ir} = \left(\frac{E_{ir}}{E_{in}} - \frac{E_{jr}}{E_{jn}} \right)E_{in} \qquad \forall \, CILQ > 1 \tag{A.5.2.6}$$

and

$$M_{ir} = \left(\frac{E_{jr}}{E_{jn}} - \frac{E_{ir}}{E_{in}} \right)E_{in} \qquad \forall \, CILQ < 1 \tag{A.5.2.7}$$

In the case where the purchasing sector j is defined as the household consumption sector, then (A.5.2.6) and (A.5.2.7) will coincide with equations (A.5.2.2) and (A.5.2.4).

There are also several other suggested location quotient formulations which combine the features of the LQ and $CILQ$ models in a variety of ways (Round 1978; Flegg et al. 1995), but the general principles underlying all the location quotient formulas are the same.

Both the location quotient approaches described here are based on a comparison of the regional and national employment structures. However, the minimum requirements approach (Ullman and Dacey 1960) discussed in section 5.3.3 suggests that there is no theoretical economic reason to assume that the national economic structure is the most appropriate benchmark against which regional trade predictions can be generated. For regions of similar sizes, the smallest share of sectoral employment in any single region within the appropriate size band is taken to represent the local sectoral consumption requirement for regions of that size, and all relative regional sectoral employment shares greater than this represent regional export employment. The MR method can thus be represented as

$$X_{ir} = \left(\frac{E_{ir}}{E_r} - \frac{E_{im}}{E_m} \right) E_r \qquad\qquad (A.5.2.8)$$

where m is the region with the minimum sectoral employment share, and $(E_{im}/E_m)E_r$ is local regional consumption of the output of sector i.

Following Isserman (1980) it is possible to compare this approach with that of the LQ by noting that equation (A.5.2.2) can be rearranged to give

$$X_{ir} = \left(\frac{E_{ir}}{E_r} - \frac{E_{in}}{E_n} \right) E_r \qquad\qquad (A.5.2.9)$$

Similarly, we can compare the MR approach with that of the $CILQ$ by rearranging equation (A.5.2.6) to give

$$X_{ir} = \left(\frac{E_{ir}}{E_r} - \left(\frac{E_{jr}}{E_r} \right) \left(\frac{E_{in}}{E_{jn}} \right) \right) E_r \qquad\qquad (A.5.2.10)$$

The key difference between the MR approach and the LQ approaches to determining regional trade patterns is the question of the appropriate benchmark against which regional sectoral employment patterns are compared in order to arrive at a measure of regional sectoral consumption. This is reflected in the differing constructions of the second bracketed term in each model. The MR approach adopts the sectoral employment structure of similar sizes areas as the benchmark, whereas the LQ approaches both adopt the sectoral employment structure of the national economy as the appropriate benchmark.

The debate as to the accuracy of employment-based regional trade estimates is not a new one. Assumptions (i) and (ii) above are clearly very difficult to sustain, although, using regional consumption and output indices, it is possible for the LQ method to be adapted to some extent to take account of any regional variations in productivity and consumption due to technical differences in factor allocations, tastes or transfer payments (Isserman 1977b;

Norcliffe 1983). Similarly, where assumption (iii) is not tenable, these types of models can be somewhat adjusted to take account of national sectoral trade balances which are non-zero. Where a regional LQ is greater than unity, Isserman (1977b, 1980) suggests that we can estimate regional export employment as

$$X_{ir} = \left(P_r \frac{E_{ir}}{E_{in}} - c_r \frac{E_r}{E_n} (1 - e_{in}) \right) \frac{E_{in}}{P_r} \qquad \forall \, LQ > 1 \tag{A.5.2.11}$$

where p_r is the labour productivity ratio between the region r and the nation n, c_r is the equivalent consumption ratio, and e_{in} is the ratio of national net exports to national output of sector i. This can be converted to estimate actual export values as before in by substituting P_{in} for E_{in} in equation (A.5.2.11). By similar reasoning, where the LQ value is less than unity we can write the regional import function as

$$M_{ir} = \left(c_r \frac{E_r}{E_n} - P_r \frac{E_{ir}}{E_{in}} \right) \frac{P_{in}}{P_r} \qquad \forall LQ_{ir} < 1 \tag{A.5.2.12}$$

in the case where the national economy is not a net importer. Where the national economy is net importer of the output of sector i, the appropriate adjustment of the LQ model gives

$$M_{ir} = \left(c_r \frac{E_r}{E_n} - P_r \frac{E_{ir}}{E_{in}} \right) \frac{P_{in}}{P_r} + c_r \left(\frac{E_r}{E_n} \right) M_{in} \tag{A.5.2.13}$$

where M_{in} is the national level of net imports of sector i, and this can be rearranged to give

$$M_{ir} = c_r \frac{E_r}{E_n} \left(\frac{P_{in}}{P_r} + M_{in} \right) - P_r \frac{E_{ir}}{E_{in}} P_{in} \tag{A.5.2.14}$$

This specification allows us to take account of imports into a region both from other regions as well as from other countries. The most difficult remaining problem, however, arises with assumption (iv), namely that of the absence of cross-hauling (Harris and Liu 1998). In reality, many products move repeatedly forwards and backwards across the same regional boundaries during the various stages of the production process. Similarly, the monopolistic competition models (Fujita et al. 1999) discussed in Chapter 2 predict that many of the products produced by the same industry will be moved in opposite directions between regions and locations.

Appendix 5.2.2 Constructing regional input–output tables by adjusting national tables

The use of the national employment structure as the appropriate benchmark comparison against which regional consumption indices are developed is the most common employment-based method used for estimating regional trade flows. The major reason for this is that detailed and updated input–output data often exist at the national level. Therefore national intersectoral expenditure coefficients are available which may be used as a benchmark in the construction of interregional coefficient estimates. The usual approach to constructing regional expenditure coefficients from national expenditure coefficients is by multiplying each national coefficient by the appropriate LQ value in the cases where the LQ values are less than unity, and adjusting the national coefficient downwards accordingly to give the regional equivalent. Where the $CILQ$ approach is used, the off-diagonals are adjusted in this manner, while the principal diagonals are still adjusted using the LQ approach (Smith and Morrison 1974). For regional LQ or $CILQ$ values which are greater than or equal to unity, the national coefficient is left unchanged. This means that the adjustments made according to the quotients are asymmetric in that the strength of export orientation plays no part in the determination of the trading coefficients (Round 1978).

In order to understand the rationale behind this method of estimating regional input–output coefficients, in which adjustments are made to national input–output coefficients by multiplying them by the appropriate LQs, we need to reconsider the simple adjustments which can be made to the LQ approach in order to take account to some extent for the unreality of assumptions (i), (ii), and (iii) in section A.5.2.1. If we assume for simplicity that there are no regional consumption or productivity variations per capital, from equation (A.5.2.14) we have

$$M_{ir} = \frac{E_r}{E_n}\left(P_{in} + M_{in}\right) - \frac{E_{ir}}{E_{in}}P_{in} \tag{A.5.2.15}$$

and thus

$$\frac{M_{ir}}{M_{ir} + P_{ir}} = \frac{\dfrac{E_r}{E_n}\left(P_{in} + M_{in}\right) - \dfrac{E_{ir}}{E_{in}}P_{in}}{\dfrac{E_r}{E_n}\left(P_{in} + M_{in}\right)} \tag{A.5.2.16}$$

which can be rearranged to give

$$\frac{M_{ir}}{M_{ir} + P_{ir}} = 1 - LQ_{ir}\left(\frac{P_{in}}{M_{in} + P_{in}}\right) \tag{A.5.2.17}$$

Assumption (iv) in section A.5.2.1, which rules out the existence of cross-hauling, means that the regional production of sector i, denoted as P_{ir}, equals the regional consumption of the regionally produced output of sector i, denoted as C_{ir}. Similarly, national production of sector i, denoted as P_{in}, equals the national consumption of the domestically produced output of sector i, C_{in}. Therefore the bracketed term on the right-hand side of equation (A.5.2.17) describes the national output of sector i as a proportion of total national consumption of sector i, and the left-hand-side term describes the net regional imports of sector i as a proportion of total regional consumption of sector i. However, given that

$$\frac{M_{ir}}{M_{ir} + C_{ir}} + \frac{C_{ir}}{M_{ir} + C_{ir}} = 1 \quad \text{can be written as}$$

$$\frac{M_{ir}}{M_{ir} + P_{ir}} + \frac{P_{ir}}{M_{ir} + P_{ir}} = 1 \tag{A.5.2.18}$$

we have

$$1 - \frac{P_{ir}}{M_{ir} + P_{ir}} = 1 - LQ_{ir}\left(\frac{P_{in}}{M_{in} + P_{in}}\right) \qquad (A.5.2.19)$$

In other words:

$$\frac{P_{ir}}{M_{ir} + P_{ir}} = LQ_{ir}\left(\frac{P_{in}}{M_{in} + P_{in}}\right) \qquad (A.5.2.20)$$

The right-hand bracketed term is the national average propensity to consume the domestically produced output of sector i. Therefore, by multiplying this by the appropriate LQ value, we arrive at an expression for the regional average propensity to consume the regionally produced output of sector i. Exactly the same result can also be produced if we choose to employ the $CILQ$ rather than the simple LQ. The only difference in this case is that the initial regional import function is specified as

$$M_{ir} = \left(\frac{E_{jr}}{E_{jn}} - \frac{E_{ir}}{E_{in}}\right)E_{in} + \frac{E_{jr}}{E_{jn}}M_{in} \qquad (A.5.2.21)$$

In terms of constructing a regional input–output model, the rationale for LQ adjustments to national input–output coefficients in order to produce regional coefficients therefore rests on the assumption that the national input–output coefficients accurately reflect net national sectoral trading balances. However, this is not necessarily the case. Input–output expenditure coefficient values only reflect the pattern of backward expenditure linkages and imports, and do not take into account the level of output of sectoral exports or household sectoral imports. We can see this from a stylized example.

In the simplest export base model, we can describe the domestic income generated by the exporting activity as

$$Y_i = \frac{X_i}{1 - c_i} = \frac{X_i}{m_i} \qquad (A.5.2.22)$$

where Y_i is the total domestic sectoral output, X_i is the level of domestic sectoral exports, and c_i is the domestic sectoral expenditure coefficient, which equals $1 - m_i$, where m_i is the domestic import coefficient for the backward input linkages. The total domestic sectoral import expenditure for the first round will be represented as $M_i = m_i Y_i$, and total first-round domestic production expenditure in backward linkages will be represented as $P_i = c_i Y_i$. If there are no other sectoral imports, then c_i accurately measures the first-round domestic average propensity to consume the domestically produced output of sector i weighted according to the relative total expenditure on each input as determined by the national input–output framework. This is because

$$\frac{P_i}{P_i + M_i} = \frac{c_i Y_i}{c_i Y_i + m_i Y_i} = c_i \qquad (A.5.2.23)$$

However, if there are other imports of goods produced by sector i exogenously consumed by the household sector h, we can represent these additional domestic sectoral imports as $M_i = m_i Y_h$, where $i \neq h$. Under these conditions, the total domestic propensity to consume the domestically produced output of sector i can thus be represented as

$$\frac{c_i Y_i}{c_i Y_i + m_i Y_i + m_i Y_h} \neq c_i \tag{A.5.2.24}$$

Under these conditions, observation of the input–output expenditure coefficient alone will overestimate the domestically produced and consumed output of sector i as a proportion of the total domestic consumption of sector i, irrespective of whether the region runs a sectoral balance of payments surplus in which $X_i > M_i$, a balance of payments deficit in which $X_i < M_i$, or a balance of payments equilibrium, in which $X_i = M_i$. The result of this is that the backward linkage input–output expenditure coefficients in the national table will not accurately reflect overall sectoral net trading balances, and will tend to exceed the overall domestic average propensity to consume domestically produced goods. Although the LQ assumption of the absence of cross-hauling, namely assumption (iv), is not a problem for input–output models which specifically allow for such behaviour in the first and subsequent rounds of expenditure, the LQ adjustment of national input–output coefficients suffers from the problem that cross-hauling can occur at the top level of household demand. Therefore, if we use national input–output expenditure coefficients as the benchmark against which regional input–output expenditure coefficients can be produced, this will also tend to systematically overestimate the regional domestic contribution to sectoral output, and consequently the regional multiplier (Leven 1956), irrespective of the form of location quotient employed.

Round (1978) found very little difference in the performance of a variety of LQ specifications, and although Harrigan et al. (1980) found that the simple LQ approach performed marginally better than other location quotient specifications, the general accuracy of such coefficients is open to question. In cases where survey-based regional input–output data do exist it is possible to compare the survey-based results with those that would have been predicted on the basis of employment shares. Accepting that the production of survey-based estimates itself may have required professional judgement based on relative regional sectoral shares in order to compensate for any missing information, particularly in areas such as public expenditure, construction, and household consumption, the general picture we observe is that employment-based estimates of regional trade tend to perform fairly poorly when compared with survey models (Czamanski and Malizia 1969; Schaffer and Chu 1969; Smith and Morrison 1974) or semi-survey models which employ algorithms to complete the tables (Bacharach 1970; Lahr 1993; Harris 1998).

Appendix 5.3 The general solution to the input–output model

A model such as that described by Table 5.3 can be considered in part to be a matrix of input–output expenditure coefficients. In order to see this we can follow the discussion of

Chiang (1984 pp. 117–118) and imagine a region where there are industries 1, 2, 3, ... n, each of which buys from, and sells, inputs to each other, plus an external demand sector which does not provide inputs to the local production process. The input coefficients for industries 1, 2, 3, ... n can be arranged into a matrix $A = [a_{ij}]$ thus:

$$\begin{bmatrix} a_{11} & a_{12} & a_{13} & \cdots a_{1n} \\ a_{21} & a_{22} & a_{23} & \cdots a_{2n} \\ a_{31} & a_{32} & a_{33} & \cdots a_{3n} \\ \cdot & \cdot & \cdot & \cdot \\ a_{n1} & a_{n2} & a_{n3} & \cdots a_{nn} \end{bmatrix}$$

The coefficients a_{ij} represent the requirements of input i needed in the production of one unit of output j. In the case of industries which do not supply inputs to their own industry, as in Table 5.3 above, the principal diagonals will all be zero.

If industry 1 produces outputs which are just sufficient to provide for the input requirements of each of the other industries 1, 2, 3, ... n, plus the demand requirements of the external sector, the total output of industry 1 which we denote as x_1, must satisfy the equation

$$x_1 = a_{11}x_1 + a_{12}x_2 + a_{13}x_3 \ldots.. + a_{1n}x_n + d_1 \tag{A.5.3.1}$$

where:

$a_{ij}x_j$ input demand for industry j
d_1 final demand by external sector for the output of sector 1

Rearranging (A.4.3.1) gives

$$(1 - a_{11})x_1 - a_{12}x_2 - a_{13}x_3 \ldots.. - a_{1n}x_n = d_1 \tag{A.5.3.2}$$

If the same exercise is repeated for the output of each of the sectors, we can modify the above matrix to give

$$\begin{bmatrix} (1 - a_{11}) & -a_{12} & -a_{13} & \cdots -a_{1n} \\ -a_{21} & (1 - a_{22}) & -a_{23} & \cdots -a_{2n} \\ -a_{31} & -a_{32} & (1 - a_{33}) & \cdots -a_{3n} \\ \cdot & \cdot & \cdot & \cdot \\ -a_{n1} & -a_{n2} & -a_{n3} & \cdots (1 - a_{nn}) \end{bmatrix} \begin{bmatrix} x_1 \\ x_2 \\ x_3 \\ \cdot \\ x_n \end{bmatrix} = \begin{bmatrix} d_1 \\ d_2 \\ d_3 \\ \cdot \\ d_n \end{bmatrix} \tag{A.5.3.3}$$

where the matrix on the left-hand side contains the input coefficients, and the vectors on the left- and right-hand sides contain the outputs of each sector used as inputs by other sectors, and final external demand for the outputs of each sector, respectively. If we ignore the 1s in the principal diagonals of the matrix on the left-hand side we see that this matrix is simply $-A = [a_{ij}]$. As it is, this matrix is the sum of the identity matrix I_n, with 1s in the principal diagonals and zeros elsewhere, and the matrix $-A$. In other words, we can write $(I - A)x = d$, where x represents the variable vector and d the final demand vector. The matrix $(I - A)$ is known as the 'technology matrix' and is usually denoted as $T = (I - A)$ such that $Tx = d$. As long as T is non-singular, we can find the inverse of T, denoted as T^{-1}. This now allows us always to solve the problem

$$\bar{x} = T^{-1}d \tag{A.5.3.4}$$

In other words, for any given level of the external output demand, we can calculate the input demand requirements through the successive rounds of the input–output expenditure process for any of the individual production sectors. With this information it is also straightforward to calculate the total factor earnings, as in Table 5.4, and to calculate the total regional multiplier impact of any given level of output demand.

6 Regional and interregional labour market analysis

6.1 Introduction

In this chapter, we will discuss the question of urban and regional labour markets. Once again, as with the multiplier models discussed in Chapter 5, we will see that there are some fundamental differences between the characteristics of the labour market at the regional and national levels, as well as many similarities between the two. However, these differences are not simply a question of scale, but rather an explicit question of the relationship between market-clearing processes and geography.

In Chapter 4 we discussed the differences between regional and national multiplier models. The regional multiplier models discussed in Chapter 5 all assume that the marginal costs of factor inputs are constant. In other words, we assume that the marginal and average costs of factor inputs are the same as output expands. This allows us to assume that labour, capital, and land inputs all maintain fixed unit prices independent of the level of output. In situations where there are unused factor supplies, such as where there is excess capacity in industrial facilities, or alternatively a pool of unemployed labour, these assumptions may be justified. However, there are many cases where no such reserve capacity exists. In these situations factor supplies will be somewhat limited, and the effect of this is that factor supply prices will not be constant as output expands. The market for factor inputs will therefore determine factor prices. In the case of geographical labour markets, such factor price changes may also bring about spatial changes in the allocation of these factors. This is because such price signals may also encourage factor migration between regions.

In this chapter we will see that the effects of local labour price changes on regional or urban employment can be rather complicated. Local factor price and income effects can become somewhat interrelated, with the result that we must consider the spatial problems discussed in each of the previous chapters in order to come to any coherent analysis of the issues.

In the next section we will discuss alternative views of the workings of local labour markets. In section 6.3 we will extend the argument to the question of interregional migration and factor allocation, and in section 6.4 onwards, we will discuss additional issues which affect regional labour market and migration behaviour.

6.2 Wages and labour markets

Labour markets are notoriously complex to analyse, with many labour market outcomes being the result of complex negotiations between employers and labour representatives within a bilateral monopoly framework. However, for our purposes here, in order to discuss the workings of the urban and regional labour market, it is first necessary to return to the basic microeconomic foundations of labour market behaviour. These will then be adjusted in order to allow for the particular characteristics of local urban and regional labour markets.

6.2.1 A neoclassical approach

The simplest neoclassical microeconomic approach to labour markets is based on two main principles. The first principle is that the demand for labour is a downward-sloping function. This is because the demand for labour is a derived demand, dependent on the marginal revenue product of the output of labour inputs to the production process. Firms will equate the marginal cost of labour, given by the wage rate w, with the marginal revenue product of labour. For a given capital stock and a given output market price, the marginal product of labour (MPL) falls as the quantity of labour employed increases, as determined by the law of diminishing marginal productivity. The demand for labour $D(L)$ is therefore downward sloping, as in Figure 6.1.

However, the position of the demand curve for labour can vary according to either the level of capital employed, or the price of the output good. The reason is that the marginal revenue product of labour is given by the marginal physical product of labour multiplied by the price of the output good. Assuming production factor inputs are complementary, a greater capital stock will imply a greater marginal and average level of output for any given level of labour input. As such, the demand curve for labour will be further to the right, the greater the stock of capital employed. Conversely, the lower the level of capital employed,

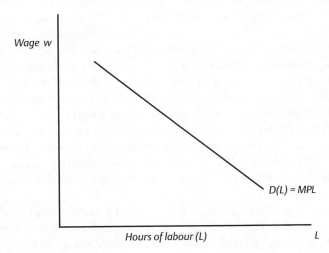

Figure 6.1 The demand for labour

the further to the left will be the demand curve for labour. Alternatively, the higher the price of the output good, the further to the right will be the demand curve for labour, for any given capital stock. Once again, the converse is true. The lower the price of the output good, the further to the left will be the demand curve for labour, for any given capital stock.

The second basic principle is that the supply of labour is upward sloping with respect to the real wage rate. This conclusion is based on an argument which is sometimes known as the 'dual decision hypothesis' (Clower 1965), in which workers use the real wage level in order to decide simultaneously on the number of hours of labour they wish to supply, the level of income they wish to earn, and the quantity of human produced goods and services they wish to consume. The dual decision hypothesis can be explained with the help of Figure 6.2.

In Figure 6.2 we assume that the individual can consume two types of utility-bearing goods, namely on the one hand, the weekly hours of leisure, and on the other hand, all human produced goods and services. The vertical axis represents the weekly quantity of hours of leisure the individual can consume H, with a fixed upper limit F, which represents a full week. The total number of labour hours supplied per week is thus $(F - H)$. The horizontal axis represents the quantity of human produced goods and services consumed by the individual I. We can now employ a standard budget constraint–indifference curve model in order to understand the supply of labour with respect to the price of labour.

In a standard indifference curve type of framework, assuming the indifference curves are convex, the object of the individual is to ensure that the price ratio between the two types of goods is just equal to their marginal rate of substitution. In Figure 6.2, the slope of the budget constraint represents the relative prices of leisure and human-produced capital goods, defined in terms of their opportunity costs with respect to each other. If, for the moment, we assume that there is a certain element of exogenous consumption even in a situation of total leisure, the origin of the budget constraint will not be on the vertical axis at

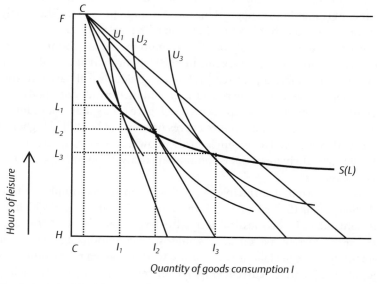

Figure 6.2 The derivation of the labour supply curve

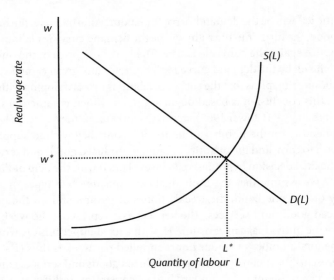

Figure 6.3 A simple model of the labour market

F, but will be somewhat shifted to the right of F, at C. As the real wage rate increases from w_1 to w_2 to w_3, the slope of the budget constraint becomes shallower, with the result that the individual consumes less leisure and more human-produced goods. Obviously, there are both price and income effects operating, in that income itself is the multiple of the wage rate and the number of hours worked. The optimum combinations of leisure and human-produced goods consumed, for different budget constraints associated with different wage levels, can be plotted as an expansion path. Given that the number of labour hours supplied is represented by $L = F - H$, we can see that as the real wage rate increases from w_1 to w_2 to w_3, the number of labour hours supplied increases from L_1 to L_2 to L_3. The supply of labour $S(L)$ is therefore assumed to be a positive function of the real wage rate.

The above argument does not rely on the assumption that all labour exhibits the same preferences. For example, we could assume that the labour market is made up of heteroge-nous individuals with different preferences. Some individuals will have a relatively higher preference for leisure, whereas others will prefer human-produced goods and services. These different preferences will be represented in Figure 6.2 by different indifference curve maps. In the former case, the indifference curves will tend to be shifted higher up whereas in the latter case they will tend to be shifted further down. However, the argument still holds that as the real wage rate increases, the optimum quantity of labour supplied by each indi-vidual will increase.

Combining these two basic principles allows us to construct a simple model of a labour market as in Figure 6.3. The real wage w^* is the market-clearing wage at which all labour L^* supplied is demanded. In neoclassical terms the level of employment L^* represents full employment at the current market wage. Under such conditions, there is no involuntary unemployment, because the labour which is not working, given by the difference between the total population T and the current employment level L^*, is regarded as being voluntar-ily unemployed.

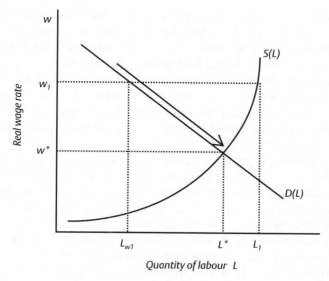

Figure 6.4 Involuntary unemployment: a neoclassical perspective

Given this logic, we can now consider conditions under which unemployment may exist in such a framework. The first reason why unemployment may exist in such a labour market is that the real wage being demanded in the labour market is simply too high. We can see this in Figure 6.4. If the real wage currently offered is w_1, this is much higher than the market-clearing equilibrium wage of w^*. The result of this is that the number of people seeking work at the current wage is L_1, whereas the quantity of labour demanded is L_{w1}. The level of involuntary unemployment is therefore $(L_1 - L_{w1})$ at the current wage w_1. The neoclassical remedy for such a situation is to allow the real wage to fall from w_1 to w^*, such that the demand for labour will increase and the supply of labour will fall until they are brought into equilibrium. The downward movement in the real wage and the relationship between the wage fall and the labour demanded is represented by the arrow in Figure 6.4.

In this schema, the only situations in which involuntary unemployment can persist is therefore where there is some sort of impediment to the free movement of real wages. In particular, in this case unemployment will persist in situations in which there is some sort of obstacle which militates against the downward adjustment of the real wage. The question therefore arises as to what are the possible impediments to the free downward movement of wages.

The first possible impediment is the existence of a trade union which maintains a monopoly over the supply of labour. The role of a trade union is in effect to set up a labour supply quota. If bargaining between trade unions and corporate management results in a labour supply quota of L_{w1} and a union real wage of w_1, the current market wage for those in employment, w_1, will be higher than the market clearing wage w^*. This is what we mean when we say that the real wage w_1 is 'too high'. Whether involuntary unemployment exists or not therefore depends on whether the trade unions are able to negotiate real wages for their members which are higher than the market-clearing wages.

The second possible impediment to the free downward movement of wages is that of a minimum wage restriction. If a minimum wage policy is instituted by a government, such that the minimum wage is set at a wage of w_1, clearly the effect of this will be to reduce employment to L_{w1} and to engender involuntary unemployment of $(L_1 - L_{w1})$. Whether involuntary unemployment exists or not therefore depends on whether the minimum wage is set at a level higher than the market-clearing real wages. Alternatively, if there is a distribution of wages according to different activities, and a minimum wage policy raises the lowest wage, it may be that average wages all move upwards as workers seek to maintain the differentials between different skill occupations. In this case we can interpret the wage in Figure 6.3 as being the average real wage. Under these conditions the argument still holds.

In both of these cases, the general neoclassical prescription will be to dismantle the obstacles which militate against the free movement of wages. This will involve legislation limiting the power of trade unions, and also the withdrawal of any minimum wage policies.

Apart from the role of trade unions and minimum wage legislation, there is a third reason for involuntary unemployment in such a framework, and this is the role of welfare payments. In order to see this we must return to Figure 6.2. In this diagram we see that there is an exogenous level of consumption even where no labour is supplied, given by the horizontal distance between F and C. If welfare payments are provided for those without employment such that the exogenous level of consumption increases, the budget constraint at C will shift even further to the right. The result of this is that the expansion path which plots all the efficient consumption points as wages increase and the budget constraint shifts to the right will be moved further to the right. The effect of this is that, compared with the situation of little or no welfare payments, in which exogenous income is very low, fewer hours are worked for any given real wage rate. In terms of our labour market diagram, Figure 6.4, this implies that the labour supply curve is therefore shifted upwards to the left. The market wage rate rises and number of people employed therefore falls below the market-clearing level. Moreover, the greater the level of welfare payments, the further to the left will be the labour supply curve, and the less will be the total number of people employed.

The neoclassical remedy for the reduced labour demand and supply is, once again, to dismantle many of these policies. As such, welfare payments will need to be reduced in absolute terms so as to have a negligible effect on market wages. Alternatively, such payments will be restricted to a very short time period, after which they will cease to be available to the individual person.

6.2.2 A Keynesian approach

The simple neoclassical labour market model described above allows for the downward movement of real wages in order to clear markets. However, an alternative approach to the labour market question comes from a Keynesian perspective, which argues that wages are 'sticky' downwards. In other words, while wages are able to move upwards over time, downward movements in wages are very difficult to bring about. This is primarily due to the existence of trade unions and the complex nature of labour bargaining processes. Under these circumstances, movements down the demand curve for labour, in which wage falls are associated with increases in labour demand, are very difficult to effect. In this situation, there is no guarantee that labour markets exhibiting involuntary unemployment can be expected to clear. The policy prescription under such conditions is therefore to attempt to expand the

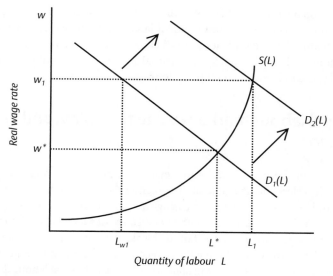

Figure 6.5 Involuntary unemployment: a Keynesian perspective

demand for labour so as to clear the excess supply of labour. The argument can be explained with reference to Figure 6.5, which is constructed on the basis of Figure 6.4.

In the Keynesian argument, a general increase in the demand for labour from D_1 to D_2 will increase the level of employment from L_{w1} to L_1 at the current wage w_1, thereby clearing the excess labour without raising the current wage level. If demand increases beyond D_2, then we will experience wage inflation. However, as long as an expansion in demand can be limited to a movement from D_1 to D_2, the labour market problem can be solved. In macro-economic terms this implies that the involuntary unemployment can be cleared without inducing any inflation.

There are many macroeconomic controversies about whether such a costless increase in demand can actually be effected feasibly or not, and these discussions centre on the questions of 'crowding out', and the relationship between labour market policy, fiscal policy, and monetary policy. It is not our intention here to enter into these debates, as these issues are widely discussed in detail elsewhere. It is worth noting, however, that until relatively recently it was fashionable in many circles within the economics profession to talk as though unemployment were entirely a matter of either market imperfections or personal choice, and to assume that the Keynesian problems associated with deficient demand and deflation no longer existed (Krugman 1999). The global financial crisis of 2008 has changed much of this thinking (Krugman 2009), and a result of the global financial crisis is that regional unemployment disparities have reappeared with a vengeance in many countries (OECD 2011). These developments have thereby reopened the debate regarding the nature of regional unemployment and the ability of regions to recover from adverse demand and employment shocks—what has become known as regional 'resilience' (Martin 2011; Fingleton et al. 2011).

It is important to understand the basic analytical principles behind the various approaches to regional labour market problems and then to apply these principles in the case of an explicitly spatial local or regional context. This will allow us to discuss the particular features of urban and regional labour markets as distinct from non-spatial analyses. As we will see, there are certain aspects of urban and regional labour markets which are rather different from standard textbook models of labour markets, at both the micro and macro levels, and an understanding of these differences is essential in order to identify the role played by geography and space in labour market behaviour.

6.3 Regional labour markets, wage flexibility, and capital utilization

The basic features of the neoclassical and Keynesian approaches to labour markets were outlined above. It is clear that the general disagreement focuses on the role that wage movements or demand changes can play in clearing involuntary unemployment. However, we can now reconsider this discussion from the perspective of a local labour market.

The neoclassical argument at the level of the local urban or regional economy is more or less the same as that at the level of the national economy, described by Figures 6.3 and 6.4. Downward labour price movements will engender increases in local labour demand for any given local capital stock. This will be reflected in terms of movements down the demand curve for labour. The simultaneous reduction in the labour supplied will bring the local labour market into equilibrium. From Chapters 2 and 5, however, we are aware that labour markets may exhibit particular features at the local level. The agglomeration arguments of Chapter 2 suggest that labour market information flows may be not be independent of geographical scale, such that local labour pools become an essential means of ensuring labour supply to firms under conditions of uncertainty. At the same time, local concentration of industry becomes an essential means of ensuring labour demand for potential skilled workers, under conditions of varying demand between sectors. Meanwhile, the multiplier arguments of Chapter 5 suggest that changes in any of the individual components of demand may have proportionately greater impacts on income than the individual demand change itself. If we combine the arguments of Chapters 2 and 5 it becomes clear that the employment effects of wage changes on the local economy can be quite complex. In order to see this we can employ Figure 6.4, in which the labour market exhibits involuntary unemployment, and using this model we can reconsider the effects of wage falls, as is done in Figure 6.6.

If we begin with the situation in which wages are at a level w_1, which is too high to clear the local labour market, we can consider the various alternative effects of local wage falls. As we have seen, the first effect is the standard neoclassical effect in which wages fall and labour demand increases, concomitant with a movement downward along the labour demand curve to the market-clearing wage and labour supply of w^* and L^* respectively. In Figure 6.6 this wage–labour supply movement is represented by the locus a.

The second effect can be understood by employing the income–expenditure multiplier model of Chapter 5, because the level of local consumption will be largely a function of the total local wage income. If we assume that all local consumption C is accounted for by wages earned locally, then in Figure 6.6 the total local consumption income can be represented as $C = w_1 L_{w1}$. If local wages begin to fall by $-\Delta w$, it may be that the immediate dominant effect on firms' perceptions is that the level of local consumption expenditure is falling by $-\Delta C = -\Delta w L_{w1}$. As we saw in Chapter 5, a change in the level of any of the components of

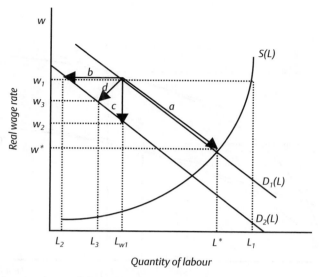

Figure 6.6 Local labour markets and downward wage movements

aggregate demand can induce a multiplier effect. Although all the multiplier changes discussed in Chapter 5 involved positive demand changes, the same types of arguments also apply to falls in any of the components of aggregate demand. Negative multiplier effects can be generated by falls in any of the individual components of aggregate demand, thereby leading to even greater reductions in income than the original demand fall. In the above situation of wage falls in the local labour market, local firms may be unwilling to increase labour demand according to the neoclassical model, and will rather seek to reduce investment expenditure by running down existing stocks of goods and cancelling future planned investment. This will also imply that firms will cancel orders from their suppliers. The combined effect of these responses to the local downward wage movements will be a negative local income multiplier effect given by $-\Delta Y = -k_r(\Delta w L_{w1})$, where k_r is the value of the regional multiplier. In terms of Figure 6.6, this contraction in local expenditure income can be represented by a downward shift to the left of the demand curve. The vertical distance of this backwards shift at the employment level of L_1 is represented by a fall in wages of $-\Delta w$ from w_1 to w_2, such that $-\Delta Y = -k_r(\Delta w L_{w1})$.

As we see in Figure 6.6, if the demand curve shifts backwards to the left, a range of wage–employment combinations also becomes possible (McCombie 1988). The actual employment effect of the wage fall depends on the labour retention policies of the local firms. If the local firms absorb the negative expenditure–income effects almost entirely through contractions of their labour stocks, rather than wage reductions to employees, the wage–employment effects will be represented by the locus b in Figure 6.6 in which we maintain a wage of w_1 but reduce employment from L_{w1} to L_2. On the other hand, if firms choose to absorb all local expenditure falls in terms of wage cuts, rather than labour reductions, the wage–employment locus will be given by c in Figure 6.6 in which we maintain the employment level at L_{w1} but reduce wages from w_1 to w_2. The final possibility is that firms will absorb the fall in local expenditure by cuts in both wages and labour

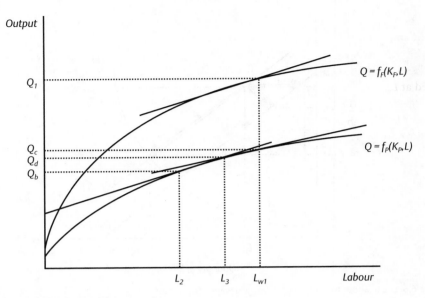

Figure 6.7 Capital utilization, output, and wages

employed, given by the locus *d* in Figure 6.6, in which wages are cut from w_1 to w_3. and employment is cut from L_{w1} to L_3.

Although the actual wage–employment locus observed in response to a local wage fall will depend on the labour retention and employment policies of the local firms, it is necessary to consider how it could be possible for the demand curve to be considered to have actually shifted downwards to the left, as proposed by the Keynesian model. The argument is that if the type of negative regional income–expenditure effect described above does indeed operate, not only will local firms cut back future planned investment and input expenditure, but they will also reduce the current level of local capital utilization. This possibility is represented by the production function diagram Figure 6.7. As we see in Figure 6.7, changes in capital utilization can be directly associated with changes in both output and wages. The argument here is that different levels of capital utilization in effect represent different regional production functions. Assuming as usual that capital and labour are complementary production factors, even temporary cutbacks in regional capital utilization in response to falling local wage income will move the local firms on to lower capacity production functions. This is because less capital is now applied to each unit of labour employed. In Figure 6.7, a reduction in the level of capital utilization from that of full capital utilization K_F to a situation of partially unused capital K_P can be represented as a move from a full-capacity regional production function in which output Q can be defined as $Q = f_F(K_F, L)$ to a lower-capacity regional production function given as $Q = f_P(K_P, L)$. The slope of the regional production functions represents the marginal product of labour, and consequently the local regional wage rate. If the local firms choose to adopt the labour retention strategy of *b*, in which wages are maintained at their existing levels, and the fall in demand is absorbed entirely in terms of labour cutbacks, in Figure 6.7 this is represented by a fall in labour demand from L_{w1} to L_2, as in Figure 6.6, and a fall in output from Q_1 to Q_b. As we see, the fact that the regional wages are unchanged at w_1 means that the slopes of the two regional production functions at these two different levels of capacity utilization, employment and output, are the same. The second case is where the labour retention strategies of the regional firms are represented by locus c is Figure 6.6. In this case, the employment level is maintained at L_{w1} but the output level falls from Q_1 to Q_c and the regional wage falls from w_1 to w_2. This is represented in Figure 6.7 by the lower slope of the regional production function at the existing employment of L_{w1}. The final alternative is where firms adopt the labour retention strategy represented by the locus d in Figure 6.6. In Figure 6.7 this is represented by a fall in output from Q_1 to Q_d, a fall in employment from L_{w1} to L_3, and a fall in the regional wage from w_1 to w_3, a wage level somewhere between w_1 and w_2.

6.4 Regional labour market adjustment

Given these general observations, it is therefore necessary at this point to consider which of the possible wage–employment and capital utilization effects described by the loci a, b, c, or d in Figure 6.6 are likely to take place in a regional labour market in response to local wage falls. In a Keynesian model of the regional labour market, as we see in Figures 6.6 and 6.7, downward movements of local wages are not possible without simultaneous backward shifts in the demand curve for local labour. The reason for this is that the negative income–expenditure effect on local firms' perceptions of local market demand is regarded as dominating any potential desire on the part of these firms to take advantage of lower wages in the form of increased labour demand. This results in the local firms cutting back the level of capital employed. In macroeconomic discussions, this particular type of negative income effect in response to a wage fall, represented by the loci b, c, or d in Figure 6.6, is sometimes known as a 'Keynes effect'. On the other hand, the willingness of firms to increase labour demand in response to a wage fall, represented by the locus a in Figure 6.6, is sometimes known in macroeconomic discussions as a 'Pigou effect'. In the neoclassical model, the Pigou effect will generally dominate any possible Keynes effect, whereas in the Keynesian model the Keynes effect will dominate any potential Pigou effect. The extent to which one effect dominates the other tends to be both a question of industrial sector and a question of time.

In the case of local regional or urban labour markets, we can argue that in the short run at least, the local firms with primarily local markets will tend to interpret local wage falls in terms of reductions in their potential output market sales revenue. These types of firms are the firms which we generally classed as 'non-basic' in our economic base discussions in Chapter 5. For the firms of this type, the negative income–expenditure effect will tend to dominate their labour demand decisions, and will generally lead to cutbacks of the type represented by the loci b, c, or d in Figure 6.6.

On the other hand, for 'basic firms' which rely primarily on regional export markets, falls in local wages will have little or no effect on their overall market outputs. For these firms, reduced local wages may mean that the area actually becomes more attractive for expanding output by employing more labour, and such firms may therefore increase their employment levels within their current levels of capital investment. This will be represented by the wage–employment locus a in Figure 6.6. As we saw in Chapter 1, reduced local labour prices may

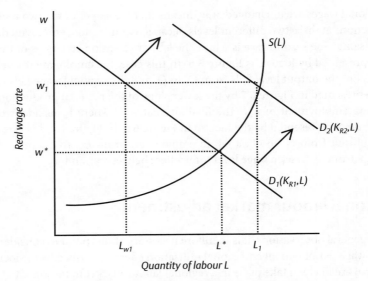

Figure 6.8 Inward investment and the regional labour market

also in the long run encourage these firms to expand their overall local capital stocks. Similarly, new immigrant firms may move into the region and this process will also increase the regional capital stock. Both of these capital expansion effects, one which takes place within existing plants and the other which results in the establishment of new plants, will be represented by a shift to the right of the labour demand curve, as the regional capital stock expands from K_{R1} to K_{R2}. As we see in Figure 6.8, the long-run result of this regional capital expansion will be to increase both the local wage and the level of regional employment. The actual extent to which the demand curves will shift outwards to the right will depend on the level and the speed of new inward investment flows.

The local effect of regional wage falls will therefore depend on the sectoral balance between the exporting and domestically oriented firms. Regional economies which are highly integrated internally, such as those which exhibit strong localization and urbanization economies as described in Chapter 3, will tend to suffer from general falls in local wages, because much of the local demand will be locally generated. On the other hand, economies which are vertically integrated, in terms of being dominated by strong hierarchical input–output expenditure linkages between locally based exporting firms and local supplier firms, will tend to benefit from local wage falls. The reason for this is that such economies will tend to become better places for immigrant mobile investment of the type discussed in Chapter 2.

There is one exception to the argument that economies which are vertically integrated, in terms of being dominated by strong hierarchical input–output expenditure linkages between locally based exporting firms and local supplier firms, will tend to benefit from local wage falls. This the case of a local economy which is dominated by strong input–output linkages between locally based exporting firms and local supplier firms, and where the initial cause of the involuntary unemployment described by Figure 6.4 is actually a contraction in the local regional export base sector itself.

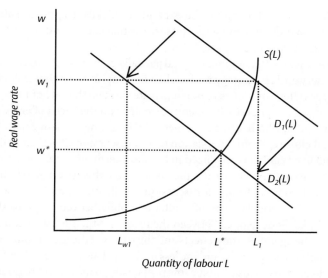

Figure 6.9 Labour market effects of a reduction in export base output demand

In such a situation, we can redraw Figure 6.4 as Figure 6.9 in which the initial level of regional labour demand is D_1, the regional market clearing wage is w_1, and the level of regional employment is L_1. Following a fall in regional export demand, the local basic sector will cut back its output. Therefore the local regional labour demand on the part of both the basic and non-basic industries will now fall from D_1 to D_2. At the existing wage of w_1, the labour employed will fall from L_1 to L_{w1} and involuntary unemployment will be given as $(L_1 - L_{w1})$. If wages are unable to fall to w^* for the kind of institutional reasons outlined in Figure 6.4, the involuntary unemployment will tend to be persistent unless there is a compensating change in the position of either the labour demand or supply curves.

In the case where the involuntary regional unemployment has been caused primarily by a general contraction in regional export demand, this will tend to indicate that the region is currently not an attractive location for new investment. This implies that in the short or medium term at least, an expansion of the regional capital stock by new immigrant investment which is sufficient to compensate for the export base contraction would appear to be unlikely. Moreover, in such a situation local business confidence will tend to be very low. This will imply that local business expansion of the type represented by the locus a in Figure 6.6 is unlikely to take place. Further local wage falls are therefore much more likely to induce further negative local income–expenditure type effects described by the loci b, c, and d in Figure 6.6.

6.4.1 Regional capital adjustment

In regional factor markets there are three particular features of local capital inputs which are somewhat different from many micro or macro discussions of factor markets. The first feature is that the regional capital stock which is combined with local labour inputs comprises largely location-specific highly durable physical capital infrastructure assets. The second feature, which is consequent on this first feature, is that regional capital can be withdrawn from production quickly, but cannot be expanded quickly. The third feature, which is a result of the combination of the first two features, is that capital withdrawal almost inevitably generates negative regional externalities.

From Chapter 2 we see that regional capital partially comprises the fixed industrial investment in machinery and technology undertaken by firms at their chosen locations. We can describe this type of investment as regional private capital. The rate of increase or decrease in the regional private capital stock depends primarily on the speed of entry or exit of firms into or out of a region, whether by new 'greenfield' investment, plant expansion, plant contraction, or plant closure. From our location theory discussions it is clear that this particular form of regional fixed capital is only fixed in the short term. Firms are able to move between alternative locations in search of greater profits such that this type of fixed capital is partially mobile in the medium term. From the discussions in Chapters 2 and 5 we can argue that the extent to which this particular type of capital is mobile between regions depends on the strength of the linkages developed between the firms and their local customers and suppliers. The stronger the agglomeration effects and the stronger the local input–output linkages, the less 'footloose' will be the firms and the less mobile will be this particular form of regional capital. In practice, many firms exhibit a low propensity to move, and regional capital infrastructure therefore tends to be rather durable.

As well as these types of private regional capital assets such as machinery and information technology capital, however, the regional capital stock will also comprise immovable assets such as non-prefabricated buildings, bridges, roads, docks, and airports. We can describe these types of capital as regional public capital assets. Much of this regional public capital stock is in the form of durable infrastructure assets which are set up at particular fixed locations. This fixed infrastructure capital is very costly to adjust and reconfigure for alternative uses, because these adjustment costs will involve construction and building engineering activities. The transactions costs involved in altering this type of capital for alternative uses are therefore very significant. Moreover, the adjustment periods for physical building capital may be further prolonged because the structure of leases and tenancies often means that capital facilities are tied up for long periods in particular uses and activities. The existing stock of regional capital is therefore composed to a large extent of physical infrastructure assets which are costly to expand or redevelop.

On the other hand, the transactions costs involved in the setting up of new capital assets may be rather less, particularly in the case of prefabricated building infrastructure and 'greenfield' developments. This general asymmetry between the development cost of new capital assets and the redevelopment costs of existing capital assets has a parallel in more general discussions of technology change. The parallel cases are what are known as 'putty-clay' models (Stoneman 1983), in which capital in its early stages of implementation is regarded as being malleable and flexible, but once it is implemented in its productive use it becomes cast and set in a very particular and inflexible form. This putty-clay metaphor successfully captures the nature of large portions of the regional capital stock. These assets tend to be adjustable only over a very long time period, and in the medium term we can regard these capital assets as being entirely fixed.

The combination of these two portions of the regional capital stock, namely the partially mobile private regional capital and the fixed regional public capital, means that in the short to medium term, the regional capital stock can only be expanded very slowly.

However, although the regional capital stock can only be expanded relatively slowly, the regional capital stock can be reduced relatively quickly. If there is a strong local negative income–expenditure effect such as described by Figure 6.6, firms may withdraw capital quickly in response to falling local wages by reducing the level of capital utilization, as we see in Figure 6.7. If such reduced capital utilization does take place, the unused excess capital ($K_F - K_P$) can be withdrawn from production very quickly simply by cutting back output, although it will not necessarily be scrapped in the short run. The reduction in investment will mean that the only form of current investment still undertaken is the depreciation expenditure on existing capital infrastructure, which is necessary to maintain it for future use. However, if the demand fall is perceived by firms not to be a short-term phenomenon, even this depreciation investment may be curtailed. In situations such as this, the capital will be withdrawn permanently from the productive process, and the firms will move permanently to a lower-capacity regional production function. As such, the fact that much of the regional productive capital is both durable and location specific means that there is something of an asymmetry in regional factor markets. Regional capital reduction can take place at a much more rapid pace than regional capital expansion. As we have seen in Figure 6.9, this is particularly a problem in the case where a region suffers an export demand fall.

In the particular case of urban and regional economies, the withdrawal of capital from the local productive process also has very specific regional implications, and the reason for this is, once again, the location specificity and durability of regional capital. To see this we must combine our two key insights, namely, that much regional capital is durable and adjustment costs are high, and also that regional capital expansion is relatively slow whereas regional capital contraction can be rapid. The combination of these observations suggests that that a rapid regional contraction will result in a physical environment characterized by derelict capital assets. The problem with this is that it can generate a negative externality in the form of a reduction in the quality of the local environment. Capital dereliction and decay can therefore play a major role in altering the attractiveness of the regional economy as a location for future investment.

An example of this is given in Figure 6.10, which is an extension of the argument given in Figure 6.9. If regional demand falls from D_1 to D_2, capital will be withdrawn from production as described by Figure 6.7. If the withdrawn capital leads to dereliction in the short to medium term, this may lead to a deterioration in the local economic environment and further reduce the attractiveness of the region as a location for investment. In the subsequent time period, demand may fall even further to D', with involuntary local unemployment at the existing wage rate of w_1 increasing from $(L_1 - L_{w1})$ to $(L_1 - L_w')$.

We can similarly reverse the argument, and imagine a demand expansion from D' to D in one time period. This could be due to the immigration of a major new immigrant firm. The consequent expansion in the regional capital stock may engender further growth in local labour demand from D to D_1 as other new firms locate in the region and local business confidence increases in general. As such, the investment and labour market decisions in the current time period depend on the investment and labour market decisions made in previous time periods in which the economic conditions may have been very different from those which currently prevail. This particular feature of the labour market, in which there is a

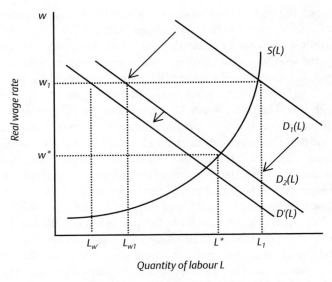

Figure 6.10 Negative interactions between capital withdrawal and labour demand

partial dependence on previous labour market and capital investment behaviour, is often known as 'hysteresis'. Yet the phenomenon of hysteresis itself in part depends on the durability and location specificity of the regional capital with which the labour is combined. Regional capital exhibits a great deal of inertia, in terms of both quantity and quality. (See Urban and Regional Example 6.1.)

⊖ Urban and Regional Example 6.1   Physical capital dereliction and time of adjustment

The regional response to demand changes is obviously in part a question of time. In economics, the definition of the 'long run' is specifically that it is the time period during which all factors are able to be adjusted, both quantitatively and qualitatively. Therefore, even where a region suffers a major decline, there must be a long-run time period during which the regional capital stock will be able to adjust so as to allow the region to expand. However, the durability of regional capital means that the adjustment time periods for regional economies can be very substantial, in comparison for example with that of an individual firm, particularly where a region suffers a decline in demand. This is evidenced by the long-term adjustment problems and capital dereliction of parts of the cities in the so-called 'rust belt' of the USA, such as Detroit, Pittsburgh, and Cleveland, or older east coast cities such as Philadelphia and Baltimore. Similarly, such capital dereliction and long-term adjustment problems exist in the former industrial cities of the UK, such as Glasgow, Sheffield, Liverpool, Manchester, and Leeds. On the other hand, because money capital funds are liquid, and new building infrastructure can often be rapidly constructed on 'greenfield' sites, regional capital expansion can often be quite a rapid process in the case where a region experiences demand expansion without facing any physical or geographical growth restrictions. Examples of this include cities in the so-called US 'sun belt', such as San Jose, Phoenix, and Atlanta.

Given that regions tend to exhibit asymmetries in terms of their ability to adjust capital stocks to increases or decreases in demand, it may be that, in many cases, a reliance on regional investment and capital changes can be a rather inefficient way of ensuring effective regional adjustment. The alternative mechanism is therefore to allow the regional supplies of labour to adjust. The relative success of these two mechanisms depends on whether the demand for labour, dependent on the regional capital stock, or the supply of labour, dependent on migration behaviour, is more quickly able to adjust to changing regional economic conditions.

6.5 Wages and interregional labour migration

As we have seen in the above sections, the individual region has limited internal wage adjustment capabilities, particularly in response to adverse demand changes. However, there is a mechanism which operates at the interregional level which can allow the region to adjust more rapidly to such changes. This mechanism is that of interregional labour migration. There are three broad types of interregional migration mechanism associated with wage levels, namely the disequilibrium model, the equilibrium model, and the endogenous human-capital model. We will discuss each of these models here in turn.

6.5.1 The disequilibrium model of interregional labour migration

The 'disequilibrium' model is the most commonly adopted model of interregional labour migration. In order to understand the basic nature of this mechanism we can use Figure 6.11 to examine the labour migration responses between two regions A and B. We can consider the case where region A has suffered a demand contraction while region B has experienced a simultaneous demand expansion. Such a shift in relative interregional demand could be brought about by a change in the tastes of consumers in preference for the outputs produced by region B rather than those produced by region A. The price of the output of region B will rise whereas the price of region A's outputs will fall. The result is that the marginal revenue product of labour in region B increases while that of labour in region A falls. This is reflected in the shifts in the respective labour demand schedules for each region.

In Figures 6.11a and b, let the real wage in region A be denoted as w_A, and the real wage in region B be denoted as w_B. We assume initially that the regions are in equilibrium, in the sense that real wages are the same in both regions. In other words, we assume that $w_A = w_B$. Let us also assume for simplicity that the levels of employment in both regions are the same. In other words, we assume that $L_A = L_B$.

If the demand for labour in region A decreases from D_A to D_{A1} while the demand for labour in region B increases from D_B to D_{B1}, the real wage in region A will fall to w_{A1}, and the real wage in region B will rise to w_{B1}. Similarly, the level of employment in region A will fall to L_{A1}, and the level of employment in region B will rise to L_{B1}. The interregional difference in employment is given by $(L_{B1} - L_{A1})$, and the interregional difference between the two real wages will be $(w_{B1} - w_{A1})$. It is this difference, or alternatively, this 'disequilibrium', between the real wages attainable in the two regions that will encourage labour to migrate from region A to region B. This is why this particular model of migration is known as a 'disequilibrium' mechanism.

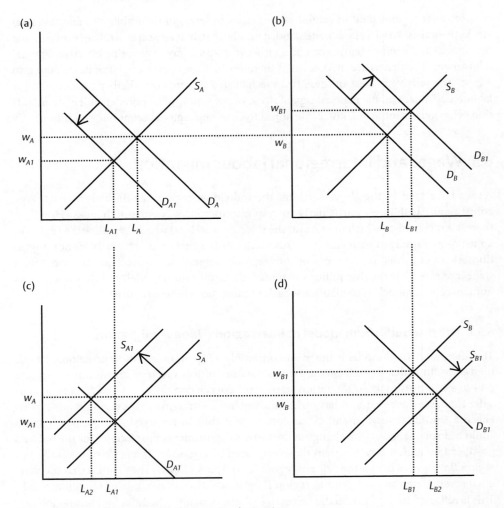

Figure 6.11 Disequilibrium model of interregional migration

As we see in Figures 6.11c and d, this migration behaviour will shift the labour supply in region A to the left from S_A to S_{A1}, and to the right in region B from S_B to S_{B1}. As more people enter region B, the available local labour supply expands, thereby reducing the marginal productivity of labour and the local wage rate in region B. Similarly, assuming that the regional capital stocks have remained unchanged, from the law of diminishing marginal productivity we know that the reduced labour supply remaining in region A will experience a relative increase in its marginal product. This process of migration will continue until the falling real wage in region B and the rising real wage in region A are brought back into equilibrium at the original regional wages of $w_A = w_B$. Once this has been achieved, the interregional migration of labour from region A to region B will cease. Although real wages will have been brought back into equilibrium between the regions at their original levels, the total quantity of labour employed in each region will

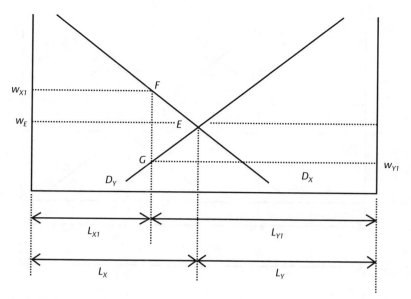

Figure 6.12 The welfare gains associated with interregional migration

have changed from the original situation. In the new equilibrium, the total quantity of labour employed in region A will have fallen in two stages from L_A to L_{A1}, and then from L_{A1} to L_{A2}, while regional wages will have fallen and risen in two stages from w_A to w_{A1} and then from w_{A1} to w_A, respectively. Meanwhile, in region B, the total quantity of labour employed will have risen in two stages from L_B to L_{B1}, and then from L_{B1} to L_{B2}, while regional wages will have risen and fallen in two stages from w_A to w_{A1} and then from w_{A1} to w_A, respectively. In the new equilibrium situation in which there is no interregional migration, region B will now be much larger than region A, whereas initially the two regions were the same size.

The process of interregional labour migration can be shown to be efficient from the point of view of the economy as a whole. In order to see this we can employ Figure 6.12, in which the labour demand curves for two regions X and Y of identical capital stocks are superimposed on each other by reversing the labour demand curve for region Y horizontally from left to right. In other words, we can read the labour demand curve of region X from left to right as normal, and read the labour demand curve of region Y from right to left. We can begin with a situation in which there is a high marginal product and real wage in region X of w_{X1} for a low level of employment in region X of L_{X1}, represented in Figure 6.12 by F. Meanwhile there is a low marginal product and real wage in region Y of w_{Y1} for a high level of employment in region Y of L_{Y1}, represented in Figure 6.12 by G. The total level of employment in the economy is given by L_N, where $L_N = (L_{X1} + L_{Y1})$. If one marginal unit of labour now transfers from region Y to region X, the individual person achieves an increase both in their marginal product and their real wage of $(w_{X1} - w_{Y1})$. This marginal transfer of labour between the regions marginally increases the wage in region Y by Δw_{Y1} and reduces the wage in region X by Δw_{X1}. At the same time, the labour employed in region Y falls to $(L_{X1} - 1)$ and the labour employed in region X increases to

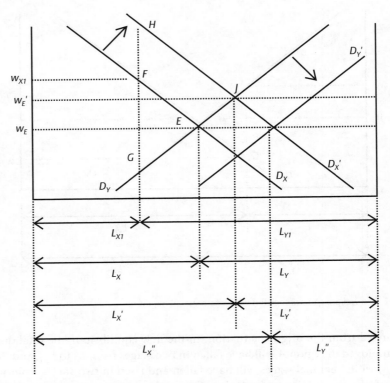

Figure 6.13 Interregional labour equilibrium with different capital stocks

$(L_{X1} + 1)$. However, there is still an interregional difference in regional marginal products given by $(w_{X1} - \Delta w_{X1}) - (w_{Y1} - \Delta w_{Y1})$ and for the next person who migrates from region Y to region X, $(w_{X1} - \Delta w_{X1}) - (w_{Y1} - \Delta w_{Y1})$ represents the increase in their real wage. Interregional migration will take place from region Y to region X until real wages are equalized in both regions at w_E, and labour employment in each region is given as $(L_X = L_Y)$, as represented in Figure 6.12 by E. As before, the total national employment is given as $L_N = (L_X + L_Y)$.

The difference between the marginal products attainable in each region at the existing regional labour employment levels not only represents the real wage increase available to the marginal migrant. This difference also represents the foregone national output which is not produced if labour migration is not allowed to take place. Therefore the area EFG can be regarded both as the deadweight loss to society due to a lack of interregional migration, and the Pareto efficiency gain to society associated with interregional migration.

Although in Figure 6.12 the argument is constructed by assuming each region X and Y initially exhibits an identical regional capital stock with identical regional demand patterns, there is no reason why this should be the case. If the two regions initially have different capital stocks, this would simply imply that the relative positions of the regional labour demand curves from each of their respective vertical axes would change. We can see this in Figure 6.13. We assume that the interregional equilibrium was initially the same as that achieved in Figure 6.12, where regional wages are given as w_E in both regions, and labour employment in each region is given as L_X and L_Y, respectively, and where $L_X = L_Y$. If the stock of capital in region X increases, for example, due to the immigration of a new firm into the region, the demand for labour will increase in region X from D_X to $D_{X'}$. This will increase the equilibrium interregional wage to $w_{E'}$, at regional employment levels of $L_{X'}$ and $L_{Y'}$, and the Pareto efficiency gain associated with migration will increase from EFG to GHJ, at the initial disequilibrium regional labour supplies of L_{X1} and L_{Y1}.

If the capital increase in region X, on the other hand, has been due to the migration of a firm from region Y to region X, this will affect the labour demand curves in the two regions in an equal and opposite manner. In this latter case, the demand for labour in region Y will have fallen from D_Y to $D_{Y'}$, such that the equilibrium interregional wage will remain unchanged at w_E, but the new equilibrium labour supply in region X, given as $L_{X''}$, will be twice as large as that in region Y, given as $L_{Y''}$. As we see here, by comparing this result with the initial result in Figure 6.12, it is perfectly possible for the sizes of the two regions, defined in terms of their capital and labour stocks, to be quite different, although the equilibrium interregional wages are identical. At the same time, the efficiency gains associated with interregional migration are always available as long as interregional real wages are not in equilibrium.

6.5.2 The equilibrium model of interregional labour migration

The description of the interregional labour migration process given in section 6.5.1 is based on a disequilibrium model of migration. The basis of this disequilibrium model is that workers are understood to move in response to differences between the real wages payable in various regions. Empirically, this should imply that in an econometric model with regional net migration as the dependent variable, and the regional real wage as an independent variable, there would always be a significant relationship between the two variables. In particular, areas with a higher than average real wage would be expected to exhibit relatively strong net in-migration flows, whereas areas with a relatively low real wage would be expected to exhibit relatively strong net out-migration flows. However, many econometric tests do not appear to find the 'correct' results, as suggested by the disequilibrium model. There are two possible explanations for this.

The first explanation is simply that the calculation of regional real wages often suffers from severe data limitations, thereby rendering such statistical work difficult. In theoretical terms regional real wages are defined as the nominal wage payable in the region divided by the local regional cost of living. Yet, in reality, measuring regional real wages can be very complicated. The simplest cost of living indices tend to be constructed using either housing rental cost or housing purchase cost data, combined with some local price index of consumer goods. However, housing markets not only tend to exhibit significant heterogeneity across locations but are also generally subject to high cyclical volatility. This means that the real wage deflators applied to nominal local wages can be very dependent on the particular time period chosen. Therefore statistical models which look at interregional labour flows of migration over a significant time period can be subject to data whose basis is changing all of the time. In order to avoid these problems, many models simply use nominal wages as a proxy for real wages, implicitly assuming that higher nominal wages imply higher real wages. In either case, whether real or nominal wage data are used in the models, the power of many statistical tests may be weakened by these measurement problems. These data problems may therefore explain why many econometric models of migration do not appear to find the 'correct' results, as suggested by the disequilibrium model.

On the other hand, there is a second and more fundamental critique of the disequilibrium model of migration, known as the 'equilibrium' model of migration (Graves 1980, 1993). The equilibrium model of migration argues that there are no 'correct' results as such in the relationship between net migration and real wages, as suggested by the disequilibrium model. The reason for this is that as well as being a reward for labour services in the production process, wages are also perceived to be a partial compensation for amenity differences. This is because residence in one area or another implies that the bundle of environmental amenity goods consumed by residents differs by location, and utility is gained from the consumption of these goods. In areas of high amenity, workers may be willing to accept lower wages for any given overall level of utility. On the other hand, in areas of poor environmental quality, workers may require higher wages to attain any given level of utility. The overall equilibrium migration argument is based on the consumption models of Roback (1982) and Tiebout (1956) applied to the case of labour mobility, and these models are discussed in Appendix 6.1.

If this compensation argument is correct, in a country with heterogeneous regions, comparing real wages across regions on the basis of either nominal wage indices or nominal wages deflated by local cost of living indices will not tell us very much about the relative utilities of the workers in each of the regions. As such, we cannot assume any particular migration motives for workers between any two regions unless we can explicitly account for such amenity differences. This leaves us with enormous empirical problems, in that we would have to calculate environmental indices for all locations and incorporate these into our local real wage indices in order to produce appropriate regional real wage data. The problem the equilibrium migration arguments also then raise is that the construction of appropriate interregional consumption indices based on a common basket of goods becomes extremely difficult, for the very reason that different locations mean that different baskets of environmental goods are consumed. Moreover, the logical limit of this argument is that we would also have to account for all consumption differences by location, whether according to natural or human-produced environmental differences.

As we saw in Appendix 3.3 to Chapter 3, the models of Fujita et al. (1999) allow for utility to be related to the local variety of consumption opportunities. Similarly, the Glaeser et al. (2001) and Gottlieb and Glaeser (2006) arguments suggest that all sorts of urban consumption amenities are related to urban cultural and leisure services. These in turn can also be considered as environmental amenity variations, albeit human-produced ones, and strictly speaking these would also need to be added to the natural environmental variations to provide a complete local amenity index. Immediately it therefore becomes clear that the econometric problems involved in these issues are very significant indeed. Notwithstanding these difficulties, however, in the US case at least, one amenity variable appears to be significant in determining migration patters over time, and this is the mean January temperature (Partridge 2010), and as we see in Box 6.1, there is some limited evidence that similar issues operate within individual European countries (Cheshire and Magrini 2006).

BOX 6.1 Equilibrium versus disequilbrium models

The debate between the appropriateness of the disequilibrium model of migration versus the equilibrium model of migration is still not entirely resolved. Research in the early 1990s (Evans 1990, 1993; Hunt 1993) argued that in reality most empirical work generally supported the view that the disequilibrium model of migration better captured the process of migration. More recently, however, empirical assessments have increasingly swung in favour of equilibrium model of migration, at least on the basis of US evidence (Partridge 2010); although once again, doubts have been raised as to what exactly is meant by amenities in this case (Storper and Kemeny 2012). In contrast, data from other parts of the world suggest that the amenity effects on migration may be much smaller (Cheshire and Magrini 2006), and may also differ between long- and short-distance migration (Biagi et al. 2011). However, the equilibrium model does caution us to fundamentally consider exactly what the motives for migration are and to understand that real wage differences across regions are the result of a variety of complex interrelated issues. The evidence from different countries suggests that in the majority of cases, the disequilibrium nature of the relationship between real wages and migration will dominate the equilibrium nature of the relationship, although in some cases such as the US the results will be reversed (Partridge 2010).

6.5.3 The endogenous human-capital model of migration

A third approach to analysing the nature of interregional labour migration is based on the consideration of the microeconomic characteristics of individual migrants themselves. The basis of this argument is known as the human-capital (HK) model of migration, and is a development of the standard model of human capital first widely discussed by Becker (1964). A simple model of human capital is given in Appendix 6.2, applied to the case of migration (Faggian and McCann 2009a). However, the broad arguments of the model of human capital, and their relationship to labour migration, can be understood quite quickly.

The basic human-capital argument is that rational and well-informed individuals will invest in personal education and training in order to increase their stock of skills, defined here as human capital, in order to maximize their expected lifetime utility, defined here in terms of their lifetime income plus job satisfaction. Education and training tend to be undertaken before employment commences fully, so the costs of such activities are generally borne at an early stage in the career of an individual, whereas the employment earnings will accrue over the career history of the individual. At the same time, different lifetime incomes will be earned in different occupations and the cost of training in different skills will differ between different occupations. The individual worker therefore has to consider what is their optimum mode of employment to aspire to, and, consequently, what is the optimum level of personal education to invest in initially. Given good information on expected wages and labour training costs, as we see in Appendix 6.2, such a calculation is perfectly possible using standard present-value discounting techniques. The general assumptions are that the higher the human capital of the individual, the relatively higher will have been the costs of their education in general, due to the extended time involved in training. At the same time, the higher the human capital of the individual, the relatively higher will be their expected wage, due to their increased marginal productivity.

However, given that educational investment must generally take place before any long-term career develops, there is always an element of risk in the educational investment decision, in that the actual lifetime earnings may differ from those which were initially expected.

From the perspective of urban and regional labour market behaviour, the problem is to understand the relationship between migration behaviour and the maximization of expected wages within the human-capital framework. In order to do this, we must combine the standard human-capital theory outlined above with what is known as 'search theory' (Molho 1986). The basic premise of search theory is that labour will only consider accepting a job if the wage offered is greater than, or equal to, a particular personal minimum acceptable wage, known as a 'reservation' wage. Individuals will continue with a process of job search in which job positions are considered sequentially until one offers a wage which at least matches the individual's reservation wage. From human-capital theory, we know that greater human capital generally involves greater initial education costs, and also greater potential wages due to higher skills. Therefore the reservation wage tends to increase for individuals with greater levels of human capital. This means that the higher the human capital of the individual, the greater will be the length of the job search process. However, in terms of regional labour market behaviour, the combination of human-capital theory with job-search theory also has a direct implication. The implication is that higher human-capital individuals will tend to search for employment opportunities over a wider geographical area than those with lower human capital in order to find employment opportunities offering wages at least equal to their higher reservation wage. In the cases where such employment opportunities are found and taken up, the result will be that the higher human-capital individuals will be more likely to have migrated over greater geographical distances than the lower human-capital individuals. In order to maximize the returns to their human capital, higher human-capital individuals therefore tend to be more migratory than lower human-capital individuals, both for reasons of recovering their initial costs of the human-capital acquisition, and for attaining their expected wages. At the same time, we can also argue that higher human-capital individuals will also be better informed of alternative employment opportunities across regions via easier personal access to informal employment networks. Once again, this will tend to increase the migratory nature of higher human-capital individuals.

There is now an increasing body of evidence on this issue (Faggian and McCann 2006, 2009a,b,c; Faggian et al. 2006, 2007a,b; McCann et al. 2010) which indeed suggests that higher human-capital individuals migrate both further and more frequently than lower human-capital individuals. This is particularly noticeable in the case of university graduates, whose combination of skills and youth allows for the highest rates of wage enhancement (Mincer 1974), as long as they move to the locations affording the best opportunities.

The argument that higher human-capital individuals will tend to be more migratory than lower human-capital individuals has profound implications for our understanding of the disequilibrium model of migration. In order to see this we can consider Figures 6.14a, b, c, and d, which are a modification of Figures 6.11a, b, c, and d. In Figures 6.14a and b, we assume initially that the real wage in region A, denoted as w_A, and the real wage in region B, denoted as w_B, are equal, as are the equilibrium employment levels in each region, denoted as L_A and L_B, respectively. As in Figures 6.11a and b, if the demand for labour in region A decreases from D_A to D_{A1}

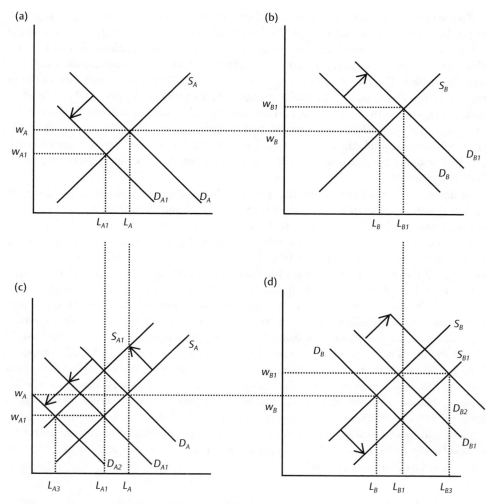

Figure 6.14 A cumulative model of interregional migration

while the demand for labour in region B increases from D_B to D_{B1}, the real wage in region A will fall to w_{A1}, and the real wage in region B will rise to w_{B1}. Similarly, the level of employment in region A will fall to L_{A1}, and the level of employment in region B will rise to L_{B1}. As before, in Figures 6.11c and d, the interregional wage disequilibrium of $(w_{B1} - w_{A1})$ encourages labour to migrate from region A to region B, resulting in a labour supply shift in region A to the left from S_A to S_{A1}, and to the right in region B from S_B to S_{B1}. However, the human-capital argument above suggests that the most migratory individuals who most efficiently respond to regional wage signals will tend to be the most highly educated workers. If we assume, therefore, that high human-capital individuals migrate relatively quickly, whereas low human-capital individuals migrate relatively slowly, the effect of this selective migration can be understood as altering the relative regional labour demand in favour of the expanding region.

To see this we can consider the outward shift in the labour supply S_B to S_{B1} in region B as tending to imply an increase in the supply of human capital within the region. If we consider the regional capital stock as comprising both physical capital and also human capital, the average and marginal product of the regional capital stock will have increased. The effect of this will be to further shift the labour demand curve in region B from D_{B1} to D_{B2}. Conversely, in region A, the reduced supply of labour from S_A to S_{A1} will tend to mean a decrease in the supply of human capital within the region. Once again, if we consider the regional capital stock as comprising both physical capital and human capital, the average and marginal product of the regional capital stock can be considered to have decreased. The labour demand curve in region A will shift further to the left.

In this particular selective migration process, the total quantity of labour employed in region A will have fallen in two stages from L_A to L_{A1}, and then from L_{A1} to L_{A3}, while regional wages will have fallen from w_A to w_{A1}. Meanwhile, in region B, the total quantity of labour employed will have risen in two stages from L_B to L_{B1}, and then from L_{B1} to L_{B3}, while regional wages will have risen from w_A to w_{A1}. Obviously, this process may continue cumulatively beyond the two stages identified here, and there is no particular unique interregional wage–employment equilibrium position towards which the regions will converge. The reason for this is that region B is enjoying agglomeration economies, and, as we know, any model in which there are economies of scale may have multiple equilibrium outcomes. Recent evidence from the USA suggests that if we consider the case of urban amenities rather than natural amenities, the evidence does indeed tend to support human-capital explanations of urban growth rather than amenity explanations (Shapiro 2007; Gottlieb and Glaeser 2008). The limits of the cumulative process described are the same as the limits to agglomeration discussed in Chapter 3. Such a cumulative process of local growth and decline may eventually reach a point where region B begins to exhibit agglomeration diseconomies of scale. In this case the cumulative processes, as represented by Figures 6.14c and d, will begin to be replaced by the equilibrating processes represented by Figures 6.11c and d.

6.5.4 Additional comments on wages and migration

Although we cannot specify over how long such a cumulative process of migration may take place, from our discussions in Chapters 3 and 5 there are several additional points we can make. The first is that the ability of the migration process to eradicate localized regional unemployment problems depends on whether the migration process is an equilibrating or a cumulative process. If migration is highly selective in terms of the human capital of migrants, the differences in regional performance may be exacerbated by the migration process itself.

A second issue which we have not discussed here is the question of the housing market. The structure of the housing market may sometimes generate impediments to the migration process. For example, if there are asymmetric demand shocks between regions, such as in Figures 6.11 and 6.14, this may engender significant movements in local real-estate prices. For workers with mortgages, this may mean that movement from weak regions to buoyant regions becomes a question of access to capital, rather than access to a job. If local house prices have fallen significantly, a worker may not be able to cover the mortgage value of the house from its sale, nor fund the deposit required for a mortgage in the more expensive region. Therefore, even if alternative superior job offers are available in more buoyant regions, the worker will be unable to leave the weaker region (Bover et al. 1989). In such a situation, only intraregional job moves within the same metropolitan region, which do not involve a change of residence, will be possible for the worker. As well as the workings of the private housing market, another potential obstacle to interregional migration comes from public sector housing policies. In some cases, subsidies to publicly provided housing may reduce the likelihood of migration (Hughes and McCormick 1981; Minford et al. 1988) by artificially increasing the real wages of those with state housing. In such cases, workers may be much less responsive to interregional wage signals.

The third point concerning migration is the problem of understanding whether the acquisition of a higher-wage job is the result of, or a cause of, migration behaviour. Many arguments suggest that, for many people, the availability of employment opportunities causes migration to take place as a response to job acquisition, rather than as part of the job-search process itself. The major evidence in support of this is that the levels of interregional migration in many countries tend to be highly pro-cyclical. In other words, as the national economy expands, the availability of jobs increases, and the levels of interregional migration tend to increase. On the other hand, as the economy contracts and employment opportunities diminish, the levels of interregional migration tend to fall. The result of this is that, in many countries, the differences between regional unemployment rates tend to fall as the economy expands and tend to increase as the economy contracts (Gordon 1985), although the evidence for this is can be rather difficult to interpret (Hemmings 1991).

An additional alternative approach is to interpret the regional wage arguments outlined above in terms of the expected wages earned by migrants, rather than the actual wages. Expected wages are the wages earned on acquiring a job multiplied by the probability of actually gaining employment in the relevant sector in the respective region. This is the classic Harris and Todaro (1970) argument which is familiar in the development economics literature (Thirlwall 1994). From the arguments in Chapter 3, this would imply that there may be situations where migration will tend to take place from peripheral areas to central higher-order areas, even though actual real wages in the central urban areas may be lower than those earned in the peripheral areas. Such cases will arise where central urban areas are achieving agglomeration economies of scale. The reason for this is that the probability of finding appropriate employment is much higher in the central urban areas, thereby allowing real wages earned to be lower. Net migration flows between the regions will continue until the expected wage is equalized between the regions. In the above scenario, if economic growth tends to originate in the dominant central areas, for the reasons outlined in Chapter 3, this will imply that the central areas initially grow faster than the peripheral regions. Migration will take place from the peripheral regions to the centre, although over time the net migration levels will fall as the peripheral regions begin to grow and close the gap with the core regions. In contrast, at the aggregate macroeconomic level, as the economy as a whole contracts, the migration flows will fall because the overall availability of jobs in the central core destination regions will fall.

An interesting final aspect of all of these migration models, as discussed in Box 6.2, is that fact that the vast majority of people do not migrate, and that interregional migration rates in many countries have been falling, even before the financial crisis of 2008.

BOX 6.2 Why so many people do not migrate

A final issue in terms of wage-related models of migration that we need to consider is the extent to which people do *not* move. The majority of households do not relocate interregionally or internationally, such that when they do relocate, it tends to be within the same broad locality or region. Indeed, there is some evidence that over recent years interregional migration rates have actually been *falling* even in the USA (Partridge et al. 2012). One possible reason for this observation is that as greater numbers of the workforce develop generic (knowledge-related) employment skills such as skills in accounting, finance, sales and marketing, or human resource management, workers become much less tied to particular industrial or commercial sectors than they were in previous decades. The implication here is that it becomes increasingly easy for workers to replace movements between places with movements between sectors. As such, employment changes can increasingly be associated with movements across industrial and commercial sectors within the same geographical location and within the same occupational set, rather than movements within industrial sectors but between different places. If households have a preference to stay in their localities (Mellander and Florida 2011), due to the strength of social ties and social capital they experience in these places, then increases in generic skills may reduce migration levels. Indeed, there is a large literature in cultural geography which argues that 'sense of place' (Vanclay et al. 2010) is a very highly valued phenomenon, and relates to all cultural, heritage, and landscape characteristics which give people meaning from living in a particular location, and this concept obviously relates very closely to the attachment value argument discussed in Chapter 4. These issues imply that households often have a preference not to relocate and such a tendency towards inertia may be enhanced by the ability to switch between sectors using generic skill sets.

A second reason, as we will discuss in more detail in Chapter 8, is that as a response to globalization and technological change, the spatial distribution of activities may increasingly become more segmented geographically, with places becoming increasingly different in terms of the types of employment activities and occupations that they offer, irrespective of the industry or commercial sector (Duranton and Puga 2005). Once again, this implies that once workers have found their ideal employment regions, given their particular individual skill sets, they will be increasingly less likely to relocate. This spatial self-sorting and self-selection appears to be an increasingly widespread phenomenon, as is the growth of generic skills, all of which points to reduced mobility. However, it also points to a more complex dynamics, in that initial or early-career migration levels may be high (Faggian and McCann 2006, 2009a,b,c; Faggian et al. 2006, 2007a,b; McCann et al. 2010), followed by reduced, or at least highly selective, subsequent mobility patterns, aspects of which are captured by the 'escalator' model discussed in section 6.6.2.

A third issue regarding the reasons for low levels of interregional mobility relates to what is known as the Roy (1951) model of migration (Borjas 2008). This is discussed in detail in Appendix 6.3, and is an argument which originates from observations of international migration flows. However, the profound insight of the Roy (1951) model, which can also be applied to interregional mobility, is that individuals may not necessarily migrate in response to differences in absolute wage levels of even real wage levels. Rather, individual migration may also depend on one's relative status in society, in terms of the level of local equality and inequality in the domicile region. The implication here is that different *types* of migrant will tend to dominate different migration flows between different sets of regions in different contexts for rather different reasons in different contexts. A natural result of this model is that high-income individuals will often *not* migrate to higher-wage locations, for very rational reasons, even in situations of very good information and awareness.

6.6 Non-wage-related models of interregional migration

Each of the above models of migration depends primarily on the relationship between regional wages and employment levels. There are, however, two major models of migration which are primarily independent of wage levels. These models are known as the gravity model of migration and the life-cycle model of migration. Both of these models suggest that migration will take place even though wages or expected wages, or amenity-adjusted wages, are in equilibrium. The major difference here is that these two models focus on gross migration and not net migration, as is the case with the models described above in sections 6.5.1 to 6.5.3.

6.6.1 The gravity model of migration

The gravity model formula has been frequently applied both to intraregional migration and to interregional migration. The implicit basis of the argument when it is applied to interregional migration is that random business fluctuations will lead to certain continuous flows of job terminations and job vacancies which are uncorrelated across both time or space. The result of this is that there will always be individuals willing and able to migrate between regions at any one time, even if interregional wages are in equilibrium. Of interest to us, however, is the level of interregional migration flows between regions, and this is where the gravity model can be instructive. The gravity model of migration suggests that the level of migration between any two areas is directly related to the population sizes of the areas, and inversely related to the distance between the areas. The gravity model of migration can be expressed by the general formula:

$$M_{AB} = G \frac{P_A P_B}{(d_{AB})^\alpha} \tag{6.1}$$

whereby P_A and P_B represent the population sizes of the two city-regions, and d_{AB} represents the distance between the two locations, and the parameters G and α are constants to be determined. Although the model appears to be a direct analogy from the physical laws of gravity attraction between any two objects, there is, however, a reasoning behind the model based on both probability and economics. In order to understand this we must consider the justifications for the numerator and denominator terms of equation (6.1) separately.

The structure of the numerator term is based on the argument that the expected number of moves by individuals to or from any region will be directly related to the population sizes of the regions. In order to see this we can consider the case where the total national population is given as P_N, and the total number of interregional migration moves per time period is given as M_N. Here, the average number of interregional migration moves per person per year is thus given as M_N/P_N. In terms of out-migration, if we assume that all people in the country are homogeneous in terms of their propensity to migrate, the expected total number of out-migrants generated by area A will be given by $(M_N/P_N)P_A$. Therefore, for any given population migration propensity, the total number of out-migration moves from any area A will be positively related to the total number of people in the area P_A. Meanwhile, if the relative size of any particular potential destination region B is given by P_B/P_N, the expected total number of in-migrants per time period to region B from region A will be given as $((M_N/P_N)P_A)(P_B/P_N)$, which gives $(M_N P_A P_B)/(P_N P_N)$. Similarly, if the relative size of any particular potential destination region B is given by P_B/P_N, the expected total number of in-migrants to area B from all other regions will be given by $M_N(P_B/P_N)$. The contribution of this in-migration to region B which is accounted for by out-migration from region A will be therefore be given by $(M_N(P_B/P_N)(P_A/P_N))$, which gives $(M_N P_A P_B)/(P_N P_N)$, as above. Therefore, in equation (6.1) we can interpret the migration flows between regions A and B as being a product of P_A and P_B, and multiplied by a constant G, where $G = M_N/(P_N P_N)$.

The argument so far has implicitly assumed that migration between any pair of regions is equally likely as migration between any other pair of regions. However, we can argue that the spatial transactions costs involved under conditions of uncertainty, as discussed in Chapter 2, suggests that this will not be so. The agglomeration and spatial information acquisition arguments in Chapter 2 suggest that migration between contiguous areas will be much more likely than between distant regions. This argument is sometimes known as 'distance deterrence' (Gordon 1978), and implies that the likelihood of migration between any two locations will be inversely related to the distance between them, given as d_{AB}. However, there is no reason to expect that the inverse relationship between the interregional migration probability and the distance should be linear. Therefore we can specify the distance function in the denominator in terms of $(d_{AB})\alpha$, to allow for any non-linearities. Combining these two distinct approaches in the construction of the numerator and denominator terms gives us the general expression (6.1). This can be used to provide indications of migration flows between regions, even under conditions of real-wage equilibrium between regions.

Gravity models can also be made much more complex than this simple description by introducing more complex behavioural assumptions (Wilson 1974; Isard et al. 1998). At the same time, the multiplicative nature of equation (6.1) means that where simple models of this form are used for estimating interregional flows across all regions, the aggregate flows do not necessarily sum to the total flows in the system. In order to adjust for this, the models must be 'doubly constrained' so as to ensure the correct total flows into and out of each region (Isard et al. 1998).

In terms of our regional labour market discussions, however, the general observation to come out of these gravity models is that interregional migration flows are in part spatially determined, in the sense that the likelihood of migration is a function of distance. This also implies that interregional adjustments to labour market shocks may also be in part spatially determined. This is because the efficiency of the migration process as a regional labour market adjustment mechanism will itself depend on the distance between the local labour market in question and any other local labour market. More central regions, which are closer to a larger number of other centres of population, may find it easier to adjust to local negative demand shocks by means of out-migration flows, whereas geographically peripheral regions may only adjust much more slowly. In other words, the ability of regions to successfully adjust to negative demand shocks may also depend simply on the location of the regions in question.

As well as labour mobility, the gravity model approach is also used for analysing a range of different flows between places, including trade flows (Anderson and van Wincoop 2003, 2004) and traffic flows.

6.6.2 **The life-cycle model of migration**

Migration may also exhibit something of a life-cycle nature. For example, young school and college graduates may tend to migrate towards large primal cities in order to gain better access to high-quality employment. This migration takes place because such young job-seekers assume that their best long-term employment prospects will be served by acquiring a job in such a central location. The majority of their working life may be spent at such a location, although eventually the worker will seek to move out of the major city to a smaller, more geographically peripheral, settlement. This may include migration to regions of higher environmental quality and lower wages (Plane 1983). In the dominant urban centres, such out-migrants will be continually replaced by new young and generally highly educated in-migrants. Meanwhile, on the other hand, the peripheral areas will consistently see an out-migration of such young workers and a continuous in-migration of older workers accepting lower wages than they previously accepted. This has been described as an 'escalator' phenomenon (Fielding 1992). As long as the generation of high-quality employment opportunities tends to be dominated by the central higher-order urban areas, such a process will continue indefinitely. These life-cycle effects on migration will tend to take place over and above the wage-migration mechanism outlined in sections 6.5 to 6.5.3, and their effect will be to systematically alter the demographic profile and labour force composition between particular regions. In addition, the nature of these life-cycle effects is conditioned on the personal migration history of the individual. People who migrated early, or who have previously migrated far or frequently, tend to remain more migratory over their life cycle (DaVanzo and Morrison 1981). The reason is that breaking the psychological ties with the home location, the attachment value or the sense of place, allows them to more easily respond to wage signals with migration. As such, they tend to exhibit enhanced lifetime earnings. In contrast, those who return home at the earliest possible opportunity (DaVanzo 1983) tend to exhibit lower lifetime earnings, precisely because their social ties become more embedded and reinforced at an earlier stage in their lives, and these become harder to break over time, thereby reducing the ability of the individual to realize their wage-earning potential via migration. This is not to say that local social ties are bad because they inhibit migration, or that migration is bad because it breaks social ties. It is simply important to note that the decisions to migrate or not to migrate both involve choices and trade-offs which depend on personal and household preferences as well as the spatial distribution of employment opportunities.

6.7 **Conclusions**

Local urban and regional labour markets can exhibit particular features which are somewhat different from national discussions of the labour market. The hierarchical relationships between the regional export base sectors and the locally oriented sectors of a region will mediate demand shocks, and the regional responses to such shocks will depend on the structure of these relationships. Where demand shocks are positive, regions can respond by expanding their local capital stock, either through the expansion of local investment or through the immigration of capital from other regions. On the other hand, in some situations, the fixity and durability of local regional capital, and the hierarchical demand interactions between the regional export base and non-basic sectors, together militate against any potential downward adjustment of local wages to market-clearing levels. Both local market clearing and local involuntary unemployment are possible consequences of this downward wage rigidity. The actual result depends on the interaction between the employment retention policies of local firms, the expectations of local firms, and the speed of response of external investors to changes in the local economic conditions.

All regions exhibit the additional labour market adjustment mechanism of interregional migration. As we have seen, there are various interpretations of the relationship between regional wages and migration flows. The most common assumption is that of the disequilibrium model, in which migration will take place as a response to real-wage differences between regions. If all regional economies exhibit constant returns to scale, the process of interregional migration will itself lead to a restoration of the interregional wage equilibrium. Moreover, we have shown that this process maximizes the welfare to society by reducing any deadweight loss associated with an inefficient interregional spatial pattern of labour. On the other hand, where differences in human capital exist, the process of migration itself may cause certain regions to experience agglomeration economies at the expense of others. In this situation, a process of cumulative growth is possible. This is the subject of Chapter 7.

Finally, over and above all of the equilibrium–disequilibrium issues surrounding regional labour markets and migration, there are certain characteristics of migration flows dependent on demographic and geographical issues, which occur irrespective of regional wage levels.

Discussion questions

6.1 Is regional unemployment primarily the result of local labour prices being 'too' high? What would be the various possible consequences of reducing local wages?

6.2 Explain how interregional migration may solve local unemployment problems.

6.3 In what ways is interregional migration related to national economic efficiency?

6.4 How is human capital related to migration and under what conditions may interregional migration actually exacerbate local unemployment problems?

6.5 What role do environmental amenities play in determining interregional equilibrium wages? How does this affect our understanding of whether migration is an 'equilibrium' or a 'disequilibrium' phenomenon?

6.6 What other non-wage-related approaches do we have for analysing interregional migration patterns?

6.7 What economic reasons are there for explaining why most people choose not to migrate between regions?

6.8 What other economic reasons are there which limit interregional migration?

Appendix 6.1 The Roback (1982)–Tiebout (1956) model of consumption

The Roback (1982) model of amenities and consumption preferences implies that consumers will be willing to pay more in order to be able to consume higher-quality environmental amenities. This will be manifested by higher local land prices, and this observation is the basis of many hedonic models of real-estate valuation (Cheshire and Sheppard 1995, 1998), in which the value of the local environment is captured in the house-prices values. Turning the argument around, the real-estate values are therefore also an indirect measure of the quality of the environment. There is also a real-wage implication here. Higher local land prices with the same nominal wage imply a lower real wage regarding the consumption of non-amenity household goods and services. In labour supply terms the corollary is that workers will be willing to work for lower nominal wages in higher natural amenity-rich environments, and these lower nominal wages translate into lower real wages for a given level of local living costs. As such, the level of observed wages in particular locations is a result of both a reward for local labour services and also a compensation for local amenity variations.

In order to convert these ideas into a migration framework we also have to employ what is known as the Tiebout (1954) hypothesis. The Tiebout (1954) hypothesis posits that if people are free to move, they will 'vote with their feet', in that they will move so as to maximize *total* utility, of which the utility derived from wages and incomes earned in employment is one very important component. In the original Tiebout (1954) hypothesis it was assumed that the other utility-generating amenities which must be considered in location and migration decisions include the bundles of public services and public goods which are offered by local municipal authorities. As these often differ according to residential location, Tiebout (1954) argued that households will assess the combined utility available from both the employment possibilities which are accessible and the public services on offer in each location in their household location decisions. If we now also incorporate the natural amenities highlighted in the Roback (1982) model into Tiebout's (1954) argument, there is one additional assumption we also need to include in order to motivate our framework, namely that amenities are highly income-elastic consumption goods, such that as society as a whole becomes wealthier, the importance of amenity consumption increases.

With these various assumptions, the Roback (1982)–Tiebout (1954) model of consumption argues that combinations of demand and supply shifts will have predictable wage–employment effects. As such, observation of the combined wage and employment shifts proves to be an indirect way of assessing the impacts of amenities and other issues which affect consumption. In order to see this we can consider the differences between the upper and lower parts of Figure A.6.1.1.

In both cases we observe that the equilibrium labour demand and supply has increased from L_1 to L_2. However, in the case depicted in the upper part of the figure, the outward shift of the demand curve is due to firms and employers increasing their intermediate labour input demand. The result of this is a rising wage from w_1 to w_2. In contrast, in the case depicted in the lower part of the figure, the increase in the quantity of labour demanded and supplied is associated with a wage fall from w_1 to w_2.

In terms of local intra-urban or intraregional effects, the rising labour demand curves of Figure A.6.1.1 could be associated with any form of improvement in local employment demand conditions which encourages firms to take on more labour, ranging from tax breaks to local inward investment stimuli to increasing local agglomeration economies. Similarly, the outward shift of the labour supply curves in Figure A.6.1.1 could be associated with any improvements in the local employment conditions, ranging from improvements in the quality of the local working environment to increased long-term job security associated with changes in the local industry and sectoral composition, or to an improved provision of public goods, exactly as Tiebout (1954) argued.

In terms of *inter*regional adjustments, however, the argument is slightly different. Over time, changes in technology and employment modes increasingly allow households to move and work and different locations. If natural environmental amenities are highly income-elastic goods, the Roback (1982)–Tiebout (1954) framework implies that as societies become richer over time, holding demand levels constant, households will increasingly move from amenity-poor to amenity-rich environments, and therefore labour supply will shift outwards in areas where amenities are higher, and will fall in areas with

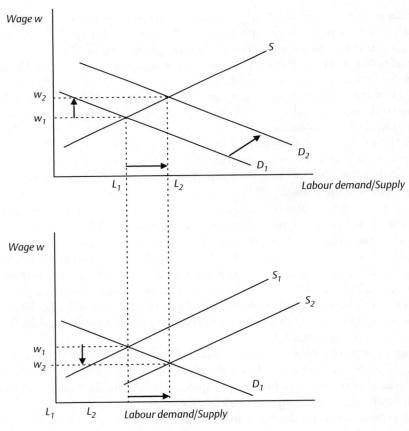

Figure A.6.1.1 Demand and supply shifts and wages

low amenities. The observed increasing employment in amenity-rich environments will be associated with falling real wages due to increased local competition for land, as depicted in Figure A.6.1.1. In contrast, the employment falls in amenity-poor regions will be associated with real-wage increases, because local land prices will fall, given the level of local nominal wages.

In order to fully account for these labour supply shifts it is of course necessary to control for the effects of demand changes, and there are various models which attempt to do this (Partridge 2010). In addition, these models can be used to estimate the strength of the effects of different migration influences. Data from the USA suggest that the environmental-amenity impacts of mid-winter temperature on mobility are consistent and significant, with households preferring to move towards warmer climates (Partridge 2010). However, the Roback (1982)–Tiebout (1954) model only works when mobility levels are very high, as is the case in the USA, in which the interregional labour markets may not be too far from equilibrium. In contexts with much lower levels of labour mobility, such as the EU or Japan, the models appear to be much less relevant (Cheshire and Magrini 2006). In these other cases, other cultural and institutional factors may be at least as important. Other US evidence also casts doubt on the wage equalization assumption even allowing for amenity variations (Storper and Kemeny 2012).

Appendix 6.2 The model of human capital

The model of human capital HK investment can be understood in terms of standard discounting techniques applied to investments in general. If we denote any future annual income stream at time t which can be earned by an investment as R_t, and we denote the discount rate as i, and the initial cost of undertaking the investment today as C_0, the simplest present value Π calculation of the investment can be defined as

$$\Pi = \sum_{t=1}^{n} \frac{R_t}{(1 + i)^t} - C_0 \sum_{t=1}^{n} R_t (1 + i)^{-t} - C_0 \tag{A.6.2.1}$$

The present value of the investment is the discounted sum of all the future income streams from time period $t = 1$ onwards. In the model specification given by (A.6.2.1) we are assuming that the future annual revenues R_t are paid at the end of each year, beginning at the end of year 1. In other words, the revenue payments which are discounted here are discrete payments.

In the case where revenues are paid continuously, however, it is necessary for us to convert (A.6.2.1) so as to discount the continuous income stream. In this case the present value Π of the investment can be defined (Chiang 1984) as

$$\Pi = \int_0^n R(t) e^{-rt} dt - C_0 \tag{A.6.2.2}$$

If we apply this model to human-capital investments, the initial cost of the investment C_0 will be represented by the initial employment training costs. These training costs will comprise the sum of any tuition fees paid plus the opportunity costs of the current income foregone during the period of training. The income earned from the human capital will be represented by the wages earned by working in the occupation for which the individual trained. If we denote the wage earned on commencing employment as W, we can rewrite (A.6.2.2) as

$$\Pi = \int_0^n W(t)e^{-rt}dt - C_0 \qquad\qquad (A.6.2.3)$$

Over the lifetime of employment, wages tend to increase over time as workers become more experienced and senior in their chosen occupations. In order to allow for the effect of the growth in wages over time in the present value model, we note that the current wage at any time period in the future t can be written as

$$W(t) = We^{\alpha t} \qquad\qquad (A.6.2.4)$$

where α is the rate of growth of wages. Therefore equation (A.6.2.3) can be adjusted to allow for continuous wage growth thus:

$$\Pi = \int_0^n W(t)e^{(\alpha-r)}dt - C_0 \qquad\qquad (A.6.2.5)$$

The basic model can be further developed to allow for costs which are incurred in a continuous manner over time, and for wage growth which changes over time.

In migration literature, the fundamental issue raised by the model of human capital is how the relationship between the costs of human-capital investment, as represented here by C_0, and the future wages earned, $W(t)$, are mediated. In particular, the wages payable for human-capital investments depend on workers moving to the locations of the appropriate employment. If the market is perfectly efficient, then workers will be matched with appropriate jobs at all locations, with expected real wages for each occupation being equal at all locations. As such, workers will be indifferent between alternative locations, and variations in workers' spatial patterns will depend only on the distribution of different types of activities and occupations. Following the logic of Borts and Stein (1964), as we will see in Chapter 7, spatial equilibrium actually implies that spatial distributions across activities, firms types, and sectors will tend to become more similar as they converge, the limit of which is that all regions exhibit the same production function. In contrast, however, if information transmission improves with human capital, and constraints to migration also fall with human capital, then we would expect differential migration propensities and variations in market-clearing mechanisms between different educational and income groups. Migrants with good information will more readily move to the locations in which the discounted net income stream of their employment is the highest, as this will maximize their long-term real earning potential, and there will develop clear spatial sorting according to skills. The human capital embodied in this selective migration process points heavily towards processes of cumulative rather than convergent regional growth.

Appendix 6.3 The Roy (1951) model of migration

The Roy (1951) model of migration based on rates of return to human capital was originally developed in the context of people moving between different countries. The basic Roy (1951) insight was that absolute wage-earning-level differences only determine the levels of migration, and do not determine migration *types*. The types of migrant are determined by relative inequality, and Borjas (1987) provided a theoretical framework for how such self-selection mechanisms work.

In order to help explain this insight, we can first consider high-income, but egalitarian, countries with high progressive taxes such as many European countries, Australia, or Canada. The rate of return to human capital in Canada or Europe is relatively lower for high-skilled workers in comparison with the USA. This is because in more unequal societies, the rate of return to human capital for high-skilled workers can be very high indeed. As such, high-skilled workers have an incentive to migrate to, or to remain in, more unequal societies, where their skills are rewarded relatively more highly, while low-skilled workers have an incentive to migrate away from more unequal societies to more egalitarian societies (Borjas 2008). Figures A.6.3.1–A.6.3.4 are all constructed from the perspective of the origin region.

If we take two countries A and B, and country A is more equal than country B, the returns to human capital for migrants above the skill level S_K are relatively greater in country B than in country A, and for skills sets below S_K the returns to human capital are relatively higher in country A than in country B. If this is the case, then the migrants from country A (say for example Canada) to country B (say for example the USA) will tend to be primarily high-skill

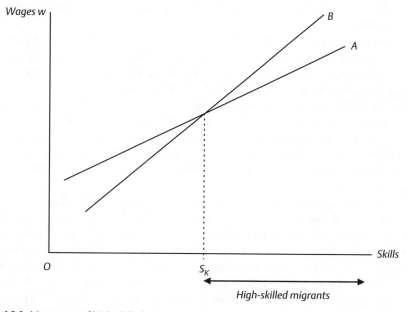

Figure A.6.3.1 Movement of high-skilled migrants

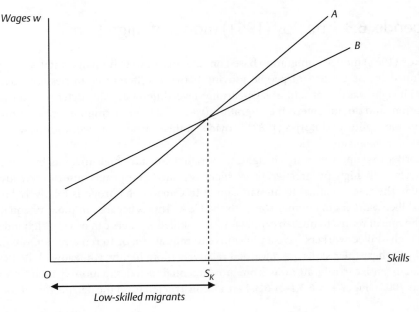

Figure A.6.3.2 Movement of low-skilled migrants

migrants with skills levels above S_K. This type of migration is described as 'positive' migration from country or region A to country or region B.

We can also consider a different situation, described in Figure A.6.3.2, in which the origin country A (for example Mexico) is a more unequal society than country B (for example the USA). In this case migration from A to B will comprise primarily 'negative' migration of low-skill workers.

We can now reframe the Roy (1951) model into an interregional migration model in order to see how wage-income changes affect the skills composition of interregional migrants.

If the wage income available in region B increases in general relative to region A, such that the relationship between wage incomes and skills there is now given by B', the minimum skills levels of 'positive' out-migrants from A to B actually falls from S_K to $S_{K'}$. More people move away from A to B and these increasing outflows are associated with a falling average skill composition of the migrant. In contrast, if the wage incomes in region B fall to B'', the minimum skills levels of 'positive' out-migrants from A to B rises from S_K to $S_{K''}$, such that falling outflows are associated with a rising average skill composition of out-migrants.

Similarly, if the wage income available in region A increases in general relative to region B, such that the relationship between wage incomes and skills is now given by A', the minimum skills levels of 'positive' out-migrants from A to B actually increases from S_K to $S_{K''}$. Fewer people move away from A to B and these decreasing outflows are associated with a rising average skill composition of the migrant. In contrast, if the wage incomes in region A fall to A'', the minimum skills levels of 'positive' out-migrants from A to B falls from S_K to $S_{K'}$, such that the increasing outflows are associated with a falling average skill composition of the out-migrants.

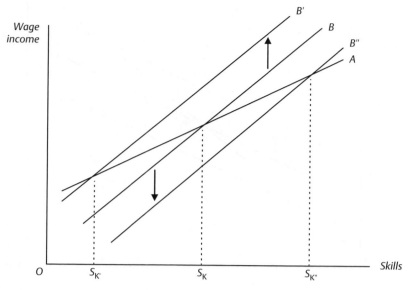

Figure A.6.3.3 The effect of changing incomes in the destination region

Similar arguments can be constructed for the case where the origin region *A* is more unequal than the potential destination region *B*, as depicted in Figure A.6.3.2. In this case rising incomes in *A* (or falling incomes in *B*) lead to lower outflows of 'negative migrants' and a falling average skills level of the out-migrants, while, in contrast, rising incomes in *B* (or falling incomes in *A*) increase the outflows of 'negative' migrants and raise the average skill sets of the migrants.

We can also apply this Roy–Borjas type of logic to the case of interregional migration with some additional assumptions, and, in particular, the assumption that clustering and agglomeration have either a levelling effect and a narrowing of inequality, or a segregation effect and in increase in inequality.

If we recall the issues we discussed in Chapter 2 on agglomeration, we see that core and dominant cities tend to be prosperous, buoyant, large, and diverse, and as such they also offer good environments for entrepreneurship, innovation, job searching, job changing, job matching, knowledge spillovers, and learning. One of the manifestations of these places is that many highly skilled people compete with one another in the same place, and this competition drives up living costs and lowers real wages. However, workers will still tend to remain in these locations for Harris–Todaro reasons, as these types of locations maximize the long-term employment possibilities and the expected wage for any given nominal wage paid. However, as well as a wage effect, this type of competitive clustering also often has a social levelling effect on many skilled people. While superstar workers do indeed emerge from these urban competitions in the form of prominent business leaders, the employment trajectories of many highly skilled individuals in large urban areas actually tend to settle down to something of an equilibrium in which their performance and outcomes are little different from most of their middle-class and suburban-living peers in the same place. It is

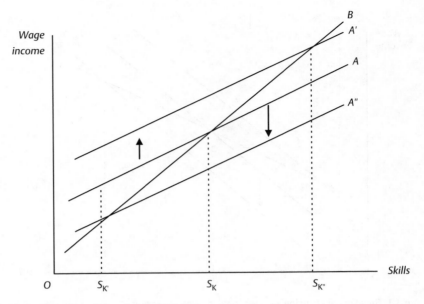

Figure A.6.3.4 The effect of changing incomes in the origin region

true that their employment status tends to exhibit a high nominal wage in comparison with the national average and also in comparison with the national average of their skills peers. Similarly, they also exhibit a high overall expected wage by national standards due to the low likelihood of facing long-term unemployment. In addition, in the USA these areas are also associated with higher real wages as well as higher nominal wages (Storper and Kemeny 2012). In contrast, however, the high degree of local skills competition implies that many such urban residents exhibit little or no wage premium in comparison with a large proportion of the local population, and in particular those living in the same neighbourhoods, while also exhibiting low wages in comparison with the urban elites.

In contrast, for the small number of highly skilled individuals who do find gainful and stable employment in smaller towns and cities, these people exhibit very high local standing in terms of both real wages and social status. Such people are often found in occupations such as law, dentistry, banking, medicine, and education, as well as in business and governmental activities. These people tend to exhibit lower nominal wages by the national standards of their skills peers but high real wages due to the relatively low local living costs. At the same time members of local elites often exhibit very high real wages in comparison with the local population in general, and this is due to the relatively high local monopoly power afforded by operating in a small and specialized environment which limits the number of potential competitors.

Local social status and influence are both likely to be part of the overall utility associated with work, and local social status and influence are also likely to be correlated with local real wages. If cities do indeed play a social levelling role as described above, this implies that high-skilled workers from an outlying non-core region *A* will not wish to move to the core city-region *B*, because their overall real income and real social status will fall with such a movement. This is one possible reason, in addition to local attachment value and sense of place, why widespread migration of high-skilled workers will often not take place from rural to urban areas, from peripheral to core areas, from small towns to large cities: these types of migration imply that a 'someone' with a high local status in a small place becomes an anonymous 'no one' in a large place. In marked contrast, a low-skill 'no one' in a small place has a greater chance of becoming 'someone' in an anonymous place, or at the very least remaining an anonymous 'no one' in a large place, but with a higher real wage.

These types of 'melting-pot' urban social dynamics which operate in large cities reflect some of the insights of a range of commentators including Jane Jacobs (1961) and Peter Hall (1998), among others, and offer the social reasons why many low-skilled people move to cities to escape the social and economic progression limitations they face due to the monopoly or monopsony power of local elites. They also underpin many of the explanations as to why people moved from Europe to North America and Australasia in the nineteenth century. However, the lack of social dynamism and the existence of many entrenched social and economic monopoly positions also explain why many high-skilled individuals embedded in locally elite positions do *not* move to more prosperous locations. The key to these insights is derived from the social capital arguments outlined in Chapter 7.

On the other hand, if core cities are characterized by increasing segregation and inequality above the levels evident in non-core regions and rural areas, this itself may deter the migration of lower-skilled groups from outer areas to core areas while increasing the mobility of high-skilled groups to the core cities.

In general, these arguments tend not to apply to new university graduates who are highly mobile precisely because they are not yet sufficiently established in their careers or community social hierarchies, and move in order to establish their careers. However, these arguments do apply very much more to workers who are well established in their careers and also in a particular community.

If increasing inequality is also associated with increasing crime, then the picture becomes even more complex, with crime increasing the degrees of local residential segregation along the lines discussed in Chapter 4, thereby reducing immigration of lower skills groups.

Furthermore, these arguments also have a cyclical effect. If core regions expand first through the business cycle with peripheral regions responding with a time-lag, as is often observed, this is reflected in a shift from B to B' in Figure A.6.3.2 or a shift from A to A'' in Figure A.6.3.3. Increasing core–periphery migration is associated with falling skills levels of migrants. However, as the positive effects of the business cycle continue to expand and spread, and peripheral regions begin to catch up, this is reflected in a shift from B to B'' in Figure A.6.3.2 or a shift from A to A' in Figure A.6.3.3. Falling core–periphery migration is associated with increasing skills levels of migrants.

However, irrespective of the stage of the business cycle, what we observe is that the most skilled people tend *not* to migrate once they are established in their jobs and communities.

7 Regional growth, factor allocation, and balance of payments

7.1 Introduction

The object of this chapter is to discuss the nature of regional growth and to provide an analysis of the various potential mechanisms by which regional growth takes place. Economic growth is a complex process, and as with labour markets and multipliers, the analysis of this issue at the regional level is somewhat different from that at the national level. Various hints as to the possible causes and consequences of regional growth have been provided in Chapters 1–6. In Chapter 1 we see that growth may take place via the location behaviour of firms, as the immigration of firms into a region increases the host region's stock of capital and employment. In Chapter 2 we see that such industrial location and relocation behaviour may also contribute to the development of localized agglomeration economies. In situations where these agglomeration economies arise, growth becomes possible at particular locations. In other words, growth is location specific. This may have implications for the size distribution of urban centres, and as we see from Chapter 3, the extent of the localized growth will also affect local land and real-estate prices. In Chapter 4 it was argued that the specifically local impacts of localized growth also depend on the sectoral origin of the growth, and the strength of the linkages between each of the local industrial sectors. Taken together, these conclusions suggest that the various regional impacts of growth will depend on both the sectoral and the spatial industrial structure of the economy.

On the other hand, we may initially perceive that the specifically local effects are relatively unimportant, in that the national or international economy as a whole will benefit from such localized growth. This is because any localized efficiency benefits will be spread via private sector trading relationships and also public sector redistributive fiscal mechanisms to the rest of the economy. However, the effects of localized growth on individual regions may be quite diverse, depending on the time required for any localized growth effects to be transmitted to the rest of the spatial economy. As we see in Chapter 5, differences in migration propensities between individuals with differing human-capital assets may militate against an even and rapid dissemination of growth benefits to all regions via labour market adjustment mechanisms. Moreover, the efficiency of labour migration as an equilibrating mechanism itself may depend on the strength of the national economy. Similarly, in periods of recession, the negative environmental effects of dereliction associated with the durability of fixed capital in declining regions may militate against an even and rapid dissemination of growth benefits to all regions via capital adjustment mechanisms. Therefore, as well as interregional differences in sectoral and spatial industrial structures, the spatial dissemination of the benefits of localized growth may depend on the extent to which the aggregate economy as a whole is buoyant.

In order to discuss the various issues associated with regional growth we will adopt two broad analytical perspectives. The first perspective, which is broadly neoclassical in nature, focuses on the questions relating to the spatial allocation of production factors, and the interrelationships which exist between factor allocation and technological change. This is the most common approach adopted in analyses of regional growth. The second approach, which is broadly Keynesian in nature, focuses on questions relating to interregional income flows, and discusses regional growth behaviour in terms of a balance of payments frame-work. Conceptually, these two frameworks are fundamentally different from each other, with the result that they produce somewhat different conclusions as to the nature, causes, and consequences of regional growth. Each approach can throw some light on different particular aspects of the nature of the regional growth process. However, there is also a variety of situations in which the two approaches can be made broadly consistent with each other, thereby providing a wide-ranging perspective on the nature of the regional growth process. We will begin by discussing the neoclassical approach to regional growth, factor allocation, and technological change, and in the subsequent sections we will contrast these arguments with the Keynesian approach.

7.2 Neoclassical regional growth

The neoclassical approach to macroeconomic growth has developed on the basis of the original insights of Solow (1956) and Swan (1956). These arguments have subsequently been applied to the case of regions, and the neoclassical approach to regional growth has two major components. The first component concerns the question of the regional alloca-tion and migration of production factors. The analysis of this issue is based on two analytical frameworks known as the 'one-sector' and 'two-sector' models of factor allocation, respec-tively. The second component concerns the question of the nature of the relationship between production factors and technological change, and this is generally analysed within a production function framework. The neoclassical growth models assume that the econ-omy is competitive, in the sense that factors are paid according to their marginal products, and also that factors are quickly able to be reallocated so as to be employed in their most productive use. In sections 7.2.1 to 7.2.3 we will initially discuss and compare the two mod-els relating to the regional allocation of factors, and then we will use the general conclusions of these models to motivate our production function approach.

7.2.1 The one-sector model of regional factor allocation and migration

The neoclassical one-sector model of regional factor allocation and migration is based on the law of variable factor proportions. In other words, the marginal productive properties of factors are perceived to depend on the relative quantities of each of the factors employed.

The basic principle underlying this comes from the law of diminishing productivity, which states that, holding one factor constant, the marginal product of the variable factor falls as a greater quantity of the variable factor is employed. The assumption here is that the variable factor is combined with the fixed factor in the production process, and it is the application of the variable factor to the fixed factor which gives rise to the diminishing marginal productivity of the variable factor. We will initially discuss the case where all factors are freely mobile between regions, and then compare this with the situation where there is a certain amount of interregional factor immobility.

In the case of capital and labour, for a fixed capital stock, the higher the level of labour employment, the lower will be the marginal product of labour. In other words, as the quantity of labour increases relative to the quantity of capital employed, the lower will be the marginal product of labour. Similarly, for a fixed quantity of labour, the higher the level of capital employed, the lower will be the marginal product of capital. In other words, as the quantity of capital increases relative to the quantity of labour employed, the lower will be the marginal product of capital. As we see, in the case of two factors, the law of diminishing marginal productivity holds for either factor, as long as the other factor is held constant. Moreover, we can extend the argument to more than two factors. For example, if we hold a third factor constant, such as land, and add successive quantities of both capital and labour, the marginal products of both capital and labour will fall.

For reasons of analytical simplicity, however, in the following sections we will assume that all production activities are the result of the combination of two factors. These two factors are a composite factor capital, denoted as K, which contains all non-labour inputs, and all labour inputs, denoted as factor L. We assume that in general, capital K and labour L are complementary inputs, and the relative quantities of capital and labour employed can be defined in terms of a capital–labour ratio K/L. Using this notation, the arguments above concerning the application of the law of diminishing marginal productivity to the complementary factor inputs can be specified in very general terms. If the quantity of capital is high relative to the quantity of labour employed, in other words the K/L ratio is high, the marginal product of capital will be low and the marginal product of labour will be high. Conversely, if the quantity of capital is low relative to the quantity of labour employed, in other words the K/L ratio is low, the marginal product of capital will be high and the marginal product of labour will be low.

These arguments can now be translated into a regional context. We can imagine the case of a country comprising two regions A and B, in which the capital–labour ratio in region A is higher than that in region B, such that

$$\frac{K_A}{L_A} > \frac{K_B}{L_B} \tag{7.1}$$

where:

K_A quantity of capital employed in region A

L_A quantity of labour employed in region A

K_B quantity of capital employed in region B

L_B quantity of labour employed in region B

In a situation such as that described by equation (7.1), the marginal product of capital in region A will be lower than the marginal product of capital in region B. Meanwhile, the marginal product of labour in region A will be higher than the marginal product of labour in region B. In other words, assuming that production factors are paid according to their marginal productivities, marginal profits will be higher in region B while wages will be higher in region A. If factors are mobile, the different regional capital–labour ratios will encourage labour to migrate from region B to region A, and capital to migrate from region A to region B. The difference in the regional capital–labour ratios therefore encourages the two factors to migrate in opposite directions, in order to earn higher factor rewards. The two factors will continue to migrate in opposite directions as long as there is still a difference in the regional capital–labour ratios. This process of interregional factor migration will therefore only cease when the capital–labour ratios in both regions are the same, such that

$$\frac{K_A}{L_A} = \frac{K_B}{L_B} \tag{7.2}$$

In this interregional equilibrium situation, wages are the same in both regions and marginal profits are the same in both regions. The interregional adjustment mechanism, in which factors migrate in opposite directions until capital–labour ratios are equalized across regions, is known as the 'one-sector' neoclassical model of factor allocation and migration.

The conclusions of the one-sector model can be discussed from the perspective of aggregate national efficiency and welfare. In order to do this we can employ an Edgeworth–Bowley box in which the factor employment levels and output of both regions are represented.

The Edgeworth–Bowley box in Figure 7.1 represents the two regions A and B. The output of region A is represented by the isoquants which originate at A, and higher levels of output are represented by isoquants which are further to the right. Similarly, the output of region B is represented by the isoquants which originate at B, and higher levels of output are represented by isoquants which are further to the left. The total level of capital in the economy is K_N, and is represented by the vertical height of the Edgeworth–Bowley box. Assuming that all factors are employed, K_N comprises the sum of the capital employed in both regions. In other words, $K_N = (K_A + K_B)$. Meanwhile, the total level of labour in the economy is L_N, and is represented by the horizontal length of the Edgeworth–Bowley box. Assuming that all factors are employed, L_N comprises the sum of the labour employed in both regions. In other words, $L_N = (L_A + L_B)$.

If the regional factor allocation is initially at point C, the quantity of capital employed in region A is given by K_{AC}, and the quantity of labour employed in region A is given by L_{AC}. Similarly, at point C, the quantity of capital employed in region B is given by K_{BC}, and the quantity of labour employed in region A is given by L_{AC}. With the particular interregional factor allocation at C, the level of output of region A is given by the isoquant Q_{A2} and the level of output of region B is given by the isoquant Q_{B3}. As we see in Figure 7.1, the capital–labour ratio in region A is much higher than that in region B. Therefore, from the logic of the one-sector model, a reallocation of factors between the regions can effect a Pareto efficiency gain. The reason for this is that a factor reallocation between regions, in which capital moves from the high capital–labour ratio region (region A) to the low capital–labour ratio

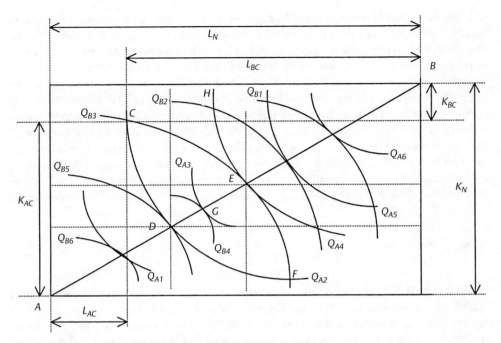

Figure 7.1 One-sector interregional Edgeworth–Bowley box

region (region B), will increase the marginal productivity of the mobile capital. Similarly, a factor reallocation between regions, in which labour moves from the low capital–labour ratio region (region B) to the high capital–labour ratio region (region A), will increase the marginal productivity of the mobile labour. This process of factor migration and reallocation, in which the marginal products of both mobile factors are increased, must therefore necessarily increase aggregate national output.

One-sector factor migration will continue until the capital–labour ratios are equal in both regions, as represented by equation (7.2) above. Once the capital–labour ratios in each region are the same, the process of factor reallocation and migration will cease, because there will be no interregional differences in factor rewards. In other words, when regional capital–labour ratios are equalized there will be no further potential Pareto efficiency gains associated with the increasing marginal productivities of migrant factors. In other words, all the possible Pareto efficient interregional factor allocations must exhibit the same capital–labour ratios. Within an Edgeworth–Bowley box framework, this argument implies that where all factors are mobile, the contract curve which links all the Pareto efficient interregional factor allocations must be a straight line, as in Figure 7.1.

For example, if factors which are initially allocated at C are reallocated to a point D, the total output of region A will remain the same at Q_{A2}, but the output of region B will have increased from Q_{B3} to Q_{B5}. At point D, the capital–labour ratios of both regions are equal. Alternatively, if the factors which are initially allocated at C are reallocated to a point E, the total output of region B will remain the same at Q_{B3}, but the output of region A will have increased from Q_{A2} to Q_{A4}. At point E, the capital–labour ratios of both regions are equal, and are also identical to the capital–labour ratios at D. Finally, if the factors which are initially allocated at C are reallocated to a point G, the total output of region B will increase from Q_{B3} to Q_{B4}, and the output of region A will increase from Q_{A2} to Q_{A3}. Each of these three possible interregional factor reallocations represents a Pareto efficiency gain. More generally, beginning at position C, the reallocation of factors between regions to any point on the boundary of, or within. the area defined by $CDEF$ represents a Pareto welfare gain with respect to the factor allocation at point C. However, only points on the straight-line contract curve within this area of potential Pareto efficiency gains, defined as DGE, represent Pareto efficient factor allocations. The line DGE represents the 'core' of the economy, given the initial allocation at C.

The same logic regarding the Pareto gains associated with interregional factor reallocations can also be applied to any other inefficient initial factor allocation, such as points H and J in Figure 7.1. In each case, there will be an area of potential efficiency gains which itself must contain a 'core' of Pareto efficient factor allocations. The straight-line contract curve therefore represents all the possible Pareto efficient core allocations. If the interregional contract curve is a straight line, this also means that the regional expansion paths are both linear and identical. In other words, the regional production functions are identical. Assuming constant returns to scale, this implies that both regional production functions must be homogeneous of degree one.

If the contract curve is a straight line, the interregional production possibility frontier must also be a straight line, as in Figure 7.2 (Borts and Stein 1964). Pareto efficient points such as D and E in Figure 7.1 will be on the production possibility frontier, as shown in Figure 7.2, whereas inefficient points such as C in Figure 7.1 will be inside the production possibility frontier.

The slope of the production possibility curve is known as the marginal rate of transformation, and is given by the ratio of the marginal costs of production. In the case of Figure 7.2 we can write this as $MRT_{AB}, = (MC_A/MC_B)$, where MRT_{AB} represents the marginal rate

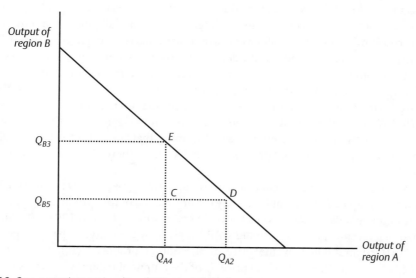

Figure 7.2 One-sector interregional production possibility frontier

of transformation of the output of region A for region B, and MC_A and MC_B represent the marginal costs of output expansion in regions A and B. The fact that the interregional production possibility curve in the one-sector model is a straight line comes from the fact that the contract curve is a straight line, whereby reallocations of factors between regions have exactly equal and opposite impacts on the outputs of the regions. This also implies that, from the perspective of production, the output of each region can therefore be regarded as a perfect substitute for the output of the other region. In other words, when output is expanded in one region and contracted in another region due to the transfer of both factors between the two regions (as represented by a movement along the contract curve), the marginal rate of increase in output of the expanding region will be exactly equal to the marginal rate of output reduction of the contracting region. Therefore, in the absence of output price changes, for a given national capital and labour stock, the total national output of the economy will remain constant irrespective of the factor allocation position on the contract curve. As such, in the situation where both factors are completely mobile, as long as we are on the straight-line contract curve with identical regional capital–labour ratios, the total output value of the economy will be independent of the regional distribution of activities.

7.2.2 The two-sector model of regional factor allocation and migration

In the one-sector model of regional factor allocation, factors flow in the opposite direction in order to earn their highest rewards. However, there are certain situations in which factors can flow in the same direction. This is possible where the regional production functions are somewhat different from each other, and such a case is analysed within the framework of a 'two-sector' model.

We can modify the one-sector example above to allow for the case of two regions A and B, producing different outputs with different production functions. More particularly, we can assume that region A's output production tends to be relatively capital intensive and regions B's output is relatively labour intensive. In this situation the interregional Edgeworth–Bowley box will exhibit a concave contract curve, as depicted in Figure 7.3.

In this case, we can imagine that the demand for the output of region A increases, due to a change in domestic consumer tastes or an increase in external export demand in favour of the output of region A, without any equivalent change in favour of the output of region B. As we see in Figure 7.4a, this increased demand pushes up the price of region A's goods from P_{A1} to P_{A2}, and the output of region A increases from Q_{1A} to Q_{2A} as the existing stocks of factors are employed more intensively. Assuming that the output price of region B's output is unchanged, the output price of region A's output therefore rises relative to that of region B.

As we know, the marginal revenue product of capital (MP_K) is given by the marginal physical product of capital (MPP_K) multiplied by the price of the output produced (P_o), assuming that the output goods market is competitive. In other words, $MP_K = (MPP_K \times P_o)$. Similarly, the marginal revenue product of labour (MP_L) is given by the marginal physical product of labour (MPP_L) multiplied by the price of the output produced (P_o). In other words, $MP_L = (MPP_L \times P_o)$. Therefore, if the price P_A of the output of region A increases relative to the price P_B of the output of region B, this implies that the marginal product of capital

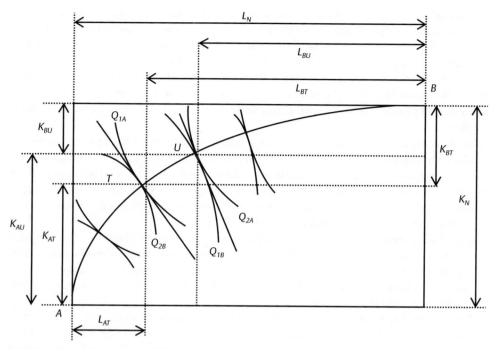

Figure 7.3 Two-sector interregional Edgeworth–Bowley box

employed in region A is now higher than the marginal product of capital employed in region B. By the same argument, if the price of the output of region A increases relative to region B, this also implies that the marginal revenue product of labour employed in region A is now higher than the marginal revenue product of labour employed in region B. In notation:

$$MP_K^A > MP_K^B \text{ and } MP_L^A > MP_L^B$$

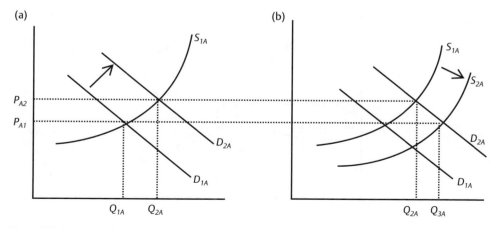

Figure 7.4 Output market adjustment for expanding region

This would suggest that both capital and labour will migrate from region B to region A in order to earn the higher factor rewards in region A. The effect of this factor migration, in which both factors move in the same direction, is to move the supply curve of region A to the right from S_{1A} to S_{2A}, as in Figure 7.4b. The increased supply consequently leads to a further increase in the output of region A from Q_{2A} to Q_{3A}. However, this increased output supply also leads to a fall in the price P_A of the output of region A from P_{A2} to P_{A1}. This fall in the output price will now reduce the marginal revenue product of both capital and labour employed in region A.

At the same time, as the output of region B falls from Q_{1B} to Q_{2B}, the price of the output produced by region B will have risen due to the contraction in the supply of the goods produced by region B, associated with the out-migration of both factors from region B. In Figure 7.5, this is represented by the backwards shift of region B's supply curve for output goods. This rise in the output price in region B will increase the marginal revenue product of both the capital and labour still employed in region B.

Therefore, as region A's output prices fall and region B's output prices rise, the marginal products of capital in regions A and B converge. Similarly, the marginal products of labour in regions A and B converge. The process of factor migration, in which both factors move in the same direction, will continue until the marginal products of both factors are equalized across the two regions.

The actual point at which the two-sector migration will cease cannot be determined without additional information concerning the regional price elasticities of demand and supply. However, assuming that the initial interregional factor allocation is Pareto efficient, such as at point T in Figure 7.3, the long-run effect of the 'two-sector' unidirectional factor migration can be depicted as a shift from point T to point U. Given that the contract curve is concave, the relative price of capital with respect to labour in both regions will be lower at point U than at point T. In Figure 7.3 we can see this change in relative factor prices by observing the change in slope of the marginal rate of substitution, which is perpendicular to the contract curve. However, for both capital and labour, the marginal factor products and factor rewards will be equalized across both regions.

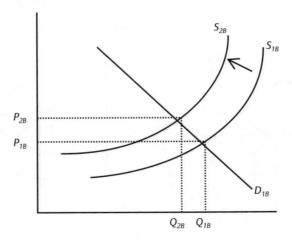

Figure 7.5 Output market adjustment for contracting region

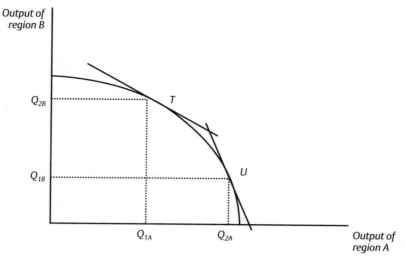

Figure 7.6 Two-sector interregional production possibility frontier

In the two-sector model of interregional factor allocation, the two regions are assumed to produce different products with different production functions. The production of one region, region A, is capital intensive and the production of the other region, region B, is labour intensive. This implies that the marginal rate of transformation of production between the two regions is constantly changing according to the level of output in each region. This is represented in Figure 7.6 by a concave production possibility frontier, in which a movement along the interregional contract curve from T to U is represented by a movement down the production possibility frontier.

The fact that the contract curve in the two-sector model is curved implies that the real-location of factors from one region to another changes the relative rates at which the output of one region can be expanded while the output of the other region can be contracted, due to the factor reallocations. In other words, the marginal rate of transformation between the regions is always changing, and this is why the production possibility frontier is also convex to origin, as discussed in any intermediate microeconomics textbook.

7.2.3 The relationship between the one-sector and the two-sector regional models

The slope of the production possibility frontier represents the marginal rate of transformation between the two outputs, and is given by the ratio of the marginal costs of production of the two goods at that particular output mix. In the one-sector interregional model, as we see in Figure 7.2, the interregional production possibility frontier is a straight line. This implies that the ratio of the marginal costs of production between the two regions is both constant and independent of the level of output in each region. In effect, the two regions exhibit production functions which are identical to each other in terms of their factor proportions. However, this is quite different from the case of the two-sector model, where the regional production functions are fundamentally different from each other in terms of their factor proportions. This is reflected by the fact that the ratio of the marginal costs of production between the two regions is constantly changing and depends on the level of output in each region. The shape of both the contract curve and the production possibility frontier in the two-sector model is familiar in simple general equilibrium frameworks and models of international trade based on comparative advantage. On the other hand, the linear shape of both the contract curve and the production possibility frontier in the one-sector model is somewhat different from that in other models. This leaves us with the problem of determining which of these two model approaches better captures the fundamental nature of the regional factor allocation process.

In order to answer the question whether the one-sector model or the two-sector model approach better captures the fundamental nature of the regional factor allocation process, there are several points to be made. The first point is that different regions within a single country are generally assumed to be much more open to each other than different countries are to each other. This is because regional economies generally function within a common currency regime, a common legal system, a common language system, a common political and institutional system, and a common cultural framework. The common framework within which regions trade with each other, relative to national differences in trading environments, therefore implies that regions are generally much more open to each other than countries are to each other. Although there are certain location-specific activities which cannot be replicated in all regions, such as land-based activities within the primary industries of mining and extraction, and also some water-borne activities relating to ports and river freighting, the vast majority of production activities can be largely replicated in any region of a country. This is because, in a broadly competitive market environment, both capital and labour are much more mobile across regions within countries than between countries. For example, interregional labour mobility within the USA is much greater than international labour mobility between the countries of the European Union. At the same time, interregional labour mobility within European Union countries is greater than the labour mobility between European Union countries. Following the arguments of Chapters 1–6, we can argue that this relatively greater openness extends not only to mutual regional trading relationships, but also to factor mobility between regions.

As we have seen, the actual regional spatial distribution of activities will depend on the spatial patterns of the market and supply areas. However, even allowing for these variations, there are significantly fewer reasons why regional production functions should be different from each other, in comparison with the production functions of different countries, at least when defined in terms of their factor proportions. Regions generally exhibit maximum factor mobility, relative to countries, and on this argument, interregional economic systems will tend to approximate more closely the one-sector model than the two-sector model. In terms of our two region examples above, the interregional allocation of factors is generally better represented by Figures 7.1 and 7.2 rather than Figures 7.3 and 7.6, except where regional output is dominated by location-specific land-based primary industries.

In order to illustrate the logic of this argument we can imagine a hypothetical case of two separate countries A and B, which subsequently merge into a single country of two regions. In Figure 7.7, in the initial time period during which the countries are separate, the respective production relationships are represented by point V. At this factor allocation, country

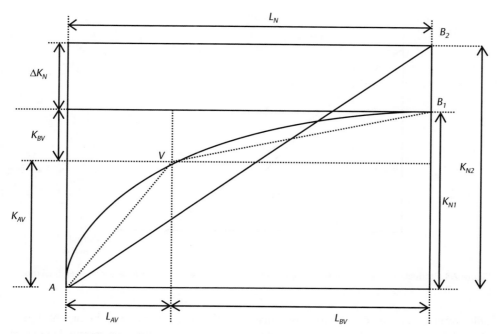

Figure 7.7 Edgeworth–Bowley box adjustment from a two-sector to a one-sector interregional model

A exhibits a capital-intensive production function which employs K_{AV} units of capital and L_{AV} units of labour, while country B exhibits a labour-intensive production function employing K_{BV} units of capital and L_{BV} units of labour. The two countries produce different goods and then trade according to Ricardian principles of comparative advantage.

In the subsequent time period, the two countries merge into a single country of two regions A and B. This encourages factors to flow between both regions in order to effect an efficient interregional factor allocation. If the production functions of the two regions continue to be quite different, due to location-specific land-based characteristics, the new interregional contract curve will be represented by the two-sector concave contract curve AB_1. On the other hand, if the vast majority of factors are mobile, the factor flows will be primarily of a one-sector nature, in that capital will flow from region A to region B, and labour will migrate from region B to region A. These one-sector flows will mean that the interregional contract curve will tend to become less concave, the long-run result of which is for the contract curve to become linear. In Figure 7.7 this is represented by the contract curve AB_2. Most analyses of interregional economic integration assume that, in the long run, the one-sector model of interregional factor flows will be the primary mode of regional factor reallocation, and will dominate any two-sector adjustments.

At the same time as encouraging the reallocation of existing factors, the process of regional economic integration is also assumed to encourage additional mutual trading links between the regions. Assuming the total population of the two areas remains more or less constant, this interregional trade creation effect will generate additional national capital stocks. In our Edgeworth–Bowley box analysis we can represent this capital expansion

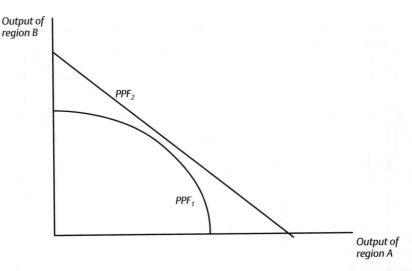

Figure 7.8 Production possibility frontier adjustment from a two-sector to a one-sector interregional model

effect by an extension to the vertical dimensions of the box. The extent of the capital expansion which occurs with the process of regional economic integration is represented in Figure 7.7 by $\Delta K_N = (K_{N2} - K_{N1})$, and the level of capital growth associated with this trade creation effect is given by $(\Delta K_N / K_{N1})$.

The transition process associated with the regional economic integration therefore has two main features. The first feature is the interregional reallocation of factors according to the principles of the one-sector model, which leads to a general flattening of the contract curve, such that the capital–labour ratios tend towards being equalized across both regions. The second feature, concomitant with the factor reallocation, is an expansion in the capital stock of the area of economic integration. The combination of these two integration effects is assumed to generate regional economic growth. In Figure 7.7 the change in the contract curve associated with the combination of these effects is represented by the transition in the contract curve from AB_1 to AB_2. The effect of these changes in the contract curve can also be represented by changes in both the shape and the position of the interregional production possibility frontier. As we see in Figure 7.8, the process of regional economic integration encourages the production possibility frontier both to shift outwards from its initial position PPF_1, and to become flatter. The long-run result of this process is that the interregional production possibility frontier will become linear, as represented by PPF_2 in Figure 7.8. Even in the absence of a growth in the labour stock, regional growth therefore comes from two different sources. These two sources are the interregional reallocation of existing factor stocks, and the increase in capital stocks associated with any trade creation effect. The long-run outcome of this one-sector regional integration process is a tendency towards regions with similar production functions and similar capital–labour ratios, in which regional rates of return to capital will converge, as will regional wage rates. As such, comparative advantage between regions tends to disappear as an explanation for regional production behaviour, and is superseded by explanations based on factor mobility.

The process of one-sector regional economic integration and factor reallocation described here forms the basis of many assumptions about economic growth in areas currently undergoing economic integration. An example of such an area is the European Union. In the case of the Europe Union, the separate national economies have become progressively more integrated over the last half-century. This integration process has involved the progressive reduction of border tariffs and the removal of restrictions to trade and factor migration. This integration process was given an additional spur at the beginning of the 1990s, with the introduction of a common EU passport system, which allows for the free migration of labour between all EU nations for reasons of employment. Such institutional arrangements ought to allow for a one-sector reallocation of factors across the EU, as well as some potential regional trade and capital creation effects. If this one-sector argument is indeed correct, over time we should observe a tendency towards regional convergence within the EU. Evidence supporting this one-sector argument was first provided by Barro and Sala-i-Martin (1992, 1995). They suggested that the level of dispersion across the EU regions of real income per head had fallen over time, a process which they termed 'σ convergence'. Barro and Sala-i-Martin also found evidence to suggest that there is a negative relationship between the rate of growth in income per head and the initial level of income per head, a process which they term 'β convergence'. Although there has been much debate as to the appropriateness of the data employed by Barro and Sala-i-Martin and the interpretation of their results (Cheshire and Carbonaro 1995, 1996; Fingleton and McCombie 1998; Martin and Sunley 1998; Button and Pentecost 1999; Durlauf and Quah 1999), these tests of σ and β convergence are primarily motivated by the theoretical conclusions of the one-sector model of interregional factor allocation and growth.

7.3 Regional growth accounting and production function analysis

The above sections lead to the general neoclassical conclusion that regional integration processes will lead to a one-sector reallocation of factors across regions. The long-run implications of this process will be that all regional production functions will tend to converge, such that regional capital–labour ratios will converge across regions, as will regional capital returns and regional wages, and regional expansion paths will also all be linear. Output growth will increase as factors are allocated more efficiently, and this process itself may generate additional growth via trade creation effects. Analytically these conclusions are useful because, at least in principle, they allow us to model the sources of regional growth within a rather straightforward production function framework. To do this we can employ a Cobb–Douglas production function, which is defined as

$$Q_t = AK^\alpha L^\beta \qquad\qquad (7.3)$$

where:

Q_t regional output at time t

t time

A constant

K regional capital stock

L regional labour stock

α share of capital in the regional economy

β share of capital in the regional economy

The Cobb–Douglas production function has two useful properties. The first property is that the factor shares are represented by the relative contributions of profits and wages to the total factor payments in the economy. In the Cobb–Douglas production function these shares are represented by α and β, respectively. If the factor shares are approximately constant, this also implies that the capital–labour ratios are approximately constant. The second property of the Cobb–Douglas production function is that if $\alpha + \beta = 1$, production exhibits constant returns to scale, in terms of the relationship between the total output produced and the total quantities of input factors employed. A given quantity of capital and labour will produce a given quantity of output, the value of which is defined as a constant multiple A of the total value of the inputs. Therefore doubling the quantity of both factor inputs employed will simply double the total level of output produced, *ceteris paribus*. The relationship between the level of output and the level of factor inputs is therefore independent of the total quantity of inputs employed or outputs produced. If this is so, it implies that the sum of the indices α plus β must equal one. In other words, $\beta = (1 - \alpha)$. Our Cobb–Douglas model (7.3) must therefore be modified accordingly.

A second modification required to equation (7.3) concerns the question of time. Over time, the relationship between total output and inputs is not static, in the sense that new production techniques and technologies become available which increase the efficiency of the production process. The adoption and implementation of these new production techniques and technologies is known as 'innovation', and this process of innovation means that over time the level of output increases for any given stock of factor inputs. For our purposes, we will define this process of applying new techniques and technologies under the general heading of 'technology'. As such, technology represents the sets of production, organization, information, and communications blueprints which are available to all firms, and which mediate the relationship between the input factors employed and the outputs produced. We denote the level of technology by the technological index ϕ. Assuming that the level of technology increases over time, we can incorporate a simple technological trajectory $e^{\phi t}$ into the Cobb–Douglas function which allows for increases in technology over time t.

Our modified Cobb–Douglas function, which incorporates both constant returns to scale and technological change over time, now has the form

$$Q_t = Ae^{\phi t}K^{\alpha}L^{1-\alpha} \tag{7.4}$$

The one-sector interregional factor allocation model discussed in the previous sections implies that all regions will converge towards the same production function with the same constant capital–labour ratios. In the Cobb–Douglas function (7.4) the constant capital–labour ratio is given by $(\alpha/1 - \alpha)$. Therefore, assuming that aggregate regional production across markets and industries can be regarded as perfectly competitive, the process of interregional factor reallocation should lead to all regions exhibiting the same Cobb–Douglas production function. In other words, if we can model the production function of one region, we can model the production function of all regions within the same economic system.

With this production function methodology we are now able to consider how the growth of regional output is related to changes in the various inputs to the production process. In order to convert our regional production function into a model of regional growth we can convert equation (7.4) into natural logarithms and then differentiate with respect to time. The details of this are given in Appendix 7.1. By these steps we can convert equation (7.4) into a regional growth accounting expression:

$$\dot{Q}_t = \phi + \alpha\dot{K}_t + (1 - \alpha)\dot{L}_t \qquad (7.5)$$

where $\dot{Q}_t$, $\dot{K}_t$, $\dot{L}_t$, represent the rates of growth of output, capital, and labour at time t, respectively.

This growth accounting expression (7.5) states that the rate of growth of regional output at time t is the sum of the rates of growth of the input factors (capital and labour), weighted according to their relative contributions to the economy, plus the level of technology ϕ. In these growth accounting terms, the level of technology represents the contributions to regional growth which cannot be accounted for simply by changes in the optimally combined stocks of regional capital and labour. As such, the term ϕ is sometimes referred to as the 'Solow residual' or the 'growth of total factor productivity'. As we see in Appendix 7.1, the growth accounting methodology of equation (7.5) can be shown to predict that, in general, wage growth depends on the growth in the capital–labour ratio and also the level of technology. Moreover, in a long-run steady-state situation in which profit rates are constant, wage growth depends simply on the level of technology.

One of the features that we often observe, however, is that the level of technology is not ubiqituous, nor does it necessarily spread quickly or evenly. As we see in Box 7.1, technology diffusion is often seen to exhibit an 'S-shape' over time. Shortly, we will also apply these ideas to geography, where similar results are often observed.

The major movement beyond the traditional growth accounting-type framework was provided by the 'endogenous growth theory' models, initially associated with the work of Romer (1986, 1987a) and later by Lucas (1988), and involves accounting for growth within an orthodox neoclassical growth accounting framework, while at the same time dispensing with the need for an exogenous technology residual (McCombie and Thirlwall 1994). The approach assumes that increasing specialization increases output, and as such, output is defined as a function of the number of units of specialized capital goods, rather than simply as an aggregate capital stock. Under certain assumptions concerning monopolistic competition and the role of product variety, in a manner similar to NEG models of Chapter 3, Romer shows that the production function can be expressed as

$$Q_t = AL^\beta K \qquad (7.6)$$

BOX 7.1 Regional technology diffusion and endogenous growth

From the point of view of growth accounting described by equation (7.5), we know that neoclassical regional growth depends on the changes in the regional factor stocks and the level of regional technology. Assuming that factors are mobile, there can be no systematic long-run differences in the growth rates of factors across regions, so any observed growth differences associated with differences in regional factor stocks can only be short- or medium-term adjustments to a Pareto-efficient factor allocation. On the other hand, from our growth accounting approach we can also suggest that different regions may differ in terms of their growth performance according to systematic differences in the level of regional technology ϕ. However, in order to understand how this might come about, it is necessary for us to consider exactly what we mean by 'technology', and to determine how technological differences may be related to geography.

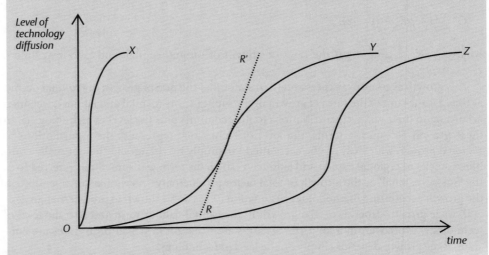

Figure 7.9 Technology diffusion over time

We have defined technology as the complete set of production, organization, information, and communications blueprints which are available to all firms, and which mediate the relationship between the input factors employed and the outputs produced. However, there is a general consensus that, in reality, the application of new technology across all firms, industries, and regions is not a process which takes place instantaneously, as is assumed by the model of perfect competition. In fact, the cumulative diffusion of technology over time tends to exhibit an 'S-shaped' form (Gomulka 1971; Dosi 1988), where technology diffusion refers to the time taken for a particular invention or innovation to be adopted across all firms, sectors, or regions. This cumulative 'S-shaped' form is represented in Figure 7.9 by the curve OY. As we see, the rate of technological diffusion is initially very low, although it is gradually increasing. After a while, the rate of technology diffusion reaches its maximum, represented by the slope RR' in Figure 7.9, after which it begins to slow. Eventually, the technology will have been spread throughout all firms, sectors, and regions, such that the rate of additional technology diffusion approaches zero.

The general assumptions of the neoclassical one-sector theoretical model are that in an environment of perfectly competitive markets and factor mobility, the level of technology will be dispersed through all sectors and all regions in the economy instantaneously. However, in reality,

---

BOX 7.1 Continued

if we assume that markets are broadly competitive, the one-sector model implies that technologal diffusion takes place at the maximum possible rate, such that complete technological diffusion is reached almost immediately. In terms of Figure 7.9 this implies that the technology diffusion process is represented by the curve *OX*. This assumption itself implies that there will be no systematic long-run differences in the level of regional technology, and that the growth benefits associated with new technology will be maximized in all regions. On the other hand, these neoclassical conclusions may initially appear to contradict some of the agglomeration conclusions of Chapter 2, which suggested that growth may be localized for long periods because certain technological advantages tend to remain in particular locations. Similarly, Chapter 6 suggested that growth possibilities may vary geographically according to persistent differences in the spatial distribution of human capital. In terms of Figure 7.9 these arguments would imply that technology diffusion in reality tends to exhibit a trajectory best represented by the curve *OZ*, such that systematic differences in regional technology, and consequently regional growth, would appear to be possible. Therefore the arguments of both Chapters 2 and 6 may appear to be somewhat at odds with the long-run conclusions of the one-sector neoclassical model. There have been many recent analytical developments in production function analysis which attempt to reconcile localized growth with neoclassical competitive market conditions. These various developments are generally grouped under the headings of 'new growth theory' or 'endogenous growth theory'.

---

and transforming equation (7.6) into a logarithmic form and differentiating with respect to time gives

$$\dot{Q}_t = \beta \dot{L}_t + \dot{K}_t \tag{7.7}$$

where $\beta = (1 - \alpha)$ as above. The argument here is that all growth is accounted for in terms of the growth of inputs, with they key issue being the level of specialized capital inputs and the associated benefits of labour specialization. As we have seen in Chapter 3, one of the arguments underlying the agglomeration model is that of increasing location-specific specialization. If such specialization is indeed place specific, then the endogenous growth model implies that the benefits of this growth will also tend to be localized.

Romer (1987b) discusses a second potential source of endogenous growth, which is the stock of knowledge. In order to account for this we can write a production function as

$$Q_t = f(K,L,E)g(N) \tag{7.8}$$

where E represents firm-specific knowledge, N represents generally available knowledge, and f and g are functional relationships. If we assume that N increases at the same rate as E, which itself increases at the same rate as K, and we also assume that F is a Cobb–Douglas functional relationship, total output can be written as

$$Q_t = f(K,L)g(K) = (L^{1-\alpha}K^\alpha)K^\psi \tag{7.9}$$

The increasing returns are external to the firm, and this ensures that a competitive equilibrium is preserved (McCombie and Thirlwall 1994). In growth rate terms equation (7.9) becomes

$$\dot{Q}_t = (1 - \alpha)\dot{L}_t + (\alpha + \psi)\dot{K}_t \tag{7.10}$$

If $(\alpha + \psi)$ is equal to one, growth will be constant. However, if $(\alpha + \psi)$ is greater than one, growth will be continuously positive and cumulative, and if $(\alpha + \psi)$ is less than one, growth will decline.

Both of these Romer models conclude that the portion of output growth which would be considered as a technology residual in the neoclassical model can be attributed entirely to capital acquisition. In the former case, this is because knowledge growth is assumed to increase directly in line with the level of specialized capital stock, whereas in the latter case it is because of the assumption that knowledge increases with the level of capital inputs.

Lucas (1988) also discusses knowledge inputs, but instead the focus of his model is on the level of human capital, rather than firm-specific capital. In his approach, we assume that workers spend a fraction of their time u acquiring human capital H. Following our discussion in Chapter 6 we assume that human capital increases the productivity of the individual person. However, Lucas assumes that this 'internal' effect H also has an 'external' effect J, which benefits all other workers. With these assumptions we can write our production function as

$$Q_t = (uHL)^{1-\alpha} K^\alpha J^\varphi \tag{7.11}$$

If we also assume that the external human-capital effect J is equal to the internal human-capital effect H, equation (7.11) can be rewritten as

$$Q_t = (uH^\theta L)^{1-\alpha} K^\alpha \tag{7.12}$$

where $\theta = (1 - \alpha + \gamma)/(1 - \alpha)$. In order to make growth endogenous, this model requires us to define the growth of human capital as

$$\frac{dH}{dt} = H^\rho v(1 - u) \tag{7.13}$$

where ρ and v are constants, with ρ being greater than or equal to one, such that there are no diminishing returns to the generation of human capital. If we take the simplest case where ρ is equal to one, the rate of growth of human capital defined by equation (7.13) is a constant λ. This allows us to rewrite equation (7.12) as

$$Q_t = (uL_q e^{\lambda t})^{1-\alpha} K^\alpha \tag{7.14}$$

where L_q represents the number of units of labour at a given level of efficiency and quality and is given by $L_q = H^\theta L$. As such, a given number of units of labour of increasing human capital can be regarded as equivalent to an increasing number of units of labour of a fixed efficiency and quality. In growth rate terms equation (7.14) becomes (McCombie and Thirlwall 1994)

$$\dot{Q}_t = (1 - \alpha)(\lambda + \dot{L}_t) + \alpha \dot{K}_t = (1 - \alpha)(\dot{L}_q)_t + \alpha \dot{K}_t \qquad (7.15)$$

This model concludes that the portion of output growth which would be considered as a technology residual in the neoclassical model can be attributed entirely to labour through human-capital acquisition.

These various models of endogenous growth provide different insights into the possible sources of cumulative growth. For our purposes, we can relate each of these potential sources of cumulative growth to spatial arguments (Nijkamp and Poot 1998). The Romer models suggest that endogenous growth can arise due to an increasing variety of specialized capital goods, or an increasing knowledge base associated with these capital goods and the associated externality effects of information spillovers. Meanwhile, the Lucas model suggests that endogenous growth can arise due to private investments in human capital, the benefits of which also spill over to the surrounding environment. However, identifying empirically whether or not localized growth takes place, and isolating the sources of such growth, is very difficult because, by definition, such effects are positive externalities. In order to circumvent these problems, various indirect methods have been employed to empirically measure systematic growth differences across regions according to location-specific technology effects. Analyses have attempted to examine if there are any systematic differences in the spatial extent of information flows by testing for variations in the spatial distribution of patent citations (Jaffe et al. 1993), variations in the spatial distribution of research and development activities (Iammarino and Cantwell 2000), or variations in the spatial distribution of technology-related infrastructure such as universities (Acs et al. 1992). Most of these indirect methods provide support for the arguments relating to agglomeration externalities, in that there are various localized technological effects which do not diffuse quickly across space.

A weakness of aspatial endogenous growth theory, however, is that without diminishing returns to either capital or human-capital accumulation, growth will be implausibly explosive. If we apply this logic to regional development, it would imply that all activities will converge to one single location. However, as we saw in Chapter 2, the spatial nature of the economy can provide brakes on any such explosive process. This is because providing for spatial markets inherently involves the problem of overcoming space. Moreover, congestion effects are always associated with industrial clustering in space, and beyond a certain point, these negative externalities can work against cumulative clustering. The balance of these positive and negative externality effects will lead to factor reallocations in which long-run real returns to factors across space will still tend towards equalization.

Although endogenous growth agglomeration models are not consistent with all development becoming localized at a single point, they are, on the other hand, perfectly consistent with the notion that new innovations may persistently tend to originate at the same locations, even in an environment in which markets are broadly competitive. As we saw in Chapter 2, this type of argument comes from the application of product-cycle arguments to the agglomeration models. The localized positive externality effects in the areas in which the innovations originate will generate appreciations in local real-estate prices, such that, in the long run, real returns to factors will tend to be equalized across regions. On the other hand, however, a permanent disequilibrium in nominal factor returns is perfectly possible, in which certain innovative regions always exhibit higher nominal factor prices. These areas will tend to be the central dominant cities and regions of the spatial economy, while the more geographically and economically peripheral regions of the economy will tend to exhibit lower nominal, but much more equal, real factor returns. Short- or medium-term localized growth effects in space are therefore perfectly consistent with an underlying one-sector model of interregional factor allocation. However, long-term localized growth is not consistent with a one-sector model of regional factor allocation, because geographically localized congestion costs will become evident. At the same time, as we see from the location models discussed in Chapters 1 and 3, systematic centre–periphery differences in nominal returns to factors can be perfectly consistent with a one-sector model of factor allocation.

7.4 Keynesian perspectives on regional growth and balance of payments

An alternative approach to the analysis of regional growth comes from a broadly Keynesian perspective, and involves discussions of the role played by interregional income flows. In Chapter 6, we saw that the local intraregional linkages between firms and factors within a region, and the relationship between these local linkages and external demand stimuli from outside of the region, can be modelled, at least in principle, by a regional multiplier analysis based on income flows. A key feature which distinguishes these Keynesian regional models from national multiplier models is that the treatment of the relationship between local investment expenditure and local regional income at the regional level is somewhat different in nature from that at the national level. In particular, regional government expenditure flows tend to run counter to regional income, whereas private sector investment tends to be very sensitive to local regional income, independent of national economic conditions.

Assuming that private sector investment levels are higher than public sector investment flows, this means that the funds locally available for current investments are dependent on current income levels. The importance of this observation lies in the fact that higher current levels of local investment expenditure imply that the regional capital stock can be more effectively expanded and upgraded. From our discussion of endogenous growth in section 7.3.1 above, it was argued that the quality of local inputs in general may be a function of the stock of local capital. Moreover, following the endogenous growth models relating to human-capital investments, and allied with our discussions in Chapters and 5 relating to local specialized inputs and human capital, the observation that the future local capital stock is a function of current local income would therefore suggest that future growth may be constrained by current income levels.

As well as this, we also see from Chapter 5, however, that current income–expenditure levels are constrained by the level of output demand. In the case of regions, we generally assume that much of a region's output is consumed outside of the region. As such, local regional expenditure is constrained by the level of regional export income earned. This is the basis of the Keynesian approach to regional growth, which posits that regional growth is constrained by a regional balance of payments constraint. While there are some commentators who would question the validity of a balance of payments discussion applied to regions (Richardson 1978), the fact that we attempt to discuss interregional trade patterns means that there must be equivalent interregional income and capital flows (Dow 1982, 1987, 1997; Hess and van Wincoop 2000; Ramos 2007; Crocco et al. 2010). Moreover, from a Keynesian perspective, the justification for such an analytical approach is that these income flows may themselves have additional monetary effects, which are in addition to any real-income effects associated with spatial factor adjustments.

This argument that interregional income flows may themselves have additional monetary effects, which are in addition to any real-income effects associated with spatial factor adjustments, is well understood by observers of the varying fortunes of the different members countries of the eurozone in the aftermath of the 2008 global financial crisis. Previously solvent nations with low public deficits and debts such as Spain, and high-growth and dynamic countries such as Ireland, were caught in a downward spiral of capital outflows and rising interest rates. These crises were primarily due to earlier excesses in real-estate bank lending to developers in the prosperous and rapidly growing regions of their countries, where price expectations had been overshooting (see section A.4.3.2). The result of this was that profitable business in these previously prosperous regions, as well as firms in other regions and also in other countries, all started to face increasingly severe credit constraints which were largely unrelated to the performance of the individual firm. The real-estate asset sales required by many investors to repay their loans then had further adverse effects on the capital borrowing ability of other firms in the areas where the sales were concentrated. Spatial factor adjustments are clearly not the only determinant of regional performance. Monetary flows are also important.

7.4.1 The balance of payments approach to regional growth

In order to understand the logic behind the balance of payments approach to regional growth, we can once again consider the simple regional income–expenditure model of the type discussed in Chapter 5.

$$Y_r = (C_r + I_r + G_r) + (X_r - M_r) \tag{7.16}$$

The first three terms on the right-hand side of equation (7.16) represent the components of aggregate demand associated with the domestic activity within the regional economy, and we can group these under the heading of 'regional domestic absorption' A_r. Meanwhile the last two components on the right-hand side of equation (7.16) represent the components of aggregate regional demand associated with the interregional traded sector. In general terms, from (7.16) we can write

$$(Y_r - A_r) = (X_r - M_r) \tag{7.17}$$

where $(Y_r - A_r)$ is equal to the net acquisition of assets from other regions.

In order to see why the difference between regional income and regional domestic absorption is the net acquisition of assets from other regions, we must begin with a discussion of a balance of payments model at a national level, and then translate this argument to the case of regions. At a national level the simplest balance of payments model can be defined as

$$CA_N + KA_N + BOF_N = 0 \tag{7.18}$$

where:

CA_N balance of payments on the national current account

KA_N balance of payments on the national capital account

BOF_N balance of official national financing

In a simple model of national balance of payments as represented by equation (7.18), the first two terms on the left-hand side represent the net flows of income from economic activities. The balance of payments on the current account represents the net money flows from all trade in goods and services, plus the net flows of interest and dividends from all assets held overseas by domestic citizens, and all overseas-owned domestic assets. The balance of payments on the current account is therefore much broader than simply the balance of trade, which refers only to the trade in goods. If the current account is in surplus, this means that the country is building up domestic money holdings, which originate as overseas currency and are then denominated in the domestic currency. The price of the home currency will rise relative to the foreign currency. Meanwhile, the balance of payments on the capital account represents a country's net acquisition of foreign assets via international financial lending and borrowing, and represents domestic citizens' net gain in titles to overseas-located wealth. If the capital account is in surplus, this implies that inflows of money from other countries used to purchase domestic assets are greater than outflows of money used to purchase assets in other countries. Together, the balance of payments on the current and capital accounts represents the net total balance of payments surplus. The balance of official financing is the amount required to keep the internationally earned income and expenditure accounts balanced, and is equal to the net difference in the demand and supply for the domestic currency in the foreign exchange markets.

$$CA_N + KA_N = -BOF_N \tag{7.19}$$

If we rearrange equation (7.18) to give (7.19), we can see that if the left-hand side of (7.19) is positive, the country is regarded as running a balance of payments surplus, and if the left-hand side of equation (7.19) is negative, the country is regarded as running a balance of payments deficit. If a country is running a balance of payments surplus, it must be either increasing its stock of foreign assets, or alternatively reducing its indebtedness to foreign citizens. On the other hand, where a country is running a balance of payments deficit, it must be either reducing its stock of foreign assets, or alternatively increasing its indebtedness to foreign citizens. These wealth adjustments are mediated via transactions in the international currency markets.

In the case of interregional trade, because all transactions within a common currency regime are denominated in the same currency, there can be no official financing as such. Moreover, we know that regions do not have customs or trade barriers. However, in principle, we can still write a balance of payments expression for a region, the key feature of which is that the right-hand side of equation (7.19) must always be zero when applied to regions (Ramos 2007). In interregional terms therefore, our balance of payments expression must be

$$CA_R + KA_R = 0 \tag{7.20}$$

where:

CA_R balance of payments on the regional current account
KA_R balance of payments on the regional capital account

which rearranges to

$$CA_N = -KA_N \tag{7.21}$$

In other words, the net surplus in a region's trade in goods and services with other regions, given by $(X_r - M_r)$ in equation (7.17), is balanced by the region's net acquisition of assets from other regions, given by $(Y_r - A_r)$ in equation (7.17). For example, if a regional exporting industry is very successful, this implies that the income generated by the exports can be used both to import goods and services from other regions and also to buy more assets in other regions. These asset purchases will include real-estate assets in other regions as well as share acquisitions in firms located in other regions. Similarly, if a region is running a balance of payments deficit, it must be financed by net sales of domestically held assets to buyers from other regions. If a region is running a balance of payments equilibrium, in means that the net acquisition of assets from other regions is zero. The problem with balance of payments surpluses or deficits is that they cannot continue indefinitely. In particular, if a region is experiencing a balance of payments deficit, there will only be a finite stock of domestically held assets and properties within the region which can be sold to external buyers in order to finance the regional deficit. Therefore a region cannot maintain a long-run balance of payments deficit. This implies that, as well as the level of domestic absorption, the level of regional income that it is possible to maintain in the long run depends on the level of regional exports.

In order to see this we can consider a country comprising two regions A and B, whereby region A exhibits weak investment demand while region B exhibits strong investment demand. By definition, regions do not have any independent control over monetary issues, as these are determined by the central banking authorities. Therefore the rate of interest prevailing in any one region is equal to the rate of interest in any other region. As such, we can regard the individual region as a small open economy in which the LM curve is horizontal.

In Figure 7.10, the rate of interest in both regions is given as r^*. At this rate of interest, in region A the local investment component of regional domestic absorption is only sufficient

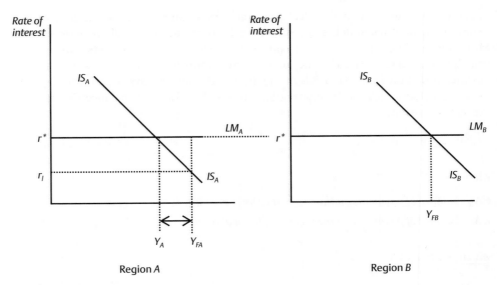

Figure 7.10 Regional investment levels

to generate a regional income level of Y_A. If the investment income required to generate full local employment is given by Y_{FA}, the local shortfall in labour market demand, expressed in terms of income, is given by $(Y_{FA} - Y_A)$. Meanwhile, in region B, the level of local investment is just sufficient to generate a level of regional income which clears the labour market at the prevailing rate of interest. Therefore a simple comparison of the differences between the situations in the two regions would suggest that the labour market in region A would clear if there were a fall in the local interest rate from r^* to r_I, whereas for region B, if rates fell below r^*, the local labour supply constraints would lead to localized inflation. However, without an independent currency we know that, by definition, regions do not have the ability to adjust local interest rates. Therefore, if the monetary authorities presiding over both regions are charged with maintaining price stability, they will ensure that interest rates are kept at a level of r^* so as to maximize the total employment level in the two regions. This will mean that the buoyant region maintains full employment whereas the depressed region exhibits a local labour demand shortfall.

One way of alleviating this labour market imbalance is for unemployed labour to migrate from region A to region B. However, as we see in Chapter 6, there are many conditions under which interregional labour market adjustment processes are rather inefficient. In the absence of local currency and interest rate adjustments, if a region cannot generate internal investment levels I_R^*, the only other mechanism a region has for expanding is through an expansion in its exports. This is explained by Figure 7.11, which represents a fixed-price model of the regional macroeconomy without currency or interest rate adjustments, the upper right-hand quadrant contains our familiar income–expenditure diagram.

In this particular case, we are assuming that the level of internally generated regional domestic investment I_R^* is constant, as are the externally determined regional interest rates r^*. By reading from right to left in the upper left-hand quadrant of Figure 7.11, we can observe the inverse relationship between regional domestic investment and interest rates.

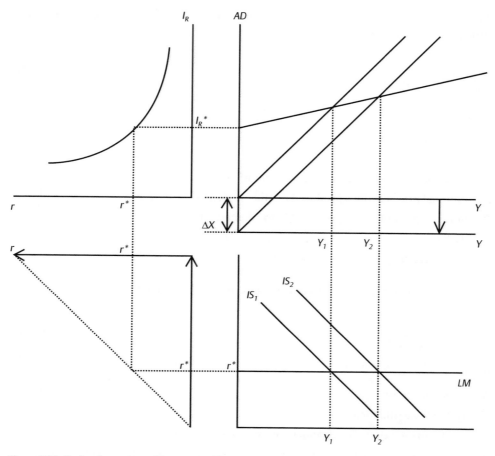

Figure 7.11 Regional exports and investment

The lower left-hand quadrant simply plots interest rates against interest rates, and the lower right-hand quadrant represents the individual regional investment market as in Figure 7.10. As we see in the income–expenditure model, as regional exports increase, we can model the resulting income increase for a given level of domestic investment $I_R{}^*$ and interest rates r^* by adjusting the origin and x-axis vertically downwards by exactly the amount of the export increase ΔX. The increase in exports provides for an increase in regional income from Y_1 to Y_2, which at the prevailing rate of interest implies that domestic regional investment increases from IS_1 to IS_2. At current interest rates, the increase in regional exports therefore generates increases in regional investment due to a general increase in regional income. This possibility has already been raised in our discussion of an export base 'super multiplier' in Chapter 4. In Keynesian regional models, the level of regional exports consequently plays a key role in determining the level of domestic investment which is sustainable, in situations where local currency and interest rates adjustments are not possible.

What we have not yet considered, however, is the question of what determines the level of regional exports, sustainable investment, and income in the long run. In order to discuss this, we can write a simple general long-run regional import demand function as (Thirlwall 1980; McCombie and Thirlwall 1994)

$$M_r = aY_r^\pi \left(\frac{P_f}{P_r} e \right)^\mu \tag{7.22}$$

where:

M_r regional imports

Y_r regional income

π regional income elasticity of demand for imports

P_f nominal price of goods produced in other regions

P_r nominal price of goods produced in the domestic region

e exchange rate

μ price elasticity of demand for imports

Similarly, we can write a simple long-run regional export demand function as

$$X_r = bZ^\varepsilon \left(\frac{P_r}{eP_f} \right)^\eta \tag{7.23}$$

where:

X_r regional exports

Z rest of the world income

ε world income elasticity of demand for exports of region r

η price elasticity of demand for the exports of region r by rest of the world

These import and export demand functions simply say that the level of imports and exports depends on both the price and income elasticities of the goods, as well as on the relative prices of domestic and externally produced goods, subject to the respective exchange rate movements. If we transform these two functions into natural logarithms and then differentiate with respect to time, in a manner analogous to sections 7.3 and 7.3.1, we can derive expressions describing import and export growth rates, respectively. Our import growth rate expression becomes

$$(\dot{M}_r)_t = \pi(\dot{Y}_r)_t + \mu[(\dot{P}_f)_t + \dot{e}_t - (\dot{P}_r)_t] \tag{7.24}$$

and our export growth rate expression becomes

$$(\dot{X}_r)_t = \varepsilon(\dot{Z})_t + \eta[(\dot{P}_r)_t - \dot{e}_t - (\dot{P}_f)_t] \tag{7.25}$$

where growth rates at time t are denoted by a dot superscript.

In the long run, we know that a region cannot run a balance of payments deficit. Therefore the level of long-run regional import growth which is continuously sustainable depends on the region's growth in exports, plus the relative changes in domestic and external production costs and prices, subject to exchange rate changes. In other words,

$$\dot{M}_r = \dot{X}_r + [\dot{P}_r - \dot{P}_f - \dot{e}]$$

(7.26)

Inserting equations (7.24) and (7.25) into equation (7.26) gives

$$\dot{Y}_r = \frac{\varepsilon \dot{Z} + (1 + \eta + \mu)[\dot{P}_r - \dot{P}_f - \dot{e}]}{\pi}$$

(7.27)

When these Keynesian (or more strictly post-Keynesian) types of balance of payments models are applied to the case of regions, it is generally assumed that the relative price effects contained in the square numerator bracket of equation (7.27) are relatively unimportant. There are three major reasons for these assumptions. The first reason is that regions do not exhibit the capacity to make independent currency adjustments. Second, it is assumed that most prices are set in oligopolistic industries, which ensure relative price stability between competing producers, even in the face of cost changes (Lavoie 1992; Davidson 1994). Third, it is assumed that geographical transactions costs and spatial competition mean that differences in nominal prices between regions also remain relatively stable over long periods. Under these assumptions, the long-run regional equilibrium balance of payments expression reduces to

$$\dot{Y}_r = \frac{\varepsilon \dot{Z}}{\pi} = \frac{\dot{X}_r}{\pi}$$

(7.28)

In other words, the maximum balance of payments constrained long-run growth rate of a region is equal to the long-run growth in world income, multiplied by the ratio of the world income elasticity of demand for the exports of the region divided by the regional income elasticity of demand for imports. This in turn is equal to the long-run rate of growth of regional exports, divided by the regional income elasticity of demand for imports.

The long-run growth of regional income is therefore determined by the ratio of the income elasticities of demand for the region's exports and for its imports. This depends on the qualitative mix of production sectors in a region. If a region is dominated by the production of high-value-added, highly income-elastic and low- price elasticity goods, its export growth will tend to be consistently strong over time, for any given patterns of regional imports. Similarly, if a region is dominated by industries with strong local linkages, its import growth will tend to be relatively low over time, for any given pattern of exporting. A combination of highly income-elastic exports and a low regional income elasticity of demand for imports will therefore tend to allow a high long-run level of regional growth, even allowing for the fact that growth may be constrained by a balance of payments constraint.[1]

---

[1] The 'Thirlwall's law' argument assumes that there is hysteresis in terms of the export sales and import demand functions of the regions due to the industrial, technological, and institutional history of the region. A closely related argument which reverses the causality in these models comes from the '45 degree rule' of Krugman (1989), whereby population growth influences the variety of output. See McCombie and Thirlwall (1994) for a detailed discussion of the relationship between the two approaches.

7.4.2 **The Verdoorn law and cumulative causation**

The final component of Keynesian or post-Keynesian regional growth theory concerns the question of economies of scale. In this approach, the analysis of economies of scale centres on the so-called 'Verdoorn law', which posits a positive relationship between the rate of growth of labour productivity and the growth of output. The Verdoorn relationship is given by

$$\dot{\rho} = a + b\dot{Q} \tag{7.29}$$

where ρ represents the rate of growth of labour productivity, and Q represents the rate of growth of output. Based on empirical observations, the 'Verdoorn law' assumes that the value of a is approximately 2 per cent, and that the value of b, the Verdoorn coefficient, is 0.5 per cent. These values can be shown to be broadly consistent with a neoclassical production in which the indices a plus b sum to 1.33 (McCombie and Thirlwall 1994).

If we use the notation employed above in sections 7.3 and 7.3.1, we can rewrite equation (7.29) as

$$(\dot{Q} - \dot{L}) = a + b\dot{Q} \tag{7.30}$$

Initial observation of equation (7.30) suggests that econometric estimation of the relationship posited by equation (7.29) will exhibit a simultaneity problem, because the term representing the rate of growth of output appears on both sides of the equation. While the treatment of this issue has been the subject of much debate (Kaldor 1975; Rowthorne 1975; McCombie and Thirlwall 1994; Scott 1989), the general assumption in post-Keynesian models is that the direction of causation is explicitly from right to left (Felipe 1998). In other words, increasing output growth is regarded as engendering dynamic economies of scale in production, via both 'learning by doing' effects on the part of labour (Arrow 1962), and also the increased capital accumulation effects associated with easy credit availability in conditions of expanding output. If the assumption of Verdoorn dynamic economies of scale is now included in our discussion of regional balance of payments constraints, by following the diagrammatic approach of Dixon and Thirlwall (1975) we can indicate the various regional growth trajectories which are possible under a regime of cumulative causation.

In Figure 7.12, we observe a set of conditions which gives rise to a constant regional output growth rate. In the upper right-hand quadrant we see that the regional export growth rate is x, and with an income elasticity of regional demand for imports given by π_1, this leads to a balance of payments constrained output growth rate of q. Via the Verdoorn effect, in the upper left-hand quadrant we see that this output growth engenders local labour productivity growth of h. In the lower left-hand quadrant we see that this itself leads to quality-adjusted real-price reductions of regional output, which fall at a rate of s. As we discussed above, in these models we assume that relative prices remain more or less the same across regions. However, for given output prices, labour productivity gains will be realized in terms of real quality improvements. Moreover, these regional output quality improvements will be transmitted in the lower right-hand quadrant to increases in regional export growth x, the actual extent of which will depend on the income elasticity of demand for the region's

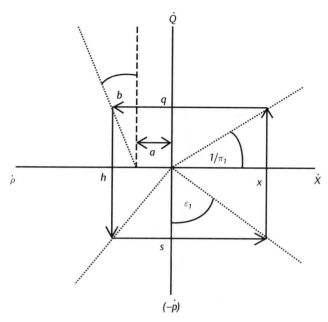

Figure 7.12 Steady-state regional growth

exports ε_1. In this particular case the export growth will itself lead to a steady-state regional output growth rate of q. As we see from Figure 7.12, however, there is no particular equilibrium steady-state rate of regional growth towards which the region will converge.

In these Keynesian type models, there is no reason why steady-state regional growth should be automatic. For example, if a region is characterized by a dense clustering of industries which exhibit agglomeration economies, the region will tend to produce highly innovative outputs and will also purchase large quantities of its input requirements from within the local regional economy. This will imply that the income elasticity of demand for the region's outputs will tend to be greater than under the case of steady-state growth, and also that the regional income elasticity of demand for imports will be relatively low. In the case of imports, we can compare this situation with that of the steady-state growth rate of Figure 7.12, by shifting upwards the line in the upper right-hand quadrant of Figure 7.13, which represents the inverse of the income elasticity of demand for imports, from $1/\pi_1$ to $1/\pi_2$. Similarly, in the case of exports, we can shift outwards the line in the lower right-hand quadrant of Figure 7.13, which represents the income elasticity of demand for the region's exports, from ε_1 to ε_2. As we see, in such a set of circumstances, the combination of highly income-elastic exports, a low income elasticity of regional imports, and increasing returns to scale can give rise to cumulative growth. The actual rate of regional growth depends on the particular values of the regional import and export elasticities.

Similarly, we can envisage the opposite type of situation, in which a region is dominated by the production of relatively low income elasticity exports, while at the same time being very dependent on imports. For example, this type of situation could occur in a relatively low-demand peripheral region which has suffered severe industrial decline and the loss of

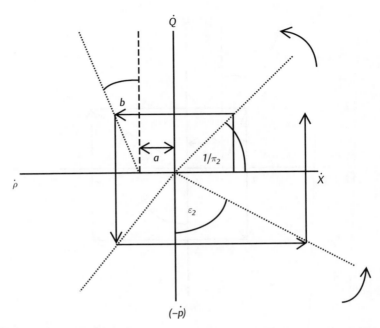

Figure 7.13 Cumulative regional growth

many local firms, and which has subsequently experienced employment growth in establishments which are relatively 'footloose'. In this case, the level of expenditure in the local economy by both the new and old firms will tend to be very small. Moreover, if both the new and old firms in the region are specialized in the production of rather standardized 'mature' products, the income elasticity of demand for the region's exports will be very low.

In the case of imports, we can compare this situation with that of the steady-state growth rate of Figure 7.12 by shifting downwards the line in the upper right-hand quadrant of Figure 7.14, which represents the inverse of the income elasticity of demand for imports, from $1/\pi_1$ to $1/\pi_3$. Similarly, in the case of exports, we can shift inwards the line in the lower right-hand quadrant of Figure 7.13, which represents the income elasticity of demand for the region's exports, from ε_1 to ε_3. As we see, in such a set of circumstances, the combination of low income elasticity exports, a high income elasticity of regional imports, and increasing returns to scale can give rise to cumulative decline. As above, the actual rate of regional decline depends on the particular values of the regional import and export elasticities.

These Keynesian and post-Keynesian approaches to regional growth differ fundamentally from neoclassical models in their basic assumptions. In particular, these models do not require the assumption that factors are paid according to their marginal products. Nor do they require the assumption that production exhibits constant returns to scale with respect to input factors. However, in a similar manner to models of endogenous growth, these models imply that there is no particular long-run rate of growth towards which a region is expected to converge. The actual regional growth rates will therefore depend on the extent to which agglomeration economies or diseconomies are operative (McCombie and Roberts 2007) and also on careful interpretation of what the underlying agglomeration

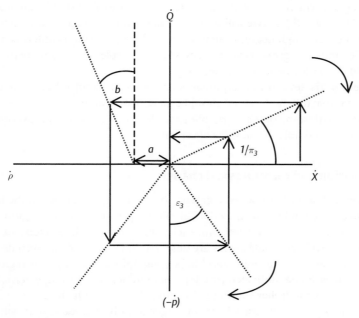

Figure 7.14 Cumulative regional decline

model formulations actually imply (Felipe and McCombie 2012). Moreover, in terms of regional growth these Keynesian and neoclassical models can be shown to produce largely equivalent results, such that the interpretation of empirical observations of regional development can be shown to be made consistent with either approach (Fingleton and McCombie 1998).

7.5 Convergent growth or divergent growth?

The models set out in the previous sections provide us with very different views of the regional economic system. The neoclassical models imply convergence and tendency towards equilibrium positions, whereas both the endogenous growth and Keynesian-type models imply processes of cumulative causation. With such an array of diverse arguments and implications it is necessary to try to draw up an inventory of what we nowadays understand from these various insights.

Within an interregional setting we know from the new economic geography (NEG) models of Chapter 3 that spatially concentrated growth can be cumulative for long periods. Obviously localized growth cannot be explosive and infinite, because in that case all individuals will end up living in the same locality, a point made by Solow (1994). As we saw in Chapter 1, and as will also be discussed in later chapters, this is indeed a situation towards which some developing countries are moving. However, most countries exhibit multiple different agglomerations with varying fortunes; some experience growth and others decline (OECD 2009a). Similarly, many other regions with few or no concentrations of urban activity, or regions which are mixed urban–rural regions, exhibit significant growth as well as decline (OECD 2009b). As we will see in Chapter 8, the most recent evidence appears to suggest that there is a high degree of heterogeneity between regions in terms of both their characteristics and their growth experiences, with no simple relationship between the type of region and the performance of the region.

Over recent years several new arguments and lines of enquiry have emerged to help explain why it is that different regions should experience different growth rates, and here we will briefly deal with some of these arguments under the headings of innovation and technological change, and different notions of capital.

7.5.1 Innovation and technological change

One argument is that rather than convergence between regions per se, in the long run we observe 'convergence clubs' (Quah 1997). The clubs represent groups of regions whose fortunes appear to be highly correlated with each other. Some of these 'clubs' of regions are observed to grow strongly while others are observed to grow slowly or even decline. These different clubs of regions are often found to be geographically contiguous regions and this observation can easily be motivated by adopting arguments regarding externalities, localized spillovers, and multiplier mechanisms (Fingleton 1997; Quah 1997). What is more complicated, however, is the case where convergence clubs include regions which are neither geographically contiguous nor even in some cases geographically close to each other.

It may be the case that non-contiguous regions are similar in the types of industries which dominate them, largely competing in the same global markets, and their similar fortunes in the global markets lead to convergence-type performance outcomes. However, these outcomes are little more than a statistical artefact due to the similarity of the regions. More fundamentally, convergence clubs can be understood by the fact that regions are linked not just by geographical distance and accessibility, but also by 'knowledge' distance and accessibility (Boschma 2005). Two regions which are at a significant geographical distance from each other may be strongly interconnected due to the characteristics of the firms, industries, and occupations in the respective regions. The interconnections may be related to different types of input–output and interfirm linkages, and these interactions may be in the form of movements of goods, people, ideas, and knowledge between the regions. Whatever the mode of connection, the point is that the regions are connected, and whatever gives rise to innovation and growth in one region will often be translated to other regions as well. The reason is that many regions are 'related' to each other in technological as well as geographical terms, and this has important implications in terms of our understanding of how innovation and growth processes operate between regions.

Neither the Romer (1986, 1987a, b) nor the Lucas (1988) models are set in geographical space. However, translating these into explicitly spatial regional growth terms can be understood, at least in principle, by way of the knowledge spillover arguments of Chapter 3 in the case of the Romer (1986, 1987a, b) models, and the human-capital migration arguments of Chapter 6 in the case of the Lucas (1988) model.

From a regional perspective, a rather more indirect connection to regional growth can also be derived from the work of Aghion and Howitt (1992, 2009). The departure point for the models of Aghion and Howitt (2009) is that at its most basic level, growth is driven neither by efficient factor allocation and pricing, nor by competition, specialization, and variety. Rather, their models are based on the assumption that growth is driven fundamentally by Schumpeterian (1934) processes of creative destruction, characterized by risk-taking, entrepreneurship, and innovation. The mechanisms at work in these Schumpeterian-type competition processes still include the knowledge spillover, input variety, and human-capital elements evident in other endogenous growth models. However, in these innovation models, competition takes place in an environment where technological change makes possible fundamental shifts in the nature of competition. Rather than growth converging in the long run to something akin to a pre-ordained growth path, in these models economic growth follows different trajectories, depending on the technological breakthroughs which take place and the innovations thereby engendered. Growth or decline can be cumulative over long periods, depending on whether a particular economy is best placed to take advantage of the newly emerging dominant technologies.

To the extent that growth is convergent, this takes place via technological diffusion. However, the speed and pattern of technological diffusion may differ substantially between regions, and the cumulative impacts of the lock-in (David 1981) and hysteresis effects associated with existing technologies, sectors, occupations, and skills may dominate the diffusion effects, thereby leading to unequal growth.

In terms of regions, these arguments suggest that the observed differences in regional growth can be largely attributed to differences in the technological profile of different places. These different technological profiles are argued to lead to differences in the ability of different regions to connect with, and relate to, the newly emerging and most competitive technologies, and there are two aspects to this. First, the ability of a region to develop and lead the newly emerging technologies is itself assumed to be conditioned on the region's existing industrial structure, with leading agglomerations perceived to be at a consistent advantage over other regions for all the arguments outlined in Chapters 2 and 3. Second, the ability of a 'follower' region to build on the technological developments in other leading regions depends on how closely related are the technological profiles between the leading and lagging regions.

Regions which are technologically further away from a leading region will have more limited opportunities to experience growth from spillovers, irrespective of how far the regions are apart in geographical terms. Convergence clubs often comprise groups of regions which are closely related in terms of technological distance, as well as groups of regions which are closely related in terms of geographical distance. As such, a region's ability to grow in response to the growth of other regions is conditional on its own technological history and how this is related to the technological history of other growing or declining regions.

As we see in Box 7.2, the extent to which a region's technologies are closely related to the other emerging technologies is known as the 'related variety' argument.

These Schumpeterian–Darwinian types of argument suggest that the clues to differing regional performance, and also the observation that different groups of regions appear to exhibit similar but differing growth trajectories, lie in different notions of distance (Boschma 2005), with technological distance playing a role which in many cases may be just as important as geographical distance. Obviously, within spatially concentrated arenas, the channels via which knowledge and technology transmission mechanisms operate are largely the

---

BOX 7.2 Technological diversification and related variety

A subtly different but just as important additional insight which also emerges from this argument is that a region's ability to grow is also conditioned on its own technological development history. In particular, a region's growth potential is likely to be stronger in technological fields which are closer and more related to a region's existing dominant technologies than in technological fields with little or no connections to the region's existing technological profile. This 'related variety' (Frenken et al. 2007) argument, which is a combination of the Schumpeterian arguments outlined above and also the Darwinian thinking outlined in Chapter 2, contends that the most promising trajectories or pathways for a region's growth are found by diversifying into technologies which are closely related to the existing dominant technologies, because this allows regional assets to more easily shift between technologies by building on the region's existing skills and capabilities. The related variety argument nowadays underpins much of the current regional growth thinking in evolutionary economics (Frenken and Boschma 2007; Boschma and Frenken 2011), and there is now strong empirical evidence (Boschma and Iammarino 2009; Neffke et al. 2011; Boschma et al. 2012) supporting this observation. Inflows of new firms and the founding of new local firms are both observed to be systematically higher in fields which are technologically diversified but also closely related to the existing dominant fields of the region, while outflows of firms or firm failures are more likely in sectors unrelated to the existing regional technological profile (Neffke et al. 2011). Indeed, the evidence suggests that the impact of this technological relatedness argument is even more pronounced at the regional scale that at the national scale (Boschma et al. 2012).

---

clustering and knowledge spillover mechanisms described in Chapters 2 and 3. However, where firms or regions are not adjacent to each other, within the modern globalizing economy context, other transmission mechanisms must operate. Some commentators point to informal 'pipelines' (Bathelt et al. 2004) of knowledge flows between highly skilled and creative (Florida 2002a,b) workers who are not working within the formal boundaries of individual corporate or buyer–supplier groupings, while other arguments suggest that formal institutions with established global connections and systems such as multinational firms (McCann and Acs 2011) and universities are far more important for converting geographical distance into knowledge proximity. Separating these various notions of distance is difficult, however, because geographical proximity and technological proximity are likely to be highly correlated, because of all of the location theory arguments examined in Chapters 2 and 3. What we can say is that the formal corporate knowledge transmission systems largely reflect the industrial complex model of Chapter 3 whereas the informal 'pipeline' system closely resembles the social network model of Chapter 3. Moreover, both geographical and technological dimensions of distance are also likely to be correlated with 'institutional proximity', defined in terms of the similarity and the connectedness of the institutional and governance systems.

7.5.2 Alternative notions of capital

Since the late 1980s in particular we have seen a subtle but fundamental shift in our notions and understanding of what input production factors are, from primarily a stock concept to much more of a flow concept. As we have already seen in many parts of this book, production factors such as labour L, land R, and capital K are traditionally represented in our models as being defined or measured in terms of stock values or quantities. However, the *stocks* of input resources provide *flows* of production services, and these flows are related to the stocks. Broadly, larger stocks of factor resources imply larger flows of the services of the resources into the production process, and this argument underpins the growth accounting-type framework outlined in Appendices 7.1 and 7.2. However, as we have already seen in Chapter 6 and in this chapter, labour services are nowadays not seen in terms of simple stocks of labour, defined in terms of the number of worker-hours L, but rather in terms of human capital HK, a concept which includes a mix of both the *quality* as well as the quantity of the labour services provided. More importantly for our purposes here is that fact that moving from L to HK implies not only that the concept of labour has shifted, but the concept of *capital* has also shifted. Our notion of capital has shifted from an emphasis on level of stocks and flows of non-human and non-land input services to an emphasis on the quality as well as the quantity of the stocks and flows of services which are not purely L or purely K as traditionally understood. The concept of human capital HK clearly incorporates flows related to both our previous traditional notions of L and K.

This subtle shift in our understanding of the nature of input factors implies that the relationships between input factors are also rather more complex than has traditionally been understood. In particular, factors cannot always be easily separated in a manner which is reflected in the construction of isoquants or bid-rent curves, and then simply added together in a manner equivalent to stock valuations. In microeconomic language, this means that factors cannot always be treated as being both additive and separable. The reason is that it is often the interactions or interrelationships between the factors that are critical for growth and development. Approaches which emphasize these interrelationships are often known as *systems* models, and such approaches are now more or less the mainstream approaches in much of the literature discussing innovation (Porter 1990), creativity (Andersson et al. 2011), well-being (Stiglitz et al. 2009), and environment (Stern 2007). For our purposes here, what is important is to recognize that the concept of capital itself has shifted, and this shift has major implications for how we discuss the various elements of growth and development.

7.5.3 Institutions and social capital

Since the early 1990s much of the recent thinking about economic growth and development has centred on the role played by institutions and governance systems (Tabellini 2010; Acemoglu and Johnson 2006). Much of this thinking was spurred by the opening up of the modern global economy, as described in Chapter 1 and to be discussed further in Chapter 8, in which newly emerging BRICS and former socialist economies entered the capital- and market-based economic system. Many of these countries exhibited very few of the institutions within which markets in advanced countries operated. In the most minimalist sense institutions here can be understood as all the formal legal architecture within which economic activities operate. This would include issues relating to the clarity and security of property rights, the ability to enforce contracts, and the separation of the legal and political arenas. More recently, the argument has been extended to include the extent to which the legal and political system interferes with commercial activities, including issues such as the number of days to start a business, the extent of the regulations with which firms must comply, the ease of capital movements, the restrictions and limitations on asset ownership, the levels of taxation, and the degrees to which 'side-payments' or bribes must be paid (Heritage Foundation 2009; World Bank 2009). This represents a subtle shift from an emphasis on the formal architecture of the institutional structure to the behavioural aspects of the institutional system. The argument here is that the operation and performance of an institutional system is not merely a question of the design of the system, but also a question of how all the actors, stakeholders, and interested parties in the system interact with each other. This structure-system shift in our understanding of the role played by institutions in growth and development also reflects the more general shift in emphasis from a stock to a flow way of understanding of the role played by factor inputs in general, as discussed above.

In the case of institutions, one of the most important developments in our understanding centres on the role of what is known as *social capital*. The concept of social capital relates to all the social norms, social rules, and social conventions operating within a society. The concept was first elaborated many decades ago within the sociological literature, but two seminal books by Putnam (1993, 1996) have brought the arguments into both mainstream economics and political science. More specifically for our purposes, these arguments have very strong urban and regional implications (Westlund 2006).

Putnam's (1993) initial argument was based on a historical analysis of the different regions of Italy, and his contention was that the huge differences in growth and development between the north and south of Italy are largely a result of the fact that the north of Italy has good institutions which people trust, whereas in the south this is not the case. The reasons for these differences in trust are related to the *governance* history of the regions, and Putnam's point is that the historically determined social capital has very long-lasting implications in terms of the relationships between individuals, households, government, and commerce. Broadly, the less that individuals trust the formal legal and government institutions, the lower will be the levels of economic development, while the more that they trust institutions, the more they will invest and take commercial risks. Social trust and economic activity are argued to be highly correlated over time. The levels of social trust are manifested in terms of the willingness of people to actively engage in voluntary and social activities without fear of being undermined by opportunistic behaviour (Williamson 1975) of others. Public and not-for-profit participation is therefore interpreted as an index of social trust, and is argued to be correlated with profit-making activities.

The long-term development of a region is therefore seen to be intrinsically related to the institutional history of the region, but institutions here are understood not just in terms of formal and legal institutions, but also the informal institutions of social norms, values, and rules. In particular, it is the interactions between formal and informal institutions which govern the relationships between individuals, households, firms, and the local state.

The second aspect of the social capital model (Putnam 1996) is that communities manifest social capital in different ways, and the benefits of, and possibilities associated with, these different social-capital manifestations also have impacts on the economic development of different communities. Broadly, there are two types of social capital, namely *bonding* capital and *bridging* capital. Bonding capital is the social capital, the social 'glue', which holds local communities together and helps them to be 'resilient' in times of adversity (Fingleton et al. 2012). Small isolated communities tend to be very homogeneous in terms of ethnicity, values, and identity, and these attributes tend to foster community and a sense of belonging, values closely related to the attachment values discussed in Chapter 4 and the place-based arguments to be discussed in Chapter 10. Somewhat differently, bridging capital is the social capital which allows communities to engage with and connect with other communities, many of which are socially, culturally, or ethnically different. Large cosmopolitan urban areas or university cities tend to be relatively weaker in terms of bonding capital, because of the constant turnover of diverse people, but relatively stronger in terms of bridging capital. The advantage of bonding capital is the increased resistance to adverse regional economic shocks due to the local institutional embeddedness, whereas the advantage of bridging capital is institutional adaptability to new economic possibilities, and the ability to learn from other regions.

Finally, and also related to these social-capital and institutional issues, there is some evidence recently emerging which suggests that long-run growth is also related to levels of inequality, with the former decreasing as the latter increase (Berg and Ostry 2011). The ability of economic growth to be maintained may also depend on the extent to which a wide section of society benefits from the growth possibilities. Obviously, interregional mobility, and the human-capital self-selection issues discussed in Chapter 6, makes these interrelationships very complex. What we have not yet discussed is the extent to which interregional inequality itself affects overall growth. We will return to this issue in Chapter 10.

7.6 Conclusions

This chapter has discussed the various analytical approaches we have for understanding the nature of regional growth and development. The most common approaches adopted by analysts are long-run neoclassical models, which distinguish between growth due to factor allocation processes and growth which is due to technological change. The two broad types of these models are the one-sector model and the two-sector model, of which it was argued that the first is regarded as the 'true' long-run model of regional factor allocation. The long-run result of these regional allocation and reallocation processes is a tendency towards interregional convergence in terms of factor proportions and rates of return. The outcomes of regional factor allocation processes are therefore seen to be somewhat different from the factor allocation assumptions which underlie models of international trade and comparative advantage. The assumptions and conclusions of these neoclassical models were then employed within production function analysis in order to discuss questions of the contribution of technology to regional growth, as distinct from growth due to factor reallocation. However, this is a complex problem, and more recent endogenous growth approaches have focused on the role played by qualitative differences in the stocks of capital and labour inputs, in order to account for variations in regional performance. These various neoclassical models were subsequently contrasted with Keynesian and post-Keynesian approaches to regional growth analysis, approaches which centre on the notion of a regional balance of payments constraint. The assumption here is that regional export levels act as a long-run constraint on regional growth by limiting the maximum level of inward income–expenditure flows into the region. Under conditions in which local factor price adjustments are regarded as of minor importance, regional growth is perceived as primarily dependent on a region's particular mix of industries and local linkages. Therefore, where economies of scale are also present, these models imply that there is no particular reason to expect interregional convergence.

The implications of the technological, institutional, and social-capital arguments for growth theory are still being investigated. However, it is fair to say that the related variety, institutional and social-capital arguments, tend to emphasize specific systemic factors within the local economic system as determining regional growth, whereas the neoclassical and macro-derived endogenous growth models tend to see largely system-wide features as playing the dominant role. In the case of the spatial distribution of innovation, Doloreux and Shearmur (2012) examine the relative importance of the role played by institutional–endogenous features versus the role played by spatial optimization behaviour, of the type outlined by McCann (2007). Their findings suggest that both played a role, with both local and system-wide factors influencing the local outcomes. In other words, outcomes were neither local nor global, but a mixture of each. Regional growth is therefore neither largely exogenous, as implied by traditional growth accounting framework, nor largely endogenous, as implied by the endogenous growth approach. Nor is it simply a matter of factor allocation and mobility. Rather, it is a mixture of all these influences, and heavily influenced by technology, institutions, and social capital.

Discussion questions

7.1 What is the relationship between the neoclassical one-sector model of interregional factor allocation and the nature of regional production functions?

7.2 In what ways does the direction of factors flows in a two-sector neoclassical model of interregional factor allocation differ from that of a one-sector neoclassical model of interregional factor allocation?

7.3 How are we to understand the term 'technology' within a neoclassical growth framework, and how can we model the relationship between 'technology' and regional factor stocks?

7.4 What are the regional economic implications of endogenous growth models? Are there any limits to these mechanisms in the regional context?

7.5 To what extent are regions limited in their growth potential by a balance of payments constraint? How can such a constraint be relaxed?

7.6 What are the implications of the 'Verdoorn law' of regional growth?

7.7 What role does innovation play in regional growth and how is the concept of 'related variety' connected to innovation advantages?

7.8 What role do institutions and social capital play in local growth and development?

Appendix 7.1 The Cobb–Douglas production function and growth accounting

Our Cobb–Douglas regional production function is defined as

$$Q_t = Ae^{\phi t}K^{\alpha}L^{1-\alpha} \qquad\qquad (A.7.1.1)$$

If we take the natural logarithm of this function, we have

$$\ln Q = \ln A + \phi t + \alpha \ln K + (1 - \alpha)\ln L \tag{A.7.1.2}$$

Differentiating equation (A.7.1.2) with respect to time t, we have

$$\frac{1}{Q}\frac{dQ}{dt} = \phi + \frac{\alpha}{K}\frac{dK}{dt} + \frac{(1 - \alpha)}{L}\frac{dL}{dt} \tag{A.7.1.3}$$

which can be rewritten as

$$\dot{Q}_t = \phi + \alpha\dot{K}_t + (1 - \alpha)\dot{L}_t \tag{A.7.1.4}$$

where Q_t, K_t, L_t represent the rates of growth of output, capital, and labour at time t, respectively.

We know that wages depend on labour productivity, and the growth of wages will therefore be related to the growth of labour productivity. In order to investigate the exact nature of these relationships, we can take the growth in labour from both sides of equation (A.7.1.4) in order to arrive at an expression for the growth of labour productivity thus:

$$\dot{Q}_t - \dot{K}_t = \phi + \alpha\dot{K}_t - \dot{K}_t - \dot{L}_t - \alpha\dot{L}_t \tag{A.7.1.5}$$

which rearranges to

$$\dot{Q}_t - \dot{L}_t = \phi + \alpha(\dot{K}_t - \dot{L}_t) \tag{A.7.1.6}$$

The left-hand side of equation (A.7.1.6) represents the rate of growth of labour productivity at time t, and is given as the sum of the level of technology, plus the growth in the capital–labour ratio, weighted by the factor share of capital. As we see in Appendix 7.2, the rate of growth of labour productivity represents the rate of growth of wages. These conclusions are exactly in agreement with our one-sector model of factor allocation.

We can also adopt a similar approach to investigate the sources of profit growth. However, in order to do this we take the rate of growth of capital from both sides of equation (A.7.1.4) to arrive at an expression for the rate of growth of capital productivity thus:

$$\dot{Q}_t - \dot{K}_t = \phi + \alpha\dot{K}_t - \dot{K}_t + \dot{L}_t - \alpha\dot{L}_t \tag{A.7.1.7}$$

which can be rearranged to give

$$\dot{Q}_t - \dot{K}_t = \phi + (1 - \alpha)(\dot{L}_t - \dot{K}_t) = \dot{r}_t \tag{A.7.1.8}$$

The left-hand side of equation (A.7.1.8) represents the rate of growth of capital productivity at time t, and is given as the sum of the level of technology, plus the growth in the labour–capital ratio, weighted by the factor share of labour. As we see in Appendix 7.2, the rate of growth of labour productivity represents the rate of growth of profits. Once again, these conclusions are exactly in agreement with our one-sector model of factor allocation.

In order to consider the sources of growth in a steady-state situation in which the rate of growth of profits is zero, we can set profit growth to zero when the rate of growth of the output–capital ratio is zero. In other words we have

$$\dot{Q}_t = \dot{K}_t \tag{A.7.1.9}$$

which allows equation (A.7.1.8) to be rewritten as

$$0 = \phi + (1 - \alpha)(\dot{L}_t - \dot{Q}_t) = \dot{r}_t \tag{A.7.1.10}$$

which can be rearranged to give

$$0 = \phi + (\alpha - 1)(\dot{Q}_t - \dot{L}_t) = \dot{r}_t \tag{A.7.1.11}$$

This implies that

$$\dot{w}_t = \dot{Q}_t - \dot{L}_t = \frac{\phi}{1 - \alpha} \tag{A.7.1.12}$$

In other words, in a steady-state situation in which the rate of growth of profits is zero, the rate of growth of labour productivity and wages depends simply on the level of technology and the factor share of labour in the economy.

Appendix 7.2 Proof of the relationship between wage growth and labour productivity growth in the Cobb–Douglas framework

The wage paid to labour w is equal to the marginal product of labour MP_L, and is given by the marginal physical product of labour MPP_L, multiplied by the price of the output P_x produced. Within the Cobb–Douglas production function, the index of labour β, given as $\beta = (1 - \alpha)$, is defined as the partial elasticity of output with respect to the input labour:

$$(1 - \alpha) = \frac{\Delta Q/Q}{\Delta L/L} = \frac{\Delta Q}{Q} \times \frac{L}{\Delta L} = \frac{\Delta Q}{\Delta L} \times \frac{L}{Q} \tag{A.7.2.1}$$

Therefore, $\beta = (1 - \alpha) = MP_L/AP_L$, where MP_L is the marginal product of labour, and AP_L is the average product of labour. As such, the wage w, which is given by the marginal product of labour, is given by $w = (1 - \alpha)AP_L$.

Similarly, the profit rate paid to capital r is equal to the marginal product of capital MP_K, and is given by the marginal physical product of capital MPP_K, multiplied by the price of the output P_x produced. Within a Cobb–Douglas production function, the index of capital, α, is defined as the partial elasticity of output with respect to the input capital:

$$\alpha = \frac{\Delta Q/Q}{\Delta K/K} = \frac{\Delta Q}{Q} \times \frac{K}{\Delta K} = \frac{\Delta Q}{\Delta K} \times \frac{K}{Q} \qquad \text{(A.7.2.2)}$$

Therefore $\alpha = MP_K/AP_K$, where MP_K is the marginal product of capital, and AP_K is the average product of capital. As such, the profit rate r, which is given by the marginal product of capital, is given by $r = \alpha AP_K$.

Part II

Globalization: Cities, Regions, and Economic Policy

8 Economic geography and economic history

8.1 Introduction to urbanization, industrialization, and globalization

Over recent years we have become increasingly aware of the power of modern globalization in influencing and shaping almost all aspects of our lives. The central elements of this book, namely cities and regions, are increasingly understood as playing a key role in driving globalization processes. At the same time, the fortunes of cities and regions are also often argued to be more than ever subject to the impacts of globalization. Yet are these relationships between the fortunes of cities, regions, and globalization new phenomena? Why are these issues important for urban and regional economic analysis, models, and methods? And what is 'globalization' and when did it begin?

These are complex questions, but providing some answers is very important in demonstrating why the study of urban and regional economics is in many ways more important and timely than ever before. The models and methods discussed in Part I of this book can be applied in many real-world contexts to analyse specific issues and mechanisms. However, the power and applicability of the insights provided also rest on our awareness of the broader backdrop and changing global context in which urban and regional matters take place. This is the topic dealt with in Chapters 9–11.

How we answer the above questions depends in part on how we view globalization and on the perspectives that we adopt (McCann 2008). Globalization can be considered from the perspective of cultural issues, political issues, historical issues, geographical issues, or economic issues, and can be understood as either a largely new phenomenon or as an ongoing process (Steger 2003; MacGillivray 2006). For our purposes in this book we interpret globalization in terms of economics and geography, and this perspective means that we focus on the relationships between globalization, industrialization, and urbanization. As we will see, the importance of studying the economics of cities and regions is that they play a crucial role in long-run economic development. However, the long-run role played by cities and regions in economic growth is one that has evolved over time. At various stages in history the changing relationships between trade, growth, and urbanization have both challenged and defined the notion of a city, a region, and even the concept of what it is to be a nation. Importantly for our purposes, these relationships have changed again over the last few decades in response to the modern era of globalization. An understanding of these recent changes is therefore essential in order to position the models and methods examined in Part I of this book.

As with all models, urban and regional economic models are by nature always at least partially abstract, but they are designed to capture aspects of the structure and processes of change of very concrete phenomena. The aim of Part II of this book is to develop an understanding of the impacts of globalization on both the long-run and current development of cities and regions, and to see how best to use the models discussed in Part I to analyse these developments. This is best done by building on all the material in Part I and then applying it within an explicitly historical as well as a geographical context.

While the logic of Part I is built around the theoretical models and methods in which factors are assumed to move, relocate, or adjust more or less instantly, it is also important to realize that the structure of many of the regions and cities we observe actually evolves gradually over time. Cities and regions as we perceive them today are in part products of the built environment, as well as being in part constructions of the social, institutional, and natural environment. These constructions typically change very slowly, but in some cases they can change quire rapidly, as witnessed by the rapid urban and regional transformations currently taking place in countries such as China. However, these transformation processes are not new, and a good knowledge of economic history helps us understand the processes by which cities and regions emerge and change over time.

In order to provide a solid understanding of the context out of which today's cities and regions have emerged, we begin here by examining the relationship between industrialization, urbanization and the economic performance of the countries in which they are located. In particular, we examine how these relationships have evolved during the various stages of globalization which have taken place since the late Middle Ages. Box 8.1 examines urbanization in the late Middle Ages, and the subsequent sections then examine the changing relationships between urbanization and industrialization and globalization which emerged over the following centuries. As we will see, the interrelationship between industrialization, urbanization, and economic growth was an ongoing and fairly direct relationship in which the world's most industrialized states were generally the most urbanized states and also the wealthiest states in the world. This relationship continued more or less unabated during each century since the transition from the late Middle Ages to the early Renaissance right up to the end of the nineteenth century and the beginning of the twentieth century.

As we will see in this chapter, the period when the relationship between urbanization, industrialization, and economic performance was at its zenith was between the late nineteenth century and the early twentieth century, and this was also the period during which many of the seminal authors referred to in this book, such as Marshall (1890), Weber (1909), Christaller (1933), Ohlin (1933), and Hoover (1937), were making their ground-breaking observations, developing their analyses, and producing their most famous texts, on which many of today's models and methods are built.

However, the middle years of the twentieth century also saw something of a hiatus in this urbanization–industrialization–economic development relationship, in that the middle years of the twentieth century were a period of anti-globalization, and in some countries also a period of anti-urbanization. Later on, during the second half of the twentieth century, the long-run relationship between industrialization, urbanization, and economic

BOX 8.1 Cities in the middle ages

The relationship between cities and economic development is one of the most important relationships in human history (Hall 1998; Glaeser 2011). In Europe and Asia Minor, cities and city-states were all central to the rise of the classical world cultures and empires of the Greeks, Persians, Phoenicians, and Romans. After the collapse of the Roman Empire in Western Europe, in the early Middle Ages European urbanization stalled and retreated, as did economic development in general. Urbanization and economic development only maintained their previous levels in Europe and Asia Minor within the Byzantine Empire, with Constantinople (Istanbul) being Europe's largest city during this period. In comparison with Constantinople, large cities were non-existent in Europe, and even medium-sized settlements were few and far between. In Charlemagne's coronation year of 800, while the population of Constantinople was 250,000, the only cities in Western Christendom with more than 30,000 inhabitants were Rome with 50,000, Thessalonica with 40,000, Naples with 30,000, and Verona with 30,000 (Chandler 1987). A similar picture also emerges in Islamic Southern Europe, the largest city of which was Cordova with 160,000, and whose second city was Seville with 35,000 (Chandler 1987). While most of Europe was characterized primarily by very small settlements, other parts of the Islamic world had already experienced major urbanization throughout the Middle Ages. By the year 1000 Baghdad was the global centre of technology and learning, and the largest city in the world with 1.2 million inhabitants (Modelski 2003). It was three times as large as the next largest city, Cordova, which, with 450,000 inhabitants (Chandler 1987; Modelski 2003), was still by far the largest city in Western Europe. The relationship between urbanization and economic development was therefore already evident in the Islamic world long before it emerged in Western Europe. Apart from Constantinople, all the world's other major cities were in the much larger and much richer far-eastern Asian cultures and empires of China, India, and Japan.

In Christendom, it was only during the later Middle Ages and the early Renaissance that urbanization became an integral part of the economic development of Europe, and the precursor to the later era of industrialization, urbanization, and globalization. The gradual shift towards urbanization and industrialization began to emerge in Western Europe from the thirteenth to fifteenth centuries onwards, a period characterized nowadays as the transition between the late Middle Ages and the early Renaissance. In the early fourteenth century the largest city in Europe was Paris, with a population of 228,000, and Europe's largest city was also the capital of Western Europe's largest country, France. Western Europe's second-largest city at this time was the city-state of Venice with a population of 110,000, which was uniquely placed to exploit trade links with the Byzantine Empire, the richest part of the Mediterranean world. However, the growth of Venice reflected a more general pattern of city-state growth during this transition period, in which various city-states grew to economic pre-eminence on the basis of trade networks, including Florence, Lisbon, and Antwerp (Alesina and Spolaore 2003), and the Hanseatic League cities in Northern Europe, led by the city of Lübeck. The rise of these city-states was associated with rapid wealth creation, and by the early fourteenth century, Venice's budget alone was approximately equal to that of the whole of Spain, and only 20 per cent less than the whole of France (Alesina and Spolaore 2003). The fourteenth- and fifteenth-century flourishing of these city-states as the centres of commerce in trading networks was also reflected in the growing relationships between urbanization, industrialization, and trade, and these relationships were most notable in Italy and the Low Countries. However, at this stage the trade relations driving the cities' commercial activities were almost entirely within Europe and the Mediterranean world, and cannot really be understood in terms of globalization.

development once again emerged, but in a rather different form from the patterns observed before the early twentieth century. In the second half of the twentieth century, the broadly positive relationship between urbanization, industrialization, and economic development was much more focused on developing rather than developed countries.

Moreover, from an urban and regional perspective there do appear to be many aspects of today's era of globalization which are not only new, but also totally different from anything experienced in earlier eras. This suggests that while on the one hand the globalization we experience today can be understood as part of an ongoing and longstanding historical process, on the other hand modern globalization can also be understood as a radical departure from earlier trends. Therefore, in order to understand the urban and regional patterns we observe today, it is necessary to consider all these features.

This chapter discusses the evolving long-run characteristics of the relationship between urbanization, industrialization, and globalization. The chapter concludes with an introduction to the major features of the most recent era of globalization, which began in the late 1980s, a period in which the relationship between industrialization and urbanization again evolved in different ways. Chapter 9 will deal with these contemporary issues in detail, while the policy responses will be discussed in Chapter 10, on the basis of all the analytical insights provided in earlier chapters.

8.2 Globalization, urbanization, industrialization: the sixteenth to the nineteenth century

The emerging relationship between urbanization, industrialization, and economic development, which initially commenced in Western Europe the late fourteenth and early fifteenth centuries, was associated with the development of European-wide trade links. Over the following centuries, however, these relationships between urbanization and industrialization also became increasingly associated with globalization. Most observers would regard globalization as beginning in the late fifteenth and sixteenth centuries.

Friedman (2007) suggests that the first era of globalization really begins with the arrival of Christopher Columbus in the Americas in 1492 and the ensuing and rapid expansion of the Spanish and Portuguese empires (Benjamin 2009). The westward colonial expansion of Spain to the Americas after Columbus's arrival in the New World in 1492 proceeded rapidly throughout the sixteenth century, with increasing transatlantic movements of people, goods, and precious metals. Similarly, after Vasco da Gama had identified the eastward trade routes through the Indian Ocean in 1498 and Cabral's discovery of Brazil in 1500, Portugal also rapidly expanded its sugar-producing colony in South America, in addition to its African colonies and Asian trading outposts (Findlay and O'Rourke 2007; Benjamin 2009). Meanwhile, the Spanish also developed the their first trade routes with the East by sailing westwards across the Pacific between the New World and Asia, after claiming the Philippines in 1542, although effective occupation only began from 1564 onwards (Findlay and O'Rourke 2007).

In terms of the economic geography of globalization, the major characteristic of the Spanish and Portuguese empires was that it was the first time that European countries had developed overseas empires in non-adjacent regions. However, globalization is an evolving process, and from a historical perspective other developments along the road to globalization also include: the fifteenth-century invention of double-entry book-keeping and the banking systems in the Italian city-states of Florence, Venice, and Sienna; the seventeenth-century invention of the joint-stock company in the Netherlands; the seventeenth-century growth of underwriting and insurance markets in the financial markets of London; the eighteenth-century industrialization and expansion of Great Britain and the subsequent industrialization of other parts of the world (Ferguson 2008).

In terms of economic geography, it seems at first sight curious that globalization should begin in Europe. We know from the various arguments in this book that city size and the size of the (home) market are all related to economic performance, and this would appear to favour the Asian empires. Therefore it appears strange that while the world's largest and richest cities and empires were all originally outside Western Europe, the initial processes of globalization and industrialization should be primarily a European phenomenon. Yet in many ways it was the very fragmentation of Europe into different kingdoms and city-states which encouraged competition between states (Ferguson 2011), whereas the larger and monolithic governance structures of the Asian empires inhibited this. As such, it is not simply city size or even the size of the country which drives development, but also the issue of international competition and governance. For this reason, many other scholars would perceive globalization in the modern sense as beginning with the competition between the major trading companies. These trading companies were the early form of multinational corporations, and in many ways were the paramount agents of globalization (Ferguson 2008), with the country playing a much lesser role.

On this argument, the founding of the VOC Dutch East India Company in 1602 (Ferguson 2008) and the establishment of similar types of companies in both England and France marks a watershed in globalization. The reason is that the founding of the Dutch East India Company was the first time in which the public raising of investment share capital was also integrated with processes of trade creation, international migration, foreign direct investment, and national–colonial expansion. These highly organized, sophisticated and very powerful trading companies emerged as the first major joint-stock-issuing multinational corporations, and it was these trading organizations which spearheaded the early globalizing processes of the major European nations.

The Dutch Republic embarked on its first major wave of colonial expansions during the latter decades of the sixteenth century, vying with the Portuguese for supremacy in the spice trade routes to the East around the Cape of Good Hope (Findlay and O'Rourke 2007). The Dutch set up colonies in South Africa, South Asia, the East Indies, and with Japan at Deshima Island outside Nagasaki in 1571. By the early seventeenth century the Dutch had overtaken the Portuguese as the principal power in the eastern trade routes, and throughout the seventeenth century the Dutch themselves were soon followed, first by the British and then by the French, in competing economically and militarily for access to these trading and colonizing opportunities. At the centre of this emerging global competition were the trading companies of each country.

In terms of economic geography, the evolution in trade and globalization processes was also reflected in terms of the evolution in urbanization patterns. As we see in Table 8.1, by the beginning of the sixteenth century, the Low Countries and Northern Italy were by far the most urbanized parts of Western Europe. This level of urbanization reflected the growth of successful city-states and their associated European and Mediterranean trade networks during the previous two centuries. In these regions, the proportion of the total population living in cities of over 10,000 was more than twice that of any other part of Western Europe.

Table 8.1 Urbanization and industrialization indices

1500 urban index	1600 urban Index	1700 urban index (industry index in 1750)	1800 urban index (industry index in 1800)	1890 urban index (industry index in 1860)	(Industry index 1913)
Belgium 21.1	Netherlands 24.3	Netherlands 33.6 (9)[1]	Netherlands 28.8 (10)	England & Wales 61.9 (64)	USA (126)
Netherlands 15.8	Italy 15.1	Belgium 23.9 (9)	England & Wales 20.3 (16)	Scotland 50.3 (64)	UK (115)
Italy 12.4	Portugal 14.1	England & Wales 13.3 (10)	Belgium 18.9 (10)	Belgium 34.5 (28)	Belgium (88)
Spain 6.1	Spain 11.4	Italy 13.2 (8)	Scotland 17.3 (16)	Netherlands 33.4 (28)	Switzerland (87)
France 4.2	Belgium 8.8	Portugal 11.5	Italy 14.6 (8)	Germany 28.2 (15)	Germany (85)
England & Wales 3.1	France 5.9	France 9.2 (9)	Spain 11.1 (7)	Spain 26.8 (11)	Sweden (67)
Germany 3.2	England & Wales 5.8	Spain 9.0 (7)	France 8.8 (9)	France 25.9 (20)	France (59)
Portugal 3.0	Germany 4.1	Scotland 5.3 (10)	Portugal 8.7	Italy 21.2 (10)	Canada (46)
Scotland 1.6	Scotland 3.0	Germany 4.8 (8)	Ireland 7.7 (10)	Ireland 17.6 (64)	Austria (32)
Switzerland 1.5	Switzerland 2.5	Scandinavia 4.0 (7)	Germany 5.5 (8)	Switzerland 16.0 (26)	Italy (26)
Scandinavia 0.9	Scandinavia 1.4	Ireland 3.4 (10)	Scandinavia 4.6 (8)	Scandinavia 13.2 (15)	Spain (22)
Ireland 0.0	Ireland 0.0	Switzerland 3.3 (7)	Switzerland 3.7 (10)	Portugal 12.7	Russia (20)
Western Europe 5.8	**Western Europe 7.9**	**Western Europe 9.5**	**Western Europe 10.2**	**Western Europe 29.6**	
China 3.8	China 4.0	China n.a. (8)	China 3.8 (6)	China 4.4 (4)	China (3)
Japan 2.9	Japan 4.4	Japan n.a. (7)	Japan 12.3 (7)	Japan 16.0 (7)	Japan (20)

Urban (urbanization) index: population living in cities of at least 10,000 inhabitants as a percentage of total population (Maddison 2007a, p. 43)

Industry (industrialization) index: levels of industrialization in the UK in 1900 = 100 (Findlay and O'Rourke 2007 p. 323)

Source: Maddison (2007a); Findlay and O'Rourke (2007)

Note: Industry indices for the Netherlands are those for Belgium; those for England and Wales, Scotland and Ireland are for the UK as a whole; those for Scandinavia are for Sweden.

In terms of individual cities, at this time, Paris, the capital of Western Europe's largest country, also remained Western Europe's largest city with 245,000 inhabitants (Chandler 1987). However, following the transatlantic expansion of the Spanish and Portuguese empires in the fifteenth century, both Spain and Portugal experienced increasing domestic urbanization. Within Spanish territory Paris was now closely rivalled by Naples with 224,000 inhabitants (Chandler 1987). More noticeably, a century of Spanish globalizing activities also meant that by 1600, along with Seville, Milan, and Palermo, the kingdom of Spain now also contained five of the ten largest cities in Western Europe. All these cities contained over 100,000 inhabitants, the other five being London, Lisbon, Venice, Prague, and Rome (Chandler 1987).

By the beginning of the eighteenth century the relationship between industrialization, urbanization, and globalization had become firmly established in all the growing colonial powers. The process of rapidly increasing urbanization, which had already been experienced by Spain and Portugal in the previous century, was now also observed on an even greater scale in the Low Countries during the seventeenth-century Dutch era of colonial expansion (Ferguson 2008). As we see in Table 8.1 and Table 8.2, by 1700 the century-long rise of the Dutch Republic and the global growth of Dutch trade had resulted in the Low Countries becoming by far the most densely urbanized region of Western Europe.

Table 8.2 The world's largest cities in 1700

1700	City population 000s	Country population 000s	GDP $000s^2	GDP per capita $
Istanbul (Constantinople)	700			565 (0) (Other Asia average)
Edo (Tokyo)	688	27,000	15,390	570 (9.6)
Beijing (Peking)	650	138,000	82,800	600 (0)
London	550	8,565	10,709	1,250 (28.3)
Paris	530	21,471	19,539	910 (17.2)
Ahmadabad	380	165,000	90,750	550 (0)
Osaka	380	27,000	15,390	570 (9.6)
Isfahan	350			565 (other Asia average)
Kyoto	350	27,000	15,390	570 (9.6)
Hangzhou (Hangchow)	303	138,000	82,800	600 (0)
Amsterdam	210	1,900	4,047	2,130 (54.2)
Naples	207	13,300	14,630	1,100 (0)
Guangzhou (Canton)	200	138,000	82,800	600 (0)
Aurangabad	200	165,000	90,750	550 (0)
Lisbon	188	2,000	1,638	854 (10.4)
World		603,410	371,369	615 (3.7)

Sources: City population data (Chandler 1987); country population, GDP and GDP per capita data (Maddison 2006)
Note: All GDP and GDP per capita $ values are given in 1990 Geary–Khamis dollars (Maddison 2006).

Amsterdam now emerged as the third-largest Western European city, after London and Paris. It is no accident that these three largest Western European cities were also the home locations of the East India and West India trading companies of England, the Netherlands, and France (Findlay and O'Rourke 2007), all of which were in the vanguard of the globalizing activities of these countries.

As we see in Table 8.2, the outcome of these interrelated processes of urbanization, industrialization, and early globalization is that the largest fifteen cities in the world in 1700 ranged in population from Constantinople (Istanbul) at 700,000 to Lisbon at 188,000. Nine of the world's fifteen largest cities were in Asia, with five being located in Western Europe, as well as Constantinople, which is at the crossroads of Europe and Asia. The large and ancient civilizations of China, India, and Japan were reflected in the size of their major cities. Only the two largest cities of Western Europe, London and Paris, were of comparable size to the very largest Asian cities, and these were the capital cities of the two largest European nations, Great Britain and France.

Table 8.2 also shows that many of the major cities of Europe in 1700 were of the same order of magnitude as many of the other largest cities in Asia. This may appear surprising given that the populations and economies of China and India were far larger than for any other countries. Yet clues as to why the European and Asian cities were of the same order of magnitude comes from the fact that the national per capita GDP of the dominant European cities' own countries was already of the order of two to four times that of the major Asian economies.[1] As a result of the seventeenth-century long 'Golden Era' of Dutch global pre-eminence, by 1700 productivity in the Netherlands was almost twice that of any other country. This suggests that while the size of a major city appears to be partly related to size of the country in which it is located, city size also appears to be related to the productivity of the country in which it is located, exactly as agglomeration arguments imply.

The dominance of the Dutch economy, built as it was around the relationships between its trading cities and its colonial empire, became increasingly overtaken by other expanding empires. The eighteenth century was the period which witnessed the increasing global pre-eminence of the empires of Great Britain, France, Russia, and Austria, all of which challenged the earlier dominance of the Dutch Empire. As with the Dutch, Spanish, and Portuguese empires in the previous centuries, these newly emerging empires experienced a similar growing relationship between urbanization, city size, industrialization, and globalization throughout the eighteenth century. As we see in Table 8.3, by 1800 six of the world's largest fifteen cities were now located in Western Europe, and most notably, these included Moscow and Vienna. The growth of these cities during the eighteenth century coincided with the growth and modernization of Russian Empire under Peter the Great and Catherine the Great, and also that of the Austrian Empire under the Habsburg Monarchy.

Of these rising empires, whose eighteenth-century globalization processes were all associated with industrialization and urbanization, the emerging superpower was Great Britain.

---

[1] Pomeranz (2000) argues that the labour productivity gap between the European and Asian economies was very much lower than the Maddison (2006, 2007a, b) figures would imply. However, these disagreements do not alter the basic argument here.

Table 8.3 The world's largest cities in 1800

1800	City population 000s (% growth 1700–1800)	Country population 000s 1820 (% growth 1700–1820)	GDP $000s 1820 (% growth 1700–1820)	GDP per capita $1820 (% growth 1700–1820)
Beijing (Peking)	1,100 (69.2)	381,000 (276)	228,600 (276)	600 (0)
London	861 (56.5)	21,239 (247)	36,232 (338)	1,706 (36.4)
Guangzhou (Canton)	800 (400)	381,000 (276)	228,600 (276)	600 (0)
Tokyo (Edo)	685 (0)	31,000 (14.8)	20,739 (34.7)	669 (17.3)
Istanbul (Constantinople)	570 (–18.5)	25,147 (West Asia)	15,269 (West Asia)	607 (West Asia) (0)
Paris	547 (3.2)	31,250 (14.6)	35,468 (182)	1,135 (24.7)
Naples	430 (208)	20,176 (15.2)	22,535 (54)	1,117 (15.4)
Hangzhou (Hangchow)	387 (27.7)	381,000 (276)	228,600 (276)	600 (0)
Osaka	383 (0)	31,000 (14.8)	20,739 (34.7)	669 (17.3)
Kyoto	377 (108)	31,000 (14.8)	20,739 (34.7)	669 (17.3)
Moscow	248 (217)	54,765 (264) (USSR)	37,678 (232)	688 (12.6)
Soochow	243 (173)	381,000 (276)	228,600 (276)	600 (0)
Lucknow	240 (400)	209,000 (26.6)	111,417 (26.6)	533 (–3.1)
Lisbon	237 (26)	3,297 (64.8)	3,043 (85.7)	923 (12.7)
Vienna	231 (220)	3,369 (34.7)	4,104 (65.2)	1,218 (18.6)
World		1,041,092 (72.5)	694,442 (86.9)	667 (8.4)

Sources: as for Table 8.2

This was the period during which Britain underwent the first phase of its industrial revolution. Rapid mechanization, capitalization, and urban–rural migration, particularly after 1750, all followed on from the widespread adoption of steam power based on large-scale coal extraction, the introduction of the first generation of large-scale factory production systems, and the spatial transformations enforced by the land enclosure movement. As we see in Table 8.1, by 1800 Britain was the most industrialized country in the world, and as the industrial transformation accelerated, so did the urban transformation.

At this time, the growth of urbanization in England, Wales, and Scotland was much greater than in any other areas of Europe, apart from the Low Countries, which are now the Netherlands and Belgium. As well as generally increasing urbanization, the onset of the industrial revolution in Britain was also associated with a rapid increase in the size of its capital city, London. By 1800 London had become the second-largest city in the world, and some 57 per cent larger than Western Europe's second-largest city, Paris. For almost two centuries London and Paris had been very similar in size, but during the eighteenth century France had undergone significantly less technological and industrial change than Britain, and this was also reflected in much lower levels of urbanization in general and the smaller size of its capital city.

The period between 1800 and 1850 was a period of increasing urbanization and industrialization in both North-Western Europe and the USA, with the advent of railways spearheading these changes. As we see in Table 8.1, by the middle of the nineteenth century, the level of industrialization in Great Britain was more than double that of any other nation. As we see in Table 8.4, the result of this was that in 1850 UK per capita gross domestic product

Table 8.4 The world's largest cities in 1850

1850	City population 000s (% change 1800–1850)	Country population 000s (% change 1820–1850)	GDP $000s (% change 1820–1850)	GDP per capita $ (% change 1820–1850)
London	2,320 (269)	27,181 (27.9)	63,342 (74.8)	2,330 (36.5)
Beijing (Peking)	1,648 (49.8)	412,000 (8.1)	247,200 (8.1)	600 (0)
Paris	1,314 (240)	36,350 (16.3)	58,039 (63.6)	1,597 (40.7)
Guangzhou (Canton)	875 (9.3)	412,000 (8.1)	247,200 (8.1)	600 (0)
Istanbul (Constantinople)	785 (37.7)	30,286 [1870 West Asia] (20.4)	22,468 [1870 West Asia] (47.1)	742 [1870 West Asia] (31.3)
Tokyo (Edo)	780 (13.8)	32,000 (18.5)	25,393 [1870] (22.4)	737 [1870] (10.1)
New York	645 (1023)	23,580 (236)	42,583 (426.6)	1,806 (43.6)
Mumbai (Bombay)	575 (410)	235,800 (12.8)	134,882 [1870] (21.1)	533 [1870] (0)
St Petersburg	502 (228)	73,750 [USSR] (34.6)	83,646 [1870] (52.7)	943 [1870] (37.1)
Berlin	446 (259)	33,746 (35.9)	48,178 (79.6)	1,428 (32.6)
Hangchow (Hangchow)	434 (12.1)	412,000 (8.1)	247,200 (8.1)	600 (0)
Vienna	426 (84.4)	3,950 (17.2)	6,519 (58.8)	1,650 (35.5)
Philadelphia	426 (626)	23,580 (236)	42,583 (426.6)	1,806 (43.6)
Liverpool	422 (555)	27,181 (27,181 (27.9))	63,342 (74.8)	2,330 (36.5)
Naples	414 (−3.8)	24,460 (21.2)	33,019 (46.5)	1,350 (20.8)
World [1870]		1,270,014 (21.9)	1,101,369 (58.6)	867 (29.9)

Sources: as for Table 8.2

(GDP), a measure of a country's output and wealth per capita, was the highest in the world and London was by then the world's largest city. The industrialization of France, a process which started in earnest many decades after Britain, allied with increasing French colonial expansion, meant that by 1850 Paris was by now the third-largest city in the world. Significantly, for the first time, cities in North America, most notably New York, appear in the list of the world's fifteen largest cities, although as we see in Table 8.1 the level of industrialization in the USA at this stage was still far below that of the UK, and more or less equivalent to those of France (Findlay and O'Rourke 2007).

The overall rate of growth of the Western world's largest cities was increasing during these years of continuing industrialization and colonial expansion. During the fifty years between 1800 and 1850, ten out of the world's fifteen largest cities had experienced faster growth than their equivalently ranked city in 1800 had experienced during the previous hundred years. Yet, by 1850, only six of the world's fifteen largest cities were in Asia. These changes in the scale of the major cities therefore also point to a geographical shift in the nature of urbanization. In particular, the change in global city rankings between 1800 and 1850 reflects the fact that rapid industrialization was taking place primarily in the European and North American economies, rather than in the major Asian economies, which remained largely rural.

During the first four centuries of the globalizing processes which took place from the beginning of the sixteenth century to the turn of the twentieth century, the period with the fastest growth of industrialization and urbanization was the very end of the era, spanning the second half of the nineteenth century and continuing right up to the eve of the First World War. As we see in Table 8.1, during the fifty years leading up to the Second World War, while the levels of industrialization in the UK and France had doubled, in the USA and Germany they had increased some six-fold. Between 1820 and 1913 these enormous increases in the level of industrialization were also associated with rapidly increasing inequality between the different parts of the world, with the rich industrialized North Atlantic economies along with British off-shoots (Maddison 2006) such as Australia and New Zealand all rapidly pulling away from the rest of the world (Findlay and O'Rourke 2007).

In terms of cities and urbanization, this period of enormous industrialization also coincided with what until then was the era with the most rapid rates of urbanization the world had ever known. As we see in Table 8.1, the global urbanization rates had tripled during the nineteenth century. By comparing Table 8.5 with Table 8.4, we see that the outcome of this was that during the fifty years between 1850 and 1900, eleven out of the world's fifteen largest cities had experienced faster growth than their equivalent-ranked city in 1850 had experienced between 1800 and 1850. By now, the world's largest cities reflected the economies with both the highest levels of per capita productivity and also productivity growth, with twelve out of the world's fifteen largest cities now being either in Western Europe or the

Table 8.5 The world's largest cities in 1900

1900	City population 000s (% change 1850–1900)	Country population 000s (% change 1850–1900)	GDP $000s (% change 1850–1900)	GDP per capita $ (% change 1850–1900)
London	6,480 (279)	41,155 (51.4)	184,861 (291)	4,492 (92.7)
New York	4,242 (657)	76,391 (323)	312,499 (734)	4,091 (226)
Paris	3,330 (253)	40,598 (11.7)	116,747 (201)	2,876 (80)
Berlin	2,707 (606)	54,388 (61.2)	162,335 (336)	2,985 (209)
Chicago	1,717 [1858–1900] (1717)	76,391 (323)	312,499 (734)	4,091 (226)
Vienna	1,698 (398)	5,973 (51.2)	17,213 (264)	2,882 (74.6)
Tokyo	1,497 (91.9)	44,103 (37.8)	52,020 (204)	1,180 (60.1)
St Petersburg	1,439 (286)	124,500 [USSR] (68.8)	154,049 (84)	1,237 (31.1))
Manchester	1,435 (348)	41,155 (51.4)	184,861 (291)	4,492 (92.7)
Philadelphia	1,418 (332)	76,391 (323)	312,499 (734)	4,091 (226)
Birmingham	1,248 (424)	41,155 (51.4)	184,861 (291)	4,492 (92.7)
Moscow	1,120 (300)	124,500 [USSR] (68.8)	154,049 (84)	1,237 (31.1)
Beijing (Peking)	1,100 (−33.2)	400,000 (−3.0)	218,074 (−11.8)	545 (−9.2)
Kolkata (Calcutta)	1,085 (262)	284,000 (20.4)	170,466 (26.4)	599 (12.4)
Boston	1,075 (514)	76,391 (323)	312,499 (734)	4,091 (226)
World [1913]		1,791,020 (41.0)	2,704,782 (246)	1,510 (74.2)

Sources: as for Table 8.2

USA. The fastest-growing large city in the world was Chicago, the dominant railway hub for the mid-West and a city in the vanguard the rapid westward expansion of the USA. Chicago grew from 100,000 in 1858 to over 1.7million in 1900. There were now sixteen cities in the world with populations of over one million people (PWC 2009).

A relationship evident in the Western nations between the productivity and scale of the economy and the size of the dominant cities was also emerging in Asia. By 1900 the largest city in the rest of the world was Tokyo, located in what was by now Asia's most productive economy. Japan had experienced rapid industrialization and modernization following the Meiji restoration of 1868, which had re-opened the Japanese economy to international trade and investment after three centuries of autarky. By 1900 Japan was already emerging as one of the world's richest economies. Apart from the Beijing, which was actually contracting, the only major exception to these general patterns in the nineteenth century was that of the Indian cities of Lucknow, Mumbai, and Kolkata, all transhipment points, ports, as well as military garrisons for the British East Indian Company. As such, the growth of these cities can be understood primarily in relation to the enormous growth of the British Empire during the nineteenth century.

8.3 Globalization, urbanization, and industrialization in the twentieth century

The evidence presented so far all points to a clear positive relationship between industrialization, urbanization, and globalization, a relationship which was ongoing from the early sixteenth century right up to the beginning of the twentieth century. Urbanization was an unambiguous indicator of industrialization and the largest cities were all in the richest countries. Not surprisingly therefore, as we see in Table 8.6, by 1925, as the dominant city of the world's dominant economy, New York had emerged as the world's largest city. Moreover, by now, fourteen of the world's fifteen largest cities were located in Europe, the USA, or Japan. Only Buenos Aires, which was the world's fastest-growing major city in the early part of the twentieth century, was outside these regions, and this too was located in what at the time was a very wealthy country. In 1925, all the world's largest cities were in the richest and largest economies.

This longstanding relationship between urbanization, industrialization, and globalization had been well established for so long that it is not surprising that, as we have already seen in this book, this was also precisely the period when the first scholars who were seriously interested in the economics of cities and regions, including Alfred Marshall (1890), Alfred Weber (1909), Walter Christaller (1933), Bertil Ohlin (1933), were making their groundbreaking observations and writing their seminar works. Cities had emerged as the economic engines at the heart of the emerging global nation-empire trading systems, and there was nothing to suggest that these relationships between urbanization, industrialization, and globalization would change. Yet, after an era of four centuries of largely uninterrupted globalization processes, there did indeed begin a period of anti-globalization in many of the richer countries.

This reversal in the long-run historical processes (Ferguson 2008) of urbanization was a result of changes in the processes of globalization, which themselves were a result of the

Table 8.6 The world's largest cities in 1925

1925	City population 000s (% change 1900–1925)	Country population 000s (% change 1900–1925)	GDP $000s (% change 1900–1925)	GDP per capita $ (% change 1900–1925)
New York	7,774 (83.2)	116,284 (52.2)	730,545 (233)	6,282 (53.5)
London	7,742 (19.5)	45,059 (9.48)	231,806 (25.4)	5,144 (14.5)
Tokyo	5,300 (354)	59,522 (86.0)	112,209 (216)	1,885 (59.7)
Paris	4,800 (44.1)	40,610 (11.7)	169,197 (44.9)	4,166 (44.8)
Berlin	4,013 (48.2)	63,166 (87.2)	223,082 (37.4)	3,532 (18.3)
Chicago	3,564 (208)	116,284 (52.2)	730,545 (233)	6,282 (53.5)
Ruhr	3,400 (443)	63,166 (87.2)	223,082 (37.4)	3,532 (18.3)
Buenos Aires	2,410 (299)	10,358 (221)	40,597 (233)	3,919 (53.5)
Osaka	2,219 (228)	59,522 (86.0)	112,209 (314)	1,885 (18.3)
Philadelphia	2,085 (47)	116,284 (52.2)	730,545 (216)	6,282 (53.5)
Vienna	1,865 (9.8)	6,582 (10.2)	22,161 (233)	3,367 (204)
Boston	1,764 (64.1)	116,284 (52.2)	730,545 (28.7)	6,282 (53.5)
Moscow	1,764 (57.5)	158,983 (27.2)(USSR)	231,886 [1928] (50.5)	1,370 [1928] (10.0)
Manchester	1,725 (20.2)	45,059 (9.48)	231,806 (25.4)	5,144 (14.5)
Birmingham	1,700 (36.2)	45,059 (9.48)	231,806 (25.4)	5,144 (14.5)

Sources: as for Table 8.2

global economic disruption engendered by the two world wars, the intervening Depression of the 1930s, and the reconstruction of the global economic system under the highly regulated international trade architecture of the Bretton-Woods system. In the inter-war years, all major economies increasingly re-oriented their trade patterns primarily to within the sphere of their own colonial systems (Findlay and O'Rourke 2007). The outcome of this period of anti-globalization was that countries became largely closed to each other, and the importance of international economic linkages and transmission mechanisms fell relatively in comparison with the importance of domestic mechanisms. In economic terms, the impacts of these reversals were that the ratio of world trade to global GDP fell during the period 1929–1950, and barely recovered until the 1970s (Fischer 2003), while the ratio of foreign assets to global GDP declined from 1914 onwards and was not attained again until 1980 (Crafts 2004).

This period of anti-globalization and the massive global contraction of trade and foreign investment on the part of the rich countries also coincided with a fall in the importance of urban growth as an economic engine in many of these same countries. As we have already seen, urbanization had always been closely associated with industrialization, and as economic growth and trade fell, so therefore did the growth of urbanization. In the rich industrialized countries the urbanization growth rates of the largest cities slowed down during the first half of the twentieth century. As we see in Table 8.7, of the world's largest cities in 1950, only six out of the world's fifteen largest cities had experienced faster growth between 1925 and 1950 than their equivalent-ranked city in 1925 had experienced between 1900 and 1925. Apart from the rapid growth of Los Angeles, in terms of the industrialized countries, the overall global city rankings remained relatively stable between 1925 and 1950.

Table 8.7 The world's largest cities in 1950

1950	City population 000s (% change 1925–1950)	Country population 000s (% change 1925–1950)	GDP $000s (% change 1925–1950)	GDP per capita $ (% change 1925–1950)
New York	12,463 (60.3)	152,271 (30.9)	1,455,916 (99.3)	9,561 (52.2)
London	8,860 (14.4)	50,127 (11.2)	347,850 (50.1)	6,939 (34.8)
Tokyo	7,000 (32.1)	83,805 (40.8)	160,966 (43.4)	1,921 (1.9)
Paris	5,900 (22.9)	41,829 (3.0)	220,492 (30.3)	5,271 (26.5)
Shanghai	5,407 (360)	546,815 (13.8)	239,903 (10.0)	439 (–21.9)
Moscow	5,100 (289)	179,571[USSR] (12.9)	510,243 (220)	2,841 (207)
Buenos Aires	5,000 (207)	17,150 (65.6)	85,524 (210)	4,987 (27.2)
Chicago	4,906 (37.6)	152,271 (30.9)	1,455,916 (99.3)	9,561 (52.2)
Ruhr	4,900 (44.1)	68,375 (8.2)	265,354 (18.9)	3,881 (9.9)
Kolkata (Calcutta)	4,800 (345)	359,000 (12.2)	222,222 (30.3)	619 (–11.4)
Los Angeles	3,986 (347)	152,271 (30.9)	1,455,916 (99.3)	9,561 (52.2)
Berlin	3,707 (–7.7)	68,375 (8.2)	265,354 (18.9)	3,881 (9.9)
Osaka	3,341 (50.6)	83,805 (40.8)	160,966 (43.4)	1,921 (1.9)
Philadelphia	2,900 (39.1)	152,271 (30.9)	1,455,916 (99.3)	9,561 (52.2)
Mexico City	2,872 (372)	28,485 (53.3)	67,368 (223)	2,365 (73.1)
World (1950)		2,524,324	5,329,719	2,111 (40) (1913–1950)

Sources: as for Table 8.2

The period characterized by the 1930s Depression and the Second World War can therefore in many ways be considered as marking the end of the first major phase of global urbanization, which from the early seventeenth century to 1950 had been dominated by Europe and North America. This initial phase of urbanization and industrialization had led to an increase in the global number of urban dwellers from fifteen million to over 400 million, and an increase in the global urbanization index from 10 per cent to 52 per cent (UNFPA 2007).

In contrast to the previous four centuries of increasing globalization, industrialization, and urbanization, the immediate post-Second World War period can be regarded as marking the start of the second phase of global urbanization (UNFPA 2007, a phase which is qualitatively quite different in nature to the earlier periods or urbanization. Since 1950, not only has the urbanization rate increased globally, but this second phase of global urbanization has been dominated by the rise of urbanization in developing countries (Satterthwaite 2005). In 1950, only eleven out of the largest thirty cities in the world were from developing countries (PWC 2009). By 1975, over 75 of the 190 urban agglomerations with over one million inhabitants were from the developing countries (Chandler 1987). As we see in Table 8.8, the result of these new forms of urbanization meant that by 1975 seven of the world's fifteen largest cities, namely Mexico City, São Paulo, Buenos Aires, Rio de Janeiro, Cairo, Shanghai, and Calcutta, were in developing countries, and between 1950 and 1975, eleven of these mega-cities had experienced faster growth than their equivalent-ranked city in 1950 had experienced between 1925 and 1950.

Table 8.8 The world's largest cities in 1975

1975	City population 000s (% change 1950–1975)	Country population 000s (% change 1950–1975)	GDP $000s (% change 1950–1975)	GDP per capita $ (% change 1950–1975)
Tokyo	23,000 (328)	111,573 (33.1)	1,265,661 (786)	11,344 (590)
New York	17,150 (37.6)	215,973 (41.8)	3,516,825 (241)	16,284 (70.3)
Osaka	15,500 (464)	111,573 (33.1)	1,265,661 (786)	11,344 (590)
Mexico City	11,339 (395)	60,828 (213)	312,998 (465)	5,146 (216)
Moscow	10,700 (209)	254,519 [USSR] (41.7)	1,561,399 (306)	6,135 (216)
London	10,500 (18.5)	56,215 (12.1)	665,984 (91.4)	11,847 (225)
São Paulo	10,041 (451)	108,824 (204)	455,918 (510)	4,190 (257)
Paris	9,400 (59.3)	52,758 (26.1)	699,106 (317)	13,773 (261)
Los Angeles	8,960 (225)	215,973 (41.8)	3,516,825 (241)	16,284 (70.3)
Buenos Aires	8,498 (69.9)	26,082 (52.1)	211,850 (247)	8,122 (62.8)
Cairo	8,400 (305)	36,952 (74.3)	52,501 (272)	1,421 (56.1)
Rio de Janeiro	8,328 (290)	108,824 (204)	455,918 (510)	4,190 (251)
Shanghai	8,000 (47.9)	916,395 (67.6)	800,876 (339)	874 (99.1)
Kolkata (Calcutta)	7,875 (64.0)	607,000 (69.1)	544,683 (245)	897 (44.9)
Seoul	7,500 (483)	35,281 (69.2)	111,548 (695)	3,162 (411)
World		4,065,408	16,644,898	4,094 (93.9)

Sources: as for Table 8.2

Between 1975 and 2000 the global process of urbanization accelerated even more. The number of cities in the world with a population of more than one million went from 115 in 1960 to 416 in 2000 (Venables 2006) and by the year 2000, there were over 140 cities globally with populations of over two million inhabitants (Le Gales 2002). The number of cities of more than 4 million the increased between 1960 and 2000 from 18 to 53 (Venables 2006) and by 2000 nineteen cities had populations of over ten million (Le Gales 2002). The number of cities with more than 12 million inhabitants had increased from 1 to 11 during the four decades between 1960 and 2000 (Venables 2006).

The effect of all of these changes was that, by 2008, at 3.3 billion, the number of people living in urban areas across the world had for the first time passed 50 per cent of the global population (OECD 2007; UNFPA 2007, and this process of increasing urbanization was common to both the industrialized and the industrializing world. But in the developing world the rate of urbanization was far more dramatic than in the developed world. By 2005 the developing world's urban population of 2.4 billion accounted for approximately three-quarters of the global urban population (World Bank 2008; UNFPA 2007. The proportion of the population in the low- and middle-income countries of the developing world which lived in urban areas had increased from 37 per cent to 44 per cent between 1990 and 2005, while during the same period the proportion of the population in developing countries living in cities of over one million inhabitants had increased from 14 per cent to 17 per cent (World Bank 2008).

The result of all of these changes was that, by the year 2000, as we see in Table 8.9, ten of the world's fifteen largest cities were from the developing world, and this tendency towards

Table 8.9 The world's largest cities in 2000

2000	City population 000s (% change 1975–2000)	Country population 000s (% change 1975–2000)	GDP $000s (% change 1975–2000)	GDP per capita $ (% change 1975–2000)
Tokyo	29,896 (30.0)	126,737 (13.6)	2,589,320 (204)	20,431 (80.0)
New York	24,719 (44.1)	270,561 (25.2)	7,394,598 (210)	27,331 (67.8)
Seoul	20,674 (275)	46,898 (30.7)	624,582 (559)	13,317 (421)
Mexico City	19,081 (68.3)	98,553 (62.0)	655,910 (209)	6,665 (29.5)
São Paulo	17,396 (73.2)	169,897 (56.0)	926,918 (203)	5,459 (30.2)
Manila	16,740 (310)	79,376 (78.5)	181,886 (201)	2,291 (12.9)
Los Angeles	15,807 (76.4)	270,561 (25.2)	7,394,598 (210)	27,331 (67.8)
Mumbai	15,769 (223)	991,691 (63.3)	1,803,172 (3.31)	1,818 (202)
Djakarta	15,086 (284)	207,429 (58.9)	628,753 (3.2)	3,031 (201)
Osaka	15,039 (–3.0)	126,737 (13.6)	2,589,320 (204)	20,431 (80.0)
Delhi	13,592 (309)	991,691 (63.3)	1,803,172 (3.31)	1,818 (202)
Kolkata (Calcutta)	12,619 (60.2)	991,691 (63.3)	1,803,172 (3.31)	1,818 (202)
Buenos Aires	12,297 (44.7)	36,235 (39.2)	334,314 (57.8)	9,219 (13.2)
Shanghai	11,960 (49.5)	1,252,704 (36.6)	4,082,513 (509)	3,259 (372)
Cairo	11,633 (38.4)	66,050 (78.7)	140,546 (339)	2,128 (89.8)
World [1998]		5,907,680 (45.3)	33,725,631 (202)	5,709 (39.4)

Sources: as for Table 8.2

Note: The figures reported here are for conurbations, and come from the GEOPOLIS database, rather than just city administrative boundaries. Therefore New York City (five boroughs) has only 7.549 million, the greater New York area has 18.7 million(OECD 2006), and the total New York conurbation (including Philadelphia) has over 24 million inhabitants. Similarly, depending on the source used and methods of defining urban areas, London city has only 7.4 million inhabitants (OECD 2006) but the London conurbation has a population of 8.5 million according to the *World Urbanization Prospects* (2008) (http://esa.un.org/unup/p2k0data.asp), a population of over 9.66 million according to GEOPOLIS, or a population of 11.22 million according to the *World Gazatteer* (www.world-gazatteer.com). Other city size estimates for the twentieth century are available from Satterthwaite (2005) and PWC (2009). More recent standardized figures for OECD urban areas have been published by the OECD, which allow for differences in density and also commuting patterns (OECD 2012)

mega-cities in the developing world was not specific to one or two countries, in that these ten cities were located in eight different countries. More recently, PWC (2009) estimated that 21 out of the 30 largest cities in the world in 2007 were located in developing or newly industrializing countries.

Moreover, all the evidence suggests that the rate of urbanization in the developing world will continue to increase even faster relative that that of the developed world. The recent annual growth of the urban population in low- and middle-income countries in the developing world between 1990 and 2005 was 2.6 per cent, while that in high-income countries was only 1.1 per cent (World Bank 2008). United Nations predictions suggest that the global urban population will increase to 4.9 billion by 2030, of which 3.9 billion will be in the developing world (UNFPA 2007). As such, the level of urbanization in the developing world will increase by 60 per cent between 2000 and 2030, which is some 3.75 times greater than the urbanization rate in the developed world over the same period.

This unprecedented urbanization is not simply a result of population growth, in that over the same period, the global rural population is expected to actually decrease (UNFPA 2007 PWC 2009). The role of urban scale and centrality appears to be becoming ever more critical as sources of economic growth. Over the last three decades, the increasing importance played by cities as engines of national, regional, and global economic growth is demonstrated by the fact that the proportion of people living in urban areas has increased in all parts of the global economy (Richardson and Bae 2005). Between 1950 and 2030, the total urbanization index of the developing world is predicted to increase from 18 per cent to 56 per cent (UNFPA 2007, with the majority of this increasing urbanization taking place in Asia and Africa. By 2030, Asia and Africa will account for 80 per cent of the global urban population (UNFPA 2007). China alone expects its urban population to double by 2030 (Venables 2006).

Estimates and forecasts of the future growth trends for city sizes, city output levels, and city productivity performance in different parts of the global economy are provided by various organizations, including PWC (2009), MGI (2009, 2010, 2011a, b, 2012) and OECD (2012). Of course cities vary enormously in terms of geographical structures and commuting patterns, and the development of standardized measurement criteria is very important (OECD 2012) in order to ensure comparability. But much of the evidence points in the same direction, namely that the world is becoming more urbanized, and that cities play an increasingly important role in the global economy. The increasing role of cities is also associated with improvements in education and indicators of health and well-being, as it has been throughout history (Glaeser 2011).

The interrelationships between city size, education, health, and well-being, however, are by no means straightforward (Burdett et al. 2011), and these relationships are particularly problematic in the case of very large cities. While on the one hand very large cities contribute significantly to economic development, the mega-cities of the developing world pose major challenges in terms of poverty reduction, environmental degradation, health care, and housing, and in many of these cities the challenges are becoming more acute (Burdett et al 2011). In contrast, in Europe, well-being and quality of life indicators are generally higher in smaller and mid-size urban centres, many of which are, by the standards of North America and the developing countries, actually small cities (European Commission 2010). However, the relationship between city size and social and health issues are very complex and the possible policy responses to these types of problems, as they relate to cities and regions, are discussed in Chapter 10. At this stage we focus on certain key features of modern cities and modern urbanization processes.

8.4 Recent features of urbanization and globalization

As well as increasing urbanization in developing countries, a major feature of the most recent era of globalization has been the re-emergence of the importance of cities, or particular cities, even within many of the rich advanced economies. While the post-war period of urbanization was dominated by the developing world, urbanization processes also re-emerged in many parts of the developed world. During the post-Second World War Bretton-Woods era, the growth in urbanization once again started to re-emerge. While there were globally 67 cities with over one million inhabitants (Chandler 1987) in 1950, as we have seen, by 1975 there were 190 urban agglomerations with over one million inhabitants (Chandler 1987). The USA alone accounted for 25 of these million-plus agglomerations, Western Europe accounted for 34, and Warsaw Pact Europe accounted for fifteen (Chandler 1987). Urbanization among the rich countries was therefore dominated by the USA. The proportion of the US population living in cities increased at a higher rate in the post-war era than during the inter-war period, and among the other rich countries urbanization and the growth of mega-cities also emerged in both Japan and South Korea during the post-Second World War era.

In other rich countries, however, the population actually fell in many cities. This was particularly the case for many traditional industrial cities which declined in population during this era as manufacturing exhibited an urban–rural drift. In Europe this was particularly noticeable in the traditional manufacturing heartlands of the UK (Fothergill et al. 1985) and Germany, while in both the USA (Glaeser 2005) and Europe (Sassen 2006) many of the very largest cities saw population declines in the core parts of the agglomerations. From the late 1970s similar trends were evident in many of the USA's mid-Western cities, and particularly those which had been specialized in traditional manufacturing and heavy engineering. While many of these urban restructuring processes were associated with absolute population declines within the core city areas, in the outer urban areas it was a different story. Many of these inner urban population declines reflected processes of urban decentralization in which residents took advantage of new transportation technologies to relocate to suburban locations. Large numbers of people moved from inner-city locations to more suburban locations or to satellite towns and cities, the result of which was that many metropolitan areas actually increased in terms of their geographical areal coverage, irrespective of whether their total population levels were falling or increasing. As such, these urban decentralization processes often tended to be associated with ever-increasing commuting distances into the urban centres, issues which we now know have contributed to climate change.

As many cities expanded in terms of their geographical areas, there also emerged new types of commuting patterns in which residents no longer commuted to central-city locations, but increasingly were employed in suburban or satellite locations. By the 1980s many urban planners, architectural historians, and sociologists were confidently espousing the emerging trends towards so-called 'post-industrial' residential patterns of living, whereby changes in technologies and work practices meant that workers would increasingly become freed from the requirements of proximity and accessibility. It was assumed that workers would increasingly become free to choose where to live and work on the basis of their lifestyle and amenity preferences, rather than according to the traditional requirements of their employers for proximity and density. The results of these new-found freedoms would be that cities would decline in importance as geography became less important. However, as we see in Box 8.2, in reality, very different spatial outcomes are also likely, giving rise to spatial concentration.

Many of the urban decentralization trends evident in the 1970s and 1980s went into reverse during the 1990s when increasing urbanization was not only observed in developing countries, but once again was also observed in many advanced and rich countries. On many indicators, cities appear to have once again re-emerged in economic importance (Glaeser 1998; Glaeser and Gottlieb 2009) at precisely the moment when the arguments of many com-

BOX 8.2 Is the world becoming 'flat' or is proximity becoming more important?

Over the last three decades suggestions that geographical proximity is becoming progressively less important have been commonplace. In 1992 O'Brien (1992) announced the 'end of geography' and in 1997 Frances Cairncross (1997) announced the 'death of distance'. However, the idea that technological improvements mean that geography and distance have become of little or no importance goes back to the early 1980s (Warf 1995; Gaspar and Glaeser 1998). As we have seen, in the 1980s these arguments were also bolstered by observations of an urban–rural shift and a drift away from city centres to surrounding areas. In 2007, however, these increasingly popular arguments were given an enormous boost with the publication of Thomas Friedman's influential bestselling book *The World is Flat*. In this book and its two subsequently updated editions, Friedman (2007) argues that the world is becoming rapidly flatter. His notion of 'flat' implies that we increasingly observe greater similarity and greater homogeneity between people in different parts of the world, and he bases his argument on ten major political economy and technological phenomena. These phenomena are: the fall of the Berlin Wall; the advent of the world wide web; the development of work-flow software; the advent of uploading and file sharing; the advent of outsourcing; the rise of off-shoring; the development of supply-chaining; the rise of third-party dedicated internal logistics operations; the rise of information availability via search engines; and the development of wireless technology. Taken together, he argues that since the year 2000 these ten phenomena have been rapidly reshaping the world in a way which is qualitatively and quantitatively different from previous eras of globalization. While, as we have seen, other commentators have defined the process of globalization using different time markers (Crafts 2004; MacGillivray 2006; Steger 2003), Friedman's book has been singularly influential simply in terms of its popularity, and the extent to which his ideas influence thinking in the political and commercial arenas therefore requires a careful and critical evaluation. Yet what is strange about the arguments that geography is becoming less important due to the recent technological advances and institutional developments is that this also implies that cities must become relatively less important. The reason is that, on this argument, the economic importance of proximity and accessibility will be reduced, and therefore the need for people and firms to be spatially concentrated in the same places will fall.

The evidence presented in this book and elsewhere, however, suggests that the reality of economic geography is almost entirely the opposite. As we have seen in this chapter, mega-urbanization is increasing in developing countries. Yet urbanization is also increasing in rich countries. In the developed world, the total urban population in 2005–2006 was estimated to be of the order of 800 million, in other words approximately one-quarter of the global urban population of 3.2 billion (World Bank 2008). By 2007, 53 per cent of the OECD population lived in urban areas, and this figure rises to almost 80 per cent if less densely populated intermediate urban areas are included (OECD 2007). The proportion of the population living in urban areas in high-income countries increased from 71 per cent to 73 per cent between 1990 and 2005 (World Bank 2008), and by 2002 the OECD contained 78 metropolitan urban regions with over 1.5 million inhabitants. The United Nations expects the urban population of the developed world to increase between 2000 and 2030 by some 16 per cent from 870 million in 2000 to 1.01 billion in 2030 (UNFPA 2007). In many ways, geography is becoming more important than ever as an economic issue.

mentators would suggest that they should be dying, or at least significantly diminishing in importance. Why this should be the case is a result of the shocks associated with the new era of globalization, an era which began at the end of the 1980s, and which instilled a complex set of technological and institutional transformations which have changed all aspects of the economic geography of the global economy. Some of these changes will be outlined here, and we will return to these issues in much more detail in Chapters 9 and 10. As we will see, the actual urban and regional economic changes taking place in the modern era of globalization are very complex, and no simple worldwide urban and regional pattern has been emerging.

8.5 Modern globalization: global firms, global regions, and global cities

The modern era of globalization can be considered on many dimensions to have arisen during the period 1989–1994, and as such is approximately still only less than three decades old. The period 1989–1994 was a period which witnessed enormous institutional transformations, including: the fall of the Berlin Wall in 1989; the accelerated opening up of the Chinese economy after 1989; the reintegration of South Africa into the global system after the release of Nelson Mandela in 1990; the second industrial reforms which took place in 1991 in both India and Indonesia; the creation of the European Single Market in 1991/1992; the establishment of the North American Free Trade Agreement (NAFTA) in 1994; the adoption of the new constitution of Brazil in 1988 and the flotation of its new currency, the real, in 1994. All these institutional changes led to a transformation in the global economy.

The opening up of the so-called BRIICS group of countries, namely of Brazil, Russia, India, Indonesia, China, and South Africa (OECD 2008), meant that these large-population nations for the first time began to play a very major role in the global labour market. Since 1990 the opening up of the former transition economies has brought some 260 million new workers into the global labour market, China some 760 million new workers, and India another 440 million new workers (Venables 2006). As such, a major difference between the current phase of globalization and all previous eras of globalization is simply in terms of both the speed and the order of magnitude of the changes (Crafts 2004; MacGillivray 2006). From the perspective of labour market integration, the period 1989–1994 represented the largest shift in global labour markets in economic history, with approximately one-third of the global labour market for the first time emerging into the global economic system within a very short time period.

The global institutional changes encouraged the rapid integration of these huge countries into the global economy and provided an enormous range of new possibilities for both the supply of cheap labour and for new consumption opportunities. These possibilities and opportunities were magnified and accelerated by the invention in 1991 of the world wide web (www) interface based on the http protocol which was developed by Tim Berners-Lee. This technological breakthrough for the first time allowed many different technological developments to be integrated into a single electronic platform. Many different transportation and communications technologies had been developing apace over the two or three decades before the 1990s, most notably technologies such as containerization (Levinson 2006), GPS global positioning systems, mobile phone technologies, electronic file sharing, but the invention of the world wide web allowed these technologies to be integrated and exploited in a vast array of new ways which were unimaginable only a few years earlier.

The major beneficiaries of these combined institutional and technological transformations were those companies which already had the skills and knowledge to exploit these transformations, namely multinational companies. The competitive advantages of multinational firms are precisely that they are able to exploit any emerging global market opportunities by developing highly integrated global supply, marketing, and control systems, and by also controlling these global systems very tightly so that they are best able to exploit their corporate knowledge. The modern era of globalization has proved to be an enormous boost to these firms, which have responded to the transformations by an enormous increase in the extent to which they outsource and off-shore many of their activities. Multinational enterprises (MNEs) are now in the vanguard of the current phase of globalization, connecting cities and regions to a higher degree than ever before in terms of all kinds of flows of knowledge, human capital, investment finance, goods, and services (McCann and Acs 2011).

In this modern era of globalization the geographical behaviour of these multinational firms and global corporations exhibits two dominant characteristics. First, multinational firms, rather than being completely global in outlook, are actually overwhelmingly regional in nature, in the sense that their sales, investments, and R&D are dominated by the same 'super-regions' or blocs or groupings of adjacent countries in which their parent companies are located (Rugman 2000, 2005). The spatial patterns of all forms of their cross-border investments tend to be concentrated in the same super-regions from which the multinational firms emerge. For example, if we take the case of the three major global super-regional blocs of countries in the global economy, namely those of NAFTA (USA, Canada and Mexico), the European Union, and East Asia, we find that the average same-regional sales share of the world's top 500 companies is over 70 per cent (Rugman 2005). In other words, a US multinational firm will typically conduct over 70 per cent of its activities within the NAFTA arena, while a French multinational firm will typically conduct over 70 per cent of its activities within the European Union. Similar evidence from patent citation data suggests that firms typically gain the vast majority of their knowledge within the local region and the same country (Peri 2005). At the same time, the geographical patterns of the bilateral investment treaties and double taxation treaties are also very spatially concentrated (UNCTAD 2003), thereby reinforcing the regionalizing trends of the global companies. These observations all suggest that modern globalization is more accurately described as 'global regionalism'.

The second geographical aspect of the concentration of multinational activities is that knowledge-related activities, in particular, tend to be concentrated in certain key 'global cities' within these same super-regions from which the firm emanates, and there is much evidence of the increasing role of global cities (Sassen 1994, 2002; Taylor 2004; Ni and Kresl 2010) in the international economy. The analysis of global cities suggests that in the current phase of globalization, the links between a city and other parts of the global economy are a key determinant of the city-region's performance.

In this particular geographical literature, which draws heavily on sociological approaches, the importance and influence of a city in the global economic system are discussed in terms of the extent of its global 'connectivity' (Sassen 2002), where 'connectivity' refers not only to the various aspects of the knowledge and information exchanges which take place between particular locations, but also to the discretionary decision-making power to act on those knowledge exchanges (Ni and Kresl 2010). As such, global connectivity may be manifested via a variety of mechanisms, such as corporate headquarter functions, corporate decision-making linkages, human-capital mobility patterns, trade linkages, transport linkages, financial linkages, and asset management roles (Taylor 2004; Sassen 2006). Network analyses of trade and knowledge indicators imply that there has emerged a new core–periphery hierarchical structure to international trading patterns (Kali and Reyes 2006; Reyes et al. 2009), and the knowledge reach of technologically leading regions is already far greater than for other regions (Peri 2005). It is argued that by locating in these centres global firms will therefore increasingly reap the economic rents associated with their knowledge assets via the exploitation of the genuinely global production, communication, and financial networks (Coleman 1996; Cohen 1998; Zook 2005) which are facilitated by these global city systems. Estimates suggest that, since 1990, one-third of economic growth in the USA was accounted for by its multinational companies (MGI 2010b). Understanding the location behaviour of these firms is therefore also critical for understanding the geography of economic growth. We will return to these issues in much more detail in Chapter 9.

In the current era of globalization, two of the most important features of the emerging urban and regional patterns of economic activity therefore appear to be a trend towards the development of cross-border global regions, and also the growing importance of the global cities embedded within these global regions. This suggests that globalization involves a newly emerging economic geography of cities and regions in which proximity and accessibility are still essential features. But the key difference between the economic relationships afforded by recent technological and institutional changes and earlier eras of globalization is that the critical scale of the relationships which operate nowadays between cities, regions, and nations has increased dramatically. Yet modern technological and institutional changes do not imply that the world is getting flatter, and nor do they imply that growing cities are the solution to development problems. Rather, these changes imply that the geography of urban and regional economies is nowadays evolving in complex and heterogeneous ways, due to ongoing processes of international economic integration, technological development, and institutional reforms.

For our purposes at this stage it is sufficient to note six features of the relationship between globalization, urbanization, and industrialization:

(i) There has been a clear long-run relationship between increasing urbanization, industrialization, and globalization since the early sixteenth century, a relationship which was stalled in many rich countries during the early twentieth century.

(ii) The long-run relationship between globalization and urbanization has re-emerged in the developed world in the latter decades of the twentieth century, after having been stalled or even going in reverse for many deacdes in some rich countries.

(iii) The re-emergence or urbanization in rich countries is associated with the reintegration of the global economy after decades of anti-globalization processes.

(iv) Rising urbanization and the growth of mega-cities in the developing world has been a major feature of the second phase of global urbanization, a phase which began after the Second World War and continues to this day.

(v) The modern era of globalization is associated with the super-regional processes of integration between groups of neighbouring countries, leading to global regionalism rather than globalization.

(vi) At the core of the newly emerging super-regions are global cities, cities whose trade linkages are dominated by the presence of multinational companies.

These six features demonstrate why understanding the economic role of cities and regions is critical for understanding economic growth and trade. However, simple parallels across history have to be treated carefully. In many ways, at first sight the features of modern globalization appear reminiscent of earlier eras of globalization. In particular, modern globalization appears to have much in common with the late nineteenth-century and early twentieth-century period during which many of the most influential early writers on urban and regional issues were writing about the importance of cities and agglomeration. However, as we will see in Chapter 9, in many ways the modern era of globalization is also quite different from earlier eras, and an understanding of these differences also changes how we view the long-run national and international economic role played by cities and regions in today's global economy.

8.6 Conclusions

The emergence of global firms, global cities, and global regions provides the modern backdrop and context in which we examine urban and regional economics. The enormous changes wrought by modern globalization since the early 1990s, in which national economies have again opened up to each other in much more profound ways than ever before, requires us to consider the role and performance played by cities and regions at the sub-national level in the light of the behaviour of global cities and global regions operating at the international level. Cities and regions are again at centre stage in many discussions of growth and development, and this reinforces the timeliness of studying urban and regional economics. However, while the focus on cities and regions has re-emerged, this does not necessarily imply that economic growth is simply about agglomeration economies driving the growth of the largest cities and the richest countries, as it was at the beginning of the twentieth century. While this may be the case nowadays in developing countries, the fact that so few of the world's largest cities are in advanced and rich countries suggests that in these countries the picture may be rather more complex. In many ways our economic thinking is heavily shaped by the models and methods we employ, many of which were originally developed in the light of the early twentieth-century experience of cities. Yet, as we will see in Chapter 9, for many wealthy countries urban scale no longer appears to be as good an indicator of growth and development as it was in previous eras, whereas in poor and developing countries this relationship still seems to hold. Understanding these complex emerging patterns therefore requires us to consider all the analytical issues discussed in Part I of this book in the light of the long-run global trends discussed in this chapter. These issues are the topics discussed in Chapter 9. Finally, the changes due to modern globalization regarding the role played by cities and regions in economic development also require us to rethink many of the traditional debates regarding urban and regional policy. As we will see in Chapter 10, the thinking surrounding urban and regional economic policy has evolved rapidly over recent years as the application of the theoretical tools discussed in this book to the new global realities is providing new insights, new challenges, and new opportunities.

Discussion questions

8.1 Discuss the emerging long-run relationships between globalization, urbanization, and industrialization which were evident in different parts of the world between the sixteenth century and the early twentieth century.

8.2 Why are the urban size observations of the early twentieth century important for understanding the nature of today's urban and regional economic theory?

8.3 What were the reasons for the long period of anti-globalization which was evident in much of the twentieth century? Discuss how this affected the growth of cities.

8.4 Can you describe the long-run patterns of urban development in your own country?

8.5 Discuss the ways in which the global urbanization patterns in the second half of the twentieth century differ from those in previous eras.

8.6 What are the major characteristics of the world's largest cities today?

8.7 What are the major characteristics of the largest cities in your own country and how important do you think they are for your own country's national economic development?

8.8 In what ways has your understanding of the processes driving national and international economic growth changed by discussing the economics of cities and regions?

9 Cities and regions in the modern global economy

9.1 Introduction

As we saw in Chapter 8, there is a great deal of evidence that cities are now once again playing an increasingly important role in the economic development of many countries. In particular, as we saw in Chapter 2, in the modern era of globalization there is much evidence to suggest that the increasing importance of cities and agglomeration economies is related to the production and acquisition of knowledge activities. However, in spite of many popular descriptions, this does not necessarily imply that cities are generally growing, or indeed that cities are the dominant engines of today's national economic growth. As we will see in this chapter, the picture is far more complex than this. The role played by cities and regions is different in different contexts, and is also changing in different ways in different situations.

In this chapter we will examine why cities and regions have re-emerged in importance during the modern era of globalization, an era which began in the late 1980s. We will examine the particular features of these newly emerging city-region roles, and discuss the economic implications of these for national and regional development. The key here is to understand the changing role played by the transactions costs of geography, or what we can call *spatial transactions costs*. In Chapters 1 to 4 we discussed various aspects of spatial transactions costs, such as transport costs, logistics costs, knowledge exchanges, and information costs, and an understanding of these costs is essential for understanding location behaviour in cities, region, and clusters. For our purposes here, however, it is also critical for us to understand that over recent decades the nature and levels of the spatial transactions costs have fundamentally changed in ways which were previously unimaginable, and these changes have had profound impacts on all aspects of the relationships between cities, regions, and countries.

The chapter begins with a description of different types of spatial transactions costs and an examination of the changes in these over recent years. A simple model which builds directly on the material in Chapters 1 to 4 is presented, and this is used to explain how a combination of rising and falling spatial transactions costs means that the geography of the economy becomes more uneven, more spiky, and less flat. After examining the empirical evidence on these matters, we then use the theoretical models and the empirical evidence to capture the modern emergence of global cities and global regions and their various features.

9.2 Different types of spatial transactions costs

The costs associated with engaging in, and coordinating, economic activities and market mechanisms across geography can be termed *spatial transactions costs*. Different types of spatial transactions costs have been changed by modern globalization in different ways, and it is important to understand these changes.

A particular subset of spatial transactions costs are those costs which are directly related to the costs of moving goods or information across space. These costs are dependent on communications and transportation technologies, and as a combined group we can refer to these as *spatial transmission costs*. As we discussed in detail in Chapters 1 to 4, transportation costs are the simplest expression of spatial transactions costs, but other spatial transactions costs involve the acquisition and transmission of knowledge and information across space, and these are extremely important in the modern economy. In order to understand the ways in which spatial transactions costs have changed over recent years we need to split up spatial transactions costs into three different types.

The first type of spatial transactions costs are the transactions costs associated with moving goods across geographical space. These are classic transportation costs. The second type are the transactions costs associated with moving knowledge and information across geographical space, and for the purposes of this book we will call these knowledge–information transmission costs. Both the first and second types of spatial transactions costs, namely transportation costs and knowledge–information transmission costs, are explicitly geographical in their construction, in that the costs incurred by these transactions always depend on the geographical distance covered. The third type of spatial transactions costs are the transactions costs associated with movements across national borders. These are typically in the form of customs charges or tariffs, which are the institutional costs associated with a particular border crossing.

These border tariffs and trade barriers are central to models of international economics. Since the late 1980s, the international institutional changes outlined in Chapter 8 which have progressively opened up international markets mean that the levels of these tariffs are generally falling. These falling trade barriers allow for greater degrees of openness and integration between countries, and increase the possibilities for trade, outsourcing, offshoring and multinationalism. In some cases the falls in tariffs are quite significant and in some cases they are very slow; the rate of change depends on progress of the trade negotiations taking place within international arenas such as the World Trade Organization, the European Union, and NAFTA, along with numerous individual bilateral arrangements between particular countries regarding specific industrial sectors.

However, these tariff costs are not explicitly defined in geographical terms in the same way as the first two sets of spatial transactions costs, in the sense that tariffs are not defined to vary systematically with the distance travelled before or after arriving at a particular institutional border. As such, from the perspective of urban and regional economics we can consider border tariff costs as fundamentally aspatial in nature, although explicitly geographical in terms of their implementation (McCann 2005). The result of these differences is that falling cross-border trade tariffs are not particularly related to the unevenness of the global spatial economy described in this chapter, whereas the first two types of spatial transactions costs are essential elements of the explanations for the unevenness and spikiness that we observe.

In the following sections, which draw heavily on McCann (2007, 2008), we consider mainly the changes in the first and second types of spatial transactions costs, namely those transactions costs which are explicitly dependent on distance, while at the same time assuming that tariffs are in general falling slowly worldwide, or at least are not increasing. What we will observe in the following sections is that spatial *transmission* costs have fallen dramatically over recent years, but that this does not necessarily also imply that spatial *transactions* costs have fallen. Indeed, much evidence suggests the exact opposite, namely that many forms of spatial transactions costs have risen. It is the combination of falling spatial transmission costs and rising spatial transactions costs which over recent years has favoured certain places over others. This is the issue to which we now turn.

9.2.1 **Falling spatial transactions costs**

Since the late 1980s we have seen dramatic improvements in the ability of decision-makers to coordinate activities across space. The primary reason for these improvements has been the enormous technological developments in information and communications technologies. Information technologies employing digital, satellite, and fibre-optic technologies allow for vastly greater quantities of information to be transmitted across space at much lower costs than was previously imaginable, even just a couple of decades ago. These developments have both increased the market access for individual firms and meant that complex operations across diverse locations can now be managed both more efficiently and effectively than was previously possible.

For industries competing on knowledge and trading primarily in information, such as finance, advertising, marketing, and tourism, modern information technologies provide entirely new possibilities for the supply of information-based services across a global market space. The level of global market access has therefore increased dramatically for huge numbers of firms trading in knowledge and information-based services, many of which are in dominant 'knowledge hub cities and regions' (OECD 2011b). At the same time, these improved technologies also allow decision-makers to undertake the coordination of complex spatial arrangements of activities in ways which were previously not possible. Probably the most noticeable outcome of these new possibilities and opportunities is the increased offshoring and outsourcing of many types of activities in both manufacturing and service industries.

In service industries notable examples of this include international accounting, whereby New York and London banks transfer their book-keeping requirements overnight to firms in Ireland or India, in order to have them updated in time for the opening of the money markets the next day. Other examples include Silicon Valley firms which subcontract software development activities to firms in Bangalore, India, while maintaining daily contact and control of the Indian software development process from California. These observations all imply that knowledge–information transmission costs must have fallen dramatically over recent decades (McCann 2008).

In manufacturing, advanced communications and control technologies have been widely applied to the management of supply chains, to production and just-in-time (JIT) inventory scheduling control systems, and to logistics and distribution operations. The types of firms which particularly benefit from these technologies are those firms requiring the precise coordination of complex networks of production and distribution operations across large geographical distances, and these firms operate in many different sectors. Examples here include firms employing advanced roll-on, roll-off trucking and containerization technologies (Levinson 2006), rapid-turnaround shipping, the widespread use of sophisticated global positioning systems, and the increased speed and efficiency of all forms of air transport technologies.

The various communications and transportation developments allied with increased outsourcing and offshoring have allowed production systems and corporate organizational networks to be greatly disaggregated spatially across both regions and countries. These observations therefore all point to dramatic falls over recent decades in both the costs of transmitting information across space and of moving goods or people across space. All these transport and movement costs can collectively be termed *spatial transmission* costs, and almost all of the available evidence suggests that they have unambiguously fallen, contributing to a Friedman-type 'flattening' of the spatial economy, as described in Box 8.2.

9.2.2 Rising spatial transactions costs

The theoretical argument that spatial transactions costs have increased while spatial transmission costs have fallen is that improvements in information technologies themselves increase the quantity, variety, and complexity of the knowledge handled and information produced. The increased quantity, variety, and complexity of the knowledge handled and information produced itself increases the costs associated with acquiring and then transacting this knowledge across space. This is because much of the information will originally have emerged from knowledge which is of a non-standardized tacit nature, as discussed in Chapter 2, and the acquisition and transmission of the type of information produced from tacit knowledge increasingly requires greater levels of face-to-face contact in order to maintain mutual trust and understanding (Gaspar and Glaeser 1998; Storper and Venables 2004).

Following the arguments in Chapters 2 and 7, one way of thinking about this is to assume that firms in advanced economies are increasingly competing in terms of high knowledge content, high value-added, and shorter product life cycles, services, and activities, precisely so as to avoid the increasing competition from the newly developing countries. The increased importance of shorter product life cycles is also associated with an increased importance of face-to-face contact in order to transact the knowledge required for producing and marketing these products. As such, for many of these types of knowledge-intensive activities the required frequency of face-to-face interaction will have increased over recent years (Storper and Venables 2004; McCann 2007) because the time (opportunity) costs associated with not having continuous face-to-face contact will also have increased with the quantity, variety, and complexity of the information produced (McCann 2007). Similar arguments apply to the speed and frequency of manufacturing and logistics operations (McCann 1993, 1998) and also to social capital interactions (McCann et al. 2010).

In location theory terms, the outcome is that, in equilibrium, the optimized frequency of interaction and transactions across space will have increased (McCann 2007; Rietveld and

Vickerman 2004). This in turn increases the spatial transactions costs for any given distance over which communication and interaction take place (McCann 2007). The features of these interactions also lead to a natural sorting of firms according to the types of knowledge exchanges and innovation outcomes they generate (Doloreux and Shearmur 2010). As advanced economies increasingly shift towards competition- and production-based knowledge-intensive activities where product life cycles are becoming shorter, these time costs become ever more important, the associated costs of distance increase, and a more pronounced spatial sorting of innovation activities naturally emerges.

Another way of thinking about this is to assume that lower transport costs imply that firms will increasingly switch to the production of higher-quality customized goods (Duranton and Storper 2007), for which the costs of providing a given level of service quality not only becomes more costly with distance, but whose sensitivity to distance is greater than for standardised products (Duranton and Storper 2008). This is akin to a knowledge-service quality version of the iceberg model discussed in Appendix 3.3. However, the question remains as to why firms would adopt this strategy. Following the Palander–Hotelling framework in Chapter 1, one argument is that this is a rational strategy for redefining and using space to bolster a local monopoly position, and avoiding competition from newly emerging economies which produce more standardized, cheaper and lower-value-added goods and services. However, there are also counter-arguments which would suggest that rational firms ought to exploit falling information transmission costs to maximize their global economies of scale, as many high-technology multinational firms already do.

Whichever theoretical approach we adopt, however, these arguments all suggest that as advanced industrialized economies increasingly shift into the production of goods and services embodying complex knowledge and information, spatial *transactions* costs as a whole will have increased in many sectors and activities, even though the spatial *transmission* costs of moving information, goods, and people have fallen. As we see in Box 9.1, the reason is that while the costs of transmitting information, shipping goods, or transporting people have fallen dramatically, the costs of transacting knowledge via human-capital interactions (Glaeser and Kohlhase 2004) have actually risen.

BOX 9.1 The empirical evidence regarding changes in spatial transactions costs

There is a great deal of empirical evidence to support the argument that many types of spatial transactions costs have risen while many types of spatial transmission costs have fallen, and this evidence comes from four broad arenas.

1. The first broad set of empirical evidence comes from the usage patterns of information and communications technologies. Gaspar and Glaeser (1998) find that the closer people are geographically to each other, the more they interact using information technologies. Moreover, the extent of this interaction is also associated with the local density of the urban area, such that large dense urban areas exhibit the greatest internal communications per head (Gaspar and Glaeser 1998). Anecdotal evidence in support of this argument also comes from the fact that many of the industries which are most dependent on information technologies, such as the advanced semiconductor-electronics industry (Arita and McCann 2000, 2006) and the international financial services industry,

BOX 9.1 Continued

are themselves among the most geographically concentrated industries in the world. Even Internet transactions exhibit this localization behaviour (Blum and Goldfarb 2006). These observations therefore suggest that while for many activities information and communications technologies and face-to-face contact are likely to be substitutes, there are also therefore many activities or roles for which information and communications technologies and face-to-face contact are actually very strong complements. The complementarity effect will reinforce the advantages of agglomeration and clustering, and will point towards interregional divergence, whereas the substitution argument will point towards spatial dispersion and convergence. Evidence from foreign direct investment in high knowledge-intensive activities (Nachum and Zaheer 2005) appears to be consistent with the complementary argument, whereas low knowledge-intensive activities use information technology as substitutes for face-to-face interaction. Even IT services markets themselves exhibit this dual nature, with some activities being closely related to the need for face-to-face contact whereas others are largely independent of this need (Arora and Forman 2007). Moreover, those activities for which face-to-face contact and information and communications technologies are complements appear to be those located in urban areas with extensive transportation infrastructure (Haynes et al. 2006). Further evidence which is also suggestive of this complementarity effect in knowledge activities comes from the fact that the frequency of airline business travel between major cities has increased more or less in line with the growth in telecommunications usage between such cities (Gaspar and Glaeser 1998). Given that many cities are increasingly being dominated by high human-capital individuals (Berry and Glaeser 2005), the implication of these various observations is that the importance of engaging in face-to-face activities is positively associated with the degree of knowledge embodied in the activities.

2. The second broad set of empirical evidence comes from trade modelling. Empirical research on distance costs finds that distance effects are not only persistent (Disdier and Head 2007), but also that these persistent effects cannot be explained simply by observing the behaviour of shipping costs. Using a meta-analysis, Disdier and Head (2007) find that bilateral trade exhibits an average elasticity of 0.9 with respect to distance, which implies that on average bilateral trade is nearly inversely proportional to distance. Given that a 1 per cent rise in the share of GDP accounted for by exports is associated with a per capita income increase of up to 1 per cent (Frankel and Romer 1999), this average elasticity of trade with respect to distance suggests that there are very large proximity–productivity effects. Moreover, the importance of accessibility is not falling over time. Disdier and Head (2007) find that although distance effects declined slightly between 1870 and 1950, after 1950 they began to rise again. More recently, and using a similar indirect approach, Boulhol and de Serres (2010) confirmed that the implied international trade costs have indeed increased over the last two decades for many types of international transactions. All these empirical observations are therefore fundamentally at odds with the flat-world assumptions.

The most likely explanation for these persistent distance effects is associated with the issue of the costs of time associated with geographical transactions costs (McCann 2011). For the shipment of goods, time in transit is costly, being up to as much as 0.5 per cent of the value of the goods shipped per day (Hummels 2001). Moreover, Hummels (2001) and Deardorff (2003) suggest that the influence of time on trade is increasing. The high and increasing cost of time in transit of goods shipments comes partly from the costs of carrying stock and also from the likelihood that long transit times reduce the reliability and predictability of deliveries (McCann 1998; Venables 2006). Time in transit also makes firms slower to respond to changing demand conditions or cost levels (Venables 2006) and in ever more rapidly changing markets with shorter life cycles these costs become ever more significant. Indeed, since the early 1980s, the opportunity costs of time appear to have increased for both household and industrial consumers (Piore and Sabel 1984; Best 1990). Consumer demand requirements are becoming ever

BOX 9.1 **Continued**

more sophisticated and exhibit an increasing preference for retail services characterized by reliability, timeliness, and quality of service. Both modern household and industrial consumers now require a level of service customization and delivery speed which is only possible by employing more frequent shipments of goods (McCann 1998). In analytical terms the effect of rising shipment frequencies is to make the costs of distance increase. This is because the total economic distance, which is a multiple of the geographical distance and the frequency of interaction (McCann 1993, 1998, 2007), increases. These increases in economic distance costs are nowadays a result of the almost universal trend towards just-in-time (JIT) type systems of shipments, which allow for total quality management (TQM) principles to be applied on the basis of minimum inventory supply chains (Schonberger 1996) for all types of goods movements. Over the last three decades these JIT logistics and distribution systems have spread progressively from the Japanese automotive industry into almost all modes of global manufacturing, retailing, and distribution. Moreover, these trends towards rising shipment frequencies and increasing distance costs are accentuated not only by the increasing sophistication of consumer preferences for customization and variety, but also by the advanced logistics systems responding to them. Both the increasing customization preferences and the advanced logistics capabilities are themselves facilitated by the recent advances in communications and transportation technologies, and this is particularly important for the shipment of high-value goods. Airfreight now accounts for a third of US imports by value and 25 per cent of African exports (Venables 2006), and for the USA, the value of time saved by airfreight and containerization has been estimated as some 12–13 per cent of the value of the goods (Hummels 2001).

3. The third broad set of empirical evidence comes from industry observations of logistics operations. Logistics costs are the combined costs of all the transportation, storage, and inventory-handling costs associated with moving goods across geographical space, and these are not only much greater than transport costs, but also are related to the costs of both time and space (McCann 1993, 1998). The importance of increasingly advanced logistics operations within the economy is increasing as firms place a growing emphasis on aiming to reduce the time in transit, and there are four pieces of evidence to support this.

   (i) Relative to the value of output (Shonberger 1996), the average inventory levels for almost all manufacturing and distribution sectors in the developed world have fallen dramatically since the 1980s. This implies that the average lead times of goods shipments have fallen over recent years, with a concomitant increase in goods-shipment frequencies. It is this increasing shipment frequency in response to increasing time costs which increases the costs of distance (McCann 2007).

   (ii) By carefully disentangling the various components of transport costs, Hummels (1999) demonstrates that for many sectors, the proportion of global output which is accounted for by the combination of logistics and transportation activities has not fallen over recent decades. More specifically, while the transportation cost component of bulk materials has indeed generally fallen, in the case of manufactured goods there is evidence that this proportion has actually increased over recent decades, in spite of the improvement in transportation and logistics technologies (Hummels 1999).

   (iii) There is much evidence for a 'home bias' in trade at the interregional level as well as at the international level (Hillberry and Hummels 2003, 2008; Chen 2004). In particular, industries which are very dependent on JIT shipments have tended to reorganize their trade patterns in favour of geographically close suppliers and customers (McCann and Fingleton 1996; McCann 1998). Moreover, this behaviour is even evident in industries in which the product value–weight ratios are extremely high and for which transport costs typically account for less

BOX 9.1 Continued

than 1 per cent of value (McCann and Fingleton 1996). In other words, increasing localization behaviour is present even in the very industries which proponents of the flat-world thesis would have deemed it to be entirely unnecessary.

(iv) The result of the increased importance of reducing the time in transit via the use of advanced logistics activities means that logistics activities are much more significant than simply the costs of transportation. While transport costs for many industries rarely amount to more than 5 per cent of the value of the goods, advanced logistics services accounted for 16 per cent of global GDP in 2000 and 18 per cent of European GDP (Leinbach and Capineri 2007) and these activities are also increasing in importance in the modern economy. During the 1990s, the growth rate for the logistics sector as a whole was of the order of 6 per cent per annum (Leinbach and Capineri 2006) and between 1987 and 1995 there was a 60 per cent increase in outsourced dedicated third-party logistics operations (Chatterji and Tsai 2006). The reason why these logistics services account for a much greater share than transport costs alone would suggest, and also why their share of GDP is growing and not falling as declining transport costs would imply, is that for goods shipments the costs of distance are very much greater than simply transport costs (McCann 1998). Distance costs include all the costs associated with holding and handling inventories, as the optimized levels of inventories held are calculated by minimizing the total costs of moving and not moving (i.e. the holding of) goods (McCann 1998). In situations where the value–weight ratio of goods is very high, such as in the electronics industry, the very low share of transport costs hides the fact that most of the distance costs are actually hidden the inventory capital costs (McCann 1998; McCann and Fingleton 1996). In contrast, in the case of low value–weight ratio goods such as coal, the distance costs are mostly manifested in terms of relatively high share of transport costs.

9.3 Economic geography is spiky and uneven

The arguments in the above sections suggest that over recent decades many types of spatial transactions costs have increased at exactly the same time as many types of spatial transmission costs have decreased. While at first these arguments may appear to be rather contradictory or paradoxical, these apparently conflicting conclusions can be easily reconciled by using the arguments outlined in Chapters 2 and 3, and applying them to the type of theoretical framework discussed in Chapter 4. The combination of these two opposing forces in different contexts generates increasing unevenness, increasing spikiness, or more technically increasing convexity, and this can be explained with the help of two diagrams (McCann 2008).

Figure 9.1 depicts a one-dimensional model of the economy in which the economic geography comprises three city-regions spanning a distance AB. In this particular spatial economy there are three cities, X, Y, and Z. Cities X and Z are larger than city Y, and all three cities exhibit two types of production, namely high-value goods and services H and low-value goods and services L.

Following the arguments in Chapter 4, the associated bid-rent curves for the production of each respective good produced by each city are denoted in Figure 9.1 as BR_{XH} for the

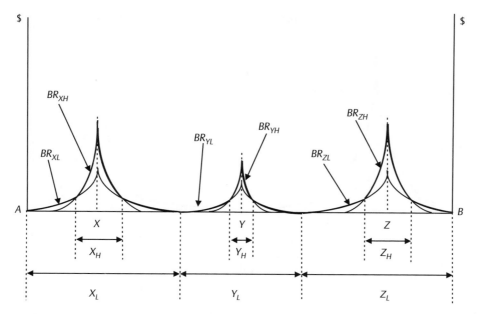

Figure 9.1 A three-city-region one-dimensional economy

high-value goods produced in city X, BR_{XL} for the low-value goods produced in city X, BR_{YH} for the high-value goods produced in city Y and BR_{YL} for the low-value goods produced in city Y, BR_{ZH} for the high-value goods produced in city Z and BR_{ZL} for the low-value goods produced in city Z, respectively. As cities X and Z are larger than city Y, this implies that there is both a larger local regional hinterland market and also more competition for each good in cities X and Z than in Y. The result is that at the central-city market locations of X and Z, land prices are higher for the production of each good H and L than at Y, and the bid-rent curves for both goods H and L produced by X and Z extend further than those associated with Y.

The urban and regional economic geography of the economy AB is such that the spatial production area for good L in city Y, denoted as Y_L, accounts for the less than one-third of the total economic geography of production of the low-value good L. Meanwhile, cities X and Z each account for more than one-third of the economic geography of production of the low-value good L, with the respective production areas denoted as X_L and Z_L. In addition, city Y also has a very small local regional production area Y_H for good H, while cities X and Z have much larger local regional production areas, denoted as X_H and Z_H, for the high-value good H. Following the arguments in Chapter 4, the equilibrium land prices at each location in the global economy AB are given by the envelope of the individual local bid-rent curves, depicted in Figure 9.1 in bold.

Figure 9.2 depicts the situation in response to the types of globalizing and localizing trends discussed above. As we have seen, falling spatial transmission costs apply primarily to low-value goods and services which are relatively standardized in nature and whose product life cycles are not very short. The falling spatial transmission costs for these goods

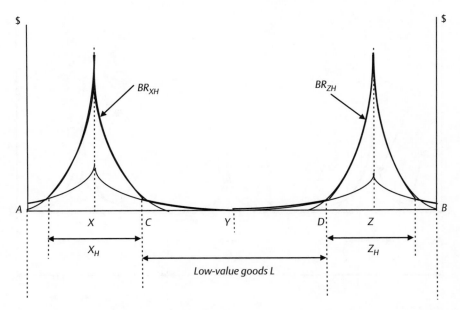

Figure 9.2 Globalization, productivity, and spatial concentration

mean that the equilibrium bid-rent curves for the production of these goods becomes shallower. In Figure 9.2, the shallower-sloping bid-rent functions for the production of low-value goods and services L imply that such activities can be profitably undertaken in all locations. This is the spatial analogy of Friedman's (2007) flat-world argument discussed in Box 8.2. However, from urban and regional economics we know that this is not the end of the story. The reason is that the actual distribution of production and activities depends on the interaction between this flattening effect and the other opposing localization trends discussed above.

If we consider the localizing tendencies operating with regard to the production of high-value non-standardized goods and services H, the face-to-face arguments above imply that the production of these goods and services will benefit from location-specific agglomeration economies. The existence of agglomeration economy advantages as well as increasing spatial transactions costs in the production of high-value goods and services H means that the land in the major urban areas X and Z is increasingly dominated by the production of these high-value goods. Cities X and Z expand outwards, the production of high-value goods is concentrated in just two locations X and Z, and the bid-rent functions associated with the production of these high-value goods become steeper. The production location Y, which previously had a local dominance in both the production of low-value L and high-value H goods for its own hinterland area, now disappears as an independent production centre. Instead, the whole region between C and D now continues to function simply as a location for producing low-value goods and services L.

The region CD corresponds to what Leamer (2007) describes as the 'flat terrain' of the global economy, while X and Z correspond to what he describes as the 'hills and mountains' of the global economy. As Fujita et al. (1999) demonstrate, the reason for this is that when agglomeration economies are allied with falling spatial transmission costs, the existence of agglomeration economies can lead to situations in which intermediate production locations such as Y disappear altogether. This is partly because the previous economic *raison d'être* of the former intermediate production location now disappears, and also because the low distance costs now no longer provide any possibility for local producers to be 'protected' by distance from the producers in the major urban centres. The local and regional producers lose their limited local monopoly power, as described in Chapter 1, and the result is that the core central locations dominate the spatial economy.

The equilibrium land prices at each location in the global economy AB are given by the envelope of the individual bid-rent curves, and once again, as with Figure 9.1, these are depicted in Figure 9.2 in bold. As we see, the envelope rental curves are now far more curved than previously. In particular, they are now far more *convex*, to use the urban economic terminology. Assuming that land prices and labour prices are highly correlated, because of the need to maintain local real wages at competitive levels, as described in Chapter 6, we can assume that the envelope land-price curves also closely resemble the spatial variations in both local incomes and local productivity levels.

The model predicts that differences between the major centres and the relatively smaller centres will therefore tend to increase, as both wages and real-estate prices increase in the core-city regions. This is not to say that all major centres will increase relative to smaller centres, as it will also depend on the range of technologies and industries evident in particular cities, as different industries and technologies rise and fall over time. However, the arguments outlined above do imply that the modern globalization processes will have led to increasing differences between the fortunes of regions and cities even within the same country. This is because particular major urban centres will have benefited from the increasing scale advantages associated with being nodes in global trade networks.

The new economic geography (NEG) frameworks (Krugman and Venables 1995; Fujita et al. 1999) discussed in Chapter 3 also demonstrate that in the presence of agglomeration economies exactly the same type of result can be generated in a situation where the border tariffs between countries of different sizes are reduced or removed, even where international factor mobility is limited or non-existent. As we discussed in Chapter 8, in the modern global economy, the dramatic changes in spatial transactions costs driven by developments in transport and communications technologies have also taken place at a time of widespread falls in trade and tariff barriers associated with institutional reforms relating to integrated market areas such as the EU and NAFTA, as well as to taxation and investment. As such, the combination of both technological changes and cross-border institutional changes reinforces the whole process towards unevenness, spikiness, and convexity.

9.3.1 Spatial equilibrium and geographical variations in productivity

Within this same analytical framework we can also consider the effects of these various changes in spatial transactions costs on the distribution of income and productivity. However, in order to do this it is first necessary to consider three aspects of the framework.

First, we recall from Chapter 4 that the definitions of the bid-rent curves constructed here are that firms within each industry are able to generate equal profits across space. As such, by combining this observation with the arguments in Chapter 1, we know that the envelope land-price gradient represents the interregional equilibrium-wage gradient which equalizes the rates of return on capital, due to spatial competition both within and between sectors.

Second, as land prices increase towards the core city-regional centres, in order to maintain gainful employment at those locations the firms must pay higher nominal wages so as to maintain real wages. The sum of the wages paid plus the land prices paid therefore increases as we move towards the centre of the city-region. However, given that the envelope land-price curve described the situation in which we observe the generation of equal profits (rates of return on capital) across space, then it becomes clear that the sum of the wages paid plus the land prices paid plus the profits earned also increases as we move towards the city-region centre. This is very important because the sum of these factor payments reflects the total GDP of the location, and the GDP divided by the number of workers employed at that location defines the labour productivity of the location. In other words, what these diagrams demonstrate is that for an interregional spatial price equilibrium to hold, the productivity levels must also increase as we move towards the core centre of the city-region.

Third, we also know from Chapter 4 that the density of employment and activity increases as we move towards the city centre, precisely because the cost of land and local real-estate space increases. If we combine this third observation with the above two observations, then it becomes clear that the spatial patterns of employment density closely reflect the spatial patterns of labour productivity per square metre and also the spatial patterns of total output per square metre.

To be precise, there are slight differences between the spatial distribution of employment density, labour productivity per square metre, and total output per square metre, due to the bid-rent factor substitution arguments described in Chapter 4. However, even allowing for these factor substitution issues, all three features are very closely related, and the extent to which they differ is only small, depending on the substitutability properties of the firms' production functions and the degree of inter-industry competition for space.

Mapping employment-density and land-price distributions across space therefore allows us to map the geographical distribution of labour productivity and total output. Excellent three-dimensional maps are produced by the OECD (2009b) in which these spikes emerge naturally and are clearly evident in all countries, irrespective of whether they are defined according to GDP per square metre, GDP per capita per square metre, employment per square metre, wages per square metre, or land prices per square metre.

Taking all these various analytical observations on board, the arguments provided by the transition from Figure 9.1 to Figure 9.2 and the OECD (2009b) maps therefore imply that in the modern era of globalization the economy has become more uneven, more spiky, and more convex, and the manifestations of this have been increasing differences between regions in terms of population distribution, productivity, and total output, all driven by competition based on the need for proximity in order to generate, acquire, exchange, and transact knowledge (Caniels 2000).

There is wide-ranging evidence in favour of these analytical arguments, and this comes from the fact that cities and densely populated regions are observed to be the locations associated with higher productivity levels (Ciccone and Hall 1996; Rosenthal and Strange 2004; Fingleton 2003b; Glaeser and Gottlieb 2009), higher levels of innovation and entrepreneurship (Acs 2002; Van Oort 2004), higher levels of creativity (Florida 2002a, b), higher levels of human capital (Berry and Glaeser 2005), and the major centres of learning and research (Anselin et al. 1997).

However, the experience of urban growth over the last two decades since the start of modern globalization does not imply that all urban areas are growing, nor that economic growth is primarily an urban issue. Nor does it imply that productivity growth is intrinsically related to large cities continuing to grow larger. The picture is much more complex. In order to see this we must first discuss the case of the large capital and dominant cities located in the core regions of each country, and then we must consider the behaviour and performance of the non-core regions, including regions which are not primarily urban.

9.4 The economic performance of today's cities and regions

The current technological and institutional changes which have taken place since the late 1980s have led to major changes in spatial transactions costs, the effects of which, as we have already seen, have favoured certain types of places over others. Some regions will be of increasing economic importance while others will be of declining economic importance. The emergence and re-emergence of major cities in many parts of the global economy, as outlined in Chapter 8, is one part of this story. Cities and densely populated regions emerge in the peaks depicted in Figure 9.2, often at the expense of other intervening regions. However, this diagrammatic description of the arguments regarding the recent geographical effects of changes in transactions and transmission costs does not imply that divergence will continue to increase between all regions as large global cities gain at the expense of other types of regions and cities.

In reality, any new rounds of unevenness which are generated by the current phase of globalization are superimposed on the previous inherited spatial structure (Warf 1995). As such, the urban and regional legacy of the history of economic development will also alter the local impacts of globalization. This superposition of different effects may lead to increasing interregional divergence in some cases and to increasing interregional convergence in other cases, depending exactly on which new industries develop where and in which regions firms choose to locate their new investments. In other words, the actual outcomes of these changes on any particular region or country will depend on the structure and history of the region, the experience of the neighbouring regions or countries, the existing spatial structure, and the actual scale of the local technological and institutional changes. In reality, the balance of these two opposing effects encouraging convergence and divergence is really a matter of observation and empirics rather than of theory, and this is the issue to which we now turn.

As we saw in Chapter 8, we are now witnessing an unprecedented level of urban growth which is taking place at the global scale (PWC 2009; MGI 2011a). This suggests that in many parts of the world it is becoming increasingly important for firms and people to be clustered together. In the newly emerging and developing countries in particular, this appears to be an almost ubiquitous phenomenon (MGI 2009, 2010, 2011b). In developing countries, both the increasing levels of overall urbanization and the growth of mega-cities are most marked (MGI 2011a), and over the next two decades the vast majority of economic growth in developing countries is expected to come from cities (MGI 2011; PWC 2009). In the developing world cities, the patterns of clustering relate to both the high-skilled and highly educated workers, and also to very large numbers of the poorest and lowest-educated groups.

Similar patterns of regional factor reallocation in favour of large and dominant cities took place on both sides of the Atlantic during the 1990s. Within Europe, investment capital and information became more concentrated in capital cities and large urban centres during the 1990s (Rodríguez-Pose 1998), as it did in the USA (Glaeser 2011). Moreover, empirical evidence at the US county level (Partridge et al. 2007) and European sub-national regional level (Caniels and Verspagen 2003) over the same period has also shown that local growth was directly related to an area's proximity to major urban centres. Either a location in, or good access to, major urban centres is important for productivity performance on both sides of the Atlantic.

In advanced countries, urban clustering is most notably associated with the spatial concentration of particular types of high-knowledge firms and high-knowledge workers. This effect appears to be very strong in the case of the USA. Following the human- capital–migration arguments in Chapters 6 and 7, recent US evidence suggests that not only is there an increasing share of university-educated human capital living and working in cities (Berry and Glaeser 2005), but that this proportion of university-educated workers is also correlated with the existing human-capital stock and both are correlated with the growth of the city (Glaeser and Shapiro 2003). The result of this is that US cities are actually becoming more dissimilar in terms of their human-capital composition. In the USA there is no evidence of the levels of high-school human capital playing any role whatsoever in city growth (Shapiro 2006), whereas the evidence regarding role played by tertiary-educated workers is very strong. Similar evidence for the UK (Faggian and McCann 2006, 2009) also points to a clear link between tertiary-educated human-capital migration and regional performance.

The reasons for the productivity premium of today's cities are therefore not just scale related, but are also related to composition effects. In particular, the increasing interregional mobility of highly skilled human capital appears to be a key driving force underlying the reasons why interregional divergence has been reappearing in many countries over the last two decades, after the previous four decades which had been characterized primarily by interregional convergence (Berry and Glaeser 2005).

Of the industrialized countries, the USA is the most urbanized large country, followed by Japan and Korea, and Canada, Australia, and the Netherlands on a much smaller scale (OECD 2011b). The USA is more urbanized than Western Europe, and US cities on average are larger than European cities. An estimated over 84 per cent of the US economy is accounted for by the output of cities with over 150,000 people, whereas the equivalent share for Western Europe is 64 per cent (MGI 2012). Moreover, US cities exhibit a 35 per cent GDP per capita premium relative to non-urban areas within the USA, whereas the equivalent for Western European cities is 30 per cent (MGI 2012; McCann and Acs 2011). Productivity gains driven by urbanization and large city growth still appear to be ongoing in the USA (Glaeser and Gottlieb 2009).

The reasons why US cities outperform European cities are complex, and are likely to be a mixture of scale-related, composition-related, and policy-related factors. US cities on average are larger than European cities, and the US economy is more urbanized than Europe (MGI 2012). But city size and urbanization alone cannot account for productivity differences. On the one hand, in terms of city size, the urban hierarchy arguments of Chapter 3 suggest that the roles and functions of cities also relate to their relative position in the national urban system. On this criterion, US cities are not particularly large relative to US national populations, in comparison to many other OECD countries. On the other hand, in terms of urbanization, much of Europe outperforms Japan and Korea in terms of productivity, although both Japan and Korea are far more urbanized than almost anywhere in Europe, and many of the most productive parts of Northern Europe exhibit small cities and low population densities. As such, differences in urban scale, differences in the levels of urbanization, and differences in interregional adjustment processes cannot entirely account for the transatlantic differences in urban productivity.

A quite different literature on the transatlantic productivity gap (Timmer et al. 2010; Ortega-Argilés 2012) suggests that the productivity advantage of the USA over Europe was primarily that the US economy was much more efficient in terms of the generation and diffusion of new technologies throughout the economy during the 1990s and 2000s than Europe. These sectoral and technology-based arguments emphasize the greater integration of pan-US markets, and the role of US multinational companies in particular (MGI 2010), in promoting technology transmission across the economy, rather than the more fragmented pan-European markets. As such, these arguments emphasize transmission mechanisms associated with firms, sectors, and technologies, rather than cities and regions.

What is still very unclear is exactly how these various industry, sector, and technology issues relate to urban and regional issues. Are US markets more integrated because US cities are bigger? Are US cities larger because US markets are more integrated? What is the relationship between either of these phenomena and the role of US multinational firms? These issues are still to be resolved. Moreover, other arguments emphasize the growth role played by the entrepreneurship and innovation effects of small firms, many of which benefit from being in cities and having connections to multinational firms. How each of these different firm, sector, and technology issues relate to urban productivity and growth issues is still to be investigated, but clues as to how they might be connected come from the cluster–transactions costs arguments in Chapter 2.

In Chapter 2 we saw that there are alternative mechanisms for knowledge exchange and transmission in which the location priorities for large firms differ from those of small firms. For small firms the local context, including access to local large firms, is likely to be important as a source of both market knowledge and inputs. In contrast, for large firms a wider national and global context is likely to be more important for market knowledge, while the local environment serves to improve knowledge of specific inputs. However, large firms will also seek inputs from a wider spatial extent. Therefore the knowledge spillover, knowledge exchange, and knowledge transmission effects operating within places, between places, within sectors, and between sectors will also depend on the organizational make-up of the firms. It is likely that both urban-regional scale and urban-regional connectivity will become important, and we will now deal with each of these issues in turn.

9.4.1 Scale and productivity in capital and dominant cities

We know from the theoretical arguments in Chapters 2, 3, and 4 that productivity and city size are related. Indeed, in Chapter 8 we see that cities and densely populated regions have been a crucial element of national wealth generation since the early seventeenth century. However, the relationship between urban scale and national wealth is no longer the simple story of urban scale that it was when Marshall (1890) and Weber (1909) were writing, and this requires us to interpret our theoretical frameworks carefully in the light of the evidence.

The most economically powerful cities in the world are primarily contained within the rich countries. According to PWC (2009), 23 out of the 30 largest GDP cities in the world in 2008 were in the advanced countries, with only seven from the newly industrializing countries. However, when it comes to labour productivity, defined in terms of GDP per capita, the advanced and rich countries of the world contain all the world's highest-productivity cities.

Recent estimates of US urban areas suggest that a doubling of city size is associated with a productivity increase of some 3–8 per cent (Rosenthal and Strange 2004). As such, moving from a city of 50,000 to one of 5 million would be predicted to increase productivity by more than 50 per cent (Venables 2006). OECD (2006) data, however, suggest that while US cities are on average very large and also very productive, there is no general law which states that urban scale is empirically related to urban productivity. Indeed, outside the USA, the relationship is actually negative for very large cities.

Many of these world's highest-productivity cities are not mega-cities or even very large cities (OECD 2006). Of the world's 75 highest-productivity cities (including Singapore, Hong Kong, and cities in Taiwan and Israel) in 2006, 29 are what the OECD (2006) classifies as 'small metro areas' of fewer than 3 million inhabitants; 32 are what the OECD (2006) classifies as 'medium to large metro areas' of between 3 and 6.99 million inhabitants; and only 14 are mega-cities of at least 7 million inhabitants. Overall, among OECD countries, the relationship between the size of cities and their GDP per capita productivity appears to exhibit something of an inverted-U-shaped relationship (OECD 2006).

Very large cities appear to exhibit diseconomies of scale associated with increasing congestion and rising land and labour costs relative to the small to medium-sized cities. Among the OECD countries there is no simple relationship between city size and city growth. In both the developed and developing world (MGI 2011), very large cities have not outperformed smaller cities at all since the mid-1990s. In fact, over recent decades, more cities in the developed world have actually shrunk in size than the number of cities that have grown (UN-HABITAT 2008; Dijkstra et al. 2012). Intermediate-sized cities and regions are increasingly seen as drivers of growth. Most of the forecast growth of the US economy over the coming decades is expected to come from growth in intermediate-sized cities (MGI 2012), and this is also the case for many emerging parts of the world (MGI 2011).

Following on from our earlier observations, however, there appear to be qualitative differences between places. Across the OECD, higher-income cities are actually outgrowing lower-income cities, irrespective of their population scale (OECD 2006), and many of these high-growth cities are small and medium-sized cities. Among the rich countries, 12 out of the 15 most entrepreneurial cities are small to medium-sized cities (Acs et al. 2008), while 11 out of the world's 15 most competitive cities are small to medium sized (COL 2008). Nowadays, in the advanced economies, urban productivity is clearly not just a matter of scale as it was a century ago. In rich countries today, knowledge, creativity, innovation, and connectivity appear to be far more important for productivity than simply urban scale. As our cluster–transactions costs discussion in Chapter 2 explains, different organizational and spatial arrangements are possible for promoting knowledge activities.

These observations all point to a very different set of conclusions regarding the relationship between urban scale, growth, and productivity than many of the arguments outlined in Chapter 3 appear to suggest. Observations of urban productivity premia do not necessarily imply that urban scale will automatically increase in all parts of the world in a manner depicted by Figures 9.1 and 9.2. The reason is that economic growth, both nationally and regionally, is not driven by productivity levels, but by rates of return on capital. In these figures the rates of return on capital are equalized in order to describe the economic geography of the types of spatial price equilibrium conditions which have become evident over the last two decades. However, there is no reason why this should continue. It depends on the changes in spatial transactions costs. Indeed, evidence from the OECD (2009b) suggest that if Figures 9.1 and 9.2 are transformed into growth rates, many of the spikes will become flat or even depressions, while many of the flat areas will become spikes.

In OECD countries in particular, urban productivity is now relatively much less associated with urban scale than it was in previous eras, except for the cases of the USA, Japan, and Korea, and also, on a very much smaller scale, Canada, Australia, and New Zealand. In the rest of the OECD the picture is far more heterogeneous, with small and medium-sized cities operating in the vanguard of productivity and productivity growth (Dijkstra et al. 2012).

Although during the twentieth century cities grew in absolute scale all over the world, most of the world's most productive cities are nowadays classed as either small cities, medium-sized cities, or large cities, rather than as mega-cities. For rich countries and also across a whole range of country sizes, the optimum size for cities in rich countries seems nowadays to be largely similar to the optimal size of the world's largest cities in the early part of the twentieth century. Over the last sixty or seventy years there appears to have been a major change from what used to be a fairly simple and direct relationship between city size, city productivity, and national economic performance to something which is now much more complex. The relationship between urban scale and productivity is neither linear nor continually increasing, and nowadays other urban features also appear to be important for city performance, most notably connectivity.

9.4.2 Connectivity in capital and dominant cities

As Porter (1990) points out, it is not regions which compete, but the firms which are located in the regions. As such, the clues as to why particular cities are highly productive must lie in the types of firms which are located there and how their activities relate to wider global market changes. In terms of the modern era of globalization, the various arguments above suggest that there have been qualitative changes in the role played by cities in the industrialized world, changes which favour the competitive advantages associated with cities as centres of knowledge. This is particularly the case for cities in the developed world. However, the scale and pace of modern globalization suggests that the individual city is much less of a reference point for determining competitive advantages than it would have been in previous eras when markets were more dominated by domestic and national issues.

For firms which invest heavily in knowledge assets, in order to generate the required returns to their knowledge investments, many of the knowledge-based firms located in today's cities must capture markets which extend well beyond the borders of their own country. Traditionally, the returns to investing in activities related to foreign markets were generated by exports. However, as we have already seen, one of the key features of the current phase of globalization is that there is now an increasing premium associated with face-to-face contact with foreign customers, suppliers, or collaborators (McCann 2007, 2008, 2011). In global markets this implies that the global engagement facilitated by direct international investment is becoming relatively far more important than exporting as a means of global engagement (McCann 2008, 2011). Qualitative differences in the role played by modern cities as centres of communication and engagement are therefore critical for understanding the modern economy.

As we saw in Chapter 8, one of the most widely discussed manifestations of the modern relationship between cities and the global economy comes from the increasingly important role played by so-called 'global cities' (Sassen 1994, 2002; Taylor 2004; Ni and Kresl 2010). The increasing relative dominance of these global cities appears to be associated with the density of knowledge (Simmie 2004) and information technology assets employed in the city (Sassen 2002; Button et al. 2006). As such, these global cities are argued to act as the 'knowledge hubs' (OECD 2011a) of the worldwide trade, migration, knowledge, and information networks linking all parts of the global economy. Research suggests that many of the dominant interactions of these cities are with other similar globally oriented cities in other countries, rather than with other cities in the same country. There is also evidence that the performance of these dominant global cities has also been playing an increasingly important role even with respect to their own hinterland national and continental economies (HMT-DTI 2001, 2003; BTRE 2004; Col 2005a, 2006; 2007c; Glaeser 2005).

The connectivity performance of these global cities is largely related to the scale of the global engagement of the companies located there, and, in particular, to the globally competitive multinational firms located there (Ni and Kresl 2010; McCann and Acs 2011). Given that multinationals accounted for almost one-third of US economic growth over the last two decades, global cities are therefore perceived to play a very significant role in the modern global economy.

It is useful to try to provide a sense of how important these issues of connectivity are in different settings, and there are various different systems of global city rankings which aim to rank cities according to their degrees of global connectivity (Taylor 2004; Taylor et al. 2008). These global city ranking systems include the *Mastercard Worldwide Centres of Commerce* rankings (Mastercard 2008), the *Global Cities Competiveness* rankings (Ni and Kresl 2010), and the *Global Financial Centres* rankings (COL 2009; Long Finance 2012). All these different ranking systems are based on a wide variety of connectivity data such as corporate headquarter functions, corporate decision-making linkages, human-capital mobility patterns, trade linkages, transport linkages, financial linkages, and asset management roles. These are analysed using different weighting measures, algorithms. and multivariate methods, and all three ranking systems provide composite indicators of the level of global connectivity of different cities viewed from different perspectives. The first two systems cover a range of measures of global connectivity, whereas the last focuses specifically on financial activities.

Not surprisingly, there is a very close correspondence between the level of global connectivity of the cities via their multinational corporations and their GDP per capita (OECD 2006; MGI 2011; McCann and Acs 2011) and this observation is consistent with the argument that the cities with the highest levels of global connectivity are also largely the world's most productive cities. Indeed, global connectivity has been found to be the single most important feature of a global city competitive position (Ni and Kresl 2010).

That is not to say that small and medium-sized companies are not important for growth; nor does it imply that agglomeration is not important. On the contrary, as we saw in Chapters 3 and 7, small entrepreneurial start-ups are critical for innovation and growth, and agglomeration is often crucial for promoting their success (Acs 2002; Van Oort 2004). However, the arguments outlined in Chapters 2 and 8, and also in this chapter, all imply that in the current era of globalization the probability of success for small and medium-sized firms will be higher in those same city-regions which are also the most globally connected, because of the potential spillovers from, and global market opportunities associated with, locally based multinationals. This is exactly what has been found by Aitken et al. (1979); Andersson (2009); and Johansson and Loof (2009).

In the modern global economy, what becomes very clear is that urban scale is only part of the story of how regions compete. The global connectivity of cities is now also a critical part of the story, in a way that has not been the case in previous eras of globalization. As we saw in Chapter 8, in earlier decades cities were still primarily the economic engines of the domestic economy, and as global markets developed the major cities also played a role in servicing these markets. Today, however, the causality is somewhat reversed, with global cities responding primarily to global changes, and much less so to domestic influences. This implies that for countries with global cities situated in them, the relationship between the global city and other more domestically oriented cities will exhibit a relationship similar to the economic base relationships discussed in Chapter 5. However, in this relationship, city size is not necessarily the key issue because urban scale is no longer a key indicator of the performance of a global city. More important for global city performance is the nature of the activities which are undertaken there and the degree of connectivity provided by the firms operating these. As we have seen here, infrastructure provision is one part of a broader story, a story which we saw in Chapter 7 is not simply captured by measures of diversity. As we discuss in Box 9.2, the modern relationship between urban productivity and globalization is related to all the qualitative attributes of cities which foster connectivity and international engagement.

BOX 9.2 Evidence for the importance of urban connectivity

There is a range of empirical evidence which suggests that the importance of major urban nodes (Limtanakool et al. 2007) within the global city networks is reinforced by the existence of hubs within the global air (Col 2002; Burghouwt 2005), rail, and marine transportation systems (Leinbach and Capineri 2007). Following the arguments outlined above regarding the modern importance of frequent and rapid face-to-face contact in knowledge-intensive activities (McCann 2007, 2011), one key aspect of this notion of connectivity for global cities is that of the relationship between the location of major corporate headquarter functions and the spatial structure of global intercontinental airline linkages.

Recent evidence from European regions suggests that the location decisions of corporate headquarters are closely linked to the availability of direct intercontinental flights (Bel and Fageda 2008). While proximity to large markets and specialist suppliers is also important, as might be expected, neither the

BOX 9.2 Continued

size of the city, the sectoral diversity of the city, the size of the country, nor the size of the city relative to the country have any real significance for these headquarter location choices. As such, in the modern European context of the European Union Single Market, urban scale and national scale alone appear to be much less important as location determinants for key corporate knowledge functions than the structure of global airline networks (Bel and Fageda 2008). Moreover, this conclusion is arrived at even after controlling for the fact that the structure of the airline networks will itself be related to the location behaviour of these headquarter functions.

Similar observations which also point to the critical role played by airline systems in facilitating face-to-face contact come from Button et al. (1999) and Wickham and Vecchi (2008). Button et al. (1999) examined the relationship between US high-technology employment and the location of hub airports. They found that proximity to a hub airport increases local high-technology employment, and that it is the former which drives the latter. The reason for this is that proximity to hub airports allows companies in general, but small companies in particular, to easily access a much wider market, thereby reducing the constraints associated with a lack of scale (Wickham and Vecchi 2008). Moreover, the importance of hub airport access appears to dominate any role played by local cluster institutions, a finding which is consistent with the Bel and Fageda (2008) finding that the size of the city is not significant once airline hub connectivity is controlled for.

Following the arguments in Chapters 3, 4, and 6, these connectivity arguments suggest that the reasons for these empirical findings are that the spatial network structure of global airline system (Grubesic et al. 2008, 2009) largely determines the nature and geographical patterns of knowledge flows embodied in the types of high-human-capital individuals who have the discretionary power to act on that knowledge. In particular, the empirical observations suggest that the spatial network structure of global airline systems determines the ease and frequency (McCann 2007) with which high-level business and corporate decision-makers are able to engage in direct face-to-face contact with other such decision-makers from other locations (Aguilera 2008; McCann 2008). As such, in the modern global economy, global hub airport functions are critical for facilitating the types of higher-order knowledge flows which result in investment decisions being made.

Greater proximity to such infrastructure should therefore increase both the likelihood of investment being forthcoming in the nearby regions and the resulting level of innovations generated by the regions (McCann and Acs 2011). Indeed, these examples of the role played by hub airports are useful as serving to highlight the difference between simply 'connectedness', defined in terms of the architecture of transport and communications infrastructure, and the much broader concept of 'connectivity', which is a behavioural concept incorporating the ability of individuals and firms to make investment decisions at particular locations. The transport systems architecture facilitates the knowledge-related behavioural responses, but the latter are conditioned by many other issues as well. Connectivity is a much broader concept than connectedness, because it also incorporates many intangible attributes of commerce, decision-making, and corporate organization, issues which from Chapters 7 and 8 we nowadays know to be very important for growth.

9.5 Non-core regions, intermediate regions, and peripheral regions

All the discussions so far have tended to centre on the role of the global cities and leading knowledge regions. The cities and regions are defined by the OECD (2011a) as the large 'knowledge hubs'. These also tend to be the cities and regions which attract the most interest from researchers, policy analysts, and journalists. However, these places are not typical by definition. Even in their own countries these types of places tend not to be the norm but rather the exception. Most regions do not exhibit these advantageous combinations of characteristics of high scale, high diversity, high productivity and high connectivity. Casual observation tells us that regions vary greatly in size, population, population density, knowledge content, innovation performance, employment and migration patterns, land and real-estate prices, institutional and governance systems, natural and rural amenities, and climate. This raises the question as to whether there are any patterns emerging in terms of the more typical regions which are not the knowledge hubs.

The major evidence on these matters has been generated from analyses of the OECD regional database (OECD 2006, 2009a,b, 2011a,b, 2012), which provides almost two decades multi-country regional data disaggregated at different spatial and governance levels. Analyses of these data show four broad patterns:

(i)   In terms of productivity the spiky and uneven nature of the regional economy implied by Figures 9.1 and 9.2 is confirmed for almost all countries.

(ii) The distribution of growth performance across regions within countries and also across countries exhibits a regular pattern.

(iii) The share of national and international economic growth accounted for by the big 'knowledge hub' (OECD 2011a) or global city-regions discussed in the previous sections is between 20 per cent and 30 per cent, depending on the scale of spatial disaggregation, and that this share remains fairly constant across both countries and time. As such, between 70 per cent and 80 per cent of economic growth comes from other types of regions.

(iv) Nowadays, the high-growth regions in most countries are generally *not* the big urban hubs (MGI 2010), nor even urban areas in general (OECD 2009a, 2011c), but other various types of regions (Dijkstra et al. 2012), many of which are even lagging regions (OECD 2012).

With regard to the second and third points, we can explain these issues by following the OECD logic applied initially in the case of a country. First, each region's absolute economic growth contribution x_r is calculated as the product of the region's individual GDP growth rate g_r multiplied by the ratio of the region's output GDP_r. In other words, we have $x_r = w_r g_r$ where $w_r = GDP_r$. Once the absolute economic growth share of every region x_r is calculated, the natural logarithm of the individual regional growth x_r is plotted for every region along the horizontal axis, while the vertical axis plots the natural logarithm of the rank order R_r of the region, defined according to the GDP size of the region GDP_r, in a manner similar to the rank-size-rule diagram of Figure 3.8.

In terms of the OECD growth analysis, the observed shapes for regional growth distributions which seem to hold in almost all countries are rather more concave in nature than the −1 slopes of Zipf's law depicted in Figure 3.8. These distributions exhibit a negative downward-sloping shape, the slope of which becomes steeper as we move down and to the right towards the cases of the very largest regions. Moreover, exactly the same logic can also be applied to regions across groups of countries, such as across the EU or the OECD (OECD 2011c), and the shapes remain largely unchanged.

Typically, some 20 per cent of a nation's economic growth is accounted for by less than 5 per cent of its regions, depicted in Figure 9.3 as zone *A*, towards 60 per cent of a nation's growth is

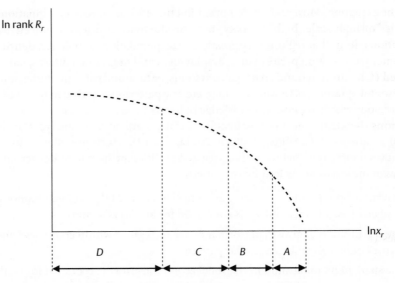

Figure 9.3 Power law relationships for regional growth and rank

accounted for by some 30 per cent of its regions, depicted in Figure 9.3 as zone *B*, some 20 per cent of a nation's growth by 50 per cent of its regions, depicted as zone *C*, and negligible contribution to a nation's total economic growth is made by some 15 per cent of regions, depicted in Figure 9.3 as zone *D*. Again, these resulting shapes also appear to hold for pooled sets of regions across group of countries. Note that regions tend to be very densely clustered along the curve in zones *B* and *C* whereas in zones *A* and *D* they tend to be much more thinly spread out. Appendix 9.2 provides a detailed explanation of how to interpret such distributions.

Following the logic of the OECD (2011c) regional growth distributions, the reason why the regional growth patterns are as they are is that many regions which are not predominantly urban in nature are also currently experiencing strong growth. Regions which are predominantly rural in nature and also regions which contain a mixture of urban and rural environments, what the OECD terms predominantly *intermediate* regions, are also growing, and often more rapidly than urban regions (OECD 2009a,b,c). OECD economic growth is not primarily an urban phenomenon, nor is it primarily a phenomenon associated with global cities (OECD 2011a,b). It is a complex picture, in which the patterns of regional growth which are greater than, equal to, or less than their respective national growth rates differ very little between urban, intermediate, or rural regions (OECD 2009a). In terms of rural areas, the largest differences are between rural areas which are very remote from intermediate or urban areas and those which are not so remote from intermediate or urban areas, with remote regions tending to face problems of depopulation and decline (Partridge et al. 2008).

The major patterns that we observe among OECD countries are that during the first decade of the modern era of globalization during the 1990s it was urban areas which systematically grew faster than intermediate regions, which in turn grew faster than rural regions. Since the turn of the twenty-first century the ordering has reversed in many places, with rural and intermediate areas in many countries now growing faster than urban areas. This reversal in regional growth patterns, whereby non-core regions are growing faster in terms of both total output and labour productivity growth than core regions, was first observed by Broersma and Van Dijk (2008), and is a pattern now widely observed (OECD 2009a). The current growth productivity performance of regions does not present the same spiky picture as depicted in Figures 9.1 and 9.2, which are based on absolute productivity levels. Many lower-productivity regions are now the fastest-growing regions such that the productivity and output growth rate spikes are often in different locations and regions from the spikes in absolute productivity (OECD 2009b).

The long-run effects of these emerging trends remain to be seen. What is important for our purposes, however, is to note that during the first decade of the current era of globalization, namely the 1990s, it was cities, and in particular global city-regions, which seem to have been the major beneficiaries of the massive international transformations taking place. Indeed, the role of large cities is still a major feature of development among the BRIICS countries (McCann 2009). However, the major impacts of these global transformations increasingly appear to be spreading to other types of regions within the industrialized countries. Nowadays growth and development are rather more regional issues within OECD countries than they are urban issues, while the long-run effects of these transformations and developments in the newly emerging countries remain to be seen.

9.6 Conclusions

Modern globalization presents a complex picture of economic geography, in which the current roles of cities and regions are evolving in various ways. The evidence regarding the development of networks of global cities points to the conclusion that in many ways geographical proximity has become increasingly important since the advent of the modern era of globalization since the late 1980s, even as transportation and communications technologies improve. The location behaviour of knowledge-intensive firms is critical, and firms already embedded in networks connected with these firms will more easily achieve major returns from globalization. As such, location in knowledge centres will therefore continue to be critical for high-value activities, and the arguments in Chapters 2 and 7 suggest that this spatial knowledge concentration will be even stronger for the service industries, because they are so dependent on trust relations.

While the rate of convergence between advanced economies has also slowed down since the 1980s (Cappelen et al. 2003; Greunz 2003), the importance of key urban areas within the global economy has increased. The result of all these changes is that over the last few decades, while between-country inequality has been falling (Crafts 2004), within-country inequality has actually been increasing since the 1980s (Brakman and van Marrewijk 2008). More recently, however, we have also started to witness the increasingly important role for intermediate regions, rural regions, and non-core regions in driving economic growth within many countries. This is a new reality which poses quite different challenges to much of what the urban-focused literature discusses. Over the coming decades, many of the major new growth opportunities and challenges will be evident in regions which are not the highest-productivity centres. This suggests that many of the advantages to core cities which arose out of the advent of the modern era of globalization are waning, and new opportunities are arising in many non-core regions.

Moreover, the arguments sketched out here are not in any way restricted to advanced industrialized economies. The importance of large cities in globalization appears to be particularly pertinent in the case of many developing countries, as witnessed by the rising international importance of centres such as Shanghai, Mumbai, Moscow, Johannesburg, Jakarta, and São Paulo. The increasing urbanization of these countries is associated with rising incomes, but these large developing BRIICS countries have also been experiencing rapidly rising interregional inequality to a much greater degree than the rich countries. As with the advanced economies, over the coming decades much of the economic growth of these countries is also forecast to take place in intermediate centres. However, intermediate-sized cities in many of these countries are far larger than those in advanced economies. Whether rural or smaller intermediate regions in these countries also emerge in a similar manner to many of the OECD countries remains to be seen.

Discussion questions

9.1 Discuss the major institutional, technological, and organization features which have rapidly transformed the global economy since the late 1980s.

9.2 Many people believe that the world is becoming 'flatter'. In terms of the economics of cities and regions, do you agree with this view? If so, why? If not, why not?

9.3 Discuss the contemporary relationship between globalization, urbanization, and industrialization which has emerged in rich countries since the late 1980s.

9.4 What is the current relationship between the wealth of a city, its size, and its global or regional connectivity?

9.5 How do you think that the current relationship between globalization, urbanization, and industrialization has reshaped the economic geography of your own country?

9.6 How do you think that the current relationship between globalization, urbanization, and industrialization has reshaped the economic geography of other countries? Give examples from different countries.

9.7 Do you think that this relationship is starting to change again in different countries?

9.8 Discuss the economic growth performance of predominantly rural regions and predominantly intermediate (mixture of urban and rural) regions in your country.

Appendix 9.1 Interpreting convergence–divergence considering the spatial units

The outcomes of the transition from Figure 9.1 to Figure 9.2 can imply either divergence or convergence, depending on the spatial units employed. In Figure 9.1, if the areas denoted as X_L, Y_L, and Z_L define the borders of three separate national market areas within the global economy AB, the transition from the environment depicted in Figure 9.1 to the environment depicted in Figure 9.2 would imply that the differences between the countries had increased, resulting in an international income or productivity divergence. On the other hand, if there were originally only two countries, whereby one country contained only city-region X while the other country contained both city-regions Y and Z, the transition from the environment depicted in Figure 9.1 to the environment depicted in Figure 9.2 would imply that the differences between the two countries had decreased, resulting in international income and productivity convergence. At the same time, irrespective of the areal definitions employed, the transition from Figure 9.1 to Figure 9.2 implies that the distribution of city sizes would become more concentrated and the surviving city sizes more similar, such that the rank-size exponent discussed in Chapter 3 would move above unity. The reason is that many of the intermediate and intervening locations denoted here as Y will disappear while the surviving locations X and Z will become more similar.

As we see with this example, the empirical outcomes regarding convergence or divergence depend in part on the definition of the spatial units, as defined by the cartographical patterns of national or regional borders. In statistical terms this reflects a well-known issue in spatial statistics and spatial econometrics raised in Chapter 3 known as the modifiable areal unit problem (MAUP) (Openshaw and Taylor 1979). We therefore note that the relationship between the cartographical pattern of borders and the spatial distribution of cities does affect empirical observations, and the interpretation of convergence or divergence issues must therefore be treated carefully.

Appendix 9.2 Interpreting cumulative regional growth patterns

In order to understand exactly what the curve depicted in Figure 9.3 means, we first need to understand how the OECD regional data are constructed. Below the national territorial level TL1, the OECD regional database (OECD 2011b) employs two different territorial scales at a sub-national level known as TL2 and TL3. These units are defined primarily according to the level of governance and public administration. TL1 is the national spatial area under the auspices of the national level of government. TL2 is the second tier of government below the national level, such as US states, German Länder, Japanese Prefectures, or French Départements, while TL3 is again the next level of governance in each country below the TL2 level.

This OECD diagrammatic approach to growth modelling is similar to the logic that we would use to construct diagrams of the rank-size rule and Zipf's law as depicted in Figure 3.8. As we saw in Chapter 3, in the case of constructing diagrams of the rank-size rule we would plot the natural logarithm of the urban population scale along the horizontal axis and along the vertical axis we would plot the natural logarithm of the rank order of the population of the urban region, with smaller cities having higher values. If Zipf's law holds, as it does in many countries, we would observe a downward-sloping distribution of plotted points displaying a slope whose gradient is close to –1. Therefore, if the OECD TL2 or TL3 spatial units of public administration in each country happened to closely reflect the geography of functional regions, then in terms of their population scales the spatial governance units would also closely reflect the rank-size distribution, with a downward-sloping straight line exhibiting a slope of –1.

If labour productivity is exactly equal in all regions, the downward-sloping curve which plots the log of the regional rank R_r against the log of regional GDP_r will also exhibit a gradient of –1. However, we know from Chapter 3 that larger functional (city)-regions often also exhibit greater population density as well as greater population scales. This means that local land prices and nominal wages are higher in larger and more densely populated city-regions, and according to the arguments earlier in the chapter, will also be associated with higher levels of labour productivity than in smaller centres. This would tend to make the gradient of the log GDP_r curve shallower as the size of the city-region increases, thereby making the curve rather more convex than linear, in a manner akin to the shape of a bid-rent curve, with the upper part of the curve exhibiting a gradient of –1, and thereafter becoming increasingly shallow. The more convex the slope, the more important the agglomeration effects.

In contrast, the institutional and governance structure of countries tends to counterbalance this effect. Administrative regions often reflect groupings of several smaller population centres in a manner which is designed explicitly to counteract the political power of the dominant city, and to allow for a more even institutional architecture. This grouping of cities and intervening rural areas into administrative regions will tend to make the slope of a curve plotting the log of the regional rank size against the log of the regional size rather more concave, irrespective of whether the regional size is measured in terms of population or GDP. As such, in terms of log rank–log size distributions these institutional issues will tend to militate against the convexity issue determined by scale-productivity differences.

We can control for these institutional issues by plotting the natural log of the rank of the scale against the natural log of the scale, where scale is defined either as regional GDP_r or in terms of regional growth rates g_r. We know that TL2 or TL3 regional governance and administrative levels do not always accurately reflect functional regions, and nor does labour productivity vary according to population density and population size. Therefore a plot of the natural logarithm of the administrative regional rank size R_r against the natural log if its size, where size is defined either according to $GDP_r = w_r$ or defined according to regional growth rates g_r, will not exactly reflect the –1 slope of Zipf's law, even if Zipf's law does approximately hold in terms of city population sizes.

Using regional data pooled across the European countries and also across time, it becomes clear that the log rank–log size graphs, whereby size is defined either as regional output GDP_r or as regional GDP growth rates g_r, exhibit distributions which are similar in shape to Zipf's law distributions in that they are downward sloping and approximately linear over a large extent (Dijsktra et al. 2012). However, the major differences between these distributions and Zipf's law are that these two distributions both exhibit slopes which are noticeably steeper than –1 and which also become curved and then flat for small values of size variable. As such, they are more concave than the Zipf's law distributions.

These distributions therefore allow us to depict the distribution of regional economic output (in other words the weighting components w_r) and also the distribution of regional growth rates g_r, which are a result of the interrelationships between the economic geography of the state and national–regional administrative and governance logic of the state. The patterns which become evident tend to hold for almost all countries, and, as we have just seen, the approach can also be applied to pooled groups of administrative regions across countries.

If all administrative regions of a country grow at the same rate g_r, we know that the curve which plots the natural logarithm of the regional rank R_r of $w_r = GDP_r$ against the natural logarithm of the regional growth contributions $x_r = w_r g_r$ will have exactly the same shape as the curve which plots the natural logarithm of the regional rank R_r of $w_r = GDP_r$ against the natural logarithm of regional output $w_r = GDP_r$. Therefore, if the curves do not have the same shape, we know that growth rates g_r differ across administrative regions. More specifically, if agglomeration effects are widespread and dominant, the curves plotting the natural logarithm of the rank R_r of the regional output $w_r = GDP_r$ against the natural logarithm of the regional growth contributions $x_r = w_r g_r$ will be more convex and flatter than the curves plotting the natural logarithm of the rank R_r of the regional output $w_r = GDP_r$ against the natural logarithm of the regional output $w_r = GDP_r$. In contrast, if the curves plotting the natural logarithm of the rank R_r of the regional output $w_r = GDP_r$ against the natural logarithm of the regional growth contributions $x_r = w_r g_r$ are more concave and steeper than the curves plotting the natural logarithm of the rank R_r of regional output $w_r = GDP_r$ against the natural logarithm of the regional output $w_r = GDP_r$, it becomes clear that the reason must be that many intermediate output size regions are growing faster than large output regions.

This is exactly what we do see (Dijsktra et al. 2012). The curve plotting the natural logarithm of the rank R_r of the regional output $w_r = GDP_r$ against the natural logarithm of the regional growth contributions $x_r = w_r g_r$ is very clearly concave, and more so than the curve plotting the relationship between the rank R_r of regional output $w_r = GDP_r$ against the natural logarithm of the regional output $w_r = GDP_r$. The reason for this becomes clear if we plot the log of the rank of GDP_r against the log of the regional growth rate g_r. Here there is no real systematic pattern, with all types of regions exhibiting fast, slow, and average growth rates, except for the fact that many intermediate types of regions are performing relatively well. Growth rate and growth shares therefore do not systematically favour large urban areas (OECD 2009a,b).

10 Modern urban and regional economic policy analysis

10.1 Introduction to the modern urban and regional policy context

Urban and regional economic policy is distinct from other forms of public sector economic policy, in that it is explicitly related to questions of geography. Both the motivation for, and the implementation of, urban and regional economic policy are specifically spatial in nature, and decisions as to whether to undertake policy intervention depend on the performance of the local economic environment. However, our perception of what is 'local' will itself determine the nature of the policy, its implementation and its evaluation. This is because the definition of a 'local economic environment' may extend from the spatial scale of an individual suburban area to that of an urban metropolitan area, and to the even larger spatial scales of a city-plus-hinterland regional economy, or even a regional economy comprising more than one city.

We know that economic indicators of average employment, unemployment, income levels, house prices, or various other indices of social deprivation will differ according to the definition of the spatial areas used in order to calculate them. Therefore our assessment of the performance of the 'economic environment' will also depend on the spatial scale adopted to define what is 'local'. In other words, the criteria against which any possible policy intervention will be considered or assessed will also depend on the spatial definition of the local economic environment.

For this reason, urban and regional economic policy is generally broken down into two distinct groups of policies and initiatives. First, there are various initiatives which are focused specifically on the urban economic environment and targeted at the urban or sub-urban spatial scale. We will refer to these policies under the general heading of 'urban policy'. Second, there is a range of initiatives which are targeted at the much broader regional spatial scale, and we will refer to these policies under the general heading of 'regional policy'. The first major distinction between urban economic policy and regional economic policy is therefore simply the spatial extent of their focus and implementation, with regional policy being applied over a much greater spatial scale than urban policy.

The spatial scale, however, is not the only distinction between urban and regional economic policies. The second distinction between these two groups of spatial policies is the nature of the policies which can be implemented. All urban and regional economic poli-cies are motivated by the desire to improve the local economic environment. However, the extent to which particular policies can be considered as viable candidates for imple-mentation will once again depend on the spatial definition of the local environment. For example, while policies encouraging 'gentrification' can be considered as candidates for economic development at the urban or suburban level, they would clearly be inappropri-ate as economic policies at the regional scale because their impacts would tend to be too localized. Similarly, large-scale regional policy, based for example on industrial reloca-tion incentives, would be inappropriate as economic policies at the suburban scale, and often largely inappropriate even at the urban scale, because their impacts would tend to be too widespread. In other words, the justification for the particular spatial economic polices adopted will in part also depend on the spatial area which is the object of the policy.

The third distinction between urban and regional policies concerns institutional issues. The different spatial scales over which these different policies are applied imply that the governmental and administrative frameworks within which such policies are implemented must also be different. This is because the geographical areas which are the focus of the spa-tial policies may cross different administrative boundaries. The implementation of such policies may therefore require cross-border agreements and cooperative arrangements between neighbouring local government bodies. This is particularly the case for regional policy, which usually spans different administrative areas, but generally much less so for urban policy, which is normally implemented at the level of a single urban municipal level of government.

The fourth distinction between urban and regional economic policies, and an issue we are particularly concerned with here, relates to the different analytical approaches which can be adopted in order to understand and evaluate such policies.

All the various spatial economic models we have discussed in this book are implicitly constructed at different spatial scales. The Weber–Moses models discussed in Chapter 1 are primarily discussed in terms of an interregional framework, in which major production facilities search for optimum production-location arrangements over broad spatial scales. On the other hand, the models of spatial competition discussed in Chapter 1, such as the Hotelling framework, can be considered either at an interregional regional scale if we are discussing large production facilities, or at an urban or suburban scale if we are considering small retail establishments. In Chapters 2 and 4 the models of industrial clustering, agglom-eration, and urban land use which are discussed are explicitly framed at the level of an indi-vidual city. This is in contrast, however, to the central-place models of the urban system by Christaller, Losch, and the more recent work of Krugman (1991) and Fujita et al. (1999), all of which are discussed in Chapter 3, and which are obviously constructed at the interre-gional scale. The regional multiplier models discussed in Chapter 5 are all framed at the city-region and interregional scale, as are the labour employment and migration models discussed in Chapter 6. Finally, the factor allocation, growth, and balance of payments mod-els discussed in Chapter 7 are all framed at the interregional level.

The fact that each of these models is implicitly constructed at a different spatial scale sug-gests that different models will be appropriate for different geographical scales of urban and regional policy analysis. In other words, the appropriate analytical technique, or combina-tion of analytical techniques, to employ to deal with a particular policy issue will depend on the object of the policy and the spatial scale of its implementation. Obviously, all the urban and regional economic issues discussed in this book have implications for urban and regional policy. However, in general there are also differences in the analytical underpinnings of each policy agenda and differences in the emphasis given to particular approaches. For example, on the one hand, urban policy issues tend to be closely related to matters of land use, local labour commuting, and the impacts of localized externalities, both positive and negative, while on the other hand, regional policy issues tend to be more related to the issues regarding the interregional mobility of labour and firms, and also the impacts of institutional and technological changes.

As we have seen in Part I of this book, over the last two or three decades there have been many modern developments in urban and regional economic theory which build on and greatly extend the insights of the earlier seminal theoretical frameworks also discussed in this book. In particular, our understanding of the mechanics of urban and regional growth has advanced significantly. At the same time, as we have also seen in Chapters 8 and 9, over the last two or three decades there have also been fundamental transformations in the global economy. These changes have enormous implications for the economic role of cities and regions within national and international economic contexts. In particular, the role of cities and regions in fostering economic growth appears to be increasing relative to the role played by countries and nation-states. At the same time, the traditional differences in the analytical emphasis of the various urban and regional debates have also been somewhat blurred ad reoriented following the recent impacts of globalization on cities and regions, impacts which tend to transcend all spatial scales.

This chapter will discuss the policy challenges relating to each of these spatial scales by examining the policy issues relating first to cities, second to regions, and third to national policy. The first section of the chapter will examine urban economic policy matters. The second section will examine traditional regional policy matters, and the third section will discuss the new debates which have emerged regarding the nature, rationale, and role of regional policy. As we will see, these new debates have profound impacts in terms of our understanding of development policy per se, and the outcomes of these debates will shape regional development policy for many years to come.

10.2 Urban economic policy

Economic policies which are implemented specifically at the urban level generally involve attempts to improve the attractiveness of city or of suburban areas as locations for investment, commerce, and housing. However, in order for such a policy to be successful it is necessary to target the initiative towards the types of investment sectors which are regarded as being sensitive to economic or environmental variations even at the localized urban or suburban scale. The sectors which are generally regarded as the most sensitive to such small spatial-scale variations are the real-estate and property development sectors. Urban economic policies therefore tend to focus on the relationship between the real-estate and property development sectors, and the rest of the local urban economy. In particular, urban policies usually attempt to alter the relative attractiveness of certain areas for property development in order to favour less developed locations. In order to achieve this, urban policies invariably involve relaxations or changes to the institutional or legal framework within which local economic development takes place. This is because real-estate and property development market transactions take place within complex legal and institutional frameworks which differ between countries and states. By changing these institutional arrangements in favour of development at particular locations, public policy may be used to guide the spatial pattern of private sector investment in order to achieve pre-ordained goals. As such, the logic of urban policy is determined primarily by political priorities, and the focus of such policies tends to be on changing the nature of the local built environment.

From the point of view of economic analysis, any such urban policies will have welfare implications for different individual social groups as well as for the economy as a whole. The welfare impacts of such policies must be considered in order to arrive at a reasonable evaluation of the success or otherwise of such policies. In order to see this we can consider two types of spatial policies, both of which are commonly employed within the urban built environment.

10.2.1 **Urban zoning policies**

One of the policies frequently employed by urban, regional, and land-use planners in many countries is that of the geographical zoning of activities. In this type of policy, different types of activities are only permitted to take place at particular urban locations. In other words, the land-use planning system is underpinned by the legal system, and this institutional arrangement determines where particular types of investment and development activities may be be undertaken within the city. Moreover, by defining the size of the zones in two-dimensional space, the land-use planning system determines both the location and the level of supply of urban development land for each activity or range of activities. What the system cannot do, however, is control the price of the development land. This is determined by the interaction of the current demand for land at the particular zoned location by the permitted industry, and the supply of the land at that particular location. Therefore, in order to understand the price effects of such a policy it is first necessary to consider the results of a competitive situation in which there is no such policy intervention, and then use this as the benchmark case against which the policy effects can be considered.

In order to consider the effects of a land-use zoning policy with respect to the situation of no such policy, we can adopt the bid-rent model discussed in Chapter 4. The bid-rent model allows us to compare the land-price gradient with respect to distance under conditions of either free competition or with land-zoning schemes. As in Chapter 3, the bid-rent model assumes that the location of the city centre, which is assumed to be the central business district M, is given, and that local land prices are determined by accessibility and factor proportions considerations. We can consider the case of a city comprising three major industrial activities, namely a service sector, a manufacturing sector, and a retail and distribution sector. In terms of land and built environment facilities, these three industry groups will require offices, factory, and workshop facilities, and shops and warehouse facilities, respectively. If we adopt the initial assumptions of Figure 4.8 in Chapter 4 relating to the trade-off between accessibility and space requirements, we can assume that the service sector will be the most oriented towards the city centre, with the manufacturing sector adjacent to this sector, and the retail sector located on the edge of the city. This is depicted again in Figure 10.1.

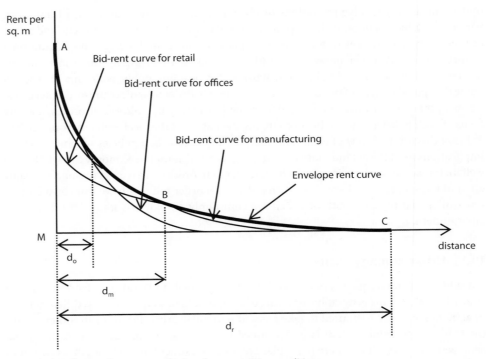

Figure 10.1 Industry urban rent gradient under competitive conditions

Under these conditions, competition for land will imply that the service sector offices will be located between the city centre M and a distance d_o from the city centre. The manufacturing sector factories and workshops will be located in the concentric ring of land around the service sector, at a distance between d_o and d_m from the city centre. Finally, the retail and distribution sector will be located in the concentric ring of land around the manufacturing sector, at a distance between d_m and d_r from the city centre. The actual urban land-rent gradient is given by the shaded envelope rent gradient ABC which is just tangent to the highest bid-rent curve at each location. As we see, the urban land-rent gradient will be a smooth downward-sloping function which is convex to the origin M.

We can now compare this competitive result with a situation in which the urban land is zoned. For example, we can imagine a situation in which the local metropolitan urban government decides not to allow manufacturing activities to be located as close to the city centre as they would be under free competition. Such a decision might be taken for reasons of preserving or enhancing the aesthetic quality of the city centre, or alternatively because of concerns about the negative effects of local environmental pollution. In this situation, the local urban planning authorities may decide to permit only retail activities to take place immediately adjacent to the city centre where the service sector activities take place. As such, the zoning policy is organized so as to act as a buffer between the city centre and the manufacturing activities. In Figure 10.2, this retail zone is defined as the area between distances d_1 and d_2 from the city centre M. At the same time, the local urban planning authorities may also decide that the more peripheral suburban areas which are largely residential,

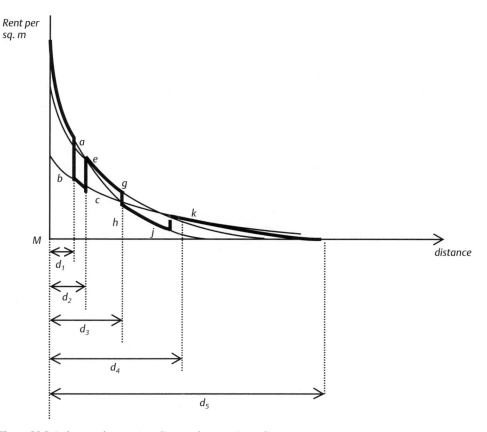

Figure 10.2 Industry urban rent gradient under a zoning policy

and in particular those areas which are occupied by middle- and higher-income house-holds, should not contain manufacturing activities. Manufacturing should only be allowed to take place in the one particular area which is specifically zoned for such activities. In order to effect this, the authorities may specify that the manufacturing zone cannot extend any further than distance d_3 from the city centre. Meanwhile, to compensate for the loss of service sector space available in the city due to the presence of the inner retail zone, the local authorities may only permit service sector activities to take place in the area between distances d_3 and d_4 from the city centre. Beyond this zone the planning system may permit a mixed use of retail or service sector activities.

In a situation such as this, the actual urban land gradient will be serrated (Evans 1985) as well as downward sloping, and is given in Figure 10.2 by the bold line. In order to consider the welfare effects of the planning policy we can compare the area under the rent gradient in the case where the zoning policy is implemented and in the case where there is no such policy. Where no zoning policy is in effect and the land market is competitive, the actual urban land rent gradient is given by the envelope rent gradient in Figure 10.1. As we see in Figure 10.2, the difference between the area under the competitive rent gradient and the area under the serrated rent gradient is represented by the sum of the areas *abce* plus *ghjk*.

These two areas together represent the total loss of urban rental revenue which results from the urban land being occupied at the zoned locations by activities which are unable to pay the maximum rent attainable under the competitive conditions. Given that Figure 10.2 is a one-dimensional diagram, the actual total revenue lost to the urban economy due to the zoning policy can be calculated by rotating the one-dimensional model through 360 degrees. This total revenue loss represents the opportunity cost of the zoning policy, and as such reflects the welfare loss to the urban economy of the planning policy.

The key point to come from the above argument is that urban planning policies inevitably have welfare implications. However, in the analytical assessment of the model described by Figures 10.1 and 10.2 we assume that the price mechanism is broadly efficient. Yet a true assessment of the implications of these policies also depends on our perception of the efficiency of the land-price mechanism to correctly price amenity goods. In the situation described by Figures 10.1 and 10.2, we have assumed that the reason for the implementation of zoning policies is that government authorities implicitly believe that the land market exhibits externalities which are not correctly priced by the market mechanism. In particular, the aesthetic aspects of the central city environment are assumed to be undervalued by private sector cost considerations, such that the profitability of individual manufacturing activities will take precedence over the perceived positive benefits associated with an attractive civic centre. If it is perceived that first- or second-best solutions are neither possible nor appropriate policy responses to the perceived market failure in this context, the government authorities simply resort to a quota mechanism, in which a quantity constraint is imposed on the amount of land available at particular locations, and land is allocated by a process of rationing. Which particular development schemes are undertaken will depend on a property developer acquiring planning permission from the local government authority. By adopting such planning schemes, the government authorities are therefore ruling out direct comparisons of the form represented by a comparison of Figures 10.1 and 10.2, because it is assumed that the private sector land prices given in Figure 10.1 do not accurately reflect marginal social benefits. This is the justification for such interventionist policies.

10.2.2 Urban regeneration policies

A feature of the type of land-use planning policies described above is that changes in the market environment are brought about by changes in the legal and institutional environment in which the local land market works. Moreover, such policies are implemented in conditions where government authorities believe that the market mechanism will lead to socially inefficient results due to the presence of externalities. However, there are also situations in which the implementation of such policies may have undesirable welfare effects. As an example of this problem we can consider the case of urban regeneration schemes, which are popular recent initiatives both in North American cities such as Philadelphia and Boston, and also in European cities such as London, Manchester, and Rotterdam. These schemes have been designed specifically to encourage the redevelopment of the downtown urban areas, and to counter the out-migration and depopulation of many central city areas. Many large urban areas have faced a consistent outward drift of both people and activities over the last three or four decades as people and businesses have moved to smaller urban centres. The reasons for this so-called 'urban–rural shift' may be connected, first, with improvements in production, communications, and transport technology, which reduce the importance of a central urban location for many firm activities. Second, as incomes rise, the increased preference by households for space and better-quality environments has encouraged an out-migration of many people to more peripheral, but still accessible, locations. Third, the fixity of the urban capital stock, as discussed in Chapter 6, may limit the ability of firms to reconfigure or expand their land-holdings in central urban areas relative to greenfield locations. Taken together, these various effects have tended to reduce the attractiveness of central urban areas for many people and businesses. The combinations of these trends has often led to the creation of urban wastelands described by Figure 4.15 in which land immediately adjacent to the urban centre is left undeveloped and derelict. However, for many civic government authorities, such trends are regarded as also leading to the additional localized problems of deprivation, poverty, and crime.

In order to improve both the aesthetic aspect of the central urban area and the conditions of the people living close to the derelict areas, many urban authorities have implemented urban regeneration schemes. In these schemes, the legal and institutional environment within which the urban land market operates is altered in favour of the disadvantaged area. As mentioned above, for reasons of congestion, it is generally assumed that most manufacturing types of activities do not wish to find central urban locations. Similarly, many urban authorities generally do not wish such activities to be located centrally for the reasons discussed above. Therefore these urban regeneration schemes tend to be focused on the real-estate markets of the residential sector and service sector, as these are generally regarded as the sectors most sensitive to urban environmental variations. In other words, these schemes are usually targeted towards the local development of housing and office properties.

As with the case of the urban zoning policies discussed above, we can adopt the bid-rent model or urban land allocation in order to analyse the welfare effects of urban redevelopment schemes. In order to do this, we will consider the situation in an urban area which initially experiences an area of downtown dereliction close to the city centre. In this 'no-man's land' area the price of real estate is zero, as no individuals wish to live there and no businesses wish to locate there under the current economic and environmental conditions. This initial situation can be represented by Figure.10.3, which is also constructed on the basis of the argument in section 4.4.2 in Chapter 4. In Figure 10.3, we assume for simplicity that there are only two income groups, a low-income group and a high-income group. The low-income group lives close to the urban centre within a radius of d_l from the centre. The high-income group lives at a distance beyond d_z from the city centre. However, because of the preference of the high-income group not to live close to the low-income group, there is an area of dereliction between d_l and d_z. In the area of dereliction, the economic prospects are so low that, even with market rents at zero, investment there is not profitable.

In situations where local civic authorities attempt to rectify the situation described in Figure 10.3, by improving the general aesthetic environment around the city centre, local civic planning authorities engage in a range of policies to influence the local real-estate market behaviour. These policies can take a range of forms such as relaxations of local planning or zoning restrictions, direct real-estate or tax subsidies to developers, indirect subsidies to developers such as special public infrastructure or public transportation provision, or joint ventures between public and private sector bodies in underwriting such schemes. However, the basic logic common to all such urban regeneration schemes is an attempt to change the

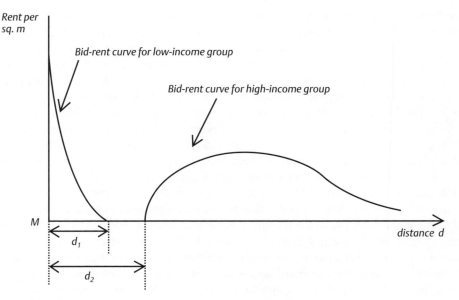

Figure 10.3 Derelict urban land

institutional environment in which the local real-estate market works, in order to effect changes in the physical environment of the local area. The reason for this, as we have seen in Chapter 3, is that the area of dereliction is due to the perverse upward-sloping behaviour of the bid-rent curves of high-income groups, due to the externalities associated with social perceptions. Therefore these urban policies aim to alter the perceptions of the higher-income groups in order to encourage real-estate investment by this group in the city centre.

The effects of such policies can be depicted in Figure 10.4 according to the argument in section 4.4.1 and the description given in Figure 4.12. If the redevelopment of the local city centre area goes ahead, this area will now become attractive for a certain portion of the high-income group which has a relatively high preference for accessibility to the city, but which previously was unwilling to pay for this due to the poor local environment. For simplicity we will characterize this group as a high-income group comprising primarily young people, but this group may also include dual-income households. The bid-rent curve of this group will tend to be very steep. On the other hand, the older people within the high-income group or those with young children will still generally have a higher preference for space in order to provide for the needs of their dependants. As such, their bid-rent curve will remain very shallow. The redevelopment of the downtown area will mean that the single perverse bid-rent curve of the high-income group depicted in Figure 10.3 will now be split into two different downward-sloping convex bid-rent curves for the two distinct high-income groups. As we see in Figure 10.4, the result of this is that the area within a radius of d_y from the central business district M will be occupied by young high-income earners. Similarly, the older high-income group will be located beyond a distance d_h from the city centre. Meanwhile, the low-income group will be located in the area between d_y and d_h from the city centre.

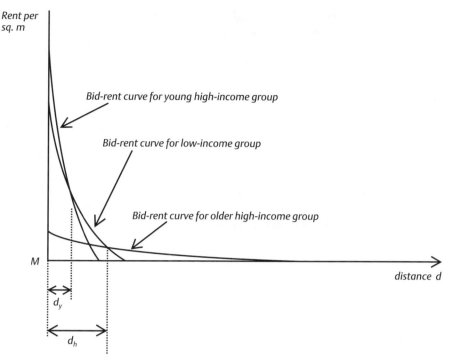

Figure 10.4 Residential land-use effects of urban regeneration schemes

We can compare the area of habitation of the low-income group before and after the urban regeneration scheme by considering the difference between Figures 10.3 and 10.4. As we see, for the same bid-rent curve, the low-income group is now constrained to live in a smaller area of occupation after the redevelopment scheme than before the scheme. The reason is that both the land immediately adjacent to the city centre and the land on the outer fringes of the area of low-income occupation are now allocated by the price mechanism to the two high-income groups. In this situation, the low-income group as a whole will have suffered a welfare loss with respect to the high-income group. This is because in the situation where the incomes and preferences of the low-income group, which are embodied in their bid-rent curve, remain unchanged, many of the low-income people will no longer be able to live in the city and will lose their residences in order to make way for the high-income group. As such, they will be forced to leave the city.

Alternatively, if the low-income population of the city remains stable, because as we discussed in Chapter 5 the ability of the low-income groups to migrate may be very limited, the low-income population will now be constrained to a greater residential density of living. Following the arguments in section 4.4 of Chapter 4, the individual bid-rent curve of the low-income group, as depicted in Figures 10.3 and 10.4, indicates the rent per square metre which people are willing to pay at different locations in order to maintain a given level of utility, where utility is partly a function of the total land area consumed. If at any location the total land area consumed falls for any given rent per square metre payable, the total utility of the individual household must fall. In terms of bid-rent analysis this utility fall is represented by an upward shift in the bid-rent curve for the low-income group. As we see in Figure 10.5, this upward shift in the bid-rent curve for the low-income group after the redevelopment scheme will be represented by an increase in the rent per square metre payable by the low-income group at any location. Competition in the real-estate market implies that the low-income group will now increase their area of habitation from the area between the distances d_y and d_h from the city centre to the area between the distances $d_{l'}$ and $d_{l''}$ from the city centre. As such, the low-income group will increase their area of habitation, relative to the situation described by Figure 10.4, by encroaching on the area of habitation of both of the high-income groups. However, this increase in habitation area is paid for by an increase in dwelling density on the part of the low-income group, the result of which is an upward shift in the bid-rent function of the low-income group. The low-income group unambiguously suffers a welfare loss due to the urban redevelopment scheme. These complex welfare-reallocation issues are inherent in most urban gentrification schemes, as discussed in Box 10.1.

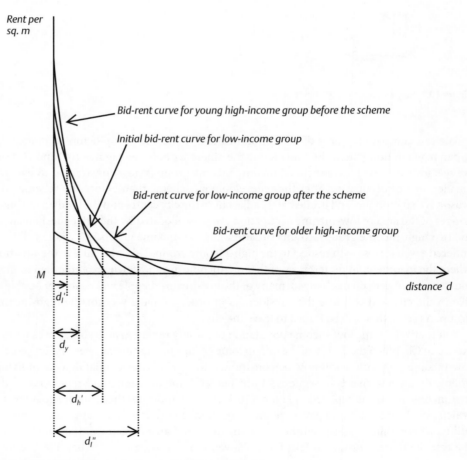

Figure 10.5 Welfare effects of urban regeneration schemes

BOX 10.1 Urban gentrification

The discussion of urban redevelopment schemes presented here is intended to provide an illustrative example of the complex welfare effects involved in any urban policy initiative. In cases where high-income groups are encouraged to move back into the central areas of the city via improvements in the physical environment of the city, this process is often known as 'gentrification'. In some cases the process of gentrification takes place naturally within the market mechanism as developers search for new profitable ventures. Many parts of old established cities such as London, New York, and Paris, which have subsequently enjoyed localized employment growth due to agglomeration effects in certain sectors such as finance, have recently experienced significant levels of gentrification. However, in many cities, and in particular in cities which are not enjoying such localized agglomeration effects, the market process alone cannot lead to gentrification. In these situations, public policy intervention is required if it is believed that the encouragement of such processes is a good thing from a social point of view. However, as we have seen here, such urban redevelopment schemes have an unfortunate consequence, in that the people who often benefit from these schemes are high-income groups, whereas the people who suffer welfare losses are low-income groups. Yet advocates of these policies do not regard these initiatives simply as attempts to change the geographical residential patterns of society. Nor do they promote these schemes as being only beneficial to the high-income groups. These policies are generally carried out in the implicit belief that by encouraging the redevelopment of the downtown areas, localized agglomeration benefits can be realized in the long run due to the clustering of tertiary activities and high-income groups in the city centre. In other words, by the careful targeting of particular schemes planners hope to use selective public intervention to encourage localized growth.

It is often argued by proponents of urban gentrification schemes that the localized growth effects will benefit all local people via the generation of local employment opportunities, the improvement in the local physical environment, and also improvements in the local social environment. Education, expectations, peer-group effects, and individual household behaviour all play a role in influencing the impacts of urban gentrification schemes on lower socioeconomic groups. However, the manner in which these effects and mechanisms operate on lower-income groups is probably rather different from the effects which influence higher-income groups. If urban gentrification means that wider area labour market demand conditions improve, the positive effects on the local labour market may filter down to the lower socioeconomic groups (Overman 2002). However, the extent of these potentially positive economic effects also depends on the spatial composition of the lower socioeconomic groups. Some evidence suggests that there are negative peer-externality effects associated with clusters of lower socioeconomic groups which may militate against the spreading of these employment effects (Overman 2002). On the other hand, there are arguments which suggest that the clustering of low-income groups may help job-search processes among the lower socioeconomic groups (Cheshire 2009). By separating out the spatial (neighbourhood) aspects of these processes from the household (intergenerational education) aspects of these processes Pattachini and Zenou (2011) suggests that the local social environment does indeed play an important role in the long-term fortunes of individuals. If urban gentrification reduces the spatial concentrations of low-income groups and promotes socioeconomic mixing, these may generate positive impacts on the lowest-income groups. If, however, clusters of low-income households remain, this will militate against potentially beneficial effects of gentrification. As we have already seen in Chapters 2 and 3, the clustering of activities and people is not always a sufficient condition for the development of localized agglomeration economies. The same is also true for lower-income groups. Indeed, the evidence points rather the other way, in that the clustering of low-income groups militates against the generation of positive spillover effects. Therefore any hypothesized beneficial gentrification–agglomeration effects accruing to the low-income groups as compensation for the welfare losses described here may be purely speculative (Cheshire 2009). In the absence of any such agglomeration effects, welfare losses will unambiguously accrue to the low-income groups, whereas the high-income groups will be the major beneficiaries of the urban redevelopment schemes.

10.2.3 **Greenbelts**

Land-use allocations take place within land-use planning systems which vary enormously across countries (OECD 2010a). In some countries of relatively high spatial population densities, such as the Netherlands, South Korea, and the UK, land use and land allocation at both the national and local levels are organized primarily within a system of 'greenbelts'. A greenbelt is a zone of land surrounding an urban area in which urban development is not permitted under any circumstances. In other words, the greenbelt forms a concentric ring around the city which clearly defines the outer edge of the urban area. The logic of the greenbelt policy is to limit the outward expansion of the urban areas in order to preserve and protect the intervening rural land. The motive for such a restrictive policy is that in densely populated countries and regions, the preservation of rural areas is often perceived to be a national priority, because of the relative scarcity of rural land. From this perspective, the value of the rural area is defined primarily in terms of aesthetic and archaeological arguments, rather than simply in economic terms. Therefore, in order to ensure that all people have relatively easy access to local rural areas, strictly enforced limits are placed on the expansion of urban areas. Implicitly, such a policy assumes that the private land market mechanism will not appropriately value the preservation of rural environmental amenities in terms of their social costs and benefits, and that urban development activities will be priced only with respect to private costs and benefits. As such, the rationale for greenbelts is an externality problem. On the other hand, such a policy inevitably also has welfare implications.

   In order understand the logic for a greenbelt policy we can consider Figure 10.6, in which a region comprises two major urban centres with their respective central business districts

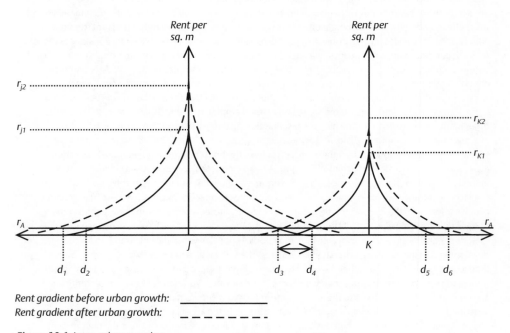

Rent gradient before urban growth: ——————

Rent gradient after urban growth: — — — — — —

Figure 10.6 Inter-urban merging

located at J and K. We assume that the nominal wage incomes earned at the central business location J are higher than the nominal wage incomes earned at K. As such, the competitive market rental price per square metre r_{J1} of land at J is higher than the competitive market rental price per square metre r_{K1} of land at K. Following the arguments in section 4.4.1 of Chapter 4, the convex envelope rent gradients of each urban area comprise the individual bid-rent functions of the different income groups employed at each urban centre. If the agricultural land rent is given as r_A at all locations, and the land market is competitive, the urban area centred on J will be larger than the urban area centred on K. The urban area centred on J extends from location d_2 to d_3, and the urban area centred on J extends from location d_4 to d_5. The agricultural areas are the areas to the left of d_2, to the right of d_5, and the area between locations d_3 and d_4. In other words, at the prevailing incomes r_{J1} and r_{K1} earned in urban activities at J and K, respectively, the two urban areas are still separated by an area of rural activities. The actual land-rent gradient is represented by the bold line in Figure 10.6.

If, for example, due to agglomeration economies, the nominal incomes payable at J and K increase over time by 50 per cent to r_{J2} and r_{K2}, respectively, both of the urban areas will expand. In this case, the new land-rent gradient is given in Figure 10.6 by the perforated bold line. As we see, the urban area centred on J will now extend to a location d_1 to the left of J, and the urban area centred on J will now extend to a location d_6 to the right of K. The area between J and K will now all be taken up by urban development such that the intervening urban area will disappear. As such, the new merged urban area will now extend continuously from d_1 to d_6.

In order to avoid the merging of urban centres over time, for the reasons outlined above, the land-use planning authorities may enforce a strict greenbelt policy to preserve the existing urban boundaries. The effects of such a policy can be seen in Figure 10.7. In this case, the land-use planning system implements a greenbelt around the urban area centred on J, such that urban development is not permitted beyond locations d_2 and d_3, and a second greenbelt around K, such that urban development is not permitted beyond locations d_4 and d_5. In this situation, if the cities grow over time due to agglomeration economies, the increased number of locally employed people will be constrained to live in the same urban areas. This will reduce the average living area of each household. Consequently the bid-rent curve for each individual urban household will shift upwards to a higher level than would be the case in the situation where growth is accommodated in a competitive land market without a greenbelt policy. The result of this is that the envelope-rent gradient will move upwards and the market price payable per square metre will increase at all locations within the urban area to higher levels than would be the case without the greenbelt. In Figure 10.7, the actual rent gradient under conditions of urban growth after the imposition of the greenbelt policy is given by the bold line, and the rent gradient under conditions of urban growth without a greenbelt policy is given by the bold perforated line. On the urban–rural boundaries at points d_2, d_3, d_4, and d_5, there are significant discontinuities in the land rent payable, and these will continue to exist as long as the greenbelt restrictions remain in place. From the perspective of living costs, all urban dwellers suffer a welfare loss due to the imposition of the greenbelt policy.

From the arguments outlined in section 4.4.2 of Chapter 4, it is also possible that the negative welfare effects of a greenbelt policy may be exacerbated by the expectation that the environment at the urban fringe will be preserved indefinitely. If environmental amenities

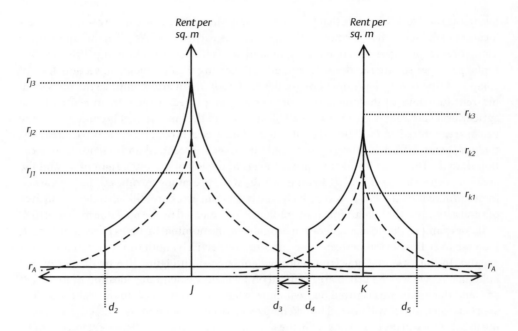

Rent gradient with the greenbelt policy: ————————
Rent gradient without the greenbelt policy: — — — — — — — -

Figure 10.7 The land-price effects of a greenbelt policy

are relatively localized and it is perceived that the greenbelt policy will be maintained in the long term, this implies that the persons who are resident on the urban fringes will always enjoy superior environmental amenities in comparison with those who are resident closer to the city centre. If low-income groups are constrained to remain close to the urban centre for the reasons discussed in sections 4.4.1 and 4.4.2 of Chapter 4, this implies that only the high-income groups will enjoy these environmental benefits at their residential locations. As we see in Figure 10.8, the effect of this will be to cause the bid-rent curves of the higher-income groups to become upward sloping as we move towards the urban fringe, such that the envelope urban rent gradient will now become U-shaped. Under these circumstances, the discontinuities between the urban and rural land prices at the urban fringes will become even more marked. Meanwhile, the major beneficiaries of the greenbelt policy will be the high-income households living on the edges of the urban areas.

10.3 **Regional economic policy**

The role of, nature of, and rationale for regional economic policy have all recently undergone a major rethinking in many parts of the world. The rethinking has been spurred by the enormous changes associated with modern globalization that were discussed in detail in

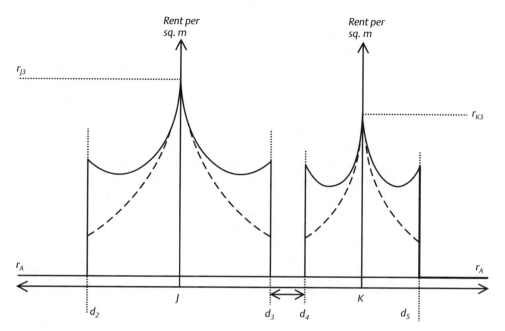

Figure 10.8 Local environmental effects of a greenbelt policy

Chapter 9. Such a process of rethinking has uncovered many complex issues and led to a fundamental reassessment of many of the assumptions on which traditional regional policy was based. In addition, this has also led to a redefining of the modern approaches to regional policy, and a reconsideration of the analytical underpinnings of such policies. Sections 10.3.1 to 10.3.3 will discuss insights from the traditional approaches to regional policy, and section 10.4 will introduce the new debates in regional policy. As we will see in section 10.4, many of the traditional insights and justifications for traditional regional policy approaches are still valid, but they also need to be updated and adapted in the light of the more recent reconsiderations discussed in section 10.4.

10.3.1 **Traditional regional policies**

Economic policies implemented at the regional level often involve attempts to improve the attractiveness of particular regions as locations for investment. In particular, regional policies attempt to improve the relative attractiveness of investment in less developed regions. In this sense these regional policies are similar to some of the urban regeneration policies discussed below. However, a key difference between regional policies and urban policies is that the industrial sectors towards which regional polices have traditionally been targeted have tended to be quite different from those targeted at the urban scale. The reason for this is that, following the arguments in Chapter 1, the types of firms which traditionally have been generally regarded as being the most sensitive to large-scale spatial cost and price variations are not the real-estate and property development sectors, but rather the manufacturing and distribution sectors, along with some other types of commercial service sectors carrying out rather routine standardized activities.

As with urban policy, in order to achieve these goals traditional regional policies involve relaxations or changes to the institutional or legal framework within which local economic development takes place. However, the local economic development impacts of regional policy can differ significantly across both sectors and regions. Therefore it is necessary for us to consider carefully the size and the spatial pattern of any possible local regional development effects. Regional policies tend to be implemented partly or wholly via the provision of public sector funds, and funding tends to be granted in selected lagging areas which are chosen as candidates for regional financial aid. However, given that regional policy typically involves public funds, it is also important to consider the social marginal costs and benefits of such a regional policy, relative to the situation where no such policy has been initiated. Counterfactual impact assessment is therefore essential.

The most common types of regional policies are supply-side policies, which attempt to improve the environment for local investment by upgrading the quality of the local production factor inputs. In particular, supply-side regional policies tend to focus on the factor inputs which are location specific. In an interregional economy in which both capital and labour are mobile, the only production factor inputs which are location specific are natural raw material inputs, land, and local infrastructure inputs, while certain segments of the labour market are partly immobile. Given that raw material locations cannot be affected by policy intervention, the focus of regional policy tends to be primarily on increasing the quality and variety of local infrastructure inputs or on the subsidizing of specific labour input costs, such as labour retraining or upskilling costs. These are generally indirect ways of reducing real local input costs. An alternative, but rather less commonly used approach nowadays, is for regional policy to focus on directly reducing the cost of local land inputs. We can consider each of these approaches individually.

In the case of regional policies which attempt to upgrade the quality and variety of local inputs, the major focus often traditionally tends to be on the improvement of local transportation infrastructure (Vickerman 1991). The expected effect of these policies is primarily to reduce the costs of accessibility to the region in question. Therefore improvements are generally sought in key strategic elements of the local transport infrastructure which connect the individual region in question to other parts of the interregional economy.

There are two reasons for this overall approach. The first is that transportation inputs are regarded as essential inputs into almost all industrial and commercial activities, irrespective of whether it is goods or people that are being moved. On the basis of the production function discussions in Chapter 7, improvements in transportation infrastructure inputs can be considered as increases in the level of regional technology. For example, a road-building programme initiated in a particular lagging region will generally reduce the delivered prices of all outputs produced in the region at any location. Assuming a broadly competitive market, this will increase the overall level of regional outputs sold both within the region and also to customers in other regions. This output expansion on the part of existing local firms is a desired effect of regional policy. Therefore improvements in these transportation inputs should improve the total factor productivity of almost all local regional industrial activities which are trading interregionally. One of the intended effects of this type of infrastructure-based regional policy is therefore to encourage an expansion of the existing local industrial base by enhancing its productivity.

The second desired effect of this type of traditional approach to regional policy is to encourage the immigration of more firm investment into a region. For industries which are relatively mobile, spatial variations in transport costs may significantly affect the attractiveness of different regions as locations for investment. If the upgrading of transport infrastructure can alter the relative costs of transportation and accessibility in favour of less developed locations, it is hoped that this will encourage further immigrant inward investment. As such, an intended effect of these types of regional policies is to encourage an expansion of the local industrial base via inflows of additional capital. However, whether or not such a policy actually has the desired local effects depends on the relationship between the provision of the transportation infrastructure, changes in transport costs, and the marginal price and revenue effects of the transport cost changes on both domestic firms and firms which are geographically mobile.

Following the arguments in Chapter 1, one possible effect of transport cost reductions can be understood as increasing the likelihood of a firm relocation into a particular region for any given set of interregional labour and land prices. However, competition in factor markets would imply that any transport cost savings will soon be countered by increases in local factor prices, such that a permanent advantage cannot be maintained by this policy. Therefore, whether the transport infrastructure improvements will encourage external firms at all to invest in that region also depends in part on whether firms will substitute in favour of inputs produced in that region.

We can analyse the potential effects of such a policy by comparing the conclusions to the Weber and Moses arguments in Chapter 1. As we see in these sections, the location effect of reductions in transport costs in particular regions depends on the location-production substitution possibilities of firms. If firms have zero or only limited input substitution possibilities, localized reductions in transport costs can be efficiently absorbed into firms' cost schedules by moving away from the area in which transport costs are reduced in order to reduce relatively higher transport costs associated with other locations. This is a classic Weber-type result. As such, the regional policy will have exactly the opposite effect from what was intended. Alternatively, if firms have a wide range of Moses-type substitution possibilities, they will most efficiently absorb the localized transport costs reductions by substituting in favour of the lower-delivered-price goods of the region in question. This will also encourage the firm to move towards the area of lower transport costs, thereby having the desired effect of increasing the immigration of firms into the area. This is a classic Moses-type result, entirely in keeping with the objectives of the regional policy.

From the foregoing discussion we see that the local regional development effects of traditional regional policy initiatives based on transport infrastructure provision can actually be rather hard to predict. If firms are able to substitute between inputs fairly easily, transport cost reductions should encourage competition in all regions along the lines of a one-sector model framework. However, if input substitution is not so easy, the results can be very complex. Furthermore, improvements in transportation infrastructure can also have additional regional effects. As we see in Chapters 1 and 3, transport costs over space in part act like a tariff barrier, protecting less efficient local firms from external competition (Krugman 1991). As transport costs are reduced by regional policy infrastructure improvements, this means that some local firms will no longer continue to exist. Krugman and Venables (1990) have shown that if agglomeration economies operate in some locations, the negative 'shadow' effects on the less developed region can be very significant unless there are major compensating local wage falls. Therefore the spatial impacts of policies to improve regional and interregional transportation infrastructure must be evaluated carefully.

Similar lines of reasoning can also be applied to the case of subsidies provided to certain aspects of labour inputs. If retraining or upskilling is partly subsidized, the aim is to increase the efficiency of the firms receiving the subsidy. These efficiency increases ought to be translated into real falls in the costs of production and increases in profitability for the subsidized firms. This is the local productivity effect. In addition, the subsidies should also encourage the immigration of firms into the regions eligible for the subsidies, and this is the substitution effect. Again, however, as with the transport infrastructure example, the actual impacts of these labour-training subsidies depend on how sensitive is the overall output performance of the firm to these subsidies, and also how geographically mobile they are in response to the subsidy opportunities.

Similar types of arguments also hold for policies such as 'enterprise zones', which encourage immigrant investment into a region via indirect land-price reductions. Such policies operate via the direct or indirect subsidizing of immigrant investment into a region via rental subsidies, local land tax rebates, or public subsidies for land assembly, land reclamation or conversion, or local infrastructure provision (Swales 1997, 2009). These types of policies are nowadays often also combined with various financial incentives for local and regional government authorities to undertake local development activities. Such financial incentives typically allow the local and regional authorities to borrow additional capital against the expected incomes earned from the 'enterprise zone' via what are known as tax incremental finance (TIF) schemes, in which the additional revenues raised by the operation of the enterprise zone are largely tax free over a long period. Examples of these types of approaches are discussed in Hague et al. (2011), while the types of systems and approaches used in regional planning in different parts of the world are discussed in Brail (2008), Faludi (2008), and Seltzer and Carbonell (2011).

10.3.2 The project-based welfare effects of regional policy

Where traditional regional policy is based on the provision of local transportation infrastructure or labour retraining or upskilling subsidies, we can consider from a social perspective whether the particular regional policy project, action, or intervention should be undertaken in an economically weaker, relatively peripheral, or sparsely populated regional economy. On national social welfare grounds, the road-building example described in Box 10.2 calls into question the justification for these types of regional economic policy actions or interventions. This is because although new road infrastructure may significantly improve the economic welfare conditions in the sparsely populated and peripheral region, the net benefits of such public expenditure, as calculated on an individual project-by-project basis, would have been greater in the central region because far more people would have benefited from access to the infrastructure. A slightly different but related argument also holds for the case of labour-training subsidies provided under a regional policy umbrella. If labour-training schemes incur fixed costs in setting up the schemes, it may be the case that

BOX 10.2 The distributional effects of transport investment

Imagine a case where there is a region which is geographically peripheral, and which also exhibits a small and highly scattered population of relatively low density. In such a region, a particular regional policy project, action, or intervention such as the provision of new high-speed road infrastructure will significantly reduce the average travel time between any two regional locations. This reduction in travel time will reduce transport costs associated with business transactions, and will therefore significantly reduce the marginal costs of all outputs produced and consumed within the region. However, these significant reductions in the marginal costs of output provision will only be realized across a rather limited number of commercial transactions, simply because the total regional population is small. On the other hand, if the new road infrastructure is built in a large and densely populated region which already has a large road network, the new road infrastructure will only lead to a small reduction in average travel times between locations. As such, this will only slightly reduce the marginal costs of all outputs produced and consumed within the region. However, in this case the small individual marginal cost reductions will be realized across a very large number of commercial transactions.

In order to compare these two effects we can construct Figure 10.9, in which the total efficiency welfare gains from the total number of transactions in the high-density region T_H and the low-density region T_L are compared with the cost of the individual transactions. For simplicity, we assume that the initial transport costs associated with intraregional transactions are given by C in both regions. If the new transport infrastructure is now introduced into the low-density region, the large marginal cost fall associated with reduced transport costs implies that the transport costs are now at a much lower level of C_L. This large reduction in transport costs significantly reduces the marginal cost of all individual transactions which take place over space, and consequently induces an increase in the total number of local business transactions. The total social welfare gain associated with this increase in business transactions is represented by the increase from Q to Q_L. On the other hand, if the new transport infrastructure is now introduced into the densely populated region, the fall in the marginal cost of individual business transactions from C to C_H is only small. This is because the transport infrastructure is already both dense and extensive, and therefore the potential reduction in transport costs for each

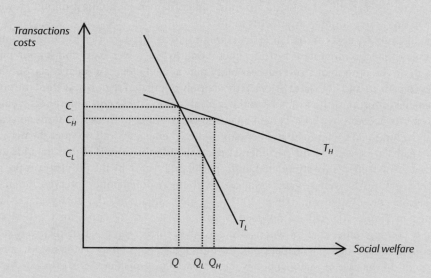

Figure 10.9 The welfare-efficiency effects of regional infrastructure

BOX 10.2 Continued

individual business transaction over space is only small. However, this small efficiency gain in the marginal cost of an individual business transaction is realized over a large number of transactions. Therefore the increase in the total social welfare which is induced by the transport cost fall is large, and in Figure 10.9 is given by the increase from Q to Q_H. The result of this is that the marginal social benefit of the transportation infrastructure may actually be higher in the large and densely populated central region than in the small and sparsely populated region.

This example indicates a common feature of economic phenomena which is often overlooked in economics textbooks, namely that the welfare impacts of public policy interventions not only have explicitly spatial aspects, but that these spatial aspects will themselves determine the absolute size of the welfare impacts. As such, differences in the location of public policy initiatives will result in both different spatial welfare distributions and also in differences in the absolute size of welfare impacts, as calculated on a project-by-project basis. Variations in the density and spatial distributions of populations and markets therefore require us to consider the welfare effects of public policy initiatives very carefully.

more people are able to gain access to such schemes if they are targeted at large firms rather than at small firms, or alternatively targeted at densely populated central regions rather than at geographically peripheral regions.

In terms of cost–benefit analysis, on a project-by-project basis the value of an individual regional policy project depends on both the marginal benefit to the individual benefiting from the project and also the number of individuals affected by the project. Such valuations would generally tend to favour densely populated central regions. As such, it would therefore appear that if the example in Box 10.2 of a road-building programme in the peripheral region were indeed initiated, the justification for such a policy could therefore only be provided primarily on political or social grounds, rather than on economic grounds. However, there are two major counter-arguments to this.

First, the relative costs of road infrastructure provision may be much lower in peripheral economies than in congested central regions due to the lower land and labour prices, although on the other hand lower accessibility may actually increase such costs. Similarly, congestion effects and high land prices in the densely populated region may limit the potential benefits of further infrastructure in the central region. These cost differences would all be taken into account in a cost–benefit analysis, and in either of these situations an evaluation of the long-run social costs and benefits of the scheme may indicate that the net social welfare gains are greater in the peripheral region than in the central region. In addition, if localized growth effects are stimulated in the peripheral region by the provision of the public infrastructure, the welfare gains associated with the regional policy intervention may be very significant (Houghwout 1998, 2002). In such situations, the cost-welfare curves depicted in Figure 10.9 will be reversed, with the cost–welfare curve for the peripheral region becoming rather shallow whereas that for the central region will be relatively steep.

Second, the cost–benefit calculation of the individual project may be too narrow a reference point. In the case of regional policy, broader welfare considerations associated with a set of policy interventions rather than just the return on the moneys invested in an individual project may be required. In this case, a project-by-project-based cost–benefit approach to evaluating regional policy will be too narrow, and a broader approach, which allows for coordination and networks effects and price changes, becomes more appropriate (Grimes 2013). Under these conditions, a portfolio real-options-based approach which captures these broader effects is more appropriate for considering these system-wide types of impacts (Grimes 2013). These issues are discussed in more detail in section 10.4.2.

The welfare evaluation of a regional policy therefore requires not only a cost–benefit analysis (Sassone and Schaffer 1978; Pearce and Nash 1981; Layard and Glaister 1994) of all the potential economic and environmental impacts of the policy, but also an explicitly spatial discussion as to the broader distributional and network impacts of the policy (Graham 2007a, b; Venables 2007). Geography plays a role in determining both the absolute size and the spatial distribution of the economic impacts of public policy initiatives. At the same time, the impacts of the policy must also be considered against what the objectives of the policy are. Therefore the success of regional policies must be evaluated carefully with respect to the intentions of the policy and the explicitly spatial outcomes of the policy.

10.3.3 **The macroeconomic effects of regional policy**

As well as considering the effect of regional policy from an individual project-by-project microeconomic welfare perspective, we can also consider the rationale for regional policy from a broader macroeconomic perspective. In Chapter 7 it was argued that at the prevailing interest rates, it is possible for regional investment levels to be insufficient to clear local regional involuntary unemployment. In the analysis presented in Chapter 7, which was based on a small open-economy macroeconomic model, the interest rates are determined exogenously of the individual region. However, national interest rates are in part also determined by demand pressures in buoyant regions. In regions which are experiencing full employment, local nominal wages and nominal land prices will be high, and the associated local labour and land supply shortages will continuously be a potential source of inflationary pressure in the local regional economy. Therefore, in order to avoid localized inflation pressures turning into macroeconomic inflation, local regional demand cannot be allowed to expand beyond the full employment level. This also limits the extent to which demand in other regions can grow. The regional implications of this are depicted in Figure 10.10.

In Figure 10.10 we compare the cases of two regions A and B, where region A is a buoyant region with full employment, and region B is a depressed region with involuntary unemployment. We can consider the case of region A which is depicted in the four upper quadrant sections. In the upper right quadrant we can see that the level of regional income is Y_{A1}. As we see in the upper left quadrant, this level of regional aggregate demand requires labour inputs which just ensure a full regional employment level of L_{AF}. At the particular interest rate i^* which just ensures that the price level P in the buoyant region remains constant at P^*, the full regional employment demand levels Y_{A1} are just sustained by the local regional investment schedule IS_{A1}. In other words, full employment is maintained in the buoyant region without incurring local inflation. On the other hand, at the prevailing rate of interest i^*, in region B, depicted by the lower four quadrants, the regional investment schedule IS_{B1} is insufficient to maintain a full employment local income level Y_{B3} and only allows for a level of regional income of Y_{B1}. This lower level of regional income only requires labour inputs of L_{B1} such that the level of local regional unemployment is given by $(L_{BF} - L_{B1})$. The

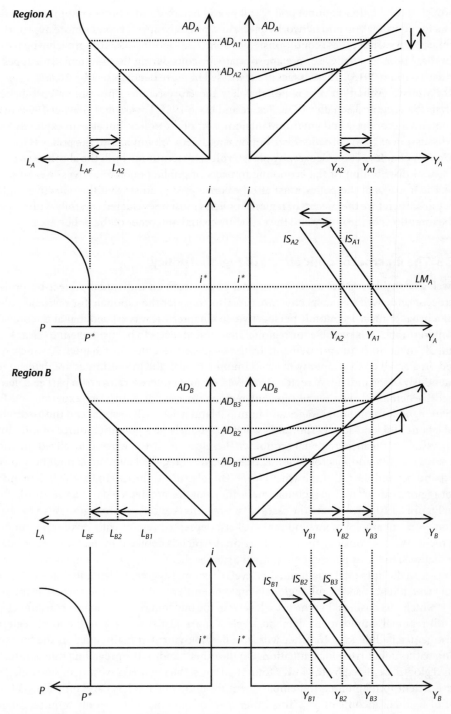

Figure 10.10 The macroeconomic effects of regional policy

unemployment in the depressed region B continues because, at the prevailing interest rate, local investment levels are unable to generate local demand sufficient to clear the local labour market. If interregional migration flows are not sufficient to clear all local regional labour markets quickly, and the interest rate cannot be reduced below i^*, the situation is maintained indefinitely.

At this point, we must consider why the interest rate will be set and maintained at i^*. One of the features of the mutually open and interconnected interregional economy is that price rises originating in one region can be transmitted very quickly to prices rises in other regions. In the case of a national economy in which one buoyant region of the economy is consistently close to facing local supply shortages, the national monetary authorities may decide to set national interest rates in order to just avoid local labour and land-price inflation in the buoyant region. The reason for this is that the monetary authorities fear that lower interest rates will engender local inflation in region A, which in turn will immediately be transmitted to the rest of the national economy. Although interest rate falls will be beneficial for the depressed regions, in that local investment and employment levels will rise, the land supply constraints in region A limit the downward movement of interest rates. Moreover, this is the case irrespective of the phase the national business cycle at which the national economy finds itself. The buoyant region therefore consistently acts as a 'bottleneck' region, and constrains the demand levels in the less buoyant regions. In this particular regional economic system, unemployment in the less buoyant region is maintained in order to preserve price stability in region A, and, consequently, price stability in the national economy. In other words, not only are differences in the individual local regional demand and employment conditions in part a result of the macroeconomic policy, but at the same time the macroeconomic policy is itself partly a result of the differences in the regional demand and supply conditions.

In situations where buoyant regions act as regional bottlenecks, regional policy can have a role to play in encouraging growth and employment in less buoyant regions without incurring inflationary pressures. In order to understand the logic of this argument we must compare the local employment demand conditions in the two regions. As we see in Figure 10.10, the prevailing local investment and labour demand conditions in the less buoyant region are constrained by the factor supply constraints and inflationary pressure in the buoyant region. However, regional policy can act so as to encourage the diversion of demand from the buoyant region A to the less buoyant region B. Regional policy tools, such as the provision of infrastructure and real-estate subsidies in the less buoyant region, which in addition may sometimes be applied in tandem with land-use planning restrictions in the buoyant region A, can effect a diversion of investment flows away from region A and towards region B. The manifestations of this will be the migration of new immigrant firms to region B in preference to region A, and the expansion of existing firms of facilities in region B in preference to region A. This investment diversion effect can be represented in Figure 10.10 by the reduction in local investment flows in region A at the prevailing interest rate i^* from IS_{A1} to IS_{A2}, and an expansion in local investment flows in region B at the prevailing interest rate from IS_{B1} to IS_{B2}. The reduction in investment in region A will lead to a fall in local regional income from Y_{A1} to Y_{A2}, and the consequent reduction in regional aggregate demand from AD_{A1} to AD_{A2} will lead to a fall in local labour employment from the full regional employment level of L_{AF} to a lower employment level of L_{A1}. The local unemployment shortfall caused by the diversion of investment away from the buoyant region is therefore given by $(L_{AF} - L_{A2})$. (However, as we will see shortly, this unemployment does not actually take effect.) In the less buoyant region B, the increase in local investment associated with the regional policy diversion effect increases the local regional income from Y_{B1} to Y_{B2}, and the consequent increase in regional aggregate demand from AD_{B1} to AD_{B2} will lead to an increase in local labour employment from L_{B1} to L_{B2}. The local unemployment shortfall caused by the diversion of investment into the buoyant region is now given by $(L_{BF} - L_{B2})$ and is exactly the same as the apparent local unemployment shortfall $(L_{AF} - L_{A2})$ in region A. In this situation, the current local price level in region A is unaffected either by the reduction in investment in region A or the expansion in investment in region B. Moreover, the aggregate demand in both regions can now be allowed to expand without causing any inflation in region A. In region A aggregate regional demand can be allowed to expand to its original level of AD_{A1} which was maintained before the application of the regional policy. At this level of aggregate regional demand region A will exhibit local full employment income, investment, and labour demand levels of Y_{A1}, IS_{A1}, and L_{AF}, respectively, at the prevailing interest rate i^* which just ensures price stability at P^* in region A. Similarly, in region B aggregate regional demand can be allowed to expand from AD_{B2} to AD_{B3}. At this level of aggregate regional demand region B will exhibit local full employment income, investment, and labour demand levels of Y_{B3}, IS_{B3}, and L_{BF}, respectively, at the prevailing interest rate i^* which just ensures price stability at P^* in region A.

This positive macroeconomic expansion effect across both regions compensates for the negative diversion effect in the buoyant region A, and is additional to the positive diversion effect in the less buoyant region B. In other words, the diversion of investment associated with the regional policy allows regional income and aggregate demand in both regions to be maintained at levels which ensure full local employment in both regions, without engendering inflation in the bottleneck region. As such, the argument here is that one role of regional policy is therefore to circumvent many of the regional bottleneck problems associated with different regional investment levels in a situation where common interregional interest rates are set primarily with respect to the demand conditions in the buoyant regions. Therefore, if the policy is implemented successfully, the net result of the regional policy diversion effect, plus the macroeconomic expansion effect in each of the two regions, is to allow for full employment aggregate demand to be maintained in both regions under a stable macroeconomic monetary regime. On this argument regional policy can be implemented without leading to 'crowding out'.

10.4 New debates in regional policy

As we have seen in this book, the last two or three decades have witnessed many advances in the theory of urban and regional economics. Moreover, our awareness of the impacts of modern globalization on cities and regions, and also the role played by cities and regions in driving modern globalization, have all increased dramatically. In contrast, apart from some of the financial incentive initiatives alluded to in section 10.3.1, the practice and implementation of regional development policy has remained largely static until very recently.

In developing countries, policy interventions at the national and regional level have continued to be based largely on growth thinking derived from the 1950s analyses of Solow

(1956), Swan (1956), Hirschmann (1958), and Rostow (1959), with little serious attention paid to questions of economic geography, knowledge spillovers, or the complex interactions between these two issues and institutional issues. Consequently, urban and regional policy in most developing countries has barely moved beyond road-building and infrastructure provision, with little serious attention paid to the social and environmental consequences of these interventions. Broader distributional and developmental issues first raised by Myrdal (1957) have been largely ignored at both the regional and urban levels, with the focus being on encouraging the efficient working of market mechanisms.

Rather differently, in developed countries regional policies tended to be organized in a top–down hierarchical fashion and at a national level. Such policies were understood as being largely redistributive in nature, operating primarily by encouraging firms to relocate to weaker regions via subsidies and tax breaks. These policies have tended to be primarily sectoral in nature, in that they focused on providing incentives to those particular industries which were perceived as being most responsive to such relocation incentives. Meanwhile, in the case of cities, as we have already seen, over the last two or three decades urban policies in advanced countries have tended to focus either on issues related to gentrification processes or on issues relating to zoning and land-use restrictions. In these policies, distributional issues are almost entirely ignored, and little explicit acknowledgement has been afforded to the relationship between the changes in the local institutional or governance issues and the social cohesion or segregation impacts of the urban redevelopment schemes.

In terms of regional and urban policy, this state of affairs has remained largely static for many decades, in spite of the major analytical and political economy transformations which have been witnessed over the last two decades. However, there are real signs that all this is about to start changing, and there are two reasons for this, one of which is realpolitik in nature and one of which is analytical in nature.

First, in terms of realpolitik, the global financial crisis of 2008 and the ongoing economic disruption caused by this has alerted people in all countries to various weaknesses in many of the current systems of economic regulation, coordination, and governance. The scale and complexity of modern globalization processes and their impacts on development have moved well beyond the accepted conventional 'Washington consensus' wisdom regarding optimal development policies (Stiglitz 2002; Fine 2003; Rodrik 2006), a line of thinking which had assumed that market deregulation and establishment of well-defined property rights were more or less sufficient to foster economic growth. Indeed, these weaknesses were seen to put many processes of development in many countries in jeopardy (Spence and Leipziger 2010) because it has become apparent that the scale of economic shocks in today's globalized world can undo and often undermine the mechanisms by which many policy initiatives were assumed to work.

Second, in analytical terms, 2009 and 2010 saw the publication of five very influential reports on the role of, nature of, and the rationale for regional development policies. These five reports have reignited many long-dormant debates and forced a rethinking of many of our assumptions. These five reports are the *World Development Report* (World Bank 2009), the Barca Report, *An Agenda for a Reformed Cohesion Policy* (Barca 2009), two reports published by the OECD entitled *How Regions Grow* (OECD 2009a) and *Regions Matter* (OECD 2009b), and the 2010 Local Development report of the Corporación Andina de Fomento (CAF 2010). All these five reports appear to deal with largely similar analytical and policy issues. However, the policy conclusions that they come to are fundamentally different in nature.

The highly influential *World Development Report* (World Bank 2009) adopts what is known as a 'space-blind' approach and comes to what seem to be very different policy conclusions from the other four 'place-based' reports published by the European Commission, the OECD, and the CAF. We can also add to this suite of major reports an earlier report published by the European Commission, namely the influential *Agenda for a Growing Europe* (Sapir et al. 2004). In some sense this report can be regarded as being space blind, inasmuch as it was not focused on regional issues but more on sectoral matters. However, the arguments and recommendations in the report did potentially have regional implications, so it is worth discussing it here.

The fact that such high-level reports come to fundamentally different conclusions regarding the case for, and role of, regional development policy suggests that the issues are both very much alive and very complex. At the very least, the debate is far from being straightforward and requires a consideration of a range of fundamental and interrelated issues, all of which have already been referred to in this book.

The reason why there are two broadly different policy camps, with the *World Development Report* and the Sapir et al. (2004) report in the 'space-blind' camp and the other four reports in the 'place-based' camp, is that they reflect two fundamentally different approaches to interpreting urban and regional empirical evidence. These differences in empirical interpretation themselves reflect deep-seated differences in analytical positions. The reports derive their arguments and insights from different elements of the theoretical literature, all of which are referred to in the various chapters of this book. As such, the reports emphasize different aspects of the theoretical literature as best reflecting the dominant underlying urban and regional growth mechanisms, and the result of these different emphases is that the recommended policy responses are quite different.

While the space-blind and place-based approaches have long intellectual traditions, both approaches have also recently undergone major changes. From the perspective of regional development, an awareness of these analytical differences is extremely important. After years of a development policy consensus which had changed little in five decades, the debates opened up by these reports will determine the trajectory of regional and urban development policy in many parts of the world over the coming decades. We now examine each approach in detail.

10.4.1 The space-blind approach

The space-blind approach to regional development policy as it is currently presented (Gill 2010) derives its inspiration and analytical underpinning from a mix of the new economic geography models as discussed in Chapter 3 and the Borts and Stein (1964) models discussed Chapter 7. The basic premise of the space-blind approach is that agglomeration leads to productivity growth, and therefore the optimal development policies are therefore those that encourage factor migration to the larger and more densely populated regions so as to derive the agglomeration advantages.

Following the original arguments of Winnick (1966), the World Bank (2009) suggests that there is a dichotomy, a conflict, between 'place prosperity' and 'people prosperity', and argues that policies which focus on places or regions will automatically inhibit migration and factor adjustment, thereby working against the interests of society as a whole. The World Bank therefore recommends that the most effective way of generating efficiency is by adopting a model of development which is 'spatially blind', where 'spatially blind' in this sense means that the policies 'are designed without explicit consideration to space' (World Bank 2009, p. 24).

For a basic space-blind model to be optimal from a social welfare perspective it is necessary for factors to be allocated across space in a manner consistent with the underlying assumptions and conditions of the one-sector model of Borts and Stein (1964). All that is required to motivate these arguments is that spatial variations in demand are responded to by factor mobility, so as to equalize rates of return on capital and real wages. As we saw in Chapter 7, if demand increases in one region relative to another, this localized demand expansion increases the returns to all factors in that region, relative to other regions. The factor returns stimulate the in-migration of all factors into the high-demand region and out-migration from low-demand regions. Assuming that the underlying mechanisms are not infinitely cumulative, the process continues until factor returns are once again equalized in all regions. These one-sector factor allocation and migration mechanisms are also assumed to underpin the more recent welfare-maximizing processes described by the long-run neoclassical interregional convergence models (Barro and Sala-i-Martin 1992), as discussed in Chapters 6 and 7.

Early space-blind arguments (Winnick 1966) assume long-run processes of interregional economic convergence, and as such do not require us to make any assumptions regarding the long-run role of agglomeration. However, unlike the earlier long-run convergence models, the contemporary space-blind approach also assumes that agglomeration processes are fundamental aspect of the economic landscape. As such, if there are localized agglomeration processes operating in the destination regions, these are assumed to operate in a manner which is consistent with a combination of the new economic geography and agglomeration theories discussed in Chapter 3 and the endogenous growth models of Romer (1986) and Lucas (1988).

Yet it is important to note here that while these modern space-neutral models usually tend to refer to the importance of fostering agglomeration, the rationale behind these space-blind models is not based on arguments about agglomeration. Rather, these space-blind arguments are actually underpinned simply by the two-sector factor allocation model of Borts and Stein (1964), as discussed in Chapter 7, and as such do not require agglomeration arguments per se.

We know that not all locations at all time periods are conducive for fostering the increasing returns mechanisms associated with agglomeration. As such, agglomeration cannot simply be a matter of geographical clustering. There must be a demand component to the agglomeration formation process. If the mechanics of agglomeration processes in part reflect such demand shocks, the two-sector model therefore implies that the agglomeration processes should be allowed to run their course until interregional factor returns are equalized, and the economy once again settles down to a one-sector model of interregional convergence. In other words, from an aggregate national welfare and efficiency perspective, encouraging these agglomeration-increasing returns processes is regarded as being inherently good for growth. Therefore, whatever policy regime promotes interregional factor mobility and the spatial reallocation of firms, people, and activities is seen as the optimal development policy approach.

Following this approach, in terms of policy recommendations, however, only a very minimalist and limited role for public intervention is therefore called for. This is because it is assumed that policy-makers have no idea what the efficient spatial allocation of factors would look like (Glaeser and Gottlieb 2008). Therefore a free market factor-mobility mechanism, as determined by market signals of regional wages and regional rates of return on capital, is regarded as being the best way to ensure that the right factors are located in the right places doing the right things. The invisible hand of the market should be left to decide of its own accord which places people ought to migrate towards, and this process is likely to lead to convergence processes operating between lagging areas.

Underlying these arguments, the *World Development Report* explicitly follows a view of economic history which reflects the arguments of Rostow (1959) and Williamson (1965), and which assumes that the urbanization-growth trajectories of today's emerging economies largely mirror the urbanization-growth processes experienced by today's rich countries in earlier eras. Applying these Rostow–Williamson arguments within a space-blind framework implies that if factors follow market signals so as to maximize national growth and welfare, then economic development will naturally be unbalanced. Economic growth is automatically assumed to be associated with rising income inequality and spatial concentration, and only at much later stages in development will income equality and spatial equalization processes become evident. The *World Development Report* therefore argues that any policy-related attempts aimed at promoting growth in weaker regions by countering these un-equalizing and concentrating flows will actually undermine national growth and prosperity (World Bank 2009) and prolong poverty.

Instead of regional policy approaches which aim to promote equality between regions, the *World Development Report* proposes a 'development in 3-D' idea as its policy system, whereby 'development in 3-D' is based on the three development dimensions of density, distance, and division. The solutions that the World Bank proposes to deal with the perceived challenges associated with each of these three dimensions are three 'I's, namely institutions, infrastructure, and interventions (Barca et al. 2012). Each development dimension is argued to have its own I-solution, and these are mapped according to the following framework:

- Regarding the development dimension of population *density*, the World Bank recommends that institutions should be geared to fostering greater urban density or agglomeration in situations where the current levels of urbanization are too low.

- Regarding the development dimension of *distance*, the World Bank recommends increasing the provision of connective infrastructure so as to overcome distance problems.

- Regarding the development challenges associated with overcoming *division*, the World Bank recommends spatially targeted interventions to overcome institutional and governance divisions (World Bank 2009, pp. 23–24).

The underlying argument of the World Bank approach is that promoting factor mobility to urban concentrations is the optimal development model for most countries. This is because it is assumed that these factor adjustment processes will guarantee the widest range of employment opportunities for all people, thereby improving the lives of the maximum number of people irrespective of where they come from.

Note at this stage also that these World Bank arguments are assumed to hold in spite of the inefficiencies and irreversibilities associated with Harris–Todaro-type migration processes, as discussed in Chapter 6, and the widespread evidence of squalour, oppression, and environmental degradation in the barrios, favelas, slums, and shanty towns of the developing world's mega-cities.

A second major report which can also be considered in many ways space neutral is the highly influential independent Sapir et al. (2004) report, *An Agenda for a Growing Europe*. Although this report was primarily concerned with the reforms of the European Union budget, and closely linked to debates regarding the so-called Lisbon Agenda for EU economic growth policy, the Sapir Report came to conclusions that were not too dissimilar from those of the World Bank (2009).

The Sapir et al. report recommended that in order to promote intra-EU convergence, the major focus of EU policy should be that of the poorer new accession countries, and any European regional policy, or more precisely EU Cohesion Policy, should be targeted at the level of countries, or EU Member States, as they are known, rather than at the level of the region. Along with the *World Development Report*, the Sapir et al. (2004) report also recommended that there should be an agenda for institutional and governance reform in these new-accession countries, along with additional sector policies focused on the development and adoption of information and communications technologies (ICTs) across the whole of Europe and other knowledge-based sectors. As such, the Sapir et al. report shares some features of the *World Development Report* in that the authors of both see their reports as being essentially space neutral, with a primary emphasis on institutional reform (Barca et al. 2012).

However, there are also some fundamental differences between these two reports. First, there is no explicit urban and regional economics or economic geography in the Sapir et al. report. The report makes no comments or recommendations regarding optimal urban or regional growth patterns and the likely mechanisms to achieve these. In contrast, economic geography and urban and regional economic thinking is fundamental to the *World Development Report* and policy recommendations regarding the likely mechanisms to achieve optimal spatial allocations are very explicit. Second, the Sapir et al. report advocates funding to less developed parts of Europe, whereas the *World Development Report* largely eschews such policies. Finally, the *World Development Report* takes no position whatsoever on the sectoral policies related to ICTs, whereas these are central issues in the Sapir et al. report (Barca et al. 2012).

10.4.2 **The place-based approach**

In contrast to the two space-blind reports discussed above, the remaining four reports (Barca 2009; OECD 2009a, b; CAF 2010) adopt a fundamentally different position, known as the place-based approach. Modern place-based arguments explicitly acknowledge the role of agglomeration, networks, and factor mobility in driving growth and development (Barca 2011), and in no sense would regard place-based thinking as focused primarily on ensuring interregional equalization. Instead, modern place-based arguments perceive that the mechanisms underpinning the workings of places—both cities and regions—are not simply a matter of production factors moving between places, but rather also depend on the ways in which the institutional context co-evolves with the factor movements. Modern place-based arguments therefore emphasize the interrelationships between the institutional frameworks within which factor movements operate or do not operate, as these are perceived to critically influence the development challenges and opportunities facing each region.

The analytical basis of these four place-based reports is therefore that the local context really does matter for development, and that the interrelationships between institutions, governance, and geography—all of which heavily influence a 'sense of place' (Vanclay et al. 2008)—do shape both the development potential for the region in question, and also for other regions. In modern terminology, a 'sense of place' relates to all the aspects of social (Putnam 1993), cultural (Beugelsdijk and Maseland 2011), creative (Florida 2002), entrepreneurial (Fritsch 2011), and institutional capital, which are specific to a particular place. These elements are assumed to be in addition to human capital, and are seen as fundamentally contributing to the character and vitality of a locality and the well-being (Stiglitz et al. 2009) of its citizens. The modern place-based approach therefore assumes that if properly mobilized, these local features can be used to foster and maximize the local economic development potential of the region. No claims whatsoever are made regarding interregional convergence or equalization (Barca 2011).

The modern place-based argument builds on and extends the traditional place-based arguments, although early place-based arguments had little or no institutional or governance dimensions. The traditional place-based approach, the details of which are discussed in Appendix 10.1, argues that the true values of weaker regions are systematically underpriced while those of stronger regions are systematically overpriced. As such, the value of place which is embodied in the one-sector and two-sector neoclassical adjustment models explained in Chapter 7, as well as in the space-blind arguments examined above, is argued to be systematically biased in favour of the stronger regions. The traditional place-based approach therefore cautions against using the one-sector and two-sector models alone as indicators of the true social welfare value of growing regions or of declining regions. The same argument holds even when we also incorporate agglomeration arguments into one-sector and two-sector models.

Modern place-based approaches extend these valuation and mispricing arguments to argue that all aspects which contribute to the value of the local regional context, where context here is understood in terms of all of its social, cultural, and institutional characteristics, need to be considered in order to understand the value and development potential of a region. The configuration of these various regional characteristics can prove to be either positive or negative, and the modern place-based approach emphasizes the role played by underdevelopment traps due to poor institutional configurations in limiting or inhibiting the growth potential of certain regions. The place-based approach therefore emphasizes the important role of policy for finding ways to tap under-utilized local potential and to circumvent these development traps.

The four place-based reports (Barca 2009; OECD 2009a, b; CAF 2010) therefore argue that development strategies should not be space neutral, but rather should be explicitly placed based and highly contingent on context so as to tap any under-utilized local capacity and to overcome poor or inappropriate institutional configurations. This is because modern place-based arguments assume that the mobilization of local elements necessary for promoting development requires an explicit consideration of the relationship between institutional and governance issues and economic geography, relationships which are assumed to differ significantly between places. The major differences between the traditional approaches to regional policy discussed in section 10.3 and the modern place-based approaches to regional policy are summarized in Table 10.1.

As we see in Table 10.1, the traditional approaches to regional policy discussed so far tended to operate under a national architecture in which the policy was dictated by central government, which decided on the subsidies to be made available and the firms and industries which were to receive the subsidies. The logic of such policies tended to be built around influencing the location and geographical investment decisions of particular industrial sectors, encouraging these firms either to relocate or to maintain their locations in particular regions. Local and regional government generally had little or no major role or influence on the logic or the design of these policies, other than acting as advocates for the particular local firms, industries, or sectors aiming to attract regional subsidies.

In contrast, as we see in Table 10.1, modern place-based approaches to regional policy emphasize the importance of designing appropriate institutional systems, whereby regional policy aims to foster participation between central and local government, and between the public, private, and civil society sectors. The aim is to design policies with local skills, expertise, and capabilities in mind, in order to foster endogenous local development processes based on the potential of a particular region. Most importantly, the aim is to design policies which provide bundles of public goods specifically tailored to the specific challenges of the region, and to do this in a manner which encourages the engagement of as many local actors as possible. The focus is on promoting transparency regarding policy intentions, objectives, monitoring, and evaluation, and applying the policies in the most appropriate geographical

Table 10.1 Traditional and modern approaches to regional policy

	Traditional regional policy	Modern regional policy
Objectives	Compensating temporarily for location disadvantages of lagging regions	Tapping into under-utilized potential in all regions to enhance development in all regions
Unit of intervention	Administrative units	Functional economic areas
Strategies	Sectoral approach	Integrated development projects
Tools	Subsidies and state aids	Mix of hard capital (infrastructure) and soft capital (business support, credit availability, networking systems)
Actors	Central government	Multi-level governance involving different tiers or levels of local, regional, and national government working in partnership and alongside the private and civil society sectors

Source: OECD (2009b)

unit given the economic conditions. This typically requires the policy to be implemented with different administrative jurisdictions working in tandem.

Local interventions are seen as essential in order to take advantage of the institutional features and to engage local stakeholders, because only local elements are assumed to have the specifically local knowledge required to achieve many of the desired and intended outcomes of these policies. At the same time, it is also important that the search for local policy solutions does not inadvertently empower entrenched local monopoly positions. Therefore finding the right types, mixes, and coordination systems between local and national interventions to best mobilize and empower local institutions to act for the common good is the central aim of modern place-based approaches. Zoellick (2012) argues that these types of interventions are aimed at 'crowding in' investment, in marked contrast to space-blind approach which perceives such interventions as 'crowding out' investment. Examples of many types of local development policies and tools used to 'crowd in' local investment are given in Pike et al. (2006, 2010) and Hague et al. (2011).

The four placed-based reports (Barca 2009; OECD 2009a,b; CAF 2010) all conclude that the objective of development intervention should be to promote growth in all regions, as all regions display growth and development potential (OECD, 2009a). These reports perceive place-based and people-based strategies as being the same thing and so involving no real trade-off whatsoever between supporting weaker regions and enhancing national growth. All four reports therefore argue that one of the answers to development problems is the promotion of integrated policies for each territory, which not only pay special attention to the different features and needs of each region, but which are synchronized and coordinated between all regions. These reports all emphasize the potential role of local and regional governments and institutions in driving the development process and stress the potential of both hard and soft infrastructure (such as innovation advice, business credit and support schemes, university–business relationships) as key factors in promoting sustainable development (CAF, 2010).

The four place-based reports also all caution against adopting stylized agglomeration-based economic geography theories as true reflections of reality, with the OECD reports pointing out that non-core regions contribute the majority of economic growth in many countries, and that the growth contribution of non-core regions is increasing across the OECD (OECD 2009a, b; 2011b). As a whole, across the OECD urban regions, rural regions and intermediate regions actually show no real differences in their propensity to outperform, underperform, or maintain parity in terms of growth rates with their own national growth rates. As such, OECD growth is not necessarily an urban story and the benefits of agglomeration in many advanced OECD countries actually appear to be waning (Dijkstra et al. 2012). Even in the case of China, regional growth is heavily related to a decentralized governance system rather than simply to the size of cities (Xu 2011), and understanding these central–local governance relationships is critical for understanding Chinese regional growth. As such, an overemphasis on core regions and massive agglomeration will not pick up most growth effects in the economy.

From a place-based perspective a space-blind sectoral approach is consequently regarded as being unrealistic, because by ignoring the interaction between geography and institutions the actual effects of space-blind policies are largely unknown. What appear to be apparently space-blind policies will often have explicitly spatial effects, many of which will be unintended effects, and the aims of the policy itself may well be undermined unless the spatial aspects are explicitly accounted for. In contrast, by taking account of these complexities and specificities, the place-based approach emphasizes the role which policy can play in the provision of public goods in a manner which is appropriately tailored to the local requirements of the region. The application of the place-based argument would therefore appear to be particularly appropriate to the context in which economies are experiencing major transitions towards new equilibria, a phenomenon very common in the current era of globalization, and in which the short-run and medium-term transition processes may heavily influence the long-run outcomes (Thissen and Van Oort 2010).

10.5 The differences between space-blind and place-based approaches

The publication of these highly influential reports within such a short time period means that after decades of little or no change in policy thinking, development scholars and practitioners all over the world are proposing, and are also therefore confronted with, two radically different regional development policy paradigms, namely the space-blind and the place-based regional development policy approaches (McCann and Rodríguez-Pose 2011; Barca et al. 2012). However, these differences also provide clues as to the complexity of the problems which today's regional development policies must confront.

Local and regional development policy is not about drawing lines or zones on a map, but rather about engaging with the complex interrelationships between institutions, geography, and economic development (Pike et al. 2010; Barca 2011). Both the space-blind and the place-based approaches acknowledge the importance of agglomeration effects, network effects, and other mechanisms leading to spatial spillovers. Both approaches acknowledge the types of spatial interactions examined in detail throughout this book, and the importance of factor mobility in allowing economies to adjust to new and emerging conditions (Barca 2011). The differences between the two approaches therefore relate primarily to how they perceive the interactions between institutions, factor mobility, and decision-making processes, and the different emphases that they give to particular issues.

There are four major areas of contention, namely: the interactions between geography and institutions; the nature of long-term development processes; the nature of national–regional decision-making processes; and the nature of intentions versus outcomes of a policy.

10.5.1 The interactions between geography and institutions

The place-based approach puts major emphasis on the influence of institutions in shaping not only local economic geography, but also the ability of regions to adjust to changing economic circumstances. In particular, the place-based approach assumes that many regional institutional features, and some of the various dimensions of regional 'capital' including institutional and physical capital, are largely immobile. A region's ability to adjust to external macroeconomic shocks is therefore regarded as being contingent on how local institutional systems respond, and in particular to outflows of mobile factors and losses of human capital. This ability of regions to respond is itself argued to be in part dependent on the national institutional and governance architecture, and the autonomy given to local institutions to implement flexible and locally designed policy responses. This is because the place-based approach assumes that the institutional relationships linking national, regional, and local levels of governance are central to regional adjustment processes. Increasing regional inequality is argued to lead primarily to increasing interregional dependency in which weaker regions increasingly become dependent on fiscal transfers from stronger regions. This dependency itself can lead to increasing political polarization and paralysis of many aspects of national–regional governance (Barca et al. 2012). For this reason, the place-based approach argues that when policies are properly designed on the basis of partnerships between local and national policy-makers, local policy design and delivery is the best way to foster appropriate institutional reform which is in the national interest (Barca et al. 2012). In the place-based approach, interregional inequality is therefore directly linked to national performance, an argument closely related to the observations of Berg and Ostry (2011) and Moretti (2012). In contrast, the space-blind approach is largely silent as to the relationship between regional inequality, institutional reform, and factor adjustment. Rather, the space-blind approach assumes that factor mobility is the primary adjustment mechanism, and what it sees as impediments to this process, such as local development and regional policies, should be removed.

10.5.2 The nature of long-term development processes

The space-blind argument assumes that long-term development processes are largely linear and unchanging. Space-blind approaches assume that what is occurring today in Manila or Lagos is more or less the same process which occurred in London, Paris, or New York in the nineteenth century, as described in Chapter 8. This view is based on the arguments associated with Rostow (1959) and the Williamson curve (1965), which suggests that in the early stages of growth disparities increase, subsequently levelling off at a later stage. Today the space-blind approach puts at centre stage the prioritizing of large-scale agglomeration in driving national development. In contrast, the place-based approaches contend that there is no automatic relationship between the stages of development and the level of geographic concentration (Barca 2009; Garcilazo et al. 2010; OECD 2011b), with development processes displaying different features and patterns at different stages and in different eras of development (Barca et al. 2012).

10.5.3 The nature of national–regional decision-making processes

Both the space-blind approach and the place-based approach argue that institutional systems and appropriate institutional reform are important for development. However, the explicit discussion of these matters is very limited in space-blind arguments. Institutional matters are largely discussed in the space-blind approach in terms of removing supply-side restrictions, and in particular constraints associated with land-use zoning and greenbelts discussed earlier in this chapter. Where other forms of decision-making are discussed, this is primarily in terms of ensuring the provision of infrastructure and public goods in the growing major agglomerations, which are the same regions emphasized by the space-blind approach.

In contrast, because long-run growth outcomes cannot be known in advance, the place-based approach contends that decision-making processes regarding the regional provisions of public goods and infrastructure, in particular, are the result of the national–political influence of capital or dominant city elites, which will always advocate the further provision of local public goods such as infrastructure in their own capital city or dominant city locations (Kim 2011; Barca et al. 2012). Importantly, these political decisions themselves heavily influence subsequent factor mobility decisions. The place-based approach therefore argues that many aspects of regional development consequently reflect a circular process in which powerful elites within the capital or dominant cities use their preferential institutional positions to ensure that infrastructure and public-good provision always favours the dominant centres. Moreover, the bias in favour of capital or dominant city goods' provision is stronger the more dominant the dominant city and the more centralized the state. The place-based approach therefore perceives regional adjustment as much less of a market-driven process than the space-blind approach contends, and in reality is much more of a political-bargaining process.

In the case of the *World Development Report*, the analysis is *de facto* also based on the assumption that the state knows best where to locate investments so as to foster private sector responses, a position which is rather contradictory given that free market mechanisms are based on the assumption that the state does not know best. In contrast, the place-based approach assumes that regional policy can enhance development and economic potential. In comparative-static terms, recent welfare economics has demonstrated that in the types of multi-level governance and institutional settings which are typical in almost all countries, the welfare effects of regional policies are often actually Pareto enhancing (Ferrara 2010). In dynamic terms, modern place-based approaches contend that all the public, private, and civil society sectors contain knowledge, which, if properly extracted and coordinated, can be used to help to maximize local development potential.

10.5.4 The intentions versus the outcomes of policies

The place-based approach argues that if some aspects of apparently space-blind policies are spatially targeted (for example in order to help overcome problems of division or to enhance infrastructure), then by definition the policy cannot be space blind because the targeting is at a particular place. Similarly, if policies are designed to encourage factor mobility, then these directions of mobility will *de facto* be to particular places or types of places, irrespective of whether or not *de jure* that was the intention of the 'space-blind' policy. As such, it becomes clear that the concept of space blindness depends on whether the spatial outcomes are or are not expected, are or are not considered, and are or are not intended to be influenced by the policy.

The place-based approach argues that if the spatial outcomes are expected, considered, intended, or fostered by a policy, then by definition space-blind policies are explicitly place based, and attempts to describe them as otherwise hides the intentions of the policy and the relationship between the policy and the outcomes. The reason is that in the end someone has to decide what to do and where, and failing to make explicit the intentions or the outcomes of the policy both exacerbates the circular political-bargaining process described above and hinders realistic policy evaluation.

As we have just seen, the bias in favour of the provision of public goods in capital or dominant city locations is stronger the more dominant the dominant city and the more centralized the state. Moreover, over time the greater the economic primacy of the dominant city relative to other regions, the more dependent the non-core regions become on fiscal redistributions away from the dominant city. Over time this can have serious inter-regional and institutional consequences, because the residents and government authorities of the dominant city will become increasingly less willing to accept rising levels of fiscal redistribution away from the dominant city towards other regions. Geography and spatial adjustment processes can undermine governance systems if the institutional consequences of the factor adjustments are not explicitly accounted for in terms of the policy intentions and outcomes.

10.5.5 Insights into the nature of regional and national development challenges

Having acknowledged above that there are both major areas of agreement as well as fundamental differences of interpretation between the space-blind and place-based approaches (Barca 2011), we must now consider whether in reality the space-blind approaches are fundamentally inconsistent or incompatible with place-based approaches. Advocates of the space-blind approach (Winnick 1966; World Bank 2009) argue that space-blind approaches are 'people-based' approaches, and that there is a trade-off between 'people-based' approaches and place-based approaches. In contrast, the place-based approach assumes that place-based and people-based approaches are entirely complementary to each other, and see no fundamental dichotomy, trade-off, or conflict between processes of spatial factor adjustment and the promotion of local development initiatives.

The differences between the space-blind and place-based approaches can be understood in terms of different views regarding: the relationships between institutions and geography; the nature of historical urbanization–development processes; and the relationship between welfare provision and labour mobility. Making explicit these different views is important for our understanding of the nature of local and regional development processes more generally.

10.5.5.1 Different views regarding institutions and geography

The place-based approach argues that the relationship between institutions and geography is always present, and finding ways to use policy measures to overcome institutional bottlenecks related to geography is also an important 'people-based' agenda which is central to the place-based approach. The place-based approach argues that the relationships between geography and institutions are both ever present and varied, and finding ways to overcome the negative aspects of these relationships as well as harnessing their positive aspects is essential to place-based thinking. As such, unlike the space-blind approach, the place-based approach sees no dichotomy between people-based and place-based approaches.

A careful assessment of the shifting positions of the World Bank demonstrates that there are in reality no simple dichotomies operating, as implied by Winnick's (1966) 'people-based' versus 'place-based' characterization. Over the last three or four decades, the orthodox

World Bank position has been fundamentally that context does not matter, where context is defined by place-specific social, cultural, technological, or industrial characteristics, and that well-functioning institutions and market mechanisms are all that is required for growth. This has been a longstanding view of the World Bank, which has often been referred to as the 'Washington consensus'. However, to say, as the *World Development Report* (2009) now does, that national growth in many countries is to be fostered by massive urban growth via spatial factor adjustment mechanisms, irrespective of the spatial outcomes, ironically acknowledges precisely the opposite. This is an admission that context really does matter, because if context did not matter, then the institutional reforms alone would indeed be sufficient for growth, without recourse to making any comments or recommendations regarding cities. Moreover, other publications by the World Bank (World Bank 2003, 2010; Swinburn et al. 2006; Zoellick 2012) adopt a much more place-based line of argument emphasizing the need for fostering partnership with the intended beneficiaries, the importance of engagement of local stakeholders, and the fostering of a broad notion of development and growth including sustainability and inclusiveness. This is because it is becoming increasingly apparent that long-term institutional reform can only be ensured via partnership and collaboration between the external actors (funding agencies) and the local actors (intended beneficiaries) built around results-based development programmes which employ monitoring and evaluation (Sachs 2011, 2012). As such, these publications are rather different from the space-blind approach of the *World Development Report* (2009), and suggest that the real relationships between geography and institutions are in reality much more complex than the simple space-blind arguments imply, and that there is no simple dichotomy between 'people-based' and 'place-based' approaches.

The reason why large-scale urban growth is recommended by the *World Development Report* is that the growth of large cities is seen by the space-blind advocates as being the best way of solving the problems associated with the generation, acquisition, and sharing of knowledge and resources (McCann and Rodríguez-Pose 2011). Importantly, if very large cities are needed, it is not only because the institutions in the country do not work properly, but also because they cannot reasonably be reformed, due to the entrenched and longstanding self-interests of the major urban–political elites. Major urban expansion may therefore be the only realistic growth option in nations with little or no realistic possibilities for institutional reform or development (McCann and Rodríguez-Pose 2011), particularly where countries are too small or fragmented to sustain home market effects (Collier 2006; Venables 2010) required for growth. However, the place-based approach argues that this is just one solution among various possibilities, and that in many other regions and countries other approaches may be preferable.

The shifting World Bank position in a sense also reflects a more general debate within both economic geography and development studies regarding the role of institutions versus geography in economic development (Sachs 2003; Rodrik et al. 2004). While some people take partisan positions on this, it may well be the case that in reality it is the relationships between geography and institutions, and how these vary across space, that are the essential issues. It is easy to think of places where reform has not taken place and where development has not occurred, and this is the typical case discussed in the literature. However, it is also possible to think of places such as New Zealand where the institutional reforms have been excellent but the economic geography outcomes have been adverse, precisely because the reform of the institutions acted in a manner similar to falling trade costs (McCann 2009). The point is that the relationships between economic geography, institutions, and development are complex, and also they vary across geography. These observations suggest that context, in the sense of the role of place as determined by social, cultural, and legal issues, really does matter, and contrary to the *World Development Report*, other World Bank and related publications (Zoellick 2012) also reflect thinking which has a great deal in common with place-based approaches.

10.5.5.2 Different views regarding historical urbanization–development processes

In terms of long-run urbanization and development processes, as we saw in Chapters 8 and 9, development processes within the rich world are highly heterogeneous. The dynamics of knowledge generation and diffusion, innovation, and growth differ substantially between Europe and the USA (Crescenzi et al., 2007), and significant differences can be observed both within and across countries in the developed world. Moreover, the place-based arguments contend that there is no theoretical reason why the uneven spatial concentration of activity should also imply that development in rich countries today should be associated with increasing agglomeration. Indeed, as we saw in Chapters 8 and 9, much of the available evidence actually suggests the opposite. For rich countries, productivity and growth are nowadays often more associated with smaller rather than with very large cities, and in many countries the benefits of agglomeration actually appear to be close to being exhausted or are declining (OECD 2006).

The problem is that simple parallels across history do not capture the complex nature of development. History really does matter for context, and there are fundamental differences in the contexts in which economic development takes place (Barca et al. 2012). As we saw in Chapter 8, before the First World War the fifteen largest cities in the world, the mega-cities of their day, were all in the eight richest countries in the world (McCann and Acs 2011). These were countries which by the standards of the time already had the most developed institutional architectures of any countries then in existence, and which were the dominant players in their colonial empire systems, ensuring access to precious resources from other poorer parts of their empire systems. This was also the time period which heavily influenced the writings of many of the seminal publications which have shaped modern urban and regional economic analysis. Today, however, apart from North America, Japan, and Korea, the majority of the world's largest cities are in the developing world, in countries with very limited institutional architectures to speak of, with no out-migration outlets for overpopulation, and in which access to resources largely depends on global companies from other richer countries and international political agreements negotiated primarily by other richer nations. The institutional context today in which mega-cities operate is fundamentally different from the context in which they operated in the nineteenth century.

10.5.5.3 Different views regarding welfare provision and labour mobility

The differing regional policy recommendations between space-neutral and place-based approaches also raise complex issues related to the nature and extent of interregional labour mobility and the case for the provision of all forms of locally provided welfare funding per se, not just regional policy funding (Partridge and Rickman 2006). The logic of the space-blind arguments is the removal of all welfare payments, because the provision, monitoring, and delivery of such payments are place specific, according to the national–regional governance architecture. The second-best solution is to pay people to move. These arguments are discussed in detail in Appendix 10.2, and the assessment of these arguments is closely related to the regional mispricing issues raised by traditional place-based arguments, all of which are discussed in detail in Appendix 10.1.

In contrast to the space-blind position, as well as both the traditional and modern place-based responses already discussed in this chapter, the argument against these types of space-blind conclusions becomes even more powerful when we consider the fact that governance systems are also place based by definition. The relationship between the national and local state requires governance and political systems to respond appropriately to the preferences of the local median voter. This in turn requires national policies to take seriously into consideration the preferences and well-being of local residents, and also the tolerance of society for inequality therefore also becomes a central issue in the discussions (Ferrara 2010). The modern place-based approach contends that what are ostensibly space-blind decision-making process are in reality the outcomes of political-bargaining power, and interregional adjustment mechanisms based on apparently space-blind logic which foster the increasing dominance of certain places over others may actually contribute to national institutional sclerosis and in-built political tensions which may undermine donor preferences. The logic of interregional spatial adjustments may therefore generate other more profound problems unless the intentions and likely outcomes of the apparently space-blind policies are made explicit from the start.

10.6 Conclusions

This chapter began by discussing the various major types of specific initiatives traditionally undertaken under the broad heading of urban policy. As we have seen, a major difference between urban polices and regional policies is the spatial scale over which the policies are implemented and assumed to take effect. The intended impacts of urban policies are expected to take place over a much smaller spatial scale than those of regional policies. These different spatial scales, however, also mean that the types of policies adopted and the criteria against which the policies will be evaluated are also different. In the case of urban policies, the dominant issue which will determine whether or not a policy is implemented is the nature of the local environment at the suburban level. The notion of 'environment' here relates to both the physical built environment and the local social and economic environment. The real-estate market is generally the target of urban policies, and the implementation of these policies generally involves relaxations or changes in the institutional framework within which the local real-estate market operates. All such urban policies have welfare impacts, which are realized in terms of changes in the prices of real-estate assets at different locations. Moreover, the nature and scale of these welfare impacts can be quite different for different income groups. Urban policies can therefore have welfare distribution effects, and for urban and regional economists an evaluation of the benefits of urban policies cannot take place without an assessment of these welfare distribution effects.

Traditional regional policies, on the other hand, simultaneously focus both on encouraging indigenous regional investment growth and on attracting new immigrant investment into a region from outside. As far as the latter approach is concerned, these polices tend to operate over a much larger spatial scale than urban policies, and aim to encourage the migration of firm capital over rather large distances. The focus of regional polices traditionally tends to be on the provision of local regional infrastructure and also, in some cases, the subsidizing of local real-estate inputs. As with urban policies, however, these regional policies will obviously have social welfare impacts, the size and spatial distribution of which will depend on the responsiveness of indigenous and immigrant firms to the regional policy initiatives.

Traditional regional polices have also been understood as partly playing a macroeconomic efficiency role in situations where aggregate inflation is very sensitive to the local 'bottleneck' supply conditions in particular core regions. The argument here is that output can be maintained while avoiding some of the location-specific real-estate-induced influences on macroeconomic crowding out. The economic justification for using regional policy as an anti-inflationary device therefore rests on the assumption that underlying land-market imperfections mean that deregulation of land and planning regimes is not sufficient to counter these bottleneck problems. Obviously land-market deregulation may contribute to alleviating such bottlenecks, but, as we saw in Chapter 4, land markets are notoriously complex and highly efficient, and responsive land-supply adjustments cannot necessarily be assumed.

As we have also seen in this chapter, however, recent debates have thrown a completely new light on the reasons for regional performance differences and also on the possible policy solutions. More complex discussions regarding the role of space-blind versus place-based approaches to regional development policy have been reviewed. As we see, new insights into the nature of social and institutional capital are argued by the place-based approach to be key issues in regional development, whereas the space-neutral approach emphasizes interregional factor mobility and the spatial allocation of factors as being dominant. The latter approach therefore recommends removing anything which distorts the market or limits factor mobility, and at the urban level this would imply the removal of greenbelts and many forms of urban zoning. In contrast, the place-based approach would view these issues as second-order problems, with the interactions between factor mobility and governance and institutional issues as being dominant. Local development initiatives underpinned by the provision of specifically tailored local public goods would therefore be encouraged, as long as these initiatives were also designed so as to correctly align the incentives of all stakeholders, and to avoid the enhancement of local monopoly or monopsony positions. Whereas traditional regional policy was in part argued to be justified on the basis of reducing 'crowding-out' effects associated with local bottlenecks, modern regional policy is intended to encourage the 'crowding-in' effects (Zoellick 2012) of investment.

These arguments relating to regional development actually relate to even wider policy issues. As we will see in Appendices 10.1 and 10.2, while the space-blind approach suggests that no regional assistance funding should be provided in weaker regions, the ultimate logic of the space-blind approach is actually that no welfare funding should be provided whatsoever, including unemployment assistance, health, or educational services. This is because the provision of welfare and the identification of the appropriate recipients are almost entirely place-specific policies, and as such they are regarded by the space-blind approach as fundamentally inhibiting migration and factor reallocation. The space-blind arguments imply that only efficiency considerations should ever matter, and not equity considerations.

Discussion questions

10.1 What are the economic motives underlying downtown urban redevelopment policies? Using standard models, discuss the welfare effects of such schemes on different local income groups.

10.2 Are urban 'greenbelt' policies justified on economic and welfare grounds?

10.3 Is regional policy required during recessions when all regions are suffering unemployment?

10.4 The best regional policy is simply a freer market in land, labour, and capital. Do you agree with this statement?

10.5 What issues do we need to consider in order to evaluate the effectiveness of a regional policy which is based on the provision of transport infrastructure?

10.6 To what extent does regional policy have a role to play in alleviating regional inflationary 'bottlenecks'?

10.7 Discuss the differences between a 'space-blind' and a 'place-based' approach to regional economic development policy.

10.8 In what ways has the thinking behind the logic, nature, and role of regional policy changed over recent years?

Appendix 10.1 The value and (mis)pricing of places

The early place-based arguments on which modern place-based arguments are built are based on the assumption that the value of places and localities is larger than simply a use or consumption value of the region (Bolton 1992), and a simple neoclassical logic therefore often involves mispricing. Whereas the use value (to firms) or consumption value (to households) of a region had traditionally been the only form of valuation contained in the orthodox neoclassical factor adjustment model, in contrast, the early place-based approaches argued that regions and localities have additional values which go beyond the use or consumption values. These are existence values, options values, and the values associated with donor preferences, as well as other additional mispricing arguments, all of which are succinctly explained by Bolton (1992).

The existence values of places

The first additional type of value of a place above just the use or consumption value is the existence value. Existence values associated with a sense of place in a region are the values that individuals or communities in one region attach to the well-being of individuals or communities in a second region. In order for this existence value to exist (Bolton 1992), it is not necessary for the individual members of the first region even to go to the second region, let alone to move to the second region. All that is required is for the individuals in the first region to know that the well-being of other communities is intact and is not declining.

The option values of places

The second additional value associated with a sense of place is the option value of a place. This is the value ascribed by an individual person or firm to a possible future option to migrate there. The more places there are with vibrant and vital local communities, the greater will be the number and variety of potentially attractive options available for future migration for all individuals. Such migration possibilities may occur in response to changing job opportunities (foreseen or unforeseen), and also changing preferences associated with, for example, age and income.

As we have seen in Chapters 8 and 9, the changing economic geography of firms and occupations has been a major feature of the last two decades in all countries. Similarly, as we saw in Chapter 6, changes in residence associated with highly income-elastic preferences for amenities are also increasing rapidly. The ability to adjust and adapt to these changes is of both real and increasing value to individuals in all regions, and the greater the number of vibrant regions, the greater will be the variety of options available for future migration choices for all individuals.

While these arguments may at first appear to be rather esoteric, in fact modern survey-based econometric techniques allow us to rigorously estimate both the existence values and the option values of places. These existence and option value arguments are also closely related to the attachment value arguments discussed in Chapter 4. However, they are different from the attachment value argument, in that whereas the attachment values are local, the values here extend well beyond the locality itself to observers in *other* places.

Donor preferences

A different light can also be shed on these issues by considering the preferences of the donors, and the easiest way to understand this is by considering international aid (Bolton 1992). We can begin by assuming that the pure equity motive results in individuals supporting government assistance to other individuals facing hardship, and there are two ways of achieving this. First, the moneys could be simply transferred to individuals who are able to spend the funds where and when they wish. However, we know from studies of donor preferences that even for pure equity reasons, donors rarely prefer open-ended monetary transfers with no conditions attached. The consumption or investment behaviour of the recipients is acknowledged to be of importance to the donors, so that the moneys tied up in the transfers are not squandered but are used constructively for reducing some of the hardships faced by the recipients. Donor preferences generally prefer that the recipients use the funds constructively in their own locations, so as to partially correct for the local hardships. At the same time, the preference by donors is to give the funds to a non-corrupt government, charity, aid organization, or development agency, rather than to individuals. This is both to ensure that the moneys are spent in an accountable manner according to good governance principles and to allow for the pooling of resources so as to achieve scale impacts from the expenditure.

As is clear, the donor preferences argument works against the migration-voucher argument described above. The reason is that the funding is provided by the donors in the wealthier regions in order to assist the recipients in their own countries or regions. Donors would generally not pay for the recipients to move to the countries of the donors.[1] This is also true in terms of intra-national mobility, and the argument holds at the level of both interregional mobility and intra-urban mobility. If we consider regional policy in terms of income transfers from donors in more prosperous regions to recipients in less prosperous regions, then by the same logic the residents of prosperous areas will not pay for residents of less favoured regions to move to their locations. The donor preferences argument works against the migration-voucher argument, and where redistributive funding is supported on equity grounds, the donor preferences argument supports funding which is place specific in the less favoured regions.

What is important here is the fact that donor preferences exist in favour of providing funding in other people's regions in order to foster development and to help other people to maintain or enhance their livelihoods in their regions, rather than using the moneys donated to encourage people to migrate to the donors' regions. This suggests that place does have a value significantly above use or consumption, a value which is not only defined in terms of the attachment value and sense-of-place value of the residents—relating to all their various social, cultural, and economic dimensions of the place—but also in terms of the value placed on the well-being of residents of *other* regions.

In addition to these different valuations of place which go above and beyond use values, there are three other regional mispricing issues which the place-based approach implies should be taken into account in valuing regions, but which are largely ignored in the inter-regional equilibrium arguments.

(i)   The traditional place-based argument suggests that the capital costs associated with public intervention in declining regions are systematically overstated (Bolton 1992). One aspect of this is a second-best argument regarding downwardly rigid local wages in declining regions, as discussed in Chapter 6. Such sticky wages overstate the true opportunity costs of utilizing the local human capital in these regions, and therefore underestimate the potential value of such interventions. A second aspect of this argument is that if the provision of infrastructure capital and other public utilities is priced according to average costs, then the fact that the marginal costs will be lower

---

[1] A rare exception here is the case of the UK, where migrants were subsidized in the post-war decades to move to countries such as Australia and other former British empire dominions. These schemes were largely funded by the recipient countries aiming at rapid population growth and were a response to their perceived vulnerability due to their small populations in the aftermath of the Second World War. At the same time the origin countries, and by far the most important one was the UK, but also other European nations, all faced post-war food and housing shortages. The UK families paid only ten pounds per family for a one-way no-return ticket to relocate and were known as 'ten pound poms'. Such migration subsidies and allocations were primarily restricted to migrants who were perceived to be ethnically and culturally close to the residents of the receiving countries (Clark 1963).

than the average costs in the declining region means that the costs of providing public goods in these regions will be once again systematically overstated. Conversely, these same arguments imply that the opportunity costs of utilizing human capital in growing regions will be systematically underestimated and the net benefits overstated (Bolton 1992). Following our discussion in Chapters 5 and 6, if the level of mis-specification is both systematic and significant, as Laurilla (2004, 2011) implies, then the interregional distribution of activities may well be fundamentally inefficient.

(ii) Because of the long discounting period over which infrastructure should be priced, new infrastructure in expanding regions should not be developed until it is clear that the declining regions will not recover in the long run. Otherwise, infrastructure capital allocation decisions will be inefficient as they will be made with respect to time periods which are too short (Bolton 1992). If this is indeed the case, as such decisions are often taken for shorter-term political rather than long-run economic reasons, the true opportunity costs of infrastructure expenditure in the declining region will be understated and the benefits in growing regions will be overstated.

(iii) If we expand our concept of capital to include the intangible forms of capital such as social capital, cultural capital, institutional capital, creative capital, and entrepreneurial capital, then valuations based only on physical and human capital will seriously underestimate the long-run opportunity costs of the processes of decline.

As these various arguments all make clear, the value of a place is therefore systematically larger than the values ascribed to places by factor adjustment models based only on the use and consumption values of places. However, the extent to which they alter the orthodox factor adjustment framework depends on the importance of these other valuations and mis-pricing issues. If the level of undervaluation or mispricing is small, we could argue that the neoclassical one-sector factor adjustment model will generate interregional factor distributions which are close to efficient distributions.

Appendix 10.2 Space-blind approaches and the provision of welfare payments

We can begin to examine the relationship between space-blind arguments and arguments regarding the provision of welfare payments and services by initially assuming that regional policy or place-based funding is purely redistributional in nature. This is obviously a view which the place-based approach contends is long since out of date, but one which serves as a useful analytical starting point here.

A pure market-driven position is to argue that unemployed or underemployed people in less economically favoured regions should not be provided with any form of employment, social housing, or welfare assistance whatsoever. The argument here is that because these forms of assistance are generally provided in a place-specific manner as dictated by the central–local governance structures, it is assumed that these welfare subsidies adversely distort the responses of local labour supply curves, as discussed in Chapter 6. In particular, these subsidies may inhibit labour mobility from weaker to stronger regions, and the removal of any such assistance should therefore encourage the out-migration of these people to more prosperous regions.

The argument obviously contains many elements in common with the thinking underlying space-blind proposals of the *World Development Report* (2009). However, the argument can be even further extended along lines used by the space-blind logic to advocate infrastructure provision in capital cities. Specifically, if we acknowledge that the value to an individual of being in a particular location may have more than simply a use value in production or consumption, as is explained in Appendix 10.1, then a second-best suggestion, and in some sense a twist on the argument above, is that unemployed or underemployed individuals in less favoured locations should be paid to migrate to more prosperous regions via some sort of system of vouchers which can only be cashed in when the recipient gains employment in a more prosperous region (Glaeser and Gottlieb 2008).

This second-best argument implicitly concedes that the recipients have a place attachment value which is more than simply a use value. If such people will not migrate with zero local assistance, then their motives for non-migration are clearly more than simply monetary issues, and presumably related to the opportunity costs they would incur due to a loss of their local attachment value regarding family, identity, and sense of place. A voucher system would therefore only work if (along with the wage from the new job) it were to compensate the recipients for their attachment value losses from leaving their origin regions, while at the same time costing less than the additional taxation revenues associated with productivity gains in the destination regions.

However, without any knowledge of these attachment values, the optimal values of the vouchers become unclear and the design and monitoring of such a system becomes highly problematic. As we saw in Chapter 4, evidence from land assembly operations in fragmented markets suggests that compensation systems are plagued with problems of opportunism, 'hold-out', and adverse selection. In the case of migration voucher systems the issues are even more complex. Ass we saw in Chapter 6, on the one hand lower-skilled workers often have higher attachment values than higher-skilled workers, but on the other hand, as we also saw in Appendix 6.3, many high-skilled workers often prefer not to migrate from weaker regions for fear of losing their social and institutional status. Therefore the pricing of the vouchers and the monitoring of the system may well face severe problems of adverse selection. Moreover, the voucher system works against the donor preferences argument outlined in Appendix 10.1.

Bibliography

Introduction

Alonso, W. (1964), *Location and Land Use*, Harvard University Press, Cambridge, MA.

Borts, G. H., and Stein, J. L. (1964), *Economic Growth in a Free Market*, Columbia University Press, New York.

Chinitz, B. (1961), 'Contrast in Agglomeration: New York and Pittsburgh', *American Economic Review*, 51, 279–89.

Christaller, W. (1933), *Die Zentralen Orte in Suddeutschland*, Fischer, Jena, trans. by C. W. Baskin (1966), *Central Places in Southern Germany*, Prentice-Hall, Englewood Cliffs, NJ.

Fujita, M. (1989), *Urban Economic Theory*, Cambridge University Press, Cambridge.

Greenhut, M. L. (1970), *A Theory of the Firm in Economic Space*, Appleton Century Crofts, New York.

Hoover, E. M. (1948), *The Location of Economic Activity*, McGraw-Hill, New York.

Hotelling, H. (1929), 'Stability in Competition', *Economic Journal*, 39, 41–57.

Isard, W. (1956), *Location and the Space Economy*, John Wiley, New York.

Isard, W., Azis, I. J., Drennan, M. P., Miller, R. E., Saltzman, S., and Thorbecke, E. (1998), *Methods of Interregional and Regional Analysis*, Ashgate, Brookfield, VT.

Krugman, P. (1991), *Geography and Trade*, MIT Press, Cambridge, MA.

Lösch, A. (1954), *The Economics of Location*, Yale University Press, New Haven, CT.

Marshall, A. (1890), *Principles of Economics* (1st edn), Macmillan, London.

Marshall, A. (1920), *Principles of Economics* (8th edn), Macmillan, London.

Moses, L. N. (1958), 'Location and the Theory of Production', *Quarterly Journal of Economics*, 78, 259–72.

Palander, T. (1935), *Beiträge zur Standortstheorie*, Almqvist and Wiksells Boktryckeri, Uppsala, Sweden.

Perroux, F. (1950), 'Economic Space, Theory and Applications', *Quarterly Journal of Economics*, 64, 89–104.

Porter, M. E. (1990), *The Competitive Advantage of Nations*, Free Press, New York.

Vernon, R. (1960), *Metropolis 1985*, Harvard University Press, Cambridge, MA.

Weber, A. (1909), *Über den Standort der Industrien*, trans. Friedrich, C. J. (1929), *Alfred Weber's Theory of the Location of Industries*, University of Chicago Press, Chicago, IL.

Chapter 1

Akerlof, G. A. (1970), 'The Market for "Lemons": Quality Uncertainty and the Market Mechanism', *Quarterly Journal of Economics*, 84.3, 488–500.

Alchian, A. A. (1950), 'Uncertainty, Evolution and Economic Theory', *Journal of Political Economy*, 58, 211–21.

Arthur, W. B. (1994), *Increasing Returns and Path Dependence in the Economy*, University of Michigan Press, Ann Arbor, MI.

Baumol, W. J. (1959), *Business Behaviour, Value and Growth*, Macmillan, New York.

Becker, G. S. (1996), *Accounting for Tastes*, Harvard University Press, Cambridge, MA.

Boschma, R., and Martin, R. (2010) (eds), *Handbook of Evolutionary Economic Geography*, Edward Elgar, Cheltenham.

Carlton, D. W., and Perloff, J. M. (2006), *Modern Industrial Organization* (4th edn), Addison-Wesley, New York.

Cyert, R. M., and March, J. G. (1963), *A Behavioural Theory of the Firm*, Prentice-Hall, Englewood Cliffs, NJ.

d'Aspremont, C., Gabszewicz, J. J., and Thisse, J. F. (1979), 'On Hotelling's Stability in Competition', *Econometrica*, 47.5, 1145–50.

Delgado, M., Porter, M. E., and Stern, S. (2010), 'Clusters and Entrepreneurship' *Journal of Economic Geography*, 10.4, 495–518.

Eswaran, M., Kanemoto, Y., and Ryan, D. (1981), 'A Dual Approach to the Locational Decision of the Firm', *Journal of Regional Science*, 21.4, 469–89.

Hotelling, H. (1929), 'Stability in Competition', *Economic Journal*, 39, 41–57.

Lancaster, K. (1971), *Consumer Demand: A New Approach*, Columbia University Press, New York.

Laundhart, W. (1885), *Mathematische Begründung der Volkswirtschaftslehre*, B. G. Taubner, Leipzig.

McCann, P. (1993), 'The Logistics-Costs Location-Production problem', *Journal of Regional Science*, 33.4, 503–16.

McCann, P. (1997), 'Logistics-Costs and the Location of the Firm: A One-Dimensional Analysis', *Location Science*, 4, 101–16.

McCann, P., (1998), *The Economics of Industrial Location: A Logistics-Costs Approach*, Springer, Heidelberg.

McCann, P. (2001), 'A Proof of the Relationship between Optimal Vehicle Size, Haulage Length and the Structure of Distance-Transport Costs' *Transportation Research A*, 35.8, 671–93.

McCann, P. (2007), 'Sketching out a Model of Innovation, Face-to-Face Interaction and Economic Geography', *Spatial Economic Analysis*, 2.2, 117–34.

Miller, S. M., and Jensen, O. W. (1978), 'Location and the Theory of Production', *Regional Science and Urban Economics*, 8, 117–28.

Miron, J. R. (2010), *The Geography of Competition: Firms, Prices and Competition*, Springer, Heidelberg.

Moses, L. N. (1958), 'Location and the Theory of Production', *Quarterly Journal of Economics*, 78, 259–72.

Palander, T. (1935), *Beiträge zur Standortstheorie*, Almqvist and Wiksells Boktryckeri, Uppsala, Sweden.

Rawstron, E. M. (1958), 'The Principles of Industrial Location', *Transactions and Papers of the Institute of British Geographers*, 25, 132–42.

ReVelle, C. (1987), 'Urban Public Facility Location', in Mills, E. S., *Handbook of Regional and Urban Economics Volume 2: Urban Economics*, North-Holland, Amsterdam.

Sakashita, N. (1968), 'Production Function, Demand Function, and Location Theory of the Firm', *Papers and Proceedings of the Regional Science Association*, 20, 109–22.

Salop, S. C. (1979), 'Monopolistic Competition with Outside Goods', *Bell Journal of Economics*, 10.1, 141–56.

Simon, H. A. (1952), 'A Behavioural Model of Rational Choice', *Quarterly Journal of Economics*, 52, 99–118.

Simon, H. A. (1959), 'Theories of Decision-Making in Economics and Behavioural Science', *American Economic Review*, 49, 253–83.

Weber, A. (1909), *Über den Standort der Industrien*, trans. by Friedrich, C. J. (1929), *Alfred Weber's Theory of the Location of Industries*, University of Chicago Press, Chicago, IL.

Chapter 2

Abreu, M., Faggian, A., Comunian, R., and McCann, P. (2012), '"Life is Short, Art is Long": The Persistent Wage Gap between Bohemian and non-Bohemian Graduates and Occupations', (2012), *Annals of Regional Science*, 49.2, 305–21.

Acs, Z. J. (2002), *Innovation and the Growth of Cities*, Edward Elgar, Cheltenham.

Alchian, A. A. (1950), 'Uncertainty, Evolution, and Economic Theory', *Journal of Political Economy*, 58.3, 211–21.

Arita, T., and McCann, P. (2000), 'Industrial Alliances and Firm Location Behaviour: Some Evidence from the US Semiconductor Industry', *Applied Economics*, 32, 1391–403.

Arthur, W. B. (1991), *Increasing Returns and Path Dependence in the Economy*, University of Michigan Press, Ann Arbor, MI.

Aydalot, P., and Keeble, D. (1988), *Milieux Innovateurs en Europe*, GREMI, Paris.

Baumol, W. J. (1959), *Business Behaviour, Value and Growth*, Macmillan, New York.

Becattini, G., Bellandi, M. and De Propris, L. (2009), *A Handbook of Industrial Districts*, Edward Elgar, Cheltenham.

Boschma, R., and Martin, R. (2010) (eds), *Handbook of Evolutionary Economic Geography*, Edward Elgar, Cheltenham.

Boudeville, J. R. (1966), *Problems of Regional Planning*, Edinburgh University Press, Edinburgh.

Breschi, S., and Malerba, F. (2005) (eds), *Clusters, Networks, and Innovation*, Oxford University Press, Oxford.

Castells, M., and Hall, P. G. (1994), *Technopoles of the World: The Making of 21st Century Industrial Complexes*, Routledge, New York.

Caves, R. E. (2000), *Creative Industries: Contracts between Art and Commerce*, Harvard University Press, Cambridge, MA.

Chiang, A. C. (1984), *Fundamental Methods of Mathematical Economics*, McGraw-Hill, Singapore.

Chinitz, B. (1961), 'Contrasts in Agglomeration: New York and Pittsburgh', *American Economic Review*, 51, 279–89.

Chinitz, B. (1964), 'City and Suburb', in Chinitz, B. (ed.), *City and Suburb: The Economics of Metropolitan Growth*, Prentice-Hall, Englewood Cliffs, NJ.

Comunian, R., Faggian, A., Li, C. Q. (2010), 'Unrewarded Careers in the Creative Class: The Strange Case of Bohemian Graduates', *Papers in Regional Science*, 89.2, 389–410.

Cyert, R. M., and March, J. G. (1963), *A Behavioural Theory of the Firm*, Prentice-Hall, Englewood Cliffs, NJ.

de Groot, H. L. F., Poot, J., and Smit, M. (2009), 'Agglomeration Externalities, Innovation and Regional Growth: Theoretical Perspectives and Meta-Analysis', in Cappello, R., and Nijkamp, P., *Handbook of Regional Growth and Development Theories*, Edward Elgar, Cheltenham, 256–81.

Delgado, M., Porter, M. E., and Stern, S. (2010), 'Clusters and Entrepreneurship', *Journal of Economic Geography*, 10.4, 495–518.

Duranton, G., and Puga, D. (2001), 'Nursery Cities: Urban Diversity, Process Innovation, and the Life Cycle of Products', *American Economic Review* 91.5, 1454–77.

Duranton, G., and Puga, D. (2004), 'Micro-Foundations of Urban Agglomeration Economies', in Henderson, J. V., and Thisse, J.-F. (eds), *Handbook of Regional and Urban Economics, Vol IV: Economic Geography*, Elsevier, Amsterdam.

Florida, R. (2002), *The Rise of the Creative Class*, Basic Books, New York.

Florida, R. (2005), *The Flight of the Creative Class: The New Competition for Global Talent*, Harper Business, New York.

Frenken, K., Van Oort, F. G, and Verburg, T. (2007), 'Related Variety, Unrelated Variety and Regional Economic Growth', *Regional Studies*, 41, 685–97.

Glaeser, E. L. (2008), *Cities, Agglomeration and Spatial Equilibrium*, Oxford University Press, Oxford.

Glaeser, E. L. (ed.) (2010), *Agglomeration Economics*, University of Chicago Press, Chicago, IL.

Glaeser, E. L. (2011), *Triumph of the City: How Our Greatest Invention Makes Us Richer, Smarter, Greener, Healthier, and Happier*, The Penguin Press, New York.

Glaeser, E. L., Kallal, H., Scheinkman, J. A., and Shleifer, A. (1992), 'Growth in Cities', *Journal of Political Economy*, 100.6, 1126–51.

Glaeser, E. L., Kolko, J., and Saiz, A. (2001), 'Consumer City', *Journal of Economic Geography*, 1.1, 27–50.

Glaeser, E. L., and Gottlieb, J. D. (2006), 'Urban Resurgence and the Consumer City', *Urban Studies*, 43.8, 1275–99.

Gordon, I. R., and McCann, P. (2000), 'Industrial Clusters: Complexes, Agglomeration and /or Social Networks', *Urban Studies*, 37.3, 513–32.

Gordon, I. R., and McCann, P. (2005), 'Innovation, Agglomeration and Regional Development', *Journal of Economic Geography*, 5.5, 523–43.

Granovetter, M. (1973), 'The Strength of Weak Ties', *American Journal of Sociology*, 78, 1360–80.

Granovetter, M. (1985), 'Economic Action and Social Structure', *American Journal of Sociology*, 91, 481–510.

Granovetter, M. (1991), 'The Social Cohesion of Economic Institutions', in Etzoni, A., and Lawrence, R. (eds), *Socio-Economics: Towards a New Synthesis*, Armonk, New York.

Granovetter, M. (1992), 'Problems of Explanations in Economic Sociology', in Nohria, N., and Eccles, R. (eds), *Networks and Organizations: Form and Action*, Harvard Business School Press, Cambridge, MA.

Grindley, P. C., and Teece, D. J. (1997), 'Licensing and Cross-Licensing in Semiconductors and Electronics', *California Management Review*, 39.2, 8–41.

Haug, P. (1986), 'US High Technology Multinationals and Silicon Glen', *Regional Studies*, 20, 103–16.

Henderson, J. V., Kuncoro, A., and Turner, M. (1995), 'Industrial Development in Cities', *Journal of Political Economy*, 103, 1067–85.

Hoover, E. M. (1937), *Location Theory and the Shoe and Leather Industries*, Harvard University Press, Cambridge, MA.

Hoover, E. M. (1948), *The Location of Economic Activity*, McGraw-Hill, New York.

Iammarino, S., and McCann, P. (2006), 'The Structure and Evolution of Industrial Clusters: Transactions, Technology and Knowledge Spillovers', *Research Policy*, 35, 1018–36.

Isard, W., and Kuenne, R. E. (1953), 'The Impact of Steel upon the Greater New York–Philadelphia Industrial Region', *Review of Economics and Statistics*, 35, 289–301.

Jacobs, J. (1960), *The Economy of Cities*, Random House, New York.

Keeble, D., and Wilkinson, F. (1999), 'Collective Learning and Knowledge Development in the Evolution of High Technology SMEs in Europe', *Regional Studies*, 33.4, 295–303.

Krugman, P. (1991a), *Geography and Trade*, MIT Press, Cambridge, MA.

Mameli, F., Faggian, A., and McCann, P. (2008), 'Employment Growth in Italian Local Labour Systems: Issues of Model Specification and Sectoral Aggregation', *Spatial Economic Analysis*, 3.3, 343–59.

Markusen, A. (1985), *Profit Cycles, Oligopoly, and Regional Development*, MIT Press, Cambridge, MA.

Markusen, A. (2006), 'Urban Development and the Politics of a Creative Class: Evidence from a Study of Artists', *Environment and Planning A*, 38, 1921–40.

Marshall, A. (1890), *Principles of Economics* (1st edn), Macmillan, London.

Marshall, A. (1920), *Principles of Economics* (8th edn), Macmillan, London.

McCann, P. (1995a), 'Rethinking the Economics of Location and Agglomeration', *Urban Studies*, 32.3, 563–77.

McCann, P. (1995b), 'Journey and Transactions Frequency: An Alternative Explanation of Rent-Gradient Convexity', *Urban Studies*, 32.9, 1549–57.

McCann, P. (1997), 'How Deeply Embedded is Silicon Glen? A Cautionary Note', *Regional Studies*, 31.7, 695–703.

McCann, P. (2005), 'Transport Costs and New Economic Geography', *Journal of Economic Geography*, 5.3, 305–18.

McCann, P., and Arita, T. (2006), 'Clusters and Regional Development: Some Cautionary Observations from the Semiconductor Industry', *Information Economics and Policy*, 18.2, 157–80.

McCann, P., and Fingleton, B. (1996), 'The Regional Agglomeration Impact of Just-In-Time Input Linkages: Evidence from the Scottish Electronics Industry', *Scottish Journal of Political Economy*, 43.5, 493–518.

McCann, P., Poot, J., and Sanderson, L. (2010), 'Migration, Relationship Capital and International Travel: Theory and Evidence', *Journal of Economic Geography*, 10.3, 361–87.

Moses, L. N. (1958), 'Location and the Theory of Production', *Quarterly Journal of Economics*, 78, 259–72.

Ohlin, B. (1933), *Interregional and International Trade*, Harvard University Press, Cambridge, MA.

Parr, J. B. (1999a), 'Growth-Pole Strategies in Regional Economic Planning: A Retrospective View. Part 1. Origins and Advocacy', *Urban Studies*, 36.7, 1195–215.

Parr, J. B. (1999b), 'Growth-Pole Strategies in Regional Economic Planning: A Retrospective View. Part 2. Implementation and Outcome', *Urban Studies*, 36.8, 1247–68.

Pavitt, K. (1984), 'Sectoral Patterns of Technical Change: Towards a Taxonomy and a Theory', *Research Policy*, 13, 343–73.

Perroux, F. (1950), 'Economic Space, Theory and Applications', *Quarterly Journal of Economics*, 64, 89–104.

Polèse, M. (2009), *The Wealth and Poverty of Nations: Why Cities Matter*, University of Chicago Press, Chicago, IL.

Porter, M. E. (1985), *Competitive Advantage: Creating and Sustaining Superior Performance*, Free Press, New York.

Porter, M. E. (1990), *The Competitive Advantage of Nations*, Free Press, New York.

Porter, M. E. (1998a), 'Clusters and the New Economics of Competition', *Harvard Business Review*, 76.6, 77.

Porter, M. E. (1998b), 'Competing Across Locations', in Porter, M. E. (ed.), *On Competition*, Harvard Business School Press, Cambridge, MA.

Putnam, R. (1996), *Bowling Alone: The Collapse and Revival of American Community*, Simon and Schuster, New York.

Rawstron, E. M. (1958), 'The Principles of Industrial Location', *Transactions and Papers of the Institute of British Geographers*, 25, 132–42.

Richardson, H.W. (1978), *Regional Economics*, University of Illinois Press, Urbana, IL.

Salop, S. C. (1979), 'Monopolistic Competition with Outside Goods', *Bell Journal of Economics*, 10.1, 141–56.

Saxenian, A. (1994), *Regional Advantage: Culture and Competition in Silicon Valley and Route 128*, Harvard University Press, Cambridge, MA.

Schumpeter, J. A. (1934), *The Theory of Economic Development*, Harvard University Press, Cambridge, MA.

Scott, A. J. (1998), *New Industrial Spaces*, Pion, London.

Scott, A. J. (2000), *The Cultural Economy of Cities*, Sage, London.

Simmie, J. (1988), 'Reasons for the Development of "Islands of Innovation": Evidence from Hertfordshire', *Urban Studies*, 35.8, 1261–89.

Simon, H. A. (1952), 'A Behavioural Model of Rational Choice', *Quarterly Journal of Economics*, 52, 99–118.

Simon, H. A. (1959), 'Theories of Decision-Making in Economics and Behavioural Science', *American Economic Review*, 49, 253–83.

Suarez-Villa, L. and Walrod, W. (1997), 'Operational Strategy, R&D and Intra-metropolitan Clustering in a Polycentric Structure: The Advanced Electronics Industries of the Los Angeles Basin', *Urban Studies*, 34, 1343–80.

UN (United Nations) (1992), *World Urbanization Prospects 1992*, Department of Economic and Social Development, United Nations Secretariat, New York.

Van Oort, F. G. (2004), *Urban Growth and Innovation: Spatially Bounded Externalities in the Netherlands*, Ashgate, Aldershot.

Vernon, R. (1960), *Metropolis 1985*, Harvard University Press, Cambridge, MA.

Vernon, R. (1966), 'International Investment and International Trade in the Product Cycle', *Quarterly Journal of Economics*, 80, 190–207.

Weber, A. (1909), *Über den Standort der Industrien*, trans. by Friedrich, C. J. (1929), *Alfred Weber's Theory of the Location of Industries*, University of Chicago Press, Chicago, IL.

Williamson, O. E. (1975), *Markets and Hierarchies*, Free Press, New York.

Chapter 3

Amiti, M. (1998), 'New Trade Theories and Industrial Location in the EU: A Survey of Evidence', *Oxford Review of Economic Policy*, 14, 45–53.

Anselin, L. (1988), *Spatial Econometrics: Methods and Models*, Kluwer Academic Publishers, Dordrecht.

Audretsch, D., and Feldman, M. P. (1996), 'R&D Spillovers and the Geography of Innovation and Production', *American Economic Review*, 86, 630–40.

Baldwin, R., Forslid, R., Martin, P., Ottaviano, G., and Robert-Nicoud, F. (2003), *Economic Geography and Public Policy*, Princeton University Press, Princeton, NJ.

Batty, M. (2005), *Cities and Complexity: Understanding Cities with Cellular Automata, Agent-Based Models, and Fractals*, MIT Press, Cambridge, MA.

Beavon, K. S. O. (1977), *Central Place Theory: A Reinterpretation*, Longman, London.

Black, D., and Henderson, V. (1999), 'Spatial Evolution of Population and Industry in the United States', *American Economic Review: Papers and Proceedings*, 89.2, 321–7.

Blair, J. P. (1995), *Local Economic Development: Analysis and Practice*, Sage, Thousand Oaks, CA.

Bosker, M., and Garretsen, J. H. (2010), 'Trade Costs in Empirical New Economic Geography', *Papers in Regional Science*, 89.3, 485–511.

Brakman, S., Garretsen, H., and Van Marrewijk, C. (2009), *A New Introduction to Geographical Economics*, Cambridge University Press, Cambridge, MA.

Christaller, W. (1933), *Die Zentralen Orte in Suddeutschland*, Fischer, Jena, trans. by Baskin, C. W. (1966), *Central Places in Southern Germany*, Prentice-Hall, Englewood Cliffs, NJ.

Combes, P.-P. (2000), 'Economic Structure and Local Growth: France 1984–(1993)', *Journal of Urban Economics*, 47, 329–55.

Combes, P.-P., Mayer, T., and Thisse J.-F. (2008), *Economic Geography: The Integration of Regions and Nations*, Princeton University Press, Princeton, NJ.

De Groot, H. L. F., Poot, J., and Smit, M. (2009), 'Agglomeration Externalities, Innovation and Regional Growth: Theoretical Perspectives and Meta-Analysis', in Cappello, R., and Nijkamp, P. (eds), *Handbook of Regional Growth and Development Theories*, Edward Elgar, Cheltenham.

Dewhurst, J. H. L., and McCann, P. (2002), 'A Comparison of Measures of Industrial Specialisation for Travel-To-Work Areas in Great Britain 1981–97', *Regional Studies*, 36.5, 541–51.

Dixit, A. K., and Stiglitz, J. E. (1977), 'Monopolistic Competition and Optimum Product Diversity', *American Economic Review*, 67.3, 297–308.

Duranton, G. (2007), 'Urban Evolutions: The Fast, the Slow, and the Still', *American Economic Review*, 97.1, 197–221.

Duranton, G., and Overman, H. G. (2005), 'Testing for Localization Using Micro-Geographic Data', *Review of Economic Studies*, 72, 1077–106.

Duranton, G., and Puga, D. (2000), 'Diversity and Specialisation in Cities: Why, Where and When Does it Matter?', *Urban Studies*, 37.3, 533–55.

Ellison, G., and Glaeser, E. L. (1997), 'Geographic Concentration in US Manufacturing Industries: A Dartboard Approach', *Journal of Political Economy*, 105, 889–927.

Ellison, G., Glaeser, E. L., and Kerr, W. R. (2010), 'What Causes Industry Agglomeration? Evidence from Coagglomeration Patterns', *American Economic Review*, 100.3, 1195–213.

Fingleton, B. (2005), 'Beyond Neoclassical Orthodoxy: A View Based on the New Economic Geography and UK Regional Wage Data', *Papers in Regional Science*, 84.3, 351–75.

Fingleton, B. (2010), 'The Empirical Performance of the NEG with Reference to Small Areas', *Journal of Economic Geography*, 11.2, 267–79.

Fingleton, B., and Fischer, M. (2010), 'Neoclassical Theory versus New Economic Geography: Competing Explanations of Cross-Regional Variation in Economic Development', *Annals of Regional Science*, 44, 467–91.

Fingleton, B., and McCann, P. (2007), 'Sinking the Iceberg? On the Treatment of Transport Costs in New Economic Geography', in Fingleton, B. (ed.), *New Directions in Economic Geography*, Edward Elgar, Cheltenham.

Fotheringham, A. S., Brunsdon, C., and Charlton, M. (2000), *Quantitative Geography: Perspectives on Spatial Data Analysis*, Sage, London.

Fotheringham, A. S., Brunsdon, C., and Charlton, M. (2002), *Geographically Weighted Regression: The Analysis of Spatially Varying Relationships*, Wiley, London.

Fujita, M., Krugman, P., and Venables, A. J. (1999a), *The Spatial Economy*, MIT Press, Cambridge, MA.

Fujita, M., Krugman, P., and Mori, T. (1999b), 'On the Evolution of Hierarchical Urban Systems', *European Economic Review*, 43, 209–51.

Fujita, M., and Krugman, P. (1995), 'When is the Economy Monocentric? von Thunen and Chamberlin Unified', *Regional Science and Urban Economics*, 18, 87–124.

Fujita, M., and Thisse, J.-F. (2002), *Economics of Agglomeration: Cities, Industrial Location, and Regional Growth*, Cambridge University Press, Cambridge.

Gabaix, X. (1999a), 'Zipf's Law and the Growth of Cities', *American Economic Review: Papers and Proceedings*, 89.2, 129–32.

Gabaix, X. (1999b), 'Zipf's Law for Cities: An Explanation', *Quarterly Journal of Economics*, 114.3, 739–67.

Glaeser, E. L., Kallal, H. D., Scheinkman, J. A., and Shleifer, A. (1992), 'Growth in Cities', *Journal of Political Economy*, 100, 1126–52.

Guimarães, P., Figueiredo, O., and Woodward, D. (2007), 'Measuring the Localization of Economic Activity: A Parametric Approach', *Journal of Regional Science*, 47, 753–74.

Greenhut, M. L. (1970), *A Theory of the Firm in Economic Space*, Appleton Century Crofts, New York.

Greenhut, M. L., and Ohta, H. (1975), *Theory of Spatial Pricing and Market Areas*, Duke University Press, Durham, NC.

Haining, R. (2003), *Spatial Data Analysis: Theory and Practice*, Cambridge University Press, Cambridge.

Harris, C. D. (1954), 'The Market as a Factor in the Localization of Industry in the United States', *Annals of the Association of American Geographers*, 44, 315–48.

Henderson, J. V., and Thisse, J.-F (2004), *Handbook of Regional and Urban Economics Vol. 4: Cities and Geography*, Elsevier, Amsterdam.

Henderson, J. V., Kuncoro, A., and Turner, M. (1995), 'Industrial Development in Cities', *Journal of Political Economy*, 103, 1067–85.

Hoare, A. G. (1975), 'Linkage Flows, Locational Evaluation and Industrial Geography', *Environment and Planning A*, 7, 241–58.

Holmes, T. J. (1999), 'Scale of Local Production and City Size', *American Economic Review: Papers and Proceedings*, 89.2, 317–20.

Hoover, E. M., and Giarratani, F. (1985), *An Introduction to Regional Economics* (3rd edn), Alfred A. Knopf, New York.

Kittiprapas, S., and McCann, P. (1999), 'Industrial Location Behaviour and Regional Restructuring within the Fifth "Tiger" Economy', *Applied Economics*, 31, 37–51.

Krugman, P. (1991a), *Geography and Trade*, MIT Press, Cambridge, MA.

Krugman, P. (1991b), 'Increasing Returns and Economic Geography', *Journal of Political Economy*, 99, 483–99.

Krugman, P. (1993), 'On the Number and Location of Cities', *European Economic Review*, 37, 293–8.

Krugman, P., and Venables, A. J. (1995), 'Globalization and the Inequality of Nations', *Quarterly Journal of Economics*, 110.4, 857–80.

LeSage, J., and Pace, R. K. (2009), *Introduction to Spatial Econometrics*, Chapman and Hall, Boca Raton, FL.

Lever, W. F. (1972), 'Industrial Movement, Spatial Association and Functional Linkages', *Regional Studies*, 6, 371–84.

Lever, W. F. (1974), 'Manufacturing Linkages and the Search for Suppliers', in Hamilton, F. E. (ed.), *Spatial Perspectives on Industrial Organization and Decision-Making*, John Wiley, London.

Lösch, A. (1944), *Die Räumliche Ordnung der Wirtschaft*, Fischer, Jena, trans. by Woglom, W. H. (1954), *The Economics of Location*, Yale University Press, New Haven, CT.

Mameli, F., Faggian, A., and McCann, P. (2008), 'Employment Growth in Italian Local Labour Systems: Issues of Model Specification and Sectoral Aggregation', *Spatial Economic Analysis*, 3.3, 343–59.

Marshall, J. N. (1987), 'Industrial Change, Linkages and Regional Development', in Lever, W. F. (ed.), *Industrial Change in the United Kingdom*, Longman, Harlow.

Maurel, F. and S'Edillot, B. (1999), 'A Measure of the Geographic Concentration of French Manufacturing Industries', *Regional Science and Urban Economics*, 29.5, 575–604.

McCann, P. (1995a), 'Rethinking the Economics of Location and Agglomeration', *Urban Studies*, 32.3, 563–77.

McCann, P. (1995b), 'A Proof of the Relationship between Optimal Vehicle Size, Haulage Length and the Structure of Distance-Transport Costs', *Transportation Research A*, 35.8, 671–93.

McCann, P. (2005), 'Transport Costs and New Economic Geography', *Journal of Economic Geography*, 5.3, 305–18.

McCann, P. (2007), 'Sketching out a Model of Innovation, Face-to-Face Interaction and Economic Geography', *Spatial Economic Analysis*, 2.2, 117–34.

Menon, C. (2012), 'The Bright Side of MAUP: Defining New Measures of Industrial Agglomeration', *Papers in Regional Science*, 91.1, 3–28.

Mills, E. S. (1972), *Urban Economics*, Scott, Foresman and Co., Glenview, IL.

Mills, E. S., and Hamilton, B. W. (1994), *Urban Economics* (5th edn), HarperCollins, New York.

Mundell, R. A. (1957), 'The Geometry of Transport Costs in International Trade Theory', *Canadian Journal of Economics and Political Science*, 23, 331–48.

Samuelson, P. A. (1952), 'The Transfer Problem and Transport Costs: The Terms of Trade when Impediments are Absent', *Economic Journal*, 62, 278–304.

OECD (2012a), *Redefining 'Urban': A New Way to Measure Metropolitan Areas*, Organisation for Economic Cooperation and Development, Paris.

Openshaw S., and Taylor P. J. (1979), 'A Million or So Correlation Coefficients: Three Experiments on the Modifiable Areal Unit Problem' in Wrigley, N. (ed.), *Statistical Applications in the Spatial Sciences*, Pion, London.

Parr, J. B. (1997), 'The Law of Retail Gravitation: Insights from Another Law', *Environment and Planning A*, 29, 1477–95.

Parr, J. B. (2002), 'The Location of Economic Activity: Central Place Theory and the Wider Urban System', in McCann, P. (ed.), *Industrial Location Economics*, Edward Elgar, Cheltenham.

Quah, D. (2001), 'The weightless economy in economic development', in Pohoja, M. (ed.), *Information Technology, Productivity, and Economic Growth*, Oxford University Press, Oxford.

Redding, S .J., and Venables, A. J. (2004), 'Economic Geography and International Inequality', *Journal of International Economics*, 62, 53–82.

Reilly, W. J. (1929), *Methods for the Study of Retail Relationships*, University of Texas Press, Austin, TX.

Reilly, W. J. (1931), *The Law of Retail Gravitation*, Knickerbocker Press, New York, republished 1953, Pilsbury Publishers, New York.

Richardson, H. W. (1978), *Regional Economics*, University of Illinois Press, Urbana, IL.

Schabenberger, O., and Gotway, C. A. (2005), *Statistical Methods for Spatial Data Analysis*, Boca Raton, FL.

Stelder, D. (2002), 'Geographic Grids in "New Economic Geography" Models', in McCann, P. (ed.), *Industrial Location Economics*, Edward Elgar, Cheltenham.

Stelder, D. (2005), 'Where do Cities Form? A Geographical Agglomeration Model for Europe', *Journal of Regional Science*, 45, 657–79.

Van Oort, F. G. (2004), *Urban Growth and Innovation: Spatially Bounded Externalities in The Netherlands*, Ashgate, Aldershot.

Venables, A. J. (1996), 'Equilibrium Locations of Vertically Linked Industries', *International Economic Review*, 37.2, 341–59.

Zipf, G. (1949), *Human Behavior and the Principle of Least Effort*, Addison-Wesley, New York.

Chapter 4

Alonso, W. (1964), *Location and Land Use*, Harvard University Press, Cambridge, MA.

Alonso, W. (1971), 'The Economics of Urban Size', *Papers and Proceedings of the Regional Science Association*, 26, 67–83.

Ball, M., Lizieri, C., and MacGregor, B. D. (1998), *The Economics of Commercial Property Markets*, Routledge, London.

Button, K. J. (1993), *Transport Economics*, Edward Elgar, Cheltenham.

Capozza, D. R., and Helsey, R. W. (1989), 'The Fundamentals of Land Prices and Urban Growth', *Journal of Urban Economics*, 26, 295–306.

Chiang, A. C. (1984), *Fundamental Methods of Mathematical Economics*, McGraw-Hill, Singapore.

DiPasquale, D., and Wheaton, W. C. (1996), *Urban Economics and Real Estate Markets*, Prentice-Hall, Englewood Cliffs, NJ.

Dynarski, M. (1986), 'Residential Attachment and Housing Demand', *Urban Studies*, 23.1, 11–20.

Evans, A. W. (1973), *The Economics of Residential Location*, Macmillan, London.

Evans, A. W. (1983), 'The Determination of the Price of Land', *Urban Studies*, 10.2, 119–29.

Evans, A. W. (1985), *Urban Economics*, Macmillan, London.

Hall, P., and Pain, K. (eds) (2006), *The Polycentric Metropolis: Learning from Mega-City Regions in Europe*, Earthscan, London.

Laurila, H. (2004), 'Urban Governance, Competition and Welfare', *Urban Studies*, 41.3, 683–96.

Laurila, H. (2011), 'Optimisation of City Size', *Urban Studies*, 48.4, 737–47.

McCann, P. (1993), 'The Logistics-Costs Location-Production problem', *Journal of Regional Science*, 33.4, 503–16.

McCann, P. (1995), 'Journey and Transactions Frequency: An Alternative Explanation of Rent-Gradient Convexity', *Urban Studies*, 32.9, 1549–57.

McCann, P., (1998), *The Economics of Industrial Location: A Logistics-Costs Approach*, Springer, Heidelberg.

McCann, P. (2007), 'Sketching out a Model of Innovation, Face-to-Face Interaction and Economic Geography', *Spatial Economic Analysis*, 2.2, 117–34.

Mills, E. S. (1969), 'The Value of Urban Land', in Perloff, H. (ed.), *The Quality of the Urban Environment*, Resources for the Future, Washington, DC.

Mills, E. S. (1972), *Urban Economics*, Scott, Foresman and Co., Glenview, IL.

Muth., R. (1969), *Cities and Housing: The Spatial Pattern of Urban Residential Land Use*, University of Chicago Press, Chicago, IL.

Ricardo, D. (1821), *On the Principles of Political Economy and Taxation* (3rd edn), republished by John Murray, London.

Riguelle, F., Thomas, I., and Verhetsel, A. (2007), 'Measuring Urban Polycentrism: a European Case Study and its Implications', *Journal of Economic Geography*, 7, 193–215.

Salop, S. C. (1979), 'Monopolistic Competition with Outside Goods', *Bell Journal of Economics*, 10.1, 141–56.

Takayama, A. (1993), *Mathematical Economics* (2nd edn), Cambridge University Press, Cambridge.

von Thunen, J. H. (1826), *Der Isolierte Staat in Beziehung auf Landtschaft und Nationalökonomie*, Hamburg, trans. by Wartenberg, C. M. (1966), *Von Thunen's Isolated State*, Pergamon Press, Oxford.

Chapter 5

Amiti, M. (1998), 'New Trade Theories and Industrial Location in the EU: A Survey of Evidence', *Oxford Review of Economic Policy*, 14, 45–53.

Anderson, J. E., and van Wincoop, E. (2003), 'Gravity with Gravitas: A Solution to the Border Puzzle', *American Economic Review*, 93.1, 170–92.

Anderson, J. E., and van Wincoop, E. (2004), 'Trade Costs', *Journal of Economic Literature*, 43.3, 691–751.

Bacharach, M. (1970), *Biproportional Matrices and Input–Output Change*, Cambridge University Press, Cambridge.

Batey, P. W., and Madden, M., (1981), 'Demographic–Economic Forecasting within an Activity–Commodity

Framework: Some Theoretical Considerations and Empirical Results', *Environment and Planning A*, 13, 1067–83.

Batey, P., Bazzazan, F., and Madden, M. (2001), 'Dynamic Extended Input–Output Models: Some Initial Thoughts', in Felsenstein, D., McQuaid, R., McCann, P., and Shefer, D. (eds), *Public Investment and Regional Development: Essays in Honour of Mass Madden*, Edward Elgar, Cheltenham.

Billings, R. B. (1969), 'The Mathematical Identity of the Multipliers derived from the Economic Base Model and the Input–Output Model', *Journal of Regional Science*, 9.3, 471–3.

Black, P. A. (1981), 'Injection Leakages, Trade Repercussions and the Regional Income Multiplier', *Scottish Journal of Political Economy*, 28.3, 227–35.

Blair, J. P. (1995), *Local Economic Development: Analysis and Practice*, Sage, Thousand Oaks, CA.

Chiang, A. C. (1984), *Fundamental Methods of Mathematical Economics*, McGraw-Hill, Singapore.

Czamanski, S., and Malizia, E. (1969), 'Applicability and Limitations in the Use of Input–Output Tables for Regional Studies', *Papers and Proceedings of the Regional Science Association*, 23, 66–75.

Dow, S. C. (1982), 'The Regional Composition of the Money Multiplier Process', *Scottish Journal of Political Economy*, 29.1, 22–44.

Dow, S. C. (1987), 'The Treatment of Money in Regional Economics', *Journal of Regional Science*, 27.1, 13–24.

Dow, S. C., and Rodriguez-Fuentes, C. J. (1997), 'Regional Finance: A Survey', *Regional Studies*, 31.9, 903–20.

Duranton, G., and Puga, D. (2000), 'Diversity and Specialisation in Cities: Why, Where and When Does it Matter?', *Urban Studies*, 37.3, 533–55.

Flegg, A. T., Webber, C. D., and Elliot, M. V. (1995), 'On the Appropriate Use of Location Quotients in Generating Regional Input–Output Tables', *Regional Studies*, 29, 547–62.

Fujita, M., Krugman, P., and Venables, A. J. (1999), *The Spatial Economy*, MIT Press, Cambridge, MA.

Harrigan, F. H., McGilvray, J. W., and McNicoll, I. H. (1980), 'A Comparison of Regional and National Technical Structures', *Economic Journal*, 90, 795–810.

Harris, R. I. D. (1998), 'The Impact of the University of Portsmouth on the Local Economy', *Urban Studies*, 34.4, 605–26.

Harris, R. I. D., and Liu, A. (1998), 'Input–Output Modelling of the Urban and Regional Economy: The Importance of External Trade', *Regional Studies*, 32.9, 851–62.

Hartman, L. M., and Seckler, D. (1967), 'Towards the Application of Dynamic Growth Theory to Regions', *Journal of Regional Science*, 7, 167–73.

Hewings, G. J. D., Sonis, M., Madden, M., and Kimura, Y. (eds) (1999), *Understanding and Interpreting Economic Structure*, Springer, Heidelberg.

Hoover, E. M., and Giarratani, F. (1985), *An Introduction to Regional Economics* (3rd edn), Alfred A. Knopf, New York.

Isard, W., Azis, I. J., Drennan, M. P., Miller, R. E., Saltzman, S., and Thorbecke, E. (1998), *Methods of Interregional and Regional Analysis*, Ashgate, Brookfield, VT.

Isserman, A. M. (1977a), 'The Location Quotient Approach to Estimating Regional Economic Impacts', *American Institute of Planners Journal*, 43, 33–41.

Isserman, A. M. (1977b), 'A Bracketing Approach for Estimating Regional Economic Impact Multipliers and a Procedure for Assessing their Accuracy', *Environment and Planning A*, 9, 1003–11.

Isserman, A. M. (1980), 'Estimating Export Activity in a Regional Economy: A Theoretical and Empirical Analysis of Alternative Methods', *International Regional Science Review*, 5, 155–84.

Karaska, G. J. (1968), 'Variation of Input–Output Coefficients for Different Levels of Aggregation', *Journal of Regional Science*, 8.2, 215–27.

Lahr, M. L. (1993), 'A Review of the Literature Supporting the Hybrid Approach to Constructing Regional Input–Output Models', *Economic Systems Research*, 5, 277–92.

Lahr, M. L. (2001), *Input–Output Analysis: Frontiers and Extension*, Palgrave, Basingstoke.

Leontief, W. W. (1953), 'Interregional Theory' in Leontief, W. W. (ed.), *Studies in the Structure of the American Economy*, Oxford University Press, New York.

Levacic, R., and Rebmann, A. (1982), *Macroeconomics: An Introduction to Keynesian–Neoclassical Controversies*, Macmillan, Basingstoke.

Leven, C. L. (1956), 'Measuring the Economic Base', *Papers of the Regional Science Association*, 2.1, 250–58.

Lichtenberg, R. M. (1960), *One-Tenth of a Nation*, Harvard University Press, Cambridge, MA.

McCombie, J. S. L., and Thirlwall, A. P. (1994), *Economic Growth and the Balance-of-Payments Constraint*, Macmillan, Basingstoke.

McGregor, P., Partridge, M. D., and Rickman, D. S. (2010), 'Innovations in Regional Computable General Equilibrium (CGE) Modellling', *Regional Studies*, 44.10, 1307–10.

Miller, R. E. (1998), 'Regional and Interregional Input–Output Analysis', in Isard, W., Azis, I. J., Drennan, M. P., Miller, R. E., Saltzman, S. and Thorbecke, E. (eds), *Methods of Interregional and Regional Analysis*, Ashgate, Brookfield, VT.

NOMIS, National on-Line Manpower Information Service, University of Durham, Durham.

Norcliffe, G. B. (1983), 'Using Location Quotients to Estimate the Economic Base and Trade Flows', *Regional Studies*, 17.3, 161–8.

Round, J. I. (1978), 'An Interregional Input–Output Approach to the Evaluation of Nonsurvey Techniques', *Journal of Regional Science*, 18.2, 179–94.

Schaffer, W., and Chu, K. (1969), 'Nonsurvey Techniques for Constructing Regional Interindustry Models', *Papers and Proceedings of the Regional Science Association*, 23, 35–50.

Sinclair, M. T. and Sutcliffe, C. M. S. (1978), 'The First Round of the Keynesian Regional Income Multiplier', *Scottish Journal of Political Economy*, 25.2, 177–85.

Sinclair, M. T., and Sutcliffe, C. M. S. (1983), 'Injection Leakages, Trade Repercussions and the Regional Income Multiplier: An Extension', *Scottish Journal of Political Economy*, 30.3, 275–86.

Smith, P., and Morrison, W. I. (1974), *Simulating the Urban Economy*, Pion, London.

Thorne, E. M. F. (1969), 'Regional Input–Output Analysis', in Orr, S. C., and Cullingworth, J. B., *Regional and Urban Studies*, George Allen and Unwin, London.

Ullman, E., and Dacey, M. (1960), 'The Minimum Requirements Approach to the Urban Economic Base', *Papers and Proceedings of the Regional Science Association*, 6, 174–94.

Weiss, S. J., and Gooding, E. C. (1968), 'Estimation of Differential Employment Multipliers in a Small Regional Economy', *Land Economics*, 44, 235–44.

Wilson, J. H. (1977), 'Impact Analysis and Multiplier Specification', *Growth and Change*, 8, 42–6.

Chapter 6

Anderson, J. E., and van Wincoop, E. (2003), 'Gravity with Gravitas: A Solution to the Border Puzzle', *American Economic Review*, 93.1, 170–92.

Anderson, J. E., and van Wincoop, E. (2004), 'Trade Costs', *Journal of Economic Literature*, 43.3, 691–751.

Becker, G. S. (1964), *Human Capital: A Theoretical and Empirical Analysis with Special Reference to Education*, Chicago University Press, Chicago, IL.

Biagi, B., Faggian, A., and McCann, P. (2011), 'Long and Short Distance Migration in Italy: The Role of Economic, Social and Environmental Characteristics', *Spatial Economic Analysis*, 6.1, 111–31.

Borjas, G. J. (1987), 'Self-Selection and the Earnings of Immigrants', *American Economic Review*, 77, 531–53.

Borjas, G. J. (2008), *Labour Economics* (4th edn), McGraw-Hill, New York.

Borts, G. H., and Stein, J. L. (1964), *Economic Growth in a Free Market*, Columbia University Press, New York.

Bover, O., Muellbauer, J., and Murphy, A. (1989), 'Housing, Wages and UK Labour Markets', *Oxford Bulletin of Economics and Statistics*, 51.2, 97–136.

Cheshire, P. C., and Magrini, S. (2006), 'Population Growth in European Cities: Weather Matters—but Only Nationally', *Regional Studies*, 40.1, 23–37.

Cheshire, P. C., and Sheppard, S .J. (1995)), 'On the Price of Land and the Value of Amenities', *Economica*, 62, 247–67.

Cheshire, P. C., and Sheppard, S. J. (1998), 'Estimating the Demand for Housing, Land, and Neighbourhood Characteristics', *Oxford Bulletin of Economics and Statistics*, 60.3, 357–82.

Chiang, A. C. (1984), *Fundamental Methods of Mathematical Economics*, McGraw-Hill, Singapore.

Christopherson, S., Michie, J., and Tyler, P. (2010), 'Regional Resilience: Theoretical and Empirical Perspectives', *Cambridge Journal of Regions, Economy and Society*, 3.1, 3–10.

Clower, R. W. (1965), 'The Keynesian Counter-Revolution: A Theoretical Appraisal', in Hahn, F. H., and Brechling, F. (eds), *The Theory of Interest Rates*, Macmillan, London.

DaVanzo, J. (1976), 'Differences between Return and Nonreturn Migration: An Econometric Analysis', *International Migration Review*, 13–27.

DaVanzo, J., and Morrison, P. A. (1981), 'Return and Other Sequences of Migration in the U.S.', *Demography*, 18, 85–101.

DaVanzo, J. (1983), 'Repeat Migration in the United States: Who Moves Back and Who Moves On?', *Review of Economics and Statistics*, 65, 552–9.

Duranton, G., and Puga, D. (2005), 'From Sectoral to Functional Urban Specialisation', *Journal of Urban Economics*, 57.2, 343–70.

Evans, A. W. (1990), 'The Assumption of Equilibrium in the Analysis of Migration and Interregional Differences', *Journal of Regional Science*, 30.4, 515–31.

Evans, A. W. (1993), 'Interregional Equilibrium: A Transatlantic View', *Journal of Regional Science*, 33.1, 89–97.

Faggian, A., and McCann, P. (2006), 'Human Capital Flows and Regional Knowledge Assets: A Simultaneous Equation Approach', *Oxford Economic Papers*, 58.3, 475–500.

Faggian, A., and McCann, P. (2009a), 'Human Capital, Graduate Migration and Innovation in British Regions', *Cambridge Journal of Economics*, 33.2, 317–33.

Faggian, A., and McCann, P. (2009b), 'Universities, Agglomerations and Graduate Human Capital Mobility', *TESG Journal of Economic and Social Geography*, 100.2, 210–23.

Faggian, A., and McCann, P. (2009c), 'Human Capital and Regional Development', in Capello, R., and Nijkamp, P. (eds), *Regional Dynamics and Growth: Advances in Regional Economics*, Edward Elgar, Cheltenham.

Faggian, A., McCann, P., and Sheppard, S. J. (2006), 'An Analysis of Ethnic Differences in UK Graduate Migration', *Annals of Regional Science*, 40.2, 461–71.

Faggian, A., McCann, P., and Sheppard, S. J. (2007a), 'Some Evidence that Women are More Mobile than Men: Gender Differences in UK Graduate Migration Behaviour', *Journal of Regional Science*, 47.3, 517–39.

Faggian, A., McCann, P., and Sheppard, S. J. (2000b), 'Human Capital, Higher Education and Graduate Migration: An Analysis of Scottish and Welsh Students', *Urban Studies*, 44.13, 2511–28.

Faggian, A., Corcoran, J., and McCann, P. (2010), 'Human Capital in Remote and Rural Australia: The Role of Graduate Migration', *Growth and Change*, 41.2, 192–220.

Fingleton, B., Garretsen, H., and Martin, R. (2012), 'Recessionary Shocks and Regional Employment: Evidence on the Resilience of U.K. Regions', *Journal of Regional Science*, 52.1, 109–33.

Fielding, A. J. (1992), 'Migration and the Metropolis: Recent Research on the Causes and Consequences of Migration to the Southeast of England', *Progress in Human Geography*, 17.2, 195–212.

Fujita, M., Krugman, P., and Venables, A. J. (1999), *The Spatial Economy*, MIT Press, Cambridge, MA.

Glaeser, E. L., Kolko, J., and Saiz, A. (2001), 'Consumer City', *Journal of Economic Geography*, 1.1, 27–50.

Gordon, I. R. (1978), 'Distance Deterrence and Commodity Values', *Environment and Planning A*, 10, 889–900.

Gordon, I. R. (1985), 'The Cyclical Sensitivity of Regional Employment and Unemployment Differentials', *Regional Studies*, 19.2, 95–110.

Gottlieb, J. D., and Glaeser, E. L. (2006), 'Urban Resurgence and the Consumer City', *Urban Studies*, 43.8, 1275–99.

Graves, P. E. (1980), 'Migration and Climate', *Journal of Regional Science*, 20.2, 227–37.

Graves, P. E. (1983), 'Migration with a Composite Amenity: The Role of Rents', *Journal of Regional Science*, 23.4, 541–6.

Hall, P. (1998), *Cities in Civilisation*, Weidenfeld and Nicolson, London.

Harris, J. R., and Todaro, M. P. (1970), 'Migration, Unemployment and Development: A Two-Sector Analysis', *American Economic Review*, 60.1, 126–42.

Hemmings, P. J. (1991), 'Regional Earnings Differences in Great Britain: Evidence from the New Earnings Survey', *Regional Studies*, 25.2, 123–33.

Hughes, G., and McCormick, B. (1981), 'Do Council House Policies Reduce Migration between Regions?', *Economic Journal*, 91, 919–37.

Hunt, G. L. (1993), 'Equilibrium and Disequilibrium Migration Modelling', *Regional Studies*, 27.4, 341–9.

Isard, W., Azis, I. J., Drennan, M. P., Miller, R. E., Saltzman, S., and Thorbecke, E. (1998), *Methods of Interregional and Regional Analysis*, Ashgate, Brookfield, VT.

Jacobs, J. (1960), *The Economy of Cities*, Random House, New York.

Krugman, P. (1999), *The Return of Depression Economics*, Norton, New York.

Krugman, P. (2009), *The Return of Depression Economics and the Crisis of 2008*, Norton, New York.

Martin, R. (2012), 'Regional Economic Resilience, Hysteresis and Recessionary Shocks', *Journal of Economic Geography*, 12.1, 1–32.

McCann, P., Poot, J., and Sanderson, L. (2010), 'Migration, Relationship Capital and International Travel: Theory and Evidence', *Journal of Economic Geography*, 10.3, 361–87.

McCombie, J. S. L. (1988), A Synoptic View of Regional Growth and Unemployment: I—The Neoclassical Theory', *Urban Studies*, 25, 267–81.

Mellander, C., Florida, R., and Stolarick, K. (2011), 'Here to Stay—The Effects of Community Satisfaction on the Decision to Stay', *Spatial Economic Analysis*, 6.1, 5–24.

Mincer, J. (1974), *Schooling, Experience, and Earnings*, Columbia University Press, New York.

Minford, P., Ashton, P., and Peel, M. (1988), 'The Effects of Housing Distortions on Unemployment', *Oxford Economic Papers*, 40, 322–45.

Molho, I. (1986), 'Theories of Migration: A Review', *Scottish Journal of Political Economy*, 33, 396–419.

OECD (2011), *Regions at a Glance 2011*, Organisation for Economic Cooperation and Development, Paris.

Partridge, M. D. (2010), 'The Duelling Models: NEG vs Amenity Migration in Explaining US Engines of Growth', *Papers in Regional Science*, 89.3, 513–36.

Partridge, M. D., Rickman, D. S., Olfert, M. R., and Ali, K. (2012), 'Dwindling U.S. Internal Migration: Evidence of Spatial Equilibrium', *Regional Science and Urban Economics*, 42.2, 375–88.

Plane, D. A. (1983), 'Demographic Influences on Migration', *Regional Studies*, 27.4, 375–83.

Quah, D. (1997), 'Empirics for Growth and Distribution: Polarization, Stratification, and Convergence Clubs,' *Journal of Economic Growth*, 2.1, 27–59.

Roback, J. (1982), 'Wages, Rents, and the Quality of Life', *Journal of Political Economy*, 90.6, 1257–78.

Roy, A. D. (1951), 'Some Thoughts on the Distribution of Earnings,' *Oxford Economic Papers*, 3, 135–46.

Shapiro, J. M. (2006), 'Smart Cities: Quality of Life, Productivity, and the Growth Effects of Human

Capital', *Review of Economics and Statistics*, 88.2, 324–35.

Simmie, J., and Martin, R. (2010), 'The Economic Resilience of Regions: Towards an Evolutionary Approach', *Cambridge Journal of Regions, Economy and Society*, 3.1, 27–43.

Stoneman, P. (1983), *The Economic Analysis of Technological Change*, Oxford University Press, Oxford.

Storper, M., and Kemeny, T. (2012), 'The Sources of Urban Development: Wages, Housing, and Amenity Gaps Across American Cities', *Journal of Regional Science*, 52.1, 85–108.

Tiebout, C. M. (1956), 'A Pure Theory of Local Expenditures', *Journal of Political Economy*, 64.5, 416–24.

Thirlwall, A. P. (1994), *Growth and Development* (5th edn), Macmillan, Basingstoke.

Vanclay, F., Higgins, M., and Blackshaw, A. (2008), *Making Sense of Place: Exploring Concepts and Expressions of Place Through Different Senses and Lenses*, National Museum of Australia Press, Canberra.

Wilson, A. G. (1974), *Urban and Regional Models in Geography and Planning*, Wiley, London.

Chapter 7

Acemoglu, D., and Robinson, J.A. (2000), 'Political Losers as a Barrier to Economic Development', *American Economic Review*, 90.2, 126–30.

Acemoglu, D., and Johnson, S. H. (2006a), 'De Facto Political Power and Institutional Persistence', *American Economic Review*, 96.2, 325–30.

Acemoglu, D., and Johnson, S. H. (2006b), 'Unbundling Institutions', *Journal of Political Economy*, 113.5, 949–95.

Acs, Z. J., Audretsch, D. B., and Feldman, M. A. (1992), 'Real Effects of Academic Research', *American Economic Review*, 82, 678–90.

Aghion, P., and Howitt, P. (1992), 'A Model of Growth through Creative Destruction', *Econometrica*, 60, 323–51.

Aghion, P., and Howitt, P. (2009), *The Economics of Growth*, MIT Press, Cambridge, MA.

Andersson, D. E., Andersson, Å. E., and Mellander, C. (2011) *Handbook of Creative Cities*, Edward Elgar, Cheltenham.

Arrow, K. J. (1962), 'The Economic Implications of Learning by Doing', *Review of Economic Studies*, 29, 155–73.

Arezki, R., Candelon, B., and Sy, A. N. R. (2011), 'Are There Spillover Effects from Munis?', IMF Working Paper, WP/11/290, International Monetary Fund, Washington, DC.

Barro, R. J., and Sala-i-Martin, X. (1992), 'Convergence', *Journal of Political Economy*, 100, 223–51.

Barro, R. J., and Sala-i-Martin, X. (1995), *Economic Growth*, McGraw-Hill, New York.

Bathelt, H. (2008), 'Knowledge-Based Clusters: Regional Multiplier Models and the Role of "Buzz" and "Pipelines"', in Karlsson, C. (ed.), *Handbook of Research on Cluster Theory*, Edward Elgar, Cheltenham and Northampton, MA.

Bathelt, H., Malmberg, A. and Maskell, P. (2004), 'Clusters and Knowledge: Local Buzz, Global Pipelines and the Process of Knowledge Creation', *Progress in Human Geography*, 28.1, 31–56.

Berg, A. G., and Ostry, J. D. (2011), 'Inequality and Unsustainable Growth: Two Sides of the Same Coin', IMF Staff Discussion Note, SDN/11/08, International Monetary Fund, Washington, DC.

Black, F. (2010), *Exploring General Equilibrium*, MIT Press, Cambridge, MA.

Boulier, B. L. (1984), 'What Lies behind Verdoorn's Law?', *Oxford Economic Papers*, 36, 259–67.

Borts, G. H., and Stein, J. L. (1964), *Economic Growth in a Free Market*, Columbia University Press, New York.

Boschma, R. A. (2005), 'Proximity and Innovation: A Critical Assessment', *Regional Studies*, 39.1, 61–74.

Boschma, R. A., and Iammarino, S. (2009), 'Related Variety, Trade Linkages and Regional Growth', *Economic Geography*, 85.3, 289–311.

Boschma, R., and Frenken, K. (2011), 'Technological Relatedness and Regional Branching', in Bathelt, H., Feldman, M. P., and Kogler, D. F. (eds), *Dynamic Geographies of Knowledge Creation and Innovation*, Taylor and Francis, Routledge, London.

Boschma, R. A., Minondo, A., and Navarro, M. (2012), 'Related Variety and Regional Grwoth in Spain', *Papers in Regional Science*, forthcoming.

Button, K. J., and Pentecost, E. J.,(1999), *Regional Economic Performance within the European Union*, Edward Elgar, Cheltenham.

Cantwell, J., and Iammarino, S. (2000), 'Multinational Corporations and the Location of Technological Innovation in the UK Regions', *Regional Studies*, 34.4, 317–32.

Cheshire, P., and Carbonaro, G. (1995), 'Convergence–Divergence in Regional Growth Rates: An Empty Black Box?', in Armstrong, H. W., and Vickerman, R. W. (eds) *Convergence and Divergence among European Regions*, Pion, London.

Cheshire, P., and Carbonaro, G. (1996), 'Urban Economic Growth ain Europe: Testing Theory and Policy Prescriptions', *Urban Studies*, 33.7, 1111–28.

Christopherson, S., Michie, J., and Tyler, P. (2010), 'Regional Resilience: Theoretical and Empirical Perspectives', *Cambridge Journal of Regions, Economy and Society*, 3.1, 3–10.

Crocco, M., Santos, F., and Amaral, P. (2010), 'The Spatial Structure of Financial Development in Brazil', *Spatial Economic Analysis*, 5.2, 181–203.

David, P. A. (1981), 'Clio and the Economics of QWERTY', *American Economic Review: Papers and Proceedings*, 75.2, 332–7.

Davidson, P. (1994), *Post-Keynesian Macroeconomic Theory*, Edward Elgar, Cheltenham.

Dixon, R. J., and Thirlwall, A. P. (1975), *Regional Growth and Unemployment in the United Kingdom*, Macmillan, London.

Doloreux, D., and Shearmur, R. (2012), 'Collaboration, Information and the Geography of Innovation in Knowledge Intensive Business Services', *Journal of Economic Geography*, 12.1, 79–105.

Dosi, G. (1988), 'Sources, Procedures and Microeconomic Effects of Innovation', *Journal of Economic Literature*, 26.3, 1120–71.

Dow, S. C. (1982), 'The Regional Composition of the Money Multiplier Process', *Scottish Journal of Political Economy*, 29.1, 22–44.

Dow, S. C. (1987), 'The Treatment of Money in Regional Economics', *Journal of Regional Science*, 27.1, 13–24.

Dow, S. C. (1997), 'Regional Finance: A Survey', *Regional Studies*, 31.9, 903–20.

Dow, S. C., Montagnoli, A., and Napolitano, O. (2012), 'Interest Rates and Convergence Across Italian Regions', Regional Stduies, 46.7, 893–905.

Durlauf, S. N., and Quah, D. (1999), 'The New Empirics of Economic Growth', in Taylor, J. B., and Woodford, M. (eds), *Handbook of Macroeconomics*, North-Holland, Amsterdam.

Felipe, J. (1998), 'The Role of the Manufacturing Sector in Southeast Asian Development: A Test of Kaldor's First Law', *Journal of Post Keynesian Economics*, 20.3, 463–85.

Felipe, J., and McCombie, J. S .L. (2012), 'Problems with Regional Production Functions and Estimates of Agglomeration Economies: A Caveat Emptor for Regional Scientists', *Spatial Economic Analysis*, 7.4, 461–84.

Fingleton, B. (1997), 'Specification and Testing of Markov Chain Models: An Application to Convergence in the European Union', *Oxford Bulletin of Economics and Statistics*, 59.3, 385–403.

Fingleton, B., and McCombie, J. S. L. (1998), 'Increasing Returns and Economic Growth: Some Evidence for Manufacturing from the European Union', *Oxford Economic Papers*, 51.3, 574–80.

Fingleton, B., Garretsen, H., and Martin, R. (2012), 'Recessionary Shocks and Regional Employment: Evidence on the Resilience of U.K. Regions', *Journal of Regional Science*, 52.1, 109–33.

Florida, R. (2002a), *The Rise of the Creative Class*, Basic Books, New York.

Florida, R. (2002b), *The Flight of the Creative Class: The New Competition for Global Talent*, Harper Business, New York.

Frenken, K., and Boschma, R. A. (2007), 'A Theoretical Framework for Evolutionary Economic Geography: Industrial Dynamics and Urban Growth as a Branching Process', *Journal of Economic Geography* 7.5, 635–49.

Frenken, K., Van Oort, F. G., and Verburg, T. (2007), 'Related Variety, Unrelated Variety and Regional Economic Growth', *Regional Studies*, 41.5, 685–97.

Gomulka, S. (1971), *Inventive Activity, Diffusion, and Stages of Economic Growth*, Aarhus University Press, Aarhus.

Hess, G. D., and van Wincoop, E. (eds) (2000), *Intranational and International Macroeconomics*, Cambridge University Press, Cambridge.

Heritage Foundation (2009), *2009 Index of Economic Freedom: The Link Between Economic Opportunity and Prosperity*, Heritage Books, Washington, DC.

Jaffe, A. B., Trajtenberg, M., and Henderson, R. (1993), 'Geographic Localization of Knowledge Spillovers as Evidenced by Patent Citations', *Quarterly Journal of Economics*, 108, 577–98.

Kaldor, N. (1975), 'Economic Growth and the Verdoorn Law', *Economic Journal*, 85, 891–6.

Krugman, P. (1989), 'Differences in Income Elasticities and Trends in Real Exchange Rates', *European Economic Review*, 33.5, 1031–46.

Lavoie, M. (1992), *Foundations of Post-Keynesian Economic Analysis*, Edward Elgar, Cheltenham.

Lucas, R. E. (1988), 'On the Mechanics of Economic Development', *Journal of Monetary Economics*, 22, 3–42.

Martin, R., and Sunley, P. (1998), 'Slow Convergence? The New Endogenous Growth Theory and Economic Development', *Economic Geography*, 74, 201–27.

McCann, P. (2007), 'Sketching out a Model of Innovation, Face-to-Face Interaction and Economic Geography', *Spatial Economic Analysis*, 2.2, 117–34.

McCann, P., and Acs, Z. J. (2011), 'Globalisation: Countries, Cities and Multinationals', *Regional Studies*, 45.1, 17–32.

McCombie, J. S. L., and Roberts, M. (2007), 'Returns to Scale and Regional Growth: The Static–Dynamic Verdoorn Law Paradox Revisited', *Journal of Regional Science*, 47.2, 179–208.

McCombie, J. S .L., and Thirlwall, A. P. (1994), *Economic Growth and the Balance-of-Payments Constraint*, Macmillan, Basingstoke.

Neffke, F., Henning, M., and Boschma, R. (2011), 'The Impact of Aging and Technological Relatedness on Agglomeration Externalities: A Survival Analysis', *Journal of Economic Geography*, forthcoming.

Nijkamp, P., and Poot, J. (1998), 'Spatial Perspectives on New Theories of Economic Growth', *Annals of Regional Science*, 32.1, 7–38.

OECD (2009a), *How Regions Grow: Trends and Analysis*, Organisation for Economic Cooperation and Development, Paris.

OECD (2009b), *Regions Matter: Economic Recovery, Innovation and Sustainable Growth*, Organisation for Economic Cooperation and Development, Paris.

Porter, M. E. (1990), *The Competitive Advantage of Nations*, Free Press, New York.

Putnam, R. (1993), *Making Democracy Work: Civic Traditions in Modern Italy*, Princeton University Press, Princeton, NJ.

Putnam. R. (1996), *Bowling Alone: The Collapse and Revival of American Community*, Simon and Schuster, New York.

Quah, D. (1997), 'Empirics for Growth and Distribution: Stratification, Polarization, and Convergence Clubs', *Journal of Economic Growth*, 2.1, 27–59.

Ramos, P. (2007), 'Does the Trade Balance Really Matter for Regions?', *Annals of Regional Science*, 41.1, 229–43.

Richardson, H. W. (1978), *Regional Economics*, University of Illinois Press, Urbana, IL.

Romer, P. M. (1986), 'Increasing Returns and Long-Run Growth', *Journal of Political Economy*, 94, 1002–37.

Romer, P. M. (1987a), 'Growth Based on Increasing Returns due to Specialization', *American Economic Review*, 77.2, 56–62.

Romer, P. M. (1987b), 'Crazy Explanations of the Productivity Slowdown', *National Bureau of Economic Research Macroeconomics Annual 1987*, MIT Press, Cambridge, MA.

Rowthorn, R. E. (1975), 'What Remains of Kaldor's Law?', *Economic Journal*, 85, 10–19.

Schumpeter, J. A. (1934), *The Theory of Economic Development*, Harvard University Press, Cambridge, MA.

Scott, M. (1989), *A New View of Economic Growth*, Clarendon Press, Oxford.

Shearmur, R., and Polèse, M. (2007), 'Do Local Factors Explain Local Employment Growth? Evidence from Canada, 1971–2001', *Regional Studies*, 41.4, 453–71.

Solow, R. M. (1956), 'A Contribution to the Theory of Economic Growth', *Quarterly Journal of Economics*, 70, 65–94.

Solow, R. M. (1994), 'Perspectives on Growth Theory', *Journal of Economic Perspectives*, 8, 45–54.

Stern, N. (2009), *A Blueprint for a Safer Planet: How to Manage Climate Change and Create a New Era of Progress and Prosperity*, Bodley Head, London.

Stiglitz, J. E., Sen, A., and Fitoussi, J.-P. (2009), *Commission of the Measurement of Economic Performance and Social Progress*, http://www.stiglitz-sen-fitoussi.fr/en/index.htm

Swan, T. (1956), 'Economic Growth and Capital Accumulation', *Economic Record*, 32, 334–61.

Tabellini, G. (2010), 'Culture and Institutions: Economic Development in the Regions of Europe', *Journal of the European Economic Association*, 8, 677–716.

Thirlwall, A. P. (1980), 'Regional Problems are "Balance of Payments" Problems', *Regional Studies*, 14, 419–25.

Verdoorn, P. J. (1949), 'Fattori che regolano lo sviluppo della produttivita del lavoro', *L'Industria*, 1, 3–10, trans. by Thirlwall, A. P., and Ironmonger, D., in Perkins, J., and Hoa, T. (eds) (1988), *National Income and Economic Progress: Essays in Honour of Colin Clark*, Macmillan, London.

Westlund, H. (2006), *Social Capital and the Knowledge Economy: Theory and Empirics*, Springer, Berlin.

Williamson, O. E. (1975), *Markets and Hierarchies*, Free Press, New York.

World Bank (2009), *Doing Business 2009: Comparing Regulation in 181 Countries*, Washington, DC.

World Bank (2010), *World Development Report 2010: Development and Climate Change*, World Bank, Washington, DC.

Chapter 8

Abrahamson, M. (2004), *Global Cities*, Oxford University Press, Oxford.

Alesina, A., and Spolaore, E. (2003), *The Size of Nations*, MIT Press, Cambridge, MA.

Benjamin, T. (2009), *The Atlantic World: Europeans, Africans, Indians and Their Shared History, 1400–1900*, Cambridge University Press, Cambridge.

Burdett, R., Taylor, M., and Kaasa, A. (eds) (2011), *Cities, Health and Wellbeing*, Proceedings of the Hong Kong Urban Age Conference, 16–17 November, LSE Cities, London.

Cairncross, F. (1997), *The Death of Distance: How The Communications Revolution will Change our Lives*, Orion Business Books, London.

Chandler, T. (1987), *Four Thousand Years of Urban Growth: An Historical Census*, The Edwin Mellen Press, Lampeter, UK.

Christaller, W. (1933), *Die Zentralen Orte in Suddeutschland*, Fischer, Jena, trans. by Baskin, C. W. (1966), *Central Places in Southern Germany*, Prentice-Hall, Englewood Cliffs, NJ.

Cohen, B. J. (1998), *The Geography of Money*, Cornell University Press, Ithaca, NY.

Coleman, W. D. (1996), *Financial Services, Globalization and Domestic Policy Change*, Macmillan, London.

Crafts, N. (2004), 'Globalization and Economic Growth: A Historical Perspective', *The World Economy*, 27.1, 45–58.

European Commission (2010), *Survey on Perception of Quality of Life in 75 European Cities*, Directorate General for Regional Policy, Brussels.

Ferguson, N. (2008), *The Ascent of Money: A Financial History of the World*, Allen Lane, London.

Ferguson, N. (2011), *Civilization: The West and the Rest*, Penguin Press, New York.

Findlay, R., and O'Rourke, K. (2007), *Power and Plenty: Trade, War, and the World Economy in the Second Millennium*, Princeton University Press, Princeton, NJ.

Fischer, S. (2003), 'Globalization and its Challenges', *American Economic Review: Papers and Proceedings*, 93.2, 1–30.

Foslter, R. S., Alonso, W., Meyer, J. A., and Kern, R. (1990), *Demographic Change and the American Future*, University of Pittsburgh Press, Pittsburgh, PA.

Fothergill, S., Kitson, M., and Monk, S. (1985), *Urban Industrial Decline: The Causes of Urban/Rural Contrasts in Manufacturing Employment Change*, HMSO, London.

Friedman, T.L. (2007), *The World is Flat: A Brief History of the Twenty-First Century* (3rd edn), Picador, New York.

Gaspar, J., and Glaeser, E .L. (1998), 'Information Technology and the Future of Cities', *Journal of Urban Economics*, 43, 136–56.

Glaeser, E. L. (1998), 'Are Cities Dying?', *Journal of Economic Perspectives*, 12.2, 139–60.

Glaeser, E. L. (2005), 'Urban Colossus: Why is New York America's Largest City?', *Economic Policy Review: Urban Dynamics in New York*, Federal Reserve Bank of New York, New York.

Glaeser, E. L. (2011), *Triumph of the City: How Our Greatest Invention Makes Us Richer, Smarter, Greener, Healthier, and Happier*, The Penguin Press, New York.

Glaeser, E. L. and Gottlieb, J. D. (2009), 'The Wealth of Cities: Agglomeration Economies and Spatial Equilibrium in the United States', *Journal of Economic Literature*, 47.4, 983–1028.

Hall, P. (1966), *The World Cities*, Weidenfeld and Nicolson, London.

Hall, P. (1988), *Cities of Tomorrow*, Blackwell, Oxford.

Hall, P. (1998), *Cities in Civilisation*, Weidenfeld and Nicolson, London.

Hoover, E. M. (1937), *Location Theory and the Shoe and Leather Industries*, Harvard University Press, Cambridge, MA.

Kali, R., and Reyes, J. (2006), 'The Architecture of Globalization: A Network Approach to International Economic Integration', Working Paper: Department of Economics, University of Arkansas.

Le Gales, P. (2002), *European Cities*, Oxford University Press, Oxford.

Levinson, M. (2006), *The Box: How the Shipping Container Made the World Smaller and the World Economy Bigger*, Princeton University Press, Princeton, NJ.

MacGillivray, A. (2006), *A Brief History of Globalization*, Robinson, London.

Maddison, A. (2006), *The World Economy. Volume 1: A Millennial Perspective Volume 2: Historical Statistics*, Organisation for Economic Cooperation and Development, Paris.

Maddison, A. (2007a), *Contours of the World Economy 1–2030: Essays in Macro-Economic History*, Oxford University Press, Oxford.

Maddison, A. (2007b), *Chinese Economic Performance in the Long Run, Second Edition Revised and Updated 960–2030AD*, Organisation for Economic Cooperation and Development, Paris.

Marshall, A. (1890), *Principles of Economics* (1st edn), Macmillan, London.

McCann, P. (2008), 'Globalization and Economic Geography: The World is Curved, Not Flat', *Cambridge Journal of Regions, Economy and Society*, 1.3, 351–70.

McCann, P., and Acs, Z. J. (2011), 'Globalisation: Countries, Cities and Multinationals', *Regional Studies*, 45.1, 17–32.

McDonald, J. F. (2008), *Urban America: Growth, Crisis and Rebirth*, M.E. Sharpe, New York.

MGI (2009), *Preparing for China's Urban Billion*, McKinsey Global Institute.

MGI (2010), *India's Urban Awakening: Building Inclusive Cities, Sustaining Economic Growth*, McKinsey Global Institute.

MGI (2011a), *Urban World: Mapping the Economic Power of Cities*, McKinsey Global Institute.

MGI (2011b), *Building Globally Competitive Cities: The Key to Latin American Growth*, McKinsey Global Institute.

Modelski, G. (2003), *World Cities – 3000 to 2000*, Faros 2000, Washington, DC.

Ni, P., and Kresl, P. K. (2010), *The Global Urban Competitiveness Report 2010*, Edward Elgar, Cheltenham.

O'Brien, R. (1992), *Global Financial Integration: The End of Geography*, Council on Foreign Relations Press, New York.

OECD (2006), *Competitive Cities in the Global Economy*, Organisation for Economic Cooperation and Development, Paris.

OECD (2007), *International Investment Perspectives: Freedom of Investment in a Changing World*, Organisation for Economic Cooperation and Development, Paris.

OECD (2009), *Globalisation and Emerging Economies: Brazil, Russia, India, Indonesia, China and South Africa*, Organisation for Economic Cooperation and Development, Paris.

OECD (2012), *Redefining Urban: Functional Urban Areas in OECD Countries*, Organisation for Economic Cooperation and Development, Paris.

Ohlin, B. (1933), *Interregional and International Trade*, Harvard University Press, Cambridge, MA.

Peri, G. (2005), 'Determinants of Knowledge Flows and their Effect on Innovation', *Review of Economics and Statistics*, 87.2, 308–22.

Polèse, M. (2009), *The Wealth and Poverty of Nations: Why Cities Matter*, University of Chicago Press, Chicago, IL.

PWC (2009), 'Which are the Largest City Economies in the World and Might this Change by 2025?', *UK Economic Outlook November*, Price Waterhouse Coopers, London.

Reyes, J. A., Garcia, M., and Lattimore, R. (2009), 'The International Economic Order and Trade Architecture', *Spatial Economic Analysis*, 4.1, 73–102.

Richardson, H. W., and Bae, C. H. C. (eds), *Globalization and Urban Development*; Springer, Heidelberg.

Rugman, A. (2000), *The End of Globalization*, Random House, New York.

Rugman, A. (2005), *The Regional Multinationals*, Cambridge University Press, Cambridge.

Sassen, S. (1994), *Cities in a World Economy*, Pine Forge Press, Thousand Oaks, CA.

Sassen, S. (2001), *The Global City: New York, London, Tokyo*, Princeton University Press, Princeton, NJ.

Sassen, S. (2002) (ed.), *Global Networks: Linked Cities*, Routledge, London.

Sassen, S. (2006), *Cities in a World Economy* (3rd edn), Pine Forge Press, Thousand Oaks, CA.

Satterthwaite, D. (2005), *The Scale of Urban Change Worldwide 1950–2000 and its Underpinnings*, International Institute for Environment and Development, London.

Steger, M. B. (2003), *Globalization: A Very Short Introduction*, Oxford University Press, Oxford.

Taylor, P. J. (2004), *World City Network: A Global Urban Analysis*, Routledge, London.

UNCTAD (2003), *World Investment Report: FDI Policies for Development: National and International Perspectives*, United Nations Conference on Trade and Development, United Nations, New York and Geneva.

UNDP (2009), *Human Development Report 2009: Overcoming Barriers: Human Mobility and Development*, United Nations Development Program, Palgrave Macmillan, Basingstoke.

UNFPA (2007), *State of the World's Population: Unleashing the Potential of Urban Growth*, United Nations Population Fund, New York.

Venables, A. J. (2006), 'Shifts in Economic Geography and their Causes', *Federal Reserve Bank of Kansas City Economic Review*, 91.4, 61–85.

Warf, B. (1995), 'Telecommunications and the Clustering Geographies of Knowledge Transmission in the Late 20th Century', *Urban Studies*, 32.2, 361–78.

Weber, A. (1909), *Über den Standort der Industrien*, trans. by Friedrich, C. J. (1929), *Alfred Weber's Theory of the Location of Industries*, University of Chicago Press, Chicago, IL.

World Bank (2008), *World Trade Indicators 2000: Benchmarking Policy and Performance*, Washington, DC.

Zenou, Y. (2009), *Urban Labor Economics*, Cambridge University Press, Cambridge.

Zook, M. A., (2005), *The Geography of the Internet*, Blackwell, Oxford.

Chapter 9

Abreu, M., Comunian, R., Faggian, A., and McCann, P. (2011) '"Life is Short, Art is Long": The Persistent Wage Gap between Bohemian and non-Bohemian Graduates and Occupations', *Annals of Regional Science*, forthcoming.

Acs, Z. J. (2002), *Innovation and the Growth of Cities*, Edward Elgar, Cheltenham.

Acs, Z. J., Bosma, N., and Sterberg, R. (2008), *The Entrepreneurial Advantage of World Cities: Evidence from Global Entrepreneurship Monitor Data*, Working Paper, H(2008)10, SCALES, University of Utrecht and Netherlands Ministry of Economic Affairs.

Aguilera, A. (2008), 'Business Travel and Mobile Workers', *Transportation Research A*, 42, 1109–16.

Aitken, B., Hanson, G., and Harrison, A. E. (1997), 'Spillovers, Foreign Investment, and Export Behaviour', *Journal of International Economics*, 43, 103–32.

Andersson, M. (2009), 'External Trade and Internal Geography', CESIS Working Paper, Jönköping University, Jönköping and Royal Institute of Technology, Stockholm, Sweden.

Anselin, L., Varga, A., and Acs, Z. J. (1997). 'Local Geographic Spillovers between University Research and High Technology Innovations', *Journal of Urban Economics*, 42, 442–8.

Ante, S. E. (2009), *Creative Capital: Georges Doriot and the Birth of Venture Capital*, Harvard Business School Press, Cambridge. MA.

Arita, T., and McCann, P. (2000), 'Industrial Alliances and Firm Location Behaviour: Some Evidence from the US Semiconductor Industry', *Applied Economics*, 32, 1391–403.

Arita, T., and McCann, P. (2006), 'Clusters and Regional Development: Some Cautionary Observations from the Semiconductor Industry', *Information Economics and Policy*, 18.2, 157–80.

Arora, A., and Forman, C. (2007), 'How Local are IT Services Markets? Proximity and IT Outsourcing', *Journal of Management Information Systems*, 24.2, 73–102.

Bel, G., and Fageda, X. (2008), 'Getting there Fast: Globalization, Intercontinental Flights and Location of Headquarters', *Journal of Economic Geography*, 8, 471–95.

Berry and Glaeser, E. L. (2005), 'The Divergence of Human Capital Levels across Cities', *Papers in Regional Science*, 84.3, 407–44.

Best, M. H. (1990), *The New Competition: Institutions of Industrial Restructuring*, Polity Press, Cambridge.

Blum, B. B., and Goldfarb, A. (2006), 'Does the Internet Defy the Law of Gravity?', *Journal of International Economics*, 70.2, 384–405.

Boulhol, H., and de Serres, A. (2010), 'Have Countries Escaped the Curse of Distance?', *Journal of Economic Geography*, 10.1, 113–39.

Brakman, S., and van Marrewijk, C. (2008), 'It's a Big World After All: On the Economic Impact of Location and Distance', *Cambridge Journals of Regions, Economy and Society*, 1, 411–37.

Broersma, L., and Van Dijk, J. (2008), 'The Effect of Congestion and Agglomeration on MFP-growth in Dutch Regions', *Journal of Economic Geography*, 8.2, 181–209.

BTRE (2004), *Focus on Regions 3: Taxable Income*, Bureau of Transport and Regional Economics, Canberra, Australia.

Burghouwt, G. (2005), *Airline Network Development in Europe and its Implications for Airport Planning*, Utrecht University Press, Netherlands.

Button, K., Lall, S., Stough, R., and Trice, M. (1999), 'High-Technology Employment and Hub Airports', *Journal of Air Transport Management*, 5, 53–9.

Button, K., Stough, R., Bragg, M. and Taylor, S. (2006), *Telecommunications, Transportation and Location*, Edward Elgar, Cheltenham.

Caniels, M. C. J. (2000), *Knowledge Spillovers and Economic Growth: Regional Growth Differences across Europe*, Edward Elgar, Cheltenham.

Caniels, M., and Verspagen, B. (2003), 'Spatial Distance in a Technology Gap Model', in Fingleton, B. (ed.), *European Regional Growth*, Springer, Heidelberg.

Cappelen, A., Castellacci, F., Fagerberg, J., and Verspagen, B. (2003), 'Regional Disparities in Income and Unemployment in Europe', in Fingleton, B. (ed.), *European Regional Growth*, Springer, Heidelberg.

Carlino, G. A., Chatterjee, S., and Hunt, R. M. (2007), 'Urban Density and the Rate of Invention', *Journal of Urban Economics*, 61.3, 389–419.

Chatterji, L., and Tsai, C.-M. (2006), 'Transport Logistics in the Global Economy: Spatial Implications', in Kobayashi, K., Lakshmanan, T. R., and Anderson, W. P. (eds), *Structural Change in Transportation and Communications in the Knowledge Society*, Edward Elgar, Cheltenham.

Chen, N. (2004), 'Intra-National versus International Trade in the European Union: Why Do National Borders Matter?', *Journal of International Economics*, 63, 93–118.

Ciccone, A. and Hall, R. E. (1996), 'Productivity and the Density of Economic Activity', *American Economic Review*, 86, 54–70.

COL (2002), *Aviation Services for London*, Corporation of London, London.

COL (2005a), *The Competitive Position of London as a Global Financial Centre*, Corporation of London, London.

COL (2005b), *Off-shoring and the City of London*, Corporation of London, London.

COL (2006), *The Importance of Wholesale Financial Services to the EU Economy 2006*, Corporation of London, London.

COL (2007), *The Impact of Recent Immigration on the London Economy*, Corporation of London, London.

COL (2008), *The Global Financial Centres Index 3*, Corporation of London, London.

COL (2009), *The Global Financial Centres Index 6*, Corporation of London, London.

Combes, P.-P., and Lafourcade, M. (2005), 'Transport Costs: Measures, Determinants, and Regional Policy Implications for France', *Journal of Economic Geography*, 319–49.

Crafts, N. (2004), 'Globalization and Economic Growth: A Historical Perspective', *The World Economy*, 27.1, 45–58.

Deardorff, A. (2003), 'Time and Trade: The Role of Time in Determining the Structure and Effects of International Trade with an Application to Japan', in Stern, R. M. (ed.), *Analytical Studies in US–Japan International Economic Relations*, Edward Elgar, Cheltenham.

Dijkstra, L., Garcilazo, E., and McCann, P. (2012), 'The Economic Performance of European Cities and City-Regions: Myths and Realities', *European Planning Studies*, forthcoming DOI:10.1080/09654313.(2012).716245.

Disdier, A.-C., and Head, K. (2007), 'The Puzzling Persistence of the Distance Effect on Bilateral Trade', *Review of Economics and Statistics*, 90.1, 37–48.

Doloreux, D., and Shearmur, R. (2012), 'Collaboration, Information and the Geography of Innovation in Knowledge Intensive Business Services', *Journal of Economic Geography*, 12.1, 79–105.

Duranton, G., and Storper, M. (2008), 'Rising Trade Costs? Agglomeration and Trade with Endogenous Transaction Costs', *Canadian Journal of Economics*, 41.1, 291–319.

Faggian, A., and McCann, P. (2006), 'Human Capital Flows and Regional Knowledge Assets: A Simultaneous Equation Approach', *Oxford Economic Papers*, 58.3, 475–500.

Faggian, A., and McCann, P. (2009), 'Human Capital, Graduate Migration and Innovation in British Regions', *Cambridge Journal of Economics*, 33.2, 317–33.

Fingleton, B. (ed.) (2003a), *European Regional Growth*, Springer, Heidelberg.

Fingleton, B. (2003b), 'Increasing Returns: Evidence from Local Wage Rates in Great Britain', *Oxford Economic Papers*, 55, 716–39.

Florida, R. (2002a), *The Rise of the Creative Class*, Basic Books, New York.

Florida, R. (2002b), *The Flight of the Creative Class: The New Competition for Global Talent*, Harper Business, New York.

Frankel, J. A., and Romer, D. (1999), 'Does Trade Cause Growth?', *American Economic Review*, 89.3, 379–99.

Friedman, T. L. (2007), *The World is Flat: A Brief History of the Twenty-First Century* (3rd edn), Picador, New York.

Fujita, M., Krugman, P., and Venables, A. J. (1999), *The Spatial Economy: Cities Regions and International Trade*, MIT Press, Cambridge, MA.

Garcilazo, E., and Oliveira Martins, J. (2010), 'The Contributions of Regions to Aggregate Growth', Paper Presented at the ERSA Conference, Jönköping, Sweden.

Gaspar, J., and Glaeser, E. L. (1998), 'Information Technology and the Future of Cities', *Journal of Urban Economics*, 43, 136–56.

Glaeser, E. L. (2005), 'Urban Colossus: Why is New York America's Largest City?', *Economic Policy Review: Urban Dynamics in New York*, Federal Reserve Bank of New York, New York.

Glaeser, E. L. (2011), *Triumph of the City: How Our Greatest Invention Makes Us Richer, Smarter, Greener, Healthier, and Happier*, Penguin Press, New York.

Glaeser, E. L., and Gottlieb, J. D. (2009), 'The Wealth of Cities: Agglomeration Economies and Spatial Equilibrium in the United States', *Journal of Economic Literature*, 47.4, 983–1028.

Glaeser, E. L., and Kohhase, J. (2004), 'Cities, Regions and the Decline of Transport Costs', *Papers in Regional Science*, 83.1, 197–228.

Glaeser, E. L. and Shapiro, J. M. (2003), 'Urban Growth in the 1990s: Is City Living Back?', *Journal of Regional Science*, 43.1, 139–65.

Glaeser, E. L., Scheinkman, J. A., and Shleifer, A. (1995), 'Economic Growth in a Cross Section of Cities', *Journal of Monetary Economics*, 36, 117–43.

Glaeser, E. L., Kolko, J., and Saiz, A. (2001), 'Consumer City', *Journal of Economic Geography*, 1.1, 27–50.

Gottlieb, J. D., and Glaeser, E. L. (2006), 'Urban Resurgence and the Consumer City', *Urban Studies*, 43.8, 1275–99.

Greunz, L. (2003), 'The Technology Gap and European Regional Growth Dynamics', in Fingleton, B. (ed.), *European Regional Growth*, Springer, Heidelberg.

Grubesic. T. H., Matisziw, T. C., and Zook, M. A. (2008), 'Global Airline Networks and Nodal Regions', *Geo-Journal*, 71, 53–66.

Grubesic, T. H., Matisziw, T. C., and Zook, M. A. (2009), 'Spatio-Temporal Fluctuations in the Global Airport Hierarchies', *Journal of Transport Geography*, 17.4, 264–75.

Haynes, K., Lall, S., Stough, R., and Yilmaz, S. (2006), 'Network Usage Patterns and the Substitution and Complementarity Effects between Telecommunications and Transportation: A Demand-Side Approach', in Kobayashi, K., Lakshmanan, T. R., and Anderson, W. P. (eds), *Structural Change in Transportation and Communications in the Knowledge Society*, Edward Elgar, Cheltenham.

Higgins, M. J., Levy, D., and Young, A. T. (2006), 'Growth and Convergence across the United States: Evidence from County-Level Data', *Review of Economics and Statistics*, 88.4, 671–81.

Hillberry, R., and Hummels, D. (2003), 'Intra-National Home Bias: Some Explanations', *Review of Economics and Statistics*, 85.4, 1089–92.

Hillberry, R., and Hummels, D. (2008), 'Trade Responses to Geographic Frictions: A Decomposition Using Micro-Data', *European Economics Review*, 52, 527–50.

HMT–DTI (2001), *Productivity in the UK: The Regional Dimension*, HM Treasury and Department of Trade and Industry, London.

HMT–DTI (2003), *Productivity in the UK: The Local Dimension*, HM Treasury and Department of Trade and Industry, London.

Hummels, D. (1999), 'Toward a Geography of Trade Costs', mimeo, University of Chicago, Chicago, IL.

Hummels, D. (2001), 'Time as a Trade Barrier', mimeo, Purdue University, Indiana.

Iammarino, S., and McCann, P. (2006), 'The Structure and Evolution of Industrial Clusters: Transactions, Technology and Knowledge Spillovers', *Research Policy*, 35, 1018–36.

Ioannides, Y., Overman, H. G., Rossi-Hansberg, E., and Schmidheiny, K. (2008), 'The Effect of Information and Communication Technologies on Urban Structure', *Economic Policy* 54, 201–42.

Johansson, B., and Loof, H. (2009), 'How are Non-MNEs Affected by Globalization?', *CESIS Working Paper*, Jönköping University, Jönköping and Royal Institute of Technology, Stockholm, Sweden.

Krätke, S. (2011), *The Creative Capital of Cities: Interactive Knowledge Creation and the Urbanization Economies of Innovation*, Wiley Blackwell, London.

Krugman, P. (1991), *Geography and Trade*, MIT Press, Cambridge, MA.

Krugman, P., and Venables, A. J. (1995), 'Globalization and the Inequality of Nations', *Quarterly Journal of Economics*, 110.4, 857–80.

Leamer, E. (2007), 'A Flat World, a Level Playing Field, a Small World After All, or None of the Above? A Review of Thomas L. Friedman's *The World is Flat*', *Journal of Economic Literature*, 83–126.

Leinbach, T. R., and Capineri, C. (2007), *Globalized Freight Transport: Intermodality, E-Commerce, Logistics and Sustainability*, Edward Elgar, Cheltenham.

Levinson, M. (2006), *The Box: How the Shipping Container Made the World Smaller and the World Economy Bigger*, Princeton University Press, Princeton, NJ.

Limtanakool, N., Schwanen, T., and Dijst, M. (2007), 'Ranking Functional Urban Regions: A Comparison of Interaction and Node Attribution Data', *Cities*, 24.5, 26–42.

Long Finance (2012), *Global Financial Centres Index 11*, London.

Lucas, R. E. (2000), 'Some Macroeconomics for the Twenty-First Century', *Journal of Economic Perspectives*, 14.1, 159–78.

Maddison, A. (2006), *The World Economy. Volume 1: A Millennial Perspective Volume 2: Historical Statistics*, Organisation for Economic Cooperation and Development, Paris.

Marshall, A. (1890), *Principles of Economics* (1st edn), Macmillan, London.

Mastercard (2008), *Worldwide Centers of Commerce Index*, www.mastercardworldwide.com

McCann, P. (1993), 'The Logistics-Costs Location-Production Problem', *Journal of Regional Science*, 33.4, 503–16.

McCann, P. (1998), *The Economics of Industrial Location: A Logistics Costs Approach*, Springer, Heidelberg.

McCann, P. (2005), 'Transport Costs and New Economic Geography', *Journal of Economic Geography*, 5.3, 305–18.

McCann, P. (2007), 'Sketching out a Model of Innovation, Face-to-Face Interaction and Economic Geography', *Spatial Economic Analysis*, 2.2, 117–34.

McCann, P. (2008), 'Globalization and Economic Geography: The World is Curved, Not Flat', *Cambridge Journal of Regions, Economy and Society*, 1.3, 351–70.

McCann, P. (2011), 'The Role of Industrial Clustering and Increasing Returns to Scale in Economic Development and Urban Growth', in Brooks, N., Donaghy, K., and Knaap, G. (eds), *The Oxford Handbook of Urban Economics and Planning*, Oxford University Press, Oxford.

McCann, P., and Fingleton, B. (1996), 'The Regional Agglomeration Impact of Just-In-Time Input Linkages: Evidence from the Scottish Electronics Industry', *Scottish Journal of Political Economy*, 43.5, 493–518.

McCann, P., Poot, J., and Sanderson, L. (2010), 'Migration, Relationship Capital and International Travel: Theory and Evidence', *Journal of Economic Geography*, 10.3, 361–87.

McCann, P. and Acs, Z. J. (2011), 'Globalisation: Countries, Cities and Multinationals', *Regional Studies*, 45.1, 17–32.

MGI (2009), *Preparing for China's Urban Billion*, McKinsey Global Institute.

MGI (2010), *India's Urban Awakening: Building Inclusive Cities, Sustaining Economic Growth*, McKinsey Global Institute.

MGI (2011a), *Urban World: Mapping the Economic Power of Cities*, McKinsey Global Institute.

MGI (2011b), *Building Globally Competitive Cities: The Key to Latin American Growth*, McKinsey Global Institute.

MGI (2012), *Urban America: US Cities in the Global Economy*, McKinsey Global Institute.

Nachum, L., and Zaheer, S. (2005), 'The Persistence of Distance? The Impact of Technology on MNE Motivations for Foreign Investment', *Strategic Management Journal*, 26, 747–67.

Ni, P., and Kresl, P. K. (2010), *The Global Urban Competitiveness Report 2010*, Edward Elgar, Cheltenham.

OECD (2006), *Competitive Cities in the Global Economy*, Organisation for Economic Cooperation and Development, Paris.

OECD (2007a), *International Investment Perspectives: Freedom of Investment in a Changing World*, Organisation for Economic Cooperation and Development, Paris.

OECD (2007b), *Regions at a Glance 2007*, Organisation for Economic Cooperation and Development, Paris.

OECD (2009a), *How Regions Growth: Trends and Analysis*, Organisation for Economic Cooperation and Development, Paris.

OECD (2009b), *Regions Matter: Economic Recovery, Innovation and Sustainable Growth*, Organisation for Economic Cooperation and Development, Paris.

OECD (2009c), *Regions at a Glance 2009*, Organisation for Economic Cooperation and Development, Paris.

OECD (2011a), *Regions and Innovation Policy*, Organisation for Economic Cooperation and Development, Paris.

OECD (2011b), *Regions at a Glance 2011*, Organisation for Economic Cooperation and Development, Paris.

OECD (2012), *Redefining Urban: Functional Urban Areas in OECD Countries*, Organisation for Economic Cooperation and Development, Paris.

Openshaw, S. and Taylor, P. J. (1979), 'A million or so correlation coefficients: three experiments on the modifiable areal unit problem' in Wrigley, N. (ed.), *Statistical Applications in the Spatial Sciences*, Pion, London.

Ortega-Argilés, R. (2012), 'The Transatlantic Productivity Gap: A Survey of the Main Causes', *Journal of Economic Surveys*, 26.3, 395–419.

Partridge, M. D., Rickman, D. S., Ali, K., and Olfert, M. R. (2008), 'Employment Growth in the American Urban Hierarchy: Long Live Distance', *B.E. Journal of Macroeconomics*, 8, 1–36.

Pavitt, K. (1984), 'Sectoral Patterns of Technical Change: Towards a Taxonomy and a Theory', *Research Policy*, 13, 343–73.

Piore, M. J., and Sabel, C. F. (1984), *The Second Industrial Divide: Possibilities for Prosperity*, Basic Books, New York.

Porter, M. E. (1990), *The Competitive Advantage of Nations*, Free Press, New York.

PWC, (2009), 'Which are the Largest City Economies in the World and Might this Change by 2025?', *UK Economic Outlook November (2009)*, Price Waterhouse Coopers, London.

Rodríguez-Pose, A. (1998), *The Dynamics of Regional Growth in Europe: Social and Political Factors*, Clarendon Press, Oxford.

Rietveld, P., and Vickerman, R. (2004), 'Transport in Regional Science: The "Death of Distance" is Premature', *Papers in Regional Science*, 83, 229–48.

Rosenthal, S. S., and Strange, W. C. (2004), 'Evidence on the Nature and Sources of Agglomeration Economics', in Henderson, V., and Thisse, J.-F. (eds) *Handbook of Urban and Regional Economics Vol.l 4*, North-Holland, Amsterdam.

Sassen, S. (1994), *Cities in a World Economy*, Pine Forge Press, Thousand Oaks, CA.

Sassen, S. (ed.) (2002), *Global Networks: Linked Cities*, Routledge, London.

Schonberger, R. J. (1996), *World Class Manufacturing: The Next Decade*, Free Press, New York.

Shapiro, J. M., (2006), 'Smart Cities: Quality of Life, Productivity, and the Growth Effects of Human Capital', *Review of Economics and Statistics*, 88.2, 324–35.

Simmie, J. (2004), 'Innovation and Clustering in the Globalized International Economy', *Urban Studies*, 41.5–6, 1095–112.

Storper, M., and Venables, A .J. (2004), 'Buzz: Face-to-Face Contact and the Urban Economy', *Journal of Economic Geography*, 4, 351–70.

Taylor, P. J. (2004), *World City Network: A Global Urban Analysis*, Routledge, London.

Taylor, P. J., Evans, D. M., and Pain, K. (2008), 'Application of the Interlocking Network Model to Mega-City Regions: Measuring Polycentricity Within and Beyond City-Regions', *Regional Studies*, 42.8, 1079–93.

UNDP (2009), *Human Development Report 2009: Overcoming Barriers: Human Mobility and Development*, United Nations Development Program, Palgrave Macmillan, Basingstoke.

UN-HABITAT (2008), *State of the World's Cities Report 2008/09*, United Nations-HABITAT Programme, Nairobi.

Timmer, M. P., Inklaar, R., O'Mahony, M., and Van Ark, B. (2010), *Economic Growth in Europe*, Cambridge University Press, Cambridge.

Van Oort, F. G. (2004), *Urban Growth and Innovation: Spatially Bounded Externalities in the Netherlands*, Ashgate, Aldershot.

Venables, A. J. (2006), 'Shifts in Economic Geography and their Causes', *Federal Reserve Bank of Kansas City Economic Review*, 91.4, 61–85.

Warf, B. (1995), 'Telecommunications and the Clustering Geographies of Knowledge Transmission in the Late 20th Century', *Urban Studies*, 32.2, 361–78.

Weber, A. (1909), *Über den Standort der Industrien*, trans. by Friedrich, C.J. (1929), *Alfred Weber's Theory of the Location of Industries*, University of Chicago Press, Chicago, IL.

Westlund, H. (2006), *Social Capital in the Knowledge Economy: Theory and Empirics*, Springer, Heidelberg.

Wickham, J., and Vecchi, A. (2008), 'Local Firms and Global Reach: Business Air Travel and the Irish Software Cluster', *European Planning Studies*, 16.5, 693–710.

World Bank (2008a), *World Trade Indicators 2008: Benchmarking Policy and Performance*, World Bank, Washington, DC.

World Bank (2009), *World Development Report 2009: Reshaping Economic Geography*, World Bank, Washington, DC.

Chapter 10

Alesina, A., and Glaeser, E.L. (2004), *Fighting Poverty in the US and Europe: A World of Difference*, Oxford University Press, Oxford.

Alesina, A., and Spolaore, E. (2005), *The Size of Nations*, MIT Press, Cambridge, MA.

Barca, F. (2009), *An Agenda for A Reformed Cohesion Policy: A Place-Based Approach to Meeting European Union Challenges and Expectations*, Independent Report Prepared at the Request of the European Commissioner for Regional Policy, Danuta Hübner, European Commission, Brussels.

Barca, F. (2011), 'Conclusion: Alternative Approaches to Development Policy: Intersections and Divergences', in *OECD Regional Outlook 2011*, Organisation for Economic Cooperation and Development, Paris.

Barca, F., McCann, P., and Rodríguez-Pose, A. (2012), 'The Case for Regional Development Intervention: Place-Based versus Place-Neutral Approaches', *Journal of Regional Science*, 52.1, 134–52.

Barro, R. J., and Sala-i-Martin, X. (1992), 'Convergence', *Journal of Political Economy*, 100, 223–51.

Berg, A. G., and Ostry, J. D. (2011), 'Inequality and Unsustainable Growth: Two Sides of the Same Coin', IMF Staff Discussion Note, SDN/11/08, International Monetary Fund, Washington, DC.

Beugelsdijk, S., and Maseland, R. (2011), *Culture in Economics: History, Methodological Reflections, and Contemporary Application*, Cambridge University Press, Cambridge.

Brail, R. K. (ed.) (2008), *Planning Support for Cities and Regions*, Lincoln Institute for Land Policy, Cambridge, MA.

Bolton, R. (1992), '"Place Prosperity vs People Prosperity" Revisited: An Old Issue with a New Angle', *Urban Studies*, 29.2, 185–203.

Borts, G. H., and Stein, J. L. (1964), *Economic Growth in a Free Market*, Columbia University Press, New York.

CAF (2010), *Desarrollo Local: Hacia un Nuevo Protagonismo de las Ciudades y Regiones*. Caracas: Corporación Andina de Fomento, Local Development Report of the Corporación Andina de Fomento, Caracas.

Cheshire, P. (2009), 'Policies for Mixed Communities: Faith-Based Displacement Activity?', *International Regional Science Review*, 32.3, 343–75.

Clark, M. (1963), *A Short History of Australia*, Penguin, Victoria, Australia.

Collier, P. (2006), *The Bottom Billion: Why the Poorest Countries are Failing and What Can be Done About It*, Oxford University Press, Oxford.

Crescenzi, R., Rodríguez-Pose, A., and Storper, M. (2007), 'The Territorial Dynamics of Innovation: a Europe–United States Comparative Analysis', *Journal of Economic Geography*, 7.6, 673–709.

Dijkstra, L., Garcilazo, E., and McCann, P. (2012), 'The Economic Performance of European Cities and City-Regions: Myths and Realities', *European Planning Studies*, forthcoming DOI:10.1080/09654313.2012.716245.

European Commission (2008), *Guide to Cost Benefit Analysis of Investment Projects*, European Commission Directorate General for Regional Policy, Brussels.

Evans, A. W. (1985), *Urban Economics*, Blackwell, Oxford.

Evans, A. W. (2004a), *Economics and Land Use Planning*, Blackwell, Oxford.

Evans, A. W. (2004b), *Economics, Real Estate and the Supply of Land*, Blackwell, Oxford.

Faludi, A. (2008), (ed.), *European Spatial Research and Planning*, Lincoln Institute of Land Policy, Cambridge, MA.

Ferrara, A. (2010), *Cost–Benefit Analysis of Multi-Level Government: The Case of EU Cohesion Policy and of US Federal Investment Policies*, Routledge, London.

Fine, B. (2003), 'Neither the Washington nor the Post-Washington Consensus: An Introduction', in Fine, F., Lapavitsas, C., and Pincus, J. (eds), *Development Policy in the Twenty-first Century: Beyond the Post-Washington Consensus*, Routledge, London.

Florida, R. (2002), *The Rise of the Creative Class*, Basic Books, New York.

Fritsch, M. (ed.) (2011), *Handbook of Research on Entrepreneurship and Regional Development. National and Regional Perspectives*, Edward Elgar, Cheltenham.

Fujita, M., Krugman, P., and Venables, A. J. (1999), *The Spatial Economy: Cities, Regions and International Trade*, MIT Press, Cambridge, MA.

Garcilazo, E., Oliveira Martins, J., and Tompson, W. (2010), 'Why Policies May Need to be Place-Based in Order to be People-Centred', OECD Regional Development Policy Division, Paris. Available at the website: http://www.voxeu.org/

Glaeser, E. L., and Gottlieb, J. (2006), 'Urban Resurgence and the Consumer City', *Urban Studies*, 43.8, 1275–99.

Glaeser, E. L., and Gottlieb, J. D. (2008), 'The Economics of Place-Making Policies', *Harvard Institute of Economic Research Discussion Paper No. 2166*, November.

Graham, D. J. (2007a), 'Agglomeration, Productivity and Transport Investment', *Journal of Transport Economics and Policy*, 41, 1–27.

Graham, D. J. (2007b), 'Variable Returns to Agglomeration and the Effect of Road Traffic Congestion', *Journal of Urban Economics*, 62, 103–20.

Grimes, A. (2013), 'Infrastructure and Regional Economic Growth', in Fischer, M., and Nijkamp, P. (eds), *Handbook of Regional Science*, Springer, Berlin.

Hague, C., Hague, E., and Breitbach, C. (2011), *Regional and Local Economic Development*, Palgrave, Basingstoke.

Hart, G. (2010), 'Redrawing the Map of the World? Reflections on the World Development Report 2009', *Economic Geography*, 86, 341–50.

Hirschmann, A. O. (1958), *The Strategy of Economic Development*, Yale University Press, New Haven, CT.

Houghwout, A. (1998), 'Aggregate Production Functions, Interregional Equilibrium, and the Measurement of Infrastructure Productivity', *Journal of Urban Economics*, 44.2, 216–27.

Houghwout, A. (2002), 'Public Infrastructure Investments, Productivity and Welfare in Fixed Geographic Areas', *Journal of Public Economics*. 83, 405–25.

Janssens, M., Pinelli, D., Reymen, D. C., and Wallman, S. (2009), *Sustainable Cities: Diversity, Economic Growth and Social Cohesion*, Edward Elgar, Cheltenham.

Kim, S.-J. (2011), 'Non-Market Effects on Agglomeration and their Public Policy Responses', in *OECD Regional Outlook 2011*, Organisation for Economic Cooperation and Development, Paris.

Krugman, P. (1991), *Geography and Trade*, MIT Press, Cambridge, MA.

Krugman, P. (2009), *The Return of Depression Economics and the Crisis of 2008*, Norton, New York.

Krugman, P., and Venables, A. J. (1990), 'Integration and Competitiveness of Peripheral Industry', in C. J., and J. B. (eds) *Unity and Diversity in the European Economy: The Community's Southern Frontier*, Cambridge University Press, Cambridge.

Krugman, P., and Venables, A. J. (1995), 'Globalization and the Inequality of Nations', *Quarterly Journal of Economics*, 110.4, 857–80.

Laurila, H. (2004), 'Urban Governance, Competition and Welfare', *Urban Studies*, 41.3, 683–96.

Laurila, H. (2011), 'Optimisation of City Size', *Urban Studies*, 48.4, 737–47.

Layard, R., and Glaister, S. (1994), *Cost–Benefit Analysis* (2nd edn) Cambridge University Press, Cambridge.

Lucas, R. E. (1988), 'On the Mechanics of Economic Development', *Journal of Monetary Economics*, 22.1, 3–42.

McCann, P. (2009), 'Economic Geography, Globalisation and New Zealand's Productivity Paradox', *New Zealand Economic Papers*, 43.3, 279–314.

McCann, P., and Rodríguez-Pose, A. (2011), 'Why and When Development Policy Should be Place-Based', in *OECD Regional Outlook 2011*, Organisation for Economic Cooperation and Development, Paris.

McCann, P., and Acs, Z. J. (2011). 'Globalization: Countries, Cities and Multinationals', *Regional Studies*, 45.1, 17–32.

Moretti, E. (2012). *The New Geography of Jobs*, Houghton Mifflin Harcourt, New York.

Myrdal, G. (1957), *Economic Theory and Underdeveloped Regions*, Hutchinson, London.

OECD (2006), *Competitive Cities in the Global Economy*, Organisation for Economic Cooperation and Development, Paris.

OECD (2009a). *How Regions Grow: Trends and Analysis*, Organisation for Economic Growth and Development, Paris.

OECD (2009b), *Regions Matter: Economic Recovery, Innovation and Sustainable Growth*, Organisation for Economic Growth and Development, Paris.

OECD (2009c). *Regions at a Glance 2009*, Organisation for Economic Cooperation and Development, Paris.

OECD (2010a), *Regional Development Policies in OECD Countries*, Organisation for Economic Cooperation and Development, Paris.

OECD (2010b), *Organising Local Economic Development: The Role of Development Agencies and Companies*, Organisation for Economic Cooperation and Development, Paris.

OECD (2011a), *Regions at a Glance 2011*, Organisation for Economic Cooperation and Development, Paris.

OECD (2011b), *Regional Outlook 2011*, Organisation for Economic Cooperation and Development, Paris.

Overman, H. G. (2002), 'Neighbourhood Effects in Large and Small Neighbourhoods', *Urban Studies*, 39.1, 117–30.

Partridge, M. D., and Rickman, D. S. (2006), *The Geography of American Poverty: Is there a Need for Place-Based Policies?*, Upjohn Institute, Kalamazoo, MI.

Pattachini, E., and Zenou, Y. (2011), 'Intergenerational Education Transmission: Neighborhood Quality and/or Parents' Involvement?', *Journal of Regional Science*, 51, 987–1013.

Pearce, D. W. and Nash, C. A. (1981), *The Social Appraisal of Projects: A Text in Cost–Benefit Analysis*, Macmillan, Basingstoke.

Peck, J, and Sheppard, E. (2010), 'Worlds Apart? Engaging with the World Development Report 2009: Reshaping Economic Geography', *Economic Geography*, 86, 331–40.

Pike, A., Rodríguez-Pose, A., and Tomaney, J. (2006), *Local and Regional Development*, Routledge, London.

Pike, A., Rodríguez-Pose, A., and Tomaney, J. (eds) (2010), *Handbook of Local and Regional Development*, Routledge, Abingdon.

Putnam. R. (1993), *Making Democracy Work: Civic Traditions in Modern Italy*, Princeton University Press, Princeton, NJ.

Quigley, J. M., and Raphael, S. (2005), 'Regulation and the High Cost of Housing in California', *American Economic Review*, 95.2, 323–8.

Rodrik, D. (2006), 'Goodbye Washington Consensus, Hello Washington Confusion? A Review of the World Bank's Economic Growth in the 1990s: Learning from a Decade of Reform', *Journal of Economic Literature*, 44.4, 973–87.

Rodrik, D., Subramanian, A., and Trebbi, F. (2004), 'Institutions Rule: the Primacy of Institutions over Geography and Integration in Economic Development', *Journal of Economic Growth*, 9.2, 131–65.

Romer, P. (1986), 'Increasing Returns and Long-Run Growth,' *Journal of Political Economy*, 94, 1002–37.

Rostow, W. W. (1959), 'The Stages of Economic Growth', *Economic History Review*, 12.1, 1–17.

Ruth, M. (ed.) (2006), *Smart Growth and Climate Change: Regional Development, Infrastructure and Adaptation*, Edward Elgar, Cheltenham.

Ruth, M., Donaghy, K., and Kirshen, P. (eds) (2006), *Regional Climate Change and Variability: Impacts and Responses*, Edward Elgar, Cheltenham.

Sachs, J. D. (2003), 'Institutions Don't Rule: Direct Effects of Geography on Per Capita Income', WP 9490, NBER, Cambridge, MA.

Sachs, J. D. (2011), *The Price of Civilisation: Reawakening American Virtue and Prosperity*, Random House, New York.

Sachs, J. D. (2012), 'Government, Geography and Growth: The True Drivers of Economic Development', *Foreign Affairs*, 91.5, 142–50.

Sapir, A., Aghion, P., Bertola, G., Hellwig, M., Pisani-Ferry, J., Rosati, D., Viñals, J., and Wallace, H. (2004), *An Agenda for a Growing Europe: The Sapir Report*, Oxford University Press, Oxford.

Sassone, P. G., and Schaffer, W. A. (1978), *Cost Benefit Analysis: A Handbook*, Academic Press, New York.

Seltzer, E., and Carbonell, A. (eds) (2011), *Regional Planning in America: Practice and Prospect*, Lincoln Institute of Land Policy, Cambridge, MA.

Solow, R. M. (1956), 'A Contribution to the Theory of Economic Growth', *Quarterly Journal of Economics*, 70, 65–94.

Spence, M., and Liepziger, D. (eds) (2010), *Globalization and Growth: Implications for a Post-Crisis World*, Commission on Growth and Development, International bank for Reconstruction and Development, World Bank, Washington, DC.

Stiglitz, J. (2002), *Globalization and its Discontents*, Penguin, London.

Stiglitz, J. E., Sen, A., and Fitoussi, J.-P. (2009), *Commission of the Measurement of Economic Performance and Social Progress*, http://www.stiglitz-sen-fitoussi.fr/en/index.htm

Swales, J. K. (1997), 'A Cost–Benefit Approach to the Evaluation of Regional Selective Assistance', *Fiscal Studies*, 18, 73–85.

Swales, J. K. (2009), 'A Cost–Benefit Approach to Regional Policy', in Farshchi, M., Janne, O. E. M., and McCann, P. (eds), *Technological Change and Mature Industrial Regions*, Edward Elgar Cheltenham, 237–258.

Swan, T. W. (1956), 'Economic Growth and Capital Accumulation', *Economic Record*, 32, 334–61.

Swinburn, G., Goga, S., and Murphy, F. (2006), *Local Economic Development—A Primer: Developing and Implementing Local Economic Development Strategies and Action Plans*, The World Bank and Bertelsman Stiftung, Washington, DC.

Thissen, M., and Van Oort, F. (2010), 'European Place-Based Development Policy and Sustainable Economic Agglomeration', *TESG Journal of Economic and Social Geography*, 101.4, 473–80.

Vanclay, F., Higgins, M., and Blackshaw, A. (2008), *Making Sense of Place: Exploring Concepts and Expressions of Place Through Different Senses and Lenses*, National Museum of Australia Press, Canberra.

Van Oort, F. G. (2004), *Urban Growth and Innovation: Spatially Bounded Externalities in The Netherlands*, Ashgate, Aldershot.

Venables, A. J. (2007), 'Evaluating Urban Transport Improvements: Cost-Benefit Analysis in the Presence of Agglomeration and Income Taxation', *Journal of Transport Economics and Policy*, 41.2, 173–88.

Venables, A. J. (2010), 'Economic Geography and African Development', *Papers in Regional Science*, 89.3, 469–83.

Vickerman, R. W. (ed.) (1991), *Infrastructure and Regional Development*, Pion, London.

Williamson, J. G. (1965), 'Regional Inequality and the Process of National Development: A Description of the Patterns', *Economic Growth and Cultural Change*, 13, 1–84.

Winnick, L. (1966), 'Place Prosperity vs People Prosperity: Welfare Considerations in the Geographic Redistribution of Economic Activity', in *Essays in Urban Land Economics in Honor of the Sixty- Fifth Birthday of Leo Grebler*, Real Estate Research Program, University of California Press, Los Angeles, CA.

World Bank (2003), *World Development Report 2003: Transforming Institutions, Growth and Quality of Life*, Washington, DC.

World Bank (2009), *World Development Report 2009: Reshaping Economic Geography*, World Bank, Washington, DC.

World Bank (2010), 'Innovation Policy: A Guide for Developing Countries', World Bank, Washington, DC.

Xu, C. (2011), 'The Fundamental Institutions of China's Reforms and Development', *Journal of Economic Literature*, 49.4, 1076–151.

Zoellick, R. B. (2012), 'Why We Still Need the World Bank: Looking Beyond Aid', *Foreign Affairs*, 91.2, 66–78.

Index